# B1207

*Body List*

# EASTERN COACH WORKS

## Series 2

## 10001 - 15000

PUBLISHED BY

THE PSV CIRCLE

FEBRUARY 2017

# FOREWORD

The draft for this publication was prepared by Maurice Doggett, making extensive use of ECW official records.

The assistance of Peter Bates, David Corke, Richard Gadsby, Tony Holdsworth, John Jones, Colin Martin, Peter Tulloch and Fred Ward is also acknowledged.

This publication lists all known information to January 2017.

The main section of this publication is presented in eight columns as follows:-

1. Vehicle body number
2. * if the vehicle has notes associated with it
3. Original vehicle registration mark
4. Chassis manufacturer and model
5. Chassis number
6. Seating arrangement following standard PSV Circle codes
7. Date the body was new – where known this is the date of effective first licensing or entry into service.
8. First operator / county code / fleet number (if used)

Photographs were taken or supplied by Harry Hay, Peter Henson, John May, Roy Marshall, Geoffrey Morant (courtesy Richard Morant), The Omnibus Society.

**Contents:**

**Note:**

This is one of a wide range of publications produced by the PSV Circle primarily as a service to its members. The information contained herein has been taken from the content of PSV Circle monthly News Sheets and also includes information provided from other reliable sources. Considerable time and effort is taken to ensure that the content of this publication is as complete and accurate as possible, but no responsibility can be accepted for any errors or omissions. However, please tell us if you discover any!

Any general comments, updates or corrections to this publication may be sent to the Publications Manager, PSV Circle, 4B Crown House, Linton Road, BARKING IG11 8HG or via email to publications.manager@psv-circle.org.uk.

Details of how to join The PSV Circle and a list of all our publications can be obtained (and ordered) from The PSV Circle website - www.psvcircle.org.uk or from the PSV Circle, 4B Crown House, Linton Road, BARKING IG11 8HG.

ISBN: 978-1-910767-17-7

Published by the PSV Circle.

# INTRODUCTION

The origins of the Lowestoft factory date back to 1919 when Mr E B Hutchinson (who started United Automobile Services Ltd) acquired an area of land in Laundry Lane, on which buildings were erected which not only served as a garage and workshop for the Lowestoft area fleet, but also as a bodybuilding workshop. During the 1920's, the Lowestoft premises, which became known as 'The Coach Factory', were enlarged to accommodate the increase in the company's bodybuilding activities which came to embrace bodies for other operators as well as for their own fleet.

In 1929 and after seeing his company become one of the major players in the 1920's bus and coach industry, Mr. Hutchinson sold United to the Tilling & British Automobile Traction Group (TBAT) jointly with the London & North Eastern Railway. The construction of new bodies by United continued as before, but as the result of the desire of the TBAT to rationalise the activities of its operating subsidiaries in East Anglia, a new company, the Eastern Counties Omnibus Co Ltd was registered on 14th July 1931 to take over the operations and assets of the Eastern Counties Road Car Co Ltd of Ipswich, the Ortona Motor Co Ltd of Cambridge, the Peterborough Electric Traction Co Ltd and the East Anglian area services of United. The new company came under the control of the TBAT and was managed by Tilling.

Included in the merger was United's bodybuilding factory at Lowestoft and Eastern Counties continued the construction of bodies as a separate activity from its main core business, but in mid-1933, negotiations began to sell the bodybuilding side. The suitor was Charles Roberts of Wakefield, but the deal fell through and the coach building business continued as before. By mid-1936, an average of nine single-deck bodies and one double-deck body per week were being constructed and it was decided to form a separate company to run that side of Eastern Counties' activities. Consequently, Eastern Coach Works Ltd. came into being on 1st July 1936 as a Tilling and BAT subsidiary, although the whole of the share capital of £100,000 was, at that time, owned by Eastern Counties.

The premises were further enlarged up to the outbreak of the Second World War on 3rd September 1939 to allow for increased production which continued until 28th May 1940, the effective date of an order to close the premises, in the light of the evacuation of the British Expeditionary Force from France and the threat of a German invasion along the East Coast. However, alternative premises were quickly found at Irthlingborough in Northamptonshire, in buildings formerly occupied by the United Counties Omnibus Co Ltd as a garage and here the Company built a comparatively small number of new bodies, but undertook a large amount of refurbishment, repair and overhaul of existing bodies, mainly for the Tilling Group operators. In the meantime, ECW was allowed to gradually resume activities at its Lowestoft premises so that by the end of 1945, both factories were fully committed. However, it was not until 22nd February 1946 that the first post-war body to the new standard design, on a Bristol K-type chassis was delivered, to be added to the Crosville fleet. This design was available in both highbridge and lowbridge versions, the majority being fitted to Bristol K family chassis, though a number were also built on Leyland PD1A chassis for various operators and others fitted as replacements for pre-war and utility bodies on various chassis. The premises at Irthlingborough were closed in May 1952 following the completion of almost 550 single deck bodies built during the preceding six years.

A new single-deck body followed, with the first being delivered in mid-1946. The standard configuration was a bus version seating thirty five, with rear entrance, but an express/dual-purpose version was also produced in smaller numbers. No full coach bodies were produced until May 1950 when the first of the so called 'Queen Mary' full-fronted bodies was delivered. This design was in production until the advent of the underfloor engined LS coach, but interestingly had a brief revival in 1957, when ten earlier Bristol L5G chassis were rebuilt and rebodied for use on a service along the Marine Drive at Scarborough by United Automobile. These vehicles had a modified version of the coach body design with centre entrance and bus seating.

In the Grouping division of September 1942, whereby the major regional bus operators became controlled either by the Tilling Group or the BET Group, Eastern Coach Works came under the control of the former, therefore becoming responsible for most of the body requirements of the Tilling Group operators. The Coach Factory had supplied a large number of new bodies to BET Group subsidiary companies in the pre-war and early post-war years, mostly single deckers to the standard BEF design. A few were also supplied to municipal operators and these two sectors of the industry continued to place orders for bodies in the second half of the 1940s. However, this was to be short-lived because effectively from the 1st January 1948, ECW came under the control of The British Transport Commission. This meant that ECW could no longer supply their products to non-nationalised operators although the company was allowed to complete orders from BET Group and municipal operators which had already been placed.

In 1949 ECW collaborated with Bristol in the first of several joint development exercises to produce the prototype body for the new Bristol Lodekka. This revolutionary design succeeded in creating a double-deck bus with an overall height comparable to lowbridge double-deckers of the day (around 13ft 4in), but with full-height central gangways on both decks, eliminating the need for the side-gangway of the lowbridge design, which had always caused problems in service. This first prototype was followed by a second similar vehicle which appeared the following year, which were the precursors of the production Lodekka, pre-production examples of which began to appear in 1953. The design had many features in common with earlier ECW double-deck bodies which it resembled from some angles.

By 1950 interest was growing in single-deck vehicles powered by underfloor mounted engines, which allowed an increase in seating capacity of around six. This concept was incorporated in the second new design from Bristol/ECW, the Bristol LS. In common with several other products from different manufacturers, this design incorporated a set-back front axle, with the entrance situated in the front overhang. This had the added benefit of allowing the driver much greater control over boarding and alighting. The LS is best described as a semi-integral vehicle because it did have a separate underframe incorporating the mechanical units, but required temporary stiffening prior to the fitment of the body. Two different designs of body for bus and coach applications were mounted on LS chassis, a number of operators taking a third variant using the bus shell with coach seats, which was in effect the successor to the dual-purpose bodied Bristol L vehicles, produced between 1947 and 1952. The body design as fitted to the Bristol LS was not actually the first ECW body fitted to underfloor engined chassis, because a slightly earlier and totally different, much squarer style appeared on twenty AEC Regal IV chassis for London Transport and Tillings Transport in 1951.

This publication lists bodies numbered between 10001 and 15000 produced between mid 1957 and mid 1965. The main thrust of production during this period consisted initially of double-deck bodies on Bristol Lodekka (LD series) chassis, alongside bus and coach bodies for fitment to Bristol MW and the lighter SC chassis, though a dual-purpose version of the MW bus-based body was also produced in smaller numbers. In response to economic problems of the time, during 1958 a substantial cutback in orders was experienced. The body numbers previously allocated to these orders were not reused.

During 1959 the first 'flat-floor' version of the Lodekka appeared, which again had been a joint effort between Bristol and ECW. These developed into two different designs, a rear entrance version for the Bristol FS and FL chassis, the appearance of which owed much to the earlier bodies on the LD Lodekka family. Alongside these a forward entrance version, also produced in short and long versions to suit the FSF and FLF chassis respectively. In the event far more of the forward entrance design were built, though substantial numbers of the shorter rear entrance design were produced as well.

Although rebodying was less prevalant in this period than previously, a significant number of earlier chassis were rebodied for various operators. These included a full-fronted single-deck design based on the SC style body, suitable for updating older L family chassis, often involving the lengthening of the chassis in the process. An interesting experimental design were two fibreglass bodies for fitment to Bristol SC chassis. Although no production bodies of this material were constructed, these two buses did achieve a full service life suggesting the original concept was a sound one.

Following cessation of Bristol SC production another lightweight design of body began to be produced for the new underfloor Bristol SUL4A chassis. The first of these appeared in 1960 seating thirty-six, though a shorter thirty seat version was built in small numbers for the shorter SUS4A chassis. As with the earlier SC design a coach version was also built in limited numbers for the SUL4A.

1961 saw the appearance of a radically different body design for the Bristol MW chassis, though the rear-end treatment bore a strong resemblance to the design supplied to London Transport and Tillings ten years earlier. The style initially attracted some criticism, but this tended to wane as the design evolved over the next few years. A similar looking body was developed for the new rear-engined Bristol RE chassis, the prototype of which appeared in 1963. These were built to take advantage of the new increased dimensions permitted, being 36ft x 8ft 2½in overall. The first production examples of a bus version of the Bristol RE, which would ultimately replace the MW, entered service in 1964. This design featured laterally curved windscreens and a three-window rear-end design, incorporating the emergency exit in the centre bay.

## Body Numbers

Post-war production of new bodies started a new series, known as Series 2, commencing at 1001 and continued up to 26600. Another new series was started, this time in 1951, for work involving major repairs, conversions and various modifications, including repaints, commencing at 501 with an 'R' prefix and which eventually reached R1557. These numbers were allocated mainly to existing ECW bodies but several bodies of other makes were included. In addition, ECW utilised three other separate sequences of numbers in the ' B', 'SA' and 'W' series for various types of work to existing bodies but full details of these are not available.

## Body List

| | | | | | | |
|---|---|---|---|---|---|---|
| 10001 | *997 CHN | Bristol L5G Reb | 63.112 | FDP39C | 5/57 | United AS, Darlington (DM) BGS9 |
| 10002 | *998 CHN | Bristol L5G Reb | 63.182 | FDP39C | 5/57 | United AS, Darlington (DM) BGS10 |
| 10003 | | | | | | Not built |
| 10004 | YWB 152 | Leyland PD2/20 | 570461 | H31/28R | 7/57 | Sheffield JOC (WR) C1152 |
| 10005 | YWB 153 | Leyland PD2/20 | 570463 | H31/28R | 7/57 | Sheffield JOC (WR) C1153 |
| 10006 | YWB 292 | Leyland PD2/20 | 570464 | H31/28R | 7/57 | Sheffield JOC (WR) B1292 |
| 10007 | YWB 293 | Leyland PD2/20 | 570465 | H31/28R | 7/57 | Sheffield JOC (WR) B1293 |
| 10008 | YWB 294 | Leyland PD2/20 | 570466 | H31/28R | 7/57 | Sheffield JOC (WR) B1294 |
| 10009 | UWW 739 | Bristol LD6B | 138.011 | H33/27RD | 3/58 | Keighley-West Yorkshire, Harrogate (WR) KDX69 |
| 10010 | UWW 740 | Bristol LD6B | 138.142 | H33/27RD | 11/58 | Keighley-West Yorkshire, Harrogate (WR) KDX70 |
| 10011 | UWW 741 | Bristol LD6B | 138.144 | H33/27RD | 11/58 | Keighley-West Yorkshire, Harrogate (WR) KDX71 |
| 10012 | *KLA 91 | AEC Regal III | 9621E807 | FC24F | 7/57 | Tillings Transport, London WC1 (LN) |
| 10013 | *KLA 90 | AEC Regal III | 9621E808 | FC24F | 7/57 | Tillings Transport, London WC1 (LN) |
| 10014 | *KLA 89 | AEC Regal III | 9621E809 | FC24F | 7/57 | Tillings Transport, London WC1 (LN) |
| 10015 | *KGX 941 | AEC Regal III | 9621E805 | FC24F | 7/57 | Tillings Transport, London WC1 (LN) |
| 10016 | *KGX 940 | AEC Regal III | 9621E806 | FC24F | 7/57 | Tillings Transport, London WC1 (LN) |
| 10017 | RSC 622 | Bristol MW6G | 135.032 | C38F | 3/58 | Scottish Omnibuses, Edinburgh (MN) A622 |
| 10018 | RSC 623 | Bristol MW6G | 135.033 | C38F | 3/58 | Scottish Omnibuses, Edinburgh (MN) A623 |
| 10019 | RSC 624 | Bristol MW6G | 135.048 | C38F | 3/58 | Scottish Omnibuses, Edinburgh (MN) A624 |
| 10020 | RSC 625 | Bristol MW6G | 135.049 | C38F | 3/58 | Scottish Omnibuses, Edinburgh (MN) A625 |
| 10021 | RSC 626 | Bristol MW6G | 135.057 | C38F | 3/58 | Scottish Omnibuses, Edinburgh (MN) A626 |
| 10022 | RSC 627 | Bristol MW6G | 135.058 | C38F | 3/58 | Scottish Omnibuses, Edinburgh (MN) A627 |
| 10023 | RSC 628 | Bristol MW6G | 135.078 | C38F | 3/58 | Scottish Omnibuses, Edinburgh (MN) A628 |
| 10024 | RSC 629 | Bristol MW6G | 135.079 | C38F | 3/58 | Scottish Omnibuses, Edinburgh (MN) A629 |
| 10025 | RSC 630 | Bristol MW6G | 135.100 | C38F | 4/58 | Scottish Omnibuses, Edinburgh (MN) A630 |
| 10026 | RSC 631 | Bristol MW6G | 135.101 | C38F | 4/58 | Scottish Omnibuses, Edinburgh (MN) A631 |
| 10027 | RSC 632 | Bristol MW6G | 135.106 | C38F | 4/58 | Scottish Omnibuses, Edinburgh (MN) A632 |
| 10028 | RSC 633 | Bristol MW6G | 135.107 | C38F | 4/58 | Scottish Omnibuses, Edinburgh (MN) A633 |
| 10029 | RSC 634 | Bristol MW6G | 135.111 | C38F | 4/58 | Scottish Omnibuses, Edinburgh (MN) A634 |
| 10030 | RSC 635 | Bristol MW6G | 135.112 | C38F | 5/58 | Scottish Omnibuses, Edinburgh (MN) A635 |
| 10031 | RSC 636 | Bristol MW6G | 135.113 | C38F | 4/58 | Scottish Omnibuses, Edinburgh (MN) A636 |
| 10032 | RSC 637 | Bristol MW6G | 135.114 | C38F | 4/58 | Scottish Omnibuses, Edinburgh (MN) A637 |
| 10033 | RSC 638 | Bristol MW6G | 135.115 | C38F | 5/58 | Scottish Omnibuses, Edinburgh (MN) A638 |
| 10034 | RSC 639 | Bristol MW6G | 135.120 | C38F | 5/58 | Scottish Omnibuses, Edinburgh (MN) A639 |
| 10035 | RSC 640 | Bristol MW6G | 135.121 | C38F | 5/58 | Scottish Omnibuses, Edinburgh (MN) A640 |
| 10036 | RSC 641 | Bristol MW6G | 135.122 | C38F | 6/58 | Scottish Omnibuses, Edinburgh (MN) A641 |
| 10037 | XUO 712 | Bristol MW6G | 135.063 | C41F | 3/58 | Western National, Exeter (DN) 2229 |
| 10038 | XUO 711 | Bristol MW6G | 135.064 | C41F | 3/58 | Western National, Exeter (DN) 2228 |
| 10039 | XUO 713 | Bristol MW6G | 135.070 | C41F | 3/58 | Western National, Exeter (DN) 2230 |
| 10040 | XUO 714 | Bristol MW6G | 135.071 | C41F | 3/58 | Western National, Exeter (DN) 2231 |
| 10041 | XUO 716 | Bristol MW6G | 135.072 | C41F | 3/58 | Western National, Exeter (DN) 2233 |
| 10042 | XUO 715 | Bristol MW6G | 135.073 | C41F | 3/58 | Western National, Exeter (DN) 2232 |
| 10043 | XUO 717 | Bristol MW6G | 135.086 | C41F | 5/58 | Western National, Exeter (DN) 2234 |
| 10044 | XUO 718 | Bristol MW6G | 135.093 | C41F | 5/58 | Western National, Exeter (DN) 2235 |
| 10045 | XUO 719 | Bristol MW6G | 135.098 | C41F | 5/58 | Western National, Exeter (DN) 2236 |
| 10046 | XUO 720 | Bristol MW6G | 135.099 | C41F | 5/58 | Western National, Exeter (DN) 2237 |
| 10047 | XUO 721 | Bristol MW6G | 135.126 | C41F | 6/58 | Western National, Exeter (DN) 2238 |
| 10048 | XUO 722 | Bristol MW6G | 135.132 | C41F | 6/58 | Western National, Exeter (DN) 2239 |
| 10049 | XUO 723 | Bristol MW6G | 135.133 | C41F | 6/58 | Western National, Exeter (DN) 2240 |
| 10050 | XUO 724 | Bristol MW6G | 135.134 | C41F | 7/58 | Western National, Exeter (DN) 2241 |
| 10051 | SFU 309 | Bristol LD5G | 138.263 | H33/27RD | 1/59 | Lincolnshire RCC, Bracebridge Heath (KN) 2355 |
| 10052 | SFU 310 | Bristol LD5G | 138.264 | H33/27RD | 12/58 | Lincolnshire RCC, Bracebridge Heath (KN) 2356 |
| 10053 | SFU 311 | Bristol LD5G | 138.270 | H33/27RD | 12/58 | Lincolnshire RCC, Bracebridge Heath (KN) 2357 |
| 10054 | SFU 312 | Bristol LD5G | 138.271 | H33/27RD | 12/58 | Lincolnshire RCC, Bracebridge Heath (KN) 2358 |

| | | | | | | |
|---|---|---|---|---|---|---|
| 10055 | SFU 313 | Bristol LD5G | 138.272 | H33/27RD | 12/58 | Lincolnshire RCC, Bracebridge Heath (KN) 2359 |
| 10056 | SFU 849 | Bristol MW5G | 139.143 | B45F | 1/59 | Lincolnshire RCC, Bracebridge Heath (KN) 2224 |
| 10057 | SFU 850 | Bristol MW5G | 139.144 | B45F | 12/58 | Lincolnshire RCC, Bracebridge Heath (KN) 2225 |
| 10058 | SFU 851 | Bristol MW5G | 139.145 | B45F | 1/59 | Lincolnshire RCC, Bracebridge Heath (KN) 2226 |
| 10059 | SFU 852 | Bristol MW5G | 139.146 | B45F | 1/59 | Lincolnshire RCC, Bracebridge Heath (KN) 2227 |
| 10060 | 805 FFM | Bristol MW6G | 135.094 | C39F | 4/58 | Crosville MS, Chester (CH) CMG357 |
| 10061 | 806 FFM | Bristol MW6G | 135.095 | C39F | 4/58 | Crosville MS, Chester (CH) CMG358 |
| 10062 | 807 FFM | Bristol MW6G | 135.096 | C39F | 4/58 | Crosville MS, Chester (CH) CMG359 |
| 10063 | 808 FFM | Bristol MW6G | 135.097 | C39F | 4/58 | Crosville MS, Chester (CH) CMG360 |
| 10064 | | | | | | Not built |
| 10065 | | | | | | Not built |
| 10066 | | | | | | Not built |
| 10067 | | | | | | Not built |
| 10068 | XUO 725 | Bristol MW6G | 135.076 | C41F | 3/58 | Southern National, Exeter (DN) 2215 |
| 10069 | XUO 726 | Bristol MW6G | 135.077 | C41F | 5/58 | Southern National, Exeter (DN) 2216 |
| 10070 | XUO 727 | Bristol MW6G | 135.082 | C41F | 3/58 | Southern National, Exeter (DN) 2217 |
| 10071 | XUO 728 | Bristol MW6G | 135.083 | C41F | 5/58 | Southern National, Exeter (DN) 2218 |
| 10072 | XUO 729 | Bristol MW6G | 135.108 | C41F | 5/58 | Southern National, Exeter (DN) 2219 |
| 10073 | XUO 730 | Bristol MW6G | 135.109 | C41F | 5/58 | Southern National, Exeter (DN) 2220 |
| 10074 | XUO 731 | Bristol MW6G | 135.110 | C41F | 5/58 | Southern National, Exeter (DN) 2221 |
| 10075 | XUO 732 | Bristol MW6G | 135.139 | C41F | 6/58 | Southern National, Exeter (DN) 2222 |
| 10076 | XUO 733 | Bristol MW6G | 135.140 | C41F | 6/58 | Southern National, Exeter (DN) 2223 |
| 10077 | XUO 734 | Bristol MW6G | 135.141 | C41F | 6/58 | Southern National, Exeter (DN) 2224 |
| 10078 | XUO 735 | Bristol MW6G | 135.142 | C41F | 6/58 | Southern National, Exeter (DN) 2225 |
| 10079 | XUO 736 | Bristol MW6G | 135.147 | C41F | 6/58 | Southern National, Exeter (DN) 2226 |
| 10080 | XUO 737 | Bristol MW6G | 135.148 | C41F | 7/58 | Southern National, Exeter (DN) 2227 |
| 10081 | | | | | | Not built |
| 10082 | | | | | | Not built |
| 10083 | | | | | | Not built |
| 10084 | PDL 514 | Bristol MW6G | 135.102 | C39F | 5/58 | Southern Vectis, Newport (IW) 314 |
| 10085 | PDL 515 | Bristol MW6G | 135.103 | C39F | 5/58 | Southern Vectis, Newport (IW) 315 |
| 10086 | 215 HRO | Bedford RLH | 28597 | Mobile Lab | 3/59 | British Railways 1033S |
| 10087 | RSC 642 | Bristol LD6G | 138.032 | H33/27R | 3/58 | Scottish Omnibuses, Edinburgh (MN) AA642 |
| 10088 | RSC 643 | Bristol LD6G | 138.033 | H33/27R | 3/58 | Scottish Omnibuses, Edinburgh (MN) AA643 |
| 10089 | RSC 644 | Bristol LD6G | 138.034 | H33/27R | 3/58 | Scottish Omnibuses, Edinburgh (MN) AA644 |
| 10090 | RSC 645 | Bristol LD6G | 138.035 | H33/27R | 3/58 | Scottish Omnibuses, Edinburgh (MN) AA645 |
| 10091 | RSC 646 | Bristol LD6G | 138.042 | H33/27R | 3/58 | Scottish Omnibuses, Edinburgh (MN) AA646 |
| 10092 | RSC 647 | Bristol LD6G | 138.043 | H33/27R | 3/58 | Scottish Omnibuses, Edinburgh (MN) AA647 |
| 10093 | RSC 648 | Bristol LD6G | 138.044 | H33/27R | 4/58 | Scottish Omnibuses, Edinburgh (MN) AA648 |
| 10094 | RSC 649 | Bristol LD6G | 138.045 | H33/27R | 4/58 | Scottish Omnibuses, Edinburgh (MN) AA649 |
| 10095 | RSC 650 | Bristol LD6G | 138.046 | H33/27R | 4/58 | Scottish Omnibuses, Edinburgh (MN) AA650 |
| 10096 | RSC 651 | Bristol LD6G | 138.047 | H33/27R | 4/58 | Scottish Omnibuses, Edinburgh (MN) AA651 |
| 10097 | RSC 652 | Bristol LD6G | 138.048 | H33/27R | 4/58 | Scottish Omnibuses, Edinburgh (MN) AA652 |
| 10098 | RSC 653 | Bristol LD6G | 138.057 | H33/27R | 4/58 | Scottish Omnibuses, Edinburgh (MN) AA653 |
| 10099 | RSC 654 | Bristol LD6G | 138.058 | H33/27R | 5/58 | Scottish Omnibuses, Edinburgh (MN) AA654 |
| 10100 | RSC 655 | Bristol LD6G | 138.059 | H33/27R | 5/58 | Scottish Omnibuses, Edinburgh (MN) AA655 |
| 10101 | RSC 656 | Bristol LD6G | 138.077 | H33/27R | 5/58 | Scottish Omnibuses, Edinburgh (MN) AA656 |
| 10102 | RSC 657 | Bristol LD6G | 138.078 | H33/27R | 5/58 | Scottish Omnibuses, Edinburgh (MN) AA657 |
| 10103 | *752 GFM | Bristol LS6B | 97.030 | B41F | 7/58 | Crosville MS, Chester (CH) SUB325 |
| 10104 | 714 JHN | Bristol MW5G | 139.215 | B45F | 2/59 | Durham District (DM) DBU14 |
| 10105 | 715 JHN | Bristol MW5G | 139.216 | B45F | 2/59 | Durham District (DM) DBU15 |
| 10106 | 716 JHN | Bristol MW5G | 139.217 | B45F | 2/59 | Durham District (DM) DBU16 |
| 10107 | GM 9271 | Bristol LD6G | 138.036 | H33/27R | 4/58 | Central SMT, Motherwell (LK) B71 |
| 10108 | GM 9272 | Bristol LD6G | 138.037 | H33/27R | 4/58 | Central SMT, Motherwell (LK) B72 |
| 10109 | GM 9273 | Bristol LD6G | 138.038 | H33/27R | 4/58 | Central SMT, Motherwell (LK) B73 |
| 10110 | GM 9274 | Bristol LD6G | 138.064 | H33/27R | 4/58 | Central SMT, Motherwell (LK) B74 |
| 10111 | GM 9275 | Bristol LD6G | 138.065 | H33/27R | 4/58 | Central SMT, Motherwell (LK) B75 |
| 10112 | GM 9276 | Bristol LD6G | 138.066 | H33/27R | 5/58 | Central SMT, Motherwell (LK) B76 |
| 10113 | GM 9277 | Bristol LD6G | 138.067 | H33/27R | 5/58 | Central SMT, Motherwell (LK) B77 |

| 10114 | GM 9278 | Bristol LD6G | 138.073 | H33/27R | 5/58 | Central SMT, Motherwell (LK) B78 |
| 10115 | GM 9279 | Bristol LD6G | 138.074 | H33/27R | 5/58 | Central SMT, Motherwell (LK) B79 |
| 10116 | GM 9280 | Bristol LD6G | 138.075 | H33/27R | 5/58 | Central SMT, Motherwell (LK) B80 |
| 10117 | GM 9281 | Bristol LD6G | 138.076 | H33/27R | 5/58 | Central SMT, Motherwell (LK) B81 |
| 10118 | GM 9282 | Bristol LD6G | 138.080 | H33/27R | 5/58 | Central SMT, Motherwell (LK) B82 |
| 10119 | GM 9283 | Bristol LD6G | 138.084 | H33/27R | 5/58 | Central SMT, Motherwell (LK) B83 |
| 10120 | GM 9284 | Bristol LD6G | 138.085 | H33/27R | 5/58 | Central SMT, Motherwell (LK) B84 |
| 10121 | GM 9285 | Bristol LD6G | 138.086 | H33/27R | 6/58 | Central SMT, Motherwell (LK) B85 |
| 10122 | GM 9286 | Bristol LD6G | 138.101 | H33/27R | 6/58 | Central SMT, Motherwell (LK) B86 |
| 10123 *GM 9287 | | Bristol LD6G | 138.102 | H33/27R | 6/58 | Central SMT, Motherwell (LK) B87 |
| 10124 | GM 9288 | Bristol LD6G | 138.103 | H33/27R | 7/58 | Central SMT, Motherwell (LK) B88 |
| 10125 | GM 9289 | Bristol LD6G | 138.110 | H33/27R | 7/58 | Central SMT, Motherwell (LK) B89 |
| 10126 | GM 9290 | Bristol LD6G | 138.111 | H33/27R | 7/58 | Central SMT, Motherwell (LK) B90 |
| 10127 | GM 9291 | Bristol LD6G | 138.112 | H33/27R | 7/58 | Central SMT, Motherwell (LK) B91 |
| 10128 | GM 9292 | Bristol LD6G | 138.119 | H33/27R | 7/58 | Central SMT, Motherwell (LK) B92 |
| 10129 | 3001 AH | Bristol SC4LK | 147.002 | B35F | 12/58 | Eastern Counties, Norwich (NK) LC554 |
| 10130 | 3002 AH | Bristol SC4LK | 147.003 | B35F | 1/59 | Eastern Counties, Norwich (NK) LC555 |
| 10131 *3003 AH | | Bristol SC4LK | 147.004 | B35F | 1/59 | Eastern Counties, Norwich (NK) LC556 |
| 10132 | LCS 341 | Bristol LD6G | 138.016 | H33/27R | 3/58 | Western SMT, Kilmarnock (AR) B1407 |
| 10133 | LCS 342 | Bristol LD6G | 138.017 | H33/27R | 3/58 | Western SMT, Kilmarnock (AR) B1408 |
| 10134 | LCS 343 | Bristol LD6G | 138.018 | H33/27R | 5/58 | Western SMT, Kilmarnock (AR) B1409 |
| 10135 | LCS 344 | Bristol LD6G | 138.083 | H33/27R | 6/58 | Western SMT, Kilmarnock (AR) B1410 |
| 10136 | LCS 345 | Bristol LD6G | 138.087 | H33/27R | 6/58 | Western SMT, Kilmarnock (AR) B1411 |
| 10137 | LCS 346 | Bristol LD6G | 138.088 | H33/27R | 6/58 | Western SMT, Kilmarnock (AR) B1412 |
| 10138 | LCS 347 | Bristol LD6G | 138.089 | H33/27R | 6/58 | Western SMT, Kilmarnock (AR) B1413 |
| 10139 | LCS 348 | Bristol LD6G | 138.120 | H33/27R | 8/58 | Western SMT, Kilmarnock (AR) B1414 |
| 10140 | LCS 349 | Bristol LD6G | 138.121 | H33/27R | 8/58 | Western SMT, Kilmarnock (AR) B1415 |
| 10141 | LCS 350 | Bristol LD6G | 138.124 | H33/27R | 8/58 | Western SMT, Kilmarnock (AR) B1416 |
| 10142 | LCS 351 | Bristol LD6G | 138.125 | H33/27R | 8/58 | Western SMT, Kilmarnock (AR) B1417 |
| 10143 | 7015 HK | Bristol MW6G | 135.104 | C39F | 5/58 | Eastern National, Chelmsford (EX) 456 |
| 10144 | 7016 HK | Bristol MW6G | 135.105 | C39F | 6/58 | Eastern National, Chelmsford (EX) 457 |
| 10145 | 7017 HK | Bristol MW6G | 139.011 | C39F | 7/58 | Eastern National, Chelmsford (EX) 458 |
| 10146 | 7018 HK | Bristol MW6G | 139.012 | C39F | 7/58 | Eastern National, Chelmsford (EX) 459 |
| 10147 | | | | | | Not built |
| 10148 | | | | | | Not built |
| 10149 | KWG 604 | Bristol LD6G | 138.093 | H33/27R | 7/58 | D Lawson Kirkintilloch (DB) RD51 |
| 10150 | KWG 605 | Bristol LD6G | 138.094 | H33/27R | 7/58 | D Lawson Kirkintilloch (DB) RD52 |
| 10151 | KWG 606 | Bristol LD6G | 138.095 | H33/27R | 7/58 | D Lawson Kirkintilloch (DB) RD53 |
| 10152 | KWG 607 | Bristol LD6G | 138.100 | H33/27R | 7/58 | D Lawson Kirkintilloch (DB) RD54 |
| 10153 | KWG 608 | Bristol LD6G | 138.107 | H33/27R | 7/58 | D Lawson Kirkintilloch (DB) RD55 |
| 10154 | KWG 609 | Bristol LD6G | 138.116 | H33/27R | 7/58 | W Alexander, Falkirk (SN) RD56 |
| 10155 | KWG 610 | Bristol LD6G | 138.117 | H33/27R | 7/58 | W Alexander, Falkirk (SN) RD57 |
| 10156 | KWG 611 | Bristol LD6G | 138.118 | H33/27R | 7/58 | W Alexander, Falkirk (SN) RD58 |
| 10157 | KWG 612 | Bristol LD6G | 138.131 | H33/27R | 9/58 | W Alexander, Falkirk (SN) RD59 |
| 10158 | KWG 613 | Bristol LD6G | 138.132 | H33/27R | 9/58 | W Alexander, Falkirk (SN) RD60 |
| 10159 | KWG 614 | Bristol LD6G | 138.138 | H33/27R | 9/58 | W Alexander, Falkirk (SN) RD61 |
| 10160 | KWG 615 | Bristol LD6G | 138.139 | H33/27R | 9/58 | W Alexander, Falkirk (SN) RD62 |
| 10161 | KWG 616 | Bristol LD6G | 138.145 | H33/27R | 9/58 | W Alexander, Falkirk (SN) RD63 |
| 10162 | KWG 617 | Bristol LD6G | 138.146 | H33/27R | 9/58 | W Alexander, Falkirk (SN) RD64 |
| 10163 | KWG 618 | Bristol LD6G | 138.152 | H33/27R | 10/58 | W Alexander, Falkirk (SN) RD65 |
| 10164 | KWG 619 | Bristol LD6G | 138.153 | H33/27R | 10/58 | W Alexander, Falkirk (SN) RD66 |
| 10165 | KWG 620 | Bristol LD6G | 138.159 | H33/27R | 10/58 | W Alexander, Falkirk (SN) RD67 |
| 10166 | KWG 621 | Bristol LD6G | 138.160 | H33/27R | 10/58 | W Alexander, Falkirk (SN) RD68 |
| 10167 | KWG 622 | Bristol LD6G | 138.164 | H33/27R | 10/58 | W Alexander, Falkirk (SN) RD69 |
| 10168 | KWG 623 | Bristol LD6G | 138.165 | H33/27R | 10/58 | W Alexander, Falkirk (SN) RD70 |
| 10169 | | | | | | Not built |
| 10170 | | | | | | Not built |
| 10171 | | | | | | Not built |
| 10172 | | | | | | Not built |
| 10173 | | | | | | Not built |
| 10174 | OPN 804 | Bristol LDS6B | 138.293 | H33/27R | 5/59 | Brighton, Hove & District (ES) 4 |
| 10175 | OPN 805 | Bristol LDS6B | 138.294 | H33/27R | 5/59 | Brighton, Hove & District (ES) 5 |
| 10176 | OPN 806 | Bristol LDS6B | 138.295 | H33/27R | 5/59 | Brighton, Hove & District (ES) 6 |
| 10177 | OPN 807 | Bristol LDS6B | 138.296 | H33/27R | 5/59 | Brighton, Hove & District (ES) 7 |

| | | | | | | |
|---|---|---|---|---|---|---|
| 10178 | OPN 808 | Bristol LDS6B | 138.297 | H33/27R | 6/59 | Brighton, Hove & District (ES) 8 |
| 10179 | OPN 801 | Bristol LDS6B | 138.298 | CO33/27R | 6/59 | Brighton, Hove & District (ES) 1 |
| 10180 | OPN 802 | Bristol LDS6B | 138.299 | CO33/27R | 6/59 | Brighton, Hove & District (ES) 2 |
| 10181 | OPN 803 | Bristol LDS6B | 138.300 | CO33/27R | 6/59 | Brighton, Hove & District (ES) 3 |
| 10182 | 811 CHU | Bristol LD6B | 138.206 | H33/25R | 11/58 | Bristol OC (GL) LC8471 |
| 10183 | 812 CHU | Bristol LD6B | 138.207 | H33/25R | 11/58 | Bristol OC (GL) LC8472 |
| 10184 | 813 CHU | Bristol LD6B | 138.208 | H33/25R | 11/58 | Bristol OC (GL) LC8473 |
| 10185 | 814 CHU | Bristol LD6B | 138.209 | H33/25R | 11/58 | Bristol OC (GL) LC8474 |
| 10186 | 815 CHU | Bristol LD6B | 138.213 | H33/25R | 11/58 | Bristol OC (GL) LC8475 |
| 10187 | 816 CHU | Bristol LD6B | 138.214 | H33/25R | 11/58 | Bristol OC (GL) LC8476 |
| 10188 | 817 CHU | Bristol LD6B | 138.225 | H33/25R | 11/58 | Bristol OC (GL) LC8477 |
| 10189 | 818 CHU | Bristol LD6B | 138.226 | H33/25R | 11/58 | Bristol OC (GL) LC8478 |
| 10190 | 819 CHU | Bristol LD6B | 138.227 | H33/25R | 11/58 | Bristol OC (GL) LC8479 |
| 10191 | 820 CHU | Bristol LD6B | 138.228 | H33/25R | 12/58 | Bristol OC (GL) LC8480 |
| 10192 | 821 CHU | Bristol LD6B | 150.005 | H33/25R | 1/59 | Bristol OC (GL) LC8490 |
| 10193 | 822 CHU | Bristol LD6B | 150.006 | H33/25R | 1/59 | Bristol OC (GL) LC8491 |
| 10194 | 823 CHU | Bristol LD6B | 150.020 | H33/25R | 1/59 | Bristol OC (GL) LC8492 |
| 10195 | 824 CHU | Bristol LD6G | 150.021 | H33/25R | 1/59 | Bristol OC (GL) LC8493 |
| 10196 | 825 CHU | Bristol LD6G | 150.027 | H33/25R | 1/59 | Bristol OC (GL) LC8494 |
| 10197 | 826 CHU | Bristol LD6B | 150.084 | H33/25R | 6/59 | Bristol OC (GL) LC8501 |
| 10198 | 827 CHU | Bristol LD6B | 150.085 | H33/25R | 6/59 | Bristol OC (GL) LC8502 |
| 10199 | 828 CHU | Bristol LD6B | 150.086 | H33/25R | 6/59 | Bristol OC (GL) LC8503 |
| 10200 | 829 CHU | Bristol LD6B | 150.087 | H33/25R | 6/59 | Bristol OC (GL) LC8504 |
| 10201 | 830 CHU | Bristol LD6B | 150.090 | H33/25R | 6/59 | Bristol OC (GL) LC8505 |
| 10202 | 831 CHU | Bristol LD6B | 150.091 | H33/25R | 6/59 | Bristol OC (GL) LC8506 |
| 10203 | 832 CHU | Bristol LD6B | 138.180 | H33/25RD | 10/58 | Bristol OC (GL) L8466 |
| 10204 | 833 CHU | Bristol LD6B | 138.181 | H33/25RD | 10/58 | Bristol OC (GL) L8467 |
| 10205 | 834 CHU | Bristol LD6G | 138.185 | H33/25RD | 10/58 | Bristol OC (GL) L8468 |
| 10206 | 835 CHU | Bristol LD6G | 138.186 | H33/25RD | 10/58 | Bristol OC (GL) L8469 |
| 10207 | 836 CHU | Bristol LD6G | 138.192 | H33/25RD | 10/58 | Bristol OC (GL) L8470 |
| 10208 | 837 CHU | Bristol LD6G | 138.193 | H33/25RD | 11/58 | Bristol OC (GL) L8481 |
| 10209 | 838 CHU | Bristol LD6G | 138.232 | H33/25RD | 12/58 | Bristol OC (GL) L8482 |
| 10210 | 839 CHU | Bristol LD6G | 138.233 | H33/25RD | 12/58 | Bristol OC (GL) L8483 |
| 10211 | 840 CHU | Bristol LD6G | 138.252 | H33/25RD | 12/58 | Bristol OC (GL) L8484 |
| 10212 | 850 CHU | Bristol LD6G | 138.253 | H33/25RD | 12/58 | Bristol OC (GL) L8485 |
| 10213 | 851 CHU | Bristol LD6G | 138.259 | H33/25RD | 12/58 | Bath Electric Tramways (SO) L8486 |
| 10214 | 852 CHU | Bristol LD6G | 138.260 | H33/25RD | 1/59 | Bath Electric Tramways (SO) L8487 |
| 10215 | 853 CHU | Bristol LD6B | 138.291 | H33/25RD | 2/59 | Bristol OC (GL) L8488 |
| 10216 | 854 CHU | Bristol LD6B | 138.292 | H33/25RD | 2/59 | Bristol OC (GL) L8489 |
| 10217 | 855 CHU | Bristol LD6G | 138.283 | H33/25RD | 2/59 | Bristol OC (GL) L8495 |
| 10218 | 856 CHU | Bristol LD6G | 138.284 | H33/25RD | 2/59 | Bath Electric Tramways (SO) L8496 |
| 10219 | 857 CHU | Bristol LD6G | 150.016 | H33/25RD | 2/59 | Bristol OC (GL) L8497 |
| 10220 | 858 CHU | Bristol LD6G | 150.017 | H33/25RD | 2/59 | Bristol OC (GL) L8498 |
| 10221 | 859 CHU | Bristol LD6G | 150.018 | H33/25RD | 3/59 | Bristol OC (GL) L8499 |
| 10222 | 860 CHU | Bristol LD6G | 150.019 | H33/25RD | 3/59 | Bristol OC (GL) L8500 |
| 10223 | | | | | | Not built |
| 10224 | 286 HFM | Bristol LD6G | 138.182 | H33/27RD | 11/58 | Crosville MS, Chester (CH) DLG950 |
| 10225 | *287 HFM | Bristol LD6G | 138.183 | H33/27RD | 11/58 | Crosville MS, Chester (CH) DLG951 |
| 10226 | 288 HFM | Bristol LD6G | 138.184 | H33/27RD | 11/58 | Crosville MS, Chester (CH) DLG952 |
| 10227 | 289 HFM | Bristol LD6G | 138.187 | H33/27RD | 11/58 | Crosville MS, Chester (CH) DLG953 |
| 10228 | 290 HFM | Bristol LD6G | 138.215 | H33/27RD | 12/58 | Crosville MS, Chester (CH) DLG954 |
| 10229 | 291 HFM | Bristol LD6G | 138.216 | H33/27RD | 12/58 | Crosville MS, Chester (CH) DLG955 |
| 10230 | 292 HFM | Bristol LD6G | 138.217 | H33/27RD | 12/58 | Crosville MS, Chester (CH) DLG956 |
| 10231 | 612 HFM | Bristol LD6B | 138.218 | H33/27RD | 12/58 | Crosville MS, Chester (CH) DLB963 |
| 10232 | 613 HFM | Bristol LD6B | 138.219 | H33/27RD | 12/58 | Crosville MS, Chester (CH) DLB964 |
| 10233 | 614 HFM | Bristol LD6B | 138.220 | H33/27RD | 12/58 | Crosville MS, Chester (CH) DLB965 |
| 10234 | 615 HFM | Bristol LD6B | 138.234 | H33/27RD | 12/58 | Crosville MS, Chester (CH) DLB966 |
| 10235 | 616 HFM | Bristol LD6B | 138.235 | H33/27RD | 12/58 | Crosville MS, Chester (CH) DLB967 |
| 10236 | 617 HFM | Bristol LD6B | 138.239 | H33/27RD | 12/58 | Crosville MS, Chester (CH) DLB968 |
| 10237 | 293 HFM | Bristol LD6G | 138.246 | H33/27RD | 12/58 | Crosville MS, Chester (CH) DLG957 |
| 10238 | 294 HFM | Bristol LD6G | 138.247 | H33/27RD | 12/58 | Crosville MS, Chester (CH) DLG958 |
| 10239 | 295 HFM | Bristol LD6G | 138.248 | H33/27RD | 12/58 | Crosville MS, Chester (CH) DLG959 |
| 10240 | *296 HFM | Bristol LD6G | 138.254 | H33/27RD | 12/58 | Crosville MS, Chester (CH) DLG960 |
| 10241 | 297 HFM | Bristol LD6G | 138.261 | H33/27RD | 1/59 | Crosville MS, Chester (CH) DLG961 |

| 10242 | 298 HFM | Bristol LD6G | 138.262 | H33/27RD | 1/59 | Crosville MS, Chester (CH) DLG962 |
|---|---|---|---|---|---|---|
| 10243 | 618 HFM | Bristol LD6B | 150.001 | H33/27RD | 2/59 | Crosville MS, Chester (CH) DLB969 |
| 10244 | 619 HFM | Bristol LD6B | 150.002 | H33/27RD | 2/59 | Crosville MS, Chester (CH) DLB970 |
| 10245 | 620 HFM | Bristol LD6B | 150.003 | H33/27RD | 2/59 | Crosville MS, Chester (CH) DLB971 |
| 10246 | 623 HFM | Bristol LD6B | 150.047 | H33/27RD | 3/59 | Crosville MS, Chester (CH) DLB974 |
| 10247 | 621 HFM | Bristol LD6B | 150.044 | H33/27RD | 3/59 | Crosville MS, Chester (CH) DLB972 |
| 10248 | 622 HFM | Bristol LD6B | 150.045 | H33/27RD | 3/59 | Crosville MS, Chester (CH) DLB973 |
| 10249 | 624 HFM | Bristol LD6B | 150.048 | H33/27RD | 3/59 | Crosville MS, Chester (CH) DLB975 |
| 10250 | 625 HFM | Bristol LD6B | 150.055 | H33/27RD | 3/59 | Crosville MS, Chester (CH) DLB976 |
| 10251 | 632 HFM | Bristol LD6B | 150.076 | H33/27RD | 6/59 | Crosville MS, Chester (CH) DLB983 |
| 10252 | 633 HFM | Bristol LD6B | 150.077 | H33/27RD | 6/59 | Crosville MS, Chester (CH) DLB984 |
| 10253 | 634 HFM | Bristol LD6B | 150.078 | H33/27RD | 6/59 | Crosville MS, Chester (CH) DLB985 |
| 10254 | 635 HFM | Bristol LD6B | 150.097 | H33/27RD | 7/59 | Crosville MS, Chester (CH) DLB986 |
| 10255 | 636 HFM | Bristol LD6B | 150.098 | H33/27RD | 7/59 | Crosville MS, Chester (CH) DLB987 |
| 10256 | 637 HFM | Bristol LD6B | 150.099 | H33/27RD | 7/59 | Crosville MS, Chester (CH) DLB988 |
| 10257 | 638 HFM | Bristol LD6B | 150.129 | H33/27RD | 7/59 | Crosville MS, Chester (CH) DLB989 |
| 10258 | 639 HFM | Bristol LD6B | 150.130 | H33/27RD | 7/59 | Crosville MS, Chester (CH) DLB990 |
| 10259 | 626 HFM | Bristol LD6B | 150.067 | CO33/27RD | 7/59 | Crosville MS, Chester (CH) DLB977 |
| 10260 | 627 HFM | Bristol LD6B | 150.068 | CO33/27RD | 7/59 | Crosville MS, Chester (CH) DLB978 |
| 10261 | 628 HFM | Bristol LD6B | 150.072 | CO33/27RD | 7/59 | Crosville MS, Chester (CH) DLB979 |
| 10262 | 629 HFM | Bristol LD6B | 150.073 | CO33/27RD | 7/59 | Crosville MS, Chester (CH) DLB980 |
| 10263 | 630 HFM | Bristol LD6B | 150.074 | CO33/27RD | 6/59 | Crosville MS, Chester (CH) DLB981 |
| 10264 | 631 HFM | Bristol LD6B | 150.075 | CO33/27RD | 6/59 | Crosville MS, Chester (CH) DLB982 |
| 10265 | VAO 383 | Bristol LD6G | 138.061 | H33/27RD | 3/58 | Cumberland MS, Whitehaven (CU) 383 |
| 10266 | VAO 384 | Bristol LD6G | 138.062 | H33/27RD | 4/58 | Cumberland MS, Whitehaven (CU) 384 |
| 10267 | VAO 385 | Bristol LD6G | 138.063 | H33/27RD | 6/58 | Cumberland MS, Whitehaven (CU) 385 |
| 10268 | VAO 386 | Bristol LD6G | 138.068 | H33/27RD | 6/58 | Cumberland MS, Whitehaven (CU) 386 |
| 10269 | VAO 387 | Bristol LD6B | 150.058 | H33/27R | 3/59 | Cumberland MS, Whitehaven (CU) 387 |
| 10270 | VAO 388 | Bristol LD6B | 150.060 | H33/27R | 3/59 | Cumberland MS, Whitehaven (CU) 388 |
| 10271 | VAO 389 | Bristol LD6B | 150.063 | H33/27R | 3/59 | Cumberland MS, Whitehaven (CU) 389 |
| 10272 | 351 LPU | Bristol LD5G | 138.199 | H33/27R | 10/58 | Eastern National, Chelmsford (EX) 1545 |
| 10273 | 352 LPU | Bristol LD5G | 138.200 | H33/27R | 10/58 | Eastern National, Chelmsford (EX) 1546 |
| 10274 | 353 LPU | Bristol LD5G | 138.201 | H33/27R | 10/58 | Eastern National, Chelmsford (EX) 1547 |
| 10275 | 354 LPU | Bristol LD5G | 138.240 | H33/27R | 11/58 | Eastern National, Chelmsford (EX) 1548 |
| 10276 | 355 LPU | Bristol LD5G | 138.241 | H33/27R | 11/58 | Eastern National, Chelmsford (EX) 1549 |
| 10277 | 356 LPU | Bristol LD5G | 138.242 | H33/27R | 11/58 | Eastern National, Chelmsford (EX) 1550 |
| 10278 | 357 LPU | Bristol LD5G | 138.243 | H33/27R | 12/58 | Eastern National, Chelmsford (EX) 1551 |
| 10279 | 358 LPU | Bristol LD5G | 150.007 | H33/27R | 1/59 | Eastern National, Chelmsford (EX) 1552 |
| 10280 | 359 LPU | Bristol LD5G | 150.012 | H33/27R | 1/59 | Eastern National, Chelmsford (EX) 1553 |
| 10281 | 360 LPU | Bristol LD5G | 150.106 | H33/27R | 5/59 | Eastern National, Chelmsford (EX) 1554 |
| 10282 | XEL 541 | Bristol LD6G | 138.194 | H33/27R | 10/58 | Hants & Dorset, Bournemouth (HA) 1407 |
| 10283 | XEL 542 | Bristol LD6G | 138.195 | H33/27R | 10/58 | Hants & Dorset, Bournemouth (HA) 1408 |
| 10284 | XEL 543 | Bristol LD6G | 138.255 | H33/27RD | 12/58 | Hants & Dorset, Bournemouth (HA) 1409 |
| 10285 | XEL 544 | Bristol LD6G | 138.256 | H33/27RD | 12/58 | Hants & Dorset, Bournemouth (HA) 1410 |
| 10286 | XEL 545 | Bristol LD6B | 138.289 | H33/27RD | 1/59 | Hants & Dorset, Bournemouth (HA) 1411 |
| 10287 | XEL 546 | Bristol LD6B | 138.290 | H33/27RD | 1/59 | Hants & Dorset, Bournemouth (HA) 1412 |
| 10288 | XEL 547 | Bristol LD6G | 150.030 | H33/27RD | 3/59 | Hants & Dorset, Bournemouth (HA) 1413 |
| 10289 | XEL 548 | Bristol LD6G | 150.038 | H33/27RD | 4/59 | Hants & Dorset, Bournemouth (HA) 1414 |
| 10290 | XEL 549 | Bristol LD6B | 150.107 | H33/27RD | 5/59 | Hants & Dorset, Bournemouth (HA) 1415 |
| 10291 | XEL 550 | Bristol LD6B | 150.131 | H33/27RD | 6/59 | Hants & Dorset, Bournemouth (HA) 1416 |
| 10292 | SFU 304 | Bristol LD5G | 138.202 | H33/27RD | 10/58 | Lincolnshire RCC, Bracebridge Heath (KN) 2350 |
| 10293 | SFU 305 | Bristol LD5G | 138.203 | H33/27RD | 10/58 | Lincolnshire RCC, Bracebridge Heath (KN) 2351 |
| 10294 | SFU 306 | Bristol LD5G | 138.204 | H33/27RD | 11/58 | Lincolnshire RCC, Bracebridge Heath (KN) 2352 |
| 10295 | SFU 307 | Bristol LD5G | 138.229 | H33/27RD | 11/58 | Lincolnshire RCC, Bracebridge Heath (KN) 2353 |
| 10296 | SFU 308 | Bristol LD5G | 138.230 | H33/27RD | 11/58 | Lincolnshire RCC, Bracebridge Heath (KN) 2354 |
| 10297 | SFU 314 | Bristol LD5G | 150.013 | H33/27RD | 1/59 | Lincolnshire RCC, Bracebridge Heath (KN) 2360 |
| 10298 | SFU 315 | Bristol LD5G | 150.014 | H33/27RD | 1/59 | Lincolnshire RCC, Bracebridge Heath (KN) 2361 |

| | | | | | | |
|---|---|---|---|---|---|---|
| 10299 | SFU 316 | Bristol LD5G | 150.015 | H33/27RD | 1/59 | Lincolnshire RCC, Bracebridge Heath (KN) 2362 |
| 10300 | SFU 317 | Bristol LD5G | 150.113 | H33/27RD | 6/59 | Lincolnshire RCC, Lincoln (LC) 2363 |
| 10301 | SFU 318 | Bristol LD5G | 150.114 | H33/27RD | 6/59 | Lincolnshire RCC, Lincoln (LC) 2364 |
| 10302 | 213 ANN | Bristol LD6G | 138.188 | H33/25RD | 11/58 | Mansfield District (NG) 516 |
| 10303 | 214 ANN | Bristol LD6G | 138.189 | H33/25RD | 11/58 | Mansfield District (NG) 517 |
| 10304 | 215 ANN | Bristol LD6G | 138.273 | H33/25RD | 12/58 | Mansfield District (NG) 518 |
| 10305 | 216 ANN | Bristol LD6G | 138.274 | H33/25RD | 12/58 | Mansfield District (NG) 519 |
| 10306 | 259 HNU | Bristol LD6G | 138.236 | H33/25RD | 12/58 | Midland General, Langley Mill (DE) 474 |
| 10307 | 260 HNU | Bristol LD6G | 138.237 | H33/25RD | 12/58 | Midland General, Langley Mill (DE) 475 |
| 10308 | 261 HNU | Bristol LD6G | 138.238 | H33/25RD | 12/58 | Midland General, Langley Mill (DE) 476 |
| 10309 | PDL 516 | Bristol LD6G | 138.104 | H33/27R | 6/58 | Southern Vectis, Newport (IW) 556 |
| 10310 | PDL 517 | Bristol LD6G | 138.105 | H33/27R | 6/58 | Southern Vectis, Newport (IW) 557 |
| 10311 | PDL 518 | Bristol LD6G | 138.106 | H33/27R | 6/58 | Southern Vectis, Newport (IW) 558 |
| 10312 | PDL 519 | Bristol LD6G | 138.108 | H33/27R | 6/58 | Southern Vectis, Newport (IW) 559 |
| 10313 | PRX 926 | Bristol LD6G | 138.190 | H33/27RD | 10/58 | Thames Valley, Reading (BE) 808 |
| 10314 | PRX 927 | Bristol LD6G | 138.191 | H33/27RD | 10/58 | Thames Valley, Reading (BE) 809 |
| 10315 | PRX 928 | Bristol LD6B | 150.008 | H33/27RD | 1/59 | Thames Valley, Reading (BE) 810 |
| 10316 | PRX 929 | Bristol LD6B | 150.009 | H33/27RD | 1/59 | Thames Valley, Reading (BE) 811 |
| 10317 | 993 GHN | Bristol LD6B | 138.196 | H33/27RD | 3/59 | United AS, Darlington (DM) BL28 |
| 10318 | 994 GHN | Bristol LD6B | 138.197 | H33/27RD | 3/59 | United AS, Darlington (DM) BL29 |
| 10319 | 995 GHN | Bristol LD6B | 138.198 | H33/27RD | 3/59 | United AS, Darlington (DM) BL30 |
| 10320 | 996 GHN | Bristol LD6B | 138.210 | H33/27RD | 3/59 | United AS, Darlington (DM) BL31 |
| 10321 | 997 GHN | Bristol LD6B | 138.221 | H33/27RD | 3/59 | United AS, Darlington (DM) BL32 |
| 10322 | 998 GHN | Bristol LD6B | 138.222 | H33/27RD | 3/59 | United AS, Darlington (DM) BL33 |
| 10323 | 999 GHN | Bristol LD6B | 138.244 | H33/27RD | 3/59 | United AS, Darlington (DM) BL34 |
| 10324 | 10 HHN | Bristol LD6B | 138.245 | H33/27RD | 3/59 | United AS, Darlington (DM) BL35 |
| 10325 | 11 HHN | Bristol LD6B | 138.249 | H33/27RD | 3/59 | United AS, Darlington (DM) BL36 |
| 10326 | 12 HHN | Bristol LD6B | 138.277 | H33/27RD | 3/59 | United AS, Darlington (DM) BL37 |
| 10327 | 13 HHN | Bristol LD6B | 138.278 | H33/27RD | 3/59 | United AS, Darlington (DM) BL38 |
| 10328 | 14 HHN | Bristol LD6B | 138.282 | H33/27RD | 3/59 | United AS, Darlington (DM) BL39 |
| 10329 | 15 HHN | Bristol LD6B | 150.039 | H33/27RD | 7/59 | United AS, Darlington (DM) BL40 |
| 10330 | 16 HHN | Bristol LD6B | 150.115 | H33/27RD | 6/59 | United AS, Darlington (DM) BL41 |
| 10331 | SBD 545 | Bristol LD6B | 138.211 | H33/27RD | 11/58 | United Counties, Northampton (NO) 545 |
| 10332 | SBD 546 | Bristol LD6B | 138.212 | H33/27RD | 11/58 | United Counties, Northampton (NO) 546 |
| 10333 | SBD 547 | Bristol LD6B | 138.223 | H33/27RD | 12/58 | United Counties, Northampton (NO) 547 |
| 10334 | SBD 548 | Bristol LD6B | 138.224 | H33/27RD | 12/58 | United Counties, Northampton (NO) 548 |
| 10335 | SBD 549 | Bristol LD6B | 138.231 | H33/27RD | 12/58 | United Counties, Northampton (NO) 549 |
| 10336 | SBD 550 | Bristol LD6B | 138.250 | H33/27RD | 3/59 | United Counties, Northampton (NO) 550 |
| 10337 | SBD 551 | Bristol LD6B | 150.004 | H33/27RD | 1/59 | United Counties, Northampton (NO) 551 |
| 10338 | SBD 552 | Bristol LD6B | 150.010 | H33/27RD | 1/59 | United Counties, Northampton (NO) 552 |
| 10339 | SBD 553 | Bristol LD6B | 150.011 | H33/27RD | 3/59 | United Counties, Northampton (NO) 553 |
| 10340 | SBD 554 | Bristol LD6B | 150.046 | H33/27RD | 4/59 | United Counties, Northampton (NO) 554 |
| 10341 | SBD 555 | Bristol LD6B | 150.088 | H33/27RD | 6/59 | United Counties, Northampton (NO) 555 |
| 10342 | SBD 556 | Bristol LD6B | 150.122 | H33/27RD | 6/59 | United Counties, Northampton (NO) 556 |
| 10343 | SWN 154 | Bristol LD6G | 138.205 | H33/27RD | 12/58 | United Welsh, Swansea (GG) 318 |
| 10344 | SWN 155 | Bristol LD6G | 138.251 | H33/27RD | 12/58 | United Welsh, Swansea (GG) 319 |
| 10345 | SWN 156 | Bristol LD6G | 150.025 | H33/27RD | 1/59 | United Welsh, Swansea (GG) 320 |
| 10346 | SWN 157 | Bristol LD6G | 150.031 | H33/27RD | 5/59 | United Welsh, Swansea (GG) 321 |
| 10347 | SWN 158 | Bristol LD6G | 150.040 | H33/27RD | 6/59 | United Welsh, Swansea (GG) 322 |
| 10348 | *SWN 159 | Bristol LD6G | 150.051 | H33/27R | 6/59 | United Welsh, Swansea (GG) 323 |
| 10349 | SWN 160 | Bristol LD6G | 150.123 | H33/27R | 6/59 | United Welsh, Swansea (GG) 324 |
| 10350 | SHR 440 | Bristol LD6G | 138.257 | H33/27RD | 12/58 | Wilts & Dorset, Salisbury (WI) 634 |
| 10351 | SHR 441 | Bristol LD6G | 138.258 | H33/27RD | 12/58 | Wilts & Dorset, Salisbury (WI) 635 |
| 10352 | 971 DAE | Bristol MW5G | 139.137 | DP41F | 12/58 | Bristol OC (GL) 2951 |
| 10353 | 972 DAE | Bristol MW5G | 139.138 | DP41F | 12/58 | Bristol OC (GL) 2952 |
| 10354 | 973 DAE | Bristol MW5G | 139.148 | DP41F | 1/59 | Bristol OC (GL) 2953 |
| 10355 | 974 DAE | Bristol MW5G | 139.149 | DP41F | 1/59 | Bristol OC (GL) 2954 |
| 10356 | 975 DAE | Bristol MW5G | 139.167 | DP41F | 1/59 | Bristol OC (GL) 2955 |
| 10357 | 976 DAE | Bristol MW5G | 139.168 | DP41F | 2/59 | Bristol OC (GL) 2956 |
| 10358 | 977 DAE | Bristol MW5G | 139.174 | B45F | 2/59 | Bristol OC (GL) G2957 |
| 10359 | 978 DAE | Bristol MW5G | 139.175 | B45F | 2/59 | Bristol OC (GL) G2958 |
| 10360 | 979 DAE | Bristol MW5G | 139.195 | B45F | 2/59 | Bristol OC (GL) 2959 |
| 10361 | 980 DAE | Bristol MW5G | 139.196 | B45F | 2/59 | Bristol OC (GL) 2960 |

| | | | | | | |
|---|---|---|---|---|---|---|
| 10362 | 981 DAE | Bristol MW5G | 139.197 | B45F | 2/59 | Bristol OC (GL) 2961 |
| 10363 | 982 DAE | Bristol MW5G | 139.198 | B45F | 4/59 | Bristol OC (GL) 2962 |
| 10364 | 983 DAE | Bristol MW5G | 139.223 | B45F | 4/59 | Bristol OC (GL) 2963 |
| 10365 | 984 DAE | Bristol MW5G | 139.224 | B45F | 4/59 | Bristol OC (GL) 2964 |
| 10366 | 985 DAE | Bristol MW5G | 139.225 | B45F | 4/59 | Bristol OC (GL) 2965 |
| 10367 | 986 DAE | Bristol MW5G | 139.232 | B45F | 5/59 | Bristol OC (GL) 2966 |
| 10368 | 987 DAE | Bristol MW5G | 139.297 | B45F | 7/59 | Bristol OC (GL) 2967 |
| 10369 | 988 DAE | Bristol MW5G | 139.298 | B45F | 7/59 | Bristol OC (GL) 2968 |
| 10370 | 3004 AH | Bristol MW5G | 139.150 | B45F | 3/59 | Eastern Counties, Norwich (NK) LL442 |
| 10371 | 3005 AH | Bristol MW5G | 139.151 | B45F | 3/59 | Eastern Counties, Norwich (NK) LL443 |
| 10372 | 3006 AH | Bristol MW5G | 139.152 | B45F | 3/59 | Eastern Counties, Norwich (NK) LL444 |
| 10373 | 3007 AH | Bristol MW5G | 139.153 | B45F | 3/59 | Eastern Counties, Norwich (NK) LL445 |
| 10374 | 3008 AH | Bristol MW5G | 139.176 | B45F | 3/59 | Eastern Counties, Norwich (NK) LL446 |
| 10375 | 3009 AH | Bristol MW5G | 139.177 | B45F | 3/59 | Eastern Counties, Norwich (NK) LL447 |
| 10376 | 3010 AH | Bristol MW5G | 139.178 | B45F | 3/59 | Eastern Counties, Norwich (NK) LL448 |
| 10377 | 3011 AH | Bristol MW5G | 139.179 | B45F | 3/59 | Eastern Counties, Norwich (NK) LL449 |
| 10378 | 3012 AH | Bristol MW5G | 139.202 | B45F | 3/59 | Eastern Counties, Norwich (NK) LL450 |
| 10379 | 3013 AH | Bristol MW5G | 139.226 | B45F | 3/59 | Eastern Counties, Norwich (NK) LL451 |
| 10380 | 3014 AH | Bristol MW5G | 139.227 | B45F | 3/59 | Eastern Counties, Norwich (NK) LL452 |
| 10381 | 3015 AH | Bristol MW5G | 152.014 | B45F | 6/59 | Eastern Counties, Norwich (NK) LL453 |
| 10382 | 3016 AH | Bristol MW5G | 152.015 | B45F | 6/59 | Eastern Counties, Norwich (NK) LL454 |
| 10383 | 3017 AH | Bristol MW5G | 152.016 | B45F | 6/59 | Eastern Counties, Norwich (NK) LL455 |
| 10384 | 3018 AH | Bristol MW5G | 152.017 | B45F | 6/59 | Eastern Counties, Norwich (NK) LL456 |
| 10385 | 3019 AH | Bristol MW5G | 152.018 | B45F | 6/59 | Eastern Counties, Norwich (NK) LL457 |
| 10386 | 3020 AH | Bristol MW5G | 152.019 | B45F | 6/59 | Eastern Counties, Norwich (NK) LL458 |
| 10387 | 201 MHK | Bristol MW5G | 139.154 | B41F | 12/58 | Eastern National, Chelmsford (EX) 464 |
| 10388 | 202 MHK | Bristol MW5G | 139.155 | B41F | 12/58 | Eastern National, Chelmsford (EX) 465 |
| 10389 | 203 MHK | Bristol MW5G | 139.156 | B41F | 12/58 | Eastern National, Chelmsford (EX) 466 |
| 10390 | 204 MHK | Bristol MW5G | 139.157 | B41F | 12/58 | Eastern National, Chelmsford (EX) 467 |
| 10391 | 205 MHK | Bristol MW5G | 139.180 | B41F | 12/58 | Eastern National, Chelmsford (EX) 468 |
| 10392 | 206 MHK | Bristol MW5G | 139.181 | B41F | 12/58 | Eastern National, Chelmsford (EX) 469 |
| 10393 | 207 MHK | Bristol MW5G | 139.187 | B41F | 12/58 | Eastern National, Chelmsford (EX) 470 |
| 10394 | 208 MHK | Bristol MW5G | 139.188 | B41F | 12/58 | Eastern National, Chelmsford (EX) 471 |
| 10395 | 209 MHK | Bristol MW5G | 139.213 | B41F | 1/59 | Eastern National, Chelmsford (EX) 472 |
| 10396 | 210 MHK | Bristol MW5G | 139.214 | B41F | 1/59 | Eastern National, Chelmsford (EX) 473 |
| 10397 | 211 MHK | Bristol MW5G | 139.218 | B41F | 1/59 | Eastern National, Chelmsford (EX) 474 |
| 10398 | 212 MHK | Bristol MW5G | 139.228 | B41F | 2/59 | Eastern National, Chelmsford (EX) 475 |
| 10399 | 213 MHK | Bristol MW5G | 139.229 | B41F | 2/59 | Eastern National, Chelmsford (EX) 476 |
| 10400 | 214 MHK | Bristol MW5G | 139.230 | B41F | 3/59 | Eastern National, Chelmsford (EX) 477 |
| 10401 | 215 MHK | Bristol MW5G | 152.010 | DP41F | 7/59 | Eastern National, Chelmsford (EX) 478 |
| 10402 | 216 MHK | Bristol MW5G | 152.011 | DP41F | 7/59 | Eastern National, Chelmsford (EX) 479 |
| 10403 | 217 MHK | Bristol MW5G | 152.012 | DP41F | 7/59 | Eastern National, Chelmsford (EX) 480 |
| 10404 | XEL 551 | Bristol MW5G | 139.139 | B45F | 12/58 | Hants & Dorset, Bournemouth (HA) 809 |
| 10405 | XEL 552 | Bristol MW5G | 139.161 | B45F | 12/58 | Hants & Dorset, Bournemouth (HA) 810 |
| 10406 | XEL 553 | Bristol MW5G | 139.162 | B45F | 12/58 | Hants & Dorset, Bournemouth (HA) 811 |
| 10407 | SFU 844 | Bristol MW5G | 139.132 | DP41F | 11/58 | Lincolnshire RCC, Bracebridge Heath (KN) 3017 |
| 10408 | SFU 845 | Bristol MW5G | 139.133 | DP41F | 11/58 | Lincolnshire RCC, Bracebridge Heath (KN) 3018 |
| 10409 | SFU 846 | Bristol MW5G | 139.134 | DP41F | 11/58 | Lincolnshire RCC, Bracebridge Heath (KN) 3019 |
| 10410 | SFU 847 | Bristol MW5G | 139.135 | DP41F | 11/58 | Lincolnshire RCC, Bracebridge Heath (KN) 3020 |
| 10411 | SFU 848 | Bristol MW5G | 139.136 | DP41F | 11/58 | Lincolnshire RCC, Bracebridge Heath (KN) 3021 |
| 10412 | SFU 853 | Bristol MW5G | 139.191 | B45F | 1/59 | Lincolnshire RCC, Bracebridge Heath (KN) 2228 |
| 10413 | SFU 854 | Bristol MW5G | 139.192 | B45F | 1/59 | Lincolnshire RCC, Bracebridge Heath (KN) 2229 |
| 10414 | SFU 855 | Bristol MW5G | 139.231 | B45F | 2/59 | Lincolnshire RCC, Lincoln (LC) 2230 |
| 10415 | SFU 856 | Bristol MW5G | 152.004 | B45F | 6/59 | Lincolnshire RCC, Lincoln (LC) 2231 |
| 10416 | UAX 556 | Bristol MW6G | 139.158 | B45F | 1/59 | Red & White, Chepstow (MH) U159 |
| 10417 | UAX 557 | Bristol MW6G | 139.159 | B45F | 1/59 | Red & White, Chepstow (MH) U259 |
| 10418 | UAX 558 | Bristol MW6G | 139.160 | B45F | 1/59 | Red & White, Chepstow (MH) U359 |

| | | | | | | | |
|---|---|---|---|---|---|---|---|
| 10419 | UAX 559 | Bristol MW6G | 139.182 | B45F | 2/59 | Red & White, Chepstow (MH) | U459 |
| 10420 | UAX 560 | Bristol MW6G | 139.183 | B45F | 2/59 | Red & White, Chepstow (MH) | U559 |
| 10421 | UAX 561 | Bristol MW6G | 139.184 | B45F | 3/59 | Red & White, Chepstow (MH) | U659 |
| 10422 | UAX 562 | Bristol MW6G | 139.207 | B45F | 3/59 | Red & White, Chepstow (MH) | U759 |
| 10423 | UAX 563 | Bristol MW6G | 139.208 | B45F | 3/59 | Red & White, Chepstow (MH) | U859 |
| 10424 | UAX 564 | Bristol MW6G | 139.209 | B45F | 3/59 | Red & White, Chepstow (MH) | U959 |
| 10425 | UAX 565 | Bristol MW6G | 139.219 | B45F | 3/59 | Red & White, Chepstow (MH) | U1059 |
| 10426 | UAX 566 | Bristol MW6G | 139.220 | B45F | 3/59 | Red & White, Chepstow (MH) | U1159 |
| 10427 | UAX 567 | Bristol MW6G | 139.233 | B45F | 3/59 | Red & White, Chepstow (MH) | U1259 |
| 10428 | UAX 568 | Bristol MW6G | 139.234 | B45F | 3/59 | Red & White, Chepstow (MH) | U1359 |
| 10429 | UAX 569 | Bristol MW6G | 152.013 | B45F | 8/59 | Red & White, Chepstow (MH) | U1459 |
| 10430 | 523 JHN | Bristol MW5G | 139.140 | B45F | 3/59 | United AS, Darlington (DM) | BU523 |
| 10431 | 524 JHN | Bristol MW5G | 139.163 | B45F | 3/59 | United AS, Darlington (DM) | BU524 |
| 10432 | 525 JHN | Bristol MW5G | 139.164 | B45F | 3/59 | United AS, Darlington (DM) | BU525 |
| 10433 | 526 JHN | Bristol MW5G | 139.165 | B45F | 3/59 | United AS, Darlington (DM) | BU526 |
| 10434 | 527 JHN | Bristol MW5G | 139.166 | B45F | 3/59 | United AS, Darlington (DM) | BU527 |
| 10435 | *928 JHN | Bristol MW5G | 139.193 | B45F | 3/59 | United AS, Darlington (DM) | BU528 |
| 10436 | *929 JHN | Bristol MW5G | 139.194 | B45F | 3/59 | United AS, Darlington (DM) | BU529 |
| 10437 | *930 JHN | Bristol MW5G | 139.199 | B45F | 3/59 | United AS, Darlington (DM) | BU530 |
| 10438 | *931 JHN | Bristol MW5G | 139.200 | B45F | 3/59 | United AS, Darlington (DM) | BU531 |
| 10439 | *932 JHN | Bristol MW5G | 139.235 | B45F | 3/59 | United AS, Darlington (DM) | BU532 |
| 10440 | *933 JHN | Bristol MW5G | 139.236 | B45F | 3/59 | United AS, Darlington (DM) | BU533 |
| 10441 | *934 JHN | Bristol MW5G | 139.237 | B45F | 3/59 | United AS, Darlington (DM) | BU534 |
| 10442 | *935 JHN | Bristol MW5G | 139.299 | B45F | 7/59 | United AS, Darlington (DM) | BU535 |
| 10443 | *936 JHN | Bristol MW5G | 139.300 | B45F | 7/59 | United AS, Darlington (DM) | BU536 |
| 10444 | SRP 134 | Bristol MW6G | 139.116 | DP41F | 1/59 | United Counties, Northampton (NO) | 134 |
| 10445 | SRP 135 | Bristol MW6G | 139.117 | DP41F | 1/59 | United Counties, Northampton (NO) | 135 |
| 10446 | SRP 136 | Bristol MW6G | 139.128 | DP41F | 1/59 | United Counties, Northampton (NO) | 136 |
| 10447 | TBD 137 | Bristol MW6G | 139.129 | DP41F | 4/59 | United Counties, Northampton (NO) | 137 |
| 10448 | SWN 150 | Bristol MW6G | 139.169 | B41F | 1/59 | United Welsh, Swansea (GG) | 113 |
| 10449 | SWN 151 | Bristol MW6G | 139.170 | B41F | 2/59 | United Welsh, Swansea (GG) | 114 |
| 10450 | SWN 152 | Bristol MW6G | 139.221 | B41F | 3/59 | United Welsh, Swansea (GG) | 115 |
| 10451 | SWN 153 | Bristol MW6G | 139.222 | B41F | 3/59 | United Welsh, Swansea (GG) | 116 |
| 10452 | 901 AUO | Bristol MW5G | 139.141 | B45F | 12/58 | Western National, Exeter (DN) | 2603 |
| 10453 | 902 AUO | Bristol MW5G | 139.142 | B45F | 12/58 | Western National, Exeter (DN) | 2604 |
| 10454 | 903 AUO | Bristol MW5G | 139.147 | B45F | 12/58 | Western National, Exeter (DN) | 2605 |
| 10455 | 904 AUO | Bristol MW5G | 139.171 | B45F | 2/59 | Western National, Exeter (DN) | 2606 |
| 10456 | 905 AUO | Bristol MW5G | 139.172 | B45F | 2/59 | Western National, Exeter (DN) | 2607 |
| 10457 | 906 AUO | Bristol MW5G | 139.173 | B45F | 2/59 | Western National, Exeter (DN) | 2608 |
| 10458 | 907 AUO | Bristol MW5G | 139.201 | B45F | 3/59 | Western National, Exeter (DN) | 2609 |
| 10459 | 908 AUO | Bristol MW5G | 139.211 | B45F | 3/59 | Western National, Exeter (DN) | 2610 |
| 10460 | 909 AUO | Bristol MW5G | 139.212 | B45F | 3/59 | Western National, Exeter (DN) | 2611 |
| 10461 | 910 AUO | Bristol MW5G | 139.238 | B45F | 3/59 | Western National, Exeter (DN) | 2612 |
| 10462 | 911 AUO | Bristol MW5G | 139.239 | B45F | 3/59 | Western National, Exeter (DN) | 2613 |
| 10463 | 912 AUO | Bristol MW5G | 152.002 | B45F | 6/59 | Western National, Exeter (DN) | 2614 |
| 10464 | 913 AUO | Bristol MW5G | 152.003 | B45F | 6/59 | Western National, Exeter (DN) | 2615 |
| 10465 | 914 AUO | Bristol MW5G | 152.020 | B45F | 7/59 | Western National, Exeter (DN) | 2616 |
| 10466 | 915 AUO | Bristol MW5G | 152.021 | B45F | 7/59 | Western National, Exeter (DN) | 2617 |
| 10467 | 916 AUO | Bristol MW5G | 152.022 | B45F | 7/59 | Western National, Exeter (DN) | 2618 |
| 10468 | 917 AUO | Bristol MW5G | 152.023 | B45F | 7/59 | Western National, Exeter (DN) | 2619 |
| 10469 | 262 HNU | Bristol MW6G | 139.114 | DP43F | 5/59 | Midland General, Langley Mill (DE) | 264 |
| 10470 | 263 HNU | Bristol MW6G | 139.115 | DP43F | 5/59 | Midland General, Langley Mill (DE) | 265 |
| 10471 | 264 HNU | Bristol MW6G | 139.118 | DP43F | 5/59 | Midland General, Langley Mill (DE) | 266 |
| 10472 | 265 HNU | Bristol MW6G | 139.119 | DP43F | 5/59 | Midland General, Langley Mill (DE) | 267 |
| 10473 | 266 HNU | Bristol MW6G | 139.120 | DP43F | 5/59 | Midland General, Langley Mill (DE) | 268 |
| 10474 | 267 HNU | Bristol MW6G | 139.121 | DP43F | 5/59 | Midland General, Langley Mill (DE) | 269 |
| 10475 | 268 HNU | Bristol MW6G | 139.122 | DP43F | 5/59 | Midland General, Langley Mill (DE) | 270 |
| 10476 | 269 HNU | Bristol MW6G | 139.123 | DP43F | 5/59 | Midland General, Langley Mill (DE) | 271 |
| 10477 | 270 HNU | Bristol MW6G | 139.124 | DP43F | 5/59 | Midland General, Langley Mill (DE) | 272 |
| 10478 | 271 HNU | Bristol MW6G | 139.125 | DP43F | 5/59 | Midland General, Langley Mill (DE) | 273 |
| 10479 | 937 JHN | Bristol MW5G | 152.001 | DP41F | 7/59 | United AS, Darlington (DM) | BU537 |
| 10480 | TBD 138 | Bristol MW6G | 139.185 | DP41F | 5/59 | United Counties, Northampton (NO) | 138 |
| 10481 | TBD 139 | Bristol MW6G | 139.186 | DP41F | 5/59 | United Counties, Northampton (NO) | 139 |
| 10482 | TBD 140 | Bristol MW6G | 139.291 | DP41F | 6/59 | United Counties, Northampton (NO) | 140 |

| | | | | | | |
|---|---|---|---|---|---|---|
| 10483 | TBD 141 | Bristol MW6G | 139.292 | DP41F | 6/59 | United Counties, Northampton (NO) 141 |
| 10484 | WWU 269 | Bristol MW6G | 139.126 | DP41F | 5/59 | West Yorkshire RCC, Harrogate (WR) EUG72 |
| 10485 | WWU 270 | Bristol MW6G | 139.127 | DP41F | 5/59 | West Yorkshire RCC, Harrogate (WR) EUG73 |
| 10486 | WWU 271 | Bristol MW6G | 139.130 | DP41F | 5/59 | West Yorkshire RCC, Harrogate (WR) EUG74 |
| 10487 | WWU 272 | Bristol MW6G | 139.131 | DP41F | 5/59 | West Yorkshire RCC, Harrogate (WR) EUG75 |
| 10488 | 565 JFM | Bristol SC4LK | 147.005 | B35F | 1/59 | Crosville MS, Chester (CH) SSG625 |
| 10489 | 566 JFM | Bristol SC4LK | 147.006 | B35F | 1/59 | Crosville MS, Chester (CH) SSG626 |
| 10490 | 568 JFM | Bristol SC4LK | 147.007 | B35F | 3/59 | Crosville MS, Chester (CH) SSG627 |
| 10491 | 569 JFM | Bristol SC4LK | 147.008 | B35F | 3/59 | Crosville MS, Chester (CH) SSG628 |
| 10492 | VAO 391 | Bristol SC4LK | 147.001 | B35F | 1/59 | Cumberland MS, Whitehaven (CU) 391 |
| | | | | | | |
| 10493-631 | | | | | | Not built |
| | | | | | | |
| 10632 | VAO 390 | Bristol MW6G | 135.149 | C39F | 6/58 | Cumberland MS, Whitehaven (CU) 390 |
| 10633 | *JAO 837 | Leyland PS1/1 | 494241 | FB35F | 12/58 | Cumberland MS, Whitehaven (CU) 35 |
| 10634 | YNG 779 | Bristol MW5G | 135.135 | C39F | 6/58 | Eastern Counties, Norwich (NK) LS779 |
| 10635 | YNG 780 | Bristol MW5G | 135.136 | C39F | 6/58 | Eastern Counties, Norwich (NK) LS780 |
| 10636 | YNG 781 | Bristol MW5G | 135.137 | C39F | 6/58 | Eastern Counties, Norwich (NK) LS781 |
| 10637 | YNG 782 | Bristol MW5G | 135.138 | C39F | 6/58 | Eastern Counties, Norwich (NK) LS782 |
| 10638 | YNG 783 | Bristol MW5G | 135.150 | C39F | 6/58 | Eastern Counties, Norwich (NK) LS783 |
| 10639 | YNG 784 | Bristol MW5G | 139.001 | C39F | 6/58 | Eastern Counties, Norwich (NK) LS784 |
| 10640 | YNG 785 | Bristol MW5G | 139.002 | C39F | 7/58 | Eastern Counties, Norwich (NK) LS785 |
| 10641 | YNG 786 | Bristol MW5G | 139.003 | C39F | 7/58 | Eastern Counties, Norwich (NK) LS786 |
| 10642 | YNG 787 | Bristol MW5G | 139.004 | C39F | 7/58 | Eastern Counties, Norwich (NK) LS787 |
| | | | | | | |
| 10643-49 | | | | | | Not built |
| | | | | | | |
| 10650 | RFU 687 | Bristol MW6G | 139.013 | C39F | 7/58 | Lincolnshire RCC, Bracebridge Heath (KN) 2813 |
| 10651 | RFU 688 | Bristol MW6G | 139.014 | C39F | 7/58 | Lincolnshire RCC, Bracebridge Heath (KN) 2814 |
| 10652 | ORX 631 | Bristol MW6G | 135.069 | C34F | 3/58 | Thames Valley, Reading (BE) 800 |
| 10653 | ORX 632 | Bristol MW6G | 135.074 | C34F | 3/58 | Thames Valley, Reading (BE) 801 |
| 10654 | ORX 633 | Bristol MW6G | 135.075 | C34F | 4/58 | Thames Valley, Reading (BE) 802 |
| 10655 | ORX 634 | Bristol MW6G | 135.089 | C32F | 4/58 | Thames Valley, Reading (BE) 803 |
| 10656 | 301 GHN | Bristol LS6B | 119.201 | C34F | 6/58 | United AS, Darlington (DM) BUC1 |
| 10657 | 302 GHN | Bristol LS6B | 119.202 | C34F | 6/58 | United AS, Darlington (DM) BUC2 |
| 10658 | 303 GHN | Bristol LS6B | 119.203 | C34F | 6/58 | United AS, Darlington (DM) BUC3 |
| 10659 | 304 GHN | Bristol LS6B | 119.204 | C34F | 6/58 | United AS, Darlington (DM) BUC4 |
| 10660 | 305 GHN | Bristol LS6B | 119.205 | C34F | 6/58 | United AS, Darlington (DM) BUC5 |
| 10661 | RWN 883 | Bristol MW6G | 139.005 | C39F | 7/58 | United Welsh, Swansea (GG) 2 |
| 10662 | RWN 884 | Bristol MW6G | 139.006 | C39F | 7/58 | United Welsh, Swansea (GG) 3 |
| 10663 | RWN 885 | Bristol MW6G | 139.007 | C39F | 7/58 | United Welsh, Swansea (GG) 4 |
| 10664 | | | | | | Not built |
| 10665 | VWU 232 | Bristol MW6G | 135.145 | C39F | 7/58 | West Yorkshire RCC, Harrogate (WR) CUG21 |
| 10666 | VWU 233 | Bristol MW6G | 135.146 | C39F | 7/58 | West Yorkshire RCC, Harrogate (WR) CUG22 |
| 10667 | VWU 234 | Bristol MW6G | 139.008 | C39F | 7/58 | West Yorkshire RCC, Harrogate (WR) CUG23 |
| 10668 | | | | | | Not built |
| 10669 | | | | | | Not built |
| 10670 | | | | | | Not built |
| 10671 | RHR 852 | Bristol MW6G | 135.143 | C39F | 6/58 | Wilts & Dorset, Salisbury (WI) 701 |
| 10672 | RHR 853 | Bristol MW6G | 135.144 | C39F | 6/58 | Wilts & Dorset, Salisbury (WI) 702 |
| 10673 | RMR 524 | Bristol MW6G | 139.009 | C39F | 7/58 | Wilts & Dorset, Salisbury (WI) 703 |
| 10674 | RMR 736 | Bristol MW6G | 139.010 | C39F | 7/58 | Wilts & Dorset, Salisbury (WI) 704 |
| 10675 | RMR 992 | Bristol MW6G | 139.020 | C39F | 7/58 | Wilts & Dorset, Salisbury (WI) 705 |
| 10676 | RMR 995 | Bristol MW6G | 139.021 | C39F | 7/58 | Wilts & Dorset, Salisbury (WI) 706 |
| | | | | | | |
| 10677-700 | | | | | | Not built |
| | | | | | | |
| 10701 | 801 LFM | Bristol SC4LK | 141.041 | C33F | 3/58 | Crosville MS, Chester (CH) CSG621 |
| 10702 | 802 LFM | Bristol SC4LK | 141.042 | C33F | 3/58 | Crosville MS, Chester (CH) CSG622 |
| 10703 | 803 LFM | Bristol SC4LK | 141.043 | C33F | 3/58 | Crosville MS, Chester (CH) CSG623 |
| 10704 | 804 LFM | Bristol SC4LK | 141.044 | C33F | 3/58 | Crosville MS, Chester (CH) CSG624 |
| 10705 | | | | | | Not built |

| | | | | | | |
|---|---|---|---|---|---|---|
| 10706 | | | | | | Not built |
| 10707 | | | | | | Not built |
| 10708 | | | | | | Not built |
| 10709 | RFU 689 | Bristol SC4LK | 141.045 | C33F | 4/58 | Lincolnshire RCC, Bracebridge Heath (KN) 2611 |
| 10710 | RFU 690 | Bristol SC4LK | 141.046 | C33F | 4/58 | Lincolnshire RCC, Bracebridge Heath (KN) 2612 |
| 10711 | RFU 691 | Bristol SC4LK | 141.047 | C33F | 4/58 | Lincolnshire RCC, Bracebridge Heath (KN) 2613 |
| 10712 | RFU 692 | Bristol SC4LK | 141.048 | C33F | 4/58 | Lincolnshire RCC, Bracebridge Heath (KN) 2614 |
| 10713 | RFU 693 | Bristol SC4LK | 141.049 | C33F | 4/58 | Lincolnshire RCC, Bracebridge Heath (KN) 2615 |
| 10714 | RFU 694 | Bristol SC4LK | 141.050 | C33F | 5/58 | Lincolnshire RCC, Bracebridge Heath (KN) 2616 |
| 10715 | RPN 12 | Bristol FS6B | 155.020 | H33/27R | 4/60 | Brighton, Hove & District (ES) 12 |
| 10716 | RPN 13 | Bristol FS6B | 155.021 | H33/27R | 4/60 | Brighton, Hove & District (ES) 13 |
| 10717 | | | | | | Not built |
| 10718 | | | | | | Not built |
| 10719 | | | | | | Not built |
| 10720 | *JUO 985 | Bristol L6B Reb | 67.034 | FB39F | 8/58 | Southern National, Exeter (DN) 1220 |
| 10721 | *JUO 980 | Bristol L6B Reb | 65.008 | FB39F | 9/58 | Western National, Exeter (DN) 1215 |
| 10722 | *JUO 978 | Bristol L6B Reb | 65.027 | FB39F | 9/58 | Southern National, Exeter (DN) 1213 |
| 10723 | *JUO 982 | Bristol L6B Reb | 65.073 | FB39F | 9/58 | Southern National, Exeter (DN) 1217 |
| 10724 | *JUO 988 | Bristol L6B Reb | 67.168 | FB39F | 9/58 | Southern National, Exeter (DN) 1223 |
| 10725 | *JUO 979 | Bristol L6B Reb | 65.046 | FB39F | 9/58 | Western National, Exeter (DN) 1214 |
| 10726 | *JUO 989 | Bristol L6B Reb | 67.169 | FB39F | 9/58 | Southern National, Exeter (DN) 1224 |
| 10727 | *JUO 986 | Bristol L6B Reb | 67.076 | FB39F | 9/58 | Southern National, Exeter (DN) 1221 |
| 10728 | *JUO 984 | Bristol L6B Reb | 65.079 | FB39F | 9/58 | Southern National, Exeter (DN) 1219 |
| 10729 | *JUO 981 | Bristol L6B Reb | 65.009 | FB39F | 9/58 | Southern National, Exeter (DN) 1216 |
| 10730 | *JUO 983 | Bristol L6B Reb | 65.078 | FB39F | 9/58 | Southern National, Exeter (DN) 1218 |
| 10731 | *JUO 987 | Bristol L6B Reb | 67.077 | FB39F | 9/58 | Southern National, Exeter (DN) 1222 |
| 10732 | *DMO 665 | Bristol L6B Reb | 63.149 | FB39F | 6/58 | Thames Valley, Reading (BE) 795 |
| 10733 | *DMO 666 | Bristol L6B Reb | 63.178 | FB39F | 6/58 | Thames Valley, Reading (BE) 796 |
| 10734 | *DMO 667 | Bristol L6B Reb | 63.179 | FB39F | 8/58 | Thames Valley, Reading (BE) 797 |
| 10735 | *DMO 668 | Bristol L6B Reb | 63.165 | FB39F | 8/58 | Thames Valley, Reading (BE) 798 |
| 10736 | *DMO 664 | Bristol L6B Reb | 63.127 | FB39F | 8/58 | Thames Valley, Reading (BE) 794 |
| 10737 | *DMO 669 | Bristol L6B Reb | 65.018 | FB39F | 8/58 | Thames Valley, Reading (BE) 799 |
| 10738 | *JUO 944 | Bristol L6B Reb | 67.075 | FB39F | 6/58 | Western National, Exeter (DN) 1212 |
| 10739 | *JUO 934 | Bristol L6B Reb | 65.070 | FB39F | 6/58 | Western National, Exeter (DN) 1202 |
| 10740 | *HOD 27 | Bristol L6A Reb | 71.001 | FB39F | 7/58 | Western National, Exeter (DN) 1225 |
| 10741 | *JUO 939 | Bristol L6B Reb | 65.061 | FB39F | 7/58 | Western National, Exeter (DN) 1207 |
| 10742 | *JUO 938 | Bristol L6B Reb | 65.060 | FB39F | 7/58 | Western National, Exeter (DN) 1206 |
| 10743 | *JUO 932 | Bristol L6B Reb | 65.017 | FB39F | 7/58 | Western National, Exeter (DN) 1200 |
| 10744 | *JUO 937 | Bristol L6B Reb | 65.059 | FB39F | 7/58 | Western National, Exeter (DN) 1205 |
| 10745 | *JUO 936 | Bristol L6B Reb | 65.016 | FB39F | 7/58 | Western National, Exeter (DN) 1204 |
| 10746 | *JUO 933 | Bristol L6B Reb | 65.047 | FB39F | 8/58 | Western National, Exeter (DN) 1201 |
| 10747 | *JUO 943 | Bristol L6B Reb | 67.074 | FB39F | 8/58 | Western National, Exeter (DN) 1211 |
| 10748 | *JUO 940 | Bristol L6B Reb | 65.107 | FB39F | 8/58 | Western National, Exeter (DN) 1208 |
| 10749 | *JUO 942 | Bristol L6B Reb | 65.109 | FB39F | 8/58 | Western National, Exeter (DN) 1210 |
| 10750 | *JUO 941 | Bristol L6B Reb | 65.108 | FB39F | 8/58 | Western National, Exeter (DN) 1209 |
| 10751 | *JUO 935 | Bristol L6B Reb | 65.015 | FB39F | 8/58 | Western National, Exeter (DN) 1203 |
| 10752 | KWG 599 | Bristol LD6G | 150.022 | H33/27R | 2/59 | D Lawson Kirkintilloch (DB) RD71 |
| 10753 | KWG 601 | Bristol LD6G | 150.023 | H33/27R | 2/59 | D Lawson Kirkintilloch (DB) RD72 |
| 10754 | KWG 602 | Bristol LD6G | 150.024 | H33/27R | 2/59 | D Lawson Kirkintilloch (DB) RD73 |
| 10755 | KWG 603 | Bristol LD6G | 150.026 | H33/27R | 2/59 | W Alexander, Falkirk (SN) RD74 |
| 10756 | KWG 624 | Bristol LD6G | 150.028 | H33/27R | 2/59 | W Alexander, Falkirk (SN) RD75 |
| 10757 | KWG 626 | Bristol LD6G | 150.041 | H33/27R | 3/59 | W Alexander, Falkirk (SN) RD76 |
| 10758 | KWG 627 | Bristol LD6G | 150.042 | H33/27R | 3/59 | W Alexander, Falkirk (SN) RD77 |
| 10759 | KWG 628 | Bristol LD6G | 150.043 | H33/27R | 3/59 | W Alexander, Falkirk (SN) RD78 |
| 10760 | MMS 731 | Bristol LD6G | 150.049 | H33/27R | 3/59 | W Alexander, Falkirk (SN) RD79 |
| 10761 | MMS 732 | Bristol LD6G | 150.050 | H33/27R | 3/59 | W Alexander, Falkirk (SN) RD80 |
| 10762 | MMS 733 | Bristol LD6G | 150.069 | H33/27R | 3/59 | W Alexander, Falkirk (SN) RD81 |
| 10763 | MMS 734 | Bristol LD6G | 150.070 | H33/27R | 3/59 | W Alexander, Falkirk (SN) RD82 |

| | | | | | | | |
|---|---|---|---|---|---|---|---|
| 10764 | MMS 735 | Bristol LD6G | 150.071 | H33/27R | 3/59 | W Alexander, Falkirk (SN) RD83 |
| 10765 | MMS 736 | Bristol LD6G | 150.079 | H33/27R | 3/59 | W Alexander, Falkirk (SN) RD84 |
| 10766 | MMS 737 | Bristol LD6G | 150.080 | H33/27R | 3/59 | W Alexander, Falkirk (SN) RD85 |
| 10767 | MMS 738 | Bristol LD6G | 150.081 | H33/27R | 3/59 | W Alexander, Falkirk (SN) RD86 |
| 10768 | MMS 739 | Bristol LD6G | 150.082 | H33/27R | 3/59 | W Alexander, Falkirk (SN) RD87 |
| 10769 | MMS 740 | Bristol LD6G | 150.083 | H33/27R | 3/59 | W Alexander, Falkirk (SN) RD88 |
| 10770 | MMS 741 | Bristol LD6G | 150.089 | H33/27R | 3/59 | W Alexander, Falkirk (SN) RD89 |
| 10771 | MMS 742 | Bristol LD6G | 150.108 | H33/27R | 5/59 | W Alexander, Falkirk (SN) RD90 |
| 10772 | MMS 743 | Bristol LD6G | 150.109 | H33/27R | 5/59 | W Alexander, Falkirk (SN) RD91 |
| 10773 | MMS 744 | Bristol LD6G | 150.110 | H33/27R | 5/59 | W Alexander, Falkirk (SN) RD92 |
| 10774 | MMS 745 | Bristol LD6G | 150.111 | H33/27R | 4/59 | W Alexander, Falkirk (SN) RD93 |
| 10775 | MMS 746 | Bristol LD6G | 150.112 | H33/27R | 5/59 | W Alexander, Falkirk (SN) RD94 |
| 10776 | MMS 747 | Bristol LD6G | 150.116 | H33/27R | 5/59 | W Alexander, Falkirk (SN) RD95 |
| 10777 | MMS 748 | Bristol LD6G | 150.132 | H33/27R | 5/59 | W Alexander, Falkirk (SN) RD96 |
| 10778 | MMS 749 | Bristol LD6G | 150.133 | H33/27R | 5/59 | W Alexander, Falkirk (SN) RD97 |
| 10779 | MMS 750 | Bristol LD6G | 150.134 | H33/27R | 5/59 | W Alexander, Falkirk (SN) RD98 |
| 10780 | MMS 751 | Bristol LD6G | 150.135 | H33/27R | 5/59 | W Alexander, Falkirk (SN) RD99 |
| 10781 | MMS 752 | Bristol LD6G | 150.136 | H33/27R | 5/59 | W Alexander, Falkirk (SN) RD100 |
| 10782 | SWS 719 | Bristol LD6G | 150.029 | H33/27R | 2/59 | Scottish Omnibuses, Edinburgh (MN) AA719 |
| 10783 | SWS 720 | Bristol LD6G | 150.032 | H33/27R | 2/59 | Scottish Omnibuses, Edinburgh (MN) AA720 |
| 10784 | SWS 721 | Bristol LD6G | 150.033 | H33/27R | 2/59 | Scottish Omnibuses, Edinburgh (MN) AA721 |
| 10785 | SWS 722 | Bristol LD6G | 150.034 | H33/27R | 2/59 | Scottish Omnibuses, Edinburgh (MN) AA722 |
| 10786 | SWS 723 | Bristol LD6G | 150.035 | H33/27R | 2/59 | Scottish Omnibuses, Edinburgh (MN) AA723 |
| 10787 | SWS 724 | Bristol LD6G | 150.036 | H33/27R | 2/59 | Scottish Omnibuses, Edinburgh (MN) AA724 |
| 10788 | SWS 725 | Bristol LD6G | 150.037 | H33/27R | 2/59 | Scottish Omnibuses, Edinburgh (MN) AA725 |
| 10789 | SWS 726 | Bristol LD6G | 150.057 | H33/27R | 2/59 | Scottish Omnibuses, Edinburgh (MN) AA726 |
| 10790 | SWS 727 | Bristol LD6G | 150.059 | H33/27R | 2/59 | Scottish Omnibuses, Edinburgh (MN) AA727 |
| 10791 | SWS 728 | Bristol LD6G | 150.061 | H33/27R | 2/59 | Scottish Omnibuses, Edinburgh (MN) AA728 |
| 10792 | SWS 729 | Bristol LD6G | 150.062 | H33/27R | 2/59 | Scottish Omnibuses, Edinburgh (MN) AA729 |
| 10793 | SWS 730 | Bristol LD6G | 150.064 | H33/27R | 2/59 | Scottish Omnibuses, Edinburgh (MN) AA730 |
| 10794 | SWS 731 | Bristol LD6G | 150.065 | H33/27R | 2/59 | Scottish Omnibuses, Edinburgh (MN) AA731 |
| 10795 | SWS 732 | Bristol LD6G | 150.066 | H33/27R | 3/59 | Scottish Omnibuses, Edinburgh (MN) AA732 |
| 10796 | SWS 733 | Bristol LD6G | 150.095 | H33/27R | 3/59 | Scottish Omnibuses, Edinburgh (MN) AA733 |
| 10797 | SWS 734 | Bristol LD6G | 150.096 | H33/27R | 3/59 | Scottish Omnibuses, Edinburgh (MN) AA734 |
| 10798 | SWS 735 | Bristol LD6G | 150.100 | H33/27R | 3/59 | Scottish Omnibuses, Edinburgh (MN) AA735 |
| 10799 | SWS 736 | Bristol LD6G | 150.101 | H33/27R | 3/59 | Scottish Omnibuses, Edinburgh (MN) AA736 |
| 10800 | SWS 737 | Bristol LD6G | 150.117 | H33/27R | 3/59 | Scottish Omnibuses, Edinburgh (MN) AA737 |
| 10801 | SWS 738 | Bristol LD6G | 150.118 | H33/27R | 3/59 | Scottish Omnibuses, Edinburgh (MN) AA738 |
| 10802 | *SWS 739 | Bristol LD6G | 150.119 | H33/27R | 4/59 | Scottish Omnibuses, Edinburgh (MN) AA739 |
| 10803 | SWS 740 | Bristol LD6G | 150.120 | H33/27R | 4/59 | Scottish Omnibuses, Edinburgh (MN) AA740 |
| 10804 | SWS 741 | Bristol LD6G | 150.121 | H33/27R | 4/59 | Scottish Omnibuses, Edinburgh (MN) AA741 |
| 10805 | *SWS 742 | Bristol LD6G | 150.140 | H33/27R | 5/59 | Scottish Omnibuses, Edinburgh (MN) AA742 |
| 10806 | *SWS 743 | Bristol LD6G | 150.141 | H33/27R | 5/59 | Scottish Omnibuses, Edinburgh (MN) AA743 |
| 10807 | SWS 744 | Bristol LD6G | 150.142 | H33/27R | 5/59 | Scottish Omnibuses, Edinburgh (MN) AA744 |
| 10808 | *SWS 745 | Bristol LD6G | 150.143 | H33/27R | 5/59 | Scottish Omnibuses, Edinburgh (MN) AA745 |
| 10809 | MCS 750 | Bristol LD6G | 138.265 | H33/27RD | 1/59 | Western SMT, Kilmarnock (AR) B1461 |
| 10810 | MCS 751 | Bristol LD6G | 138.266 | H33/27RD | 1/59 | Western SMT, Kilmarnock (AR) B1462 |
| 10811 | MCS 752 | Bristol LD6G | 138.267 | H33/27RD | 1/59 | Western SMT, Kilmarnock (AR) B1463 |
| 10812 | MCS 753 | Bristol LD6G | 138.268 | H33/27RD | 1/59 | Western SMT, Kilmarnock (AR) B1464 |
| 10813 | MCS 754 | Bristol LD6G | 138.269 | H33/27RD | 1/59 | Western SMT, Kilmarnock (AR) B1465 |
| 10814 | MCS 755 | Bristol LD6G | 138.275 | H33/27RD | 1/59 | Western SMT, Kilmarnock (AR) B1466 |
| 10815 | MCS 756 | Bristol LD6G | 138.276 | H33/27RD | 1/59 | Western SMT, Kilmarnock (AR) B1467 |
| 10816 | MCS 757 | Bristol LD6G | 138.279 | H33/27RD | 1/59 | Western SMT, Kilmarnock (AR) B1468 |
| 10817 | MCS 758 | Bristol LD6G | 138.280 | H33/27RD | 1/59 | Western SMT, Kilmarnock (AR) B1469 |
| 10818 | MCS 759 | Bristol LD6G | 138.281 | H33/27RD | 1/59 | Western SMT, Kilmarnock (AR) B1470 |
| 10819 | MCS 760 | Bristol LD6G | 138.285 | H33/27RD | 1/59 | Western SMT, Kilmarnock (AR) B1471 |
| 10820 | MCS 761 | Bristol LD6G | 138.286 | H33/27RD | 1/59 | Western SMT, Kilmarnock (AR) B1472 |
| 10821 | MCS 762 | Bristol LD6G | 138.287 | H33/27RD | 2/59 | Western SMT, Kilmarnock (AR) B1473 |
| 10822 | MCS 763 | Bristol LD6G | 138.288 | H33/27RD | 2/59 | Western SMT, Kilmarnock (AR) B1474 |
| 10823 | MCS 764 | Bristol LD6G | 150.052 | H33/27RD | 3/59 | Western SMT, Kilmarnock (AR) B1475 |
| 10824 | MCS 765 | Bristol LD6G | 150.053 | H33/27RD | 3/59 | Western SMT, Kilmarnock (AR) B1476 |
| 10825 | MCS 766 | Bristol LD6G | 150.054 | H33/27RD | 3/59 | Western SMT, Kilmarnock (AR) B1477 |
| 10826 | MCS 767 | Bristol LD6G | 150.056 | H33/27R | 3/59 | Western SMT, Kilmarnock (AR) B1478 |
| 10827 | MCS 768 | Bristol LD6G | 150.102 | H33/27R | 3/59 | Western SMT, Kilmarnock (AR) B1479 |

| 10828 | MCS 769 | Bristol LD6G | 150.103 | H33/27R | 3/59 | Western SMT, Kilmarnock (AR) B1480 |
|---|---|---|---|---|---|---|
| 10829 | MCS 770 | Bristol LD6G | 150.104 | H33/27R | 3/59 | Western SMT, Kilmarnock (AR) B1481 |
| 10830 | MCS 771 | Bristol LD6G | 150.105 | H33/27R | 3/59 | Western SMT, Kilmarnock (AR) B1482 |
| 10831 | MCS 772 | Bristol LD6G | 150.124 | H33/27R | 5/59 | Western SMT, Kilmarnock (AR) B1483 |
| 10832 | MCS 773 | Bristol LD6G | 150.125 | H33/27R | 5/59 | Western SMT, Kilmarnock (AR) B1484 |
| 10833 | MCS 774 | Bristol LD6G | 150.126 | H33/27R | 5/59 | Western SMT, Kilmarnock (AR) B1485 |
| 10834 | MCS 775 | Bristol LD6G | 150.127 | H33/27R | 5/59 | Western SMT, Kilmarnock (AR) B1486 |
| 10835 | MCS 776 | Bristol LD6G | 150.128 | H33/27R | 5/59 | Western SMT, Kilmarnock (AR) B1487 |
| 10836 | MMS 753 | Bristol LD6G | 150.137 | H33/27R | 5/59 | W Alexander, Falkirk (SN) RD101 |
| 10837 | MMS 754 | Bristol LD6G | 150.148 | H33/27R | 5/59 | W Alexander, Falkirk (SN) RD102 |
| 10838 | MMS 755 | Bristol LD6G | 150.149 | H33/27R | 5/59 | W Alexander, Falkirk (SN) RD103 |
| 10839 | MMS 756 | Bristol LD6G | 150.150 | H33/27R | 5/59 | W Alexander, Falkirk (SN) RD104 |
| 10840 | MMS 757 | Bristol LD6G | 150.151 | H33/27R | 5/59 | W Alexander, Falkirk (SN) RD105 |
| 10841 | SWS 746 | Bristol LD6G | 150.144 | H33/27R | 5/59 | Scottish Omnibuses, Edinburgh (MN) AA746 |
| 10842 | SWS 747 | Bristol LD6G | 150.145 | H33/27R | 5/59 | Scottish Omnibuses, Edinburgh (MN) AA747 |
| 10843 | SWS 748 | Bristol LD6G | 150.152 | H33/27R | 5/59 | Scottish Omnibuses, Edinburgh (MN) AA748 |
| 10844 | SWS 749 | Bristol LD6G | 150.153 | H33/27R | 5/59 | Scottish Omnibuses, Edinburgh (MN) AA749 |
| 10845 | GM 9993 | Bristol LD6B | 150.092 | H33/27R | 3/59 | Central SMT, Motherwell (LK) B93 |
| 10846 | GM 9994 | Bristol LD6B | 150.093 | H33/27R | 3/59 | Central SMT, Motherwell (LK) B94 |
| 10847 | GM 9995 | Bristol LD6B | 150.094 | H33/27R | 3/59 | Central SMT, Motherwell (LK) B95 |
| 10848 | RPN 14 | Bristol FS6B | 155.022 | H33/27R | 4/60 | Brighton, Hove & District (ES) 14 |
| 10849 | RPN 15 | Bristol FS6B | 155.023 | H33/27R | 4/60 | Brighton, Hove & District (ES) 15 |
| 10850 | RPN 16 | Bristol FS6B | 155.024 | H33/27R | 4/60 | Brighton, Hove & District (ES) 16 |
| 10851 | RPN 17 | Bristol FS6B | 155.025 | H33/27R | 5/60 | Brighton, Hove & District (ES) 17 |
| 10852 | RPN 18 | Bristol FS6B | 155.026 | H33/27R | 4/60 | Brighton, Hove & District (ES) 18 |
| 10853 | RPN 19 | Bristol FS6B | 155.027 | H33/27R | 5/60 | Brighton, Hove & District (ES) 19 |
| 10854 | RPN 20 | Bristol FS6B | 155.028 | H33/27R | 5/60 | Brighton, Hove & District (ES) 20 |
| 10855 | SPM 23 | Bristol FS6B | 155.061 | H33/27R | 6/60 | Brighton, Hove & District (ES) 23 |
| 10856 | SPM 24 | Bristol FS6B | 155.062 | H33/27R | 6/60 | Brighton, Hove & District (ES) 24 |
| 10857 | SPM 25 | Bristol FS6B | 155.063 | H33/27R | 6/60 | Brighton, Hove & District (ES) 25 |
| 10858 | 983 EHW | Bristol LD6B | 150.222 | H33/25R | 10/59 | Bristol OC (GL) LC8528 |
| 10859 | 984 EHW | Bristol LD6B | 150.223 | H33/25R | 10/59 | Bristol OC (GL) LC8529 |
| 10860 | 985 EHW | Bristol LD6B | 150.232 | H33/25R | 10/59 | Bristol OC (GL) LC8530 |
| 10861 | 986 EHW | Bristol LD6B | 150.233 | H33/25R | 10/59 | Bristol OC (GL) LC8531 |
| 10862 | 987 EHW | Bristol LD6B | 150.234 | H33/25R | 10/59 | Bristol OC (GL) LC8532 |
| 10863 | *990 EHW | Bristol LD6B | 150.245 | H33/25R | 12/59 | Bristol OC (GL) LC8533 |
| 10864 | 991 EHW | Bristol LD6B | 150.246 | H33/25R | 12/59 | Bristol OC (GL) LC8534 |
| 10865 | 992 EHW | Bristol LD6B | 150.247 | H33/25R | 12/59 | Bristol OC (GL) LC8535 |
| 10866 | 995 EHW | Bristol FLF6B | 156.001 | H38/32F | 12/59 | Bristol OC (GL) LC8540 |
| 10867 | 571 EHY | Bristol FLF6B | 156.003 | H38/32F | 8/60 | Bristol OC (GL) LC8551 |
| 10868 | 572 EHY | Bristol FLF6B | 156.004 | H38/32F | 8/60 | Bristol OC (GL) LC8552 |
| 10869 | 573 EHY | Bristol FLF6B | 156.005 | H38/32F | 8/60 | Bristol OC (GL) LC8553 |
| 10870 | 574 EHY | Bristol FLF6B | 156.007 | H38/32F | 8/60 | Bristol OC (GL) LC8554 |
| 10871 | 575 EHY | Bristol FLF6B | 156.008 | H38/32F | 8/60 | Bristol OC (GL) LC8555 |
| 10872 | 576 EHY | Bristol FLF6B | 156.009 | H38/32F | 9/60 | Bristol OC (GL) LC8556 |
| 10873 | 577 EHY | Bristol FLF6B | 156.010 | H38/32F | 9/60 | Bristol OC (GL) LC8557 |
| 10874 | 578 EHY | Bristol FLF6B | 156.011 | H38/32F | 9/60 | Bristol OC (GL) LC8558 |
| 10875 | 579 EHY | Bristol FLF6B | 156.012 | H38/32F | 9/60 | Bristol OC (GL) LC8559 |
| 10876 | 580 EHY | Bristol FLF6B | 156.013 | H38/32F | 9/60 | Bristol OC (GL) LC8560 |
| 10877 | 581 EHY | Bristol FLF6B | 156.014 | H38/32F | 10/60 | Bristol OC (GL) LC8561 |
| 10878 | 982 EHW | Bristol LD6B | 150.221 | H33/25R | 8/59 | Cheltenham District (GL) L98 |
| 10879 | 961 EHW | Bristol LD6G | 150.155 | H33/25R | 7/59 | Bristol OC (GL) GL8507 |
| 10880 | 962 EHW | Bristol LD6G | 150.158 | H33/25R | 7/59 | Bristol OC (GL) GL8508 |
| 10881 | 963 EHW | Bristol LD6G | 150.159 | H33/25R | 7/59 | Bristol OC (GL) GL8509 |
| 10882 | 964 EHW | Bristol LD6G | 150.160 | H33/25RD | 7/59 | Bristol OC (GL) L8510 |
| 10883 | 965 EHW | Bristol LD6G | 150.172 | H33/25RD | 7/59 | Bristol OC (GL) L8511 |
| 10884 | 966 EHW | Bristol LD6G | 150.173 | H33/25RD | 7/59 | Bristol OC (GL) L8512 |
| 10885 | 967 EHW | Bristol LD6G | 150.174 | H33/25RD | 7/59 | Bristol OC (GL) L8513 |
| 10886 | 968 EHW | Bristol LD6G | 150.187 | H33/25RD | 7/59 | Bristol OC (GL) L8514 |
| 10887 | 969 EHW | Bristol LD6G | 150.188 | H33/25RD | 7/59 | Bath Electric Tramways (SO) L8515 |
| 10888 | 970 EHW | Bristol LD6G | 150.202 | H33/25RD | 7/59 | Bath Electric Tramways (SO) L8516 |
| 10889 | 431 FHW | Bristol LD6G | 154.037 | H33/25RD | 11/59 | Bristol OC (GL) L8541 |
| 10890 | 432 FHW | Bristol LD6G | 154.038 | H33/25RD | 11/59 | Bristol OC (GL) L8542 |
| 10891 | 433 FHW | Bristol LD6G | 154.039 | H33/25RD | 11/59 | Bristol OC (GL) L8543 |

| | | | | | | | |
|---|---|---|---|---|---|---|---|
| 10892 | *434 FHW | Bristol LD6G | 154.040 | H33/25RD | 11/59 | Bristol OC (GL) L8544 |
| 10893 | 435 FHW | Bristol LD6G | 154.062 | H33/25RD | 11/59 | Bristol OC (GL) L8545 |
| 10894 | 436 FHW | Bristol LD6G | 154.063 | H33/25RD | 11/59 | Bristol OC (GL) L8546 |
| 10895 | 437 FHW | Bristol FS6G | 155.007 | H33/27RD | 3/60 | Bristol OC (GL) L8547 |
| 10896 | 438 FHW | Bristol FS6G | 155.008 | H33/27RD | 3/60 | Bristol OC (GL) L8548 |
| 10897 | 439 FHW | Bristol FS6G | 155.009 | H33/27RD | 3/60 | Bristol OC (GL) L8549 |
| 10898 | 440 FHW | Bristol FS6G | 155.010 | H33/27RD | 3/60 | Bristol OC (GL) L8550 |
| 10899 | 988 EHW | Bristol LD6G | 154.001 | H33/25RD | 10/59 | Bristol OC (GL) L8536 |
| 10900 | 989 EHW | Bristol LD6G | 154.002 | H33/25RD | 10/59 | Bristol OC (GL) L8537 |
| 10901 | 993 EHW | Bristol LD6G | 154.003 | H33/25RD | 10/59 | Bristol OC (GL) L8538 |
| 10902 | 994 EHW | Bristol LD6G | 154.004 | H33/25RD | 10/59 | Bristol OC (GL) L8539 |
| 10903 | *611 LFM | Bristol LD6G | 150.164 | H33/27RD | 8/59 | Crosville MS, Chester (CH) DLG1 |
| 10904 | 612 LFM | Bristol LD6G | 150.165 | H33/27RD | 8/59 | Crosville MS, Chester (CH) DLG2 |
| 10905 | 613 LFM | Bristol LD6G | 150.203 | H33/27RD | 8/59 | Crosville MS, Chester (CH) DLG3 |
| 10906 | 614 LFM | Bristol LD6G | 150.204 | H33/27RD | 8/59 | Crosville MS, Chester (CH) DLG4 |
| 10907 | 615 LFM | Bristol LD6G | 150.205 | H33/27RD | 8/59 | Crosville MS, Chester (CH) DLG5 |
| 10908 | 624 LFM | Bristol LD6B | 150.226 | H33/27RD | 9/59 | Crosville MS, Chester (CH) DLB14 |
| 10909 | 625 LFM | Bristol LD6B | 150.227 | H33/27RD | 9/59 | Crosville MS, Chester (CH) DLB15 |
| 10910 | 626 LFM | Bristol LD6B | 150.251 | H33/27RD | 10/59 | Crosville MS, Chester (CH) DLB16 |
| 10911 | 627 LFM | Bristol LD6B | 150.252 | H33/27RD | 10/59 | Crosville MS, Chester (CH) DLB17 |
| 10912 | 628 LFM | Bristol LD6B | 154.007 | H33/27RD | 11/59 | Crosville MS, Chester (CH) DLB18 |
| 10913 | *629 LFM | Bristol LD6B | 154.008 | H33/27RD | 11/59 | Crosville MS, Chester (CH) DLB19 |
| 10914 | 630 LFM | Bristol LD6B | 154.009 | H33/27RD | 6/60 | Crosville MS, Chester (CH) DLB20 |
| 10915 | 631 LFM | Bristol LD6B | 154.010 | H33/27RD | 6/60 | Crosville MS, Chester (CH) DLB21 |
| 10916 | 616 LFM | Bristol LD6G | 154.022 | H33/27RD | 3/60 | Crosville MS, Chester (CH) DLG6 |
| 10917 | *617 LFM | Bristol LD6G | 154.023 | H33/27RD | 3/60 | Crosville MS, Chester (CH) DLG7 |
| 10918 | 618 LFM | Bristol LD6G | 154.024 | H33/27RD | 6/60 | Crosville MS, Chester (CH) DLG8 |
| 10919 | 619 LFM | Bristol LD6G | 154.025 | H33/27RD | 6/60 | Crosville MS, Chester (CH) DLG9 |
| 10920 | 632 LFM | Bristol LD6B | 154.069 | H33/27RD | 6/60 | Crosville MS, Chester (CH) DLB22 |
| 10921 | 620 LFM | Bristol LD6G | 154.073 | H33/27RD | 3/60 | Crosville MS, Chester (CH) DLG10 |
| 10922 | 621 LFM | Bristol LD6G | 154.074 | H33/27RD | 6/60 | Crosville MS, Chester (CH) DLG11 |
| 10923 | 622 LFM | Bristol LD6G | 154.099 | H33/27RD | 6/60 | Crosville MS, Chester (CH) DLG12 |
| 10924 | 623 LFM | Bristol LD6G | 154.100 | H33/27RD | 6/60 | Crosville MS, Chester (CH) DLG13 |
| 10925 | 633 LFM | Bristol FS6B | 155.005 | H33/27RD | 7/60 | Crosville MS, Chester (CH) DFB23 |
| 10926 | 634 LFM | Bristol FS6B | 155.006 | H33/27RD | 6/60 | Crosville MS, Chester (CH) DFB24 |
| 10927 | 635 LFM | Bristol FS6B | 155.018 | H33/27RD | 6/60 | Crosville MS, Chester (CH) DFB25 |
| 10928 | XAO 602 | Bristol LD6G | 150.156 | H33/27R | 7/59 | Cumberland MS, Whitehaven (CU) 394 |
| 10929 | XAO 603 | Bristol LD6G | 150.157 | H33/27R | 7/59 | Cumberland MS, Whitehaven (CU) 395 |
| 10930 | *XAO 604 | Bristol LD6B | 150.185 | H33/27RD | 9/59 | Cumberland MS, Whitehaven (CU) 396 |
| 10931 | XAO 605 | Bristol LD6B | 150.186 | H33/27RD | 9/59 | Cumberland MS, Whitehaven (CU) 397 |
| 10932 | XAO 606 | Bristol LD6B | 150.224 | H33/27RD | 9/59 | Cumberland MS, Whitehaven (CU) 398 |
| 10933 | XAO 607 | Bristol LD6B | 150.225 | H33/27RD | 9/59 | Cumberland MS, Whitehaven (CU) 399 |
| 10934 | *XAO 608 | Bristol LD6G | 150.260 | H33/27R | 9/59 | Cumberland MS, Whitehaven (CU) 400 |
| 10935 | XAO 609 | Bristol LD6G | 150.261 | H33/27R | 9/59 | Cumberland MS, Whitehaven (CU) 401 |
| 10936 | 9216 AH | Bristol LD5G | 154.026 | H33/27RD | 11/59 | Eastern Counties, Norwich (NK) LKD216 |
| 10937 | 9217 AH | Bristol LD5G | 154.027 | H33/27RD | 11/59 | Eastern Counties, Norwich (NK) LKD217 |
| 10938 | 47 PPU | Bristol LD5G | 150.166 | H33/27R | 6/59 | Eastern National, Chelmsford (EX) 1555 |
| 10939 | 48 PPU | Bristol LD5G | 150.167 | H33/27R | 7/59 | Eastern National, Chelmsford (EX) 1556 |
| 10940 | 49 PPU | Bristol LD5G | 150.228 | H33/27R | 8/59 | Eastern National, Chelmsford (EX) 1557 |
| 10941 | 50 PPU | Bristol LD5G | 150.229 | H33/27R | 8/59 | Eastern National, Chelmsford (EX) 1558 |
| 10942 | 51 PPU | Bristol LD5G | 150.253 | H33/27R | 9/59 | Eastern National, Chelmsford (EX) 1559 |
| 10943 | 52 PPU | Bristol LD5G | 154.028 | H33/27R | 10/59 | Eastern National, Chelmsford (EX) 1560 |
| 10944 | 53 PPU | Bristol LD5G | 154.029 | H33/27R | 10/59 | Eastern National, Chelmsford (EX) 1561 |
| 10945 | 54 PPU | Bristol LD5G | 154.030 | H33/27R | 10/59 | Eastern National, Chelmsford (EX) 1562 |
| 10946 | 55 PPU | Bristol LD5G | 154.075 | H33/27R | 10/59 | Eastern National, Chelmsford (EX) 1563 |
| 10947 | 56 PPU | Bristol LD5G | 154.076 | H33/27R | 10/59 | Eastern National, Chelmsford (EX) 1564 |
| 10948 | 57 PPU | Bristol LD5G | 154.077 | H33/27R | 10/59 | Eastern National, Chelmsford (EX) 1565 |
| 10949 | 58 PPU | Bristol LD5G | 154.078 | H33/27R | 10/59 | Eastern National, Chelmsford (EX) 1566 |
| 10950 | 59 PPU | Bristol LD5G | 154.079 | H33/27R | 10/59 | Eastern National, Chelmsford (EX) 1567 |
| 10951 | 60 PPU | Bristol LD5G | 154.080 | H33/27R | 10/59 | Eastern National, Chelmsford (EX) 1568 |
| 10952 | 61 PPU | Bristol FS5G | 155.035 | H33/27R | 4/60 | Eastern National, Chelmsford (EX) 1569 |
| 10953 | 62 PPU | Bristol FS5G | 155.038 | H33/27R | 4/60 | Eastern National, Chelmsford (EX) 1570 |
| 10954 | YRU 56 | Bristol LD6G | 150.179 | H33/27RD | 7/59 | Hants & Dorset, Bournemouth (HA) 1417 |
| 10955 | YRU 57 | Bristol LD6G | 150.180 | H33/27RD | 7/59 | Hants & Dorset, Bournemouth (HA) 1418 |

| | | | | | | | |
|---|---|---|---|---|---|---|---|
| 10956 | YRU 58 | Bristol LD6G | 150.181 | H33/27RD | 6/59 | Hants & Dorset, Bournemouth (HA) | 1419 |
| 10957 | YRU 59 | Bristol LD6G | 150.182 | H33/27RD | 7/59 | Hants & Dorset, Bournemouth (HA) | 1420 |
| 10958 | YRU 60 | Bristol LD6B | 150.220 | H33/27RD | 7/59 | Hants & Dorset, Bournemouth (HA) | 1421 |
| 10959 | YRU 61 | Bristol LD6B | 150.235 | H33/27RD | 8/59 | Hants & Dorset, Bournemouth (HA) | 1422 |
| 10960 | YRU 62 | Bristol LD6B | 150.236 | H33/27RD | 8/59 | Hants & Dorset, Bournemouth (HA) | 1423 |
| 10961 | YRU 63 | Bristol LD6B | 150.237 | H33/27RD | 8/59 | Hants & Dorset, Bournemouth (HA) | 1424 |
| 10962 | YRU 64 | Bristol LD6B | 150.238 | H33/27RD | 8/59 | Hants & Dorset, Bournemouth (HA) | 1425 |
| 10963 | YRU 68 | Bristol LD6B | 154.044 | H33/27RD | 10/59 | Hants & Dorset, Bournemouth (HA) | 1429 |
| 10964 | YRU 69 | Bristol LD6B | 154.055 | H33/27RD | 10/59 | Hants & Dorset, Bournemouth (HA) | 1430 |
| 10965 | *YRU 65 | Bristol LD6G | 154.031 | H33/27RD | 10/59 | Hants & Dorset, Bournemouth (HA) | 1426 |
| 10966 | YRU 66 | Bristol LD6G | 154.032 | H33/27RD | 10/59 | Hants & Dorset, Bournemouth (HA) | 1427 |
| 10967 | *YRU 67 | Bristol LD6G | 154.033 | H33/27RD | 10/59 | Hants & Dorset, Bournemouth (HA) | 1428 |
| 10968 | YRU 70 | Bristol LD6G | 154.085 | H33/27RD | 11/59 | Hants & Dorset, Bournemouth (HA) | 1431 |
| 10969 | YRU 71 | Bristol LD6G | 154.086 | H33/27RD | 11/59 | Hants & Dorset, Bournemouth (HA) | 1432 |
| 10970 | YRU 72 | Bristol LD6B | 154.093 | H33/27RD | 12/59 | Hants & Dorset, Bournemouth (HA) | 1433 |
| 10971 | YRU 73 | Bristol LD6B | 154.094 | H33/27RD | 12/59 | Hants & Dorset, Bournemouth (HA) | 1434 |
| 10972 | YRU 74 | Bristol LD6B | 154.095 | H33/27RD | 12/59 | Hants & Dorset, Bournemouth (HA) | 1435 |
| 10973 | YRU 75 | Bristol FS6B | 155.001 | H33/27RD | 2/60 | Hants & Dorset, Bournemouth (HA) | 1436 |
| 10974 | YRU 76 | Bristol FS6B | 155.033 | H33/27RD | 4/60 | Hants & Dorset, Bournemouth (HA) | 1437 |
| 10975 | YRU 77 | Bristol FS6B | 155.034 | H33/27RD | 4/60 | Hants & Dorset, Bournemouth (HA) | 1438 |
| 10976 | YEL 223 | Bristol MW6G | 139.242 | C39F | 5/59 | Hants & Dorset, Bournemouth (HA) | 864 |
| 10977 | YEL 224 | Bristol MW6G | 139.243 | C39F | 5/59 | Hants & Dorset, Bournemouth (HA) | 865 |
| 10978 | NFE 928 | Bristol LD5G | 150.175 | H33/27RD | 6/59 | Lincolnshire RCC, Lincoln (LC) | 2365 |
| 10979 | NFE 929 | Bristol LD5G | 150.176 | H33/27RD | 6/59 | Lincolnshire RCC, Lincoln (LC) | 2366 |
| 10980 | NFE 930 | Bristol LD5G | 150.206 | H33/27RD | 7/59 | Lincolnshire RCC, Lincoln (LC) | 2367 |
| 10981 | NFE 931 | Bristol LD5G | 150.207 | H33/27RD | 7/59 | Lincolnshire RCC, Lincoln (LC) | 2368 |
| 10982 | NFE 932 | Bristol LD5G | 154.005 | H33/27RD | 9/59 | Lincolnshire RCC, Lincoln (LC) | 2369 |
| 10983 | NFE 933 | Bristol LD5G | 154.006 | H33/27RD | 9/59 | Lincolnshire RCC, Lincoln (LC) | 2370 |
| 10984 | NFE 934 | Bristol LD5G | 154.052 | H33/27RD | 10/59 | Lincolnshire RCC, Lincoln (LC) | 2371 |
| 10985 | NFE 935 | Bristol LD5G | 154.053 | H33/27RD | 11/59 | Lincolnshire RCC, Lincoln (LC) | 2372 |
| 10986 | NFE 936 | Bristol FS5G | 155.011 | H33/27RD | 3/60 | Lincolnshire RCC, Lincoln (LC) | 2373 |
| 10987 | NFE 937 | Bristol FS5G | 155.012 | H33/27RD | 3/60 | Lincolnshire RCC, Lincoln (LC) | 2374 |
| 10988 | 191 BRR | Bristol LD6G | 150.230 | H33/25RD | 9/59 | Mansfield District (NG) | 520 |
| 10989 | 192 BRR | Bristol LD6G | 150.231 | H33/25RD | 9/59 | Mansfield District (NG) | 521 |
| 10990 | 193 BRR | Bristol LD6G | 154.034 | H33/25RD | 11/59 | Mansfield District (NG) | 522 |
| 10991 | 194 BRR | Bristol LD6G | 154.035 | H33/25RD | 11/59 | Mansfield District (NG) | 523 |
| 10992 | 195 BRR | Bristol LD6G | 154.036 | H33/25RD | 11/59 | Mansfield District (NG) | 524 |
| 10993 | 515 JRA | Bristol LD6G | 150.177 | H33/25RD | 7/59 | Midland General, Langley Mill (DE) | 477 |
| 10994 | 516 JRA | Bristol LD6G | 150.178 | H33/25RD | 7/59 | Midland General, Langley Mill (DE) | 478 |
| 10995 | 517 JRA | Bristol LD6G | 150.208 | H33/25RD | 8/59 | Midland General, Langley Mill (DE) | 479 |
| 10996 | 518 JRA | Bristol LD6G | 150.209 | H33/25RD | 8/59 | Midland General, Langley Mill (DE) | 480 |
| 10997 | 519 JRA | Bristol LD6G | 150.239 | H33/25RD | 9/59 | Midland General, Langley Mill (DE) | 481 |
| 10998 | 520 JRA | Bristol LD6G | 154.011 | H33/25RD | 10/59 | Midland General, Langley Mill (DE) | 482 |
| 10999 | 521 JRA | Bristol LD6G | 154.012 | H33/25RD | 10/59 | Midland General, Langley Mill (DE) | 483 |
| 11000 | 522 JRA | Bristol LD6G | 154.013 | H33/25RD | 10/59 | Midland General, Langley Mill (DE) | 484 |
| 11001 | 523 JRA | Bristol LD6G | 154.014 | H33/25RD | 10/59 | Midland General, Langley Mill (DE) | 485 |
| 11002 | 524 JRA | Bristol LD6G | 154.041 | H33/25RD | 11/59 | Midland General, Langley Mill (DE) | 486 |
| 11003 | 525 JRA | Bristol LD6G | 154.087 | H33/25RD | 12/59 | Midland General, Langley Mill (DE) | 487 |
| 11004 | 526 JRA | Bristol LD6G | 154.088 | H33/25RD | 12/59 | Midland General, Langley Mill (DE) | 488 |
| 11005 | 527 JRA | Bristol LD6G | 154.089 | H33/25RD | 12/59 | Midland General, Langley Mill (DE) | 489 |
| 11006 | 528 JRA | Bristol FS6G | 155.017 | H33/27RD | 3/60 | Midland General, Langley Mill (DE) | 490 |
| 11007 | VAX 501 | Bristol LD6G | 150.161 | H33/27RD | 7/59 | Red & White, Chepstow (MH) | L159 |
| 11008 | VAX 502 | Bristol LD6G | 150.162 | H33/27RD | 7/59 | Red & White, Chepstow (MH) | L259 |
| 11009 | VAX 503 | Bristol LD6G | 154.015 | H33/27RD | 10/59 | Red & White, Chepstow (MH) | L359 |
| 11010 | VAX 504 | Bristol LD6G | 154.042 | H33/27RD | 11/59 | Red & White, Chepstow (MH) | L459 |
| 11011 | VAX 505 | Bristol LD6G | 154.043 | H33/27RD | 11/59 | Red & White, Chepstow (MH) | L559 |
| 11012 | VAX 506 | Bristol LD6G | 154.050 | H33/27RD | 11/59 | Red & White, Chepstow (MH) | L659 |
| 11013 | VAX 507 | Bristol LD6G | 154.054 | H33/27RD | 12/59 | Red & White, Chepstow (MH) | L759 |
| 11014 | 19 AAX | Bristol FL6G | 168.024 | H37/33RD | 2/61 | Red & White, Chepstow (MH) | L1960 |
| 11015 | * 20 AAX | Bristol FL6G | 168.025 | H37/33RD | 1/61 | Red & White, Chepstow (MH) | L2060 |
| 11016 | SDL 265 | Bristol LD6G | 150.138 | H33/27R | 6/59 | Southern Vectis, Newport (IW) | 560 |
| 11017 | SDL 266 | Bristol LD6G | 150.139 | H33/27R | 6/59 | Southern Vectis, Newport (IW) | 561 |
| 11018 | *SDL 267 | Bristol LD6G | 150.146 | H33/27R | 6/59 | Southern Vectis, Newport (IW) | 562 |
| 11019 | SDL 268 | Bristol LD6G | 150.147 | H33/27R | 6/59 | Southern Vectis, Newport (IW) | 563 |

| | | | | | | | |
|---|---|---|---|---|---|---|---|
| 11020 | SDL 269 | Bristol LD6G | 150.154 | H33/27R | 6/59 | Southern Vectis, Newport (IW) 564 |
| 11021 | SMO 78 | Bristol LD6G | 150.163 | H33/27RD | 6/59 | Thames Valley, Reading (BE) 812 |
| 11022 | SMO 79 | Bristol LD6G | 150.189 | H33/27RD | 6/59 | Thames Valley, Reading (BE) 813 |
| 11023 | SMO 80 | Bristol LD6G | 150.190 | H33/27RD | 6/59 | Thames Valley, Reading (BE) 814 |
| 11024 | SMO 81 | Bristol LD6B | 150.210 | H33/27RD | 7/59 | Thames Valley, Reading (BE) 815 |
| 11025 | SMO 82 | Bristol LD6B | 150.211 | H33/27RD | 7/59 | Thames Valley, Reading (BE) 816 |
| 11026 | 442 LHN | Bristol LD6B | 150.212 | H33/27RD | 8/59 | United AS, Darlington (DM) BL42 |
| 11027 | 443 LHN | Bristol LD6B | 150.213 | H33/27RD | 8/59 | United AS, Darlington (DM) BL43 |
| 11028 | 444 LHN | Bristol LD6B | 150.214 | H33/27RD | 8/59 | United AS, Darlington (DM) BL44 |
| 11029 | 445 LHN | Bristol LD6B | 150.254 | H33/27RD | 10/59 | United AS, Darlington (DM) BL45 |
| 11030 | 446 LHN | Bristol LD6B | 150.255 | H33/27RD | 10/59 | United AS, Darlington (DM) BL46 |
| 11031 | 447 LHN | Bristol LD6B | 150.256 | H33/27RD | 10/59 | United AS, Darlington (DM) BL47 |
| 11032 | 448 LHN | Bristol LD6B | 154.056 | H33/27RD | 12/59 | United AS, Darlington (DM) BL48 |
| 11033 | 449 LHN | Bristol LD6B | 154.057 | H33/27RD | 12/59 | United AS, Darlington (DM) BL49 |
| 11034 | 450 LHN | Bristol LD6B | 154.058 | H33/27RD | 12/59 | United AS, Darlington (DM) BL50 |
| 11035 | 451 LHN | Bristol LD6B | 154.070 | H33/27RD | 12/59 | United AS, Darlington (DM) BL51 |
| 11036 | 452 LHN | Bristol LD6B | 154.081 | H33/27RD | 12/59 | United AS, Darlington (DM) BL52 |
| 11037 | 453 LHN | Bristol LD6B | 154.082 | H33/27RD | 12/59 | United AS, Darlington (DM) BL53 |
| 11038 | 454 LHN | Bristol LD6B | 154.083 | H33/27RD | 12/59 | United AS, Darlington (DM) BL54 |
| 11039 | 455 LHN | Bristol FS6B | 155.039 | H33/27RD | 5/60 | United AS, Darlington (DM) BL55 |
| 11040 | 456 LHN | Bristol FS6B | 155.040 | H33/27RD | 5/60 | United AS, Darlington (DM) BL56 |
| 11041 | TRP 557 | Bristol LD6B | 150.217 | H33/27RD | 8/59 | United Counties, Northampton (NO) 557 |
| 11042 | TRP 558 | Bristol LD6B | 150.218 | H33/27RD | 8/59 | United Counties, Northampton (NO) 558 |
| 11043 | TRP 559 | Bristol LD6B | 150.219 | H33/27RD | 9/59 | United Counties, Northampton (NO) 559 |
| 11044 | TRP 560 | Bristol LD6B | 150.257 | H33/27RD | 9/59 | United Counties, Northampton (NO) 560 |
| 11045 | TRP 561 | Bristol LD6B | 150.258 | H33/27RD | 10/59 | United Counties, Northampton (NO) 561 |
| 11046 | TRP 562 | Bristol LD6B | 150.259 | H33/27RD | 10/59 | United Counties, Northampton (NO) 562 |
| 11047 | TRP 563 | Bristol LD6B | 154.047 | H33/27RD | 11/59 | United Counties, Northampton (NO) 563 |
| 11048 | TRP 564 | Bristol LD6B | 154.048 | H33/27RD | 11/59 | United Counties, Northampton (NO) 564 |
| 11049 | TRP 565 | Bristol LD6B | 154.066 | H33/27RD | 11/59 | United Counties, Northampton (NO) 565 |
| 11050 | TRP 566 | Bristol LD6B | 154.067 | H33/27RD | 11/59 | United Counties, Northampton (NO) 566 |
| 11051 | TRP 567 | Bristol LD6B | 154.068 | H33/27RD | 12/59 | United Counties, Northampton (NO) 567 |
| 11052 | TRP 568 | Bristol LD6B | 154.090 | H33/27RD | 12/59 | United Counties, Northampton (NO) 568 |
| 11053 | TRP 569 | Bristol LD6B | 154.091 | H33/27RD | 12/59 | United Counties, Northampton (NO) 569 |
| 11054 | TRP 570 | Bristol LD6B | 154.092 | H33/27RD | 12/59 | United Counties, Northampton (NO) 570 |
| 11055 | URP 600 | Bristol FS6B | 155.013 | H33/27RD | 4/60 | United Counties, Northampton (NO) 600 |
| 11056 | URP 601 | Bristol FS6B | 155.014 | H33/27RD | 4/60 | United Counties, Northampton (NO) 601 |
| 11057 | TWN 102 | Bristol LD6G | 150.183 | H33/27RD | 8/59 | United Welsh, Swansea (GG) 325 |
| 11058 | TWN 103 | Bristol LD6G | 150.184 | H33/27RD | 8/59 | United Welsh, Swansea (GG) 326 |
| 11059 | TWN 104 | Bristol LD6G | 150.240 | H33/27RD | 9/59 | United Welsh, Swansea (GG) 327 |
| 11060 | TWN 105 | Bristol LD6G | 150.241 | H33/27RD | 9/59 | United Welsh, Swansea (GG) 328 |
| 11061 | TWN 106 | Bristol LD6G | 154.016 | H33/27RD | 10/59 | United Welsh, Swansea (GG) 329 |
| 11062 | TWN 107 | Bristol LD6G | 154.017 | H33/27RD | 10/59 | United Welsh, Swansea (GG) 330 |
| 11063 | TWN 108 | Bristol LD6G | 154.018 | H33/27RD | 10/59 | United Welsh, Swansea (GG) 331 |
| 11064 | TWN 109 | Bristol LD6G | 154.059 | H33/27RD | 12/59 | United Welsh, Swansea (GG) 332 |
| 11065 | TWN 110 | Bristol LD6G | 154.060 | H33/27RD | 12/59 | United Welsh, Swansea (GG) 333 |
| 11066 | TWN 111 | Bristol LD6G | 154.061 | H33/27RD | 12/59 | United Welsh, Swansea (GG) 334 |
| 11067 | TWN 112 | Bristol FS6G | 155.015 | H33/27RD | 4/60 | United Welsh, Swansea (GG) 335 |
| 11068 | TWN 113 | Bristol FS6G | 155.016 | H33/27RD | 4/60 | United Welsh, Swansea (GG) 336 |
| 11069 | 501 BTA | Bristol LD6G | 150.168 | H33/27RD | 7/59 | Western National, Exeter (DN) 1949 |
| 11070 | 502 BTA | Bristol LD6G | 150.169 | H33/27RD | 7/59 | Western National, Exeter (DN) 1950 |
| 11071 | 503 BTA | Bristol LD6G | 150.170 | H33/27RD | 7/59 | Western National, Exeter (DN) 1951 |
| 11072 | *504 BTA | Bristol LD6G | 150.171 | H33/27RD | 7/59 | Western National, Exeter (DN) 1952 |
| 11073 | 505 BTA | Bristol LD6G | 150.248 | H33/27RD | 9/59 | Western National, Exeter (DN) 1953 |
| 11074 | 506 BTA | Bristol LD6G | 150.249 | H33/27RD | 10/59 | Western National, Exeter (DN) 1954 |
| 11075 | 507 BTA | Bristol LD6G | 150.250 | H33/27RD | 10/59 | Western National, Exeter (DN) 1955 |
| 11076 | 508 BTA | Bristol LD6G | 154.019 | H33/27RD | 11/59 | Western National, Exeter (DN) 1956 |
| 11077 | *509 BTA | Bristol LD6G | 154.020 | H33/27RD | 11/59 | Western National, Exeter (DN) 1957 |
| 11078 | 510 BTA | Bristol LD6G | 154.021 | H33/27RD | 11/59 | Western National, Exeter (DN) 1958 |
| 11079 | 511 BTA | Bristol LD6G | 154.064 | H33/27RD | 12/59 | Western National, Exeter (DN) 1959 |
| 11080 | 512 BTA | Bristol LD6G | 154.065 | H33/27RD | 12/59 | Western National, Exeter (DN) 1960 |
| 11081 | 513 BTA | Bristol LD6G | 154.071 | H33/27RD | 12/59 | Western National, Exeter (DN) 1961 |
| 11082 | *514 BTA | Bristol LD6G | 154.072 | H33/27RD | 12/59 | Western National, Exeter (DN) 1962 |
| 11083 | 515 BTA | Bristol LD6G | 154.096 | H33/27RD | 12/59 | Western National, Exeter (DN) 1963 |

| | | | | | | |
|---|---|---|---|---|---|---|
| 11084 | 516 BTA | Bristol LD6G | 154.097 | H33/27RD | 12/59 | Western National, Exeter (DN) 1964 |
| 11085 | 517 BTA | Bristol LD6G | 154.098 | H33/27RD | 12/59 | Western National, Exeter (DN) 1965 |
| 11086 | *518 BTA | Bristol FS6G | 155.041 | H33/27RD | 5/60 | Western National, Exeter (DN) 1966 |
| 11087 | 519 BTA | Bristol FS6G | 155.042 | H33/27RD | 5/60 | Western National, Exeter (DN) 1967 |
| 11088 | YWW 73 | Bristol LD6B | 150.243 | H33/27RD | 9/59 | West Yorkshire RCC, Harrogate (WR) DX78 |
| 11089 | YWW 74 | Bristol LD6B | 154.045 | H33/27RD | 11/59 | West Yorkshire RCC, Harrogate (WR) DX79 |
| 11090 | YWW 75 | Bristol LD6B | 154.046 | H33/27RD | 11/59 | West Yorkshire RCC, Harrogate (WR) DX80 |
| 11091 | YWW 76 | Bristol LD6B | 154.049 | H33/27RD | 11/59 | West Yorkshire RCC, Harrogate (WR) DX81 |
| 11092 | YWW 78 | Bristol LD6B | 154.084 | H33/27RD | 12/59 | West Yorkshire RCC, Harrogate (WR) DX83 |
| 11093 | YWW 77 | Bristol FSF6B | 156.002 | H34/26F | 5/60 | West Yorkshire RCC, Harrogate (WR) DX82 |
| 11094 | XYG 831 | Bristol LD6B | 150.215 | H33/27RD | 11/59 | Keighley-West Yorkshire, Harrogate (WR) KDX75 |
| 11095 | XYG 832 | Bristol LD6B | 150.216 | H33/27RD | 11/59 | Keighley-West Yorkshire, Harrogate (WR) KDX76 |
| 11096 | XYG 833 | Bristol LD6B | 150.242 | H33/27RD | 11/59 | Keighley-West Yorkshire, Harrogate (WR) KDX77 |
| 11097 | 4506 WU | Bristol FS6B | 155.002 | H33/27RD | 3/60 | York-West Yorkshire, Harrogate (WR) YDX84 |
| 11098 | 4507 WU | Bristol FS6B | 155.003 | H33/27RD | 3/60 | York-West Yorkshire, Harrogate (WR) YDX85 |
| 11099 | 4508 WU | Bristol FS6B | 155.004 | H33/27RD | 3/60 | York-West Yorkshire, Harrogate (WR) YDX86 |
| 11100 | 4509 WU | Bristol FS6B | 155.019 | H33/27RD | 4/60 | York-West Yorkshire, Harrogate (WR) YDX87 |
| 11101 | 4510 WU | Bristol FS6B | 155.032 | H33/27RD | 4/60 | York-West Yorkshire, Harrogate (WR) YDX88 |
| 11102 | TMW 273 | Bristol LD6G | 150.244 | H33/27RD | 9/59 | Wilts & Dorset, Salisbury (WI) 636 |
| 11103 | UAM 941 | Bristol LD6G | 154.051 | H33/27RD | 11/59 | Wilts & Dorset, Salisbury (WI) 637 |
| 11104 | 981 EHY | Bristol MW5G | 152.037 | B45F | 8/59 | Bristol OC (GL) 2969 |
| 11105 | 982 EHY | Bristol MW5G | 152.038 | B45F | 9/59 | Bristol OC (GL) 2970 |
| 11106 | 983 EHY | Bristol MW5G | 152.039 | B45F | 9/59 | Bristol OC (GL) 2971 |
| 11107 | 984 EHY | Bristol MW5G | 152.080 | B45F | 10/59 | Bristol OC (GL) 2972 |
| 11108 | 985 EHY | Bristol MW5G | 152.081 | B45F | 10/59 | Bristol OC (GL) 2973 |
| 11109 | 986 EHY | Bristol MW5G | 152.082 | B45F | 10/59 | Bristol OC (GL) 2974 |
| 11110 | 987 EHY | Bristol MW5G | 152.083 | B45F | 10/59 | Bristol OC (GL) 2975 |
| 11111 | 988 EHY | Bristol MW5G | 152.105 | B45F | 11/59 | Bristol OC (GL) 2976 |
| 11112 | 989 EHY | Bristol MW5G | 152.112 | B45F | 11/59 | Bristol OC (GL) 2977 |
| 11113 | 990 EHY | Bristol MW5G | 152.113 | B45F | 11/59 | Bristol OC (GL) 2978 |
| 11114 | 991 EHY | Bristol MW5G | 152.114 | B45F | 11/59 | Bristol OC (GL) 2979 |
| 11115 | 992 EHY | Bristol MW5G | 152.150 | B45F | 1/60 | Bristol OC (GL) 2980 |
| 11116 | 993 EHY | Bristol MW5G | 152.151 | B45F | 2/60 | Bristol OC (GL) 2981 |
| 11117 | 994 EHY | Bristol MW5G | 152.152 | B45F | 3/60 | Bristol OC (GL) 2982 |
| 11118 | 995 EHY | Bristol MW5G | 152.153 | B45F | 3/60 | Bristol OC (GL) 2983 |
| 11119 | 347 MFM | Bristol MW6G | 152.047 | B41F | 9/59 | Crosville MS, Chester (CH) SMG371 |
| 11120 | *348 MFM | Bristol MW6G | 152.048 | B41F | 9/59 | Crosville MS, Chester (CH) SMG372 |
| 11121 | 349 MFM | Bristol MW6G | 152.049 | B41F | 10/59 | Crosville MS, Chester (CH) SMG373 |
| 11122 | 350 MFM | Bristol MW6G | 152.084 | B41F | 11/59 | Crosville MS, Chester (CH) SMG374 |
| 11123 | *351 MFM | Bristol MW6G | 152.085 | B41F | 11/59 | Crosville MS, Chester (CH) SMG375 |
| 11124 | 352 MFM | Bristol MW6G | 152.086 | B41F | 11/59 | Crosville MS, Chester (CH) SMG376 |
| 11125 | 353 MFM | Bristol MW6G | 152.087 | B41F | 11/59 | Crosville MS, Chester (CH) SMG377 |
| 11126 | 354 MFM | Bristol MW6G | 152.131 | B41F | 12/59 | Crosville MS, Chester (CH) SMG378 |
| 11127 | 355 MFM | Bristol MW6G | 152.132 | B41F | 1/60 | Crosville MS, Chester (CH) SMG379 |
| 11128 | 356 MFM | Bristol MW6G | 152.133 | B41F | 1/60 | Crosville MS, Chester (CH) SMG380 |
| 11129 | 357 MFM | Bristol MW6G | 152.134 | B41F | 1/60 | Crosville MS, Chester (CH) SMG381 |
| 11130 | 358 MFM | Bristol MW6G | 152.169 | B41F | 3/60 | Crosville MS, Chester (CH) SMG382 |
| 11131 | 359 MFM | Bristol MW6G | 152.170 | B41F | 2/60 | Crosville MS, Chester (CH) SMG383 |
| 11132 | 360 MFM | Bristol MW6G | 152.171 | B41F | 2/60 | Crosville MS, Chester (CH) SMG384 |
| 11133 | 361 MFM | Bristol MW6G | 152.172 | B41F | 3/60 | Crosville MS, Chester (CH) SMG385 |
| 11134 | 9459 AH | Bristol MW5G | 152.090 | B45F | 11/59 | Eastern Counties, Norwich (NK) LL459 |
| 11135 | 9460 AH | Bristol MW5G | 152.091 | B45F | 11/59 | Eastern Counties, Norwich (NK) LL460 |
| 11136 | 9461 AH | Bristol MW5G | 152.092 | B45F | 11/59 | Eastern Counties, Norwich (NK) LL461 |
| 11137 | 1251 EV | Bristol MW5G | 152.066 | DP41F | 9/59 | Eastern National, Chelmsford (EX) 487 |
| 11138 | 1252 EV | Bristol MW5G | 152.067 | DP41F | 9/59 | Eastern National, Chelmsford (EX) 488 |
| 11139 | 1253 EV | Bristol MW5G | 152.068 | DP41F | 9/59 | Eastern National, Chelmsford (EX) 489 |
| 11140 | 1254 EV | Bristol MW5G | 152.069 | DP41F | 9/59 | Eastern National, Chelmsford (EX) 490 |
| 11141 | 1255 EV | Bristol MW5G | 152.100 | DP41F | 10/59 | Eastern National, Chelmsford (EX) 491 |
| 11142 | 1256 EV | Bristol MW5G | 152.101 | DP41F | 10/59 | Eastern National, Chelmsford (EX) 492 |
| 11143 | 1257 EV | Bristol MW5G | 152.102 | DP41F | 10/59 | Eastern National, Chelmsford (EX) 493 |
| 11144 | 1258 EV | Bristol MW5G | 152.103 | B45F | 11/59 | Eastern National, Chelmsford (EX) 494 |

| | | | | | | |
|---|---|---|---|---|---|---|
| 11145 | 1259 EV | Bristol MW5G | 152.104 | B45F | 10/59 | Eastern National, Chelmsford (EX) 495 |
| 11146 | 1260 EV | Bristol MW5G | 152.106 | B45F | 11/59 | Eastern National, Chelmsford (EX) 496 |
| 11147 | 1261 EV | Bristol MW5G | 152.107 | B45F | 11/59 | Eastern National, Chelmsford (EX) 497 |
| 11148 *1262 EV | | Bristol MW5G | 152.108 | B45F | 11/59 | Eastern National, Chelmsford (EX) 498 |
| 11149 | 1263 EV | Bristol MW5G | 152.109 | B45F | 11/59 | Eastern National, Chelmsford (EX) 499 |
| 11150 | 1264 EV | Bristol MW5G | 152.110 | B45F | 11/59 | Eastern National, Chelmsford (EX) 500 |
| 11151 | 1265 EV | Bristol MW5G | 152.111 | B45F | 11/59 | Eastern National, Chelmsford (EX) 501 |
| 11152 | 1266 EV | Bristol MW5G | 152.173 | B45F | 2/60 | Eastern National, Chelmsford (EX) 502 |
| 11153 | 1267 EV | Bristol MW5G | 152.174 | B45F | 5/60 | Eastern National, Chelmsford (EX) 503 |
| 11154 | 1268 EV | Bristol MW5G | 152.175 | B45F | 5/60 | Eastern National, Chelmsford (EX) 504 |
| 11155 | 1269 EV | Bristol MW5G | 152.176 | B45F | 5/60 | Eastern National, Chelmsford (EX) 505 |
| 11156 | 1270 EV | Bristol MW5G | 152.177 | B45F | 5/60 | Eastern National, Chelmsford (EX) 506 |
| 11157 | 2714 EL | Bristol MW5G | 152.115 | B43F | 10/59 | Hants & Dorset, Bournemouth (HA) 812 |
| 11158 | 2715 EL | Bristol MW5G | 152.116 | B43F | 11/59 | Hants & Dorset, Bournemouth (HA) 813 |
| 11159 | 2716 EL | Bristol MW5G | 152.117 | B43F | 11/59 | Hants & Dorset, Bournemouth (HA) 814 |
| 11160 | 2717 EL | Bristol MW5G | 152.154 | B43F | 1/60 | Hants & Dorset, Bournemouth (HA) 815 |
| 11161 | 2718 EL | Bristol MW5G | 152.155 | B43F | 1/60 | Hants & Dorset, Bournemouth (HA) 816 |
| 11162 | 2719 EL | Bristol MW5G | 152.156 | B43F | 1/60 | Hants & Dorset, Bournemouth (HA) 817 |
| 11163 | YEL 225 | Bristol MW6G | 139.244 | C39F | 4/59 | Hants & Dorset, Bournemouth (HA) 866 |
| 11164 | YEL 226 | Bristol MW6G | 139.293 | C39F | 6/59 | Hants & Dorset, Bournemouth (HA) 867 |
| 11165 | NVL 613 | Bristol MW5G | 152.070 | DP41F | 9/59 | Lincolnshire RCC, Lincoln (LC) 3022 |
| 11166 | NVL 614 | Bristol MW5G | 152.071 | DP41F | 9/59 | Lincolnshire RCC, Lincoln (LC) 3023 |
| 11167 | NVL 615 | Bristol MW5G | 152.072 | DP41F | 9/59 | Lincolnshire RCC, Lincoln (LC) 3024 |
| 11168 | NVL 157 | Bristol MW5G | 152.040 | B45F | 7/59 | Lincolnshire RCC, Lincoln (LC) 2232 |
| 11169 | NVL 158 | Bristol MW5G | 152.041 | B45F | 7/59 | Lincolnshire RCC, Lincoln (LC) 2233 |
| 11170 | NVL 159 | Bristol MW5G | 152.042 | B43F | 7/59 | Lincolnshire RCC, Lincoln (LC) 2234 |
| 11171 | NVL 160 | Bristol MW5G | 152.118 | B45F | 11/59 | Lincolnshire RCC, Lincoln (LC) 2235 |
| 11172 | NVL 161 | Bristol MW5G | 152.119 | B43F | 11/59 | Lincolnshire RCC, Lincoln (LC) 2236 |
| 11173 | NVL 162 | Bristol MW5G | 152.120 | B43F | 11/59 | Lincolnshire RCC, Lincoln (LC) 2237 |
| 11174 | NVL 163 | Bristol MW5G | 152.157 | B45F | 1/60 | Lincolnshire RCC, Lincoln (LC) 2238 |
| 11175 | NVL 164 | Bristol MW5G | 152.158 | B43F | 1/60 | Lincolnshire RCC, Lincoln (LC) 2239 |
| 11176 *NVL 165 | | Bristol MW5G | 152.159 | B45F | 1/60 | Lincolnshire RCC, Lincoln (LC) 2240 |
| 11177 | NVL 168 | Bristol MW5G | 152.160 | B43F | 1/60 | Lincolnshire RCC, Lincoln (LC) 2241 |
| 11178 | VWO 215 | Bristol MW6G | 152.043 | B45F | 9/59 | Red & White, Chepstow (MH) U1559 |
| 11179 | VWO 216 | Bristol MW6G | 152.044 | B45F | 9/59 | Red & White, Chepstow (MH) U1659 |
| 11180 | VWO 217 | Bristol MW6G | 152.045 | B45F | 10/59 | Red & White, Chepstow (MH) U1759 |
| 11181 | VWO 218 | Bristol MW6G | 152.046 | B45F | 10/59 | Red & White, Chepstow (MH) U1859 |
| 11182 | VWO 219 | Bristol MW6G | 152.121 | B45F | 12/59 | Red & White, Chepstow (MH) U1959 |
| 11183 | VWO 220 | Bristol MW6G | 152.122 | B45F | 12/59 | Red & White, Chepstow (MH) U2059 |
| 11184 | VWO 221 | Bristol MW6G | 152.123 | B45F | 12/59 | Red & White, Chepstow (MH) U2159 |
| 11185 | VWO 222 | Bristol MW6G | 152.135 | B45F | 1/60 | Red & White, Chepstow (MH) U2259 |
| 11186 | VWO 223 | Bristol MW6G | 152.136 | B45F | 1/60 | Red & White, Chepstow (MH) U2359 |
| 11187 | VWO 224 | Bristol MW6G | 152.137 | B45F | 1/60 | Red & White, Chepstow (MH) U2459 |
| 11188 | VWO 225 | Bristol MW6G | 152.138 | B45F | 1/60 | Red & White, Chepstow (MH) U2559 |
| 11189 | VWO 226 | Bristol MW6G | 152.139 | B45F | 1/60 | Red & White, Chepstow (MH) U2659 |
| 11190 | VWO 227 | Bristol MW6G | 152.140 | B45F | 1/60 | Red & White, Chepstow (MH) U2759 |
| 11191 | VWO 228 | Bristol MW6G | 152.141 | B45F | 1/60 | Red & White, Chepstow (MH) U2859 |
| 11192 | VWO 229 | Bristol MW6G | 152.178 | B45F | 2/60 | Red & White, Chepstow (MH) U2959 |
| 11193 | VWO 230 | Bristol MW6G | 152.179 | B45F | 2/60 | Red & White, Chepstow (MH) U3059 |
| 11194 | VWO 231 | Bristol MW6G | 152.180 | B45F | 2/60 | Red & White, Chepstow (MH) U3159 |
| 11195 | VWO 232 | Bristol MW6G | 152.181 | B45F | 2/60 | Red & White, Chepstow (MH) U3259 |
| 11196 | 538 LHN | Bristol MW5G | 152.024 | B45F | 8/59 | United AS, Darlington (DM) BU538 |
| 11197 | 539 LHN | Bristol MW5G | 152.025 | B45F | 8/59 | United AS, Darlington (DM) BU539 |
| 11198 | 540 LHN | Bristol MW5G | 152.026 | B45F | 8/59 | United AS, Darlington (DM) BU540 |
| 11199 | 541 LHN | Bristol MW5G | 152.027 | B45F | 8/59 | United AS, Darlington (DM) BU541 |
| 11200 | 542 LHN | Bristol MW5G | 152.028 | B45F | 8/59 | United AS, Darlington (DM) BU542 |
| 11201 | 543 LHN | Bristol MW5G | 152.029 | B45F | 8/59 | United AS, Darlington (DM) BU543 |
| 11202 | 544 LHN | Bristol MW5G | 152.079 | B45F | 9/59 | United AS, Darlington (DM) BU544 |
| 11203 | 545 LHN | Bristol MW5G | 152.093 | B45F | 3/60 | United AS, Darlington (DM) BU545 |
| 11204 | 546 LHN | Bristol MW5G | 152.094 | B45F | 3/60 | United AS, Darlington (DM) BU546 |
| 11205 | 547 LHN | Bristol MW5G | 152.095 | B45F | 5/60 | United AS, Darlington (DM) BU547 |
| 11206 | 548 LHN | Bristol MW5G | 152.096 | B45F | 5/60 | United AS, Darlington (DM) BU548 |
| 11207 | 549 LHN | Bristol MW5G | 152.097 | B45F | 5/60 | United AS, Darlington (DM) BU549 |
| 11208 | 550 LHN | Bristol MW5G | 152.098 | B45F | 6/60 | United AS, Darlington (DM) BU550 |

| | | | | | | |
|---|---|---|---|---|---|---|
| 11209 | 551 LHN | Bristol MW5G | 152.099 | B45F | 6/60 | United AS, Darlington (DM) BU551 |
| 11210 | 552 LHN | Bristol MW5G | 152.124 | B45F | 6/60 | United AS, Darlington (DM) BU552 |
| 11211 | 553 LHN | Bristol MW5G | 152.125 | B45F | 3/60 | United AS, Darlington (DM) BU553 |
| 11212 | 554 LHN | Bristol MW5G | 152.126 | B45F | 6/60 | United AS, Darlington (DM) BU554 |
| 11213 | 555 LHN | Bristol MW5G | 152.127 | B45F | 6/60 | United AS, Darlington (DM) BU555 |
| 11214 | 556 LHN | Bristol MW5G | 152.128 | B45F | 6/60 | United AS, Darlington (DM) BU556 |
| 11215 | 557 LHN | Bristol MW5G | 152.129 | B45F | 6/60 | United AS, Darlington (DM) BU557 |
| 11216 | 558 LHN | Bristol MW5G | 152.130 | B45F | 6/60 | United AS, Darlington (DM) BU558 |
| 11217 | 559 LHN | Bristol MW5G | 152.142 | B45F | 6/60 | United AS, Darlington (DM) BU559 |
| 11218 | 560 LHN | Bristol MW5G | 152.143 | B45F | 6/60 | United AS, Darlington (DM) BU560 |
| 11219 | 561 LHN | Bristol MW5G | 152.144 | B45F | 6/60 | United AS, Darlington (DM) BU561 |
| 11220 | 562 LHN | Bristol MW5G | 152.145 | B45F | 6/60 | United AS, Darlington (DM) BU562 |
| 11221 | 563 LHN | Bristol MW5G | 152.146 | B45F | 6/60 | United AS, Darlington (DM) BU563 |
| 11222 | 564 LHN | Bristol MW5G | 152.147 | B45F | 6/60 | United AS, Darlington (DM) BU564 |
| 11223 | 565 LHN | Bristol MW5G | 152.148 | B45F | 6/60 | United AS, Darlington (DM) BU565 |
| 11224 | 566 LHN | Bristol MW5G | 152.149 | B45F | 6/60 | United AS, Darlington (DM) BU566 |
| 11225 | 567 LHN | Bristol MW5G | 152.161 | B45F | 6/60 | United AS, Darlington (DM) BU567 |
| 11226 | 568 LHN | Bristol MW5G | 152.162 | B45F | 3/60 | United AS, Darlington (DM) BU568 |
| 11227 | 569 LHN | Bristol MW5G | 152.163 | B45F | 3/60 | United AS, Darlington (DM) BU569 |
| 11228 | 570 LHN | Bristol MW5G | 152.164 | B45F | 6/60 | United AS, Darlington (DM) BU570 |
| 11229 | 571 LHN | Bristol MW5G | 152.165 | B45F | 6/60 | United AS, Darlington (DM) BU571 |
| 11230 | 572 LHN | Bristol MW5G | 152.166 | B45F | 6/60 | United AS, Darlington (DM) BU572 |
| 11231 | 573 LHN | Bristol MW5G | 152.167 | B45F | 6/60 | United AS, Darlington (DM) BU573 |
| 11232 | 574 LHN | Bristol MW5G | 152.168 | B45F | 6/60 | United AS, Darlington (DM) BU574 |
| 11233 | 575 LHN | Bristol MW5G | 152.182 | B45F | 6/60 | United AS, Darlington (DM) BU575 |
| 11234 | 576 LHN | Bristol MW5G | 152.183 | B45F | 6/60 | United AS, Darlington (DM) BU576 |
| 11235 | 577 LHN | Bristol MW5G | 152.184 | B45F | 6/60 | United AS, Darlington (DM) BU577 |
| 11236 | 578 LHN | Bristol MW5G | 152.185 | B45F | 6/60 | United AS, Darlington (DM) BU578 |
| 11237 | 579 LHN | Bristol MW5G | 152.186 | B45F | 6/60 | United AS, Darlington (DM) BU579 |
| 11238 | 580 LHN | Bristol MW5G | 152.187 | B45F | 6/60 | United AS, Darlington (DM) BU580 |
| 11239 | 581 LHN | Bristol MW5G | 152.188 | B45F | 6/60 | United AS, Darlington (DM) BU581 |
| 11240 | 582 LHN | Bristol MW5G | 152.189 | B45F | 6/60 | United AS, Darlington (DM) BU582 |
| 11241 | *TWN 114 | Bristol MW6G | 152.089 | B45F | 11/59 | United Welsh, Swansea (GG) 117 |
| 11242 | *TWN 115 | Bristol MW6G | 152.088 | B45F | 11/59 | United Welsh, Swansea (GG) 118 |
| 11243 | 196 BRR | Bristol MW6G | 152.052 | DP43F | 3/60 | Mansfield District (NG) 211 |
| 11244 | 197 BRR | Bristol MW6G | 152.053 | DP43F | 3/60 | Mansfield District (NG) 212 |
| 11245 | 508 JRA | Bristol MW6G | 152.005 | DP43F | 7/59 | Midland General, Langley Mill (DE) 274 |
| 11246 | 509 JRA | Bristol MW6G | 152.006 | DP43F | 7/59 | Midland General, Langley Mill (DE) 275 |
| 11247 | 510 JRA | Bristol MW6G | 152.007 | DP43F | 7/59 | Midland General, Langley Mill (DE) 276 |
| 11248 | 511 JRA | Bristol MW6G | 152.008 | DP43F | 7/59 | Midland General, Langley Mill (DE) 277 |
| 11249 | 512 JRA | Bristol MW6G | 152.009 | DP43F | 7/59 | Midland General, Langley Mill (DE) 278 |
| 11250 | 513 JRA | Bristol MW6G | 152.050 | DP43F | 6/60 | Midland General, Langley Mill (DE) 279 |
| 11251 | 514 JRA | Bristol MW6G | 152.051 | DP43F | 6/60 | Midland General, Langley Mill (DE) 280 |
| 11252 | 516 LHN | Bristol MW6G | 152.030 | DP39F | 8/59 | United AS, Darlington (DM) BUE516 |
| 11253 | 517 LHN | Bristol MW6G | 152.031 | DP39F | 8/59 | United AS, Darlington (DM) BUE517 |
| 11254 | 518 LHN | Bristol MW6G | 152.032 | DP39F | 8/59 | United AS, Darlington (DM) BUE518 |
| 11255 | 519 LHN | Bristol MW6G | 152.033 | DP39F | 8/59 | United AS, Darlington (DM) BUE519 |
| 11256 | 520 LHN | Bristol MW6G | 152.034 | DP39F | 8/59 | United AS, Darlington (DM) BUE520 |
| 11257 | 521 LHN | Bristol MW6G | 152.035 | DP39F | 8/59 | United AS, Darlington (DM) BUE521 |
| 11258 | 522 LHN | Bristol MW6G | 152.036 | DP39F | 8/59 | United AS, Darlington (DM) BUE522 |
| 11259 | 523 LHN | Bristol MW6G | 152.059 | DP39F | 6/60 | United AS, Darlington (DM) BUE523 |
| 11260 | 524 LHN | Bristol MW6G | 152.060 | DP39F | 6/60 | United AS, Darlington (DM) BUE524 |
| 11261 | 525 LHN | Bristol MW6G | 152.061 | DP39F | 6/60 | United AS, Darlington (DM) BUE525 |
| 11262 | 526 LHN | Bristol MW6G | 152.062 | DP39F | 6/60 | United AS, Darlington (DM) BUE526 |
| 11263 | 527 LHN | Bristol MW6G | 152.063 | DP39F | 6/60 | United AS, Darlington (DM) BUE527 |
| 11264 | 528 LHN | Bristol MW6G | 152.064 | DP39F | 6/60 | United AS, Darlington (DM) BUE528 |
| 11265 | 529 LHN | Bristol MW6G | 152.065 | DP39F | 6/60 | United AS, Darlington (DM) BUE529 |
| 11266 | 530 LHN | Bristol MW6G | 152.073 | DP39F | 6/60 | United AS, Darlington (DM) BUE530 |
| 11267 | 531 LHN | Bristol MW6G | 152.074 | DP39F | 6/60 | United AS, Darlington (DM) BUE531 |
| 11268 | 532 LHN | Bristol MW6G | 152.075 | DP39F | 6/60 | United AS, Darlington (DM) BUE532 |
| 11269 | 533 LHN | Bristol MW6G | 152.076 | DP39F | 6/60 | United AS, Darlington (DM) BUE533 |
| 11270 | 534 LHN | Bristol MW6G | 152.077 | DP39F | 6/60 | United AS, Darlington (DM) BUE534 |
| 11271 | 535 LHN | Bristol MW6G | 152.078 | DP39F | 6/60 | United AS, Darlington (DM) BUE535 |
| 11272 | YWT 290 | Bristol MW5G | 152.054 | DP41F | 8/59 | West Yorkshire RCC, Harrogate (WR) EUG76 |

| | | | | | | | |
|---|---|---|---|---|---|---|---|
| 11273 | YWT 291 | Bristol MW5G | 152.055 | DP41F | 8/59 | West Yorkshire RCC, Harrogate (WR) EUG77 |
| 11274 | YWT 292 | Bristol MW5G | 152.056 | DP41F | 8/59 | West Yorkshire RCC, Harrogate (WR) EUG78 |
| 11275 | YWT 293 | Bristol MW5G | 152.057 | DP41F | 8/59 | West Yorkshire RCC, Harrogate (WR) EUG79 |
| 11276 | YWT 294 | Bristol MW5G | 152.058 | DP41F | 6/60 | West Yorkshire RCC, Harrogate (WR) EUG80 |
| 11277 | 201 KFM | Bristol MW6G | 139.265 | C39F | -/59 | Crosville MS, Chester (CH) CMG361 |
| 11278 | 202 KFM | Bristol MW6G | 139.266 | C39F | 6/59 | Crosville MS, Chester (CH) CMG362 |
| 11279 | 203 KFM | Bristol MW6G | 139.267 | C39F | -/59 | Crosville MS, Chester (CH) CMG363 |
| 11280 | 204 KFM | Bristol MW6G | 139.268 | C39F | 6/59 | Crosville MS, Chester (CH) CMG364 |
| 11281 | 205 KFM | Bristol MW6G | 139.269 | C39F | 6/59 | Crosville MS, Chester (CH) CMG365 |
| 11282 | *206 KFM | Bristol MW6G | 139.270 | C39F | 6/59 | Crosville MS, Chester (CH) CMG366 |
| 11283 | 207 KFM | Bristol MW6G | 139.271 | C39F | 6/59 | Crosville MS, Chester (CH) CMG367 |
| 11284 | 208 KFM | Bristol MW6G | 139.285 | C39F | 6/59 | Crosville MS, Chester (CH) CMG368 |
| 11285 | 209 KFM | Bristol MW6G | 139.286 | C39F | 6/59 | Crosville MS, Chester (CH) CMG369 |
| 11286 | 210 KFM | Bristol MW6G | 139.287 | C39F | 6/59 | Crosville MS, Chester (CH) CMG370 |
| 11287 | XAO 600 | Bristol MW6G | 139.240 | C39F | 6/59 | Cumberland MS, Whitehaven (CU) 392 |
| 11288 | XAO 601 | Bristol MW6G | 139.241 | C39F | 6/59 | Cumberland MS, Whitehaven (CU) 393 |
| 11289 | 5788 AH | Bristol MW5G | 139.275 | C39F | 5/59 | Eastern Counties, Norwich (NK) LS788 |
| 11290 | 5789 AH | Bristol MW5G | 139.276 | C39F | 5/59 | Eastern Counties, Norwich (NK) LS789 |
| 11291 | 5790 AH | Bristol MW5G | 139.277 | C32F | 5/59 | Eastern Counties, Norwich (NK) LS790 |
| 11292 | 5791 AH | Bristol MW5G | 139.278 | C32F | 6/59 | Eastern Counties, Norwich (NK) LS791 |
| 11293 | 280 NHK | Bristol MW6G | 139.250 | C39F | 4/59 | Eastern National, Chelmsford (EX) 481 |
| 11294 | 281 NHK | Bristol MW6G | 139.251 | C39F | 4/59 | Eastern National, Chelmsford (EX) 482 |
| 11295 | 282 NHK | Bristol MW6G | 139.252 | C39F | 4/59 | Eastern National, Chelmsford (EX) 483 |
| 11296 | 283 NHK | Bristol MW6G | 139.253 | C39F | 4/59 | Eastern National, Chelmsford (EX) 484 |
| 11297 | 284 NHK | Bristol MW6G | 139.254 | C39F | 4/59 | Eastern National, Chelmsford (EX) 485 |
| 11298 | 285 NHK | Bristol MW6G | 139.255 | C39F | 4/59 | Eastern National, Chelmsford (EX) 486 |
| 11299 | YEL 227 | Bristol MW6G | 139.294 | C39F | 5/59 | Hants & Dorset, Bournemouth (HA) 868 |
| 11300 | YEL 228 | Bristol MW6G | 139.295 | C30F | 6/59 | Hants & Dorset, Bournemouth (HA) 869 |
| 11301 | YEL 229 | Bristol MW6G | 139.296 | C30F | 6/59 | Hants & Dorset, Bournemouth (HA) 870 |
| 11302 | NFE 311 | Bristol MW5G | 139.260 | C39F | 4/59 | Lincolnshire RCC, Lincoln (LC) 2815 |
| 11303 | NFE 312 | Bristol MW5G | 139.261 | C39F | 4/59 | Lincolnshire RCC, Lincoln (LC) 2816 |
| 11304 | UWO 701 | Bristol MW6G | 139.272 | C39F | 6/59 | Red & White, Chepstow (MH) UC159 |
| 11305 | UWO 702 | Bristol MW6G | 139.273 | C39F | 6/59 | Red & White, Chepstow (MH) UC259 |
| 11306 | UWO 703 | Bristol MW6G | 139.274 | C39F | 6/59 | Red & White, Chepstow (MH) UC359 |
| 11307 | UWO 704 | Bristol MW6G | 139.279 | C39F | 6/59 | Red & White, Chepstow (MH) UC459 |
| 11308 | UWO 705 | Bristol MW6G | 139.280 | C39F | 6/59 | Red & White, Chepstow (MH) UC559 |
| 11309 | UWO 706 | Bristol MW6G | 139.281 | C39F | 6/59 | Red & White, Chepstow (MH) UC659 |
| 11310 | UWO 707 | Bristol MW6G | 139.282 | C39F | 6/59 | Red & White, Chepstow (MH) UC759 |
| 11311 | UWO 708 | Bristol MW6G | 139.283 | C39F | 6/59 | Red & White, Chepstow (MH) UC859 |
| 11312 | UWO 709 | Bristol MW6G | 139.284 | C39F | 6/59 | Red & White, Chepstow (MH) UC959 |
| 11313 | UWO 710 | Bristol MW6G | 139.288 | C39F | 6/59 | Red & White, Chepstow (MH) UC1059 |
| 11314 | UWO 711 | Bristol MW6G | 139.289 | C39F | 6/59 | Red & White, Chepstow (MH) UC1159 |
| 11315 | UWO 712 | Bristol MW6G | 139.290 | C39F | 6/59 | Red & White, Chepstow (MH) UC1259 |
| 11316 | PRX 930 | Bristol MW6G | 139.256 | C34F | 4/59 | Thames Valley, Reading (BE) 804 |
| 11317 | PRX 931 | Bristol MW6G | 139.257 | C34F | 4/59 | Thames Valley, Reading (BE) 805 |
| 11318 | PRX 932 | Bristol MW6G | 139.258 | C34F | 4/59 | Thames Valley, Reading (BE) 806 |
| 11319 | PRX 933 | Bristol MW6G | 139.259 | C34F | 4/59 | Thames Valley, Reading (BE) 807 |
| 11320 | VYO 765 | Bristol MW6G | 139.245 | C39F | 4/59 | Tillings Transport, London WC1 (LN) |
| 11321 | VYO 766 | Bristol MW6G | 139.246 | C39F | 4/59 | Tillings Transport, London WC1 (LN) |
| 11322 | VYO 767 | Bristol MW6G | 139.247 | C41F | 4/59 | Tillings Transport, London WC1 (LN) |
| 11323 | VYO 768 | Bristol MW6G | 139.248 | C41F | 4/59 | Tillings Transport, London WC1 (LN) |
| 11324 | VYO 769 | Bristol MW6G | 139.249 | C41F | 4/59 | Tillings Transport, London WC1 (LN) |
| 11325 | TWN 101 | Bristol MW6G | 139.262 | C39F | 5/59 | United Welsh, Swansea (GG) 5 |
| 11326 | SWV 688 | Bristol MW6G | 139.263 | C39F | 4/59 | Wilts & Dorset, Salisbury (WI) 707 |
| 11327 | SWV 689 | Bristol MW6G | 139.264 | C39F | 4/59 | Wilts & Dorset, Salisbury (WI) 708 |
| 11328 | 190 KFM | Bristol SC4LK | 147.009 | C33F | 5/59 | Crosville MS, Chester (CH) CSG629 |
| 11329 | 191 KFM | Bristol SC4LK | 147.010 | C33F | 5/59 | Crosville MS, Chester (CH) CSG630 |
| 11330 | 192 KFM | Bristol SC4LK | 147.011 | C33F | 5/59 | Crosville MS, Chester (CH) CSG631 |
| 11331 | 193 KFM | Bristol SC4LK | 147.012 | C33F | 5/59 | Crosville MS, Chester (CH) CSG632 |
| 11332 | 194 KFM | Bristol SC4LK | 147.013 | C33F | 5/59 | Crosville MS, Chester (CH) CSG633 |
| 11333 | 195 KFM | Bristol SC4LK | 147.014 | C33F | 5/59 | Crosville MS, Chester (CH) CSG634 |
| 11334 | 196 KFM | Bristol SC4LK | 147.015 | C33F | 5/59 | Crosville MS, Chester (CH) CSG635 |
| 11335 | 197 KFM | Bristol SC4LK | 147.023 | C33F | 6/59 | Crosville MS, Chester (CH) CSG636 |
| 11336 | 198 KFM | Bristol SC4LK | 147.024 | C33F | 6/59 | Crosville MS, Chester (CH) CSG637 |

| | | | | | | |
|---|---|---|---|---|---|---|
| 11337 | 199 KFM | Bristol SC4LK | 147.025 | C33F | 6/59 | Crosville MS, Chester (CH) CSG638 |
| 11338 | 636 LFM | Bristol SC4LK | 147.029 | B35F | 7/59 | Crosville MS, Chester (CH) SSG639 |
| 11339 | 637 LFM | Bristol SC4LK | 147.030 | B35F | 9/59 | Crosville MS, Chester (CH) SSG640 |
| 11340 | 638 LFM | Bristol SC4LK | 147.031 | B35F | 7/59 | Crosville MS, Chester (CH) SSG641 |
| 11341 | 639 LFM | Bristol SC4LK | 147.043 | B35F | 11/59 | Crosville MS, Chester (CH) SSG642 |
| 11342 | 640 LFM | Bristol SC4LK | 147.044 | B35F | 11/59 | Crosville MS, Chester (CH) SSG643 |
| 11343 | 641 LFM | Bristol SC4LK | 147.045 | B35F | 11/59 | Crosville MS, Chester (CH) SSG644 |
| 11344 | 642 LFM | Bristol SC4LK | 147.046 | B35F | 11/59 | Crosville MS, Chester (CH) SSG645 |
| 11345 | 643 LFM | Bristol SC4LK | 158.005 | B35F | 3/60 | Crosville MS, Chester (CH) SSG646 |
| 11346 | 644 LFM | Bristol SC4LK | 158.006 | B35F | 3/60 | Crosville MS, Chester (CH) SSG647 |
| 11347 | 645 LFM | Bristol SC4LK | 158.007 | B35F | 3/60 | Crosville MS, Chester (CH) SSG648 |
| 11348 | 646 LFM | Bristol SC4LK | 158.008 | B35F | 3/60 | Crosville MS, Chester (CH) SSG649 |
| 11349 | 647 LFM | Bristol SC4LK | 158.011 | B35F | 6/60 | Crosville MS, Chester (CH) SSG650 |
| 11350 | 648 LFM | Bristol SC4LK | 158.012 | B35F | 6/60 | Crosville MS, Chester (CH) SSG651 |
| 11351 | 649 LFM | Bristol SC4LK | 158.013 | B35F | 5/60 | Crosville MS, Chester (CH) SSG652 |
| 11352 | 650 LFM | Bristol SC4LK | 158.014 | B35F | 5/60 | Crosville MS, Chester (CH) SSG653 |
| 11353 | XAO 610 | Bristol SC4LK | 147.022 | B35F | 6/59 | Cumberland MS, Whitehaven (CU) 402 |
| 11354 | XAO 611 | Bristol SC4LK | 147.026 | C33F | 6/59 | Cumberland MS, Whitehaven (CU) 403 |
| 11355 | 6557 AH | Bristol SC4LK | 147.027 | B35F | 6/59 | Eastern Counties, Norwich (NK) LC557 |
| 11356 | 6558 AH | Bristol SC4LK | 147.028 | B35F | 6/59 | Eastern Counties, Norwich (NK) LC558 |
| 11357 | 6559 AH | Bristol SC4LK | 147.036 | B35F | 9/59 | Eastern Counties, Norwich (NK) LC559 |
| 11358 | 6560 AH | Bristol SC4LK | 147.037 | B35F | 9/59 | Eastern Counties, Norwich (NK) LC560 |
| 11359 | 6561 AH | Bristol SC4LK | 147.038 | B35F | 9/59 | Eastern Counties, Norwich (NK) LC561 |
| 11360 | 6562 AH | Bristol SC4LK | 147.047 | B35F | 11/59 | Eastern Counties, Norwich (NK) LC562 |
| 11361 | 6563 AH | Bristol SC4LK | 147.048 | B35F | 11/59 | Eastern Counties, Norwich (NK) LC563 |
| 11362 | 6564 AH | Bristol SC4LK | 147.049 | B35F | 12/59 | Eastern Counties, Norwich (NK) LC564 |
| 11363 | 6566 NG | Bristol SC4LK | 158.031 | B35F | 6/60 | Eastern Counties, Norwich (NK) LC566 |
| 11364 | NFE 431 | Bristol SC4LK | 147.016 | B35F | 5/59 | Lincolnshire RCC, Lincoln (LC) 2461 |
| 11365 | NFE 433 | Bristol SC4LK | 147.017 | B35F | 5/59 | Lincolnshire RCC, Lincoln (LC) 2462 |
| 11366 | NFE 434 | Bristol SC4LK | 147.018 | B35F | 5/59 | Lincolnshire RCC, Lincoln (LC) 2463 |
| 11367 | NFE 435 | Bristol SC4LK | 147.019 | B35F | 5/59 | Lincolnshire RCC, Lincoln (LC) 2464 |
| 11368 | NFE 436 | Bristol SC4LK | 147.020 | B35F | 5/59 | Lincolnshire RCC, Lincoln (LC) 2465 |
| 11369 | NFE 437 | Bristol SC4LK | 147.021 | B35F | 5/59 | Lincolnshire RCC, Lincoln (LC) 2466 |
| 11370 | NFE 438 | Bristol SC4LK | 147.032 | B35F | 7/59 | Lincolnshire RCC, Lincoln (LC) 2467 |
| 11371 | NFE 439 | Bristol SC4LK | 147.033 | B35F | 7/59 | Lincolnshire RCC, Lincoln (LC) 2468 |
| 11372 | NFE 440 | Bristol SC4LK | 147.034 | B35F | 7/59 | Lincolnshire RCC, Lincoln (LC) 2469 |
| 11373 | NFE 441 | Bristol SC4LK | 147.035 | B35F | 7/59 | Lincolnshire RCC, Lincoln (LC) 2470 |
| 11374 | NFE 442 | Bristol SC4LK | 147.039 | B35F | 8/59 | Lincolnshire RCC, Lincoln (LC) 2471 |
| 11375 | NFE 443 | Bristol SC4LK | 147.040 | B35F | 9/59 | Lincolnshire RCC, Lincoln (LC) 2472 |
| 11376 | NFE 445 | Bristol SC4LK | 147.041 | B35F | 9/59 | Lincolnshire RCC, Lincoln (LC) 2473 |
| 11377 | NFE 446 | Bristol SC4LK | 147.042 | B35F | 9/59 | Lincolnshire RCC, Lincoln (LC) 2474 |
| 11378 | NFE 447 | Bristol SC4LK | 158.001 | B35F | 1/60 | Lincolnshire RCC, Lincoln (LC) 2475 |
| 11379 | NFE 448 | Bristol SC4LK | 158.002 | B35F | 1/60 | Lincolnshire RCC, Lincoln (LC) 2476 |
| 11380 | *NFE 449 | Bristol SC4LK | 158.003 | B35F | 1/60 | Lincolnshire RCC, Lincoln (LC) 2477 |
| 11381 | NFE 450 | Bristol SC4LK | 158.004 | B35F | 2/60 | Lincolnshire RCC, Lincoln (LC) 2478 |
| 11382 | NFE 451 | Bristol SC4LK | 158.009 | B35F | 2/60 | Lincolnshire RCC, Lincoln (LC) 2479 |
| 11383 | NFE 452 | Bristol SC4LK | 158.010 | B35F | 2/60 | Lincolnshire RCC, Lincoln (LC) 2480 |
| 11384 | 681 COD | Bristol SUS4A | 157.001 | B30F | 3/60 | Southern National, Exeter (DN) 609 |
| 11385 | 682 COD | Bristol SUS4A | 157.002 | B30F | 2/60 | Southern National, Exeter (DN) 610 |
| 11386 | 667 COD | Bristol SUS4A | 157.003 | B30F | 3/60 | Southern National, Exeter (DN) 611 |
| 11387 | 668 COD | Bristol SUS4A | 157.010 | B30F | 3/60 | Southern National, Exeter (DN) 612 |
| 11388 | 669 COD | Bristol SUS4A | 157.011 | B30F | 3/60 | Southern National, Exeter (DN) 613 |
| 11389 | *670 COD | Bristol SUS4A | 157.012 | B30F | 5/60 | Southern National, Exeter (DN) 614 |
| 11390 | 671 COD | Bristol SUS4A | 157.013 | B30F | 5/60 | Southern National, Exeter (DN) 615 |
| 11391 | 672 COD | Bristol SUS4A | 157.004 | B30F | 2/60 | Western National, Exeter (DN) 600 |
| 11392 | 673 COD | Bristol SUS4A | 157.005 | B30F | 2/60 | Western National, Exeter (DN) 601 |
| 11393 | 674 COD | Bristol SUS4A | 157.006 | B30F | 3/60 | Western National, Exeter (DN) 602 |
| 11394 | 675 COD | Bristol SUS4A | 157.007 | B30F | 2/60 | Western National, Exeter (DN) 603 |
| 11395 | 676 COD | Bristol SUS4A | 157.008 | B30F | 2/60 | Western National, Exeter (DN) 604 |
| 11396 | 677 COD | Bristol SUS4A | 157.009 | B30F | 3/60 | Western National, Exeter (DN) 605 |
| 11397 | 678 COD | Bristol SUS4A | 157.014 | B30F | 3/60 | Western National, Exeter (DN) 606 |
| 11398 | 679 COD | Bristol SUS4A | 157.015 | B30F | 3/60 | Western National, Exeter (DN) 607 |
| 11399 | 680 COD | Bristol SUS4A | 157.016 | B30F | 3/60 | Western National, Exeter (DN) 608 |
| 11400 | *FMO 22 | Bristol L6B Reb | 79.090 | FB39F | 4/59 | Thames Valley, Reading (BE) 818 |

| | | | | | | |
|---|---|---|---|---|---|---|
| 11401 | *FMO 24 | Bristol L6B Reb | 79.117 | FB39F | 4/59 | Thames Valley, Reading (BE) 820 |
| 11402 | *FMO 21 | Bristol L6B Reb | 79.089 | FB39F | 4/59 | Thames Valley, Reading (BE) 817 |
| 11403 | *FMO 23 | Bristol L6B Reb | 79.116 | FB39F | 4/59 | Thames Valley, Reading (BE) 819 |
| 11404 | | | | | | Not built |
| 11405 | | | | | | Not built |
| 11406 | | | | | | Not built |
| 11407 | 971 EHW | Bristol LD6B | 150.191 | H33/25R | 7/59 | Bristol OC (GL) LC8517 |
| 11408 | 972 EHW | Bristol LD6B | 150.192 | H33/25R | 7/59 | Bristol OC (GL) LC8518 |
| 11409 | 973 EHW | Bristol LD6B | 150.193 | H33/25R | 7/59 | Bristol OC (GL) LC8519 |
| 11410 | 974 EHW | Bristol LD6G | 150.194 | H33/25R | 7/59 | Bristol OC (GL) LC8520 |
| 11411 | 975 EHW | Bristol LD6G | 150.195 | H33/25R | 7/59 | Bristol OC (GL) LC8521 |
| 11412 | 976 EHW | Bristol LD6G | 150.196 | H33/25R | 7/59 | Bristol OC (GL) LC8522 |
| 11413 | 977 EHW | Bristol LD6G | 150.197 | H33/25R | 7/59 | Bristol OC (GL) LC8523 |
| 11414 | 978 EHW | Bristol LD6G | 150.198 | H33/25R | 8/59 | Bristol OC (GL) LC8524 |
| 11415 | 979 EHW | Bristol LD6G | 150.199 | H33/25R | 8/59 | Bristol OC (GL) LC8525 |
| 11416 | 980 EHW | Bristol LD6G | 150.200 | H33/25R | 8/59 | Bristol OC (GL) LC8526 |
| 11417 | 981 EHW | Bristol LD6G | 150.201 | H33/25R | 8/59 | Bristol OC (GL) LC8527 |
| 11418 | UJB 200 | Bristol FLF6B | 156.006 | CH37/28F | 11/60 | Thames Valley, Reading (BE) 834 |
| 11419 | UJB 201 | Bristol FLF6G | 169.006 | CH37/28F | 11/60 | Thames Valley, Reading (BE) 835 |
| 11420 | UJB 202 | Bristol FLF6G | 169.007 | CH37/28F | 11/60 | Thames Valley, Reading (BE) 836 |
| 11421 | UJB 203 | Bristol FLF6G | 169.008 | CH37/28F | 11/60 | Thames Valley, Reading (BE) 837 |
| 11422 | UJB 204 | Bristol FLF6G | 169.009 | CH37/28F | 11/60 | Thames Valley, Reading (BE) 838 |
| 11423 | OMS 209 | Bristol LD6G | 163.001 | H33/27R | 1/60 | W Alexander, Falkirk (SN) RD106 |
| 11424 | OMS 210 | Bristol LD6G | 163.002 | H33/27R | 1/60 | W Alexander, Falkirk (SN) RD107 |
| 11425 | OMS 211 | Bristol LD6G | 163.003 | H33/27R | 1/60 | W Alexander, Falkirk (SN) RD108 |
| 11426 | OMS 212 | Bristol LD6G | 163.004 | H33/27R | 1/60 | W Alexander, Falkirk (SN) RD109 |
| 11427 | OMS 213 | Bristol LD6G | 163.005 | H33/27R | 1/60 | W Alexander, Falkirk (SN) RD110 |
| 11428 | OMS 214 | Bristol LD6G | 163.016 | H33/27R | 1/60 | W Alexander, Falkirk (SN) RD111 |
| 11429 | OMS 215 | Bristol LD6G | 163.017 | H33/27R | 1/60 | W Alexander, Falkirk (SN) RD112 |
| 11430 | OMS 216 | Bristol LD6G | 163.018 | H33/27R | 1/60 | W Alexander, Falkirk (SN) RD113 |
| 11431 | OMS 217 | Bristol LD6G | 163.019 | H33/27R | 1/60 | W Alexander, Falkirk (SN) RD114 |
| 11432 | OMS 218 | Bristol LD6G | 163.020 | H33/27R | 1/60 | W Alexander, Falkirk (SN) RD115 |
| 11433 | OMS 219 | Bristol LD6G | 163.021 | H33/27R | 2/60 | W Alexander, Falkirk (SN) RD116 |
| 11434 | OMS 220 | Bristol LD6G | 163.022 | H33/27R | 2/60 | W Alexander, Falkirk (SN) RD117 |
| 11435 | OMS 221 | Bristol LD6G | 163.023 | H33/27R | 2/60 | W Alexander, Falkirk (SN) RD118 |
| 11436 | OMS 222 | Bristol LD6G | 163.024 | H33/27R | 2/60 | W Alexander, Falkirk (SN) RD119 |
| 11437 | OMS 223 | Bristol LD6G | 163.025 | H33/27R | 2/60 | W Alexander, Falkirk (SN) RD120 |
| 11438 | OMS 224 | Bristol LD6G | 163.051 | H33/27R | 3/60 | W Alexander, Falkirk (SN) RD121 |
| 11439 | OMS 225 | Bristol LD6G | 163.052 | H33/27R | 3/60 | W Alexander, Falkirk (SN) RD122 |
| 11440 | OMS 226 | Bristol LD6G | 163.053 | H33/27R | 3/60 | W Alexander, Falkirk (SN) RD123 |
| 11441 | OMS 227 | Bristol LD6G | 163.054 | H33/27R | 3/60 | W Alexander, Falkirk (SN) RD124 |
| 11442 | OMS 228 | Bristol LD6G | 163.055 | H33/27R | 3/60 | W Alexander, Falkirk (SN) RD125 |
| 11443 | OMS 229 | Bristol LD6G | 163.070 | H33/27R | 4/60 | W Alexander, Falkirk (SN) RD126 |
| 11444 | OMS 230 | Bristol LD6G | 163.071 | H33/27R | 4/60 | W Alexander, Falkirk (SN) RD127 |
| 11445 | OMS 231 | Bristol LD6G | 163.072 | H33/27R | 4/60 | W Alexander, Falkirk (SN) RD128 |
| 11446 | OMS 232 | Bristol LD6G | 163.073 | H33/27R | 4/60 | W Alexander, Falkirk (SN) RD129 |
| 11447 | OMS 233 | Bristol LD6G | 163.074 | H33/27R | 4/60 | W Alexander, Falkirk (SN) RD130 |
| 11448 | OMS 234 | Bristol LD6G | 163.080 | H33/27R | 5/60 | W Alexander, Falkirk (SN) RD131 |
| 11449 | OMS 235 | Bristol LD6G | 163.081 | H33/27R | 5/60 | W Alexander, Falkirk (SN) RD132 |
| 11450 | OMS 236 | Bristol LD6G | 163.082 | H33/27R | 5/60 | W Alexander, Falkirk (SN) RD133 |
| 11451 | OMS 237 | Bristol LD6G | 163.083 | H33/27R | 5/60 | W Alexander, Falkirk (SN) RD134 |
| 11452 | OMS 238 | Bristol LD6G | 163.084 | H33/27R | 5/60 | W Alexander, Falkirk (SN) RD135 |
| 11453 | BGM 96 | Bristol LD6G | 163.036 | H33/27R | 2/60 | Central SMT, Motherwell (LK) B96 |
| 11454 | BGM 97 | Bristol LD6G | 163.037 | H33/27R | 2/60 | Central SMT, Motherwell (LK) B97 |
| 11455 | BGM 98 | Bristol LD6G | 163.038 | H33/27R | 2/60 | Central SMT, Motherwell (LK) B98 |
| 11456 | BGM 99 | Bristol LD6G | 163.039 | H33/27R | 3/60 | Central SMT, Motherwell (LK) B99 |
| 11457 | BGM 100 | Bristol LD6G | 163.040 | H33/27R | 2/60 | Central SMT, Motherwell (LK) B100 |
| 11458 | BGM 101 | Bristol LD6G | 163.056 | H33/27R | 3/60 | Central SMT, Motherwell (LK) B101 |
| 11459 | BGM 102 | Bristol LD6G | 163.057 | H33/27R | 3/60 | Central SMT, Motherwell (LK) B102 |
| 11460 | BGM 103 | Bristol LD6G | 163.058 | H33/27R | 3/60 | Central SMT, Motherwell (LK) B103 |
| 11461 | BGM 104 | Bristol LD6G | 163.059 | H33/27R | 3/60 | Central SMT, Motherwell (LK) B104 |
| 11462 | BGM 105 | Bristol LD6G | 163.060 | H33/27R | 3/60 | Central SMT, Motherwell (LK) B105 |
| 11463 | BGM 106 | Bristol LD6G | 163.061 | H33/27R | 3/60 | Central SMT, Motherwell (LK) B106 |
| 11464 | BGM 107 | Bristol LD6G | 163.062 | H33/27R | 4/60 | Central SMT, Motherwell (LK) B107 |

| | | | | | | |
|---|---|---|---|---|---|---|
| 11465 | BGM 108 | Bristol LD6G | 163.063 | H33/27R | 4/60 | Central SMT, Motherwell (LK) B108 |
| 11466 | BGM 109 | Bristol LD6G | 163.064 | H33/27R | 4/60 | Central SMT, Motherwell (LK) B109 |
| 11467 | BGM 110 | Bristol LD6G | 163.065 | H33/27RD | 4/60 | Central SMT, Motherwell (LK) B110 |
| 11468 | BGM 111 | Bristol LD6G | 163.075 | H33/27RD | 4/60 | Central SMT, Motherwell (LK) B111 |
| 11469 | BGM 112 | Bristol LD6G | 163.076 | H33/27RD | 4/60 | Central SMT, Motherwell (LK) B112 |
| 11470 | BGM 113 | Bristol LD6G | 163.077 | H33/27RD | 4/60 | Central SMT, Motherwell (LK) B113 |
| 11471 | BGM 114 | Bristol LD6G | 163.078 | H33/27RD | 5/60 | Central SMT, Motherwell (LK) B114 |
| 11472 | BGM 115 | Bristol LD6G | 163.079 | H33/27RD | 5/60 | Central SMT, Motherwell (LK) B115 |
| 11473 | USC 750 | Bristol LD6G | 163.006 | H33/27RD | 12/59 | Scottish Omnibuses, Edinburgh (MN) AA750 |
| 11474 | USC 751 | Bristol LD6G | 163.007 | H33/27RD | 12/59 | Scottish Omnibuses, Edinburgh (MN) AA751 |
| 11475 | USC 752 | Bristol LD6G | 163.008 | H33/27RD | 12/59 | Scottish Omnibuses, Edinburgh (MN) AA752 |
| 11476 | USC 753 | Bristol LD6G | 163.009 | H33/27RD | 12/59 | Scottish Omnibuses, Edinburgh (MN) AA753 |
| 11477 | USC 754 | Bristol LD6G | 163.010 | H33/27RD | 12/59 | Scottish Omnibuses, Edinburgh (MN) AA754 |
| 11478 | USC 755 | Bristol LD6G | 163.011 | H33/27RD | 12/59 | Scottish Omnibuses, Edinburgh (MN) AA755 |
| 11479 | USC 756 | Bristol LD6G | 163.012 | H33/27RD | 1/60 | Scottish Omnibuses, Edinburgh (MN) AA756 |
| 11480 | USC 757 | Bristol LD6G | 163.013 | H33/27RD | 1/60 | Scottish Omnibuses, Edinburgh (MN) AA757 |
| 11481 | USC 758 | Bristol LD6G | 163.014 | H33/27RD | 1/60 | Scottish Omnibuses, Edinburgh (MN) AA758 |
| 11482 | USC 759 | Bristol LD6G | 163.015 | H33/27RD | 1/60 | Scottish Omnibuses, Edinburgh (MN) AA759 |
| 11483 | USC 760 | Bristol LD6G | 163.031 | H33/27RD | 1/60 | Scottish Omnibuses, Edinburgh (MN) AA760 |
| 11484 | USC 761 | Bristol LD6G | 163.032 | H33/27RD | 1/60 | Scottish Omnibuses, Edinburgh (MN) AA761 |
| 11485 | USC 762 | Bristol LD6G | 163.033 | H33/27RD | 1/60 | Scottish Omnibuses, Edinburgh (MN) AA762 |
| 11486 | USC 763 | Bristol LD6G | 163.034 | H33/27RD | 2/60 | Scottish Omnibuses, Edinburgh (MN) AA763 |
| 11487 | USC 764 | Bristol LD6G | 163.035 | H33/27RD | 2/60 | Scottish Omnibuses, Edinburgh (MN) AA764 |
| 11488 | USC 765 | Bristol LD6G | 163.041 | H33/27RD | 2/60 | Scottish Omnibuses, Edinburgh (MN) AA765 |
| 11489 | USC 766 | Bristol LD6G | 163.042 | H33/27RD | 2/60 | Scottish Omnibuses, Edinburgh (MN) AA766 |
| 11490 | USC 767 | Bristol LD6G | 163.043 | H33/27RD | 2/60 | Scottish Omnibuses, Edinburgh (MN) AA767 |
| 11491 | USC 768 | Bristol LD6G | 163.044 | H33/27RD | 2/60 | Scottish Omnibuses, Edinburgh (MN) AA768 |
| 11492 | USC 769 | Bristol LD6G | 163.045 | H33/27RD | 2/60 | Scottish Omnibuses, Edinburgh (MN) AA769 |
| 11493 | USC 770 | Bristol LD6G | 163.046 | H33/27RD | 3/60 | Scottish Omnibuses, Edinburgh (MN) AA770 |
| 11494 | USC 771 | Bristol LD6G | 163.047 | H33/27RD | 3/60 | Scottish Omnibuses, Edinburgh (MN) AA771 |
| 11495 | USC 772 | Bristol LD6G | 163.048 | H33/27RD | 3/60 | Scottish Omnibuses, Edinburgh (MN) AA772 |
| 11496 | USC 773 | Bristol LD6G | 163.049 | H33/27RD | 3/60 | Scottish Omnibuses, Edinburgh (MN) AA773 |
| 11497 | USC 774 | Bristol LD6G | 163.050 | H33/27RD | 3/60 | Scottish Omnibuses, Edinburgh (MN) AA774 |
| 11498 | OCS 61 | Bristol LD6G | 163.026 | H33/27RD | 2/60 | Western SMT, Kilmarnock (AR) B1557 |
| 11499 | OCS 62 | Bristol LD6G | 163.027 | H33/27RD | 2/60 | Western SMT, Kilmarnock (AR) B1558 |
| 11500 | OCS 63 | Bristol LD6G | 163.028 | H33/27RD | 2/60 | Western SMT, Kilmarnock (AR) B1559 |
| 11501 | OCS 64 | Bristol LD6G | 163.029 | H33/27RD | 2/60 | Western SMT, Kilmarnock (AR) B1560 |
| 11502 | OCS 65 | Bristol LD6G | 163.030 | H33/27RD | 2/60 | Western SMT, Kilmarnock (AR) B1561 |
| 11503 | OCS 66 | Bristol LD6G | 163.066 | H33/27RD | 5/60 | Western SMT, Kilmarnock (AR) B1562 |
| 11504 | OCS 67 | Bristol LD6G | 163.067 | H33/27RD | 5/60 | Western SMT, Kilmarnock (AR) B1563 |
| 11505 | OCS 68 | Bristol LD6G | 163.068 | H33/27RD | 5/60 | Western SMT, Kilmarnock (AR) B1564 |
| 11506 | OCS 69 | Bristol LD6G | 163.069 | H33/27RD | 5/60 | Western SMT, Kilmarnock (AR) B1565 |
| 11507 | OCS 70 | Bristol LD6G | 163.085 | H33/27RD | 6/60 | Western SMT, Kilmarnock (AR) B1566 |
| 11508 | TPN 26 | Bristol FSF6B | 167.025 | H34/26F | 1/61 | Brighton, Hove & District (ES) 26 |
| 11509 | TPN 27 | Bristol FSF6B | 167.026 | H34/26F | 1/61 | Brighton, Hove & District (ES) 27 |
| 11510 | UAP 28 | Bristol FSF6B | 167.048 | H34/26F | 2/61 | Brighton, Hove & District (ES) 28 |
| 11511 | UAP 29 | Bristol FSF6B | 167.049 | H34/26F | 2/61 | Brighton, Hove & District (ES) 29 |
| 11512 | UAP 30 | Bristol FSF6B | 167.050 | H34/26F | 2/61 | Brighton, Hove & District (ES) 30 |
| 11513 | 709 JHY | Bristol FSF6B | 167.009 | H34/26F | 11/60 | Bristol OC (GL) LC8568 |
| 11514 | 710 JHY | Bristol FSF6B | 167.010 | H34/26F | 11/60 | Bristol OC (GL) LC8569 |
| 11515 | 711 JHY | Bristol FSF6B | 167.011 | H34/26F | 11/60 | Bristol OC (GL) LC8570 |
| 11516 | 712 JHY | Bristol FSF6B | 167.012 | H34/26F | 11/60 | Bristol OC (GL) LC8571 |
| 11517 | 713 JHY | Bristol FSF6B | 167.013 | H34/26F | 11/60 | Bristol OC (GL) LC8572 |
| 11518 | 714 JHY | Bristol FSF6B | 167.014 | H34/26F | 11/60 | Bristol OC (GL) LC8573 |
| 11519 | 715 JHY | Bristol FSF6B | 167.015 | H34/26F | 11/60 | Bristol OC (GL) LC8574 |
| 11520 | 716 JHY | Bristol FSF6B | 167.016 | H34/26F | 11/60 | Bristol OC (GL) LC8575 |
| 11521 | 717 JHY | Bristol FSF6B | 167.037 | H34/26F | 2/61 | Bristol OC (GL) C6025 |
| 11522 | 718 JHY | Bristol FSF6B | 167.038 | H34/26F | 2/61 | Bristol OC (GL) C6026 |
| 11523 | 723 JHY | Bristol FSF6B | 167.039 | H34/26F | 2/61 | Bristol OC (GL) C6027 |
| 11524 | 724 JHY | Bristol FSF6B | 167.040 | H34/26F | 2/61 | Bristol OC (GL) C6028 |
| 11525 | 725 JHY | Bristol FSF6B | 167.041 | H34/26F | 2/61 | Bristol OC (GL) C6029 |
| 11526 | 704 JHY | Bristol FSF6G | 167.002 | H34/26F | 10/60 | Bristol OC (GL) LC8565 |
| 11527 | 719 JHY | Bristol FSF6G | 167.030 | H34/26F | 2/61 | Bristol OC (GL) 6020 |
| 11528 | 720 JHY | Bristol FSF6G | 167.031 | H34/26F | 2/61 | Bristol OC (GL) 6021 |

| | | | | | | | |
|---|---|---|---|---|---|---|---|
| 11529 | 721 JHY | Bristol FSF6G | 167.032 | H34/26F | 2/61 | Bristol OC (GL) 6022 |
| 11530 | 722 JHY | Bristol FSF6G | 167.033 | H34/26F | 2/61 | Bristol OC (GL) 6023 |
| 11531 | 726 JHY | Bristol FSF6G | 167.034 | H34/26F | 2/61 | Bristol OC (GL) 6024 |
| 11532 | 727 JHY | Bristol FSF6G | 167.042 | H34/26F | 2/61 | Bristol OC (GL) 6030 |
| 11533 | *728 JHY | Bristol FSF6G | 167.043 | H34/26F | 3/61 | Bristol OC (GL) 6031 |
| 11534 | 729 JHY | Bristol FSF6G | 167.044 | H34/26F | 3/61 | Bristol OC (GL) 6032 |
| 11535 | 730 JHY | Bristol FSF6G | 167.045 | H34/26F | 3/61 | Bristol OC (GL) 6033 |
| 11536 | 731 JHY | Bristol FSF6G | 167.046 | H34/26F | 3/61 | Bristol OC (GL) 6034 |
| 11537 | 732 JHY | Bristol FSF6G | 167.047 | H34/26F | 3/61 | Bristol OC (GL) 6035 |
| 11538 | 701 JHY | Bristol FSF6G | 156.019 | H34/26F | 10/60 | Bristol OC (GL) GL8562 |
| 11539 | 702 JHY | Bristol FSF6G | 156.020 | H34/26F | 10/60 | Bristol OC (GL) GL8563 |
| 11540 | 703 JHY | Bristol FSF6G | 167.001 | H34/26F | 10/60 | Bristol OC (GL) GL8564 |
| 11541 | 705 JHY | Bristol FSF6G | 156.017 | H34/26F | 11/60 | Cheltenham District (GL) L99 |
| 11542 | *706 JHY | Bristol FSF6G | 156.018 | H34/26F | 11/60 | Cheltenham District (GL) L100 |
| 11543 | 707 JHY | Bristol FSF6G | 156.015 | H34/26F | 11/60 | Bath Tramways Motor Co (SO) L8566 |
| 11544 | 708 JHY | Bristol FSF6G | 156.016 | H34/26F | 11/60 | Bath Tramways Motor Co (SO) L8567 |
| 11545 | 501 BRM | Bristol FSF6B | 167.003 | H34/26F | 10/60 | Cumberland MS, Whitehaven (CU) C404 |
| 11546 | 502 BRM | Bristol FSF6B | 167.004 | H34/26F | 10/60 | Cumberland MS, Whitehaven (CU) C405 |
| 11547 | 503 BRM | Bristol FSF6B | 167.005 | H34/26F | 11/60 | Cumberland MS, Whitehaven (CU) C406 |
| 11548 | *504 BRM | Bristol FSF6B | 167.017 | H34/26F | 11/60 | Cumberland MS, Whitehaven (CU) C407 |
| 11549 | *505 BRM | Bristol FSF6B | 167.018 | H34/26F | 11/60 | Cumberland MS, Whitehaven (CU) C408 |
| 11550 | 2057 HN | Bristol FSF6B | 167.006 | H34/26F | 11/60 | United AS, Darlington (DM) BL57 |
| 11551 | 2058 HN | Bristol FSF6B | 167.007 | H34/26F | 11/60 | United AS, Darlington (DM) BL58 |
| 11552 | 2059 HN | Bristol FSF6B | 167.008 | H34/26F | 11/60 | United AS, Darlington (DM) BL59 |
| 11553 | 2060 HN | Bristol FSF6B | 167.019 | H34/26F | 12/60 | United AS, Darlington (DM) BL60 |
| 11554 | 2061 HN | Bristol FSF6B | 167.020 | H34/26F | 12/60 | United AS, Darlington (DM) BL61 |
| 11555 | 2062 HN | Bristol FSF6B | 167.021 | H34/26F | 12/60 | United AS, Darlington (DM) BL62 |
| 11556 | 2063 HN | Bristol FSF6B | 167.022 | H34/26F | 12/60 | United AS, Darlington (DM) BL63 |
| 11557 | 2064 HN | Bristol FSF6B | 167.023 | H34/26F | 12/60 | United AS, Darlington (DM) BL64 |
| 11558 | 2065 HN | Bristol FSF6B | 167.024 | H34/26F | 12/60 | United AS, Darlington (DM) BL65 |
| 11559 | 2066 HN | Bristol FSF6B | 167.027 | H34/26F | 3/61 | United AS, Darlington (DM) BL66 |
| 11560 | 2067 HN | Bristol FSF6B | 167.028 | H34/26F | 3/61 | United AS, Darlington (DM) BL67 |
| 11561 | 2068 HN | Bristol FSF6B | 167.029 | H34/26F | 3/61 | United AS, Darlington (DM) BL68 |
| 11562 | 2069 HN | Bristol FSF6B | 167.035 | H34/26F | 3/61 | United AS, Darlington (DM) BL69 |
| 11563 | 2070 HN | Bristol FSF6B | 167.036 | H34/26F | 3/61 | United AS, Darlington (DM) BL70 |
| 11564 | 2071 HN | Bristol FSF6B | 167.051 | H34/26F | 3/61 | United AS, Darlington (DM) BL71 |
| 11565 | 2072 HN | Bristol FSF6B | 167.052 | H34/26F | 3/61 | United AS, Darlington (DM) BL72 |
| 11566 | 2073 HN | Bristol FSF6B | 167.060 | H34/26F | 3/61 | United AS, Darlington (DM) BL73 |
| 11567 | 2074 HN | Bristol FSF6B | 167.061 | H34/26F | 3/61 | United AS, Darlington (DM) BL74 |
| 11568 | 2075 HN | Bristol FSF6B | 167.062 | H34/26F | 4/61 | United AS, Darlington (DM) BL75 |
| 11569 | 2076 HN | Bristol FSF6B | 167.063 | H34/26F | 5/61 | United AS, Darlington (DM) BL76 |
| 11570 | RPN 9 | Bristol FS6B | 155.029 | CO33/27R | 5/60 | Brighton, Hove & District (ES) 9 |
| 11571 | *RPN 10 | Bristol FS6B | 155.030 | CO33/27R | 5/60 | Brighton, Hove & District (ES) 10 |
| 11572 | *RPN 11 | Bristol FS6B | 155.031 | CO33/27R | 5/60 | Brighton, Hove & District (ES) 11 |
| 11573 | *SPM 21 | Bristol FS6B | 155.087 | CO33/27R | 7/60 | Brighton, Hove & District (ES) 21 |
| 11574 | *SPM 22 | Bristol FS6B | 155.090 | CO33/27R | 7/60 | Brighton, Hove & District (ES) 22 |
| 11575 | 307 PFM | Bristol FS6G | 155.049 | H33/27RD | 6/60 | Crosville MS, Chester (CH) DFG26 |
| 11576 | *308 PFM | Bristol FS6G | 155.050 | H33/27RD | 6/60 | Crosville MS, Chester (CH) DFG27 |
| 11577 | 309 PFM | Bristol FS6G | 155.054 | H33/27RD | 6/60 | Crosville MS, Chester (CH) DFG28 |
| 11578 | 310 PFM | Bristol FS6G | 155.066 | H33/27RD | 7/60 | Crosville MS, Chester (CH) DFG29 |
| 11579 | 311 PFM | Bristol FS6G | 155.067 | H33/27RD | 7/60 | Crosville MS, Chester (CH) DFG30 |
| 11580 | 312 PFM | Bristol FS6G | 155.071 | H33/27RD | 7/60 | Crosville MS, Chester (CH) DFG31 |
| 11581 | 313 PFM | Bristol FS6G | 166.005 | H33/27RD | 9/60 | Crosville MS, Chester (CH) DFG32 |
| 11582 | 314 PFM | Bristol FS6G | 166.006 | H33/27RD | 9/60 | Crosville MS, Chester (CH) DFG33 |
| 11583 | 315 PFM | Bristol FS6G | 166.042 | H33/27RD | 5/61 | Crosville MS, Chester (CH) DFG34 |
| 11584 | 316 PFM | Bristol FS6G | 166.043 | H33/27RD | 5/61 | Crosville MS, Chester (CH) DFG35 |
| 11585 | 317 PFM | Bristol FS6G | 166.044 | H33/27RD | 5/61 | Crosville MS, Chester (CH) DFG36 |
| 11586 | 318 PFM | Bristol FS6G | 166.070 | H33/27RD | 7/61 | Crosville MS, Chester (CH) DFG37 |
| 11587 | *319 PFM | Bristol FS6G | 166.079 | H33/27RD | 7/61 | Crosville MS, Chester (CH) DFG38 |
| 11588 | 320 PFM | Bristol FS6G | 166.080 | H33/27RD | 7/61 | Crosville MS, Chester (CH) DFG39 |
| 11589 | 5601 NG | Bristol FS5G | 155.046 | H33/27RD | 6/60 | Eastern Counties, Norwich (NK) LFS1 |
| 11590 | 5602 NG | Bristol FS5G | 155.047 | H33/27RD | 6/60 | Eastern Counties, Norwich (NK) LFS2 |
| 11591 | 5603 NG | Bristol FS5G | 155.048 | H33/27RD | 6/60 | Eastern Counties, Norwich (NK) LFS3 |
| 11592 | 5604 NG | Bristol FS5G | 155.088 | H33/27RD | 7/60 | Eastern Counties, Norwich (NK) LFS4 |

| | | | | | | |
|---|---|---|---|---|---|---|
| 11593 | 5605 NG | Bristol FS5G | 155.089 | H33/27RD | 7/60 | Eastern Counties, Norwich (NK) LFS5 |
| 11594 | 5606 NG | Bristol FS5G | 166.001 | H33/27RD | 8/60 | Eastern Counties, Norwich (NK) LFS6 |
| 11595 | 5607 NG | Bristol FS5G | 166.002 | H33/27RD | 7/60 | Eastern Counties, Norwich (NK) LFS7 |
| 11596 | 5608 NG | Bristol FS5G | 166.013 | H33/27RD | 8/60 | Eastern Counties, Norwich (NK) LFS8 |
| 11597 | 5609 NG | Bristol FS5G | 166.014 | H33/27RD | 9/60 | Eastern Counties, Norwich (NK) LFS9 |
| 11598 | 5610 NG | Bristol FS5G | 166.015 | H33/27RD | 9/60 | Eastern Counties, Norwich (NK) LFS10 |
| 11599 | 5611 NG | Bristol FS5G | 166.039 | H33/27RD | 4/61 | Eastern Counties, Norwich (NK) LFS11 |
| 11600 | 5612 NG | Bristol FS5G | 166.040 | H33/27RD | 4/61 | Eastern Counties, Norwich (NK) LFS12 |
| 11601 | 5613 NG | Bristol FS5G | 166.041 | H33/27RD | 4/61 | Eastern Counties, Norwich (NK) LFS13 |
| 11602 | 5614 NG | Bristol FS5G | 166.073 | H33/27RD | 6/61 | Eastern Counties, Norwich (NK) LFS14 |
| 11603 | 5615 NG | Bristol FS5G | 166.076 | H33/27RD | 6/61 | Eastern Counties, Norwich (NK) LFS15 |
| 11604 | 5616 NG | Bristol FS5G | 166.077 | H33/27RD | 6/61 | Eastern Counties, Norwich (NK) LFS16 |
| 11605 | 5666 EL | Bristol FS6B | 155.043 | H33/27RD | 5/60 | Hants & Dorset, Bournemouth (HA) 1439 |
| 11606 | 5667 EL | Bristol FS6B | 155.044 | H33/27RD | 5/60 | Hants & Dorset, Bournemouth (HA) 1440 |
| 11607 | 5668 EL | Bristol FS6B | 155.045 | H33/27RD | 5/60 | Hants & Dorset, Bournemouth (HA) 1441 |
| 11608 | 5669 EL | Bristol FS6G | 155.079 | H33/27RD | 7/60 | Hants & Dorset, Bournemouth (HA) 1442 |
| 11609 | 5670 EL | Bristol FS6G | 155.080 | H33/27RD | 7/60 | Hants & Dorset, Bournemouth (HA) 1443 |
| 11610 | 5671 EL | Bristol FS6B | 166.003 | H33/27RD | 8/60 | Hants & Dorset, Bournemouth (HA) 1444 |
| 11611 | 5672 EL | Bristol FS6B | 166.004 | H33/27RD | 8/60 | Hants & Dorset, Bournemouth (HA) 1445 |
| 11612 | 5673 EL | Bristol FS6G | 166.016 | H33/27RD | 8/60 | Hants & Dorset, Bournemouth (HA) 1446 |
| 11613 | 5674 EL | Bristol FS6G | 166.017 | H33/27RD | 9/60 | Hants & Dorset, Bournemouth (HA) 1447 |
| 11614 | 5675 EL | Bristol FS6G | 166.018 | H33/27RD | 9/60 | Hants & Dorset, Bournemouth (HA) 1448 |
| 11615 | 5676 EL | Bristol FS6G | 166.025 | H33/27RD | 2/61 | Hants & Dorset, Bournemouth (HA) 1449 |
| 11616 | 5677 EL | Bristol FS6G | 166.026 | H33/27RD | 2/61 | Hants & Dorset, Bournemouth (HA) 1450 |
| 11617 | *5678 EL | Bristol FS6G | 166.027 | H33/27RD | 2/61 | Hants & Dorset, Bournemouth (HA) 1451 |
| 11618 | 5679 EL | Bristol FS6G | 166.084 | H33/27RD | 6/61 | Hants & Dorset, Bournemouth (HA) 1452 |
| 11619 | 5680 EL | Bristol FS6G | 166.085 | H33/27RD | 6/61 | Hants & Dorset, Bournemouth (HA) 1453 |
| 11620 | OVL 470 | Bristol FS5G | 155.068 | H33/27RD | 6/60 | Lincolnshire RCC, Lincoln (LC) 2375 |
| 11621 | OVL 471 | Bristol FS5G | 155.069 | H33/27RD | 6/60 | Lincolnshire RCC, Lincoln (LC) 2376 |
| 11622 | OVL 472 | Bristol FS5G | 155.070 | H33/27RD | 6/60 | Lincolnshire RCC, Lincoln (LC) 2377 |
| 11623 | *OVL 473 | Bristol FS5G | 155.081 | H33/27RD | 7/60 | Lincolnshire RCC, Lincoln (LC) 2378 |
| 11624 | *OVL 474 | Bristol FS5G | 155.082 | H33/27RD | 7/60 | Lincolnshire RCC, Lincoln (LC) 2379 |
| 11625 | OVL 475 | Bristol FS5G | 155.083 | H33/27RD | 7/60 | Lincolnshire RCC, Lincoln (LC) 2380 |
| 11626 | OVL 476 | Bristol FS5G | 155.084 | H33/27RD | 7/60 | Lincolnshire RCC, Lincoln (LC) 2381 |
| 11627 | OVL 477 | Bristol FS5G | 166.007 | H33/27RD | 8/60 | Lincolnshire RCC, Lincoln (LC) 2382 |
| 11628 | OVL 478 | Bristol FS5G | 166.008 | H33/27RD | 8/60 | Lincolnshire RCC, Lincoln (LC) 2383 |
| 11629 | OVL 479 | Bristol FS5G | 166.009 | H33/27RD | 8/60 | Lincolnshire RCC, Lincoln (LC) 2384 |
| 11630 | OVL 480 | Bristol FS5G | 166.053 | H33/27RD | 4/61 | Lincolnshire RCC, Lincoln (LC) 2385 |
| 11631 | OVL 481 | Bristol FS5G | 166.054 | H33/27RD | 4/61 | Lincolnshire RCC, Lincoln (LC) 2386 |
| 11632 | OVL 482 | Bristol FS5G | 166.055 | H33/27RD | 5/61 | Lincolnshire RCC, Lincoln (LC) 2387 |
| 11633 | OVL 483 | Bristol FS5G | 166.086 | H33/27RD | 6/61 | Lincolnshire RCC, Lincoln (LC) 2388 |
| 11634 | OVL 484 | Bristol FS5G | 166.087 | H33/27RD | 7/61 | Lincolnshire RCC, Lincoln (LC) 2389 |
| 11635 | 561 ERR | Bristol FS6G | 155.055 | H33/27RD | 7/60 | Mansfield District (NG) 525 |
| 11636 | 562 ERR | Bristol FS6G | 155.056 | H33/27RD | 7/60 | Mansfield District (NG) 526 |
| 11637 | 563 ERR | Bristol FS6G | 155.057 | H33/27RD | 7/60 | Mansfield District (NG) 527 |
| 11638 | 564 ERR | Bristol FS6G | 155.058 | H33/27RD | 7/60 | Mansfield District (NG) 528 |
| 11639 | 565 ERR | Bristol FS6G | 155.059 | H33/27RD | 7/60 | Mansfield District (NG) 529 |
| 11640 | 566 ERR | Bristol FS6G | 155.060 | H33/27RD | 7/60 | Mansfield District (NG) 530 |
| 11641 | 567 ERR | Bristol FS6G | 166.028 | H33/27RD | 3/61 | Mansfield District (NG) 531 |
| 11642 | 568 ERR | Bristol FS6G | 166.029 | H33/27RD | 3/61 | Mansfield District (NG) 532 |
| 11643 | 569 ERR | Bristol FS6G | 166.030 | H33/27RD | 3/61 | Mansfield District (NG) 533 |
| 11644 | 570 ERR | Bristol FS6G | 166.031 | H33/27RD | 3/61 | Mansfield District (NG) 534 |
| 11645 | 906 MRB | Bristol FS6G | 155.085 | H33/27RD | 7/60 | Midland General, Langley Mill (DE) 491 |
| 11646 | 907 MRB | Bristol FS6G | 155.086 | H33/27RD | 8/60 | Midland General, Langley Mill (DE) 492 |
| 11647 | 908 MRB | Bristol FS6G | 155.091 | H33/27RD | 9/60 | Midland General, Langley Mill (DE) 493 |
| 11648 | 909 MRB | Bristol FS6G | 155.092 | H33/27RD | 8/60 | Midland General, Langley Mill (DE) 494 |
| 11649 | 910 MRB | Bristol FS6G | 166.062 | H33/27RD | 5/61 | Midland General, Langley Mill (DE) 495 |
| 11650 | 911 MRB | Bristol FS6G | 166.063 | H33/27RD | 5/61 | Midland General, Langley Mill (DE) 496 |
| 11651 | 912 MRB | Bristol FS6G | 166.064 | H33/27RD | 6/61 | Midland General, Langley Mill (DE) 497 |
| 11652 | 913 MRB | Bristol FS6G | 166.065 | H33/27RD | 6/61 | Midland General, Langley Mill (DE) 498 |
| 11653 | 914 MRB | Bristol FS6G | 166.066 | H33/27RD | 6/61 | Midland General, Langley Mill (DE) 499 |
| 11654 | 915 MRB | Bristol FS6G | 166.067 | H33/27RD | 6/61 | Midland General, Langley Mill (DE) 500 |
| 11655 | *TDL 998 | Bristol FS6G | 155.036 | H33/27RD | 6/60 | Southern Vectis, Newport (IW) 565 |
| 11656 | TDL 999 | Bristol FS6G | 155.037 | H33/27RD | 6/60 | Southern Vectis, Newport (IW) 566 |

| | | | | | | |
|---|---|---|---|---|---|---|
| 11657 | WBD 602 | Bristol FS6B | 155.072 | H33/27RD | 7/60 | United Counties, Northampton (NO) 602 |
| 11658 | WBD 603 | Bristol FS6B | 155.073 | H33/27RD | 7/60 | United Counties, Northampton (NO) 603 |
| 11659 | WBD 604 | Bristol FS6B | 155.074 | H33/27RD | 7/60 | United Counties, Northampton (NO) 604 |
| 11660 | WBD 605 | Bristol FS6B | 155.097 | H33/27RD | 9/60 | United Counties, Northampton (NO) 605 |
| 11661 | WBD 606 | Bristol FS6B | 155.098 | H33/27RD | 9/60 | United Counties, Northampton (NO) 606 |
| 11662 | WBD 607 | Bristol FS6B | 155.099 | H33/27RD | 9/60 | United Counties, Northampton (NO) 607 |
| 11663 | WBD 608 | Bristol FS6B | 155.100 | H33/27RD | 9/60 | United Counties, Northampton (NO) 608 |
| 11664 | WBD 609 | Bristol FS6B | 166.019 | H33/27RD | 10/60 | United Counties, Northampton (NO) 609 |
| 11665 | WBD 610 | Bristol FS6B | 166.020 | H33/27RD | 10/60 | United Counties, Northampton (NO) 610 |
| 11666 | WBD 611 | Bristol FS6B | 166.056 | H33/27RD | 5/61 | United Counties, Northampton (NO) 611 |
| 11667 | WBD 612 | Bristol FS6B | 166.057 | H33/27RD | 6/61 | United Counties, Northampton (NO) 612 |
| 11668 | WBD 613 | Bristol FS6B | 166.058 | H33/27RD | 6/61 | United Counties, Northampton (NO) 613 |
| 11669 | WBD 614 | Bristol FS6B | 166.081 | H33/27RD | 7/61 | United Counties, Northampton (NO) 614 |
| 11670 | WBD 615 | Bristol FS6B | 166.082 | H33/27RD | 7/61 | United Counties, Northampton (NO) 615 |
| 11671 | WBD 616 | Bristol FS6B | 166.083 | H33/27RD | 8/61 | United Counties, Northampton (NO) 616 |
| 11672 | WCY 706 | Bristol FS6G | 155.064 | H33/27RD | 7/60 | United Welsh, Swansea (GG) 337 |
| 11673 | WCY 707 | Bristol FS6G | 155.065 | H33/27RD | 7/60 | United Welsh, Swansea (GG) 338 |
| 11674 | WCY 708 | Bristol FS6G | 166.010 | H33/27RD | 10/60 | United Welsh, Swansea (GG) 339 |
| 11675 | WCY 709 | Bristol FS6G | 166.011 | H33/27RD | 9/60 | United Welsh, Swansea (GG) 340 |
| 11676 | WCY 710 | Bristol FS6G | 166.012 | H33/27RD | 9/60 | United Welsh, Swansea (GG) 341 |
| 11677 | WCY 711 | Bristol FS6G | 166.023 | H33/27RD | 3/61 | United Welsh, Swansea (GG) 342 |
| 11678 | WCY 712 | Bristol FS6G | 166.024 | H33/27RD | 3/61 | United Welsh, Swansea (GG) 343 |
| 11679 | WCY 713 | Bristol FS6G | 166.032 | H33/27RD | 3/61 | United Welsh, Swansea (GG) 344 |
| 11680 | WCY 714 | Bristol FS6G | 166.033 | H33/27RD | 3/61 | United Welsh, Swansea (GG) 345 |
| 11681 | WCY 715 | Bristol FS6G | 166.034 | H33/27RD | 3/61 | United Welsh, Swansea (GG) 346 |
| 11682 | 9755 WU | Bristol FS6B | 155.051 | H33/27RD | 6/60 | West Yorkshire RCC, Harrogate (WR) DX97 |
| 11683 | 9756 WU | Bristol FS6B | 155.052 | H33/27RD | 6/60 | West Yorkshire RCC, Harrogate (WR) DX98 |
| 11684 | 9757 WU | Bristol FS6B | 155.053 | H33/27RD | 6/60 | West Yorkshire RCC, Harrogate (WR) DX99 |
| 11685 | 9758 WU | Bristol FS6B | 155.093 | H33/27RD | 9/60 | West Yorkshire RCC, Harrogate (WR) DX100 |
| 11686 | 9759 WU | Bristol FS6B | 155.094 | H33/27RD | 9/60 | West Yorkshire RCC, Harrogate (WR) DX101 |
| 11687 | 9760 WU | Bristol FS6B | 155.095 | H33/27RD | 10/60 | West Yorkshire RCC, Harrogate (WR) DX102 |
| 11688 | 9761 WU | Bristol FS6B | 155.096 | H33/27RD | 10/60 | West Yorkshire RCC, Harrogate (WR) DX103 |
| 11689 | 9762 WU | Bristol FS6B | 166.021 | H33/27RD | 10/60 | West Yorkshire RCC, Harrogate (WR) DX104 |
| 11690 | 9763 WU | Bristol FS6B | 166.022 | H33/27RD | 10/60 | West Yorkshire RCC, Harrogate (WR) DX105 |
| 11691 | 9764 WU | Bristol FS6B | 166.059 | H33/27RD | 5/61 | West Yorkshire RCC, Harrogate (WR) DX106 |
| 11692 | 9765 WU | Bristol FS6B | 166.060 | H33/27RD | 5/61 | West Yorkshire RCC, Harrogate (WR) DX107 |
| 11693 | 9766 WU | Bristol FS6B | 166.061 | H33/27RD | 6/61 | West Yorkshire RCC, Harrogate (WR) DX108 |
| 11694 | 9767 WU | Bristol FS6B | 166.068 | H33/27RD | 7/61 | West Yorkshire RCC, Harrogate (WR) DX109 |
| 11695 | 9768 WU | Bristol FS6B | 166.069 | H33/27RD | 7/61 | West Yorkshire RCC, Harrogate (WR) DX110 |
| 11696 | 9769 WU | Bristol FS6B | 166.074 | H33/27RD | 7/61 | West Yorkshire RCC, Harrogate (WR) DX111 |
| 11697 | 9770 WU | Bristol FS6B | 166.075 | H33/27RD | 7/61 | West Yorkshire RCC, Harrogate (WR) DX112 |
| 11698 | 9771 WU | Bristol FS6B | 166.078 | H33/27RD | 7/61 | West Yorkshire RCC, Harrogate (WR) DX113 |
| 11699 | 2223 WW | Bristol FS6B | 155.075 | H33/27RD | 8/60 | York-West Yorkshire, Harrogate (WR) YDX89 |
| 11700 | 2224 WW | Bristol FS6B | 155.076 | H33/27RD | 8/60 | York-West Yorkshire, Harrogate (WR) YDX90 |
| 11701 | 2225 WW | Bristol FS6B | 166.035 | H33/27RD | 3/61 | York-West Yorkshire, Harrogate (WR) YDX91 |
| 11702 | 2226 WW | Bristol FS6B | 166.036 | H33/27RD | 3/61 | York-West Yorkshire, Harrogate (WR) YDX92 |
| 11703 | 2227 WW | Bristol FS6B | 155.077 | H33/27RD | 8/60 | Keighley-West Yorkshire, Harrogate (WR) KDX93 |
| 11704 | 2228 WW | Bristol FS6B | 155.078 | H33/27RD | 8/60 | Keighley-West Yorkshire, Harrogate (WR) KDX94 |
| 11705 | 2229 WW | Bristol FS6B | 166.037 | H33/27RD | 3/61 | Keighley-West Yorkshire, Harrogate (WR) KDX95 |
| 11706 | 2230 WW | Bristol FS6B | 166.038 | H33/27RD | 3/61 | Keighley-West Yorkshire, Harrogate (WR) KDX96 |
| 11707 | 253 SFM | Bristol FLF6B | 169.013 | H38/32F | 2/61 | Crosville MS, Chester (CH) DFB40 |
| 11708 | 254 SFM | Bristol FLF6B | 169.020 | H38/32F | 3/61 | Crosville MS, Chester (CH) DFB41 |
| 11709 | 255 SFM | Bristol FLF6B | 169.021 | H38/32F | 3/61 | Crosville MS, Chester (CH) DFB42 |
| 11710 | 256 SFM | Bristol FLF6B | 169.022 | H38/32F | 3/61 | Crosville MS, Chester (CH) DFB43 |
| 11711 | 257 SFM | Bristol FLF6B | 169.023 | H38/32F | 3/61 | Crosville MS, Chester (CH) DFB44 |
| 11712 | 258 SFM | Bristol FLF6B | 169.024 | H38/32F | 3/61 | Crosville MS, Chester (CH) DFB45 |
| 11713 | 259 SFM | Bristol FLF6B | 169.037 | H38/32F | 3/61 | Crosville MS, Chester (CH) DFB46 |
| 11714 | 260 SFM | Bristol FLF6B | 169.038 | H38/32F | 3/61 | Crosville MS, Chester (CH) DFB47 |
| 11715 | 261 SFM | Bristol FLF6B | 169.041 | H38/32F | 3/61 | Crosville MS, Chester (CH) DFB48 |
| 11716 | 262 SFM | Bristol FLF6B | 169.042 | H38/32F | 3/61 | Crosville MS, Chester (CH) DFB49 |

| | | | | | | |
|---|---|---|---|---|---|---|
| 11717 | 263 SFM | Bristol FLF6B | 169.043 | H38/32F | 3/61 | Crosville MS, Chester (CH) DFB50 |
| 11718 | *264 SFM | Bristol FLF6B | 169.046 | H38/32F | 3/61 | Crosville MS, Chester (CH) DFB51 |
| 11719 | 265 SFM | Bristol FLF6B | 169.051 | H38/32F | 3/61 | Crosville MS, Chester (CH) DFB52 |
| 11720 | 266 SFM | Bristol FLF6B | 169.053 | H38/32F | 3/61 | Crosville MS, Chester (CH) DFB53 |
| 11721 | 506 BRM | Bristol FLF6G | 169.010 | H38/32F | 11/60 | Cumberland MS, Whitehaven (CU) C409 |
| 11722 | 507 BRM | Bristol FLF6G | 169.011 | H38/32F | 11/60 | Cumberland MS, Whitehaven (CU) C410 |
| 11723 | 508 BRM | Bristol FLF6G | 169.012 | H38/32F | 11/60 | Cumberland MS, Whitehaven (CU) C411 |
| 11724 | 509 BRM | Bristol FLF6G | 169.025 | H38/32F | 12/60 | Cumberland MS, Whitehaven (CU) C412 |
| 11725 | 510 BRM | Bristol FLF6G | 169.026 | H38/32F | 12/60 | Cumberland MS, Whitehaven (CU) C413 |
| 11726 | * 80 TVX | Bristol FLF6G | 169.002 | H38/32F | 11/60 | Eastern National, Chelmsford (EX) 1571 |
| 11727 | 81 TVX | Bristol FLF6G | 169.003 | H38/32F | 11/60 | Eastern National, Chelmsford (EX) 1572 |
| 11728 | 82 TVX | Bristol FLF6G | 169.004 | H38/32F | 11/60 | Eastern National, Chelmsford (EX) 1573 |
| 11729 | 83 TVX | Bristol FLF6G | 169.005 | H38/32F | 11/60 | Eastern National, Chelmsford (EX) 1574 |
| 11730 | 89 TVX | Bristol FLF6B | 169.032 | H38/32F | 11/60 | Eastern National, Chelmsford (EX) 1580 |
| 11731 | 90 TVX | Bristol FLF6B | 169.033 | H38/32F | 11/60 | Eastern National, Chelmsford (EX) 1581 |
| 11732 | 91 TVX | Bristol FLF6B | 169.034 | H38/32F | 11/60 | Eastern National, Chelmsford (EX) 1582 |
| 11733 | 92 TVX | Bristol FLF6B | 169.035 | H38/32F | 11/60 | Eastern National, Chelmsford (EX) 1583 |
| 11734 | 93 TVX | Bristol FLF6B | 169.036 | H38/32F | 11/60 | Eastern National, Chelmsford (EX) 1584 |
| 11735 | 84 TVX | Bristol FLF6G | 169.027 | H38/32F | 11/60 | Eastern National, Chelmsford (EX) 1575 |
| 11736 | 85 TVX | Bristol FLF6G | 169.028 | H38/32F | 12/60 | Eastern National, Chelmsford (EX) 1576 |
| 11737 | 86 TVX | Bristol FLF6G | 169.029 | H38/32F | 12/60 | Eastern National, Chelmsford (EX) 1577 |
| 11738 | 87 TVX | Bristol FLF6G | 169.030 | H38/32F | 12/60 | Eastern National, Chelmsford (EX) 1578 |
| 11739 | 88 TVX | Bristol FLF6G | 169.031 | H38/32F | 11/60 | Eastern National, Chelmsford (EX) 1579 |
| 11740 | 94 TVX | Bristol FLF6G | 169.039 | H38/32F | 12/60 | Eastern National, Chelmsford (EX) 1585 |
| 11741 | 95 TVX | Bristol FLF6G | 169.040 | H38/32F | 12/60 | Eastern National, Chelmsford (EX) 1586 |
| 11742 | 96 TVX | Bristol FLF6G | 169.050 | H38/32F | 12/60 | Eastern National, Chelmsford (EX) 1587 |
| 11743 | 97 TVX | Bristol FLF6G | 169.052 | H38/32F | 12/60 | Eastern National, Chelmsford (EX) 1588 |
| 11744 | 98 TVX | Bristol FLF6G | 169.054 | H38/32F | 12/60 | Eastern National, Chelmsford (EX) 1589 |
| 11745 | 99 TVX | Bristol FLF6G | 169.055 | H38/32F | 1/61 | Eastern National, Chelmsford (EX) 1590 |
| 11746 | *462 FTT | Bristol FLF6G | 169.017 | H38/32F | 5/61 | Southern National, Exeter (DN) 1974 |
| 11747 | *463 FTT | Bristol FLF6G | 169.018 | H38/32F | 6/61 | Southern National, Exeter (DN) 1975 |
| 11748 | *464 FTT | Bristol FLF6G | 169.019 | H38/32F | 6/61 | Southern National, Exeter (DN) 1976 |
| 11749 | *465 FTT | Bristol FLF6G | 169.048 | H38/32F | 6/61 | Southern National, Exeter (DN) 1977 |
| 11750 | *466 FTT | Bristol FLF6G | 169.049 | H38/32F | 6/61 | Southern National, Exeter (DN) 1978 |
| 11751 | 467 FTT | Bristol FLF6G | 169.014 | H38/32F | 12/60 | Western National, Exeter (DN) 1968 |
| 11752 | 468 FTT | Bristol FLF6G | 169.015 | H38/32F | 12/60 | Western National, Exeter (DN) 1969 |
| 11753 | 469 FTT | Bristol FLF6G | 169.016 | H38/32F | 1/61 | Western National, Exeter (DN) 1970 |
| 11754 | *470 FTT | Bristol FLF6G | 169.044 | H38/32F | 1/61 | Western National, Exeter (DN) 1971 |
| 11755 | 471 FTT | Bristol FLF6G | 169.045 | H38/32F | 1/61 | Western National, Exeter (DN) 1972 |
| 11756 | *472 FTT | Bristol FLF6G | 169.047 | H38/32F | 1/61 | Western National, Exeter (DN) 1973 |
| 11757 | OVL 485 | Bristol FL6G | 168.017 | H33/27RD | 12/60 | Lincolnshire RCC, Lincoln (LC) 2390 |
| 11758 | OVL 486 | Bristol FL6G | 168.018 | H33/27RD | 1/61 | Lincolnshire RCC, Lincoln (LC) 2391 |
| 11759 | OVL 487 | Bristol FL6G | 168.019 | H33/27RD | 12/60 | Lincolnshire RCC, Lincoln (LC) 2392 |
| 11760 | *OVL 488 | Bristol FL6G | 168.020 | H33/27RD | 1/61 | Lincolnshire RCC, Lincoln (LC) 2393 |
| 11761 | OVL 489 | Bristol FL6G | 168.021 | H33/27RD | 1/61 | Lincolnshire RCC, Lincoln (LC) 2394 |
| 11762 | VAX 508 | Bristol FL6G | 168.001 | H37/33RD | 1/61 | Red & White, Chepstow (MH) L160 |
| 11763 | VAX 509 | Bristol FL6G | 168.002 | H37/33RD | 1/61 | Red & White, Chepstow (MH) L260 |
| 11764 | 3 AAX | Bristol FL6G | 168.003 | H37/33RD | 1/61 | Red & White, Chepstow (MH) L360 |
| 11765 | 4 AAX | Bristol FL6G | 168.004 | H37/33RD | 1/61 | Red & White, Chepstow (MH) L460 |
| 11766 | * 5 AAX | Bristol FL6G | 168.005 | H37/33RD | 1/61 | Red & White, Chepstow (MH) L560 |
| 11767 | 6 AAX | Bristol FL6G | 168.006 | H37/33RD | 1/61 | Red & White, Chepstow (MH) L660 |
| 11768 | 7 AAX | Bristol FL6G | 168.007 | H37/33RD | 1/61 | Red & White, Chepstow (MH) L760 |
| 11769 | 8 AAX | Bristol FL6G | 168.008 | H37/33RD | 1/61 | Red & White, Chepstow (MH) L860 |
| 11770 | 9 AAX | Bristol FL6G | 168.009 | H37/33RD | 1/61 | Red & White, Chepstow (MH) L960 |
| 11771 | 10 AAX | Bristol FL6G | 168.010 | H37/33RD | 1/61 | Red & White, Chepstow (MH) L1060 |
| 11772 | 11 AAX | Bristol FL6G | 168.011 | H37/33RD | 1/61 | Red & White, Chepstow (MH) L1160 |
| 11773 | 12 AAX | Bristol FL6G | 168.012 | H37/33RD | 2/61 | Red & White, Chepstow (MH) L1260 |
| 11774 | 13 AAX | Bristol FL6G | 168.013 | H37/33RD | 1/61 | Red & White, Chepstow (MH) L1360 |
| 11775 | 14 AAX | Bristol FL6G | 168.014 | H37/33RD | 2/61 | Red & White, Chepstow (MH) L1460 |
| 11776 | 15 AAX | Bristol FL6G | 168.015 | H37/33RD | 2/61 | Red & White, Chepstow (MH) L1560 |
| 11777 | 16 AAX | Bristol FL6G | 168.016 | H37/33RD | 2/61 | Red & White, Chepstow (MH) L1660 |
| 11778 | 17 AAX | Bristol FL6G | 168.022 | H37/33RD | 2/61 | Red & White, Chepstow (MH) L1760 |
| 11779 | 18 AAX | Bristol FL6G | 168.023 | H37/33RD | 2/61 | Red & White, Chepstow (MH) L1860 |
| 11780 | 511 JHU | Bristol MW5G | 164.063 | B45F | 7/60 | Bristol OC (GL) 2989 |

| | | | | | | | |
|---|---|---|---|---|---|---|---|
| 11781 | 512 JHU | Bristol MW5G | 164.064 | B45F | 7/60 | Bristol OC (GL) 2990 | |
| 11782 | 513 JHU | Bristol MW5G | 164.065 | B45F | 7/60 | Bristol OC (GL) 2991 | |
| 11783 | 514 JHU | Bristol MW5G | 164.066 | B45F | 7/60 | Bristol OC (GL) 2992 | |
| 11784 | 515 JHU | Bristol MW5G | 164.095 | B45F | 10/60 | Bristol OC (GL) 2993 | |
| 11785 | 516 JHU | Bristol MW5G | 164.096 | B45F | 10/60 | Bristol OC (GL) 2994 | |
| 11786 | 517 JHU | Bristol MW5G | 164.097 | B45F | 10/60 | Bristol OC (GL) 2995 | |
| 11787 | 518 JHU | Bristol MW5G | 164.098 | B45F | 10/60 | Bristol OC (GL) 2996 | |
| 11788 | 519 JHU | Bristol MW5G | 164.099 | B45F | 10/60 | Bristol OC (GL) 2997 | |
| 11789 | 520 JHU | Bristol MW5G | 164.100 | B45F | 10/60 | Bristol OC (GL) 2998 | |
| 11790 | 521 JHU | Bristol MW5G | 164.121 | B45F | 11/60 | Bristol OC (GL) 2999 | |
| 11791 | 522 JHU | Bristol MW5G | 164.122 | B45F | 11/60 | Bristol OC (GL) 6000 | |
| 11792 | 523 JHU | Bristol MW5G | 164.123 | B45F | 11/60 | Bristol OC (GL) 6001 | |
| 11793 | 524 JHU | Bristol MW5G | 164.124 | B45F | 11/60 | Bristol OC (GL) 6002 | |
| 11794 | 525 JHU | Bristol MW5G | 164.125 | B45F | 11/60 | Bristol OC (GL) 6003 | |
| 11795 | 526 JHU | Bristol MW5G | 164.146 | B45F | 1/61 | Bristol OC (GL) 2504 | |
| 11796 | 527 JHU | Bristol MW5G | 164.147 | B45F | 1/61 | Bristol OC (GL) 2505 | |
| 11797 | 528 JHU | Bristol MW5G | 164.148 | B45F | 1/61 | Bristol OC (GL) 2506 | |
| 11798 | 529 JHU | Bristol MW5G | 164.149 | B45F | 1/61 | Bristol OC (GL) 2507 | |
| 11799 | 530 JHU | Bristol MW5G | 164.166 | B45F | 2/61 | Bristol OC (GL) 2508 | |
| 11800 | 531 JHU | Bristol MW5G | 164.167 | B45F | 2/61 | Bristol OC (GL) 2509 | |
| 11801 | 532 JHU | Bristol MW5G | 164.168 | B45F | 2/61 | Bristol OC (GL) 2510 | |
| 11802 | 533 JHU | Bristol MW5G | 164.169 | B45F | 2/61 | Bristol OC (GL) 2511 | |
| 11803 | 534 JHU | Bristol MW5G | 164.187 | B45F | 3/61 | Bristol OC (GL) 2512 | |
| 11804 | 535 JHU | Bristol MW5G | 164.188 | B45F | 3/61 | Bristol OC (GL) 2513 | |
| 11805 | 536 JHU | Bristol MW5G | 164.189 | B45F | 3/61 | Bristol OC (GL) 2514 | |
| 11806 | 537 JHU | Bristol MW5G | 164.190 | B45F | 3/61 | Bristol OC (GL) 2515 | |
| 11807 | 848 RFM | Bristol MW6G | 164.067 | B41F | 8/60 | Crosville MS, Chester (CH) SMG391 | |
| 11808 | 849 RFM | Bristol MW6G | 164.068 | B41F | 8/60 | Crosville MS, Chester (CH) SMG392 | |
| 11809 | 850 RFM | Bristol MW6G | 164.069 | B41F | 8/60 | Crosville MS, Chester (CH) SMG393 | |
| 11810 | 851 RFM | Bristol MW6G | 164.070 | B41F | 8/60 | Crosville MS, Chester (CH) SMG394 | |
| 11811 | 852 RFM | Bristol MW6G | 164.101 | B41F | 10/60 | Crosville MS, Chester (CH) SMG395 | |
| 11812 | 853 RFM | Bristol MW6G | 164.102 | B41F | 11/60 | Crosville MS, Chester (CH) SMG396 | |
| 11813 | 854 RFM | Bristol MW6G | 164.119 | B41F | 11/60 | Crosville MS, Chester (CH) SMG397 | |
| 11814 | 855 RFM | Bristol MW6G | 164.120 | B41F | 12/60 | Crosville MS, Chester (CH) SMG398 | |
| 11815 | 856 RFM | Bristol MW6G | 164.151 | B41F | 1/61 | Crosville MS, Chester (CH) SMG399 | |
| 11816 | 857 RFM | Bristol MW6G | 164.152 | B41F | 3/61 | Crosville MS, Chester (CH) SMG400 | |
| 11817 | 858 RFM | Bristol MW6G | 164.153 | B41F | 3/61 | Crosville MS, Chester (CH) SMG401 | |
| 11818 | 859 RFM | Bristol MW6G | 164.154 | B41F | 3/61 | Crosville MS, Chester (CH) SMG402 | |
| 11819 | 860 RFM | Bristol MW6G | 164.180 | B41F | 4/61 | Crosville MS, Chester (CH) SMG403 | |
| 11820 | 861 RFM | Bristol MW6G | 164.181 | B41F | 4/61 | Crosville MS, Chester (CH) SMG404 | |
| 11821 | 862 RFM | Bristol MW6G | 164.182 | B41F | 4/61 | Crosville MS, Chester (CH) SMG405 | |
| 11822 | 863 RFM | Bristol MW6G | 164.183 | B41F | 4/61 | Crosville MS, Chester (CH) SMG406 | |
| 11823 | 2917 HN | Bristol MW5G | 164.111 | DP41F | 5/61 | Durham District (DM) DBE17 | |
| 11824 | 2918 HN | Bristol MW5G | 164.112 | DP41F | 5/61 | Durham District (DM) DBE18 | |
| 11825 | 2919 HN | Bristol MW5G | 164.159 | DP41F | 5/61 | Durham District (DM) DBE19 | |
| 11826 | 2920 HN | Bristol MW5G | 164.160 | DP41F | 5/61 | Durham District (DM) DBE20 | |
| 11827 | 2921 HN | Bristol MW5G | 164.161 | DP41F | 5/61 | Durham District (DM) DBE21 | |
| 11828 | *2723 VX | Bristol MW5G | 164.071 | B45F | 8/60 | Eastern National, Chelmsford (EX) 512 | |
| 11829 | 2724 VX | Bristol MW5G | 164.072 | B45F | 7/60 | Eastern National, Chelmsford (EX) 513 | |
| 11830 | 2725 VX | Bristol MW5G | 164.073 | B45F | 8/60 | Eastern National, Chelmsford (EX) 514 | |
| 11831 | 2726 VX | Bristol MW5G | 164.074 | B45F | 7/60 | Eastern National, Chelmsford (EX) 515 | |
| 11832 | 2727 VX | Bristol MW5G | 164.103 | B45F | 11/60 | Eastern National, Chelmsford (EX) 516 | |
| 11833 | 2728 VX | Bristol MW5G | 164.104 | B45F | 11/60 | Eastern National, Chelmsford (EX) 517 | |
| 11834 | 2729 VX | Bristol MW5G | 164.105 | B45F | 11/60 | Eastern National, Chelmsford (EX) 518 | |
| 11835 | 2730 VX | Bristol MW5G | 164.106 | B45F | 11/60 | Eastern National, Chelmsford (EX) 519 | |
| 11836 | 2731 VX | Bristol MW5G | 164.126 | B45F | 1/61 | Eastern National, Chelmsford (EX) 520 | |
| 11837 | 2732 VX | Bristol MW5G | 164.127 | B45F | 1/61 | Eastern National, Chelmsford (EX) 521 | |
| 11838 | 2733 VX | Bristol MW5G | 164.128 | B45F | 1/61 | Eastern National, Chelmsford (EX) 522 | |
| 11839 | 2734 VX | Bristol MW5G | 164.129 | B45F | 1/61 | Eastern National, Chelmsford (EX) 523 | |
| 11840 | 2735 VX | Bristol MW5G | 164.162 | DP41F | 2/61 | Eastern National, Chelmsford (EX) 524 | |
| 11841 | 2736 VX | Bristol MW5G | 164.163 | DP41F | 3/61 | Eastern National, Chelmsford (EX) 525 | |
| 11842 | 2737 VX | Bristol MW5G | 164.164 | DP41F | 3/61 | Eastern National, Chelmsford (EX) 526 | |
| 11843 | 2738 VX | Bristol MW5G | 164.165 | DP41F | 2/61 | Eastern National, Chelmsford (EX) 527 | |
| 11844 | 2739 VX | Bristol MW5G | 164.191 | DP41F | 3/61 | Eastern National, Chelmsford (EX) 528 | |

| | | | | | | | |
|---|---|---|---|---|---|---|---|
| 11845 | 2740 VX | Bristol MW5G | 164.192 | DP41F | 3/61 | Eastern National, Chelmsford (EX) | 529 |
| 11846 | 2741 VX | Bristol MW5G | 164.193 | DP41F | 3/61 | Eastern National, Chelmsford (EX) | 530 |
| 11847 | 2742 VX | Bristol MW5G | 164.194 | DP41F | 5/61 | Eastern National, Chelmsford (EX) | 531 |
| 11848 | OVL 462 | Bristol MW5G | 164.075 | B45F | 8/60 | Lincolnshire RCC, Lincoln (LC) | 2242 |
| 11849 | OVL 463 | Bristol MW5G | 164.076 | B45F | 7/60 | Lincolnshire RCC, Lincoln (LC) | 2243 |
| 11850 | OVL 464 | Bristol MW5G | 164.107 | B45F | 10/60 | Lincolnshire RCC, Lincoln (LC) | 2244 |
| 11851 | OVL 465 | Bristol MW5G | 164.108 | B45F | 10/60 | Lincolnshire RCC, Lincoln (LC) | 2245 |
| 11852 | OVL 466 | Bristol MW5G | 164.130 | B45F | 11/60 | Lincolnshire RCC, Lincoln (LC) | 2246 |
| 11853 | OVL 467 | Bristol MW5G | 164.131 | B45F | 11/60 | Lincolnshire RCC, Lincoln (LC) | 2247 |
| 11854 | OVL 468 | Bristol MW5G | 164.170 | B45F | 2/61 | Lincolnshire RCC, Lincoln (LC) | 2248 |
| 11855 | OVL 469 | Bristol MW5G | 164.171 | B45F | 2/61 | Lincolnshire RCC, Lincoln (LC) | 2249 |
| 11856 | VJB 943 | Bristol MW6G | 164.079 | DP41F | 7/60 | Thames Valley, Reading (BE) | 852 |
| 11857 | VJB 944 | Bristol MW6G | 164.080 | DP41F | 8/60 | Thames Valley, Reading (BE) | 853 |
| 11858 | VJB 945 | Bristol MW6G | 164.132 | B41F | 11/60 | Thames Valley, Reading (BE) | 854 |
| 11859 | VJB 946 | Bristol MW6G | 164.133 | B41F | 11/60 | Thames Valley, Reading (BE) | 855 |
| 11860 | VJB 947 | Bristol MW6G | 164.144 | B41F | 12/60 | Thames Valley, Reading (BE) | 856 |
| 11861 | VJB 948 | Bristol MW6G | 164.145 | B41F | 12/60 | Thames Valley, Reading (BE) | 857 |
| 11862 | 2583 HN | Bristol MW5G | 164.060 | DP41F | 8/60 | United AS, Darlington (DM) | BUE583 |
| 11863 | 2584 HN | Bristol MW5G | 164.061 | DP41F | 8/60 | United AS, Darlington (DM) | BUE584 |
| 11864 | 2585 HN | Bristol MW5G | 164.062 | DP41F | 5/61 | United AS, Darlington (DM) | BUE585 |
| 11865 | 2586 HN | Bristol MW5G | 164.081 | DP41F | 5/61 | United AS, Darlington (DM) | BUE586 |
| 11866 | 2587 HN | Bristol MW5G | 164.082 | DP41F | 5/61 | United AS, Darlington (DM) | BUE587 |
| 11867 | 2588 HN | Bristol MW5G | 164.083 | DP41F | 5/61 | United AS, Darlington (DM) | BUE588 |
| 11868 | 2589 HN | Bristol MW5G | 164.084 | DP41F | 5/61 | United AS, Darlington (DM) | BUE589 |
| 11869 | 2590 HN | Bristol MW5G | 164.085 | DP41F | 5/61 | United AS, Darlington (DM) | BUE590 |
| 11870 | 2591 HN | Bristol MW5G | 164.086 | DP41F | 5/61 | United AS, Darlington (DM) | BUE591 |
| 11871 | 2592 HN | Bristol MW5G | 164.087 | DP41F | 5/61 | United AS, Darlington (DM) | BUE592 |
| 11872 | 2593 HN | Bristol MW5G | 164.088 | DP41F | 5/61 | United AS, Darlington (DM) | BUE593 |
| 11873 | 2594 HN | Bristol MW5G | 164.089 | DP41F | 5/61 | United AS, Darlington (DM) | BUE594 |
| 11874 | 2595 HN | Bristol MW5G | 164.090 | DP41F | 5/61 | United AS, Darlington (DM) | BUE595 |
| 11875 | 2596 HN | Bristol MW5G | 164.091 | DP41F | 6/61 | United AS, Darlington (DM) | BUE596 |
| 11876 | 2597 HN | Bristol MW5G | 164.092 | DP41F | 6/61 | United AS, Darlington (DM) | BUE597 |
| 11877 | 2598 HN | Bristol MW5G | 164.093 | DP41F | 6/61 | United AS, Darlington (DM) | BUE598 |
| 11878 | 2599 HN | Bristol MW5G | 164.094 | DP41F | 6/61 | United AS, Darlington (DM) | BUE599 |
| 11879 | 2600 HN | Bristol MW5G | 164.115 | DP41F | 6/61 | United AS, Darlington (DM) | BUE600 |
| 11880 | 2601 HN | Bristol MW5G | 164.116 | DP41F | 6/61 | United AS, Darlington (DM) | BUE601 |
| 11881 | 2602 HN | Bristol MW5G | 164.117 | DP41F | 6/61 | United AS, Darlington (DM) | BUE602 |
| 11882 | 2603 HN | Bristol MW5G | 164.109 | B45F | 12/60 | United AS, Darlington (DM) | BU603 |
| 11883 | 2604 HN | Bristol MW5G | 164.110 | B45F | 12/60 | United AS, Darlington (DM) | BU604 |
| 11884 | 2605 HN | Bristol MW5G | 164.118 | B45F | 1/61 | United AS, Darlington (DM) | BU605 |
| 11885 | 2606 HN | Bristol MW5G | 164.134 | B45F | 4/61 | United AS, Darlington (DM) | BU606 |
| 11886 | 2607 HN | Bristol MW5G | 164.135 | B45F | 4/61 | United AS, Darlington (DM) | BU607 |
| 11887 | 2608 HN | Bristol MW5G | 164.136 | B45F | 4/61 | United AS, Darlington (DM) | BU608 |
| 11888 | 2609 HN | Bristol MW5G | 164.137 | B45F | 4/61 | United AS, Darlington (DM) | BU609 |
| 11889 | 2610 HN | Bristol MW5G | 164.138 | B45F | 4/61 | United AS, Darlington (DM) | BU610 |
| 11890 | 2611 HN | Bristol MW5G | 164.139 | B45F | 4/61 | United AS, Darlington (DM) | BU611 |
| 11891 | 2612 HN | Bristol MW5G | 164.150 | B45F | 4/61 | United AS, Darlington (DM) | BU612 |
| 11892 | 2613 HN | Bristol MW5G | 164.155 | B45F | 4/61 | United AS, Darlington (DM) | BU613 |
| 11893 | 2614 HN | Bristol MW5G | 164.156 | B45F | 4/61 | United AS, Darlington (DM) | BU614 |
| 11894 | 2615 HN | Bristol MW5G | 164.157 | B45F | 5/61 | United AS, Darlington (DM) | BU615 |
| 11895 | 2616 HN | Bristol MW5G | 164.158 | B45F | 5/61 | United AS, Darlington (DM) | BU616 |
| 11896 | 2617 HN | Bristol MW5G | 164.172 | B45F | 5/61 | United AS, Darlington (DM) | BU617 |
| 11897 | 2618 HN | Bristol MW5G | 164.173 | B45F | 5/61 | United AS, Darlington (DM) | BU618 |
| 11898 | 2619 HN | Bristol MW5G | 164.174 | B45F | 5/61 | United AS, Darlington (DM) | BU619 |
| 11899 | 2620 HN | Bristol MW5G | 164.175 | B45F | 5/61 | United AS, Darlington (DM) | BU620 |
| 11900 | 2621 HN | Bristol MW5G | 164.176 | B45F | 6/61 | United AS, Darlington (DM) | BU621 |
| 11901 | 2622 HN | Bristol MW5G | 164.177 | B45F | 6/61 | United AS, Darlington (DM) | BU622 |
| 11902 | 2623 HN | Bristol MW5G | 164.178 | B45F | 6/61 | United AS, Darlington (DM) | BU623 |
| 11903 | 2624 HN | Bristol MW5G | 164.179 | B45F | 6/61 | United AS, Darlington (DM) | BU624 |
| 11904 | 2625 HN | Bristol MW5G | 164.184 | B45F | 6/61 | United AS, Darlington (DM) | BU625 |
| 11905 | 2626 HN | Bristol MW5G | 164.185 | B45F | 6/61 | United AS, Darlington (DM) | BU626 |
| 11906 | 2627 HN | Bristol MW5G | 164.186 | B45F | 6/61 | United AS, Darlington (DM) | BU627 |
| 11907 | 2628 HN | Bristol MW5G | 164.195 | B45F | 7/61 | United AS, Darlington (DM) | BU628 |
| 11908 | 2629 HN | Bristol MW5G | 164.196 | B45F | 7/61 | United AS, Darlington (DM) | BU629 |

| | | | | | | |
|---|---|---|---|---|---|---|
| 11909 | 2630 HN | Bristol MW5G | 164.197 | B45F | 7/61 | United AS, Darlington (DM) BU630 |
| 11910 | 2631 HN | Bristol MW5G | 164.198 | B45F | 7/61 | United AS, Darlington (DM) BU631 |
| 11911 | 2632 HN | Bristol MW5G | 164.199 | B45F | 7/61 | United AS, Darlington (DM) BU632 |
| 11912 | *WCY 696 | Bristol MW6G | 164.077 | B45F | 9/60 | United Welsh, Swansea (GG) 119 |
| 11913 | *WCY 697 | Bristol MW6G | 164.078 | B45F | 9/60 | United Welsh, Swansea (GG) 120 |
| 11914 | *WCY 698 | Bristol MW6G | 164.113 | B45F | 11/60 | United Welsh, Swansea (GG) 121 |
| 11915 | *WCY 701 | Bristol MW6G | 164.114 | B45F | 11/60 | United Welsh, Swansea (GG) 122 |
| 11916 | *WCY 702 | Bristol MW6G | 164.140 | B45F | 1/61 | United Welsh, Swansea (GG) 123 |
| 11917 | *WCY 703 | Bristol MW6G | 164.141 | B45F | 1/61 | United Welsh, Swansea (GG) 124 |
| 11918 | *WCY 704 | Bristol MW6G | 164.142 | B45F | 1/61 | United Welsh, Swansea (GG) 125 |
| 11919 | *WCY 705 | Bristol MW6G | 164.143 | B45F | 1/61 | United Welsh, Swansea (GG) 126 |
| 11920 | 289 HHU | Bristol MW6G | 164.022 | C39F | 5/60 | Bristol OC (GL) 2984 |
| 11921 | 290 HHU | Bristol MW6G | 164.023 | C39F | 5/60 | Bristol OC (GL) 2985 |
| 11922 | 291 HHU | Bristol MW6G | 164.024 | C39F | 5/60 | Bristol OC (GL) 2986 |
| 11923 | 292 HHU | Bristol MW6G | 164.025 | C39F | 5/60 | Bristol OC (GL) 2987 |
| 11924 | 293 HHU | Bristol MW6G | 164.026 | C39F | 5/60 | Bristol OC (GL) 2988 |
| 11925 | *302 PFM | Bristol MW6G | 164.038 | C39F | 6/60 | Crosville MS, Chester (CH) CMG386 |
| 11926 | 303 PFM | Bristol MW6G | 164.039 | C39F | 6/60 | Crosville MS, Chester (CH) CMG387 |
| 11927 | 304 PFM | Bristol MW6G | 164.040 | C39F | 6/60 | Crosville MS, Chester (CH) CMG388 |
| 11928 | 305 PFM | Bristol MW6G | 164.041 | C39F | 6/60 | Crosville MS, Chester (CH) CMG389 |
| 11929 | 306 PFM | Bristol MW6G | 164.042 | C39F | 7/60 | Crosville MS, Chester (CH) CMG390 |
| 11930 | 7792 NG | Bristol MW5G | 164.016 | C39F | 3/60 | Eastern Counties, Norwich (NK) LS792 |
| 11931 | 7793 NG | Bristol MW5G | 164.017 | C39F | 3/60 | Eastern Counties, Norwich (NK) LS793 |
| 11932 | 7794 NG | Bristol MW5G | 164.018 | C39F | 3/60 | Eastern Counties, Norwich (NK) LS794 |
| 11933 | 3384 VW | Bristol MW6G | 164.027 | C41F | 5/60 | Eastern National, Chelmsford (EX) 507 |
| 11934 | 3385 VW | Bristol MW6G | 164.028 | C41F | 5/60 | Eastern National, Chelmsford (EX) 508 |
| 11935 | 3386 VW | Bristol MW6G | 164.029 | C41F | 5/60 | Eastern National, Chelmsford (EX) 509 |
| 11936 | 3387 VW | Bristol MW6G | 164.030 | C41F | 5/60 | Eastern National, Chelmsford (EX) 510 |
| 11937 | 3388 VW | Bristol MW6G | 164.031 | C41F | 6/60 | Eastern National, Chelmsford (EX) 511 |
| 11938 | 6226 EL | Bristol MW6G | 164.043 | C30F | 6/60 | Hants & Dorset, Bournemouth (HA) 871 |
| 11939 | 6227 EL | Bristol MW6G | 164.044 | C30F | 6/60 | Hants & Dorset, Bournemouth (HA) 872 |
| 11940 | 6228 EL | Bristol MW6G | 164.045 | C30F | 6/60 | Hants & Dorset, Bournemouth (HA) 873 |
| 11941 | 6229 EL | Bristol MW6G | 164.046 | C30F | 6/60 | Hants & Dorset, Bournemouth (HA) 874 |
| 11942 | 6230 EL | Bristol MW6G | 164.047 | C30F | 6/60 | Hants & Dorset, Bournemouth (HA) 875 |
| 11943 | 615 DDV | Bristol MW6G | 164.032 | C39F | 6/60 | Southern National, Exeter (DN) 2248 |
| 11944 | 616 DDV | Bristol MW6G | 164.033 | C39F | 6/60 | Southern National, Exeter (DN) 2249 |
| 11945 | 617 DDV | Bristol MW6G | 164.034 | C39F | 6/60 | Southern National, Exeter (DN) 2250 |
| 11946 | 618 DDV | Bristol MW6G | 164.035 | C39F | 6/60 | Southern National, Exeter (DN) 2251 |
| 11947 | 619 DDV | Bristol MW6G | 164.036 | C39F | 6/60 | Southern National, Exeter (DN) 2252 |
| 11948 | 620 DDV | Bristol MW6G | 164.037 | C39F | 6/60 | Southern National, Exeter (DN) 2253 |
| 11949 | UJB 196 | Bristol MW6G | 164.001 | C34F | 5/60 | Thames Valley, Reading (BE) 830 |
| 11950 | UJB 197 | Bristol MW6G | 164.002 | C34F | 4/60 | Thames Valley, Reading (BE) 831 |
| 11951 | UJB 198 | Bristol MW6G | 164.003 | C34F | 4/60 | Thames Valley, Reading (BE) 832 |
| 11952 | UJB 199 | Bristol MW6G | 164.004 | C34F | 4/60 | Thames Valley, Reading (BE) 833 |
| 11953 | WCY 694 | Bristol MW6G | 164.013 | C39F | 4/60 | United Welsh, Swansea (GG) 6 |
| 11954 | WCY 695 | Bristol MW6G | 164.014 | C39F | 4/60 | United Welsh, Swansea (GG) 7 |
| 11955 | 7935 WU | Bristol MW6G | 164.019 | C39F | 6/60 | West Yorkshire RCC, Harrogate (WR) CUG24 |
| 11956 | 7936 WU | Bristol MW6G | 164.020 | C39F | 6/60 | West Yorkshire RCC, Harrogate (WR) CUG25 |
| 11957 | 7937 WU | Bristol MW6G | 164.021 | C39F | 6/60 | West Yorkshire RCC, Harrogate (WR) CUG26 |
| 11958 | 621 DDV | Bristol MW6G | 164.005 | C39F | 3/60 | Western National, Exeter (DN) 2242 |
| 11959 | 622 DDV | Bristol MW6G | 164.006 | C39F | 4/60 | Western National, Exeter (DN) 2243 |
| 11960 | 623 DDV | Bristol MW6G | 164.007 | C39F | 3/60 | Western National, Exeter (DN) 2244 |
| 11961 | 624 DDV | Bristol MW6G | 164.008 | C39F | 4/60 | Western National, Exeter (DN) 2245 |
| 11962 | 625 DDV | Bristol MW6G | 164.009 | C39F | 5/60 | Western National, Exeter (DN) 2246 |
| 11963 | 626 DDV | Bristol MW6G | 164.010 | C39F | 5/60 | Western National, Exeter (DN) 2247 |
| 11964 | 511 BRM | Bristol MW6G | 164.058 | DP41F | 7/60 | Cumberland MS, Whitehaven (CU) 414 |
| 11965 | 512 BRM | Bristol MW6G | 164.059 | DP41F | 7/60 | Cumberland MS, Whitehaven (CU) 415 |
| 11966 | OVL 461 | Bristol MW6G | 164.015 | C39F | 4/60 | Lincolnshire RCC, Lincoln (LC) 2817 |
| 11967 | | | | | | Not built |
| 11968 | | | | | | Not built |
| 11969 | | | | | | Not built |
| 11970 | | | | | | Not built |
| 11971 | 1536 HN | Bristol MW6G | 164.053 | DP39F | 7/60 | United AS, Darlington (DM) BUE536 |
| 11972 | 1537 HN | Bristol MW6G | 164.054 | DP39F | 7/60 | United AS, Darlington (DM) BUE537 |

| | | | | | | |
|---|---|---|---|---|---|---|
| 11973 | 1538 HN | Bristol MW6G | 164.055 | DP39F | 8/60 | United AS, Darlington (DM) BUE538 |
| 11974 | 1539 HN | Bristol MW6G | 164.056 | DP39F | 7/60 | United AS, Darlington (DM) BUE539 |
| 11975 | 1540 HN | Bristol MW6G | 164.057 | DP39F | 8/60 | United AS, Darlington (DM) BUE540 |
| 11976 | WBD 142 | Bristol MW6G | 164.048 | DP41F | 7/60 | United Counties, Northampton (NO) 142 |
| 11977 | WBD 143 | Bristol MW6G | 164.049 | DP41F | 7/60 | United Counties, Northampton (NO) 143 |
| 11978 | WBD 144 | Bristol MW6G | 164.050 | DP41F | 7/60 | United Counties, Northampton (NO) 144 |
| 11979 | WBD 145 | Bristol MW6G | 164.051 | DP41F | 7/60 | United Counties, Northampton (NO) 145 |
| 11980 | WBD 146 | Bristol MW6G | 164.052 | DP41F | 7/60 | United Counties, Northampton (NO) 146 |
| 11981 | *237 SFM | Bristol SC4LK | 158.035 | B35F | 10/60 | Crosville MS, Chester (CH) SSG664 |
| 11982 | 238 SFM | Bristol SC4LK | 172.001 | B35F | 11/60 | Crosville MS, Chester (CH) SSG665 |
| 11983 | 239 SFM | Bristol SC4LK | 172.002 | B35F | 11/60 | Crosville MS, Chester (CH) SSG666 |
| 11984 | 240 SFM | Bristol SC4LK | 172.003 | B35F | 12/60 | Crosville MS, Chester (CH) SSG667 |
| 11985 | 241 SFM | Bristol SC4LK | 172.010 | B35F | 1/61 | Crosville MS, Chester (CH) SSG668 |
| 11986 | 242 SFM | Bristol SC4LK | 172.011 | B35F | 2/61 | Crosville MS, Chester (CH) SSG669 |
| 11987 | 243 SFM | Bristol SC4LK | 172.012 | B35F | 2/61 | Crosville MS, Chester (CH) SSG670 |
| 11988 | 244 SFM | Bristol SC4LK | 172.013 | B35F | 4/61 | Crosville MS, Chester (CH) SSG671 |
| 11989 | 245 SFM | Bristol SC4LK | 172.014 | B35F | 4/61 | Crosville MS, Chester (CH) SSG672 |
| 11990 | 246 SFM | Bristol SC4LK | 172.015 | B35F | 5/61 | Crosville MS, Chester (CH) SSG673 |
| 11991 | 247 SFM | Bristol SC4LK | 172.023 | B35F | 5/61 | Crosville MS, Chester (CH) SSG674 |
| 11992 | 248 SFM | Bristol SC4LK | 172.024 | B35F | 5/61 | Crosville MS, Chester (CH) SSG675 |
| 11993 | 249 SFM | Bristol SC4LK | 172.025 | B35F | 6/61 | Crosville MS, Chester (CH) SSG676 |
| 11994 | 250 SFM | Bristol SC4LK | 172.026 | B35F | 6/61 | Crosville MS, Chester (CH) SSG677 |
| 11995 | 251 SFM | Bristol SC4LK | 172.027 | B35F | 6/61 | Crosville MS, Chester (CH) SSG678 |
| 11996 | 252 SFM | Bristol SC4LK | 172.028 | B35F | 7/61 | Crosville MS, Chester (CH) SSG679 |
| 11997 | 6567 NG | Bristol SC4LK | 158.032 | B35F | 6/60 | Eastern Counties, Norwich (NK) LC567 |
| 11998 | 6568 NG | Bristol SC4LK | 158.033 | B35F | 6/60 | Eastern Counties, Norwich (NK) LC568 |
| 11999 | 6569 NG | Bristol SC4LK | 158.034 | B35F | 7/60 | Eastern Counties, Norwich (NK) LC569 |
| 12000 | 6570 NG | Bristol SC4LK | 172.004 | B35F | 11/60 | Eastern Counties, Norwich (NK) LC570 |
| 12001 | 6571 NG | Bristol SC4LK | 172.005 | B35F | 11/60 | Eastern Counties, Norwich (NK) LC571 |
| 12002 | 6572 NG | Bristol SC4LK | 172.006 | B35F | 11/60 | Eastern Counties, Norwich (NK) LC572 |
| 12003 | 6573 NG | Bristol SC4LK | 172.007 | B35F | 11/60 | Eastern Counties, Norwich (NK) LC573 |
| 12004 | 6574 NG | Bristol SC4LK | 172.008 | B35F | 11/60 | Eastern Counties, Norwich (NK) LC574 |
| 12005 | 6575 NG | Bristol SC4LK | 172.009 | B35F | 11/60 | Eastern Counties, Norwich (NK) LC575 |
| 12006 | 6576 NG | Bristol SC4LK | 172.020 | B35F | 3/61 | Eastern Counties, Norwich (NK) LC576 |
| 12007 | 6577 NG | Bristol SC4LK | 172.021 | B35F | 3/61 | Eastern Counties, Norwich (NK) LC577 |
| 12008 | 6578 NG | Bristol SC4LK | 172.022 | B35F | 3/61 | Eastern Counties, Norwich (NK) LC578 |
| 12009 | *LAH 448E | Bristol FLF6B | 169.001 | shell | -/60 | Bristol Commercial Vehicles |
| 12010 | OVL 490 | Bristol SC4LK | 158.025 | B35F | 5/60 | Lincolnshire RCC, Lincoln (LC) 2481 |
| 12011 | OVL 491 | Bristol SC4LK | 158.026 | B35F | 5/60 | Lincolnshire RCC, Lincoln (LC) 2482 |
| 12012 | OVL 492 | Bristol SC4LK | 158.027 | B35F | 5/60 | Lincolnshire RCC, Lincoln (LC) 2483 |
| 12013 | OVL 493 | Bristol SC4LK | 158.028 | B35F | 5/60 | Lincolnshire RCC, Lincoln (LC) 2484 |
| 12014 | OVL 494 | Bristol SC4LK | 158.029 | B35F | 6/60 | Lincolnshire RCC, Lincoln (LC) 2485 |
| 12015 | OVL 495 | Bristol SC4LK | 158.030 | B35F | 6/60 | Lincolnshire RCC, Lincoln (LC) 2486 |
| 12016 | OVL 496 | Bristol SC4LK | 172.016 | B35F | 1/61 | Lincolnshire RCC, Lincoln (LC) 2487 |
| 12017 | OVL 497 | Bristol SC4LK | 172.017 | B35F | 1/61 | Lincolnshire RCC, Lincoln (LC) 2488 |
| 12018 | OVL 498 | Bristol SC4LK | 172.018 | B35F | 1/61 | Lincolnshire RCC, Lincoln (LC) 2489 |
| 12019 | OVL 499 | Bristol SC4LK | 172.019 | B35F | 1/61 | Lincolnshire RCC, Lincoln (LC) 2490 |
| 12020 | 318 EDV | Bristol SUL4A | 157.031 | B36F | 10/60 | Southern National, Exeter (DN) 616 |
| 12021 | 319 EDV | Bristol SUL4A | 157.032 | B36F | 11/60 | Southern National, Exeter (DN) 617 |
| 12022 | 320 EDV | Bristol SUL4A | 157.033 | B36F | 4/61 | Southern National, Exeter (DN) 618 |
| 12023 | 321 EDV | Bristol SUL4A | 157.034 | B36F | 5/61 | Southern National, Exeter (DN) 619 |
| 12024 | 322 EDV | Bristol SUL4A | 173.006 | B36F | 5/61 | Southern National, Exeter (DN) 620 |
| 12025 | 323 EDV | Bristol SUL4A | 173.007 | B36F | 6/61 | Southern National, Exeter (DN) 621 |
| 12026 | 324 EDV | Bristol SUL4A | 173.008 | B36F | 6/61 | Southern National, Exeter (DN) 622 |
| 12027 | 325 EDV | Bristol SUL4A | 173.009 | B36F | 5/61 | Southern National, Exeter (DN) 623 |
| 12028 | 338 EDV | Bristol SUL4A | 157.025 | B36F | 10/60 | Western National, Exeter (DN) 624 |
| 12029 | 339 EDV | Bristol SUL4A | 157.026 | B36F | 10/60 | Western National, Exeter (DN) 625 |
| 12030 | 340 EDV | Bristol SUL4A | 157.027 | B36F | 10/60 | Western National, Exeter (DN) 626 |
| 12031 | 341 EDV | Bristol SUL4A | 157.028 | B36F | 1/61 | Western National, Exeter (DN) 627 |
| 12032 | 342 EDV | Bristol SUL4A | 157.029 | B36F | 1/61 | Western National, Exeter (DN) 628 |
| 12033 | 343 EDV | Bristol SUL4A | 157.030 | B36F | 1/61 | Western National, Exeter (DN) 629 |
| 12034 | 344 EDV | Bristol SUL4A | 157.035 | B36F | 1/61 | Western National, Exeter (DN) 630 |
| 12035 | 345 EDV | Bristol SUL4A | 173.001 | B36F | 1/61 | Western National, Exeter (DN) 631 |
| 12036 | *346 EDV | Bristol SUL4A | 173.002 | B36F | 1/61 | Western National, Exeter (DN) 632 |

| 12037 | 347 EDV | Bristol SUL4A | 173.003 | B36F | 1/61 | Western National, Exeter (DN) 633 |
|-------|---------|---------------|---------|------|------|-----------------------------------|
| 12038 | 348 EDV | Bristol SUL4A | 173.004 | B36F | 1/61 | Western National, Exeter (DN) 634 |
| 12039 | 349 EDV | Bristol SUL4A | 173.005 | B36F | 1/61 | Western National, Exeter (DN) 635 |
| 12040 | 350 EDV | Bristol SUL4A | 173.010 | B36F | 2/61 | Western National, Exeter (DN) 636 |
| 12041 | 351 EDV | Bristol SUL4A | 173.011 | B36F | 3/61 | Western National, Exeter (DN) 637 |
| 12042 | 352 EDV | Bristol SUL4A | 173.012 | B36F | 3/61 | Western National, Exeter (DN) 638 |
| 12043 | 353 EDV | Bristol SUL4A | 173.013 | B36F | 3/61 | Western National, Exeter (DN) 639 |
| 12044 | 354 EDV | Bristol SUL4A | 173.014 | B36F | 3/61 | Western National, Exeter (DN) 640 |
| 12045 | 355 EDV | Bristol SUL4A | 173.015 | B36F | 3/61 | Western National, Exeter (DN) 641 |
| 12046 | *356 EDV | Bristol SUL4A | 173.016 | B36F | 4/61 | Western National, Exeter (DN) 642 |
| 12047 | 357 EDV | Bristol SUL4A | 173.017 | B36F | 3/61 | Western National, Exeter (DN) 643 |
| 12048 | 358 EDV | Bristol SUL4A | 173.018 | B36F | 3/61 | Western National, Exeter (DN) 644 |
| 12049 | 903 OFM | Bristol SC4LK | 158.015 | C33F | 5/60 | Crosville MS, Chester (CH) CSG654 |
| 12050 | 904 OFM | Bristol SC4LK | 158.016 | C33F | 5/60 | Crosville MS, Chester (CH) CSG655 |
| 12051 | 905 OFM | Bristol SC4LK | 158.017 | C33F | 5/60 | Crosville MS, Chester (CH) CSG656 |
| 12052 | 906 OFM | Bristol SC4LK | 158.018 | C33F | 6/60 | Crosville MS, Chester (CH) CSG657 |
| 12053 | 907 OFM | Bristol SC4LK | 158.019 | C33F | 6/60 | Crosville MS, Chester (CH) CSG658 |
| 12054 | 908 OFM | Bristol SC4LK | 158.020 | C33F | 6/60 | Crosville MS, Chester (CH) CSG659 |
| 12055 | 909 OFM | Bristol SC4LK | 158.021 | C33F | 6/60 | Crosville MS, Chester (CH) CSG660 |
| 12056 | 910 OFM | Bristol SC4LK | 158.022 | C33F | 6/60 | Crosville MS, Chester (CH) CSG661 |
| 12057 | 911 OFM | Bristol SC4LK | 158.023 | C33F | 6/60 | Crosville MS, Chester (CH) CSG662 |
| 12058 | 912 OFM | Bristol SC4LK | 158.024 | C33F | 7/60 | Crosville MS, Chester (CH) CSG663 |
| 12059 | *314 EDV | Bristol SUL4A | 157.021 | C33F | 4/61 | Southern National, Exeter (DN) 404 |
| 12060 | *315 EDV | Bristol SUL4A | 157.022 | C33F | 4/61 | Southern National, Exeter (DN) 405 |
| 12061 | *316 EDV | Bristol SUL4A | 157.023 | C33F | 4/61 | Southern National, Exeter (DN) 406 |
| 12062 | *317 EDV | Bristol SUL4A | 157.024 | C33F | 4/61 | Southern National, Exeter (DN) 407 |
| 12063 | 334 EDV | Bristol SUL4A | 157.017 | C33F | 10/60 | Western National, Exeter (DN) 400 |
| 12064 | 335 EDV | Bristol SUL4A | 157.018 | C33F | 5/61 | Western National, Exeter (DN) 401 |
| 12065 | 336 EDV | Bristol SUL4A | 157.019 | C33F | 5/61 | Western National, Exeter (DN) 402 |
| 12066 | 337 EDV | Bristol SUL4A | 157.020 | C33F | 5/61 | Western National, Exeter (DN) 403 |
| 12067 | *LYM 731 | AEC Regal IV | 9821E278 | C34F | 5/60 | Tillings Transport, London WC1 (LN) |
| 12068 | *LYM 728 | AEC Regal IV | 9821E275 | C34F | 5/60 | Tillings Transport, London WC1 (LN) |
| 12069 | *LYM 729 | AEC Regal IV | 9821E276 | C34F | 5/60 | Tillings Transport, London WC1 (LN) |
| 12070 | *LYM 730 | AEC Regal IV | 9821E277 | C34F | 5/60 | Tillings Transport, London WC1 (LN) |
| 12071 | *LYM 732 | AEC Regal IV | 9821E279 | C34F | 5/60 | Tillings Transport, London WC1 (LN) |
| 12072 | *KEL 65 | Bristol L6G Reb | 73.117 | FB39F | 3/60 | Hants & Dorset, Bournemouth (HA) 670 |
| 12073 | *KEL 66 | Bristol L6G Reb | 73.118 | FB39F | 3/60 | Hants & Dorset, Bournemouth (HA) 671 |
| 12074 | *JRU 66 | Bristol L6A Reb | 73.060 | FB39F | 3/60 | Hants & Dorset, Bournemouth (HA) 663 |
| 12075 | *JRU 67 | Bristol L6A Reb | 73.061 | FB39F | 3/60 | Hants & Dorset, Bournemouth (HA) 664 |
| 12076 | *JRU 68 | Bristol L6A Reb | 73.062 | FB39F | 4/60 | Hants & Dorset, Bournemouth (HA) 665 |
| 12077 | *JRU 69 | Bristol L6A Reb | 73.063 | FB39F | 4/60 | Hants & Dorset, Bournemouth (HA) 666 |
| 12078 | *WJB 223 | Bristol FLF6G | 169.056 | H38/32F | 12/60 | Thames Valley, Reading (BE) 839 |
| 12079 | WJB 224 | Bristol FLF6G | 169.057 | H38/32F | 12/60 | Thames Valley, Reading (BE) 840 |
| 12080 | WJB 225 | Bristol FLF6G | 169.058 | H38/32F | 1/61 | Thames Valley, Reading (BE) 841 |
| 12081 | WJB 226 | Bristol FLF6G | 169.059 | H38/32F | 1/61 | Thames Valley, Reading (BE) 842 |
| 12082 | WJB 227 | Bristol FLF6G | 169.060 | H38/32F | 1/61 | Thames Valley, Reading (BE) 843 |
| 12083 | WJB 228 | Bristol FLF6G | 181.004 | H38/32F | 7/61 | Thames Valley, Reading (BE) 844 |
| 12084 | WJB 229 | Bristol FLF6G | 181.005 | H38/32F | 7/61 | Thames Valley, Reading (BE) 845 |
| 12085 | WJB 230 | Bristol FLF6G | 181.006 | H38/32F | 7/61 | Thames Valley, Reading (BE) 846 |
| 12086 | WJB 231 | Bristol FLF6G | 181.007 | H38/32F | 7/61 | Thames Valley, Reading (BE) 847 |
| 12087 | WJB 232 | Bristol FLF6G | 181.012 | H38/32F | 7/61 | Thames Valley, Reading (BE) 848 |
| 12088 | WJB 233 | Bristol FLF6G | 181.049 | H38/32F | 11/61 | Thames Valley, Reading (BE) 849 |
| 12089 | WJB 234 | Bristol FLF6G | 181.050 | H38/32F | 11/61 | Thames Valley, Reading (BE) 850 |
| 12090 | WJB 235 | Bristol FLF6G | 181.051 | H38/32F | 11/61 | Thames Valley, Reading (BE) 851 |
| 12091 | RAG 389 | Bristol FL6G | 168.026 | H33/27RD | 2/61 | Western SMT, Kilmarnock (AR) B1623 |
| 12092 | RAG 390 | Bristol FL6G | 168.027 | H33/27RD | 2/61 | Western SMT, Kilmarnock (AR) B1624 |
| 12093 | RWG 359 | Bristol LD6G | 177.006 | H33/27R | 3/61 | W Alexander (Midland), Falkirk (SN) RD136 |
| 12094 | RWG 360 | Bristol LD6G | 177.007 | H33/27R | 3/61 | W Alexander (Midland), Falkirk (SN) RD137 |
| 12095 | RWG 361 | Bristol LD6G | 177.011 | H33/27R | 4/61 | W Alexander (Midland), Falkirk (SN) RD138 |
| 12096 | RWG 362 | Bristol LD6G | 177.012 | H33/27R | 4/61 | W Alexander (Midland), Falkirk (SN) RD139 |
| 12097 | RWG 363 | Bristol LD6G | 177.013 | H33/27R | 4/61 | W Alexander (Midland), Falkirk (SN) RD140 |
| 12098 | RWG 364 | Bristol LD6G | 177.014 | H33/27R | 4/61 | W Alexander (Midland), Falkirk (SN) RD141 |
| 12099 | RWG 365 | Bristol LD6G | 177.015 | H33/27R | 4/61 | W Alexander (Midland), Falkirk (SN) RD142 |
| 12100 | RWG 366 | Bristol LD6G | 177.026 | H33/27R | 5/61 | W Alexander (Midland), Falkirk (SN) RD143 |

| 12101 | RWG 367 | Bristol LD6G | 177.027 | H33/27R | 5/61 | W Alexander (Midland), Falkirk (SN) RD144 |
|---|---|---|---|---|---|---|
| 12102 | RWG 368 | Bristol LD6G | 177.028 | H33/27R | 5/61 | W Alexander (Midland), Falkirk (SN) RD145 |
| 12103 | RWG 369 | Bristol LD6G | 177.029 | H33/27R | 5/61 | W Alexander (Midland), Falkirk (SN) RD146 |
| 12104 | RWG 370 | Bristol LD6G | 177.030 | H33/27R | 5/61 | W Alexander (Midland), Falkirk (SN) RD147 |
| 12105 | RWG 371 | Bristol LD6G | 177.036 | H33/27R | 5/61 | W Alexander (Midland), Falkirk (SN) RD148 |
| 12106 *RWG 372 | | Bristol LD6G | 177.037 | H33/27R | 7/61 | W Alexander, Falkirk (SN) RD149 |
| 12107 | RWG 373 | Bristol LD6G | 177.038 | H33/27R | 5/61 | W Alexander (Midland), Falkirk (SN) RD150 |
| 12108 | RWG 374 | Bristol LD6G | 177.039 | H33/27R | 7/61 | W Alexander, Falkirk (SN) RD151 |
| 12109 | RWG 375 | Bristol LD6G | 177.040 | H33/27R | 7/61 | W Alexander, Falkirk (SN) RD152 |
| 12110 | RWG 376 | Bristol LD6G | 177.041 | H33/27R | 6/61 | W Alexander (Midland), Falkirk (SN) RD153 |
| 12111 | RWG 377 | Bristol LD6G | 177.042 | H33/27R | 6/61 | W Alexander (Midland), Falkirk (SN) RD154 |
| 12112 | RWG 378 | Bristol LD6G | 177.058 | H33/27R | 7/61 | W Alexander (Midland), Falkirk (SN) RD155 |
| 12113 | RWG 379 | Bristol LD6G | 177.059 | H33/27R | 7/61 | W Alexander (Midland), Falkirk (SN) RD156 |
| 12114 | RWG 380 | Bristol LD6G | 177.060 | H33/27R | 7/61 | W Alexander (Midland), Falkirk (SN) RD157 |
| 12115 *RWG 381 | | Bristol LD6G | 177.061 | H33/27R | 7/61 | W Alexander (Midland), Falkirk (SN) RD158 |
| 12116 *RWG 382 | | Bristol LD6G | 177.076 | H33/27R | 7/61 | W Alexander (Midland), Falkirk (SN) RD159 |
| 12117 | RWG 383 | Bristol LD6G | 177.077 | H33/27R | 7/61 | W Alexander (Midland), Falkirk (SN) RD160 |
| 12118 | CGM 123 | Bristol LD6G | 177.046 | H33/27R | 6/61 | Central SMT, Motherwell (LK) B123 |
| 12119 | CGM 124 | Bristol LD6G | 177.047 | H33/27R | 6/61 | Central SMT, Motherwell (LK) B124 |
| 12120 | CGM 125 | Bristol LD6G | 177.048 | H33/27R | 6/61 | Central SMT, Motherwell (LK) B125 |
| 12121 | CGM 126 | Bristol LD6G | 177.049 | H33/27R | 6/61 | Central SMT, Motherwell (LK) B126 |
| 12122 | CGM 127 | Bristol LD6G | 177.062 | H33/27R | 7/61 | Central SMT, Motherwell (LK) B127 |
| 12123 | CGM 128 | Bristol LD6G | 177.063 | H33/27R | 7/61 | Central SMT, Motherwell (LK) B128 |
| 12124 | CGM 129 | Bristol LD6G | 177.069 | H33/27R | 7/61 | Central SMT, Motherwell (LK) B129 |
| 12125 | WSC 845 | Bristol LD6G | 177.001 | H33/27RD | 3/61 | Scottish Omnibuses, Edinburgh (MN) AA845 |
| 12126 | WSC 846 | Bristol LD6G | 177.002 | H33/27RD | 3/61 | Scottish Omnibuses, Edinburgh (MN) AA846 |
| 12127 | WSC 847 | Bristol LD6G | 177.003 | H33/27RD | 3/61 | Scottish Omnibuses, Edinburgh (MN) AA847 |
| 12128 | WSC 848 | Bristol LD6G | 177.004 | H33/27RD | 3/61 | Scottish Omnibuses, Edinburgh (MN) AA848 |
| 12129 | WSC 849 | Bristol LD6G | 177.005 | H33/27RD | 3/61 | Scottish Omnibuses, Edinburgh (MN) AA849 |
| 12130 | WSC 850 | Bristol LD6G | 177.016 | H33/27RD | 3/61 | Scottish Omnibuses, Edinburgh (MN) AA850 |
| 12131 | WSC 851 | Bristol LD6G | 177.017 | H33/27RD | 3/61 | Scottish Omnibuses, Edinburgh (MN) AA851 |
| 12132 | WSC 852 | Bristol LD6G | 177.018 | H33/27RD | 3/61 | Scottish Omnibuses, Edinburgh (MN) AA852 |
| 12133 | WSC 853 | Bristol LD6G | 177.019 | H33/27RD | 3/61 | Scottish Omnibuses, Edinburgh (MN) AA853 |
| 12134 | WSC 854 | Bristol LD6G | 177.020 | H33/27RD | 4/61 | Scottish Omnibuses, Edinburgh (MN) AA854 |
| 12135 | WSC 855 | Bristol LD6G | 177.031 | H33/27RD | 5/61 | Scottish Omnibuses, Edinburgh (MN) AA855 |
| 12136 | WSC 856 | Bristol LD6G | 177.032 | H33/27RD | 5/61 | Scottish Omnibuses, Edinburgh (MN) AA856 |
| 12137 | WSC 857 | Bristol LD6G | 177.033 | H33/27RD | 5/61 | Scottish Omnibuses, Edinburgh (MN) AA857 |
| 12138 | WSC 858 | Bristol LD6G | 177.034 | H33/27RD | 5/61 | Scottish Omnibuses, Edinburgh (MN) AA858 |
| 12139 | WSC 859 | Bristol LD6G | 177.035 | H33/27RD | 5/61 | Scottish Omnibuses, Edinburgh (MN) AA859 |
| 12140 | WSC 860 | Bristol LD6G | 177.050 | H33/27RD | 6/61 | Scottish Omnibuses, Edinburgh (MN) AA860 |
| 12141 | WSC 861 | Bristol LD6G | 177.051 | H33/27RD | 6/61 | Scottish Omnibuses, Edinburgh (MN) AA861 |
| 12142 | WSC 862 | Bristol LD6G | 177.052 | H33/27RD | 6/61 | Scottish Omnibuses, Edinburgh (MN) AA862 |
| 12143 | WSC 863 | Bristol LD6G | 177.053 | H33/27RD | 6/61 | Scottish Omnibuses, Edinburgh (MN) AA863 |
| 12144 | WSC 864 | Bristol LD6G | 177.064 | H33/27RD | 7/61 | Scottish Omnibuses, Edinburgh (MN) AA864 |
| 12145 | WSC 865 | Bristol LD6G | 177.065 | H33/27RD | 7/61 | Scottish Omnibuses, Edinburgh (MN) AA865 |
| 12146 | WSC 866 | Bristol LD6G | 177.072 | H33/27RD | 7/61 | Scottish Omnibuses, Edinburgh (MN) AA866 |
| 12147 | WSC 867 | Bristol LD6G | 177.073 | H33/27RD | 7/61 | Scottish Omnibuses, Edinburgh (MN) AA867 |
| 12148 | WSC 868 | Bristol LD6G | 177.074 | H33/27RD | 7/61 | Scottish Omnibuses, Edinburgh (MN) AA868 |
| 12149 | WSC 869 | Bristol LD6G | 177.075 | H33/27RD | 7/61 | Scottish Omnibuses, Edinburgh (MN) AA869 |
| 12150 | RAG 394 | Bristol LD6G | 177.008 | H33/27RD | 4/61 | Western SMT, Kilmarnock (AR) B1628 |
| 12151 | RAG 395 | Bristol LD6G | 177.009 | H33/27RD | 4/61 | Western SMT, Kilmarnock (AR) B1629 |
| 12152 | RAG 396 | Bristol LD6G | 177.010 | H33/27RD | 4/61 | Western SMT, Kilmarnock (AR) B1630 |
| 12153 | RAG 397 | Bristol LD6G | 177.021 | H33/27RD | 5/61 | Western SMT, Kilmarnock (AR) B1631 |
| 12154 | RAG 398 | Bristol LD6G | 177.022 | H33/27RD | 5/61 | Western SMT, Kilmarnock (AR) B1632 |
| 12155 | RAG 399 | Bristol LD6G | 177.023 | H33/27RD | 5/61 | Western SMT, Kilmarnock (AR) B1633 |
| 12156 | RAG 400 | Bristol LD6G | 177.024 | H33/27RD | 5/61 | Western SMT, Kilmarnock (AR) B1634 |
| 12157 | RAG 401 | Bristol LD6G | 177.025 | H33/27RD | 5/61 | Western SMT, Kilmarnock (AR) B1635 |
| 12158 | RAG 402 | Bristol LD6G | 177.043 | H33/27RD | 6/61 | Western SMT, Kilmarnock (AR) B1636 |
| 12159 *RAG 403 | | Bristol LD6G | 177.044 | H33/27RD | 6/61 | Western SMT, Kilmarnock (AR) B1637 |
| 12160 | RAG 404 | Bristol LD6G | 177.045 | H33/27RD | 6/61 | Western SMT, Kilmarnock (AR) B1638 |
| 12161 | RAG 405 | Bristol LD6G | 177.054 | H33/27RD | 7/61 | Western SMT, Kilmarnock (AR) B1639 |
| 12162 | RAG 406 | Bristol LD6G | 177.055 | H33/27RD | 7/61 | Western SMT, Kilmarnock (AR) B1640 |
| 12163 | RAG 407 | Bristol LD6G | 177.056 | H33/27RD | 7/61 | Western SMT, Kilmarnock (AR) B1641 |
| 12164 | RAG 408 | Bristol LD6G | 177.057 | H33/27RD | 7/61 | Western SMT, Kilmarnock (AR) B1642 |

| | | | | | | |
|---|---|---|---|---|---|---|
| 12165 | RAG 409 | Bristol LD6G | 177.066 | H33/27RD | 8/61 | Western SMT, Kilmarnock (AR) B1643 |
| 12166 | RAG 410 | Bristol LD6G | 177.067 | H33/27RD | 8/61 | Western SMT, Kilmarnock (AR) B1644 |
| 12167 | RAG 411 | Bristol LD6G | 177.068 | H33/27RD | 8/61 | Western SMT, Kilmarnock (AR) B1645 |
| 12168 | RAG 412 | Bristol LD6G | 177.070 | H33/27RD | 8/61 | Western SMT, Kilmarnock (AR) B1646 |
| 12169 | RAG 413 | Bristol LD6G | 177.071 | H33/27RD | 8/61 | Western SMT, Kilmarnock (AR) B1647 |
| 12170 | RAG 391 | Bristol FS6G | 166.047 | H33/27RD | 5/61 | Western SMT, Kilmarnock (AR) B1625 |
| 12171 | RAG 392 | Bristol FS6G | 166.051 | H33/27RD | 5/61 | Western SMT, Kilmarnock (AR) B1626 |
| 12172 | RAG 393 | Bristol FS6G | 166.052 | H33/27RD | 5/61 | Western SMT, Kilmarnock (AR) B1627 |
| 12173 | 403 LHT | Bristol MW6G | 184.011 | C39F | 5/61 | Bristol OC (GL) 2110 |
| 12174 | *404 LHT | Bristol MW6G | 184.012 | C39F | 5/61 | Bristol OC (GL) 2111 |
| 12175 | 405 LHT | Bristol MW6G | 184.021 | C39F | 5/61 | Bristol OC (GL) 2112 |
| 12176 | *406 LHT | Bristol MW6G | 184.050 | C39F | 5/61 | Bristol OC (GL) 2113 |
| 12177 | 407 LHT | Bristol MW6G | 184.051 | C39F | 5/61 | Bristol OC (GL) 2114 |
| 12178 | 427 UFM | Bristol MW6G | 184.001 | C39F | 7/61 | Crosville MS, Chester (CH) CMG407 |
| 12179 | *428 UFM | Bristol MW6G | 184.029 | C39F | 6/61 | Crosville MS, Chester (CH) CMG408 |
| 12180 | *429 UFM | Bristol MW6G | 184.030 | C39F | 6/61 | Crosville MS, Chester (CH) CMG409 |
| 12181 | *430 UFM | Bristol MW6G | 184.070 | C39F | 6/61 | Crosville MS, Chester (CH) CMG410 |
| 12182 | 431 UFM | Bristol MW6G | 184.071 | C39F | 6/61 | Crosville MS, Chester (CH) CMG411 |
| 12183 | 432 UFM | Bristol MW6G | 184.072 | C39F | 6/61 | Crosville MS, Chester (CH) CMG412 |
| 12184 | 433 UFM | Bristol MW6G | 184.081 | C39F | 7/61 | Crosville MS, Chester (CH) CMG413 |
| 12185 | 434 UFM | Bristol MW6G | 184.082 | C39F | 7/61 | Crosville MS, Chester (CH) CMG414 |
| 12186 | 4227 VF | Bristol MW6G | 184.068 | C32F | 6/61 | Eastern Counties, Norwich (NK) LS801 |
| 12187 | 4228 VF | Bristol MW6G | 184.069 | C32F | 6/61 | Eastern Counties, Norwich (NK) LS802 |
| 12188 | 4229 VF | Bristol MW6G | 184.073 | C32F | 6/61 | Eastern Counties, Norwich (NK) LS803 |
| 12189 | 4821 VF | Bristol MW5G | 184.004 | C39F | 5/61 | Eastern Counties, Norwich (NK) LS795 |
| 12190 | 4822 VF | Bristol MW5G | 184.005 | C39F | 5/61 | Eastern Counties, Norwich (NK) LS796 |
| 12191 | 4823 VF | Bristol MW5G | 184.007 | C39F | 5/61 | Eastern Counties, Norwich (NK) LS797 |
| 12192 | 4824 VF | Bristol MW5G | 184.042 | C39F | 5/61 | Eastern Counties, Norwich (NK) LS798 |
| 12193 | 4825 VF | Bristol MW5G | 184.043 | C39F | 5/61 | Eastern Counties, Norwich (NK) LS799 |
| 12194 | 4826 VF | Bristol MW5G | 184.044 | C39F | 5/61 | Eastern Counties, Norwich (NK) LS800 |
| 12195 | 569 UVX | Bristol MW6G | 184.013 | C34F | 4/61 | Eastern National, Chelmsford (EX) 532 |
| 12196 | 570 UVX | Bristol MW6G | 184.014 | C34F | 5/61 | Eastern National, Chelmsford (EX) 533 |
| 12197 | 571 UVX | Bristol MW6G | 184.055 | C34F | 6/61 | Eastern National, Chelmsford (EX) 534 |
| 12198 | 572 UVX | Bristol MW6G | 184.056 | C34F | 6/61 | Eastern National, Chelmsford (EX) 535 |
| 12199 | 573 UVX | Bristol MW6G | 184.057 | C34F | 6/61 | Eastern National, Chelmsford (EX) 536 |
| 12200 | 1468 LJ | Bristol MW6G | 184.031 | C30F | 5/61 | Hants & Dorset, Bournemouth (HA) 876 |
| 12201 | 1469 LJ | Bristol MW6G | 184.032 | C30F | 5/61 | Hants & Dorset, Bournemouth (HA) 877 |
| 12202 | 1470 LJ | Bristol MW6G | 184.033 | C30F | 5/61 | Hants & Dorset, Bournemouth (HA) 878 |
| 12203 | 1471 LJ | Bristol MW6G | 184.063 | C30F | 6/61 | Hants & Dorset, Bournemouth (HA) 879 |
| 12204 | 1472 LJ | Bristol MW6G | 184.064 | C30F | 6/61 | Hants & Dorset, Bournemouth (HA) 880 |
| 12205 | 1473 LJ | Bristol MW6G | 184.065 | C30F | 6/61 | Hants & Dorset, Bournemouth (HA) 881 |
| 12206 | *RFE 461 | Bristol MW6G | 164.200 | C39F | 3/61 | Lincolnshire RCC, Lincoln (LC) 2818 |
| 12207 | 59 GUO | Bristol MW6G | 184.024 | C39F | 6/61 | Southern National, Exeter (DN) 2254 |
| 12208 | 60 GUO | Bristol MW6G | 184.025 | C39F | 6/61 | Southern National, Exeter (DN) 2255 |
| 12209 | 61 GUO | Bristol MW6G | 184.026 | C39F | 6/61 | Southern National, Exeter (DN) 2256 |
| 12210 | 62 GUO | Bristol MW6G | 184.060 | C39F | 6/61 | Southern National, Exeter (DN) 2257 |
| 12211 | 63 GUO | Bristol MW6G | 184.061 | C39F | 6/61 | Southern National, Exeter (DN) 2258 |
| 12212 | 64 GUO | Bristol MW6G | 184.062 | C39F | 6/61 | Southern National, Exeter (DN) 2259 |
| 12213 | 65 GUO | Bristol MW6G | 184.079 | C39F | 6/61 | Southern National, Exeter (DN) 2260 |
| 12214 | 66 GUO | Bristol MW6G | 184.080 | C39F | 6/61 | Southern National, Exeter (DN) 2261 |
| 12215 | WRX 773 | Bristol MW6G | 184.022 | C34F | 4/61 | Thames Valley, Reading (BE) 858 |
| 12216 | WRX 774 | Bristol MW6G | 184.023 | C34F | 4/61 | Thames Valley, Reading (BE) 859 |
| 12217 | WRX 775 | Bristol MW6G | 184.049 | C34F | 6/61 | Thames Valley, Reading (BE) 860 |
| 12218 | * | | | | | Not built |
| 12219 | 2 BXB | Bristol MW6G | 184.027 | C34F | 5/61 | Tillings Transport, London WC1 (LN) |
| 12220 | 3 BXB | Bristol MW6G | 184.028 | C34F | 5/61 | Tillings Transport, London WC1 (LN) |
| 12221 | 1 BXB | Bristol MW6G | 184.015 | C39F | 9/61 | Tillings Transport, London WC1 (LN) |
| 12222 | * 4 BXB | Bristol MW6G | 184.047 | C34F | 9/61 | Tillings Transport, London WC1 (LN) |
| 12223 | 5 BXB | Bristol MW6G | 184.048 | C34F | 9/61 | Tillings Transport, London WC1 (LN) |
| 12224 | 4206 HN | Bristol MW6G | 184.052 | C39F | 6/61 | United AS, Darlington (DM) BUC6 |
| 12225 | 4207 HN | Bristol MW6G | 184.053 | C39F | 7/61 | United AS, Darlington (DM) BUC7 |
| 12226 | 4208 HN | Bristol MW6G | 184.054 | C39F | 7/61 | United AS, Darlington (DM) BUC8 |
| 12227 | 4209 HN | Bristol MW6G | 184.066 | C39F | 7/61 | United AS, Darlington (DM) BUC9 |
| 12228 | 4210 HN | Bristol MW6G | 184.067 | C39F | 7/61 | United AS, Darlington (DM) BUC10 |

| | | | | | | |
|---|---|---|---|---|---|---|
| 12229 | YBD 200 | Bristol MW6G | 184.037 | C34F | 6/61 | United Counties, Northampton (NO) 200 |
| 12230 | YBD 201 | Bristol MW6G | 184.038 | C34F | 6/61 | United Counties, Northampton (NO) 201 |
| 12231 | YBD 202 | Bristol MW6G | 184.058 | C34F | 6/61 | United Counties, Northampton (NO) 202 |
| 12232 | YBD 203 | Bristol MW6G | 184.059 | C34F | 6/61 | United Counties, Northampton (NO) 203 |
| 12233 | YCY 809 | Bristol MW6G | 184.009 | C39F | 5/61 | United Welsh, Swansea (GG) 8 |
| 12234 | YCY 810 | Bristol MW6G | 184.010 | C39F | 5/61 | United Welsh, Swansea (GG) 9 |
| 12235 | 51 GUO | Bristol MW6G | 184.002 | C39F | 6/61 | Western National, Exeter (DN) 2262 |
| 12236 | 52 GUO | Bristol MW6G | 184.003 | C39F | 6/61 | Western National, Exeter (DN) 2263 |
| 12237 | 53 GUO | Bristol MW6G | 184.006 | C39F | 6/61 | Western National, Exeter (DN) 2264 |
| 12238 | 54 GUO | Bristol MW6G | 184.008 | C39F | 6/61 | Western National, Exeter (DN) 2265 |
| 12239 * | 55 GUO | Bristol MW6G | 184.045 | C39F | 6/61 | Western National, Exeter (DN) 2266 |
| 12240 | 56 GUO | Bristol MW6G | 184.046 | C39F | 6/61 | Western National, Exeter (DN) 2267 |
| 12241 | 57 GUO | Bristol MW6G | 184.074 | C39F | 6/61 | Western National, Exeter (DN) 2268 |
| 12242 | 58 GUO | Bristol MW6G | 184.075 | C39F | 6/61 | Western National, Exeter (DN) 2269 |
| 12243 | 8124 WX | Bristol MW6G | 184.034 | C39F | 5/61 | West Yorkshire RCC, Harrogate (WR) CUG27 |
| 12244 | 8125 WX | Bristol MW6G | 184.035 | C39F | 5/61 | West Yorkshire RCC, Harrogate (WR) CUG28 |
| 12245 | 8126 WX | Bristol MW6G | 184.036 | C39F | 5/61 | West Yorkshire RCC, Harrogate (WR) CUG29 |
| 12246 | 8127 WX | Bristol MW6G | 184.076 | C39F | 7/61 | West Yorkshire RCC, Harrogate (WR) CUG30 |
| 12247 | 8128 WX | Bristol MW6G | 184.077 | C39F | 7/61 | West Yorkshire RCC, Harrogate (WR) CUG31 |
| 12248 | 8129 WX | Bristol MW6G | 184.078 | C39F | 7/61 | West Yorkshire RCC, Harrogate (WR) CUG32 |
| 12249 | XMR 942 | Bristol MW6G | 184.039 | C39F | 5/61 | Wilts & Dorset, Salisbury (WI) 709 |
| 12250 | XMR 943 | Bristol MW6G | 184.040 | C39F | 5/61 | Wilts & Dorset, Salisbury (WI) 710 |
| 12251 | XMR 944 | Bristol MW6G | 184.041 | C39F | 5/61 | Wilts & Dorset, Salisbury (WI) 711 |
| 12252 | XMR 945 | Bristol MW6G | 184.083 | C39F | 7/61 | Wilts & Dorset, Salisbury (WI) 712 |
| 12253 | XMR 946 | Bristol MW6G | 184.084 | C39F | 7/61 | Wilts & Dorset, Salisbury (WI) 713 |
| 12254 | XMR 947 | Bristol MW6G | 184.085 | C39F | 7/61 | Wilts & Dorset, Salisbury (WI) 714 |
| 12255 | 1880 WA | Leyland L1 | 603155 | C41F | 4/61 | Sheffield JOC (WR) C1180 |
| 12256 | 1881 WA | Leyland L1 | 603156 | C41F | 4/61 | Sheffield JOC (WR) C1181 |
| 12257 | 1882 WA | Leyland L1 | 603169 | C41F | 4/61 | Sheffield JOC (WR) C1182 |
| 12258 | 1910 WA | Leyland L1 | 603178 | C41F | 5/61 | Sheffield JOC (WR) B1310 |
| 12259 | 1911 WA | Leyland L1 | 603168 | C41F | 5/61 | Sheffield JOC (WR) B1311 |
| 12260 | CGM 116 | Bristol FSF6G | 167.053 | H34/26F | 2/61 | Central SMT, Motherwell (LK) B116 |
| 12261 | CGM 117 | Bristol FSF6G | 167.054 | H34/26F | 3/61 | Central SMT, Motherwell (LK) B117 |
| 12262 | CGM 118 | Bristol FSF6G | 167.055 | H34/26F | 2/61 | Central SMT, Motherwell (LK) B118 |
| 12263 | CGM 119 | Bristol FSF6G | 167.056 | H34/26F | 3/61 | Central SMT, Motherwell (LK) B119 |
| 12264 | CGM 120 | Bristol FSF6G | 167.057 | H34/26F | 3/61 | Central SMT, Motherwell (LK) B120 |
| 12265 | CGM 121 | Bristol FSF6G | 167.058 | H34/26F | 3/61 | Central SMT, Motherwell (LK) B121 |
| 12266 | CGM 122 | Bristol FSF6G | 167.059 | H34/26F | 3/61 | Central SMT, Motherwell (LK) B122 |
| 12267 | VAP 31 | Bristol FSF6B | 179.001 | H34/26F | 7/61 | Brighton, Hove & District (ES) 31 |
| 12268 | VAP 32 | Bristol FSF6B | 179.002 | H34/26F | 7/61 | Brighton, Hove & District (ES) 32 |
| 12269 | VAP 33 | Bristol FSF6B | 179.003 | H34/26F | 7/61 | Brighton, Hove & District (ES) 33 |
| 12270 | VAP 34 | Bristol FSF6B | 179.012 | H34/26F | 7/61 | Brighton, Hove & District (ES) 34 |
| 12271 | VAP 35 | Bristol FSF6B | 179.013 | H34/26F | 7/61 | Brighton, Hove & District (ES) 35 |
| 12272 | WNJ 36 | Bristol FSF6B | 179.075 | H34/26F | 3/62 | Brighton, Hove & District (ES) 36 |
| 12273 | WNJ 37 | Bristol FSF6B | 179.076 | H34/26F | 3/62 | Brighton, Hove & District (ES) 37 |
| 12274 | WNJ 38 | Bristol FSF6B | 179.077 | H34/26F | 4/62 | Brighton, Hove & District (ES) 38 |
| 12275 | WNJ 39 | Bristol FSF6B | 179.078 | H34/26F | 4/62 | Brighton, Hove & District (ES) 39 |
| 12276 | WNJ 40 | Bristol FSF6B | 179.079 | H34/26F | 4/62 | Brighton, Hove & District (ES) 40 |
| 12277 | 207 NAE | Bristol FLF6G | 199.001 | H38/32F | 4/62 | Bristol OC (GL) C7039 |
| 12278 | 208 NAE | Bristol FLF6G | 199.002 | H38/32F | 4/62 | Bristol OC (GL) C7040 |
| 12279 | 209 NAE | Bristol FLF6G | 199.003 | H38/32F | 4/62 | Bristol OC (GL) C7041 |
| 12280 | 210 NAE | Bristol FLF6G | 199.004 | H38/32F | 4/62 | Bristol OC (GL) C7042 |
| 12281 | 211 NAE | Bristol FLF6G | 199.005 | H38/32F | 4/62 | Bristol OC (GL) C7043 |
| 12282 | 212 NAE | Bristol FLF6G | 199.006 | H38/32F | 4/62 | Bristol OC (GL) C7044 |
| 12283 | 213 NAE | Bristol FLF6G | 199.007 | H38/32F | 4/62 | Bristol OC (GL) C7045 |
| 12284 | 801 MHW | Bristol FSF6G | 179.022 | H34/26F | 10/61 | Cheltenham District (GL) 6036 |
| 12285 | 802 MHW | Bristol FSF6G | 179.023 | H34/26F | 10/61 | Cheltenham District (GL) 6037 |
| 12286 * | 866 NHT | Bristol FS6G | 178.001 | CO33/27R | 11/61 | Bristol OC (GL) 8576 |
| 12287 | 867 NHT | Bristol FS6G | 178.002 | CO33/27R | 11/61 | Bristol OC (GL) 8577 |
| 12288 | 868 NHT | Bristol FS6G | 178.003 | CO33/27R | 11/61 | Bristol OC (GL) 8578 |
| 12289 * | 869 NHT | Bristol FS6G | 178.004 | CO33/27R | 11/61 | Bristol OC (GL) 8579 |
| 12290 * | 806 MHW | Bristol FSF6G | 179.021 | H34/26F | 10/61 | Bath Electric Tramways (SO) 6041 |
| 12291 | 214 NAE | Bristol FLF6G | 199.008 | H38/32F | 5/62 | Bristol OC (GL) 7046 |
| 12292 | 215 NAE | Bristol FLF6G | 199.009 | H38/32F | 5/62 | Bristol OC (GL) 7047 |

| | | | | | | | |
|---|---|---|---|---|---|---|---|
| 12293 | 216 NAE | Bristol FLF6G | 199.010 | H38/32F | 5/62 | Bristol OC (GL) 7048 |
| 12294 | 217 NAE | Bristol FLF6G | 199.011 | H38/32F | 5/62 | Bristol OC (GL) 7049 |
| 12295 | 218 NAE | Bristol FLF6G | 199.022 | H38/32F | 5/62 | Bristol OC (GL) 7050 |
| 12296 | 219 NAE | Bristol FLF6G | 199.023 | H38/32F | 5/62 | Bristol OC (GL) 7051 |
| 12297 | 220 NAE | Bristol FLF6G | 199.024 | H38/32F | 6/62 | Bristol OC (GL) 7052 |
| 12298 | 221 NAE | Bristol FLF6G | 199.025 | H38/32F | 6/62 | Bristol OC (GL) 7053 |
| 12299 | 222 NAE | Bristol FLF6G | 199.026 | H38/32F | 6/62 | Bristol OC (GL) 7054 |
| 12300 | 223 NAE | Bristol FLF6G | 199.027 | H38/32F | 6/62 | Bristol OC (GL) 7055 |
| 12301 | *803 MHW | Bristol FSF6G | 179.024 | H34/26F | 10/61 | Bristol OC (GL) G6038 |
| 12302 | 804 MHW | Bristol FSF6G | 179.040 | H34/26F | 10/61 | Bristol OC (GL) G6039 |
| 12303 | 864 VFM | Bristol FSF6B | 167.068 | H34/26F | 10/61 | Crosville MS, Chester (CH) DFB54 |
| 12304 | 865 VFM | Bristol FSF6B | 179.008 | H34/26F | 10/61 | Crosville MS, Chester (CH) DFB55 |
| 12305 | 866 VFM | Bristol FSF6B | 179.035 | H34/26F | 11/61 | Crosville MS, Chester (CH) DFB56 |
| 12306 | 869 VFM | Bristol FSF6G | 179.019 | H34/26F | 11/61 | Crosville MS, Chester (CH) DFG59 |
| 12307 | 870 VFM | Bristol FSF6G | 179.020 | H34/26F | 11/61 | Crosville MS, Chester (CH) DFG60 |
| 12308 | 871 VFM | Bristol FSF6G | 179.025 | H34/26F | 11/61 | Crosville MS, Chester (CH) DFG61 |
| 12309 | 872 VFM | Bristol FSF6G | 179.026 | H34/26F | 11/61 | Crosville MS, Chester (CH) DFG62 |
| 12310 | 873 VFM | Bristol FSF6G | 179.027 | H34/26F | 11/61 | Crosville MS, Chester (CH) DFG63 |
| 12311 | 874 VFM | Bristol FSF6G | 179.028 | H34/26F | 11/61 | Crosville MS, Chester (CH) DFG64 |
| 12312 | 875 VFM | Bristol FSF6G | 179.042 | H34/26F | 1/62 | Crosville MS, Chester (CH) DFG65 |
| 12313 | 876 VFM | Bristol FSF6G | 179.043 | H34/26F | 1/62 | Crosville MS, Chester (CH) DFG66 |
| 12314 | 877 VFM | Bristol FSF6G | 179.044 | H34/26F | 1/62 | Crosville MS, Chester (CH) DFG67 |
| 12315 | *878 VFM | Bristol FSF6G | 179.045 | H34/26F | 2/62 | Crosville MS, Chester (CH) DFG68 |
| 12316 | 879 VFM | Bristol FSF6G | 179.054 | H34/26F | 3/62 | Crosville MS, Chester (CH) DFG69 |
| 12317 | 880 VFM | Bristol FSF6G | 179.059 | H34/26F | 3/62 | Crosville MS, Chester (CH) DFG70 |
| 12318 | 881 VFM | Bristol FSF6G | 179.060 | H34/26F | 4/62 | Crosville MS, Chester (CH) DFG71 |
| 12319 | 882 VFM | Bristol FSF6G | 179.061 | H34/26F | 4/62 | Crosville MS, Chester (CH) DFG72 |
| 12320 | 883 VFM | Bristol FSF6G | 179.062 | H34/26F | 4/62 | Crosville MS, Chester (CH) DFG73 |
| 12321 | 884 VFM | Bristol FSF6G | 179.067 | H34/26F | 4/62 | Crosville MS, Chester (CH) DFG74 |
| 12322 | 867 VFM | Bristol FSF6B | 179.080 | H34/26F | 5/62 | Crosville MS, Chester (CH) DFB57 |
| 12323 | 868 VFM | Bristol FSF6B | 179.081 | H34/26F | 5/62 | Crosville MS, Chester (CH) DFB58 |
| 12324 | 885 VFM | Bristol FSF6G | 197.003 | H34/26F | 6/62 | Crosville MS, Chester (CH) DFG75 |
| 12325 | 886 VFM | Bristol FSF6G | 197.004 | H34/26F | 6/62 | Crosville MS, Chester (CH) DFG76 |
| 12326 | 887 VFM | Bristol FSF6G | 197.014 | H34/26F | 6/62 | Crosville MS, Chester (CH) DFG77 |
| 12327 | 888 VFM | Bristol FSF6G | 197.015 | H34/26F | 6/62 | Crosville MS, Chester (CH) DFG78 |
| 12328 | 889 VFM | Bristol FSF6G | 197.016 | H34/26F | 6/62 | Crosville MS, Chester (CH) DFG79 |
| 12329 | 890 VFM | Bristol FSF6G | 197.024 | H34/26F | 6/62 | Crosville MS, Chester (CH) DFG80 |
| 12330 | 891 VFM | Bristol FSF6G | 197.025 | H34/26F | 6/62 | Crosville MS, Chester (CH) DFG81 |
| 12331 | 892 VFM | Bristol FSF6G | 197.026 | H34/26F | 6/62 | Crosville MS, Chester (CH) DFG82 |
| 12332 | 893 VFM | Bristol FSF6G | 197.027 | H34/26F | 6/62 | Crosville MS, Chester (CH) DFG83 |
| 12333 | *109 DRM | Bristol FS6G | 166.045 | H33/27RD | 4/61 | Cumberland MS, Whitehaven (CU) C416 |
| 12334 | 110 DRM | Bristol FS6G | 166.046 | H33/27RD | 4/61 | Cumberland MS, Whitehaven (CU) C417 |
| 12335 | 111 DRM | Bristol FS6G | 166.048 | H33/27RD | 4/61 | Cumberland MS, Whitehaven (CU) C418 |
| 12336 | 112 DRM | Bristol FS6G | 166.049 | H33/27RD | 4/61 | Cumberland MS, Whitehaven (CU) C419 |
| 12337 | 113 DRM | Bristol FS6G | 166.050 | H33/27RD | 4/61 | Cumberland MS, Whitehaven (CU) C420 |
| 12338 | 51 JAL | Bristol FSF6G | 179.006 | H34/26F | 2/62 | Mansfield District (NG) 535 |
| 12339 | * 52 JAL | Bristol FSF6G | 179.007 | H34/26F | 2/62 | Mansfield District (NG) 536 |
| 12340 | 53 JAL | Bristol FSF6G | 179.032 | H34/26F | 2/62 | Mansfield District (NG) 537 |
| 12341 | 54 JAL | Bristol FSF6G | 179.033 | H34/26F | 2/62 | Mansfield District (NG) 538 |
| 12342 | 55 JAL | Bristol FSF6G | 179.051 | H34/26F | 3/62 | Mansfield District (NG) 539 |
| 12343 | 56 JAL | Bristol FSF6G | 179.052 | H34/26F | 3/62 | Mansfield District (NG) 540 |
| 12344 | 57 JAL | Bristol FSF6G | 179.053 | H34/26F | 3/62 | Mansfield District (NG) 541 |
| 12345 | 58 JAL | Bristol FSF6G | 197.001 | H34/26F | 6/62 | Mansfield District (NG) 542 |
| 12346 | * 59 JAL | Bristol FSF6G | 197.002 | H34/26F | 6/62 | Mansfield District (NG) 543 |
| 12347 | * 60 JAL | Bristol FSF6G | 197.021 | H34/26F | 6/62 | Mansfield District (NG) 544 |
| 12348 | 441 SNU | Bristol FSF6G | 179.004 | H34/26F | 11/61 | Midland General, Langley Mill (DE) 501 |
| 12349 | 442 SNU | Bristol FSF6G | 179.005 | H34/26F | 11/61 | Midland General, Langley Mill (DE) 502 |
| 12350 | 443 SNU | Bristol FSF6G | 179.029 | H34/26F | 11/61 | Midland General, Langley Mill (DE) 503 |
| 12351 | *444 SNU | Bristol FSF6G | 179.030 | H34/26F | 11/61 | Midland General, Langley Mill (DE) 504 |
| 12352 | 445 SNU | Bristol FSF6G | 179.031 | H34/26F | 11/61 | Midland General, Langley Mill (DE) 505 |
| 12353 | 446 SNU | Bristol FSF6G | 179.046 | H34/26F | 3/62 | Midland General, Langley Mill (DE) 506 |
| 12354 | 447 SNU | Bristol FSF6G | 179.047 | H34/26F | 3/62 | Midland General, Langley Mill (DE) 507 |
| 12355 | 448 SNU | Bristol FSF6G | 179.048 | H34/26F | 3/62 | Midland General, Langley Mill (DE) 508 |
| 12356 | *449 SNU | Bristol FSF6G | 197.022 | H34/26F | 6/62 | Midland General, Langley Mill (DE) 509 |

| | | | | | | |
|---|---|---|---|---|---|---|
| 12357 | 450 SNU | Bristol FSF6G | 197.023 | H34/26F | 6/62 | Midland General, Langley Mill (DE) 510 |
| 12358 | 5099 HN | Bristol FSF6B | 167.069 | H34/26F | 11/61 | United AS, Darlington (DM) BL99 |
| 12359 | 5100 HN | Bristol FSF6B | 167.070 | H34/26F | 10/61 | United AS, Darlington (DM) BL100 |
| 12360 | 5101 HN | Bristol FSF6B | 179.014 | H34/26F | 10/61 | United AS, Darlington (DM) BL101 |
| 12361 | 5102 HN | Bristol FSF6B | 179.015 | H34/26F | 10/61 | United AS, Darlington (DM) BL102 |
| 12362 | 5103 HN | Bristol FSF6B | 179.016 | H34/26F | 11/61 | United AS, Darlington (DM) BL103 |
| 12363 | 5104 HN | Bristol FSF6B | 179.017 | H34/26F | 11/61 | United AS, Darlington (DM) BL104 |
| 12364 | 5105 HN | Bristol FSF6B | 179.018 | H34/26F | 11/61 | United AS, Darlington (DM) BL105 |
| 12365 | 5106 HN | Bristol FSF6B | 179.034 | H34/26F | 11/61 | United AS, Darlington (DM) BL106 |
| 12366 | 5107 HN | Bristol FS6B | 196.008 | H33/27R | 4/62 | United AS, Darlington (DM) BL107 |
| 12367 | 5108 HN | Bristol FS6B | 196.009 | H33/27R | 4/62 | United AS, Darlington (DM) BL108 |
| 12368 | 5109 HN | Bristol FS6B | 196.010 | H33/27R | 4/62 | United AS, Darlington (DM) BL109 |
| 12369 | 5110 HN | Bristol FS6B | 196.011 | H33/27R | 4/62 | United AS, Darlington (DM) BL110 |
| 12370 | 5111 HN | Bristol FS6B | 196.012 | H33/27R | 4/62 | United AS, Darlington (DM) BL111 |
| 12371 | 5077 HN | Bristol FLF6B | 181.033 | H38/32F | 10/61 | United AS, Darlington (DM) BL77 |
| 12372 | 5078 HN | Bristol FLF6B | 181.039 | H38/32F | 10/61 | United AS, Darlington (DM) BL78 |
| 12373 | 5079 HN | Bristol FLF6B | 181.040 | H38/32F | 10/61 | United AS, Darlington (DM) BL79 |
| 12374 | 5080 HN | Bristol FLF6B | 181.041 | H38/32F | 10/61 | United AS, Darlington (DM) BL80 |
| 12375 | 5081 HN | Bristol FLF6B | 181.042 | H38/32F | 10/61 | United AS, Darlington (DM) BL81 |
| 12376 | 5082 HN | Bristol FLF6B | 181.087 | H38/32F | 1/62 | United AS, Darlington (DM) BL82 |
| 12377 | 5083 HN | Bristol FLF6B | 181.088 | H38/32F | 1/62 | United AS, Darlington (DM) BL83 |
| 12378 | 5084 HN | Bristol FLF6B | 181.089 | H38/32F | 1/62 | United AS, Darlington (DM) BL84 |
| 12379 | 5085 HN | Bristol FLF6B | 181.099 | H38/32F | 1/62 | United AS, Darlington (DM) BL85 |
| 12380 | 5086 HN | Bristol FLF6B | 181.100 | H38/32F | 1/62 | United AS, Darlington (DM) BL86 |
| 12381 | 143 ACY | Bristol FSF6G | 167.064 | H34/26F | 10/61 | United Welsh, Swansea (GG) 349 |
| 12382 | 144 ACY | Bristol FSF6G | 167.065 | H34/26F | 10/61 | United Welsh, Swansea (GG) 350 |
| 12383 | 145 ACY | Bristol FSF6G | 167.066 | H34/26F | 10/61 | United Welsh, Swansea (GG) 351 |
| 12384 | 146 ACY | Bristol FSF6G | 167.067 | H34/26F | 10/61 | United Welsh, Swansea (GG) 352 |
| 12385 | 147 ACY | Bristol FSF6G | 179.009 | H34/26F | 10/61 | United Welsh, Swansea (GG) 353 |
| 12386 | 148 ACY | Bristol FSF6G | 179.010 | H34/26F | 10/61 | United Welsh, Swansea (GG) 354 |
| 12387 | 149 ACY | Bristol FSF6G | 179.011 | H34/26F | 10/61 | United Welsh, Swansea (GG) 355 |
| 12388 | 150 ACY | Bristol FSF6G | 179.036 | H34/26F | 11/61 | United Welsh, Swansea (GG) 356 |
| 12389 | 151 ACY | Bristol FSF6G | 179.037 | H34/26F | 11/61 | United Welsh, Swansea (GG) 357 |
| 12390 | 152 ACY | Bristol FSF6G | 179.038 | H34/26F | 11/61 | United Welsh, Swansea (GG) 358 |
| 12391 | 153 ACY | Bristol FSF6G | 179.039 | H34/26F | 11/61 | United Welsh, Swansea (GG) 359 |
| 12392 | 1117 PW | Bristol FS5G | 178.007 | H33/27RD | 11/61 | Eastern Counties, Norwich (NK) LFS17 |
| 12393 | 1118 PW | Bristol FS5G | 178.008 | H33/27RD | 11/61 | Eastern Counties, Norwich (NK) LFS18 |
| 12394 | 1119 PW | Bristol FS5G | 178.009 | H33/27RD | 11/61 | Eastern Counties, Norwich (NK) LFS19 |
| 12395 | 1120 PW | Bristol FS5G | 178.020 | H33/27RD | 11/61 | Eastern Counties, Norwich (NK) LFS20 |
| 12396 | 1121 PW | Bristol FS5G | 178.021 | H33/27RD | 11/61 | Eastern Counties, Norwich (NK) LFS21 |
| 12397 | 1122 PW | Bristol FS5G | 178.022 | H33/27RD | 11/61 | Eastern Counties, Norwich (NK) LFS22 |
| 12398 | 1123 PW | Bristol FS5G | 178.023 | H33/27RD | 11/61 | Eastern Counties, Norwich (NK) LFS23 |
| 12399 | 1124 PW | Bristol FS5G | 178.024 | H33/27RD | 11/61 | Eastern Counties, Norwich (NK) LFS24 |
| 12400 | 1125 PW | Bristol FS5G | 178.025 | H33/27RD | 11/61 | Eastern Counties, Norwich (NK) LFS25 |
| 12401 | 2926 PW | Bristol FS5G | 178.032 | H33/27RD | 2/62 | Eastern Counties, Norwich (NK) LFS26 |
| 12402 | 2927 PW | Bristol FS5G | 178.033 | H33/27RD | 2/62 | Eastern Counties, Norwich (NK) LFS27 |
| 12403 | 2928 PW | Bristol FS5G | 178.034 | H33/27RD | 2/62 | Eastern Counties, Norwich (NK) LFS28 |
| 12404 | 2929 PW | Bristol FS5G | 178.035 | H33/27RD | 2/62 | Eastern Counties, Norwich (NK) LFS29 |
| 12405 | 2930 PW | Bristol FS5G | 178.036 | H33/27RD | 2/62 | Eastern Counties, Norwich (NK) LFS30 |
| 12406 | 2931 PW | Bristol FS5G | 178.037 | H33/27RD | 2/62 | Eastern Counties, Norwich (NK) LFS31 |
| 12407 | 2932 PW | Bristol FS5G | 196.004 | H33/27RD | 2/62 | Eastern Counties, Norwich (NK) LFS32 |
| 12408 | 2933 PW | Bristol FS5G | 196.005 | H33/27RD | 2/62 | Eastern Counties, Norwich (NK) LFS33 |
| 12409 | 2934 PW | Bristol FS5G | 196.006 | H33/27RD | 2/62 | Eastern Counties, Norwich (NK) LFS34 |
| 12410 | 2935 PW | Bristol FS5G | 196.007 | H33/27RD | 2/62 | Eastern Counties, Norwich (NK) LFS35 |
| 12411 | 4377 LJ | Bristol FS6G | 166.088 | H33/27RD | 10/61 | Hants & Dorset, Bournemouth (HA) 1454 |
| 12412 | 4378 LJ | Bristol FS6G | 166.089 | H33/27RD | 11/61 | Hants & Dorset, Bournemouth (HA) 1455 |
| 12413 | 4379 LJ | Bristol FS6G | 166.090 | H33/27RD | 11/61 | Hants & Dorset, Bournemouth (HA) 1456 |
| 12414 | 4380 LJ | Bristol FS6G | 178.040 | H33/27RD | 1/62 | Hants & Dorset, Bournemouth (HA) 1457 |
| 12415 | 4381 LJ | Bristol FS6G | 178.041 | H33/27RD | 1/62 | Hants & Dorset, Bournemouth (HA) 1458 |
| 12416 | 4382 LJ | Bristol FS6G | 178.042 | H33/27RD | 1/62 | Hants & Dorset, Bournemouth (HA) 1459 |
| 12417 | 4383 LJ | Bristol FS6G | 178.043 | H33/27RD | 2/62 | Hants & Dorset, Bournemouth (HA) 1460 |
| 12418 *4384 LJ | | Bristol FS6G | 178.044 | H33/27RD | 2/62 | Hants & Dorset, Bournemouth (HA) 1461 |
| 12419 | 4385 LJ | Bristol FS6G | 196.001 | H33/27RD | 2/62 | Hants & Dorset, Bournemouth (HA) 1462 |
| 12420 | 4386 LJ | Bristol FS6G | 196.002 | H33/27RD | 2/62 | Hants & Dorset, Bournemouth (HA) 1463 |

| | | | | | | |
|---|---|---|---|---|---|---|
| 12421 | 4387 LJ | Bristol FS6G | 196.003 | H33/27RD | 2/62 | Hants & Dorset, Bournemouth (HA) 1464 |
| 12422 | RFE 473 | Bristol FS5G | 178.005 | H33/27RD | 11/61 | Lincolnshire RCC, Lincoln (LC) 2395 |
| 12423 | RFE 474 | Bristol FS5G | 178.006 | H33/27RD | 11/61 | Lincolnshire RCC, Lincoln (LC) 2396 |
| 12424 | RFE 475 | Bristol FS5G | 178.026 | H33/27RD | 11/61 | Lincolnshire RCC, Lincoln (LC) 2397 |
| 12425 | RFE 476 | Bristol FS5G | 178.027 | H33/27RD | 11/61 | Lincolnshire RCC, Lincoln (LC) 2398 |
| 12426 | RFE 477 | Bristol FS5G | 178.038 | H33/27RD | 2/62 | Lincolnshire RCC, Lincoln (LC) 2502 |
| 12427 | RFE 478 | Bristol FS5G | 178.039 | H33/27RD | 2/62 | Lincolnshire RCC, Lincoln (LC) 2503 |
| 12428 | VDL 844 | Bristol FS6G | 166.071 | H33/27RD | 5/61 | Southern Vectis, Newport (IW) 567 |
| 12429 | VDL 845 | Bristol FS6G | 166.072 | H33/27RD | 5/61 | Southern Vectis, Newport (IW) 568 |
| 12430 | 2010 YG | Bristol FS6B | 178.012 | H33/27RD | 12/61 | West Yorkshire RCC, Harrogate (WR) DX114 |
| 12431 | 2011 YG | Bristol FS6B | 178.013 | H33/27RD | 12/61 | West Yorkshire RCC, Harrogate (WR) DX115 |
| 12432 | 2012 YG | Bristol FS6B | 178.014 | H33/27RD | 12/61 | West Yorkshire RCC, Harrogate (WR) DX116 |
| 12433 | 2013 YG | Bristol FS6B | 178.015 | H33/27RD | 12/61 | West Yorkshire RCC, Harrogate (WR) DX117 |
| 12434 | 2014 YG | Bristol FS6B | 178.016 | H33/27RD | 12/61 | West Yorkshire RCC, Harrogate (WR) DX118 |
| 12435 | 2015 YG | Bristol FS6B | 178.028 | H33/27RD | 12/61 | West Yorkshire RCC, Harrogate (WR) DX119 |
| 12436 | 2016 YG | Bristol FS6B | 178.029 | H33/27RD | 12/61 | West Yorkshire RCC, Harrogate (WR) DX120 |
| 12437 | 2017 YG | Bristol FS6B | 178.045 | H33/27RD | 3/62 | West Yorkshire RCC, Harrogate (WR) DX121 |
| 12438 | 2018 YG | Bristol FS6B | 178.046 | H33/27RD | 3/62 | West Yorkshire RCC, Harrogate (WR) DX122 |
| 12439 | 2019 YG | Bristol FS6B | 178.047 | H33/27RD | 3/62 | West Yorkshire RCC, Harrogate (WR) DX123 |
| 12440 | 2020 YG | Bristol FS6B | 178.048 | H33/27RD | 3/62 | West Yorkshire RCC, Harrogate (WR) DX124 |
| 12441 | 2021 YG | Bristol FS6B | 178.049 | H33/27RD | 3/62 | West Yorkshire RCC, Harrogate (WR) DX125 |
| 12442 | 2022 YG | Bristol FS6B | 178.050 | H33/27RD | 3/62 | West Yorkshire RCC, Harrogate (WR) DX126 |
| 12443 | 2023 YG | Bristol FS6B | 178.051 | H33/27RD | 3/62 | West Yorkshire RCC, Harrogate (WR) DX127 |
| 12444 | 2027 YG | Bristol FS6B | 178.010 | H33/27RD | 12/61 | York-West Yorkshire, Harrogate (WR) YDX128 |
| 12445 | *2028 YG | Bristol FS6B | 178.011 | H33/27RD | 12/61 | York-West Yorkshire, Harrogate (WR) YDX129 |
| 12446 | 2029 YG | Bristol FS6B | 178.052 | H33/27RD | 3/62 | York-West Yorkshire, Harrogate (WR) YDX130 |
| 12447 | 2030 YG | Bristol FS6B | 178.053 | H33/27RD | 3/62 | York-West Yorkshire, Harrogate (WR) YDX131 |
| 12448 | *2031 YG | Bristol FS6B | 178.054 | H33/27RD | 3/62 | York-West Yorkshire, Harrogate (WR) YDX132 |
| 12449 | 2024 YG | Bristol FS6B | 178.017 | H33/27RD | 12/61 | Keighley-West Yorkshire, Harrogate (WR) KDX133 |
| 12450 | 2025 YG | Bristol FS6B | 178.018 | H33/27RD | 12/61 | Keighley-West Yorkshire, Harrogate (WR) KDX134 |
| 12451 | 2026 YG | Bristol FS6B | 178.019 | H33/27RD | 12/61 | Keighley-West Yorkshire, Harrogate (WR) KDX135 |
| 12452 | *813 MHW | Bristol FLF6G | 181.054 | H38/32F | 12/61 | Bristol OC (GL) C7018 |
| 12453 | 814 MHW | Bristol FLF6G | 181.055 | H38/32F | 12/61 | Bristol OC (GL) C7019 |
| 12454 | 815 MHW | Bristol FLF6G | 181.056 | H38/32F | 12/61 | Bristol OC (GL) C7020 |
| 12455 | 820 MHW | Bristol FLF6B | 181.072 | H38/32F | 1/62 | Bristol OC (GL) C7025 |
| 12456 | 821 MHW | Bristol FLF6B | 181.073 | H38/32F | 1/62 | Bristol OC (GL) C7026 |
| 12457 | 822 MHW | Bristol FLF6B | 181.074 | H38/32F | 1/62 | Bristol OC (GL) C7027 |
| 12458 | *823 MHW | Bristol FLF6B | 181.075 | H38/32F | 1/62 | Bristol OC (GL) C7028 |
| 12459 | 824 MHW | Bristol FLF6G | 181.076 | H38/32F | 12/61 | Bristol OC (GL) C7029 |
| 12460 | 203 NAE | Bristol FLF6B | 181.103 | H38/32F | 2/62 | Bristol OC (GL) C7035 |
| 12461 | 204 NAE | Bristol FLF6B | 181.104 | H38/32F | 2/62 | Bristol OC (GL) C7036 |
| 12462 | *205 NAE | Bristol FLF6B | 181.114 | H38/32F | 2/62 | Bristol OC (GL) C7037 |
| 12463 | 206 NAE | Bristol FLF6B | 181.115 | H38/32F | 2/62 | Bristol OC (GL) C7038 |
| 12464 | 807 MHW | Bristol FLF6B | 181.031 | H38/32F | 9/61 | Bristol OC (GL) 7012 |
| 12465 | 808 MHW | Bristol FLF6B | 181.032 | H38/32F | 9/61 | Bristol OC (GL) 7013 |
| 12466 | 809 MHW | Bristol FLF6B | 181.034 | H38/32F | 9/61 | Bristol OC (GL) 7014 |
| 12467 | 810 MHW | Bristol FLF6B | 181.035 | H38/32F | 9/61 | Bristol OC (GL) 7015 |
| 12468 | 811 MHW | Bristol FLF6B | 181.036 | H38/32F | 9/61 | Bristol OC (GL) 7016 |
| 12469 | 812 MHW | Bristol FLF6B | 181.037 | H38/32F | 9/61 | Bristol OC (GL) 7017 |
| 12470 | 816 MHW | Bristol FLF6B | 181.064 | H38/32F | 12/61 | Bristol OC (GL) 7021 |
| 12471 | *817 MHW | Bristol FLF6B | 181.065 | H38/32F | 12/61 | Bristol OC (GL) 7022 |
| 12472 | 818 MHW | Bristol FLF6B | 181.066 | H38/32F | 12/61 | Bristol OC (GL) 7023 |
| 12473 | 819 MHW | Bristol FLF6B | 181.067 | H38/32F | 1/62 | Bristol OC (GL) 7024 |
| 12474 | 825 MHW | Bristol FLF6B | 181.094 | H38/32F | 2/62 | Bristol OC (GL) 7030 |
| 12475 | 826 MHW | Bristol FLF6B | 181.095 | H38/32F | 2/62 | Bristol OC (GL) 7031 |
| 12476 | *827 MHW | Bristol FLF6B | 181.096 | H38/32F | 2/62 | Bristol OC (GL) 7032 |
| 12477 | 201 NAE | Bristol FLF6B | 181.097 | H38/32F | 2/62 | Bristol OC (GL) 7033 |
| 12478 | 202 NAE | Bristol FLF6B | 181.098 | H38/32F | 2/62 | Bristol OC (GL) 7034 |
| 12479 | 894 VFM | Bristol FLF6B | 181.018 | H38/32F | 10/61 | Crosville MS, Chester (CH) DFB84 |
| 12480 | 895 VFM | Bristol FLF6B | 181.019 | H38/32F | 10/61 | Crosville MS, Chester (CH) DFB85 |
| 12481 | 896 VFM | Bristol FLF6B | 181.020 | H38/32F | 10/61 | Crosville MS, Chester (CH) DFB86 |

| | | | | | | | |
|---|---|---|---|---|---|---|---|
| 12482 | 897 VFM | Bristol FLF6B | 181.021 | H38/32F | 10/61 | Crosville MS, Chester (CH) DFB87 |
| 12483 | 898 VFM | Bristol FLF6B | 181.022 | H38/32F | 10/61 | Crosville MS, Chester (CH) DFB88 |
| 12484 | 899 VFM | Bristol FLF6B | 181.029 | H38/32F | 10/61 | Crosville MS, Chester (CH) DFB89 |
| 12485 | *900 VFM | Bristol FLF6B | 181.030 | H38/32F | 10/61 | Crosville MS, Chester (CH) DFB90 |
| 12486 | 901 VFM | Bristol FLF6B | 181.058 | H38/32F | 12/61 | Crosville MS, Chester (CH) DFB91 |
| 12487 | 902 VFM | Bristol FLF6B | 181.059 | H38/32F | 12/61 | Crosville MS, Chester (CH) DFB92 |
| 12488 | 903 VFM | Bristol FLF6B | 181.068 | H38/32F | 1/62 | Crosville MS, Chester (CH) DFB93 |
| 12489 | 904 VFM | Bristol FLF6B | 181.069 | H38/32F | 1/62 | Crosville MS, Chester (CH) DFB94 |
| 12490 | 905 VFM | Bristol FLF6B | 181.085 | H38/32F | 2/62 | Crosville MS, Chester (CH) DFB95 |
| 12491 | 906 VFM | Bristol FLF6B | 181.086 | H38/32F | 2/62 | Crosville MS, Chester (CH) DFB96 |
| 12492 | 907 VFM | Bristol FLF6B | 181.107 | H38/32F | 2/62 | Crosville MS, Chester (CH) DFB97 |
| 12493 | 908 VFM | Bristol FLF6B | 181.108 | H38/32F | 2/62 | Crosville MS, Chester (CH) DFB98 |
| 12494 | 909 VFM | Bristol FLF6B | 181.109 | H38/32F | 2/62 | Crosville MS, Chester (CH) DFB99 |
| 12495 | 910 VFM | Bristol FLF6B | 181.116 | H38/32F | 2/62 | Crosville MS, Chester (CH) DFB100 |
| 12496 | 911 VFM | Bristol FLF6B | 181.121 | H38/32F | 3/62 | Crosville MS, Chester (CH) DFB101 |
| 12497 | 912 VFM | Bristol FLF6B | 181.122 | H38/32F | 3/62 | Crosville MS, Chester (CH) DFB102 |
| 12498 | 913 VFM | Bristol FLF6B | 181.123 | H38/32F | 5/62 | Crosville MS, Chester (CH) DFB103 |
| 12499 | 114 DRM | Bristol FLF6G | 181.043 | H38/32F | 7/61 | Cumberland MS, Whitehaven (CU) C421 |
| 12500 | 115 DRM | Bristol FLF6G | 181.044 | H38/32F | 7/61 | Cumberland MS, Whitehaven (CU) C422 |
| 12501 | 116 DRM | Bristol FLF6G | 181.045 | H38/32F | 7/61 | Cumberland MS, Whitehaven (CU) C423 |
| 12502 | 117 DRM | Bristol FLF6G | 181.052 | H38/32F | 12/61 | Cumberland MS, Whitehaven (CU) C424 |
| 12503 | 118 DRM | Bristol FLF6G | 181.053 | H38/32F | 12/61 | Cumberland MS, Whitehaven (CU) C425 |
| 12504 | 801 WVW | Bristol FLF6B | 181.001 | H38/32F | 7/61 | Eastern National, Chelmsford (EX) 1591 |
| 12505 | 170 XNO | Bristol FLF6B | 181.002 | H38/32F | 7/61 | Eastern National, Chelmsford (EX) 1596 |
| 12506 | 802 WVW | Bristol FLF6B | 181.003 | H38/32F | 7/61 | Eastern National, Chelmsford (EX) 1592 |
| 12507 | 803 WVW | Bristol FLF6B | 181.027 | H38/32F | 8/61 | Eastern National, Chelmsford (EX) 1593 |
| 12508 | 171 XNO | Bristol FLF6B | 181.028 | H38/32F | 8/61 | Eastern National, Chelmsford (EX) 1594 |
| 12509 | 172 XNO | Bristol FLF6B | 181.038 | H38/32F | 10/61 | Eastern National, Chelmsford (EX) 1595 |
| 12510 | 173 XNO | Bristol FLF6G | 181.046 | H38/32F | 11/61 | Eastern National, Chelmsford (EX) 1597 |
| 12511 | 174 XNO | Bristol FLF6G | 181.047 | H38/32F | 12/61 | Eastern National, Chelmsford (EX) 1598 |
| 12512 | 175 XNO | Bristol FLF6G | 181.048 | H38/32F | 12/61 | Eastern National, Chelmsford (EX) 1599 |
| 12513 | 176 XNO | Bristol FLF6G | 181.057 | H38/32F | 1/62 | Eastern National, Chelmsford (EX) 1600 |
| 12514 | 177 XNO | Bristol FLF6G | 181.060 | H38/32F | 1/62 | Eastern National, Chelmsford (EX) 1601 |
| 12515 | 178 XNO | Bristol FLF6G | 181.077 | H38/32F | 1/62 | Eastern National, Chelmsford (EX) 1602 |
| 12516 | 179 XNO | Bristol FLF6G | 181.078 | H38/32F | 1/62 | Eastern National, Chelmsford (EX) 1603 |
| 12517 | 180 XNO | Bristol FLF6G | 181.079 | H38/32F | 1/62 | Eastern National, Chelmsford (EX) 1604 |
| 12518 | 181 XNO | Bristol FLF6G | 181.080 | H38/32F | 1/62 | Eastern National, Chelmsford (EX) 1605 |
| 12519 | 182 XNO | Bristol FLF6G | 181.081 | H38/32F | 1/62 | Eastern National, Chelmsford (EX) 1606 |
| 12520 | 183 XNO | Bristol FLF6B | 181.117 | H38/32F | 1/62 | Eastern National, Chelmsford (EX) 1607 |
| 12521 | *184 XNO | Bristol FLF6B | 181.118 | CH37/18F | 2/62 | Eastern National, Chelmsford (EX) 1608 |
| 12522 | 186 XNO | Bristol FLF6B | 181.119 | CH37/18F | 3/62 | Eastern National, Chelmsford (EX) 1610 |
| 12523 | 185 XNO | Bristol FLF6B | 181.120 | CH37/18F | 2/62 | Eastern National, Chelmsford (EX) 1609 |
| 12524 | 142 HUO | Bristol FLF6B | 181.013 | H38/32F | 9/61 | Southern National, Exeter (DN) 1979 |
| 12525 | 143 HUO | Bristol FLF6B | 181.014 | H38/32F | 9/61 | Southern National, Exeter (DN) 1980 |
| 12526 | 144 HUO | Bristol FLF6B | 181.015 | H38/32F | 9/61 | Southern National, Exeter (DN) 1981 |
| 12527 | 145 HUO | Bristol FLF6B | 181.092 | H38/32F | 2/62 | Southern National, Exeter (DN) 1982 |
| 12528 | 146 HUO | Bristol FLF6B | 181.093 | H38/32F | 2/62 | Southern National, Exeter (DN) 1983 |
| 12529 | 5087 HN | Bristol FLF6B | 181.101 | H38/32F | 1/62 | United AS, Darlington (DM) BL87 |
| 12530 | 5088 HN | Bristol FLF6B | 181.102 | H38/32F | 2/62 | United AS, Darlington (DM) BL88 |
| 12531 | 5089 HN | Bristol FLF6B | 181.124 | H38/32F | 2/62 | United AS, Darlington (DM) BL89 |
| 12532 | 5090 HN | Bristol FLF6B | 181.125 | H38/32F | 2/62 | United AS, Darlington (DM) BL90 |
| 12533 | *5091 HN | Bristol FLF6B | 181.126 | H38/32F | 2/62 | United AS, Darlington (DM) BL91 |
| 12534 | 5092 HN | Bristol FLF6B | 181.127 | H38/32F | 2/62 | United AS, Darlington (DM) BL92 |
| 12535 | 5093 HN | Bristol FLF6B | 181.128 | H38/32F | 2/62 | United AS, Darlington (DM) BL93 |
| 12536 | 5094 HN | Bristol FLF6B | 181.129 | H38/32F | 2/62 | United AS, Darlington (DM) BL94 |
| 12537 | 5095 HN | Bristol FLF6B | 181.130 | H38/32F | 2/62 | United AS, Darlington (DM) BL95 |
| 12538 | 5096 HN | Bristol FLF6B | 181.131 | H38/32F | 2/62 | United AS, Darlington (DM) BL96 |
| 12539 | 5097 HN | Bristol FLF6B | 181.132 | H38/32F | 2/62 | United AS, Darlington (DM) BL97 |
| 12540 | 5098 HN | Bristol FLF6B | 181.133 | H38/32F | 2/62 | United AS, Darlington (DM) BL98 |
| 12541 | YNV 617 | Bristol FLF6B | 181.023 | H38/32F | 10/61 | United Counties, Northampton (NO) 617 |
| 12542 | YNV 618 | Bristol FLF6B | 181.024 | H38/32F | 10/61 | United Counties, Northampton (NO) 618 |
| 12543 | YNV 619 | Bristol FLF6B | 181.025 | H38/32F | 10/61 | United Counties, Northampton (NO) 619 |
| 12544 | YNV 620 | Bristol FLF6B | 181.026 | H38/32F | 10/61 | United Counties, Northampton (NO) 620 |
| 12545 | YNV 621 | Bristol FLF6B | 181.070 | H38/32F | 12/61 | United Counties, Northampton (NO) 621 |

| | | | | | | |
|---|---|---|---|---|---|---|
| 12546 | YNV 622 | Bristol FLF6B | 181.071 | H38/32F | 12/61 | United Counties, Northampton (NO) 622 |
| 12547 | YNV 623 | Bristol FLF6B | 181.090 | H38/32F | 1/62 | United Counties, Northampton (NO) 623 |
| 12548 | YNV 624 | Bristol FLF6B | 181.091 | H38/32F | 1/62 | United Counties, Northampton (NO) 624 |
| 12549 | YNV 625 | Bristol FLF6B | 181.110 | H38/32F | 2/62 | United Counties, Northampton (NO) 625 |
| 12550 | YNV 626 | Bristol FLF6B | 181.111 | H38/32F | 2/62 | United Counties, Northampton (NO) 626 |
| 12551 | YNV 627 | Bristol FLF6B | 181.112 | H38/32F | 2/62 | United Counties, Northampton (NO) 627 |
| 12552 | YNV 628 | Bristol FLF6B | 181.113 | H38/32F | 2/62 | United Counties, Northampton (NO) 628 |
| 12553 | 141 ACY | Bristol FLF6G | 181.016 | H38/32F | 9/61 | United Welsh, Swansea (GG) 347 |
| 12554 | 142 ACY | Bristol FLF6G | 181.017 | H38/32F | 9/61 | United Welsh, Swansea (GG) 348 |
| 12555 | 130 HUO | Bristol FLF6B | 181.008 | H38/32F | 9/61 | Western National, Exeter (DN) 1984 |
| 12556 | 131 HUO | Bristol FLF6B | 181.009 | H38/32F | 9/61 | Western National, Exeter (DN) 1985 |
| 12557 | 132 HUO | Bristol FLF6B | 181.010 | H38/32F | 9/61 | Western National, Exeter (DN) 1986 |
| 12558 | 133 HUO | Bristol FLF6B | 181.011 | H38/32F | 9/61 | Western National, Exeter (DN) 1987 |
| 12559 | *134 HUO | Bristol FLF6G | 181.061 | H38/32F | 2/62 | Western National, Exeter (DN) 1988 |
| 12560 | *135 HUO | Bristol FLF6G | 181.062 | H38/32F | 2/62 | Western National, Exeter (DN) 1989 |
| 12561 | *136 HUO | Bristol FLF6G | 181.063 | H38/32F | 2/62 | Western National, Exeter (DN) 1990 |
| 12562 | *137 HUO | Bristol FLF6G | 181.082 | H38/32F | 2/62 | Western National, Exeter (DN) 1991 |
| 12563 | 138 HUO | Bristol FLF6G | 181.083 | H38/32F | 2/62 | Western National, Exeter (DN) 1992 |
| 12564 | *139 HUO | Bristol FLF6G | 181.084 | H38/32F | 2/62 | Western National, Exeter (DN) 1993 |
| 12565 | *140 HUO | Bristol FLF6G | 181.105 | H38/32F | 2/62 | Western National, Exeter (DN) 1994 |
| 12566 | 141 HUO | Bristol FLF6G | 181.106 | H38/32F | 2/62 | Western National, Exeter (DN) 1995 |
| 12567 | 4388 LJ | Bristol FL6B | 168.028 | H37/33RD | 11/61 | Hants & Dorset, Bournemouth (HA) 1465 |
| 12568 | 4389 LJ | Bristol FL6B | 168.029 | H37/33RD | 11/61 | Hants & Dorset, Bournemouth (HA) 1466 |
| 12569 | 4390 LJ | Bristol FL6B | 168.030 | H37/33RD | 11/61 | Hants & Dorset, Bournemouth (HA) 1467 |
| 12570 | 4391 LJ | Bristol FL6B | 180.001 | H38/28RD | 11/61 | Hants & Dorset, Bournemouth (HA) 1468 |
| 12571 | 4392 LJ | Bristol FL6B | 180.002 | H38/28RD | 11/61 | Hants & Dorset, Bournemouth (HA) 1469 |
| 12572 | 4393 LJ | Bristol FL6B | 180.003 | H38/28RD | 12/61 | Hants & Dorset, Bournemouth (HA) 1470 |
| 12573 | 803 BWO | Bristol FS6G | 178.030 | H33/27RD | 12/61 | Red & White, Chepstow (MH) L161 |
| 12574 | 804 BWO | Bristol FS6G | 178.031 | H33/27RD | 12/61 | Red & White, Chepstow (MH) L261 |
| 12575 | 351 MHU | Bristol MW5G | 184.095 | B45F | 8/61 | Bristol OC (GL) C2516 |
| 12576 | 352 MHU | Bristol MW5G | 184.096 | B45F | 8/61 | Bristol OC (GL) C2517 |
| 12577 | 353 MHU | Bristol MW5G | 184.112 | B45F | 9/61 | Bristol OC (GL) C2518 |
| 12578 | 354 MHU | Bristol MW5G | 184.113 | B45F | 9/61 | Bristol OC (GL) C2519 |
| 12579 | 355 MHU | Bristol MW5G | 184.114 | B45F | 9/61 | Bristol OC (GL) C2520 |
| 12580 | 356 MHU | Bristol MW5G | 184.151 | B45F | 11/61 | Bristol OC (GL) 2521 |
| 12581 | 357 MHU | Bristol MW5G | 184.152 | B45F | 11/61 | Bristol OC (GL) 2522 |
| 12582 | 358 MHU | Bristol MW5G | 184.153 | B45F | 12/61 | Bristol OC (GL) 2523 |
| 12583 | 359 MHU | Bristol MW5G | 184.154 | B45F | 12/61 | Bristol OC (GL) 2524 |
| 12584 | 360 MHU | Bristol MW5G | 184.163 | B45F | 12/61 | Bristol OC (GL) 2525 |
| 12585 | 361 MHU | Bristol MW5G | 184.164 | B45F | 12/61 | Bristol OC (GL) 2526 |
| 12586 | 362 MHU | Bristol MW5G | 184.171 | B45F | 12/61 | Bristol OC (GL) 2527 |
| 12587 | 363 MHU | Bristol MW5G | 184.172 | B45F | 12/61 | Bristol OC (GL) 2528 |
| 12588 | 364 MHU | Bristol MW5G | 184.175 | B45F | 1/62 | Bristol OC (GL) 2529 |
| 12589 | 365 MHU | Bristol MW5G | 184.178 | B45F | 12/61 | Bristol OC (GL) 2530 |
| 12590 | 366 MHU | Bristol MW5G | 184.179 | B45F | 1/62 | Bristol OC (GL) 2531 |
| 12591 | 367 MHU | Bristol MW5G | 184.180 | B45F | 1/62 | Bristol OC (GL) 2532 |
| 12592 | 368 MHU | Bristol MW5G | 184.192 | B45F | 1/62 | Bristol OC (GL) 2533 |
| 12593 | 369 MHU | Bristol MW5G | 184.193 | B45F | 1/62 | Bristol OC (GL) 2534 |
| 12594 | 370 MHU | Bristol MW5G | 184.198 | B45F | 2/62 | Bristol OC (GL) 2535 |
| 12595 | 371 MHU | Bristol MW5G | 184.199 | B45F | 2/62 | Bristol OC (GL) 2536 |
| 12596 | 372 MHU | Bristol MW5G | 184.200 | B45F | 2/62 | Bristol OC (GL) 2537 |
| 12597 | 373 MHU | Bristol MW5G | 184.201 | B45F | 2/62 | Bristol OC (GL) 2538 |
| 12598 | 374 MHU | Bristol MW5G | 195.057 | B45F | 7/62 | Bristol OC (GL) 2539 |
| 12599 | 375 MHU | Bristol MW5G | 195.061 | B45F | 8/62 | Bristol OC (GL) 2540 |
| 12600 | 376 MHU | Bristol MW5G | 195.062 | B45F | 9/62 | Bristol OC (GL) 2541 |
| 12601 | 377 MHU | Bristol MW5G | 195.063 | B45F | 9/62 | Bristol OC (GL) 2542 |
| 12602 | 378 MHU | Bristol MW5G | 195.067 | B45F | 9/62 | Bristol OC (GL) 2543 |
| 12603 | 379 MHU | Bristol MW5G | 195.068 | B45F | 9/62 | Bristol OC (GL) 2544 |
| 12604 | 380 MHU | Bristol MW5G | 195.081 | B45F | 9/62 | Bristol OC (GL) 2545 |
| 12605 | 381 MHU | Bristol MW5G | 195.082 | B45F | 9/62 | Bristol OC (GL) 2546 |
| 12606 | 382 MHU | Bristol MW5G | 195.083 | B45F | 9/62 | Bristol OC (GL) 2547 |
| 12607 | 383 MHU | Bristol MW5G | 195.084 | B45F | 10/62 | Bristol OC (GL) 2548 |
| 12608 | *805 MHW | Bristol FSF6G | 179.041 | H34/26F | 10/61 | Bristol OC (GL) G6040 |
| 12609 | 804 WVW | Bristol MW5G | 184.099 | DP41F | 7/61 | Eastern National, Chelmsford (EX) 537 |

| | | | | | | |
|---|---|---|---|---|---|---|
| 12610 | 805 WVW | Bristol MW5G | 184.100 | DP41F | 7/61 | Eastern National, Chelmsford (EX) 538 |
| 12611 | 806 WVW | Bristol MW5G | 184.101 | DP41F | 8/61 | Eastern National, Chelmsford (EX) 539 |
| 12612 | 807 WVW | Bristol MW5G | 184.102 | DP41F | 8/61 | Eastern National, Chelmsford (EX) 540 |
| 12613 | 201 YVX | Bristol MW5G | 184.155 | DP41F | 2/62 | Eastern National, Chelmsford (EX) 541 |
| 12614 | 202 YVX | Bristol MW5G | 184.156 | DP41F | 3/62 | Eastern National, Chelmsford (EX) 542 |
| 12615 | 203 YVX | Bristol MW5G | 184.157 | DP41F | 3/62 | Eastern National, Chelmsford (EX) 543 |
| 12616 | 204 YVX | Bristol MW5G | 184.158 | DP41F | 3/62 | Eastern National, Chelmsford (EX) 544 |
| 12617 | 205 YVX | Bristol MW5G | 184.181 | B45F | 12/61 | Eastern National, Chelmsford (EX) 545 |
| 12618 | 206 YVX | Bristol MW5G | 184.182 | B45F | 12/61 | Eastern National, Chelmsford (EX) 546 |
| 12619 | 207 YVX | Bristol MW5G | 184.183 | B45F | 1/62 | Eastern National, Chelmsford (EX) 547 |
| 12620 | 208 YVX | Bristol MW5G | 184.184 | B45F | 1/62 | Eastern National, Chelmsford (EX) 548 |
| 12621 | 209 YVX | Bristol MW5G | 184.207 | B45F | 4/62 | Eastern National, Chelmsford (EX) 549 |
| 12622 | 210 YVX | Bristol MW5G | 184.208 | B45F | 6/62 | Eastern National, Chelmsford (EX) 550 |
| 12623 | 211 YVX | Bristol MW5G | 184.209 | B45F | 6/62 | Eastern National, Chelmsford (EX) 551 |
| 12624 | 212 YVX | Bristol MW5G | 184.210 | B45F | 6/62 | Eastern National, Chelmsford (EX) 552 |
| 12625 | MOO 174 | Bristol MW5G | 195.106 | B45F | 9/62 | Eastern National, Chelmsford (EX) 553 |
| 12626 | MOO 175 | Bristol MW5G | 195.107 | B45F | 9/62 | Eastern National, Chelmsford (EX) 554 |
| 12627 | MOO 176 | Bristol MW5G | 195.108 | B45F | 9/62 | Eastern National, Chelmsford (EX) 555 |
| 12628 | MOO 177 | Bristol MW5G | 195.112 | B45F | 9/62 | Eastern National, Chelmsford (EX) 556 |
| 12629 | RFE 462 | Bristol MW5G | 184.107 | B45F | 7/61 | Lincolnshire RCC, Lincoln (LC) 2250 |
| 12630 | RFE 463 | Bristol MW5G | 184.108 | B45F | 7/61 | Lincolnshire RCC, Lincoln (LC) 2251 |
| 12631 | RFE 464 | Bristol MW5G | 184.167 | B45F | 11/61 | Lincolnshire RCC, Lincoln (LC) 2252 |
| 12632 | RFE 465 | Bristol MW5G | 184.168 | B45F | 11/61 | Lincolnshire RCC, Lincoln (LC) 2253 |
| 12633 | RFE 466 | Bristol MW5G | 184.194 | B45F | 12/61 | Lincolnshire RCC, Lincoln (LC) 2254 |
| 12634 | RFE 467 | Bristol MW5G | 184.195 | B45F | 12/61 | Lincolnshire RCC, Lincoln (LC) 2255 |
| 12635 | RFE 468 | Bristol MW5G | 184.211 | B45F | 1/62 | Lincolnshire RCC, Lincoln (LC) 2256 |
| 12636 | RFE 469 | Bristol MW5G | 184.212 | B45F | 1/62 | Lincolnshire RCC, Lincoln (LC) 2257 |
| 12637 | 361 BAX | Bristol MW6G | 184.103 | B45F | 7/61 | Red & White, Chepstow (MH) U161 |
| 12638 | 362 BAX | Bristol MW6G | 184.104 | B45F | 7/61 | Red & White, Chepstow (MH) U261 |
| 12639 | 363 BAX | Bristol MW6G | 184.105 | B45F | 7/61 | Red & White, Chepstow (MH) U361 |
| 12640 | 364 BAX | Bristol MW6G | 184.106 | B45F | 7/61 | Red & White, Chepstow (MH) U461 |
| 12641 | 365 BAX | Bristol MW6G | 184.169 | B45F | 1/62 | Red & White, Chepstow (MH) U561 |
| 12642 | 366 BAX | Bristol MW6G | 184.170 | B45F | 12/61 | Red & White, Chepstow (MH) U661 |
| 12643 | 367 BAX | Bristol MW6G | 195.055 | B45F | 8/62 | Red & White, Chepstow (MH) U761 |
| 12644 | 368 BAX | Bristol MW6G | 195.056 | B45F | 8/62 | Red & White, Chepstow (MH) U861 |
| 12645 | 5033 HN | Bristol MW5G | 184.097 | B45F | 8/61 | United AS, Darlington (DM) BU633 |
| 12646 | 5034 HN | Bristol MW5G | 184.098 | B45F | 8/61 | United AS, Darlington (DM) BU634 |
| 12647 | 5035 HN | Bristol MW5G | 184.117 | B45F | 9/61 | United AS, Darlington (DM) BU635 |
| 12648 | 5036 HN | Bristol MW5G | 184.118 | B45F | 9/61 | United AS, Darlington (DM) BU636 |
| 12649 | 5037 HN | Bristol MW5G | 184.147 | B45F | 1/62 | United AS, Darlington (DM) BU637 |
| 12650 | 5038 HN | Bristol MW5G | 184.148 | B45F | 1/62 | United AS, Darlington (DM) BU638 |
| 12651 | 5039 HN | Bristol MW5G | 184.159 | B45F | 1/62 | United AS, Darlington (DM) BU639 |
| 12652 | 5040 HN | Bristol MW5G | 184.160 | B45F | 1/62 | United AS, Darlington (DM) BU640 |
| 12653 | 5041 HN | Bristol MW5G | 184.161 | B45F | 1/62 | United AS, Darlington (DM) BU641 |
| 12654 | 5042 HN | Bristol MW5G | 184.162 | B45F | 1/62 | United AS, Darlington (DM) BU642 |
| 12655 | 5043 HN | Bristol MW5G | 184.187 | B45F | 3/62 | United AS, Darlington (DM) BU643 |
| 12656 | 5044 HN | Bristol MW5G | 184.188 | B45F | 5/62 | United AS, Darlington (DM) BU644 |
| 12657 | 5045 HN | Bristol MW5G | 184.189 | B45F | 5/62 | United AS, Darlington (DM) BU645 |
| 12658 | 5046 HN | Bristol MW5G | 184.190 | B45F | 5/62 | United AS, Darlington (DM) BU646 |
| 12659 | 5047 HN | Bristol MW5G | 184.202 | B45F | 5/62 | United AS, Darlington (DM) BU647 |
| 12660 | 5048 HN | Bristol MW5G | 184.203 | B45F | 5/62 | United AS, Darlington (DM) BU648 |
| 12661 | 5049 HN | Bristol MW5G | 184.204 | B45F | 6/62 | United AS, Darlington (DM) BU649 |
| 12662 | 5050 HN | Bristol MW5G | 184.205 | B45F | 6/62 | United AS, Darlington (DM) BU650 |
| 12663 | 5051 HN | Bristol MW5G | 184.206 | B45F | 6/62 | United AS, Darlington (DM) BU651 |
| 12664 | 5052 HN | Bristol MW5G | 195.074 | B45F | 9/62 | United AS, Darlington (DM) BU652 |
| 12665 | 5053 HN | Bristol MW5G | 195.075 | B45F | 9/62 | United AS, Darlington (DM) BU653 |
| 12666 | 5054 HN | Bristol MW5G | 195.076 | B45F | 9/62 | United AS, Darlington (DM) BU654 |
| 12667 | 5055 HN | Bristol MW5G | 195.077 | B45F | 9/62 | United AS, Darlington (DM) BU655 |
| 12668 | 5056 HN | Bristol MW5G | 195.080 | B45F | 9/62 | United AS, Darlington (DM) BU656 |
| 12669 | 5057 HN | Bristol MW5G | 195.093 | B45F | 10/62 | United AS, Darlington (DM) BU657 |
| 12670 | 5058 HN | Bristol MW5G | 195.094 | B45F | 10/62 | United AS, Darlington (DM) BU658 |
| 12671 | 5059 HN | Bristol MW5G | 195.098 | B45F | 10/62 | United AS, Darlington (DM) BU659 |
| 12672 | 5060 HN | Bristol MW5G | 195.101 | B45F | 10/62 | United AS, Darlington (DM) BU660 |
| 12673 | 5061 HN | Bristol MW5G | 195.102 | B45F | 10/62 | United AS, Darlington (DM) BU661 |

| | | | | | | |
|---|---|---|---|---|---|---|
| 12674 | 5062 HN | Bristol MW5G | 195.103 | B45F | 10/62 | United AS, Darlington (DM) BU662 |
| 12675 | 5022 HN | Bristol MW5G | 184.109 | B45F | 8/62 | Durham District (DM) DBU22 |
| 12676 | 5023 HN | Bristol MW5G | 184.110 | B45F | 8/62 | Durham District (DM) DBU23 |
| 12677 | 5024 HN | Bristol MW5G | 184.149 | B45F | 8/62 | Durham District (DM) DBU24 |
| 12678 | 5025 HN | Bristol MW5G | 184.150 | B45F | 8/62 | Durham District (DM) DBU25 |
| 12679 | 5026 HN | Bristol MW5G | 184.173 | B45F | 9/62 | Durham District (DM) DBU26 |
| 12680 | 5027 HN | Bristol MW5G | 184.174 | B45F | 9/62 | Durham District (DM) DBU27 |
| 12681 | 5028 HN | Bristol MW5G | 184.196 | B45F | 9/62 | Durham District (DM) DBU28 |
| 12682 | 5029 HN | Bristol MW5G | 184.197 | B45F | 9/62 | Durham District (DM) DBU29 |
| 12683 | 5030 HN | Bristol MW5G | 195.088 | B45F | 10/62 | Durham District (DM) DBU30 |
| 12684 | 5031 HN | Bristol MW5G | 195.089 | B45F | 10/62 | Durham District (DM) DBU31 |
| 12685 | *135 ACY | Bristol MW6G | 184.086 | B45F | 8/61 | United Welsh, Swansea (GG) 127 |
| 12686 | *136 ACY | Bristol MW6G | 184.087 | B45F | 7/61 | United Welsh, Swansea (GG) 128 |
| 12687 | *137 ACY | Bristol MW6G | 184.088 | B45F | 7/61 | United Welsh, Swansea (GG) 129 |
| 12688 | *138 ACY | Bristol MW6G | 184.089 | B45F | 7/61 | United Welsh, Swansea (GG) 130 |
| 12689 | *139 ACY | Bristol MW6G | 184.090 | B45F | 8/61 | United Welsh, Swansea (GG) 131 |
| 12690 | *140 ACY | Bristol MW6G | 184.091 | B45F | 8/61 | United Welsh, Swansea (GG) 132 |
| 12691 | XMR 948 | Bristol MW6G | 184.119 | B43F | 8/61 | Wilts & Dorset, Salisbury (WI) 801 |
| 12692 | XMR 949 | Bristol MW6G | 184.120 | B43F | 8/61 | Wilts & Dorset, Salisbury (WI) 802 |
| 12693 | XMR 950 | Bristol MW6G | 184.165 | B43F | 11/61 | Wilts & Dorset, Salisbury (WI) 803 |
| 12694 | XMR 951 | Bristol MW6G | 184.166 | B43F | 11/61 | Wilts & Dorset, Salisbury (WI) 804 |
| 12695 | XMR 952 | Bristol MW6G | 184.176 | B43F | 12/61 | Wilts & Dorset, Salisbury (WI) 805 |
| 12696 | XMR 953 | Bristol MW6G | 184.177 | B43F | 1/62 | Wilts & Dorset, Salisbury (WI) 806 |
| 12697 | XMR 954 | Bristol MW6G | 195.069 | B43F | 8/62 | Wilts & Dorset, Salisbury (WI) 807 |
| 12698 | XMR 955 | Bristol MW6G | 195.070 | B43F | 8/62 | Wilts & Dorset, Salisbury (WI) 808 |
| 12699 | XMR 956 | Bristol MW6G | 195.099 | B43F | 9/62 | Wilts & Dorset, Salisbury (WI) 809 |
| 12700 | XMR 957 | Bristol MW6G | 195.100 | B43F | 9/62 | Wilts & Dorset, Salisbury (WI) 810 |
| 12701 | 914 VFM | Bristol MW6G | 184.123 | DP41F | 10/61 | Crosville MS, Chester (CH) EMG415 |
| 12702 | 915 VFM | Bristol MW6G | 184.124 | DP41F | 10/61 | Crosville MS, Chester (CH) EMG416 |
| 12703 | 916 VFM | Bristol MW6G | 184.125 | DP41F | 10/61 | Crosville MS, Chester (CH) EMG417 |
| 12704 | 917 VFM | Bristol MW6G | 184.126 | DP41F | 11/61 | Crosville MS, Chester (CH) EMG418 |
| 12705 | 918 VFM | Bristol MW6G | 184.132 | DP41F | 11/61 | Crosville MS, Chester (CH) EMG419 |
| 12706 | 919 VFM | Bristol MW6G | 184.133 | DP41F | 11/61 | Crosville MS, Chester (CH) EMG420 |
| 12707 | 920 VFM | Bristol MW6G | 184.134 | DP41F | 11/61 | Crosville MS, Chester (CH) EMG421 |
| 12708 | 921 VFM | Bristol MW6G | 184.135 | DP41F | 11/61 | Crosville MS, Chester (CH) EMG422 |
| 12709 | 922 VFM | Bristol MW6G | 184.137 | DP41F | 11/61 | Crosville MS, Chester (CH) EMG423 |
| 12710 | 923 VFM | Bristol MW6G | 184.138 | DP41F | 11/61 | Crosville MS, Chester (CH) EMG424 |
| 12711 | 924 VFM | Bristol MW6G | 184.139 | DP41F | 11/61 | Crosville MS, Chester (CH) EMG425 |
| 12712 | 925 VFM | Bristol MW6G | 184.140 | DP41F | 11/61 | Crosville MS, Chester (CH) EMG426 |
| 12713 | 119 DRM | Bristol MW6G | 184.121 | DP41F | 4/62 | Cumberland MS, Whitehaven (CU) 426 |
| 12714 | 120 DRM | Bristol MW6G | 184.122 | DP41F | 4/62 | Cumberland MS, Whitehaven (CU) 427 |
| 12715 | RFE 470 | Bristol MW5G | 184.092 | DP41F | 7/61 | Lincolnshire RCC, Lincoln (LC) 3025 |
| 12716 | RFE 471 | Bristol MW5G | 184.093 | DP41F | 7/61 | Lincolnshire RCC, Lincoln (LC) 3026 |
| 12717 | RFE 472 | Bristol MW5G | 184.094 | DP41F | 7/61 | Lincolnshire RCC, Lincoln (LC) 3027 |
| 12718 | 7902 WY | Bristol MW5G | 184.127 | DP41F | 5/62 | West Yorkshire RCC, Harrogate (WR) EUG81 |
| 12719 | 7903 WY | Bristol MW5G | 184.128 | DP41F | 12/61 | West Yorkshire RCC, Harrogate (WR) EUG82 |
| 12720 | 7904 WY | Bristol MW5G | 184.129 | DP41F | 6/62 | West Yorkshire RCC, Harrogate (WR) EUG83 |
| 12721 | 7905 WY | Bristol MW5G | 184.130 | DP41F | 6/62 | West Yorkshire RCC, Harrogate (WR) EUG84 |
| 12722 | 7906 WY | Bristol MW5G | 184.131 | DP41F | 6/62 | West Yorkshire RCC, Harrogate (WR) EUG85 |
| 12723 | 7907 WY | Bristol MW5G | 184.136 | DP41F | 6/62 | West Yorkshire RCC, Harrogate (WR) EUG86 |
| 12724 | 7908 WY | Bristol MW5G | 184.141 | DP41F | 6/62 | West Yorkshire RCC, Harrogate (WR) EUG87 |
| 12725 | 7909 WY | Bristol MW5G | 184.142 | DP41F | 6/62 | West Yorkshire RCC, Harrogate (WR) EUG88 |
| 12726 | 7910 WY | Bristol MW5G | 184.143 | DP41F | 6/62 | West Yorkshire RCC, Harrogate (WR) EUG89 |
| 12727 | 8001 VF | Bristol MW5G | 184.111 | B45F | 8/61 | Eastern Counties, Norwich (NK) LM462 |
| 12728 | 8002 VF | Bristol MW5G | 184.115 | B45F | 8/61 | Eastern Counties, Norwich (NK) LM463 |
| 12729 | 8003 VF | Bristol MW5G | 184.116 | B45F | 8/61 | Eastern Counties, Norwich (NK) LM464 |
| 12730 | 8004 VF | Bristol MW5G | 184.144 | B45F | 11/61 | Eastern Counties, Norwich (NK) LM465 |
| 12731 | 8005 VF | Bristol MW5G | 184.145 | B45F | 11/61 | Eastern Counties, Norwich (NK) LM466 |
| 12732 | 8006 VF | Bristol MW5G | 184.146 | B45F | 11/61 | Eastern Counties, Norwich (NK) LM467 |
| 12733 | 8007 VF | Bristol MW5G | 184.185 | B45F | 1/62 | Eastern Counties, Norwich (NK) LM468 |
| 12734 | 8008 VF | Bristol MW5G | 184.186 | B45F | 1/62 | Eastern Counties, Norwich (NK) LM469 |
| 12735 | 8009 VF | Bristol MW5G | 184.191 | B45F | 1/62 | Eastern Counties, Norwich (NK) LM470 |
| 12736 | RFE 479 | Bristol SC4LK | 172.029 | B35F | 7/61 | Lincolnshire RCC, Lincoln (LC) 2491 |
| 12737 | RFE 480 | Bristol SC4LK | 172.030 | B35F | 7/61 | Lincolnshire RCC, Lincoln (LC) 2492 |

| | | | | | | |
|---|---|---|---|---|---|---|
| 12738 | RFE 481 | Bristol SC4LK | 172.031 | B35F | 8/61 | Lincolnshire RCC, Lincoln (LC) 2493 |
| 12739 | *RFE 482 | Bristol SC4LK | 172.032 | B35F | 8/61 | Lincolnshire RCC, Lincoln (LC) 2494 |
| 12740 | RFE 483 | Bristol SC4LK | 191.001 | B35F | 8/61 | Lincolnshire RCC, Lincoln (LC) 2495 |
| 12741 | RFE 484 | Bristol SC4LK | 191.002 | B35F | 8/61 | Lincolnshire RCC, Lincoln (LC) 2496 |
| 12742 | RFE 485 | Bristol SC4LK | 191.003 | B35F | 8/61 | Lincolnshire RCC, Lincoln (LC) 2497 |
| 12743 | | | | | | Not built |
| 12744 | | | | | | Not built |
| 12745 | | | | | | Not built |
| 12746 | | | | | | Not built |
| 12747 | | | | | | Not built |
| 12748 | 423 HDV | Bristol SUL4A | 190.015 | B36F | 1/62 | Southern National, Exeter (DN) 654 |
| 12749 | 424 HDV | Bristol SUL4A | 190.016 | B36F | 1/62 | Southern National, Exeter (DN) 655 |
| 12750 | 425 HDV | Bristol SUL4A | 190.017 | B36F | 1/62 | Southern National, Exeter (DN) 656 |
| 12751 | 426 HDV | Bristol SUL4A | 190.018 | B36F | 1/62 | Southern National, Exeter (DN) 657 |
| 12752 | 427 HDV | Bristol SUL4A | 190.023 | B36F | 1/62 | Southern National, Exeter (DN) 658 |
| 12753 | 428 HDV | Bristol SUL4A | 190.024 | B36F | 2/62 | Southern National, Exeter (DN) 659 |
| 12754 | 429 HDV | Bristol SUL4A | 190.025 | B36F | 2/62 | Southern National, Exeter (DN) 660 |
| 12755 | *430 HDV | Bristol SUL4A | 190.026 | B36F | 3/62 | Southern National, Exeter (DN) 661 |
| 12756 | 431 HDV | Bristol SUL4A | 190.027 | B36F | 3/62 | Southern National, Exeter (DN) 662 |
| 12757 | 414 HDV | Bristol SUL4A | 190.010 | B36F | 10/61 | Western National, Exeter (DN) 645 |
| 12758 | 415 HDV | Bristol SUL4A | 190.011 | B36F | 10/61 | Western National, Exeter (DN) 646 |
| 12759 | 416 HDV | Bristol SUL4A | 190.012 | B36F | 10/61 | Western National, Exeter (DN) 647 |
| 12760 | *417 HDV | Bristol SUL4A | 190.013 | B36F | 11/61 | Western National, Exeter (DN) 648 |
| 12761 | 418 HDV | Bristol SUL4A | 190.014 | B36F | 11/61 | Western National, Exeter (DN) 649 |
| 12762 | 419 HDV | Bristol SUL4A | 190.019 | B36F | 1/62 | Western National, Exeter (DN) 650 |
| 12763 | 420 HDV | Bristol SUL4A | 190.020 | B36F | 11/61 | Western National, Exeter (DN) 651 |
| 12764 | 421 HDV | Bristol SUL4A | 190.021 | B36F | 1/62 | Western National, Exeter (DN) 652 |
| 12765 | 422 HDV | Bristol SUL4A | 190.022 | B36F | 1/62 | Western National, Exeter (DN) 653 |
| 12766 | 922 GUO | Bristol SUL4A | 190.006 | C33F | 7/61 | Southern National, Exeter (DN) 408 |
| 12767 | 923 GUO | Bristol SUL4A | 190.007 | C33F | 7/61 | Southern National, Exeter (DN) 409 |
| 12768 | 924 GUO | Bristol SUL4A | 190.008 | C33F | 7/61 | Southern National, Exeter (DN) 410 |
| 12769 | 925 GUO | Bristol SUL4A | 190.009 | C33F | 7/61 | Southern National, Exeter (DN) 411 |
| 12770 | 917 GUO | Bristol SUL4A | 190.001 | C33F | 6/61 | Western National, Exeter (DN) 412 |
| 12771 | 918 GUO | Bristol SUL4A | 190.002 | C33F | 6/61 | Western National, Exeter (DN) 413 |
| 12772 | 919 GUO | Bristol SUL4A | 190.003 | C33F | 6/61 | Western National, Exeter (DN) 414 |
| 12773 | 920 GUO | Bristol SUL4A | 190.004 | C33F | 6/61 | Western National, Exeter (DN) 415 |
| 12774 | 921 GUO | Bristol SUL4A | 190.005 | C33F | 6/61 | Western National, Exeter (DN) 416 |
| 12775 | *EDL 14 | Bristol L5G | 61.026 | FB35F | 5/61 | Southern Vectis, Newport (IW) 829 |
| 12776 | *EDL 15 | Bristol L5G | 61.027 | FB35F | 5/61 | Southern Vectis, Newport (IW) 830 |
| 12777 | *KEL 67 | Bristol L6G Reb | 73.119 | FB39F | 5/61 | Hants & Dorset, Bournemouth (HA) 672 |
| 12778 | *KEL 401 | Bristol L6G Reb | 73.120 | FB39F | 5/61 | Hants & Dorset, Bournemouth (HA) 673 |
| 12779 | *KEL 402 | Bristol L6G Reb | 73.121 | FB39F | 6/61 | Hants & Dorset, Bournemouth (HA) 674 |
| 12780 | *KEL 405 | Bristol L6G Reb | 73.124 | FB39F | 6/61 | Hants & Dorset, Bournemouth (HA) 677 |
| 12781 | *KEL 403 | Bristol L6G Reb | 73.122 | FB39F | 6/61 | Hants & Dorset, Bournemouth (HA) 675 |
| 12782 | *KEL 404 | Bristol L6G Reb | 73.123 | FB39F | 6/61 | Hants & Dorset, Bournemouth (HA) 676 |
| 12783 | 864 RAE | Bristol MW5G | 195.118 | B45F | 11/62 | Bristol OC (GL) 2549 |
| 12784 | 865 RAE | Bristol MW5G | 195.119 | B45F | 11/62 | Bristol OC (GL) 2550 |
| 12785 | 866 RAE | Bristol MW5G | 195.120 | B45F | 11/62 | Bristol OC (GL) 2551 |
| 12786 | 867 RAE | Bristol MW5G | 195.121 | B45F | 11/62 | Bristol OC (GL) 2552 |
| 12787 | 868 RAE | Bristol MW5G | 195.122 | B45F | 11/62 | Bristol OC (GL) 2553 |
| 12788 | 808 XFM | Bristol MW6G | 184.247 | C39F | 7/62 | Crosville MS, Chester (CH) CMG427 |
| 12789 | 809 XFM | Bristol MW6G | 184.248 | C39F | 7/62 | Crosville MS, Chester (CH) CMG428 |
| 12790 | 810 XFM | Bristol MW6G | 184.249 | C39F | 7/62 | Crosville MS, Chester (CH) CMG429 |
| 12791 | 811 XFM | Bristol MW6G | 184.250 | C39F | 7/62 | Crosville MS, Chester (CH) CMG430 |
| 12792 | 812 XFM | Bristol MW6G | 195.014 | C39F | 6/62 | Crosville MS, Chester (CH) CMG431 |
| 12793 | 813 XFM | Bristol MW6G | 195.016 | C39F | 5/62 | Crosville MS, Chester (CH) CMG432 |
| 12794 | 814 XFM | Bristol MW6G | 195.017 | C39F | 5/62 | Crosville MS, Chester (CH) CMG433 |
| 12795 | 815 XFM | Bristol MW6G | 195.040 | C39F | 6/62 | Crosville MS, Chester (CH) CMG434 |
| 12796 | 816 XFM | Bristol MW6G | 195.041 | C39F | 6/62 | Crosville MS, Chester (CH) CMG435 |
| 12797 | 817 XFM | Bristol MW6G | 195.042 | C39F | 6/62 | Crosville MS, Chester (CH) CMG436 |
| 12798 | 3804 PW | Bristol MW6G | 184.217 | C32F | 6/62 | Eastern Counties, Norwich (NK) LS804 |
| 12799 | 3805 PW | Bristol MW6G | 184.218 | C32F | 5/62 | Eastern Counties, Norwich (NK) LS805 |
| 12800 | 3806 PW | Bristol MW6G | 184.223 | C32F | 6/62 | Eastern Counties, Norwich (NK) LS806 |
| 12801 | 3807 PW | Bristol MW6G | 184.224 | C39F | 4/62 | Eastern Counties, Norwich (NK) LS807 |

| | | | | | | |
|---|---|---|---|---|---|---|
| 12802 | 3808 PW | Bristol MW6G | 184.225 | C39F | 4/62 | Eastern Counties, Norwich (NK) LS808 |
| 12803 | 3809 PW | Bristol MW6G | 184.226 | C39F | 6/62 | Eastern Counties, Norwich (NK) LS809 |
| 12804 | 3810 PW | Bristol MW6G | 184.227 | C39F | 4/62 | Eastern Counties, Norwich (NK) LS810 |
| 12805 | 3811 PW | Bristol MW6G | 195.023 | C39F | 6/62 | Eastern Counties, Norwich (NK) LS811 |
| 12806 | 3812 PW | Bristol MW6G | 195.046 | C39F | 6/62 | Eastern Counties, Norwich (NK) LS812 |
| 12807 | 3813 PW | Bristol MW6G | 195.047 | C39F | 6/62 | Eastern Counties, Norwich (NK) LS813 |
| 12808 | 3814 PW | Bristol MW6G | 195.048 | C39F | 6/62 | Eastern Counties, Norwich (NK) LS814 |
| 12809 | 3815 PW | Bristol MW6G | 195.049 | C39F | 6/62 | Eastern Counties, Norwich (NK) LS815 |
| 12810 | OO 9543 | Bristol MW6G | 184.238 | C39F | 5/62 | Eastern National, Chelmsford (EX) 557 |
| 12811 | OO 9544 | Bristol MW6G | 184.239 | C39F | 4/62 | Eastern National, Chelmsford (EX) 558 |
| 12812 | OO 9545 | Bristol MW6G | 184.240 | C39F | 4/62 | Eastern National, Chelmsford (EX) 559 |
| 12813 | OO 9546 | Bristol MW6G | 184.241 | C39F | 5/62 | Eastern National, Chelmsford (EX) 560 |
| 12814 | OO 9547 | Bristol MW6G | 195.027 | C39F | 5/62 | Eastern National, Chelmsford (EX) 561 |
| 12815 | OO 9548 | Bristol MW6G | 195.028 | C34F | 5/62 | Eastern National, Chelmsford (EX) 562 |
| 12816 | OO 9549 | Bristol MW6G | 195.029 | C34F | 5/62 | Eastern National, Chelmsford (EX) 563 |
| 12817 | OO 9550 | Bristol MW6G | 195.030 | C34F | 5/62 | Eastern National, Chelmsford (EX) 564 |
| 12818 | 7118 LJ | Bristol MW6G | 195.018 | C39F | 5/62 | Hants & Dorset, Bournemouth (HA) 882 |
| 12819 | 7119 LJ | Bristol MW6G | 195.019 | C39F | 5/62 | Hants & Dorset, Bournemouth (HA) 883 |
| 12820 | 7120 LJ | Bristol MW6G | 195.022 | C39F | 5/62 | Hants & Dorset, Bournemouth (HA) 884 |
| 12821 | 7121 LJ | Bristol MW6G | 195.033 | C39F | 5/62 | Hants & Dorset, Bournemouth (HA) 885 |
| 12822 | 7122 LJ | Bristol MW6G | 195.034 | C39F | 5/62 | Hants & Dorset, Bournemouth (HA) 886 |
| 12823 | 7123 LJ | Bristol MW6G | 195.035 | C39F | 6/62 | Hants & Dorset, Bournemouth (HA) 887 |
| 12824 | 101 CWO | Bristol MW6G | 184.219 | C39F | 4/62 | Red & White, Chepstow (MH) UC162 |
| 12825 | 102 CWO | Bristol MW6G | 184.220 | C39F | 4/62 | Red & White, Chepstow (MH) UC262 |
| 12826 | 103 CWO | Bristol MW6G | 184.221 | C39F | 4/62 | Red & White, Chepstow (MH) UC362 |
| 12827 | 104 CWO | Bristol MW6G | 184.222 | C39F | 4/62 | Red & White, Chepstow (MH) UC462 |
| 12828 | 105 CWO | Bristol MW6G | 184.228 | C39F | 4/62 | Red & White, Chepstow (MH) UC562 |
| 12829 | 106 CWO | Bristol MW6G | 184.229 | C39F | 4/62 | Red & White, Chepstow (MH) UC662 |
| 12830 | 107 CWO | Bristol MW6G | 184.230 | C39F | 4/62 | Red & White, Chepstow (MH) UC762 |
| 12831 | 108 CWO | Bristol MW6G | 184.231 | C39F | 4/62 | Red & White, Chepstow (MH) UC862 |
| 12832 | 109 CWO | Bristol MW6G | 184.232 | C39F | 4/62 | Red & White, Chepstow (MH) UC962 |
| 12833 | 110 CWO | Bristol MW6G | 195.036 | C39F | 6/62 | Red & White, Chepstow (MH) UC1062 |
| 12834 | 111 CWO | Bristol MW6G | 195.037 | C39F | 6/62 | Red & White, Chepstow (MH) UC1162 |
| 12835 | 112 CWO | Bristol MW6G | 195.038 | C39F | 6/62 | Red & White, Chepstow (MH) UC1262 |
| 12836 | 113 CWO | Bristol MW6G | 195.039 | C39F | 6/62 | Red & White, Chepstow (MH) UC1362 |
| 12837 | 282 KTA | Bristol MW6G | 195.031 | C39F | 6/62 | Southern National, Exeter (DN) 1383 |
| 12838 | 283 KTA | Bristol MW6G | 195.032 | C39F | 6/62 | Southern National, Exeter (DN) 1384 |
| 12839 | 520 ABL | Bristol MW6G | 195.008 | C39F | 4/62 | Thames Valley, Reading (BE) 866 |
| 12840 | *EDL 16 | Bristol L5G | 61.028 | FB35F | 4/62 | Southern Vectis, Newport (IW) 831 |
| 12841 | | | | | | Not built |
| 12842 | | | | | | Not built |
| 12843 | | | | | | Not built |
| 12844 | | | | | | Not built |
| 12845 | 9 DLY | Bristol MW6G | 184.244 | C34F | 5/62 | Tillings Transport, London WC1 (LN) |
| 12846 | 10 DLY | Bristol MW6G | 184.245 | C34F | 5/62 | Tillings Transport, London WC1 (LN) |
| 12847 | 11 DLY | Bristol MW6G | 184.246 | C34F | 5/62 | Tillings Transport, London WC1 (LN) |
| 12848 | * 12 DLY | Bristol MW6G | 195.001 | C34F | 5/62 | Tillings Transport, London WC1 (LN) |
| 12849 | 13 DLY | Bristol MW6G | 195.002 | C34F | 5/62 | Tillings Transport, London WC1 (LN) |
| 12850 | 253 KTA | Bristol MW6G | 184.213 | C39F | 4/62 | Western National, Exeter (DN) 2270 |
| 12851 | 254 KTA | Bristol MW6G | 184.214 | C39F | 3/62 | Western National, Exeter (DN) 1385 |
| 12852 | 255 KTA | Bristol MW6G | 184.215 | C39F | 4/62 | Western National, Exeter (DN) 1386 |
| 12853 | 256 KTA | Bristol MW6G | 184.216 | C39F | 4/62 | Western National, Exeter (DN) 1387 |
| 12854 | 257 KTA | Bristol MW6G | 184.233 | C39F | 4/62 | Western National, Exeter (DN) 1388 |
| 12855 | 258 KTA | Bristol MW6G | 184.234 | C39F | 5/62 | Western National, Exeter (DN) 1389 |
| 12856 | 259 KTA | Bristol MW6G | 184.235 | C39F | 5/62 | Western National, Exeter (DN) 1390 |
| 12857 | 260 KTA | Bristol MW6G | 184.236 | C39F | 5/62 | Western National, Exeter (DN) 1391 |
| 12858 | 261 KTA | Bristol MW6G | 184.237 | C39F | 4/62 | Western National, Exeter (DN) 1392 |
| 12859 | 262 KTA | Bristol MW6G | 195.043 | C39F | 6/62 | Western National, Exeter (DN) 1393 |
| 12860 | 263 KTA | Bristol MW6G | 195.044 | C39F | 6/62 | Western National, Exeter (DN) 1394 |
| 12861 | 264 KTA | Bristol MW6G | 195.045 | C39F | 6/62 | Western National, Exeter (DN) 1395 |
| 12862 | 265 KTA | Bristol MW6G | 195.050 | C39F | 7/62 | Western National, Exeter (DN) 1396 |
| 12863 | 266 KTA | Bristol MW6G | 195.051 | C39F | 7/62 | Western National, Exeter (DN) 1397 |
| 12864 | 9168 YG | Bristol MW6G | 195.009 | C39F | 4/62 | West Yorkshire RCC, Harrogate (WR) CUG33 |
| 12865 | 9169 YG | Bristol MW6G | 195.010 | C39F | 4/62 | West Yorkshire RCC, Harrogate (WR) CUG34 |

| | | | | | | |
|---|---|---|---|---|---|---|
| 12866 | 9170 YG | Bristol MW6G | 195.011 | C39F | 4/62 | West Yorkshire RCC, Harrogate (WR) CUG35 |
| 12867 | 673 AAM | Bristol MW6G | 195.024 | C39F | 5/62 | Wilts & Dorset, Salisbury (WI) 715 |
| 12868 | 674 AAM | Bristol MW6G | 195.025 | C39F | 5/62 | Wilts & Dorset, Salisbury (WI) 716 |
| 12869 | *675 AAM | Bristol MW6G | 195.026 | C39F | 5/62 | Wilts & Dorset, Salisbury (WI) 717 |
| 12870 | 7011 HN | Bristol MW6G | 195.003 | C34F | 5/62 | United AS, Darlington (DM) BUC11 |
| 12871 | 7012 HN | Bristol MW6G | 195.004 | C34F | 5/62 | United AS, Darlington (DM) BUC12 |
| 12872 | 7013 HN | Bristol MW6G | 195.005 | C34F | 6/62 | United AS, Darlington (DM) BUC13 |
| 12873 | 7014 HN | Bristol MW6G | 195.006 | C34F | 6/62 | United AS, Darlington (DM) BUC14 |
| 12874 | 7015 HN | Bristol MW6G | 195.007 | C34F | 6/62 | United AS, Darlington (DM) BUC15 |
| 12875 | 284 KTA | Bristol SUL4A | 190.034 | C33F | 7/62 | Southern National, Exeter (DN) 432 |
| 12876 | 285 KTA | Bristol SUL4A | 190.035 | C33F | 7/62 | Southern National, Exeter (DN) 433 |
| 12877 | *286 KTA | Bristol SUL4A | 190.037 | C33F | 7/62 | Southern National, Exeter (DN) 434 |
| 12878 | 287 KTA | Bristol SUL4A | 190.038 | C33F | 7/62 | Southern National, Exeter (DN) 435 |
| 12879 | *752 BWN | Bristol SUL4A | 190.028 | C33F | 7/62 | United Welsh, Swansea (GG) 10 |
| 12880 | 753 BWN | Bristol SUL4A | 190.029 | C33F | 7/62 | United Welsh, Swansea (GG) 11 |
| 12881 | 267 KTA | Bristol SUL4A | 190.030 | C33F | 6/62 | Western National, Exeter (DN) 417 |
| 12882 | *268 KTA | Bristol SUL4A | 190.031 | C33F | 7/62 | Western National, Exeter (DN) 418 |
| 12883 | 269 KTA | Bristol SUL4A | 190.032 | C33F | 7/62 | Western National, Exeter (DN) 419 |
| 12884 | 270 KTA | Bristol SUL4A | 190.033 | C33F | 7/62 | Western National, Exeter (DN) 420 |
| 12885 | *271 KTA | Bristol SUL4A | 190.036 | C33F | 7/62 | Western National, Exeter (DN) 421 |
| 12886 | *272 KTA | Bristol SUL4A | 190.039 | C33F | 7/62 | Western National, Exeter (DN) 422 |
| 12887 | 273 KTA | Bristol SUL4A | 190.040 | C33F | 7/62 | Western National, Exeter (DN) 423 |
| 12888 | 274 KTA | Bristol SUL4A | 190.041 | C33F | 7/62 | Western National, Exeter (DN) 424 |
| 12889 | 275 KTA | Bristol SUL4A | 190.042 | C33F | 7/62 | Western National, Exeter (DN) 425 |
| 12890 | 276 KTA | Bristol SUL4A | 190.043 | C33F | 7/62 | Western National, Exeter (DN) 426 |
| 12891 | 277 KTA | Bristol SUL4A | 190.044 | C33F | 7/62 | Western National, Exeter (DN) 427 |
| 12892 | *278 KTA | Bristol SUL4A | 190.045 | C33F | 7/62 | Western National, Exeter (DN) 428 |
| 12893 | 279 KTA | Bristol SUL4A | 190.046 | C33F | 7/62 | Western National, Exeter (DN) 429 |
| 12894 | *280 KTA | Bristol SUL4A | 190.047 | C33F | 7/62 | Western National, Exeter (DN) 430 |
| 12895 | 281 KTA | Bristol SUL4A | 190.048 | C33F | 7/62 | Western National, Exeter (DN) 431 |
| 12896 | *XPM 41 | Bristol FS6G | 196.037 | CO33/27R | 10/62 | Brighton, Hove & District (ES) 41 |
| 12897 | *XPM 42 | Bristol FS6G | 196.038 | CO33/27R | 9/62 | Brighton, Hove & District (ES) 42 |
| 12898 | XPM 43 | Bristol FS6G | 196.039 | CO33/27R | 10/62 | Brighton, Hove & District (ES) 43 |
| 12899 | XPM 44 | Bristol FS6G | 196.040 | CO33/27R | 10/62 | Brighton, Hove & District (ES) 44 |
| 12900 | 1198 FM | Bristol FS6G | 196.059 | H33/27RD | 4/63 | Crosville MS, Chester (CH) DFG119 |
| 12901 | 1199 FM | Bristol FS6G | 196.060 | H33/27RD | 4/63 | Crosville MS, Chester (CH) DFG120 |
| 12902 | 1201 FM | Bristol FS6G | 196.061 | H33/27RD | 3/63 | Crosville MS, Chester (CH) DFG121 |
| 12903 | 1207 FM | Bristol FS6B | 205.009 | H33/27RD | 4/63 | Crosville MS, Chester (CH) DFB127 |
| 12904 | 1208 FM | Bristol FS6B | 205.010 | H33/27RD | 4/63 | Crosville MS, Chester (CH) DFB128 |
| 12905 | 1202 FM | Bristol FS6G | 205.019 | H33/27RD | 4/63 | Crosville MS, Chester (CH) DFG122 |
| 12906 | 1203 FM | Bristol FS6G | 205.020 | H33/27RD | 4/63 | Crosville MS, Chester (CH) DFG123 |
| 12907 | 1204 FM | Bristol FS6G | 205.029 | H33/27RD | 5/63 | Crosville MS, Chester (CH) DFG124 |
| 12908 | *1205 FM | Bristol FS6G | 205.030 | H33/27RD | 5/63 | Crosville MS, Chester (CH) DFG125 |
| 12909 | 1206 FM | Bristol FS6G | 205.031 | H33/27RD | 4/63 | Crosville MS, Chester (CH) DFG126 |
| 12910 | 1209 FM | Bristol FS6B | 205.056 | H33/27RD | 7/63 | Crosville MS, Chester (CH) DFB129 |
| 12911 | 1211 FM | Bristol FS6B | 205.057 | H33/27RD | 6/63 | Crosville MS, Chester (CH) DFB130 |
| 12912 | 1212 FM | Bristol FS6B | 205.058 | H33/27RD | 6/63 | Crosville MS, Chester (CH) DFB131 |
| 12913 | 1213 FM | Bristol FS6B | 205.059 | H33/27RD | 7/63 | Crosville MS, Chester (CH) DFB132 |
| 12914 | 1214 FM | Bristol FS6B | 205.060 | H33/27RD | 7/63 | Crosville MS, Chester (CH) DFB133 |
| 12915 | 715 GRM | Bristol FS6B | 196.018 | H33/27RD | 10/62 | Cumberland MS, Whitehaven (CU) 555 |
| 12916 | *716 GRM | Bristol FS6B | 196.019 | H33/27RD | 10/62 | Cumberland MS, Whitehaven (CU) 556 |
| 12917 | 717 GRM | Bristol FS6B | 196.020 | H33/27RD | 10/62 | Cumberland MS, Whitehaven (CU) 557 |
| 12918 | 718 GRM | Bristol FS6B | 196.062 | H33/27RD | 12/62 | Cumberland MS, Whitehaven (CU) 558 |
| 12919 | 719 GRM | Bristol FS6B | 196.063 | H33/27RD | 12/62 | Cumberland MS, Whitehaven (CU) 559 |
| 12920 | 720 GRM | Bristol FS6B | 196.064 | H33/27RD | 12/62 | Cumberland MS, Whitehaven (CU) 560 |
| 12921 | 8036 PW | Bristol FS5G | 196.021 | H33/27RD | 10/62 | Eastern Counties, Norwich (NK) LFS36 |
| 12922 | 8037 PW | Bristol FS5G | 196.022 | H33/27RD | 10/62 | Eastern Counties, Norwich (NK) LFS37 |
| 12923 | 8038 PW | Bristol FS5G | 196.050 | H33/27RD | 10/62 | Eastern Counties, Norwich (NK) LFS38 |
| 12924 | 8039 PW | Bristol FS5G | 196.051 | H33/27RD | 10/62 | Eastern Counties, Norwich (NK) LFS39 |
| 12925 | 8040 PW | Bristol FS5G | 196.052 | H33/27RD | 10/62 | Eastern Counties, Norwich (NK) LFS40 |
| 12926 | 41 BNG | Bristol FS5G | 205.001 | H33/27RD | 12/62 | Eastern Counties, Norwich (NK) LFS41 |
| 12927 | 42 BNG | Bristol FS5G | 205.002 | H33/27RD | 12/62 | Eastern Counties, Norwich (NK) LFS42 |
| 12928 | 43 BNG | Bristol FS5G | 205.003 | H33/27RD | 12/62 | Eastern Counties, Norwich (NK) LFS43 |
| 12929 | 44 CNG | Bristol FS5G | 205.043 | H33/27RD | 5/63 | Eastern Counties, Norwich (NK) LFS44 |

| | | | | | | | |
|---|---|---|---|---|---|---|---|
| 12930 | 45 CNG | Bristol FS5G | 205.044 | H33/27RD | 5/63 | Eastern Counties, Norwich (NK) LFS45 |
| 12931 | 46 CNG | Bristol FS5G | 205.045 | H33/27R | 5/63 | Eastern Counties, Norwich (NK) LFS46 |
| 12932 | 47 CNG | Bristol FS5G | 205.046 | H33/27R | 5/63 | Eastern Counties, Norwich (NK) LFS47 |
| 12933 | 48 CNG | Bristol FS5G | 205.047 | H33/27R | 5/63 | Eastern Counties, Norwich (NK) LFS48 |
| 12934 | 49 CNG | Bristol FS5G | 205.048 | H33/27R | 5/63 | Eastern Counties, Norwich (NK) LFS49 |
| 12935 * | 50 CNG | Bristol FS5G | 205.049 | H33/27RD | 6/63 | Eastern Counties, Norwich (NK) LFS50 |
| 12936 | 51 CPW | Bristol FS5G | 205.061 | H33/27RD | 6/63 | Eastern Counties, Norwich (NK) LFS51 |
| 12937 | 52 CPW | Bristol FS5G | 205.062 | H33/27RD | 7/63 | Eastern Counties, Norwich (NK) LFS52 |
| 12938 | 53 CPW | Bristol FS5G | 205.063 | H33/27RD | 7/63 | Eastern Counties, Norwich (NK) LFS53 |
| 12939 | 54 CPW | Bristol FS5G | 205.064 | H33/27RD | 7/63 | Eastern Counties, Norwich (NK) LFS54 |
| 12940 | 55 CPW | Bristol FS5G | 205.065 | H33/27RD | 7/63 | Eastern Counties, Norwich (NK) LFS55 |
| 12941 | 7671 LJ | Bristol FS6B | 196.041 | H33/27RD | 9/62 | Hants & Dorset, Bournemouth (HA) 1471 |
| 12942 | 7672 LJ | Bristol FS6B | 196.042 | H33/27RD | 9/62 | Hants & Dorset, Bournemouth (HA) 1472 |
| 12943 | 7673 LJ | Bristol FS6B | 196.043 | H33/27RD | 9/62 | Hants & Dorset, Bournemouth (HA) 1473 |
| 12944 | 7674 LJ | Bristol FS6B | 196.044 | H33/27RD | 9/62 | Hants & Dorset, Bournemouth (HA) 1474 |
| 12945 | 7675 LJ | Bristol FS6B | 196.045 | H33/27RD | 9/62 | Hants & Dorset, Bournemouth (HA) 1475 |
| 12946 | 7676 LJ | Bristol FS6B | 196.067 | H33/27RD | 11/62 | Hants & Dorset, Bournemouth (HA) 1476 |
| 12947 | 7677 LJ | Bristol FS6B | 196.068 | H33/27RD | 11/62 | Hants & Dorset, Bournemouth (HA) 1477 |
| 12948 | 7678 LJ | Bristol FS6B | 196.069 | H33/27RD | 11/62 | Hants & Dorset, Bournemouth (HA) 1478 |
| 12949 | 7679 LJ | Bristol FS6B | 205.050 | H33/27RD | 5/63 | Hants & Dorset, Bournemouth (HA) 1479 |
| 12950 | 7680 LJ | Bristol FS6B | 205.051 | H33/27RD | 5/63 | Hants & Dorset, Bournemouth (HA) 1480 |
| 12951 | 7681 LJ | Bristol FS6B | 205.066 | H33/27RD | 7/63 | Hants & Dorset, Bournemouth (HA) 1481 |
| 12952 | TVL 305 | Bristol FS5G | 205.011 | H33/27RD | 11/62 | Lincolnshire RCC, Lincoln (LC) 2504 |
| 12953 | TVL 306 | Bristol FS5G | 205.012 | H33/27RD | 11/62 | Lincolnshire RCC, Lincoln (LC) 2505 |
| 12954 | TVL 307 | Bristol FS5G | 205.013 | H33/27RD | 11/62 | Lincolnshire RCC, Lincoln (LC) 2506 |
| 12955 | 1 EWO | Bristol FS6G | 196.046 | H33/27RD | 9/62 | Red & White, Chepstow (MH) L162 |
| 12956 | 2 EWO | Bristol FS6G | 196.047 | H33/27RD | 9/62 | Red & White, Chepstow (MH) L262 |
| 12957 | 3 EWO | Bristol FS6G | 196.048 | H33/27RD | 10/62 | Red & White, Chepstow (MH) L362 |
| 12958 | 4 EWO | Bristol FS6G | 196.049 | H33/27RD | 10/62 | Red & White, Chepstow (MH) L462 |
| 12959 | 5 EWO | Bristol FS6B | 196.070 | H33/27RD | 12/62 | Red & White, Chepstow (MH) L562 |
| 12960 * | 6 EWO | Bristol FS6G | 205.014 | H33/27RD | 1/63 | Red & White, Chepstow (MH) L662 |
| 12961 | 7 EWO | Bristol FS6G | 205.015 | H33/27RD | 12/62 | Red & White, Chepstow (MH) L762 |
| 12962 | 8 EWO | Bristol FS6B | 205.032 | H33/27RD | 5/63 | Red & White, Chepstow (MH) L862 |
| 12963 | 9 EWO | Bristol FS6B | 205.033 | H33/27RD | 5/63 | Red & White, Chepstow (MH) L962 |
| 12964 | 10 EWO | Bristol FS6B | 205.034 | H33/27RD | 5/63 | Red & White, Chepstow (MH) L1062 |
| 12965 | 11 EWO | Bristol FS6B | 205.035 | H33/27RD | 5/63 | Red & White, Chepstow (MH) L1162 |
| 12966 | 12 EWO | Bristol FS6B | 205.067 | H33/27RD | 7/63 | Red & White, Chepstow (MH) L1262 |
| 12967 | YDL 314 | Bristol FS6G | 196.029 | H33/27RD | 7/62 | Southern Vectis, Newport (IW) 569 |
| 12968 | YDL 315 | Bristol FS6G | 196.030 | H33/27RD | 7/62 | Southern Vectis, Newport (IW) 570 |
| 12969 | YDL 316 | Bristol FS6G | 196.031 | H33/27RD | 7/62 | Southern Vectis, Newport (IW) 571 |
| 12970 | YDL 317 | Bristol FS6G | 196.032 | H33/27RD | 7/62 | Southern Vectis, Newport (IW) 572 |
| 12971 | YDL 318 | Bristol FS6G | 196.033 | H33/27RD | 7/62 | Southern Vectis, Newport (IW) 573 |
| 12972 | 274 BWU | Bristol FS6B | 196.028 | H33/27RD | 11/62 | West Yorkshire RCC, Harrogate (WR) DX150 |
| 12973 | 275 BWU | Bristol FS6B | 196.034 | H33/27RD | 11/62 | West Yorkshire RCC, Harrogate (WR) DX151 |
| 12974 | 276 BWU | Bristol FS6B | 196.035 | H33/27RD | 11/62 | West Yorkshire RCC, Harrogate (WR) DX152 |
| 12975 | 277 BWU | Bristol FS6B | 196.036 | H33/27RD | 11/62 | West Yorkshire RCC, Harrogate (WR) DX153 |
| 12976 | 278 BWU | Bristol FS6B | 205.018 | H33/27RD | 12/62 | West Yorkshire RCC, Harrogate (WR) DX154 |
| 12977 | 279 BWU | Bristol FS6B | 205.036 | H33/27RD | 5/63 | West Yorkshire RCC, Harrogate (WR) DX155 |
| 12978 | 280 BWU | Bristol FS6B | 205.052 | H33/27RD | 7/63 | West Yorkshire RCC, Harrogate (WR) DX156 |
| 12979 | 281 BWU | Bristol FS6B | 205.053 | H33/27RD | 7/63 | West Yorkshire RCC, Harrogate (WR) DX157 |
| 12980 | 282 BWU | Bristol FS6B | 205.054 | H33/27RD | 7/63 | West Yorkshire RCC, Harrogate (WR) DX158 |
| 12981 | 283 BWU | Bristol FS6B | 205.055 | H33/27RD | 7/63 | West Yorkshire RCC, Harrogate (WR) DX159 |
| 12982 | 284 BWU | Bristol FS6B | 205.068 | H33/27RD | 8/63 | West Yorkshire RCC, Harrogate (WR) DX160 |
| 12983 * | 285 BWU | Bristol FS6B | 205.069 | H33/27RD | 8/63 | West Yorkshire RCC, Harrogate (WR) DX161 |
| 12984 * | 950 BWR | Bristol FS6B | 196.013 | H33/27RD | 11/62 | Keighley-West Yorkshire, Harrogate (WR) KDX136 |
| 12985 | 951 BWR | Bristol FS6B | 196.014 | H33/27RD | 11/62 | Keighley-West Yorkshire, Harrogate (WR) KDX137 |
| 12986 | 952 BWR | Bristol FS6B | 196.015 | H33/27RD | 11/62 | Keighley-West Yorkshire, Harrogate (WR) KDX138 |
| 12987 | 953 BWR | Bristol FS6B | 196.016 | H33/27RD | 11/62 | Keighley-West Yorkshire, Harrogate (WR) KDX139 |
| 12988 | 954 BWR | Bristol FS6B | 196.017 | H33/27RD | 11/62 | Keighley-West Yorkshire, Harrogate (WR) KDX140 |

| | | | | | | |
|---|---|---|---|---|---|---|
| 12989 | 955 BWR | Bristol FS6B | 205.024 | H33/27RD | 1/63 | Keighley-West Yorkshire, Harrogate (WR) KDX141 |
| 12990 | 956 BWR | Bristol FS6B | 205.025 | H33/27RD | 1/63 | Keighley-West Yorkshire, Harrogate (WR) KDX142 |
| 12991 | *957 BWR | Bristol FS6B | 205.026 | H33/27RD | 1/63 | Keighley-West Yorkshire, Harrogate (WR) KDX143 |
| 12992 | 958 BWR | Bristol FS6B | 205.027 | H33/27RD | 1/63 | Keighley-West Yorkshire, Harrogate (WR) KDX144 |
| 12993 | 959 BWR | Bristol FS6B | 205.028 | H33/27RD | 1/63 | Keighley-West Yorkshire, Harrogate (WR) KDX145 |
| 12994 | 144 CWR | Bristol FS6B | 196.065 | H33/27RD | 12/62 | York-West Yorkshire, Harrogate (WR) YDX146 |
| 12995 | 145 CWR | Bristol FS6B | 196.066 | H33/27RD | 12/62 | York-West Yorkshire, Harrogate (WR) YDX147 |
| 12996 | 146 CWR | Bristol FS6B | 205.016 | H33/27RD | 12/62 | York-West Yorkshire, Harrogate (WR) YDX148 |
| 12997 | 147 CWR | Bristol FS6B | 205.017 | H33/27RD | 12/62 | York-West Yorkshire, Harrogate (WR) YDX149 |
| 12998 | 676 AAM | Bristol FS6G | 196.023 | H33/27RD | 9/62 | Wilts & Dorset, Salisbury (WI) 638 |
| 12999 | 677 AAM | Bristol FS6G | 196.024 | H33/27RD | 9/62 | Wilts & Dorset, Salisbury (WI) 639 |
| 13000 | 678 AAM | Bristol FS6G | 196.025 | H33/27RD | 9/62 | Wilts & Dorset, Salisbury (WI) 640 |
| 13001 | 679 AAM | Bristol FS6G | 196.026 | H33/27RD | 9/62 | Wilts & Dorset, Salisbury (WI) 641 |
| 13002 | 680 AAM | Bristol FS6G | 196.027 | H33/27RD | 10/62 | Wilts & Dorset, Salisbury (WI) 642 |
| 13003 | 681 AAM | Bristol FS6G | 205.004 | H33/27RD | 11/62 | Wilts & Dorset, Salisbury (WI) 643 |
| 13004 | 682 AAM | Bristol FS6G | 205.005 | H33/27RD | 11/62 | Wilts & Dorset, Salisbury (WI) 644 |
| 13005 | *683 AAM | Bristol FS6G | 205.006 | H33/27RD | 11/62 | Wilts & Dorset, Salisbury (WI) 645 |
| 13006 | 684 AAM | Bristol FS6G | 205.007 | H33/27RD | 11/62 | Wilts & Dorset, Salisbury (WI) 646 |
| 13007 | 685 AAM | Bristol FS6G | 205.008 | H33/27RD | 11/62 | Wilts & Dorset, Salisbury (WI) 647 |
| 13008 | 686 AAM | Bristol FS6B | 205.021 | H33/27RD | 12/62 | Wilts & Dorset, Salisbury (WI) 648 |
| 13009 | 687 AAM | Bristol FS6B | 205.022 | H33/27RD | 12/62 | Wilts & Dorset, Salisbury (WI) 649 |
| 13010 | 688 AAM | Bristol FS6B | 205.023 | H33/27RD | 12/62 | Wilts & Dorset, Salisbury (WI) 650 |
| 13011 | 689 AAM | Bristol FS6B | 205.037 | H33/27R | 5/63 | Wilts & Dorset, Salisbury (WI) 651 |
| 13012 | 690 AAM | Bristol FS6B | 205.038 | H33/27R | 5/63 | Wilts & Dorset, Salisbury (WI) 652 |
| 13013 | *691 AAM | Bristol FS6B | 205.039 | H33/27R | 5/63 | Wilts & Dorset, Salisbury (WI) 653 |
| 13014 | *692 AAM | Bristol FS6B | 205.040 | H33/27R | 5/63 | Wilts & Dorset, Salisbury (WI) 654 |
| 13015 | 693 AAM | Bristol FS6B | 205.041 | H33/27R | 5/63 | Wilts & Dorset, Salisbury (WI) 655 |
| 13016 | *694 AAM | Bristol FS6B | 205.042 | H33/27R | 5/63 | Wilts & Dorset, Salisbury (WI) 656 |
| 13017 | 695 AAM | Bristol FS6B | 205.070 | H33/27R | 7/63 | Wilts & Dorset, Salisbury (WI) 657 |
| 13018 | XPM 45 | Bristol FS6G | 196.053 | H33/27R | 10/62 | Brighton, Hove & District (ES) 45 |
| 13019 | XPM 46 | Bristol FS6B | 196.054 | H33/27R | 10/62 | Brighton, Hove & District (ES) 46 |
| 13020 | XPM 47 | Bristol FS6B | 196.055 | H33/27R | 10/62 | Brighton, Hove & District (ES) 47 |
| 13021 | XPM 48 | Bristol FS6B | 196.056 | H33/27R | 10/62 | Brighton, Hove & District (ES) 48 |
| 13022 | XPM 49 | Bristol FS6B | 196.057 | H33/27R | 10/62 | Brighton, Hove & District (ES) 49 |
| 13023 | XPM 50 | Bristol FS6B | 196.058 | H33/27R | 10/62 | Brighton, Hove & District (ES) 50 |
| 13024 | 258 DCY | Bristol FSF6B | 197.028 | H34/26F | 11/62 | United Welsh, Swansea (GG) 360 |
| 13025 | 259 DCY | Bristol FSF6B | 197.029 | H34/26F | 11/62 | United Welsh, Swansea (GG) 361 |
| 13026 | 260 DCY | Bristol FSF6G | 197.030 | H34/26F | 11/62 | United Welsh, Swansea (GG) 362 |
| 13027 | 261 DCY | Bristol FSF6G | 197.031 | H34/26F | 11/62 | United Welsh, Swansea (GG) 363 |
| 13028 | 262 DCY | Bristol FSF6G | 197.032 | H34/26F | 11/62 | United Welsh, Swansea (GG) 364 |
| 13029 | 263 DCY | Bristol FSF6G | 197.033 | H34/26F | 11/62 | United Welsh, Swansea (GG) 365 |
| 13030 | 264 DCY | Bristol FSF6G | 197.034 | H34/26F | 11/62 | United Welsh, Swansea (GG) 366 |
| 13031 | 265 DCY | Bristol FSF6G | 197.035 | H34/26F | 11/62 | United Welsh, Swansea (GG) 367 |
| 13032 | 266 DCY | Bristol FSF6G | 197.036 | H34/26F | 11/62 | United Welsh, Swansea (GG) 368 |
| 13033 | 267 DCY | Bristol FSF6G | 197.042 | H34/26F | 11/62 | United Welsh, Swansea (GG) 369 |
| 13034 | 268 DCY | Bristol FSF6G | 197.043 | H34/26F | 11/62 | United Welsh, Swansea (GG) 370 |
| 13035 | 269 DCY | Bristol FSF6G | 197.044 | H34/26F | 11/62 | United Welsh, Swansea (GG) 371 |
| 13036 | 270 DCY | Bristol FSF6B | 197.045 | H34/26F | 11/62 | United Welsh, Swansea (GG) 372 |
| 13037 | 271 DCY | Bristol FSF6B | 197.046 | H34/26F | 11/62 | United Welsh, Swansea (GG) 373 |
| 13038 | 272 DCY | Bristol FSF6B | 197.047 | H34/26F | 11/62 | United Welsh, Swansea (GG) 374 |
| 13039 | 273 DCY | Bristol FSF6B | 197.048 | H34/26F | 11/62 | United Welsh, Swansea (GG) 375 |
| 13040 | 274 DCY | Bristol FSF6B | 197.049 | H34/26F | 11/62 | United Welsh, Swansea (GG) 376 |
| 13041 | 8109 HN | Bristol FSF6B | 197.037 | H34/26F | 9/62 | Durham District (DM) DBL9 |
| 13042 | 8110 HN | Bristol FSF6B | 197.038 | H34/26F | 9/62 | Durham District (DM) DBL10 |
| 13043 | 8111 HN | Bristol FSF6B | 197.039 | H34/26F | 9/62 | Durham District (DM) DBL11 |
| 13044 | 8112 HN | Bristol FSF6B | 197.040 | H34/26F | 10/62 | Durham District (DM) DBL12 |
| 13045 | 8113 HN | Bristol FSF6B | 197.041 | H34/26F | 10/62 | Durham District (DM) DBL13 |
| 13046 | *501 OHU | Bristol FLF6B | 199.032 | H38/32F | 6/62 | Bristol OC (GL) C7056 |
| 13047 | 502 OHU | Bristol FLF6B | 199.033 | H38/32F | 7/62 | Bristol OC (GL) C7057 |

| | | | | | | | |
|---|---|---|---|---|---|---|---|
| 13048 | 503 OHU | Bristol FLF6B | 199.034 | H38/32F | 7/62 | Bristol OC (GL) | C7058 |
| 13049 | 504 OHU | Bristol FLF6B | 199.035 | H38/32F | 7/62 | Bristol OC (GL) | C7059 |
| 13050 | 505 OHU | Bristol FLF6B | 199.036 | H38/32F | 7/62 | Bristol OC (GL) | C7060 |
| 13051 | 514 OHU | Bristol FLF6B | 199.167 | H38/32F | 11/62 | Bristol OC (GL) | C7069 |
| 13052 | 515 OHU | Bristol FLF6B | 199.168 | H38/32F | 11/62 | Bristol OC (GL) | C7070 |
| 13053 | 516 OHU | Bristol FLF6B | 199.169 | H38/32F | 11/62 | Bristol OC (GL) | C7071 |
| 13054 | 517 OHU | Bristol FLF6B | 199.170 | H38/32F | 11/62 | Bristol OC (GL) | C7072 |
| 13055 | 518 OHU | Bristol FLF6B | 199.171 | H38/32F | 11/62 | Bristol OC (GL) | C7073 |
| 13056 | 519 OHU | Bristol FLF6B | 208.028 | H38/32F | 2/63 | Bristol OC (GL) | C7076 |
| 13057 | *520 OHU | Bristol FLF6B | 208.029 | H38/32F | 2/63 | Bristol OC (GL) | C7077 |
| 13058 | 521 OHU | Bristol FLF6B | 208.030 | H38/32F | 2/63 | Bristol OC (GL) | C7078 |
| 13059 | 522 OHU | Bristol FLF6B | 208.031 | H38/32F | 2/63 | Bristol OC (GL) | C7079 |
| 13060 | 523 OHU | Bristol FLF6B | 208.032 | H38/32F | 4/63 | Bristol OC (GL) | C7080 |
| 13061 | 524 OHU | Bristol FLF6B | 210.017 | H38/32F | 3/63 | Bristol OC (GL) | C7081 |
| 13062 | 531 OHU | Bristol FLF6B | 210.022 | H38/32F | 3/63 | Bristol OC (GL) | C7088 |
| 13063 | 532 OHU | Bristol FLF6B | 210.023 | H38/32F | 3/63 | Bristol OC (GL) | C7089 |
| 13064 | 533 OHU | Bristol FLF6B | 210.024 | H38/32F | 3/63 | Bristol OC (GL) | C7090 |
| 13065 | 534 OHU | Bristol FLF6B | 210.025 | H38/32F | 4/63 | Bristol OC (GL) | C7091 |
| 13066 | *535 OHU | Bristol FLF6B | 210.026 | H38/32F | 4/63 | Bristol OC (GL) | C7092 |
| 13067 | 536 OHU | Bristol FLF6B | 210.028 | H38/32F | 4/63 | Bristol OC (GL) | C7093 |
| 13068 | 539 OHU | Bristol FLF6B | 210.029 | H38/32F | 4/63 | Bristol OC (GL) | C7094 |
| 13069 | 540 OHU | Bristol FLF6B | 210.030 | H38/32F | 4/63 | Bristol OC (GL) | C7095 |
| 13070 | 541 OHU | Bristol FLF6B | 210.039 | H38/32F | 4/63 | Bristol OC (GL) | C7096 |
| 13071 | *542 OHU | Bristol FLF6B | 210.040 | H38/32F | 4/63 | Bristol OC (GL) | C7097 |
| 13072 | 543 OHU | Bristol FLF6B | 210.041 | H38/32F | 4/63 | Bristol OC (GL) | C7098 |
| 13073 | 544 OHU | Bristol FLF6B | 210.042 | H38/32F | 4/63 | Bristol OC (GL) | C7099 |
| 13074 | 537 OHU | Bristol FLF6G | 199.194 | H38/32F | 12/62 | Cheltenham District (GL) | 7074 |
| 13075 | *538 OHU | Bristol FLF6G | 199.195 | H38/32F | 12/62 | Cheltenham District (GL) | 7075 |
| 13076 | *506 OHU | Bristol FLF6B | 199.126 | H38/32F | 9/62 | Bristol OC (GL) | 7061 |
| 13077 | 507 OHU | Bristol FLF6B | 199.127 | H38/32F | 9/62 | Bristol OC (GL) | 7062 |
| 13078 | 508 OHU | Bristol FLF6B | 199.128 | H38/32F | 9/62 | Bristol OC (GL) | 7063 |
| 13079 | 509 OHU | Bristol FLF6B | 199.129 | H38/32F | 9/62 | Bristol OC (GL) | 7064 |
| 13080 | 510 OHU | Bristol FLF6B | 199.130 | H38/32F | 9/62 | Bristol OC (GL) | 7065 |
| 13081 | 525 OHU | Bristol FLF6G | 210.006 | H38/32F | 2/63 | Bristol OC (GL) | 7082 |
| 13082 | 526 OHU | Bristol FLF6G | 210.007 | H38/32F | 3/63 | Bristol OC (GL) | 7083 |
| 13083 | 527 OHU | Bristol FLF6G | 210.008 | H38/32F | 3/63 | Bristol OC (GL) | 7084 |
| 13084 | 528 OHU | Bristol FLF6G | 210.009 | H38/32F | 3/63 | Bristol OC (GL) | 7085 |
| 13085 | 529 OHU | Bristol FLF6G | 210.015 | H38/32F | 3/63 | Bristol OC (GL) | 7086 |
| 13086 | *530 OHU | Bristol FLF6G | 210.016 | H38/32F | 3/63 | Bristol OC (GL) | 7087 |
| 13087 | 545 OHU | Bristol FLF6B | 210.043 | H38/32F | 5/63 | Bristol OC (GL) | 7100 |
| 13088 | 546 OHU | Bristol FLF6B | 210.044 | H38/32F | 5/63 | Bristol OC (GL) | 7101 |
| 13089 | *547 OHU | Bristol FLF6B | 210.045 | H38/32F | 4/63 | Bristol OC (GL) | 7102 |
| 13090 | 548 OHU | Bristol FLF6B | 210.046 | H38/32F | 4/63 | Bristol OC (GL) | 7103 |
| 13091 | 549 OHU | Bristol FLF6B | 210.047 | H38/32F | 4/63 | Bristol OC (GL) | 7104 |
| 13092 | 550 OHU | Bristol FLF6G | 210.060 | H38/32F | 5/63 | Bristol OC (GL) | 7105 |
| 13093 | 551 OHU | Bristol FLF6G | 210.061 | H38/32F | 5/63 | Bristol OC (GL) | 7106 |
| 13094 | 552 OHU | Bristol FLF6G | 210.062 | H38/32F | 5/63 | Bristol OC (GL) | 7107 |
| 13095 | *511 OHU | Bristol FLF6G | 199.156 | H38/32F | 10/62 | Bristol OC (GL) | G7066 |
| 13096 | 512 OHU | Bristol FLF6G | 199.157 | H38/32F | 10/62 | Bristol OC (GL) | G7067 |
| 13097 | 513 OHU | Bristol FLF6G | 199.158 | H38/32F | 10/62 | Bristol OC (GL) | G7068 |
| 13098 | 137 YFM | Bristol FLF6B | 199.081 | H38/32F | 7/62 | Crosville MS, Chester (CH) | DFB104 |
| 13099 | 138 YFM | Bristol FLF6B | 199.082 | H38/32F | 7/62 | Crosville MS, Chester (CH) | DFB105 |
| 13100 | 139 YFM | Bristol FLF6B | 199.083 | H38/32F | 7/62 | Crosville MS, Chester (CH) | DFB106 |
| 13101 | 140 YFM | Bristol FLF6B | 199.089 | H38/32F | 7/62 | Crosville MS, Chester (CH) | DFB107 |
| 13102 | 141 YFM | Bristol FLF6B | 199.090 | H38/32F | 7/62 | Crosville MS, Chester (CH) | DFB108 |
| 13103 | 142 YFM | Bristol FLF6B | 199.187 | CH37/18F | 12/62 | Crosville MS, Chester (CH) | DFB109 |
| 13104 | 143 YFM | Bristol FLF6B | 199.188 | CH37/18F | 12/62 | Crosville MS, Chester (CH) | DFB110 |
| 13105 | 144 YFM | Bristol FLF6B | 199.189 | CH37/18F | 12/62 | Crosville MS, Chester (CH) | DFB111 |
| 13106 | 145 YFM | Bristol FLF6B | 199.190 | CH37/18F | 12/62 | Crosville MS, Chester (CH) | DFB112 |
| 13107 | 146 YFM | Bristol FLF6B | 199.191 | CH37/18F | 12/62 | Crosville MS, Chester (CH) | DFB113 |
| 13108 | *147 YFM | Bristol FLF6B | 210.036 | H38/32F | 4/63 | Crosville MS, Chester (CH) | DFB114 |
| 13109 | 148 YFM | Bristol FLF6B | 210.037 | H38/32F | 4/63 | Crosville MS, Chester (CH) | DFB115 |
| 13110 | 149 YFM | Bristol FLF6B | 210.038 | H38/32F | 4/63 | Crosville MS, Chester (CH) | DFB116 |
| 13111 | 150 YFM | Bristol FLF6B | 210.052 | H38/32F | 5/63 | Crosville MS, Chester (CH) | DFB117 |

| | | | | | | | |
|---|---|---|---|---|---|---|---|
| 13112 | 151 YFM | Bristol FLF6B | 210.053 | H38/32F | 5/63 | Crosville MS, Chester (CH) DFB118 |
| 13113 | 709 GRM | Bristol FLF6G | 199.105 | H38/32F | 8/62 | Cumberland MS, Whitehaven (CU) 515 |
| 13114 | 710 GRM | Bristol FLF6G | 199.106 | H38/32F | 8/62 | Cumberland MS, Whitehaven (CU) 516 |
| 13115 | 711 GRM | Bristol FLF6G | 199.107 | H38/32F | 8/62 | Cumberland MS, Whitehaven (CU) 517 |
| 13116 | 712 GRM | Bristol FLF6G | 199.166 | H38/32F | 11/62 | Cumberland MS, Whitehaven (CU) 518 |
| 13117 | 713 GRM | Bristol FLF6G | 199.192 | H38/32F | 12/62 | Cumberland MS, Whitehaven (CU) 519 |
| 13118 | 714 GRM | Bristol FLF6G | 199.193 | H38/32F | 12/62 | Cumberland MS, Whitehaven (CU) 520 |
| 13119 | 556 BNG | Bristol FL6B | 198.001 | H38/32R | 12/62 | Eastern Counties, Norwich (NK) LFL56 |
| 13120 | 557 BNG | Bristol FL6B | 198.002 | H38/32R | 12/62 | Eastern Counties, Norwich (NK) LFL57 |
| 13121 *558 BNG | | Bristol FL6B | 198.003 | H38/32R | 1/63 | Eastern Counties, Norwich (NK) LFL58 |
| 13122 | 559 BPW | Bristol FL6B | 198.010 | H38/32R | 1/63 | Eastern Counties, Norwich (NK) LFL59 |
| 13123 | 560 BPW | Bristol FL6B | 198.011 | H38/32R | 1/63 | Eastern Counties, Norwich (NK) LFL60 |
| 13124 | 561 BPW | Bristol FL6B | 198.012 | H38/32R | 1/63 | Eastern Counties, Norwich (NK) LFL61 |
| 13125 | EOO 579 | Bristol FLF6G | 199.043 | H38/32F | 6/62 | Eastern National, Chelmsford (EX) 1611 |
| 13126 | EOO 580 | Bristol FLF6G | 199.044 | H38/32F | 6/62 | Eastern National, Chelmsford (EX) 1612 |
| 13127 | EOO 581 | Bristol FLF6G | 199.045 | H38/32F | 6/62 | Eastern National, Chelmsford (EX) 1613 |
| 13128 | EOO 582 | Bristol FLF6G | 199.050 | H38/32F | 6/62 | Eastern National, Chelmsford (EX) 1614 |
| 13129 | EOO 583 | Bristol FLF6G | 199.051 | H38/32F | 6/62 | Eastern National, Chelmsford (EX) 1615 |
| 13130 | EOO 584 | Bristol FLF6B | 199.134 | H38/32F | 8/62 | Eastern National, Chelmsford (EX) 1616 |
| 13131 | EOO 585 | Bristol FLF6B | 199.135 | H38/32F | 8/62 | Eastern National, Chelmsford (EX) 1617 |
| 13132 | EOO 586 | Bristol FLF6B | 199.136 | H38/32F | 8/62 | Eastern National, Chelmsford (EX) 1618 |
| 13133 | EOO 587 | Bristol FLF6B | 199.137 | H38/32F | 8/62 | Eastern National, Chelmsford (EX) 1619 |
| 13134 | EOO 588 | Bristol FLF6B | 199.138 | H38/32F | 9/62 | Eastern National, Chelmsford (EX) 1620 |
| 13135 | EOO 589 | Bristol FLF6B | 199.145 | H38/32F | 8/62 | Eastern National, Chelmsford (EX) 1621 |
| 13136 | EOO 590 | Bristol FLF6B | 199.146 | H38/32F | 9/62 | Eastern National, Chelmsford (EX) 1622 |
| 13137 | EOO 591 | Bristol FLF6B | 199.147 | H38/32F | 9/62 | Eastern National, Chelmsford (EX) 1623 |
| 13138 | JWC 710 | Bristol FLF6G | 199.172 | H38/32F | 11/62 | Eastern National, Chelmsford (EX) 1624 |
| 13139 *JWC 711 | | Bristol FLF6G | 199.173 | H38/32F | 11/62 | Eastern National, Chelmsford (EX) 1625 |
| 13140 | JWC 712 | Bristol FLF6G | 199.174 | H38/32F | 11/62 | Eastern National, Chelmsford (EX) 1626 |
| 13141 | JWC 713 | Bristol FLF6G | 199.175 | H38/32F | 11/62 | Eastern National, Chelmsford (EX) 1627 |
| 13142 | JWC 714 | Bristol FLF6G | 199.176 | H38/32F | 11/62 | Eastern National, Chelmsford (EX) 1628 |
| 13143 | JWC 715 | Bristol FLF6G | 199.177 | H38/32F | 11/62 | Eastern National, Chelmsford (EX) 1629 |
| 13144 | JWC 716 | Bristol FLF6G | 199.178 | H38/32F | 11/62 | Eastern National, Chelmsford (EX) 1630 |
| 13145 | JWC 717 | Bristol FLF6B | 199.196 | H38/32F | 2/63 | Eastern National, Chelmsford (EX) 1631 |
| 13146 | JWC 718 | Bristol FLF6B | 199.197 | H38/32F | 2/63 | Eastern National, Chelmsford (EX) 1632 |
| 13147 | RWC 600 | Bristol FLF6G | 208.033 | H38/32F | 1/63 | Eastern National, Chelmsford (EX) 1633 |
| 13148 | RWC 601 | Bristol FLF6G | 208.034 | H38/32F | 2/63 | Eastern National, Chelmsford (EX) 1634 |
| 13149 *RWC 607 | | Bristol FLF6B | 210.013 | CH37/18F | 4/63 | Eastern National, Chelmsford (EX) 1640 |
| 13150 | RWC 608 | Bristol FLF6B | 210.014 | CH37/18F | 4/63 | Eastern National, Chelmsford (EX) 1641 |
| 13151 | RWC 604 | Bristol FLF6B | 210.010 | CH37/18F | 3/63 | Eastern National, Chelmsford (EX) 1637 |
| 13152 *RWC 605 | | Bristol FLF6B | 210.011 | H38/32F | 1/63 | Eastern National, Chelmsford (EX) 1638 |
| 13153 | RWC 606 | Bristol FLF6B | 210.012 | H38/32F | 4/63 | Eastern National, Chelmsford (EX) 1639 |
| 13154 | RWC 602 | Bristol FLF6G | 208.035 | H38/32F | 2/63 | Eastern National, Chelmsford (EX) 1635 |
| 13155 | RWC 603 | Bristol FLF6G | 208.036 | H38/32F | 2/63 | Eastern National, Chelmsford (EX) 1636 |
| 13156 | VWC 45 | Bristol FLF6B | 210.031 | H38/32F | 3/63 | Eastern National, Chelmsford (EX) 1642 |
| 13157 | VWC 46 | Bristol FLF6B | 210.032 | H38/32F | 3/63 | Eastern National, Chelmsford (EX) 1643 |
| 13158 | VWC 47 | Bristol FLF6B | 210.033 | H38/32F | 3/63 | Eastern National, Chelmsford (EX) 1644 |
| 13159 | VWC 48 | Bristol FLF6B | 210.034 | H38/32F | 5/63 | Eastern National, Chelmsford (EX) 1645 |
| 13160 | VWC 49 | Bristol FLF6B | 210.035 | H38/32F | 3/63 | Eastern National, Chelmsford (EX) 1646 |
| 13161 *VWC 52 | | Bristol FLF6G | 210.056 | H38/32F | 4/63 | Eastern National, Chelmsford (EX) 1649 |
| 13162 | VWC 50 | Bristol FLF6G | 210.048 | H38/32F | 3/63 | Eastern National, Chelmsford (EX) 1647 |
| 13163 | VWC 53 | Bristol FLF6G | 210.057 | H38/32F | 4/63 | Eastern National, Chelmsford (EX) 1650 |
| 13164 | VWC 51 | Bristol FLF6G | 210.049 | H38/32F | 4/63 | Eastern National, Chelmsford (EX) 1648 |
| 13165 | TVL 308 | Bristol FLF6G | 199.148 | H38/32F | 7/62 | Lincolnshire RCC, Lincoln (LC) 2507 |
| 13166 | TVL 309 | Bristol FLF6G | 199.149 | H38/32F | 7/62 | Lincolnshire RCC, Lincoln (LC) 2508 |
| 13167 | TVL 310 | Bristol FLF6G | 199.150 | H38/32F | 7/62 | Lincolnshire RCC, Lincoln (LC) 2509 |
| 13168 | 241 MNN | Bristol FLF6G | 199.139 | H38/32F | 10/62 | Mansfield District (NG) 545 |
| 13169 | 242 MNN | Bristol FLF6G | 199.140 | H38/32F | 10/62 | Mansfield District (NG) 546 |
| 13170 | 243 MNN | Bristol FLF6G | 199.184 | H38/32F | 12/62 | Mansfield District (NG) 547 |
| 13171 *244 MNN | | Bristol FLF6G | 199.185 | H38/32F | 2/63 | Mansfield District (NG) 548 |
| 13172 | 245 MNN | Bristol FLF6G | 208.003 | H38/32F | 2/63 | Mansfield District (NG) 549 |
| 13173 | 246 MNN | Bristol FLF6B | 208.004 | H38/32F | 2/63 | Mansfield District (NG) 550 |
| 13174 | 247 MNN | Bristol FLF6B | 208.019 | H38/32F | 2/63 | Mansfield District (NG) 551 |
| 13175 | 248 MNN | Bristol FLF6B | 208.020 | H38/32F | 2/63 | Mansfield District (NG) 552 |

| | | | | | | | |
|---|---|---|---|---|---|---|---|
| 13176 | 250 MNN | Bristol FLF6B | 210.058 | H38/32F | 4/63 | Mansfield District (NG) 554 |
| 13177 | 249 MNN | Bristol FLF6B | 210.050 | H38/32F | 4/63 | Mansfield District (NG) 553 |
| 13178 | 526 VRB | Bristol FLF6B | 199.094 | H38/32F | 8/62 | Midland General, Langley Mill (DE) 511 |
| 13179 | *527 VRB | Bristol FLF6B | 199.095 | H38/32F | 8/62 | Midland General, Langley Mill (DE) 512 |
| 13180 | *528 VRB | Bristol FLF6B | 199.096 | H38/32F | 8/62 | Midland General, Langley Mill (DE) 513 |
| 13181 | 529 VRB | Bristol FLF6B | 199.097 | H38/32F | 8/62 | Midland General, Langley Mill (DE) 514 |
| 13182 | *530 VRB | Bristol FLF6B | 199.098 | H38/32F | 8/62 | Midland General, Langley Mill (DE) 515 |
| 13183 | *531 VRB | Bristol FLF6G | 208.012 | H38/32F | 2/63 | Midland General, Langley Mill (DE) 516 |
| 13184 | 532 VRB | Bristol FLF6G | 208.013 | H38/32F | 2/63 | Midland General, Langley Mill (DE) 517 |
| 13185 | *533 VRB | Bristol FLF6G | 208.014 | H38/32F | 2/63 | Midland General, Langley Mill (DE) 518 |
| 13186 | *534 VRB | Bristol FLF6G | 208.015 | H38/32F | 2/63 | Midland General, Langley Mill (DE) 519 |
| 13187 | *535 VRB | Bristol FLF6G | 208.016 | H38/32F | 2/63 | Midland General, Langley Mill (DE) 520 |
| 13188 | 536 BBL | Bristol FLF6B | 199.108 | H38/32F | 8/62 | Thames Valley, Reading (BE) 868 |
| 13189 | 537 BBL | Bristol FLF6B | 199.109 | H38/32F | 8/62 | Thames Valley, Reading (BE) 869 |
| 13190 | 538 BBL | Bristol FLF6B | 199.141 | H38/32F | 9/62 | Thames Valley, Reading (BE) 870 |
| 13191 | 539 BBL | Bristol FLF6B | 199.142 | H38/32F | 9/62 | Thames Valley, Reading (BE) 871 |
| 13192 | 540 BBL | Bristol FLF6B | 199.151 | H38/32F | 9/62 | Thames Valley, Reading (BE) 872 |
| 13193 | 541 BBL | Bristol FLF6B | 199.152 | H38/32F | 9/62 | Thames Valley, Reading (BE) 873 |
| 13194 | 542 BBL | Bristol FLF6B | 199.153 | H38/32F | 9/62 | Thames Valley, Reading (BE) 874 |
| 13195 | 543 BBL | Bristol FLF6G | 208.001 | H38/32F | 12/62 | Thames Valley, Reading (BE) 875 |
| 13196 | 544 BBL | Bristol FLF6G | 208.002 | H38/32F | 12/62 | Thames Valley, Reading (BE) 876 |
| 13197 | 545 BBL | Bristol FLF6G | 208.037 | H38/32F | 1/63 | Thames Valley, Reading (BE) 877 |
| 13198 | 546 BBL | Bristol FLF6G | 208.038 | H38/32F | 1/63 | Thames Valley, Reading (BE) 878 |
| 13199 | 547 BBL | Bristol FLF6G | 208.039 | H38/32F | 2/63 | Thames Valley, Reading (BE) 879 |
| 13200 | 548 BBL | Bristol FLF6G | 210.027 | H38/32F | 3/63 | Thames Valley, Reading (BE) 880 |
| 13201 | 549 BBL | Bristol FLF6G | 210.059 | H38/32F | 3/63 | Thames Valley, Reading (BE) 881 |
| 13202 | 7112 HN | Bristol FLF6B | 199.052 | H38/32F | 7/62 | United AS, Darlington (DM) BL112 |
| 13203 | 7113 HN | Bristol FLF6B | 199.053 | H38/32F | 7/62 | United AS, Darlington (DM) BL113 |
| 13204 | 7114 HN | Bristol FLF6B | 199.054 | H38/32F | 7/62 | United AS, Darlington (DM) BL114 |
| 13205 | 7115 HN | Bristol FLF6B | 199.060 | H38/32F | 7/62 | United AS, Darlington (DM) BL115 |
| 13206 | 7116 HN | Bristol FLF6B | 199.061 | H38/32F | 7/62 | United AS, Darlington (DM) BL116 |
| 13207 | 7117 HN | Bristol FLF6B | 199.159 | H38/32F | 10/62 | United AS, Darlington (DM) BL117 |
| 13208 | 7118 HN | Bristol FLF6B | 199.160 | H38/32F | 10/62 | United AS, Darlington (DM) BL118 |
| 13209 | 7119 HN | Bristol FLF6B | 199.161 | H38/32F | 10/62 | United AS, Darlington (DM) BL119 |
| 13210 | 7120 HN | Bristol FLF6B | 199.179 | H38/32F | 11/62 | United AS, Darlington (DM) BL120 |
| 13211 | 7121 HN | Bristol FLF6B | 199.180 | H38/32F | 11/62 | United AS, Darlington (DM) BL121 |
| 13212 | 7122 HN | Bristol FLF6B | 199.181 | H38/32F | 12/62 | United AS, Darlington (DM) BL122 |
| 13213 | 7123 HN | Bristol FLF6B | 208.005 | H38/32F | 2/63 | United AS, Darlington (DM) BL123 |
| 13214 | 7124 HN | Bristol FLF6B | 208.006 | H38/32F | 2/63 | United AS, Darlington (DM) BL124 |
| 13215 | 7125 HN | Bristol FLF6B | 208.007 | H38/32F | 2/63 | United AS, Darlington (DM) BL125 |
| 13216 | 7126 HN | Bristol FLF6B | 208.008 | H38/32F | 2/63 | United AS, Darlington (DM) BL126 |
| 13217 | 7127 HN | Bristol FLF6B | 208.017 | H38/32F | 2/63 | United AS, Darlington (DM) BL127 |
| 13218 | 7128 HN | Bristol FLF6B | 208.018 | H38/32F | 2/63 | United AS, Darlington (DM) BL128 |
| 13219 | 7129 HN | Bristol FLF6B | 208.040 | H38/32F | 3/63 | United AS, Darlington (DM) BL129 |
| 13220 | 7130 HN | Bristol FLF6B | 210.001 | H38/32F | 1/63 | United AS, Darlington (DM) BL130 |
| 13221 | 7131 HN | Bristol FLF6B | 210.002 | H38/32F | 3/63 | United AS, Darlington (DM) BL131 |
| 13222 | 7132 HN | Bristol FLF6B | 210.018 | H38/32F | 3/63 | United AS, Darlington (DM) BL132 |
| 13223 | 7133 HN | Bristol FLF6B | 210.019 | H38/32F | 3/63 | United AS, Darlington (DM) BL133 |
| 13224 | 7134 HN | Bristol FLF6B | 210.020 | H38/32F | 3/63 | United AS, Darlington (DM) BL134 |
| 13225 | 7135 HN | Bristol FLF6B | 210.054 | H38/32F | 4/63 | United AS, Darlington (DM) BL135 |
| 13226 | 7136 HN | Bristol FLF6B | 210.055 | H38/32F | 5/63 | United AS, Darlington (DM) BL136 |
| 13227 | 629 BRP | Bristol FLF6B | 199.116 | H38/32F | 9/62 | United Counties, Northampton (NO) 629 |
| 13228 | 630 BRP | Bristol FLF6B | 199.117 | H38/32F | 9/62 | United Counties, Northampton (NO) 630 |
| 13229 | 631 BRP | Bristol FLF6B | 199.118 | H38/32F | 9/62 | United Counties, Northampton (NO) 631 |
| 13230 | 632 BRP | Bristol FLF6B | 199.119 | H38/32F | 9/62 | United Counties, Northampton (NO) 632 |
| 13231 | 633 BRP | Bristol FLF6B | 199.120 | H38/32F | 9/62 | United Counties, Northampton (NO) 633 |
| 13232 | 634 BRP | Bristol FLF6B | 199.198 | H38/32F | 11/62 | United Counties, Northampton (NO) 634 |
| 13233 | 635 BRP | Bristol FLF6B | 199.199 | H38/32F | 11/62 | United Counties, Northampton (NO) 635 |
| 13234 | 636 BRP | Bristol FLF6B | 199.200 | H38/32F | 11/62 | United Counties, Northampton (NO) 636 |
| 13235 | 637 BRP | Bristol FLF6B | 208.021 | H38/32F | 2/63 | United Counties, Northampton (NO) 637 |
| 13236 | 638 BRP | Bristol FLF6B | 208.022 | H38/32F | 2/63 | United Counties, Northampton (NO) 638 |
| 13237 | 639 BRP | Bristol FLF6B | 210.051 | H38/32F | 5/63 | United Counties, Northampton (NO) 639 |
| 13238 | 640 BRP | Bristol FLF6B | 210.063 | H38/32F | 5/63 | United Counties, Northampton (NO) 640 |
| 13239 | 801 KDV | Bristol FLF6B | 199.062 | H38/32F | 7/62 | Western National, Exeter (DN) 1996 |

| | | | | | | |
|---|---|---|---|---|---|---|
| 13240 | 802 KDV | Bristol FLF6B | 199.063 | H38/32F | 7/62 | Western National, Exeter (DN) 1997 |
| 13241 | *803 KDV | Bristol FLF6B | 199.064 | H38/32F | 7/62 | Western National, Exeter (DN) 1998 |
| 13242 | *804 KDV | Bristol FLF6B | 199.072 | H38/32F | 7/62 | Western National, Exeter (DN) 1999 |
| 13243 | 805 KDV | Bristol FLF6B | 199.073 | H38/32F | 7/62 | Western National, Exeter (DN) 2000 |
| 13244 | 806 KDV | Bristol FLF6G | 199.131 | H38/32F | 9/62 | Western National, Exeter (DN) 2001 |
| 13245 | *807 KDV | Bristol FLF6G | 199.162 | H38/32F | 10/62 | Western National, Exeter (DN) 2002 |
| 13246 | 808 KDV | Bristol FLF6G | 199.163 | H38/32F | 10/62 | Western National, Exeter (DN) 2003 |
| 13247 | 809 KDV | Bristol FLF6B | 199.182 | H38/32F | 11/62 | Western National, Exeter (DN) 2004 |
| 13248 | 810 KDV | Bristol FLF6B | 199.183 | H38/32F | 11/62 | Western National, Exeter (DN) 2005 |
| 13249 | *811 KDV | Bristol FLF6B | 199.186 | H38/32F | 11/62 | Western National, Exeter (DN) 2006 |
| 13250 | 812 KDV | Bristol FLF6G | 208.009 | H38/32F | 1/63 | Western National, Exeter (DN) 2007 |
| 13251 | *813 KDV | Bristol FLF6G | 208.010 | H38/32F | 1/63 | Western National, Exeter (DN) 2008 |
| 13252 | 814 KDV | Bristol FLF6B | 208.011 | H38/32F | 1/63 | Western National, Exeter (DN) 2009 |
| 13253 | 815 KDV | Bristol FLF6B | 208.023 | H38/32F | 1/63 | Western National, Exeter (DN) 2010 |
| 13254 | 816 KDV | Bristol FLF6B | 208.024 | H38/30F | 1/63 | Western National, Exeter (DN) 2011 |
| 13255 | 817 KDV | Bristol FLF6B | 208.025 | H38/30F | 4/63 | Western National, Exeter (DN) 2012 |
| 13256 | *818 KDV | Bristol FLF6B | 208.026 | H38/30F | 4/63 | Western National, Exeter (DN) 2013 |
| 13257 | 819 KDV | Bristol FLF6B | 208.027 | H38/30F | 4/63 | Western National, Exeter (DN) 2014 |
| 13258 | 820 KDV | Bristol FLF6B | 210.003 | H38/30F | 4/63 | Western National, Exeter (DN) 2015 |
| 13259 | 821 KDV | Bristol FLF6B | 210.004 | H38/30F | 4/63 | Western National, Exeter (DN) 2016 |
| 13260 | 822 KDV | Bristol FLF6G | 210.005 | H38/30F | 5/63 | Western National, Exeter (DN) 2017 |
| 13261 | 823 KDV | Bristol FLF6G | 210.021 | H38/30F | 5/63 | Western National, Exeter (DN) 2018 |
| 13262 | 824 KDV | Bristol FLF6G | 210.064 | H38/30F | 5/63 | Western National, Exeter (DN) 2019 |
| 13263 | 7682 LJ | Bristol FL6G | 198.004 | H38/28RD | 12/62 | Hants & Dorset, Bournemouth (HA) 1482 |
| 13264 | 7683 LJ | Bristol FL6G | 198.005 | H38/28RD | 12/62 | Hants & Dorset, Bournemouth (HA) 1483 |
| 13265 | 7684 LJ | Bristol FL6G | 198.006 | H38/28RD | 12/62 | Hants & Dorset, Bournemouth (HA) 1484 |
| 13266 | 7685 LJ | Bristol FL6G | 198.007 | H38/28RD | 12/62 | Hants & Dorset, Bournemouth (HA) 1485 |
| 13267 | *7686 LJ | Bristol FL6G | 198.008 | H38/28RD | 12/62 | Hants & Dorset, Bournemouth (HA) 1486 |
| 13268 | 7687 LJ | Bristol FL6G | 198.009 | H38/28RD | 12/62 | Hants & Dorset, Bournemouth (HA) 1487 |
| 13269 | *MOO 178 | Bristol MW5G | 195.052 | DP41F | 7/62 | Eastern National, Chelmsford (EX) 565 |
| 13270 | *MOO 179 | Bristol MW5G | 195.053 | DP41F | 7/62 | Eastern National, Chelmsford (EX) 566 |
| 13271 | *MOO 973 | Bristol MW5G | 195.054 | DP41F | 7/62 | Eastern National, Chelmsford (EX) 567 |
| 13272 | *MOO 974 | Bristol MW5G | 195.058 | DP41F | 7/62 | Eastern National, Chelmsford (EX) 568 |
| 13273 | *MOO 975 | Bristol MW5G | 195.059 | DP41F | 7/62 | Eastern National, Chelmsford (EX) 569 |
| 13274 | *MOO 976 | Bristol MW5G | 195.060 | DP41F | 8/62 | Eastern National, Chelmsford (EX) 570 |
| 13275 | 7541 HN | Bristol MW6G | 195.064 | DP41F | 10/62 | United AS, Darlington (DM) BUE541 |
| 13276 | 7542 HN | Bristol MW6G | 195.065 | DP41F | 10/62 | United AS, Darlington (DM) BUE542 |
| 13277 | 7543 HN | Bristol MW6G | 195.066 | DP41F | 10/62 | United AS, Darlington (DM) BUE543 |
| 13278 | 7544 HN | Bristol MW6G | 195.078 | DP41F | 10/62 | United AS, Darlington (DM) BUE544 |
| 13279 | 7545 HN | Bristol MW6G | 195.079 | DP41F | 10/62 | United AS, Darlington (DM) BUE545 |
| 13280 | 8663 HN | Bristol MW5G | 195.104 | B45F | 11/62 | United AS, Darlington (DM) BU663 |
| 13281 | 8664 HN | Bristol MW5G | 195.105 | B45F | 11/62 | United AS, Darlington (DM) BU664 |
| 13282 | 8665 HN | Bristol MW5G | 195.111 | B45F | 11/62 | United AS, Darlington (DM) BU665 |
| 13283 | 8666 HN | Bristol MW5G | 195.116 | B45F | 11/62 | United AS, Darlington (DM) BU666 |
| 13284 | 8667 HN | Bristol MW5G | 195.117 | B45F | 11/62 | United AS, Darlington (DM) BU667 |
| 13285 | 7432 HN | Bristol MW6G | 195.090 | DP41F | 9/62 | Durham District (DM) DBE32 |
| 13286 | 7433 HN | Bristol MW6G | 195.091 | DP41F | 9/62 | Durham District (DM) DBE33 |
| 13287 | 7434 HN | Bristol MW6G | 195.092 | DP41F | 9/62 | Durham District (DM) DBE34 |
| 13288 | 7435 HN | Bristol MW6G | 195.095 | DP41F | 9/62 | Durham District (DM) DBE35 |
| 13289 | 147 BRP | Bristol MW6G | 195.071 | DP41F | 7/62 | United Counties, Northampton (NO) 147 |
| 13290 | 148 BRP | Bristol MW6G | 195.072 | DP41F | 7/62 | United Counties, Northampton (NO) 148 |
| 13291 | 149 BRP | Bristol MW6G | 195.073 | DP41F | 7/62 | United Counties, Northampton (NO) 149 |
| 13292 | 150 BRP | Bristol MW6G | 195.085 | DP41F | 7/62 | United Counties, Northampton (NO) 150 |
| 13293 | 151 BRP | Bristol MW6G | 195.086 | DP41F | 7/62 | United Counties, Northampton (NO) 151 |
| 13294 | 152 BRP | Bristol MW6G | 195.087 | DP41F | 10/62 | United Counties, Northampton (NO) 152 |
| 13295 | 153 BRP | Bristol MW6G | 195.096 | DP41F | 10/62 | United Counties, Northampton (NO) 153 |
| 13296 | 154 BRP | Bristol MW6G | 195.097 | DP41F | 10/62 | United Counties, Northampton (NO) 154 |
| 13297 | 155 BRP | Bristol MW6G | 195.109 | DP41F | 11/62 | United Counties, Northampton (NO) 155 |
| 13298 | 156 BRP | Bristol MW6G | 195.110 | DP41F | 10/62 | United Counties, Northampton (NO) 156 |
| 13299 | 157 BRP | Bristol MW6G | 195.113 | DP41F | 11/62 | United Counties, Northampton (NO) 157 |
| 13300 | 158 BRP | Bristol MW6G | 195.114 | DP41F | 11/62 | United Counties, Northampton (NO) 158 |
| 13301 | 159 BRP | Bristol MW6G | 195.115 | DP41F | 11/62 | United Counties, Northampton (NO) 159 |
| 13302 | 160 BRP | Bristol MW6G | 195.124 | DP41F | 11/62 | United Counties, Northampton (NO) 160 |
| 13303 | 869 RAE | Bristol MW5G | 195.123 | B45F | 11/62 | Bristol OC (GL) 2554 |

| | | | | | | |
|---|---|---|---|---|---|---|
| 13304 | 870 RAE | Bristol MW5G | 195.125 | B45F | 11/62 | Bristol OC (GL) 2555 |
| 13305 | 871 RAE | Bristol MW5G | 195.126 | B45F | 12/62 | Bristol OC (GL) 2556 |
| 13306 | 872 RAE | Bristol MW5G | 195.127 | B45F | 12/62 | Bristol OC (GL) 2557 |
| 13307 | 873 RAE | Bristol MW5G | 195.128 | B45F | 12/62 | Bristol OC (GL) 2558 |
| 13308 | 874 RAE | Bristol MW5G | 195.129 | B45F | 12/62 | Bristol OC (GL) 2559 |
| 13309 | 875 RAE | Bristol MW5G | 195.141 | B45F | 12/62 | Bristol OC (GL) 2560 |
| 13310 | 876 RAE | Bristol MW5G | 195.142 | B45F | 12/62 | Bristol OC (GL) 2561 |
| 13311 | 877 RAE | Bristol MW5G | 195.143 | B45F | 2/63 | Bristol OC (GL) 2562 |
| 13312 | *878 RAE | Bristol MW5G | 195.144 | B45F | 3/63 | Bristol OC (GL) 2018 |
| 13313 | 879 RAE | Bristol MW5G | 195.145 | B45F | 2/63 | Bristol OC (GL) 2564 |
| 13314 | 880 RAE | Bristol MW5G | 195.146 | B45F | 3/63 | Bristol OC (GL) 2565 |
| 13315 | *921 RAE | Bristol MW5G | 195.165 | B45F | 3/63 | Bristol OC (GL) 2019 |
| 13316 | *922 RAE | Bristol MW5G | 195.166 | B45F | 3/63 | Bristol OC (GL) 2020 |
| 13317 | 923 RAE | Bristol MW5G | 195.167 | B45F | 3/63 | Bristol OC (GL) 2566 |
| 13318 | 924 RAE | Bristol MW5G | 195.168 | B45F | 3/63 | Bristol OC (GL) 2567 |
| 13319 | *925 RAE | Bristol MW5G | 195.169 | B45F | 4/63 | Bristol OC (GL) 2021 |
| 13320 | *926 RAE | Bristol MW5G | 195.170 | B45F | 4/63 | Bristol OC (GL) 2022 |
| 13321 | 927 RAE | Bristol MW5G | 204.089 | B45F | 6/63 | Bristol OC (GL) 2568 |
| 13322 | 928 RAE | Bristol MW5G | 213.001 | B45F | 6/63 | Bristol OC (GL) 2569 |
| 13323 | 929 RAE | Bristol MW5G | 213.027 | B45F | 6/63 | Bristol OC (GL) 2570 |
| 13324 | 930 RAE | Bristol MW5G | 213.028 | B45F | 7/63 | Bristol OC (GL) 2571 |
| 13325 | 931 RAE | Bristol MW5G | 213.029 | B45F | 7/63 | Bristol OC (GL) 2572 |
| 13326 | 932 RAE | Bristol MW5G | 213.030 | B45F | 7/63 | Bristol OC (GL) 2573 |
| 13327 | 933 RAE | Bristol MW5G | 213.031 | B45F | 7/63 | Bristol OC (GL) 2574 |
| 13328 | 934 RAE | Bristol MW5G | 213.039 | B45F | 7/63 | Bristol OC (GL) 2575 |
| 13329 | 935 RAE | Bristol MW5G | 213.040 | B45F | 7/63 | Bristol OC (GL) 2576 |
| 13330 | 936 RAE | Bristol MW5G | 213.041 | B45F | 7/63 | Bristol OC (GL) 2577 |
| 13331 | 937 RAE | Bristol MW5G | 213.048 | B45F | 8/63 | Bristol OC (GL) 2578 |
| 13332 | 938 RAE | Bristol MW5G | 213.049 | B45F | 8/63 | Bristol OC (GL) 2579 |
| 13333 | *939 RAE | Bristol MW5G | 213.050 | B45F | 7/63 | Bristol OC (GL) 2023 |
| 13334 | 940 RAE | Bristol MW5G | 213.051 | B45F | 8/63 | Bristol OC (GL) 2580 |
| 13335 | 941 RAE | Bristol MW5G | 213.052 | B45F | 8/63 | Bristol OC (GL) 2581 |
| 13336 | 942 RAE | Bristol MW5G | 213.053 | B45F | 8/63 | Bristol OC (GL) 2582 |
| 13337 | 943 RAE | Bristol MW5G | 213.066 | B45F | 8/63 | Bristol OC (GL) 2583 |
| 13338 | 944 RAE | Bristol MW5G | 213.067 | B45F | 8/63 | Bristol OC (GL) 2584 |
| 13339 | 945 RAE | Bristol MW5G | 213.068 | B45F | 9/63 | Bristol OC (GL) 2585 |
| 13340 | 946 RAE | Bristol MW5G | 213.069 | B45F | 9/63 | Bristol OC (GL) 2586 |
| 13341 | 947 RAE | Bristol MW5G | 213.070 | B45F | 9/63 | Bristol OC (GL) 2587 |
| 13342 | 1215 FM | Bristol MW6G | 195.136 | B41F | 1/63 | Crosville MS, Chester (CH) SMG437 |
| 13343 | 1216 FM | Bristol MW6G | 195.137 | B41F | 1/63 | Crosville MS, Chester (CH) SMG438 |
| 13344 | 1217 FM | Bristol MW6G | 195.138 | B41F | 1/63 | Crosville MS, Chester (CH) SMG439 |
| 13345 | 1218 FM | Bristol MW6G | 195.139 | B41F | 1/63 | Crosville MS, Chester (CH) SMG440 |
| 13346 | 1219 FM | Bristol MW6G | 195.140 | B41F | 1/63 | Crosville MS, Chester (CH) SMG441 |
| 13347 | 1221 FM | Bristol MW6G | 195.177 | B41F | 4/63 | Crosville MS, Chester (CH) SMG442 |
| 13348 | 1222 FM | Bristol MW6G | 195.178 | B41F | 4/63 | Crosville MS, Chester (CH) SMG443 |
| 13349 | 1223 FM | Bristol MW6G | 195.179 | B41F | 5/63 | Crosville MS, Chester (CH) SMG444 |
| 13350 | 1224 FM | Bristol MW6G | 195.180 | B41F | 5/63 | Crosville MS, Chester (CH) SMG445 |
| 13351 | 1225 FM | Bristol MW6G | 195.181 | B41F | 5/63 | Crosville MS, Chester (CH) SMG446 |
| 13352 | 1226 FM | Bristol MW6G | 195.182 | B41F | 6/63 | Crosville MS, Chester (CH) SMG447 |
| 13353 | 1227 FM | Bristol MW6G | 195.183 | B41F | 6/63 | Crosville MS, Chester (CH) SMG448 |
| 13354 | 1228 FM | Bristol MW6G | 213.002 | B41F | 6/63 | Crosville MS, Chester (CH) SMG449 |
| 13355 | 1229 FM | Bristol MW6G | 213.003 | B41F | 6/63 | Crosville MS, Chester (CH) SMG450 |
| 13356 | 1231 FM | Bristol MW6G | 213.004 | B41F | 6/63 | Crosville MS, Chester (CH) SMG451 |
| 13357 | 1232 FM | Bristol MW6G | 213.005 | B45F | 6/63 | Crosville MS, Chester (CH) SMG452 |
| 13358 | 1233 FM | Bristol MW6G | 213.054 | B45F | 8/63 | Crosville MS, Chester (CH) SMG453 |
| 13359 | 1234 FM | Bristol MW6G | 213.055 | B45F | 8/63 | Crosville MS, Chester (CH) SMG454 |
| 13360 | 1235 FM | Bristol MW6G | 213.056 | B45F | 8/63 | Crosville MS, Chester (CH) SMG455 |
| 13361 | 1236 FM | Bristol MW6G | 213.057 | B45F | 8/63 | Crosville MS, Chester (CH) SMG456 |
| 13362 | 1237 FM | Bristol MW6G | 213.058 | B45F | 8/63 | Crosville MS, Chester (CH) SMG457 |
| 13363 | 1238 FM | Bristol MW6G | 213.059 | B45F | 8/63 | Crosville MS, Chester (CH) SMG458 |
| 13364 | 1239 FM | Bristol MW6G | 213.082 | B45F | 9/63 | Crosville MS, Chester (CH) SMG459 |
| 13365 | 1241 FM | Bristol MW6G | 213.083 | B45F | 9/63 | Crosville MS, Chester (CH) SMG460 |
| 13366 | 1242 FM | Bristol MW6G | 213.084 | B45F | 9/63 | Crosville MS, Chester (CH) SMG461 |
| 13367 | 1243 FM | Bristol MW6G | 213.085 | B45F | 10/63 | Crosville MS, Chester (CH) SMG462 |

| | | | | | | | |
|---|---|---|---|---|---|---|---|
| 13368 | 1244 FM | Bristol MW6G | 213.088 | B45F | 10/63 | Crosville MS, Chester (CH) SMG463 |
| 13369 | 1245 FM | Bristol MW6G | 213.089 | B45F | 10/63 | Crosville MS, Chester (CH) SMG464 |
| 13370 | 1246 FM | Bristol MW6G | 213.090 | B45F | 2/64 | Crosville MS, Chester (CH) SMG465 |
| 13371 | 1247 FM | Bristol MW6G | 213.091 | B45F | 3/64 | Crosville MS, Chester (CH) SMG466 |
| 13372 | 471 BNG | Bristol MW5G | 195.153 | B45F | 2/63 | Eastern Counties, Norwich (NK) LM471 |
| 13373 | 472 BNG | Bristol MW5G | 195.154 | B45F | 2/63 | Eastern Counties, Norwich (NK) LM472 |
| 13374 | 473 BNG | Bristol MW5G | 195.155 | B45F | 2/63 | Eastern Counties, Norwich (NK) LM473 |
| 13375 | 474 BNG | Bristol MW5G | 195.156 | B45F | 2/63 | Eastern Counties, Norwich (NK) LM474 |
| 13376 | 475 BNG | Bristol MW5G | 195.157 | B45F | 2/63 | Eastern Counties, Norwich (NK) LM475 |
| 13377 | 476 BNG | Bristol MW5G | 195.158 | B45F | 2/63 | Eastern Counties, Norwich (NK) LM476 |
| 13378 | 477 BPW | Bristol MW5G | 195.194 | B45F | 4/63 | Eastern Counties, Norwich (NK) LM477 |
| 13379 | 478 BPW | Bristol MW5G | 195.195 | B45F | 4/63 | Eastern Counties, Norwich (NK) LM478 |
| 13380 | 479 BVF | Bristol MW5G | 195.196 | B45F | 4/63 | Eastern Counties, Norwich (NK) LM479 |
| 13381 | 480 BVF | Bristol MW5G | 195.197 | B45F | 5/63 | Eastern Counties, Norwich (NK) LM480 |
| 13382 | 481 BVF | Bristol MW5G | 195.198 | B45F | 5/63 | Eastern Counties, Norwich (NK) LM481 |
| 13383 | 482 BVF | Bristol MW5G | 195.199 | B45F | 5/63 | Eastern Counties, Norwich (NK) LM482 |
| 13384 | 483 DAH | Bristol MW5G | 213.060 | B45F | 7/63 | Eastern Counties, Norwich (NK) LM483 |
| 13385 | 484 DAH | Bristol MW5G | 213.061 | B45F | 7/63 | Eastern Counties, Norwich (NK) LM484 |
| 13386 | 485 DAH | Bristol MW5G | 213.062 | B45F | 7/63 | Eastern Counties, Norwich (NK) LM485 |
| 13387 | 486 DAH | Bristol MW5G | 213.063 | B45F | 7/63 | Eastern Counties, Norwich (NK) LM486 |
| 13388 | 487 DAH | Bristol MW5G | 213.064 | B45F | 7/63 | Eastern Counties, Norwich (NK) LM487 |
| 13389 | 488 DAH | Bristol MW5G | 213.065 | B45F | 7/63 | Eastern Counties, Norwich (NK) LM488 |
| 13390 | 489 DPW | Bristol MW5G | 213.092 | B45F | 9/63 | Eastern Counties, Norwich (NK) LM489 |
| 13391 | 490 DPW | Bristol MW5G | 213.097 | B45F | 11/63 | Eastern Counties, Norwich (NK) LM490 |
| 13392 | 491 DPW | Bristol MW5G | 213.098 | B45F | 11/63 | Eastern Counties, Norwich (NK) LM491 |
| 13393 | 492 DPW | Bristol MW5G | 213.099 | B45F | 11/63 | Eastern Counties, Norwich (NK) LM492 |
| 13394 | OWC 606 | Bristol MW5G | 195.184 | B45F | 3/63 | Eastern National, Chelmsford (EX) 571 |
| 13395 | OWC 607 | Bristol MW5G | 195.185 | B45F | 3/63 | Eastern National, Chelmsford (EX) 572 |
| 13396 | OWC 608 | Bristol MW5G | 195.186 | B45F | 3/63 | Eastern National, Chelmsford (EX) 573 |
| 13397 | OWC 609 | Bristol MW5G | 195.187 | B45F | 3/63 | Eastern National, Chelmsford (EX) 574 |
| 13398 | OWC 610 | Bristol MW5G | 213.032 | B45F | 6/63 | Eastern National, Chelmsford (EX) 575 |
| 13399 | OWC 611 | Bristol MW5G | 213.033 | B45F | 6/63 | Eastern National, Chelmsford (EX) 576 |
| 13400 | 11 FAX | Bristol MW6G | 195.171 | B45F | 3/63 | Red & White, Chepstow (MH) U162 |
| 13401 | 12 FAX | Bristol MW6G | 195.172 | B45F | 3/63 | Red & White, Chepstow (MH) U262 |
| 13402 | 13 FAX | Bristol MW6G | 195.173 | B45F | 3/63 | Red & White, Chepstow (MH) U362 |
| 13403 | 14 FAX | Bristol MW6G | 195.174 | B45F | 3/63 | Red & White, Chepstow (MH) U462 |
| 13404 | 15 FAX | Bristol MW6G | 195.175 | B45F | 3/63 | Red & White, Chepstow (MH) U562 |
| 13405 | 16 FAX | Bristol MW6G | 195.176 | B45F | 3/63 | Red & White, Chepstow (MH) U662 |
| 13406 | 17 FAX | Bristol MW6G | 213.071 | B45F | 8/63 | Red & White, Chepstow (MH) U762 |
| 13407 | 18 FAX | Bristol MW6G | 213.078 | B45F | 9/63 | Red & White, Chepstow (MH) U862 |
| 13408 | 19 FAX | Bristol MW6G | 213.079 | B45F | 9/63 | Red & White, Chepstow (MH) U962 |
| 13409 | 20 FAX | Bristol MW6G | 213.080 | B45F | 9/63 | Red & White, Chepstow (MH) U1062 |
| 13410 | 21 FAX | Bristol MW6G | 213.086 | B45F | 10/63 | Red & White, Chepstow (MH) U1162 |
| 13411 | 22 FAX | Bristol MW6G | 213.087 | B45F | 10/63 | Red & White, Chepstow (MH) U1262 |
| 13412 | 751 MDV | Bristol MW5G | 204.075 | B45F | 5/63 | Western National, Exeter (DN) 2620 |
| 13413 | 752 MDV | Bristol MW5G | 204.076 | B45F | 6/63 | Western National, Exeter (DN) 2621 |
| 13414 | 753 MDV | Bristol MW5G | 204.077 | B45F | 6/63 | Western National, Exeter (DN) 2622 |
| 13415 | 754 MDV | Bristol MW5G | 213.100 | B45F | 11/63 | Western National, Exeter (DN) 2623 |
| 13416 | 755 MDV | Bristol MW5G | 213.101 | B45F | 11/63 | Western National, Exeter (DN) 2624 |
| 13417 | 756 MDV | Bristol MW5G | 213.102 | B45F | 11/63 | Western National, Exeter (DN) 2625 |
| 13418 | 8668 HN | Bristol MW6G | 195.130 | B45F | 12/62 | United AS, Darlington (DM) BU668 |
| 13419 | 8669 HN | Bristol MW6G | 195.131 | B45F | 12/62 | United AS, Darlington (DM) BU669 |
| 13420 | 8670 HN | Bristol MW6G | 195.132 | B45F | 1/63 | United AS, Darlington (DM) BU670 |
| 13421 | 8671 HN | Bristol MW6G | 195.133 | B45F | 1/63 | United AS, Darlington (DM) BU671 |
| 13422 | 8672 HN | Bristol MW6G | 195.134 | B45F | 1/63 | United AS, Darlington (DM) BU672 |
| 13423 | 8673 HN | Bristol MW6G | 195.135 | B45F | 1/63 | United AS, Darlington (DM) BU673 |
| 13424 | 8674 HN | Bristol MW6G | 195.147 | B45F | 2/63 | United AS, Darlington (DM) BU674 |
| 13425 | 8675 HN | Bristol MW6G | 195.148 | B45F | 2/63 | United AS, Darlington (DM) BU675 |
| 13426 | 8676 HN | Bristol MW6G | 195.149 | B45F | 2/63 | United AS, Darlington (DM) BU676 |
| 13427 | 8677 HN | Bristol MW6G | 195.150 | B45F | 2/63 | United AS, Darlington (DM) BU677 |
| 13428 | 8678 HN | Bristol MW6G | 195.151 | B45F | 2/63 | United AS, Darlington (DM) BU678 |
| 13429 | 8679 HN | Bristol MW6G | 195.152 | B45F | 2/63 | United AS, Darlington (DM) BU679 |
| 13430 | 8680 HN | Bristol MW6G | 195.188 | B45F | 4/63 | United AS, Darlington (DM) BU680 |
| 13431 | 8681 HN | Bristol MW6G | 195.189 | B45F | 4/63 | United AS, Darlington (DM) BU681 |

| | | | | | | | |
|---|---|---|---|---|---|---|---|
| 13432 | 8682 HN | Bristol MW6G | 195.190 | B45F | 4/63 | United AS, Darlington (DM) BU682 |
| 13433 | 8683 HN | Bristol MW6G | 195.191 | B45F | 5/63 | United AS, Darlington (DM) BU683 |
| 13434 | 8684 HN | Bristol MW6G | 195.192 | B45F | 4/63 | United AS, Darlington (DM) BU684 |
| 13435 | 8685 HN | Bristol MW6G | 195.193 | B45F | 4/63 | United AS, Darlington (DM) BU685 |
| 13436 | 8686 HN | Bristol MW6G | 204.088 | B45F | 5/63 | United AS, Darlington (DM) BU686 |
| 13437 | 8687 HN | Bristol MW6G | 213.006 | B45F | 6/63 | United AS, Darlington (DM) BU687 |
| 13438 | 8688 HN | Bristol MW6G | 213.007 | B45F | 7/63 | United AS, Darlington (DM) BU688 |
| 13439 | 8689 HN | Bristol MW6G | 213.008 | B45F | 6/63 | United AS, Darlington (DM) BU689 |
| 13440 | 8690 HN | Bristol MW6G | 213.009 | B45F | 7/63 | United AS, Darlington (DM) BU690 |
| 13441 | 8691 HN | Bristol MW6G | 213.010 | B45F | 7/63 | United AS, Darlington (DM) BU691 |
| 13442 | 8692 HN | Bristol MW6G | 213.011 | B45F | 7/63 | United AS, Darlington (DM) BU692 |
| 13443 | 8693 HN | Bristol MW6G | 213.012 | B45F | 7/63 | United AS, Darlington (DM) BU693 |
| 13444 | 8694 HN | Bristol MW6G | 213.034 | B45F | 7/63 | United AS, Darlington (DM) BU694 |
| 13445 | 8695 HN | Bristol MW6G | 213.072 | B45F | 9/63 | United AS, Darlington (DM) BU695 |
| 13446 | 8696 HN | Bristol MW6G | 213.073 | B45F | 9/63 | United AS, Darlington (DM) BU696 |
| 13447 | 8697 HN | Bristol MW6G | 213.074 | B45F | 9/63 | United AS, Darlington (DM) BU697 |
| 13448 | 8698 HN | Bristol MW6G | 213.075 | B45F | 9/63 | United AS, Darlington (DM) BU698 |
| 13449 | 8699 HN | Bristol MW6G | 213.076 | B45F | 9/63 | United AS, Darlington (DM) BU699 |
| 13450 | 8700 HN | Bristol MW6G | 213.077 | B45F | 9/63 | United AS, Darlington (DM) BU700 |
| 13451 | 8701 HN | Bristol MW6G | 213.081 | B45F | 10/63 | United AS, Darlington (DM) BU701 |
| 13452 | | | | | | Not built |
| 13453 | 9636 HN | Bristol MW6G | 204.078 | B45F | 5/63 | Durham District (DM) DBU36 |
| 13454 | 9637 HN | Bristol MW6G | 204.084 | B45F | 5/63 | Durham District (DM) DBU37 |
| 13455 | 9638 HN | Bristol MW6G | 213.035 | B45F | 6/63 | Durham District (DM) DBU38 |
| 13456 | 9639 HN | Bristol MW6G | 213.036 | B45F | 6/63 | Durham District (DM) DBU39 |
| 13457 | 9640 HN | Bristol MW6G | 213.037 | B45F | 6/63 | Durham District (DM) DBU40 |
| 13458 | 9641 HN | Bristol MW6G | 213.038 | B45F | 6/63 | Durham District (DM) DBU41 |
| 13459 | 821 BWY | Bristol MW6G | 195.159 | B45F | 2/63 | West Yorkshire RCC, Harrogate (WR) SMG13 |
| 13460 | 822 BWY | Bristol MW6G | 195.160 | B45F | 2/63 | West Yorkshire RCC, Harrogate (WR) SMG14 |
| 13461 | 823 BWY | Bristol MW6G | 195.161 | B45F | 2/63 | West Yorkshire RCC, Harrogate (WR) SMG15 |
| 13462 | 824 BWY | Bristol MW6G | 195.162 | B45F | 2/63 | West Yorkshire RCC, Harrogate (WR) SMG16 |
| 13463 | 825 BWY | Bristol MW6G | 195.163 | B45F | 2/63 | West Yorkshire RCC, Harrogate (WR) SMG17 |
| 13464 | 827 BWY | Bristol MW6G | 195.164 | B45F | 2/63 | West Yorkshire RCC, Harrogate (WR) SMG18 |
| 13465 | 827 BWY | Bristol MW6G | 195.200 | B45F | 5/63 | West Yorkshire RCC, Harrogate (WR) SMG19 |
| 13466 | 828 BWY | Bristol MW6G | 204.085 | B45F | 6/63 | West Yorkshire RCC, Harrogate (WR) SMG20 |
| 13467 | 829 BWY | Bristol MW6G | 204.086 | B45F | 6/63 | West Yorkshire RCC, Harrogate (WR) SMG21 |
| 13468 | 830 BWY | Bristol MW6G | 204.087 | B45F | 7/63 | West Yorkshire RCC, Harrogate (WR) SMG22 |
| 13469 | 831 BWY | Bristol MW6G | 213.042 | B45F | 7/63 | West Yorkshire RCC, Harrogate (WR) SMG23 |
| 13470 | 832 BWY | Bristol MW6G | 213.043 | B45F | 7/63 | West Yorkshire RCC, Harrogate (WR) SMG24 |
| 13471 | 833 BWY | Bristol MW6G | 213.044 | B45F | 7/63 | West Yorkshire RCC, Harrogate (WR) SMG25 |
| 13472 | 834 BWY | Bristol MW6G | 213.045 | B45F | 7/63 | West Yorkshire RCC, Harrogate (WR) SMG26 |
| 13473 | 835 BWY | Bristol MW6G | 213.046 | B45F | 8/63 | West Yorkshire RCC, Harrogate (WR) SMG27 |
| 13474 | 836 BWY | Bristol MW6G | 213.047 | B45F | 8/63 | West Yorkshire RCC, Harrogate (WR) SMG28 |
| 13475 | 837 BWY | Bristol MW6G | 213.093 | B45F | 11/63 | West Yorkshire RCC, Harrogate (WR) SMG29 |
| 13476 | 838 BWY | Bristol MW6G | 213.094 | B45F | 11/63 | West Yorkshire RCC, Harrogate (WR) SMG30 |
| 13477 | 839 BWY | Bristol MW6G | 213.095 | B45F | 11/63 | West Yorkshire RCC, Harrogate (WR) SMG31 |
| 13478 | 840 BWY | Bristol MW6G | 213.096 | B45F | 11/63 | West Yorkshire RCC, Harrogate (WR) SMG32 |
| 13479 | 861 RAE | Bristol SUS4A | 190.049 | B30F | 11/62 | Bristol OC (GL) 300 |
| 13480 | 862 RAE | Bristol SUS4A | 190.050 | B30F | 11/62 | Bristol OC (GL) 301 |
| 13481 | 863 RAE | Bristol SUS4A | 190.051 | B30F | 11/62 | Bristol OC (GL) 302 |
| 13482 | 807 BWR | Bristol SUL4A | 190.052 | B36F | 11/62 | West Yorkshire RCC, Harrogate (WR) SMA1 |
| 13483 | 808 BWR | Bristol SUL4A | 190.053 | B36F | 11/62 | West Yorkshire RCC, Harrogate (WR) SMA2 |
| 13484 | 809 BWR | Bristol SUL4A | 190.054 | B36F | 11/62 | West Yorkshire RCC, Harrogate (WR) SMA3 |
| 13485 | 810 BWR | Bristol SUL4A | 190.055 | B36F | 11/62 | West Yorkshire RCC, Harrogate (WR) SMA4 |
| 13486 | 811 BWR | Bristol SUL4A | 190.056 | B36F | 11/62 | West Yorkshire RCC, Harrogate (WR) SMA5 |
| 13487 | 812 BWR | Bristol SUL4A | 190.057 | B36F | 11/62 | West Yorkshire RCC, Harrogate (WR) SMA6 |
| 13488 | *KEL 406 | Bristol L6G Reb | 73.125 | FB39F | 4/62 | Hants & Dorset, Bournemouth (HA) 678 |
| 13489 | *KEL 407 | Bristol L6G Reb | 73.126 | FB39F | 4/62 | Hants & Dorset, Bournemouth (HA) 679 |
| 13490 | *KEL 408 | Bristol L6G Reb | 73.127 | FB39F | 4/62 | Hants & Dorset, Bournemouth (HA) 680 |
| 13491 | *KEL 409 | Bristol L6G Reb | 73.129 | FB39F | 5/62 | Hants & Dorset, Bournemouth (HA) 681 |
| 13492 | *KEL 410 | Bristol L6G Reb | 73.128 | FB39F | 5/62 | Hants & Dorset, Bournemouth (HA) 682 |
| 13493 | *KEL 411 | Bristol L6G Reb | 73.130 | FB39F | 5/62 | Hants & Dorset, Bournemouth (HA) 683 |
| 13494 | YWS 870 | Bristol FLF6G | 199.012 | H38/32F | 4/62 | Scottish Omnibuses, Edinburgh (MN) AA870 |
| 13495 | YWS 871 | Bristol FLF6G | 199.013 | H38/32F | 4/62 | Scottish Omnibuses, Edinburgh (MN) AA871 |

| 13496 | YWS 872 | Bristol FLF6G | 199.014 | H38/32F | 4/62 | Scottish Omnibuses, Edinburgh (MN) AA872 |
|---|---|---|---|---|---|---|
| 13497 | YWS 873 | Bristol FLF6G | 199.015 | H38/32F | 4/62 | Scottish Omnibuses, Edinburgh (MN) AA873 |
| 13498 | YWS 874 | Bristol FLF6G | 199.016 | H38/32F | 4/62 | Scottish Omnibuses, Edinburgh (MN) AA874 |
| 13499 | YWS 875 | Bristol FLF6G | 199.017 | H38/32F | 4/62 | Scottish Omnibuses, Edinburgh (MN) AA875 |
| 13500 | YWS 876 | Bristol FLF6G | 199.018 | H38/32F | 4/62 | Scottish Omnibuses, Edinburgh (MN) AA876 |
| 13501 | YWS 877 | Bristol FLF6G | 199.019 | H38/32F | 4/62 | Scottish Omnibuses, Edinburgh (MN) AA877 |
| 13502 | YWS 878 | Bristol FLF6G | 199.020 | H38/32F | 4/62 | Scottish Omnibuses, Edinburgh (MN) AA878 |
| 13503 | YWS 879 | Bristol FLF6G | 199.021 | H38/32F | 4/62 | Scottish Omnibuses, Edinburgh (MN) AA879 |
| 13504 | YWS 880 | Bristol FLF6G | 199.028 | H38/32F | 5/62 | Scottish Omnibuses, Edinburgh (MN) AA880 |
| 13505 | YWS 881 | Bristol FLF6G | 199.029 | H38/32F | 5/62 | Scottish Omnibuses, Edinburgh (MN) AA881 |
| 13506 | YWS 882 | Bristol FLF6G | 199.030 | H38/32F | 5/62 | Scottish Omnibuses, Edinburgh (MN) AA882 |
| 13507 | YWS 883 | Bristol FLF6G | 199.065 | H38/32F | 5/62 | Scottish Omnibuses, Edinburgh (MN) AA883 |
| 13508 | YWS 884 | Bristol FLF6G | 199.066 | H38/32F | 6/62 | Scottish Omnibuses, Edinburgh (MN) AA884 |
| 13509 | YWS 885 | Bristol FLF6G | 199.067 | H38/32F | 6/62 | Scottish Omnibuses, Edinburgh (MN) AA885 |
| 13510 | YWS 886 | Bristol FLF6G | 199.068 | H38/32F | 6/62 | Scottish Omnibuses, Edinburgh (MN) AA886 |
| 13511 | YWS 887 | Bristol FLF6G | 199.086 | H38/32F | 6/62 | Scottish Omnibuses, Edinburgh (MN) AA887 |
| 13512 | YWS 888 | Bristol FLF6G | 199.087 | H38/32F | 6/62 | Scottish Omnibuses, Edinburgh (MN) AA888 |
| 13513 | YWS 889 | Bristol FLF6G | 199.088 | H38/32F | 6/62 | Scottish Omnibuses, Edinburgh (MN) AA889 |
| 13514 | YWS 890 | Bristol FLF6G | 199.091 | H38/32F | 6/62 | Scottish Omnibuses, Edinburgh (MN) AA890 |
| 13515 | YWS 891 | Bristol FLF6G | 199.092 | H38/32F | 6/62 | Scottish Omnibuses, Edinburgh (MN) AA891 |
| 13516 | YWS 892 | Bristol FLF6G | 199.093 | H38/32F | 6/62 | Scottish Omnibuses, Edinburgh (MN) AA892 |
| 13517 | YWS 893 | Bristol FLF6G | 199.110 | H38/32F | 6/62 | Scottish Omnibuses, Edinburgh (MN) AA893 |
| 13518 | YWS 894 | Bristol FLF6G | 199.111 | H38/32F | 6/62 | Scottish Omnibuses, Edinburgh (MN) AA894 |
| 13519 | DGM 430 | Bristol FSF6G | 179.049 | H34/26F | 3/62 | Central SMT, Motherwell (LK) B130 |
| 13520 | DGM 431 | Bristol FSF6G | 179.050 | H34/26F | 3/62 | Central SMT, Motherwell (LK) B131 |
| 13521 | DGM 432 | Bristol FSF6G | 179.055 | H34/26F | 3/62 | Central SMT, Motherwell (LK) B132 |
| 13522 | DGM 433 | Bristol FSF6G | 179.056 | H34/26F | 3/62 | Central SMT, Motherwell (LK) B133 |
| 13523 | DGM 434 | Bristol FSF6G | 179.057 | H34/26F | 3/62 | Central SMT, Motherwell (LK) B134 |
| 13524 | DGM 435 | Bristol FSF6G | 179.058 | H34/26F | 3/62 | Central SMT, Motherwell (LK) B135 |
| 13525 | DGM 436 | Bristol FSF6G | 179.063 | H34/26F | 3/62 | Central SMT, Motherwell (LK) B136 |
| 13526 | DGM 437 | Bristol FSF6G | 179.064 | H34/26F | 3/62 | Central SMT, Motherwell (LK) B137 |
| 13527 | DGM 438 | Bristol FSF6G | 179.065 | H34/26F | 3/62 | Central SMT, Motherwell (LK) B138 |
| 13528 | DGM 439 | Bristol FSF6G | 179.066 | H34/26F | 3/62 | Central SMT, Motherwell (LK) B139 |
| 13529 | DGM 440 | Bristol FSF6G | 179.068 | H34/26F | 3/62 | Central SMT, Motherwell (LK) B140 |
| 13530 | DGM 441 | Bristol FSF6G | 179.070 | H34/26F | 3/62 | Central SMT, Motherwell (LK) B141 |
| 13531 | DGM 442 | Bristol FSF6G | 179.071 | H34/26F | 3/62 | Central SMT, Motherwell (LK) B142 |
| 13532 | DGM 443 | Bristol FSF6G | 179.072 | H34/26F | 3/62 | Central SMT, Motherwell (LK) B143 |
| 13533 | DGM 445 | Bristol FSF6G | 179.073 | H34/26F | 3/62 | Central SMT, Motherwell (LK) B145 |
| 13534 | DGM 444 | Bristol FSF6G | 179.069 | H34/26F | 4/62 | Central SMT, Motherwell (LK) B144 |
| 13535 | DGM 446 | Bristol FSF6G | 179.074 | H34/26F | 4/62 | Central SMT, Motherwell (LK) B146 |
| 13536 | DGM 447 | Bristol FSF6G | 197.005 | H34/26F | 4/62 | Central SMT, Motherwell (LK) B147 |
| 13537 | DGM 448 | Bristol FSF6G | 197.006 | H34/26F | 4/62 | Central SMT, Motherwell (LK) B148 |
| 13538 | DGM 449 | Bristol FSF6G | 197.007 | H34/26F | 4/62 | Central SMT, Motherwell (LK) B149 |
| 13539 | DGM 450 | Bristol FSF6G | 197.008 | H34/26F | 4/62 | Central SMT, Motherwell (LK) B150 |
| 13540 | DGM 451 | Bristol FSF6G | 197.009 | H34/26F | 4/62 | Central SMT, Motherwell (LK) B151 |
| 13541 | DGM 452 | Bristol FSF6G | 197.010 | H34/26F | 4/62 | Central SMT, Motherwell (LK) B152 |
| 13542 | DGM 453 | Bristol FSF6G | 197.011 | H34/26F | 4/62 | Central SMT, Motherwell (LK) B153 |
| 13543 | DGM 454 | Bristol FSF6G | 197.012 | H34/26F | 4/62 | Central SMT, Motherwell (LK) B154 |
| 13544 | DGM 455 | Bristol FSF6G | 197.013 | H34/26F | 4/62 | Central SMT, Motherwell (LK) B155 |
| 13545 | DGM 456 | Bristol FSF6G | 197.017 | H34/26F | 4/62 | Central SMT, Motherwell (LK) B156 |
| 13546 | DGM 457 | Bristol FSF6G | 197.018 | H34/26F | 4/62 | Central SMT, Motherwell (LK) B157 |
| 13547 | DGM 458 | Bristol FSF6G | 197.019 | H34/26F | 4/62 | Central SMT, Motherwell (LK) B158 |
| 13548 | DGM 459 | Bristol FSF6G | 197.020 | H34/26F | 4/62 | Central SMT, Motherwell (LK) B159 |
| 13549 | TWG 531 | Bristol FLF6G | 199.031 | H38/32F | 5/62 | W Alexander (Midland), Falkirk (SN) MRD161 |
| 13550 | TWG 541 | Bristol FLF6G | 199.037 | H38/32F | 5/62 | W Alexander (Midland), Falkirk (SN) MRD162 |
| 13551 | TWG 542 | Bristol FLF6G | 199.038 | H38/32F | 5/62 | W Alexander (Midland), Falkirk (SN) MRD163 |
| 13552 | TWG 543 | Bristol FLF6G | 199.046 | H38/32F | 5/62 | W Alexander (Midland), Falkirk (SN) MRD164 |
| 13553 | TWG 544 | Bristol FLF6G | 199.047 | H38/32F | 5/62 | W Alexander (Midland), Falkirk (SN) MRD165 |
| 13554 | TWG 545 | Bristol FLF6G | 199.048 | H38/32F | 5/62 | W Alexander (Midland), Falkirk (SN) MRD166 |
| 13555 | TWG 546 | Bristol FLF6G | 199.049 | H38/32F | 5/62 | W Alexander (Midland), Falkirk (SN) MRD167 |
| 13556 | TWG 547 | Bristol FLF6G | 199.069 | H38/32F | 5/62 | W Alexander (Midland), Falkirk (SN) MRD168 |
| 13557 | 7401 SP | Bristol FLF6G | 199.070 | H38/32F | 6/62 | W Alexander (Fife), Kirkcaldy (FE) FRD153 |
| 13558 | 7402 SP | Bristol FLF6G | 199.071 | H38/32F | 6/62 | W Alexander (Fife), Kirkcaldy (FE) FRD154 |
| 13559 | 7403 SP | Bristol FLF6G | 199.074 | H38/32F | 6/62 | W Alexander (Fife), Kirkcaldy (FE) FRD155 |

| | | | | | | | |
|---|---|---|---|---|---|---|---|
| 13560 | 7404 SP | Bristol FLF6G | 199.075 | H38/32F | 6/62 | W Alexander (Fife), Kirkcaldy (FE) FRD156 |
| 13561 | 7405 SP | Bristol FLF6G | 199.076 | H38/32F | 6/62 | W Alexander (Fife), Kirkcaldy (FE) FRD157 |
| 13562 | TWG 548 | Bristol FLF6G | 199.099 | H38/32F | 6/62 | W Alexander (Midland), Falkirk (SN) MRD169 |
| 13563 | TWG 549 | Bristol FLF6G | 199.100 | H38/32F | 6/62 | W Alexander (Midland), Falkirk (SN) MRD170 |
| 13564 | 7406 SP | Bristol FLF6G | 199.101 | H38/32F | 6/62 | W Alexander (Fife), Kirkcaldy (FE) FRD158 |
| 13565 | 7407 SP | Bristol FLF6G | 199.102 | H38/32F | 6/62 | W Alexander (Fife), Kirkcaldy (FE) FRD159 |
| 13566 | 7408 SP | Bristol FLF6G | 199.103 | H38/32F | 6/62 | W Alexander (Fife), Kirkcaldy (FE) FRD160 |
| 13567 | 7409 SP | Bristol FLF6G | 199.104 | H38/32F | 6/62 | W Alexander (Fife), Kirkcaldy (FE) FRD161 |
| 13568 | TWG 550 | Bristol FLF6G | 199.132 | H38/32F | 7/62 | W Alexander (Midland), Falkirk (SN) MRD171 |
| 13569 | TWG 551 | Bristol FLF6G | 199.133 | H38/32F | 7/62 | W Alexander (Midland), Falkirk (SN) MRD172 |
| 13570 | 7410 SP | Bristol FLF6G | 199.143 | H38/32F | 7/62 | W Alexander (Fife), Kirkcaldy (FE) FRD162 |
| 13571 | 7411 SP | Bristol FLF6G | 199.144 | H38/32F | 7/62 | W Alexander (Fife), Kirkcaldy (FE) FRD163 |
| 13572 | 7412 SP | Bristol FLF6G | 199.164 | H38/32F | 7/62 | W Alexander (Fife), Kirkcaldy (FE) FRD164 |
| 13573 | 7413 SP | Bristol FLF6G | 199.165 | H38/32F | 9/62 | W Alexander (Fife), Kirkcaldy (FE) FRD165 |
| 13574 | TCS 159 | Bristol FLF6G | 199.039 | H38/32F | 6/62 | Western SMT, Kilmarnock (AR) B1711 |
| 13575 | TCS 160 | Bristol FLF6G | 199.040 | H38/32F | 6/62 | Western SMT, Kilmarnock (AR) B1712 |
| 13576 | TCS 161 | Bristol FLF6G | 199.041 | H38/32F | 6/62 | Western SMT, Kilmarnock (AR) B1713 |
| 13577 | TCS 162 | Bristol FLF6G | 199.042 | H38/32F | 6/62 | Western SMT, Kilmarnock (AR) B1714 |
| 13578 | TCS 163 | Bristol FLF6G | 199.055 | H38/32F | 6/62 | Western SMT, Kilmarnock (AR) B1715 |
| 13579 | TCS 164 | Bristol FLF6G | 199.056 | H38/32F | 6/62 | Western SMT, Kilmarnock (AR) B1716 |
| 13580 | TCS 165 | Bristol FLF6G | 199.057 | H38/32F | 6/62 | Western SMT, Kilmarnock (AR) B1717 |
| 13581 | TCS 166 | Bristol FLF6G | 199.058 | H38/32F | 6/62 | Western SMT, Kilmarnock (AR) B1718 |
| 13582 | TCS 167 | Bristol FLF6G | 199.059 | H38/32F | 6/62 | Western SMT, Kilmarnock (AR) B1719 |
| 13583 | TCS 168 | Bristol FLF6G | 199.077 | H38/32F | 7/62 | Western SMT, Kilmarnock (AR) B1720 |
| 13584 | TCS 169 | Bristol FLF6G | 199.078 | H38/32F | 7/62 | Western SMT, Kilmarnock (AR) B1721 |
| 13585 | TCS 170 | Bristol FLF6G | 199.079 | H38/32F | 7/62 | Western SMT, Kilmarnock (AR) B1722 |
| 13586 | TCS 171 | Bristol FLF6G | 199.080 | H38/32F | 7/62 | Western SMT, Kilmarnock (AR) B1723 |
| 13587 | TCS 172 | Bristol FLF6G | 199.084 | H38/32F | 7/62 | Western SMT, Kilmarnock (AR) B1724 |
| 13588 | TCS 173 | Bristol FLF6G | 199.085 | H38/32F | 7/62 | Western SMT, Kilmarnock (AR) B1725 |
| 13589 | TCS 174 | Bristol FLF6G | 199.112 | H38/32F | 7/62 | Western SMT, Kilmarnock (AR) B1726 |
| 13590 | TCS 175 | Bristol FLF6G | 199.113 | H38/32F | 8/62 | Western SMT, Kilmarnock (AR) B1727 |
| 13591 *| TCS 176 | Bristol FLF6G | 199.114 | H38/32F | 8/62 | Western SMT, Kilmarnock (AR) B1728 |
| 13592 | TCS 177 | Bristol FLF6G | 199.115 | H38/32F | 8/62 | Western SMT, Kilmarnock (AR) B1729 |
| 13593 | TCS 178 | Bristol FLF6G | 199.121 | H38/32F | 8/62 | Western SMT, Kilmarnock (AR) B1730 |
| 13594 | TCS 179 | Bristol FLF6G | 199.122 | H38/32F | 8/62 | Western SMT, Kilmarnock (AR) B1731 |
| 13595 | TCS 180 | Bristol FLF6G | 199.123 | H38/32F | 8/62 | Western SMT, Kilmarnock (AR) B1732 |
| 13596 *| TCS 181 | Bristol FLF6G | 199.124 | H38/32F | 8/62 | Western SMT, Kilmarnock (AR) B1733 |
| 13597 | TCS 182 | Bristol FLF6G | 199.125 | H38/32F | 8/62 | Western SMT, Kilmarnock (AR) B1734 |
| 13598 | TCS 183 | Bristol FLF6G | 199.154 | H38/32F | 8/62 | Western SMT, Kilmarnock (AR) B1735 |
| 13599 | TCS 184 | Bristol FLF6G | 199.155 | H38/32F | 8/62 | Western SMT, Kilmarnock (AR) B1736 |
| 13600 | 2172 FM | Bristol MW6G | 204.043 | C39F | 3/63 | Crosville MS, Chester (CH) CMG467 |
| 13601 | 2173 FM | Bristol MW6G | 204.044 | C39F | 3/63 | Crosville MS, Chester (CH) CMG468 |
| 13602 | 2174 FM | Bristol MW6G | 204.045 | C39F | 3/63 | Crosville MS, Chester (CH) CMG469 |
| 13603 | 2175 FM | Bristol MW6G | 204.046 | C39F | 3/63 | Crosville MS, Chester (CH) CMG470 |
| 13604 | 2176 FM | Bristol MW6G | 204.047 | C39F | 3/63 | Crosville MS, Chester (CH) CMG471 |
| 13605 | 2177 FM | Bristol MW6G | 204.053 | C39F | 3/63 | Crosville MS, Chester (CH) CMG472 |
| 13606 | 2178 FM | Bristol MW6G | 204.054 | C39F | 4/63 | Crosville MS, Chester (CH) CMG473 |
| 13607 | 2179 FM | Bristol MW6G | 204.055 | C39F | 4/63 | Crosville MS, Chester (CH) CMG474 |
| 13608 | 2181 FM | Bristol MW6G | 204.056 | C39F | 5/63 | Crosville MS, Chester (CH) CMG475 |
| 13609 | 2182 FM | Bristol MW6G | 204.057 | C39F | 4/63 | Crosville MS, Chester (CH) CMG476 |
| 13610 | 2183 FM | Bristol MW6G | 204.063 | C39F | 4/63 | Crosville MS, Chester (CH) CMG477 |
| 13611 | 2184 FM | Bristol MW6G | 204.064 | C39F | 5/63 | Crosville MS, Chester (CH) CMG478 |
| 13612 | 2185 FM | Bristol MW6G | 204.065 | C39F | 5/63 | Crosville MS, Chester (CH) CMG479 |
| 13613 | 2186 FM | Bristol MW6G | 204.066 | C39F | 4/63 | Crosville MS, Chester (CH) CMG480 |
| 13614 | 2187 FM | Bristol MW6G | 204.067 | C39F | 5/63 | Crosville MS, Chester (CH) CMG481 |
| 13615 | 2188 FM | Bristol MW6G | 204.074 | C39F | 5/63 | Crosville MS, Chester (CH) CMG482 |
| 13616 | 2189 FM | Bristol MW6G | 204.079 | C39F | 5/63 | Crosville MS, Chester (CH) CMG483 |
| 13617 | 2191 FM | Bristol MW6G | 204.080 | C39F | 5/63 | Crosville MS, Chester (CH) CMG484 |
| 13618 | 2192 FM | Bristol MW6G | 204.081 | C39F | 5/63 | Crosville MS, Chester (CH) CMG485 |
| 13619 | 2193 FM | Bristol MW6G | 204.082 | C39F | 6/63 | Crosville MS, Chester (CH) CMG486 |
| 13620 | 2194 FM | Bristol MW6G | 213.018 | C39F | 6/63 | Crosville MS, Chester (CH) CMG487 |
| 13621 | 2195 FM | Bristol MW6G | 213.019 | C39F | 6/63 | Crosville MS, Chester (CH) CMG488 |
| 13622 | 2196 FM | Bristol MW6G | 213.020 | C39F | 6/63 | Crosville MS, Chester (CH) CMG489 |
| 13623 | 2197 FM | Bristol MW6G | 213.021 | C39F | 6/63 | Crosville MS, Chester (CH) CMG490 |

| | | | | | | |
|---|---|---|---|---|---|---|
| 13624 | 2198 FM | Bristol MW6G | 213.022 | C39F | 6/63 | Crosville MS, Chester (CH) CMG491 |
| 13625 | 2199 FM | Bristol MW6G | 213.023 | C39F | 6/63 | Crosville MS, Chester (CH) CMG492 |
| 13626 | 5454 FM | Bristol RELH6G | 212.011 | C47F | 1/64 | Crosville MS, Chester (CH) CRG493 |
| 13627 | 5455 FM | Bristol RELH6G | 212.016 | C47F | 1/64 | Crosville MS, Chester (CH) CRG494 |
| 13628 | 5457 FM | Bristol RELH6G | 212.017 | C47F | 2/64 | Crosville MS, Chester (CH) CRG495 |
| 13629 | 5458 FM | Bristol RELH6G | 212.018 | C47F | 2/64 | Crosville MS, Chester (CH) CRG496 |
| 13630 | 816 BNG | Bristol MW6G | 204.009 | C39F | 12/62 | Eastern Counties, Norwich (NK) LS816 |
| 13631 | 817 BNG | Bristol MW6G | 204.010 | C39F | 12/62 | Eastern Counties, Norwich (NK) LS817 |
| 13632 | 818 BNG | Bristol MW6G | 204.011 | C39F | 12/62 | Eastern Counties, Norwich (NK) LS818 |
| 13633 | 819 BNG | Bristol MW6G | 204.012 | C39F | 12/62 | Eastern Counties, Norwich (NK) LS819 |
| 13634 | 820 BNG | Bristol MW6G | 204.018 | C39F | 12/62 | Eastern Counties, Norwich (NK) LS820 |
| 13635 | 821 BNG | Bristol MW6G | 204.019 | C39F | 12/62 | Eastern Counties, Norwich (NK) LS821 |
| 13636 | 822 BNG | Bristol MW6G | 204.020 | C39F | 12/62 | Eastern Counties, Norwich (NK) LS822 |
| 13637 | 823 BNG | Bristol MW6G | 204.021 | C39F | 12/62 | Eastern Counties, Norwich (NK) LS823 |
| 13638 | 2688 RU | Bristol MW6G | 204.068 | C39F | 4/63 | Hants & Dorset, Bournemouth (HA) 888 |
| 13639 | 2689 RU | Bristol MW6G | 204.069 | C39F | 4/63 | Hants & Dorset, Bournemouth (HA) 889 |
| 13640 | 2690 RU | Bristol MW6G | 204.070 | C39F | 4/63 | Hants & Dorset, Bournemouth (HA) 890 |
| 13641 | 2691 RU | Bristol MW6G | 204.071 | C39F | 4/63 | Hants & Dorset, Bournemouth (HA) 891 |
| 13642 | 2692 RU | Bristol MW6G | 204.072 | C39F | 4/63 | Hants & Dorset, Bournemouth (HA) 892 |
| 13643 | 2693 RU | Bristol MW6G | 204.073 | C39F | 4/63 | Hants & Dorset, Bournemouth (HA) 893 |
| 13644 | 370 RNN | Bristol MW6G | 213.014 | C39F | 6/63 | Mansfield District (NG) 287 |
| 13645 | 371 RNN | Bristol MW6G | 213.015 | C39F | 6/63 | Mansfield District (NG) 288 |
| 13646 | 372 RNN | Bristol MW6G | 213.016 | C39F | 6/63 | Mansfield District (NG) 289 |
| 13647 | 373 RNN | Bristol MW6G | 213.017 | C39F | 6/63 | Mansfield District (NG) 290 |
| 13648 | 1378 R | Bristol MW6G | 204.094 | C39F | 5/63 | Midland General, Langley Mill (DE) 281 |
| 13649 | 1379 R | Bristol MW6G | 204.095 | C39F | 5/63 | Midland General, Langley Mill (DE) 282 |
| 13650 | 1380 R | Bristol MW6G | 204.096 | C39F | 5/63 | Midland General, Langley Mill (DE) 283 |
| 13651 | 1381 R | Bristol MW6G | 204.097 | C39F | 5/63 | Midland General, Langley Mill (DE) 284 |
| 13652 | 1382 R | Bristol MW6G | 204.098 | C39F | 5/63 | Midland General, Langley Mill (DE) 285 |
| 13653 | 1383 R | Bristol MW6G | 213.013 | C39F | 6/63 | Midland General, Langley Mill (DE) 286 |
| 13654 | 23 FAX | Bristol MW6G | 204.001 | C39F | 6/63 | Red & White, Chepstow (MH) UC163 |
| 13655 | 24 FAX | Bristol MW6G | 204.002 | C39F | 6/63 | Red & White, Chepstow (MH) UC263 |
| 13656 | 25 FAX | Bristol MW6G | 204.003 | C39F | 6/63 | Red & White, Chepstow (MH) UC363 |
| 13657 | 26 FAX | Bristol MW6G | 204.004 | C39F | 4/63 | Red & White, Chepstow (MH) UC463 |
| 13658 | 27 FAX | Bristol MW6G | 204.005 | C39F | 6/63 | Red & White, Chepstow (MH) UC563 |
| 13659 | 28 FAX | Bristol MW6G | 204.022 | C39F | 4/63 | Red & White, Chepstow (MH) UC663 |
| 13660 | 29 FAX | Bristol MW6G | 204.023 | C39F | 4/63 | Red & White, Chepstow (MH) UC763 |
| 13661 | 30 FAX | Bristol MW6G | 204.024 | C39F | 5/63 | Red & White, Chepstow (MH) UC863 |
| 13662 | 31 FAX | Bristol MW6G | 204.025 | C39F | 6/63 | Red & White, Chepstow (MH) UC963 |
| 13663 | 757 MDV | Bristol MW6G | 204.034 | C39F | 4/63 | Southern National, Exeter (DN) 1408 |
| 13664 | 758 MDV | Bristol MW6G | 204.035 | C39F | 5/63 | Southern National, Exeter (DN) 1409 |
| 13665 | 759 MDV | Bristol MW6G | 204.036 | C39F | 4/63 | Southern National, Exeter (DN) 1410 |
| 13666 | 760 MDV | Bristol MW6G | 204.037 | C39F | 5/63 | Southern National, Exeter (DN) 1411 |
| 13667 | 761 MDV | Bristol MW6G | 204.050 | C39F | 4/63 | Southern National, Exeter (DN) 2273 |
| 13668 | 762 MDV | Bristol MW6G | 204.051 | C39F | 4/63 | Southern National, Exeter (DN) 2274 |
| 13669 | 763 MDV | Bristol MW6G | 204.052 | C39F | 4/63 | Southern National, Exeter (DN) 2275 |
| 13670 | 764 MDV | Bristol MW6G | 204.083 | C39F | 5/63 | Southern National, Exeter (DN) 2276 |
| 13671 | 765 MDV | Bristol MW6G | 204.090 | C39F | 5/63 | Southern National, Exeter (DN) 2277 |
| 13672 | 766 MDV | Bristol MW6G | 204.091 | C39F | 5/63 | Southern National, Exeter (DN) 2278 |
| 13673 | 767 MDV | Bristol MW6G | 204.092 | C39F | 5/63 | Southern National, Exeter (DN) 2279 |
| 13674 | 768 MDV | Bristol MW6G | 204.093 | C39F | 5/63 | Southern National, Exeter (DN) 2280 |
| 13675 | NWC 14 | Bristol MW6G | 204.013 | C34F | 4/63 | Tillings Transport, London WC1 (LN) |
| 13676 | NWC 15 | Bristol MW6G | 204.014 | C39F | 4/63 | Tillings Transport, London WC1 (LN) |
| 13677 | NWC 16 | Bristol MW6G | 204.015 | C39F | 4/63 | Tillings Transport, London WC1 (LN) |
| 13678 | NWC 17 | Bristol MW6G | 204.016 | C39F | 4/63 | Tillings Transport, London WC1 (LN) |
| 13679 | *AOO 18B | Bristol RELH6G | 212.025 | C47F | 1/64 | Tillings Transport, London WC1 (LN) |
| 13680 | 276 ECY | Bristol MW6G | 204.058 | C39F | 4/63 | United Welsh, Swansea (GG) 12 |
| 13681 | 277 ECY | Bristol MW6G | 204.059 | C39F | 4/63 | United Welsh, Swansea (GG) 13 |
| 13682 | 278 ECY | Bristol MW6G | 204.060 | C39F | 4/63 | United Welsh, Swansea (GG) 14 |
| 13683 | 279 ECY | Bristol MW6G | 204.061 | C39F | 4/63 | United Welsh, Swansea (GG) 15 |
| 13684 | 280 ECY | Bristol MW6G | 204.062 | C39F | 4/63 | United Welsh, Swansea (GG) 16 |
| 13685 | 736 MDV | Bristol MW6G | 204.038 | C39F | 4/63 | Western National, Exeter (DN) 1398 |
| 13686 | 737 MDV | Bristol MW6G | 204.039 | C39F | 4/63 | Western National, Exeter (DN) 1399 |
| 13687 | 738 MDV | Bristol MW6G | 204.040 | C39F | 4/63 | Western National, Exeter (DN) 1400 |

| | | | | | | | |
|---|---|---|---|---|---|---|---|
| 13688 | 739 MDV | Bristol MW6G | 204.041 | C39F | 4/63 | Western National, Exeter (DN) | 1401 |
| 13689 | 740 MDV | Bristol MW6G | 204.042 | C39F | 4/63 | Western National, Exeter (DN) | 1402 |
| 13690 | 741 MDV | Bristol MW6G | 204.048 | C39F | 4/63 | Western National, Exeter (DN) | 1403 |
| 13691 | 742 MDV | Bristol MW6G | 204.049 | C39F | 4/63 | Western National, Exeter (DN) | 1404 |
| 13692 | 743 MDV | Bristol MW6G | 204.099 | C39F | 5/63 | Western National, Exeter (DN) | 1405 |
| 13693 | 744 MDV | Bristol MW6G | 204.100 | C39F | 5/63 | Western National, Exeter (DN) | 1406 |
| 13694 | 745 MDV | Bristol MW6G | 213.024 | C39F | 5/63 | Western National, Exeter (DN) | 1407 |
| 13695 | 746 MDV | Bristol MW6G | 213.025 | C39F | 6/63 | Western National, Exeter (DN) | 2271 |
| 13696 | 747 MDV | Bristol MW6G | 213.026 | C39F | 6/63 | Western National, Exeter (DN) | 2272 |
| 13697 | 796 CWU | Bristol MW6G | 204.028 | C39F | 5/63 | West Yorkshire RCC, Harrogate (WR) | CUG36 |
| 13698 | 797 CWU | Bristol MW6G | 204.029 | C39F | 5/63 | West Yorkshire RCC, Harrogate (WR) | CUG37 |
| 13699 | 798 CWU | Bristol MW6G | 204.030 | C39F | 5/63 | West Yorkshire RCC, Harrogate (WR) | CUG38 |
| 13700 | 799 CWU | Bristol MW6G | 204.031 | C39F | 5/63 | West Yorkshire RCC, Harrogate (WR) | CUG39 |
| 13701 | 800 CWU | Bristol MW6G | 204.032 | C39F | 5/63 | West Yorkshire RCC, Harrogate (WR) | CUG40 |
| 13702 | 801 CWU | Bristol MW6G | 204.033 | C39F | 5/63 | West Yorkshire RCC, Harrogate (WR) | CUG41 |
| 13703 | 130 AMW | Bristol MW6G | 204.006 | C39F | 11/62 | Wilts & Dorset, Salisbury (WI) | 718 |
| 13704 | 131 AMW | Bristol MW6G | 204.007 | C39F | 11/62 | Wilts & Dorset, Salisbury (WI) | 719 |
| 13705 | 132 AMW | Bristol MW6G | 204.008 | C39F | 11/62 | Wilts & Dorset, Salisbury (WI) | 720 |
| 13706 | 133 AMW | Bristol MW6G | 204.026 | DP41F | 2/63 | Wilts & Dorset, Salisbury (WI) | 721 |
| 13707 | 134 AMW | Bristol MW6G | 204.027 | DP41F | 2/63 | Wilts & Dorset, Salisbury (WI) | 722 |
| 13708 | 861 UAE | Bristol RELH6G | 212.001 | C47F | 11/63 | Bristol OC (GL) | 2115 |
| 13709 | 862 UAE | Bristol RELH6G | 212.002 | C47F | 3/64 | Bristol OC (GL) | 2116 |
| 13710 | 863 UAE | Bristol RELH6G | 212.003 | C47F | 3/64 | Bristol OC (GL) | 2117 |
| 13711 | 864 UAE | Bristol RELH6G | 212.004 | C47F | 3/64 | Bristol OC (GL) | 2118 |
| 13712 | 865 UAE | Bristol RELH6G | 212.005 | C47F | 3/64 | Bristol OC (GL) | 2119 |
| 13713 | 866 UAE | Bristol RELH6G | 212.006 | C47F | 3/64 | Bristol OC (GL) | 2120 |
| 13714 | 867 UAE | Bristol RELH6G | 212.028 | C45F | 3/64 | Bristol OC (GL) | 2121 |
| 13715 | 868 UAE | Bristol RELH6G | 212.029 | C45F | 3/64 | Bristol OC (GL) | 2122 |
| 13716 | 869 UAE | Bristol RELH6G | 212.030 | C45F | 3/64 | Bristol OC (GL) | 2123 |
| 13717 | 870 UAE | Bristol RELH6G | 212.031 | C45F | 3/64 | Bristol OC (GL) | 2124 |
| 13718 | AAH 124B | Bristol RELH6G | 212.012 | C47F | 4/64 | Eastern Counties, Norwich (NK) | RE974 |
| 13719 | AAH 125B | Bristol RELH6G | 212.023 | C47F | 4/64 | Eastern Counties, Norwich (NK) | RE975 |
| 13720 | AAH 126B | Bristol RELH6G | 212.024 | C47F | 4/64 | Eastern Counties, Norwich (NK) | RE976 |
| 13721 | *AVX 961B | Bristol RELH6G | 212.007 | C47F | 1/64 | Eastern National, Chelmsford (EX) | 578 |
| 13722 | *AVX 962B | Bristol RELH6G | 212.008 | C47F | 1/64 | Eastern National, Chelmsford (EX) | 579 |
| 13723 | *AVX 963B | Bristol RELH6G | 212.009 | C47F | 1/64 | Eastern National, Chelmsford (EX) | 580 |
| 13724 | *AVX 964B | Bristol RELH6G | 212.010 | C47F | 1/64 | Eastern National, Chelmsford (EX) | 581 |
| 13725 | *AVX 965B | Bristol RELH6G | 212.013 | C47F | 3/64 | Eastern National, Chelmsford (EX) | 582 |
| 13726 | *AVX 966B | Bristol RELH6G | 212.014 | C47F | 3/64 | Eastern National, Chelmsford (EX) | 583 |
| 13727 | *AVX 967B | Bristol RELH6G | 212.015 | C47F | 3/64 | Eastern National, Chelmsford (EX) | 584 |
| 13728 | LWC 869 | Bristol MW6G | 204.017 | C39F | 3/63 | Eastern National, Chelmsford (EX) | 577 |
| 13729 | VVL 730 | Bristol RELH6G | 212.019 | C47F | 3/64 | Lincolnshire RCC, Lincoln (LC) | 2819 |
| 13730 | VVL 731 | Bristol RELH6G | 212.020 | C47F | 3/64 | Lincolnshire RCC, Lincoln (LC) | 2820 |
| 13731 | 834 CRX | Bristol RELH6G | 212.021 | C47F | 2/64 | Thames Valley, Reading (BE) | C404 |
| 13732 | 835 CRX | Bristol RELH6G | 212.022 | C47F | 2/64 | Thames Valley, Reading (BE) | C405 |
| 13733 | 134 FCY | Bristol FS6B | 214.095 | H33/27RD | 12/63 | United Welsh, Swansea (GG) | 386 |
| 13734 | 135 FCY | Bristol FS6B | 214.096 | H33/27RD | 12/63 | United Welsh, Swansea (GG) | 387 |
| 13735 | 136 FCY | Bristol FS6B | 214.162 | H33/27RD | 5/64 | United Welsh, Swansea (GG) | 388 |
| 13736 | *OWT 241E | Bristol RELH6B | REX003 | shell | 7/63 | Bristol Commercial Vehicles | |
| 13737 | | | | | | Not built | |
| 13738 | 374 GWN | Bristol RELH6G | 212.026 | C47F | 1/64 | United Welsh, Swansea (GG) | 17 |
| 13739 | 375 GWN | Bristol RELH6G | 212.027 | C47F | 1/64 | United Welsh, Swansea (GG) | 18 |
| 13740 | AAP 51B | Bristol FS6B | 214.099 | CO33/27R | 1/64 | Brighton, Hove & District (ES) | 51 |
| 13741 | AAP 52B | Bristol FS6B | 214.100 | CO33/27R | 1/64 | Brighton, Hove & District (ES) | 52 |
| 13742 | AAP 53B | Bristol FS6B | 214.160 | CO33/27R | 4/64 | Brighton, Hove & District (ES) | 53 |
| 13743 | AAP 54B | Bristol FS6B | 214.161 | CO33/27R | 4/64 | Brighton, Hove & District (ES) | 54 |
| 13744 | 4655 AP | Bristol FS6G | 214.028 | H33/27R | 9/63 | Brighton, Hove & District (ES) | 55 |
| 13745 | 4656 AP | Bristol FS6G | 214.029 | H33/27R | 9/63 | Brighton, Hove & District (ES) | 56 |
| 13746 | 4657 AP | Bristol FS6G | 214.030 | H33/27R | 9/63 | Brighton, Hove & District (ES) | 57 |
| 13747 | BPM 58B | Bristol FS6G | 223.003 | H33/27R | 6/64 | Brighton, Hove & District (ES) | 58 |
| 13748 | BPM 59B | Bristol FS6G | 223.004 | H33/27R | 6/64 | Brighton, Hove & District (ES) | 59 |
| 13749 | 4202 FM | Bristol FS6B | 214.011 | H33/27RD | 9/63 | Crosville MS, Chester (CH) | DFB134 |
| 13750 | 4203 FM | Bristol FS6B | 214.012 | H33/27RD | 8/63 | Crosville MS, Chester (CH) | DFB135 |
| 13751 | 4204 FM | Bristol FS6B | 214.013 | H33/27RD | 9/63 | Crosville MS, Chester (CH) | DFB136 |

| | | | | | | |
|---|---|---|---|---|---|---|
| 13752 | 4205 FM | Bristol FS6B | 214.068 | H33/27RD | 11/63 | Crosville MS, Chester (CH) DFB137 |
| 13753 | 4206 FM | Bristol FS6B | 214.069 | H33/27RD | 12/63 | Crosville MS, Chester (CH) DFB138 |
| 13754 | 4207 FM | Bristol FS6B | 214.070 | H33/27RD | 1/64 | Crosville MS, Chester (CH) DFB139 |
| 13755 | 4208 FM | Bristol FS6B | 214.071 | H33/27RD | 1/64 | Crosville MS, Chester (CH) DFB140 |
| 13756 | 4209 FM | Bristol FS6B | 214.072 | H33/27RD | 1/64 | Crosville MS, Chester (CH) DFB141 |
| 13757 | 4211 FM | Bristol FS6B | 214.080 | H33/27RD | 1/64 | Crosville MS, Chester (CH) DFB142 |
| 13758 | 4212 FM | Bristol FS6B | 214.081 | H33/27RD | 1/64 | Crosville MS, Chester (CH) DFB143 |
| 13759 | 4213 FM | Bristol FS6B | 214.088 | H33/27RD | 1/64 | Crosville MS, Chester (CH) DFB144 |
| 13760 | 4214 FM | Bristol FS6B | 214.097 | H33/27RD | 1/64 | Crosville MS, Chester (CH) DFB145 |
| 13761 | 4215 FM | Bristol FS6B | 214.090 | H33/27RD | 1/64 | Crosville MS, Chester (CH) DFB146 |
| 13762 | 4216 FM | Bristol FS6B | 214.114 | H33/27RD | 1/64 | Crosville MS, Chester (CH) DFB147 |
| 13763 | 4217 FM | Bristol FS6B | 214.115 | H33/27RD | 1/64 | Crosville MS, Chester (CH) DFB148 |
| 13764 | 4224 FM | Bristol FS6G | 214.130 | H33/27RD | 5/64 | Crosville MS, Chester (CH) DFG154 |
| 13765 | 4225 FM | Bristol FS6G | 214.131 | H33/27RD | 5/64 | Crosville MS, Chester (CH) DFG155 |
| 13766 | *4226 FM | Bristol FS6G | 214.132 | H33/27RD | 5/64 | Crosville MS, Chester (CH) DFG156 |
| 13767 | 4227 FM | Bristol FS6G | 214.133 | H33/27RD | 5/64 | Crosville MS, Chester (CH) DFG157 |
| 13768 | BFM 234B | Bristol FS6B | 223.041 | H33/27RD | 10/64 | Crosville MS, Chester (CH) DFB158 |
| 13769 | BFM 235B | Bristol FS6B | 223.042 | H33/27RD | 10/64 | Crosville MS, Chester (CH) DFB159 |
| 13770 | BFM 236B | Bristol FS6B | 223.043 | H33/27RD | 10/64 | Crosville MS, Chester (CH) DFB160 |
| 13771 | BFM 237B | Bristol FS6B | 223.044 | H33/27RD | 10/64 | Crosville MS, Chester (CH) DFB161 |
| 13772 | BFM 238B | Bristol FS6B | 223.045 | H33/27RD | 10/64 | Crosville MS, Chester (CH) DFB162 |
| 13773 | 420 LAO | Bristol FS6B | 214.073 | H33/27RD | 11/63 | Cumberland MS, Whitehaven (CU) 561 |
| 13774 | 421 LAO | Bristol FS6B | 214.074 | H33/27RD | 11/63 | Cumberland MS, Whitehaven (CU) 562 |
| 13775 | AAO 573B | Bristol FS6B | 214.151 | H33/27RD | 3/64 | Cumberland MS, Whitehaven (CU) 563 |
| 13776 | AAO 574B | Bristol FS6B | 214.152 | H33/27RD | 3/64 | Cumberland MS, Whitehaven (CU) 564 |
| 13777 | BRM 79B | Bristol FS6B | 223.030 | H33/27RD | 7/64 | Cumberland MS, Whitehaven (CU) 565 |
| 13778 | 62 CPW | Bristol FS5G | 214.017 | H33/27RD | 9/63 | Eastern Counties, Norwich (NK) LFS62 |
| 13779 | 63 CPW | Bristol FS5G | 214.018 | H33/27RD | 9/63 | Eastern Counties, Norwich (NK) LFS63 |
| 13780 | 64 CPW | Bristol FS5G | 214.019 | H33/27RD | 9/63 | Eastern Counties, Norwich (NK) LFS64 |
| 13781 | 65 DNG | Bristol FS5G | 214.049 | H33/27RD | 9/63 | Eastern Counties, Norwich (NK) LFS65 |
| 13782 | 66 DNG | Bristol FS5G | 214.063 | H33/27RD | 10/63 | Eastern Counties, Norwich (NK) LFS66 |
| 13783 | 67 DNG | Bristol FS5G | 214.064 | H33/27RD | 11/63 | Eastern Counties, Norwich (NK) LFS67 |
| 13784 | * 68 DNG | Bristol FS5G | 214.065 | H33/27RD | 11/63 | Eastern Counties, Norwich (NK) LFS68 |
| 13785 | 69 DNG | Bristol FS5G | 214.066 | H33/27RD | 11/63 | Eastern Counties, Norwich (NK) LFS69 |
| 13786 | 70 DPW | Bristol FS5G | 214.082 | H33/27RD | 12/63 | Eastern Counties, Norwich (NK) LFS70 |
| 13787 | 71 DPW | Bristol FS5G | 214.083 | H33/27RD | 12/63 | Eastern Counties, Norwich (NK) LFS71 |
| 13788 | 72 DPW | Bristol FS5G | 214.084 | H33/27RD | 12/63 | Eastern Counties, Norwich (NK) LFS72 |
| 13789 | AAH 173B | Bristol FS5G | 214.102 | H33/27RD | 1/64 | Eastern Counties, Norwich (NK) LFS73 |
| 13790 | AAH 174B | Bristol FS5G | 214.103 | H33/27RD | 1/64 | Eastern Counties, Norwich (NK) LFS74 |
| 13791 | AAH 175B | Bristol FS5G | 214.111 | H33/27RD | 1/64 | Eastern Counties, Norwich (NK) LFS75 |
| 13792 | AAH 614B | Bristol FS5G | 214.121 | H33/27RD | 1/64 | Eastern Counties, Norwich (NK) LFS76 |
| 13793 | AAH 615B | Bristol FS5G | 214.122 | H33/27RD | 1/64 | Eastern Counties, Norwich (NK) LFS77 |
| 13794 | AAH 616B | Bristol FS5G | 214.123 | H33/27RD | 1/64 | Eastern Counties, Norwich (NK) LFS78 |
| 13795 | AVF 579B | Bristol FS5G | 214.173 | H33/27RD | 5/64 | Eastern Counties, Norwich (NK) LFS79 |
| 13796 | AVF 580B | Bristol FS5G | 214.174 | H33/27RD | 5/64 | Eastern Counties, Norwich (NK) LFS80 |
| 13797 | BNG 881B | Bristol FS5G | 223.018 | H33/27RD | 7/64 | Eastern Counties, Norwich (NK) LFS81 |
| 13798 | BNG 882B | Bristol FS5G | 223.019 | H33/27RD | 7/64 | Eastern Counties, Norwich (NK) LFS82 |
| 13799 | BNG 883B | Bristol FS5G | 223.020 | H33/27RD | 7/64 | Eastern Counties, Norwich (NK) LFS83 |
| 13800 | BNG 884B | Bristol FS5G | 223.021 | H33/27RD | 7/64 | Eastern Counties, Norwich (NK) LFS84 |
| 13801 | BNG 885B | Bristol FS5G | 223.022 | H33/27RD | 7/64 | Eastern Counties, Norwich (NK) LFS85 |
| 13802 | *BNG 886B | Bristol FS5G | 223.023 | H33/27RD | 7/64 | Eastern Counties, Norwich (NK) LFS86 |
| 13803 | 4688 RU | Bristol FS6G | 214.020 | H33/27RD | 8/63 | Hants & Dorset, Bournemouth (HA) 1488 |
| 13804 | 4689 RU | Bristol FS6G | 214.021 | H33/27RD | 8/63 | Hants & Dorset, Bournemouth (HA) 1489 |
| 13805 | 4690 RU | Bristol FS6G | 214.022 | H33/27RD | 9/63 | Hants & Dorset, Bournemouth (HA) 1490 |
| 13806 | 4691 RU | Bristol FS6B | 214.085 | H33/27RD | 11/63 | Hants & Dorset, Bournemouth (HA) 1491 |
| 13807 | 4692 RU | Bristol FS6B | 214.086 | H33/27RD | 11/63 | Hants & Dorset, Bournemouth (HA) 1492 |
| 13808 | 4693 RU | Bristol FS6B | 214.087 | H33/27RD | 11/63 | Hants & Dorset, Bournemouth (HA) 1493 |
| 13809 | 4694 RU | Bristol FS6B | 214.109 | H33/27RD | 12/63 | Hants & Dorset, Bournemouth (HA) 1494 |
| 13810 | 4695 RU | Bristol FS6B | 214.110 | H33/27RD | 12/63 | Hants & Dorset, Bournemouth (HA) 1495 |
| 13811 | 4696 RU | Bristol FS6B | 214.112 | H33/27RD | 12/63 | Hants & Dorset, Bournemouth (HA) 1496 |
| 13812 | 4697 RU | Bristol FS6B | 214.113 | H33/27RD | 12/63 | Hants & Dorset, Bournemouth (HA) 1497 |
| 13813 | 4698 RU | Bristol FS6B | 214.153 | H33/27RD | 3/64 | Hants & Dorset, Bournemouth (HA) 1498 |
| 13814 | 4699 RU | Bristol FS6B | 214.154 | H33/27RD | 3/64 | Hants & Dorset, Bournemouth (HA) 1499 |
| 13815 | ALJ 573B | Bristol FS6G | 223.024 | H33/27RD | 7/64 | Hants & Dorset, Bournemouth (HA) 1500 |

| | | | | | | | |
|---|---|---|---|---|---|---|---|
| 13816 | *ALJ 574B | Bristol FS6G | 223.025 | H33/27RD | 7/64 | Hants & Dorset, Bournemouth (HA) 1501 |
| 13817 | ALJ 575B | Bristol FS6G | 223.026 | H33/27RD | 8/64 | Hants & Dorset, Bournemouth (HA) 1502 |
| 13818 | ALJ 576B | Bristol FS6B | 223.031 | H33/27RD | 8/64 | Hants & Dorset, Bournemouth (HA) 1503 |
| 13819 | VFE 961 | Bristol FS5G | 214.091 | H33/27RD | 11/63 | Lincolnshire RCC, Lincoln (LC) 2512 |
| 13820 | VFE 962 | Bristol FS5G | 214.092 | H33/27RD | 11/63 | Lincolnshire RCC, Lincoln (LC) 2513 |
| 13821 | VFE 963 | Bristol FS5G | 214.169 | H33/27RD | 4/64 | Lincolnshire RCC, Lincoln (LC) 2514 |
| 13822 | VFE 964 | Bristol FS5G | 214.170 | H33/27RD | 4/64 | Lincolnshire RCC, Lincoln (LC) 2515 |
| 13823 | VFE 965 | Bristol FS5G | 214.171 | H33/27RD | 4/64 | Lincolnshire RCC, Lincoln (LC) 2516 |
| 13824 | VFE 966 | Bristol FS5G | 214.172 | H33/27RD | 4/64 | Lincolnshire RCC, Lincoln (LC) 2517 |
| 13825 | 163 HAX | Bristol FS6B | 214.052 | H33/27RD | 10/63 | Red & White, Chepstow (MH) L163 |
| 13826 | 164 HAX | Bristol FS6B | 214.053 | H33/27RD | 10/63 | Red & White, Chepstow (MH) L263 |
| 13827 | 165 HAX | Bristol FS6B | 214.054 | H33/27RD | 10/63 | Red & White, Chepstow (MH) L363 |
| 13828 | 166 HAX | Bristol FS6B | 214.093 | H33/27RD | 12/63 | Red & White, Chepstow (MH) L463 |
| 13829 | 167 HAX | Bristol FS6B | 214.094 | H33/27RD | 1/64 | Red & White, Chepstow (MH) L563 |
| 13830 | 168 HAX | Bristol FS6G | 214.116 | H33/27RD | 1/64 | Red & White, Chepstow (MH) L663 |
| 13831 | *AAX 21B | Bristol FS6G | 214.125 | H33/27RD | 3/64 | Red & White, Chepstow (MH) L763 |
| 13832 | *AAX 22B | Bristol FS6B | 223.001 | H33/27RD | 7/64 | Red & White, Chepstow (MH) L863 |
| 13833 | *AAX 23B | Bristol FS6B | 223.002 | H33/27RD | 7/64 | Red & White, Chepstow (MH) L963 |
| 13834 | *AAX 24B | Bristol FS6B | 223.032 | H33/27RD | 9/64 | Red & White, Chepstow (MH) L1063 |
| 13835 | *AAX 25B | Bristol FS6B | 223.033 | H33/27RD | 9/64 | Red & White, Chepstow (MH) L1163 |
| 13836 | 641 EBD | Bristol FS6B | 214.014 | H33/27RD | 10/63 | United Counties, Northampton (NO) 641 |
| 13837 | 642 EBD | Bristol FS6B | 214.015 | H33/27RD | 9/63 | United Counties, Northampton (NO) 642 |
| 13838 | 643 EBD | Bristol FS6B | 214.016 | H33/27RD | 10/63 | United Counties, Northampton (NO) 643 |
| 13839 | 644 EBD | Bristol FS6B | 214.036 | H33/27RD | 10/63 | United Counties, Northampton (NO) 644 |
| 13840 | 645 EBD | Bristol FS6B | 214.037 | H33/27RD | 10/63 | United Counties, Northampton (NO) 645 |
| 13841 | 646 EBD | Bristol FS6B | 214.075 | H33/27RD | 11/63 | United Counties, Northampton (NO) 646 |
| 13842 | 647 EBD | Bristol FS6B | 214.076 | H33/27RD | 11/63 | United Counties, Northampton (NO) 647 |
| 13843 | 648 EBD | Bristol FS6B | 214.077 | H33/27RD | 11/63 | United Counties, Northampton (NO) 648 |
| 13844 | 649 EBD | Bristol FS6B | 214.101 | H33/27RD | 12/63 | United Counties, Northampton (NO) 649 |
| 13845 | 650 EBD | Bristol FS6B | 214.104 | H33/27RD | 1/64 | United Counties, Northampton (NO) 650 |
| 13846 | 651 EBD | Bristol FS6B | 214.124 | H33/27RD | 2/64 | United Counties, Northampton (NO) 651 |
| 13847 | 652 EBD | Bristol FS6B | 214.126 | H33/27RD | 3/64 | United Counties, Northampton (NO) 652 |
| 13848 | 653 EBD | Bristol FS6B | 214.127 | H33/27RD | 3/64 | United Counties, Northampton (NO) 653 |
| 13849 | 654 EBD | Bristol FS6B | 214.128 | H33/27RD | 3/64 | United Counties, Northampton (NO) 654 |
| 13850 | 655 EBD | Bristol FS6B | 214.129 | H33/27RD | 3/64 | United Counties, Northampton (NO) 655 |
| 13851 | ABD 656B | Bristol FS6B | 214.181 | H33/27RD | 5/64 | United Counties, Northampton (NO) 656 |
| 13852 | ABD 657B | Bristol FS6B | 214.182 | H33/27RD | 6/64 | United Counties, Northampton (NO) 657 |
| 13853 | ABD 658B | Bristol FS6B | 223.027 | H33/27RD | 9/64 | United Counties, Northampton (NO) 658 |
| 13854 | ABD 659B | Bristol FS6B | 223.028 | H33/27RD | 8/64 | United Counties, Northampton (NO) 659 |
| 13855 | ABD 660B | Bristol FS6B | 223.029 | H33/27RD | 9/64 | United Counties, Northampton (NO) 660 |
| 13856 | ABD 661B | Bristol FS6B | 223.034 | H33/27RD | 9/64 | United Counties, Northampton (NO) 661 |
| 13857 | ABD 662B | Bristol FS6B | 223.035 | H33/27RD | 9/64 | United Counties, Northampton (NO) 662 |
| 13858 | 834 DYG | Bristol FS6B | 214.038 | H33/27RD | 10/63 | West Yorkshire RCC, Harrogate (WR) DX167 |
| 13859 | 835 DYG | Bristol FS6B | 214.039 | H33/27RD | 11/63 | West Yorkshire RCC, Harrogate (WR) DX168 |
| 13860 | 836 DYG | Bristol FS6B | 214.040 | H33/27RD | 10/63 | West Yorkshire RCC, Harrogate (WR) DX169 |
| 13861 | 837 DYG | Bristol FS6B | 214.089 | H33/27RD | 12/63 | West Yorkshire RCC, Harrogate (WR) DX170 |
| 13862 | 838 DYG | Bristol FS6B | 214.098 | H33/27RD | 12/63 | West Yorkshire RCC, Harrogate (WR) DX171 |
| 13863 | 839 DYG | Bristol FS6B | 214.117 | H33/27RD | 2/64 | West Yorkshire RCC, Harrogate (WR) DX172 |
| 13864 | 840 DYG | Bristol FS6B | 214.118 | H33/27RD | 2/64 | West Yorkshire RCC, Harrogate (WR) DX173 |
| 13865 | 841 DYG | Bristol FS6B | 214.119 | H33/27RD | 2/64 | West Yorkshire RCC, Harrogate (WR) DX174 |
| 13866 | 842 DYG | Bristol FS6B | 214.120 | H33/27RD | 2/64 | West Yorkshire RCC, Harrogate (WR) DX175 |
| 13867 | AWU 469B | Bristol FS6B | 214.183 | H33/27RD | 6/64 | West Yorkshire RCC, Harrogate (WR) DX176 |
| 13868 | AWU 470B | Bristol FS6B | 223.036 | H33/27RD | 9/64 | West Yorkshire RCC, Harrogate (WR) DX177 |
| 13869 | AWU 471B | Bristol FS6B | 223.037 | H33/27RD | 9/64 | West Yorkshire RCC, Harrogate (WR) DX178 |
| 13870 | AWU 472B | Bristol FS6B | 223.038 | H33/27RD | 9/64 | West Yorkshire RCC, Harrogate (WR) DX179 |
| 13871 | 573 EWX | Bristol FS6B | 214.067 | H33/27RD | 11/63 | Keighley-West Yorkshire, Harrogate (WR) KDX162 |
| 13872 | 574 EWX | Bristol FS6B | 214.078 | H33/27RD | 11/63 | Keighley-West Yorkshire, Harrogate (WR) KDX163 |
| 13873 | 575 EWX | Bristol FS6B | 214.079 | H33/27RD | 12/63 | Keighley-West Yorkshire, Harrogate (WR) KDX164 |
| 13874 | *AWU 467B | Bristol FS6B | 214.163 | H33/27RD | 5/64 | Keighley-West Yorkshire, Harrogate (WR) KDX165 |

| | | | | | | |
|---|---|---|---|---|---|---|
| 13875 | AWU 468B | Bristol FS6B | 223.039 | H33/27RD | 10/64 | Keighley-West Yorkshire, Harrogate (WR) KDX166 |
| 13876 | 473 BMR | Bristol FS6B | 214.105 | H33/27RD | 1/64 | Wilts & Dorset, Salisbury (WI) 664 |
| 13877 | 474 BMR | Bristol FS6B | 214.106 | H33/27RD | 1/64 | Wilts & Dorset, Salisbury (WI) 665 |
| 13878 | 475 BMR | Bristol FS6B | 214.107 | H33/27RD | 1/64 | Wilts & Dorset, Salisbury (WI) 666 |
| 13879 | 476 BMR | Bristol FS6B | 214.108 | H33/27RD | 1/64 | Wilts & Dorset, Salisbury (WI) 667 |
| 13880 | 477 BMR | Bristol FS6B | 214.189 | H33/27RD | 6/64 | Wilts & Dorset, Salisbury (WI) 668 |
| 13881 | 478 BMR | Bristol FS6B | 214.190 | H33/27RD | 6/64 | Wilts & Dorset, Salisbury (WI) 669 |
| 13882 | 479 BMR | Bristol FS6B | 214.191 | H33/27RD | 6/64 | Wilts & Dorset, Salisbury (WI) 670 |
| 13883 | AHR 245B | Bristol FS6B | 223.040 | H33/27RD | 9/64 | Wilts & Dorset, Salisbury (WI) 671 |
| 13884 | 806 SHW | Bristol FLF6B | 210.088 | H38/32F | 10/63 | Bristol OC (GL) 7113 |
| 13885 | 807 SHW | Bristol FLF6B | 210.089 | H38/32F | 10/63 | Bristol OC (GL) 7114 |
| 13886 | *808 SHW | Bristol FLF6B | 210.090 | H38/32F | 10/63 | Bristol OC (GL) 7115 |
| 13887 | 809 SHW | Bristol FLF6B | 210.091 | H38/32F | 11/63 | Bristol OC (GL) 7116 |
| 13888 | *810 SHW | Bristol FLF6B | 217.006 | H38/32F | 11/63 | Bristol OC (GL) 7117 |
| 13889 | 811 SHW | Bristol FLF6B | 217.007 | H38/32F | 11/63 | Bristol OC (GL) 7118 |
| 13890 | *822 SHW | Bristol FLF6L | 217.098 | H38/32F | 2/64 | Bristol OC (GL) 7129 |
| 13891 | 817 SHW | Bristol FLF6B | 217.079 | H38/32F | 12/63 | Bristol OC (GL) 7124 |
| 13892 | *818 SHW | Bristol FLF6B | 217.093 | H38/32F | 2/64 | Bristol OC (GL) 7125 |
| 13893 | 819 SHW | Bristol FLF6B | 217.094 | H38/32F | 2/64 | Bristol OC (GL) 7126 |
| 13894 | 820 SHW | Bristol FLF6B | 217.095 | H38/32F | 2/64 | Bristol OC (GL) 7127 |
| 13895 | 821 SHW | Bristol FLF6B | 217.096 | H38/32F | 2/64 | Bristol OC (GL) 7128 |
| 13896 | 833 SHW | Bristol FLF6B | 217.182 | H38/32F | 6/64 | Bristol OC (GL) 7140 |
| 13897 | 834 SHW | Bristol FLF6B | 217.192 | H38/32F | 7/64 | Bristol OC (GL) 7141 |
| 13898 | 835 SHW | Bristol FLF6B | 217.193 | H38/32F | 7/64 | Bristol OC (GL) 7142 |
| 13899 | 836 SHW | Bristol FLF6B | 217.195 | H38/32F | 7/64 | Bristol OC (GL) 7143 |
| 13900 | 837 SHW | Bristol FLF6B | 217.196 | H38/32F | 7/64 | Bristol OC (GL) 7144 |
| 13901 | 842 SHW | Bristol FLF6B | 224.014 | H38/32F | 8/64 | Bristol OC (GL) 7149 |
| 13902 | 801 SHW | Bristol FLF6B | 210.065 | H38/32F | 5/63 | Bristol OC (GL) C7108 |
| 13903 | 802 SHW | Bristol FLF6B | 210.066 | H38/32F | 5/63 | Bristol OC (GL) C7109 |
| 13904 | 803 SHW | Bristol FLF6B | 210.067 | H38/32F | 5/63 | Bristol OC (GL) C7110 |
| 13905 | *804 SHW | Bristol FLF6B | 210.086 | H38/32F | 10/63 | Bristol OC (GL) C7111 |
| 13906 | *805 SHW | Bristol FLF6B | 210.087 | H38/32F | 10/63 | Bristol OC (GL) C7112 |
| 13907 | 823 SHW | Bristol FLF6L | 217.119 | H38/32F | 3/64 | Bristol OC (GL) C7130 |
| 13908 | 824 SHW | Bristol FLF6L | 217.122 | H38/32F | 3/64 | Bristol OC (GL) C7131 |
| 13909 | 825 SHW | Bristol FLF6B | 217.116 | H38/32F | 2/64 | Bristol OC (GL) C7132 |
| 13910 | 826 SHW | Bristol FLF6B | 217.118 | H38/32F | 3/64 | Bristol OC (GL) C7133 |
| 13911 | *828 SHW | Bristol FLF6B | 217.126 | H38/32F | 3/64 | Bristol OC (GL) C7135 |
| 13912 | 827 SHW | Bristol FLF6B | 217.120 | H38/32F | 3/64 | Bristol OC (GL) C7134 |
| 13913 | 829 SHW | Bristol FLF6B | 217.150 | H38/32F | 4/64 | Bristol OC (GL) C7136 |
| 13914 | 830 SHW | Bristol FLF6B | 217.164 | H38/32F | 5/64 | Bristol OC (GL) C7137 |
| 13915 | 831 SHW | Bristol FLF6B | 217.165 | H38/32F | 5/64 | Bristol OC (GL) C7138 |
| 13916 | 832 SHW | Bristol FLF6B | 217.166 | H38/32F | 5/64 | Bristol OC (GL) C7139 |
| 13917 | *838 SHW | Bristol FLF6B | 224.005 | H38/32F | 7/64 | Bristol OC (GL) C7145 |
| 13918 | 839 SHW | Bristol FLF6B | 224.006 | H38/32F | 7/64 | Bristol OC (GL) C7146 |
| 13919 | *840 SHW | Bristol FLF6B | 224.007 | H38/32F | 8/64 | Bristol OC (GL) C7147 |
| 13920 | 841 SHW | Bristol FLF6B | 224.008 | H38/32F | 8/64 | Bristol OC (GL) C7148 |
| 13921 | 843 SHW | Bristol FLF6B | 224.015 | H38/32F | 8/64 | Bristol OC (GL) C7150 |
| 13922 | 844 SHW | Bristol FLF6B | 224.016 | H38/32F | 8/64 | Bristol OC (GL) C7151 |
| 13923 | 845 SHW | Bristol FLF6B | 224.017 | H38/32F | 8/64 | Bristol OC (GL) C7152 |
| 13924 | 846 SHW | Bristol FLF6B | 224.018 | H38/32F | 8/64 | Bristol OC (GL) C7153 |
| 13925 | *847 SHW | Bristol FLF6B | 224.019 | H38/32F | 8/64 | Bristol OC (GL) C7154 |
| 13926 | *AAE 51B | Bristol FLF6B | 224.020 | H38/32F | 9/64 | Bristol OC (GL) C7155 |
| 13927 | 812 SHW | Bristol FLF6G | 217.053 | H38/32F | 12/63 | Cheltenham District (GL) 7119 |
| 13928 | 813 SHW | Bristol FLF6G | 217.054 | H38/32F | 12/63 | Cheltenham District (GL) 7120 |
| 13929 | 814 SHW | Bristol FLF6G | 217.055 | H38/32F | 12/63 | Bristol OC (GL) G7121 |
| 13930 | 815 SHW | Bristol FLF6G | 217.074 | H38/32F | 12/63 | Bristol OC (GL) G7122 |
| 13931 | *816 SHW | Bristol FLF6G | 217.075 | H38/32F | 12/63 | Bristol OC (GL) G7123 |
| 13932 | AAO 37B | Bristol FLF6L | 217.123 | H38/32F | 3/64 | Cumberland MS, Whitehaven (CU) 522 |
| 13933 | AAO 38B | Bristol FLF6L | 217.124 | H38/32F | 3/64 | Cumberland MS, Whitehaven (CU) 523 |
| 13934 | AAO 39B | Bristol FLF6L | 217.125 | H38/32F | 3/64 | Cumberland MS, Whitehaven (CU) 524 |
| 13935 | *AAO 36B | Bristol FLF6G | 217.111 | H38/32F | 3/64 | Cumberland MS, Whitehaven (CU) 521 |
| 13936 | 914 THN | Bristol FLF6B | 217.066 | H38/32F | 12/63 | Durham District (DM) DBL14 |
| 13937 | 915 THN | Bristol FLF6B | 217.067 | H38/32F | 12/63 | Durham District (DM) DBL15 |

The Sheffield JOC B Fleet, being jointly owned by British Railways, was able to purchase ECW bodies. YWB 294 (1294) was one of three bodies supplied in 1957 based on Leyland PD2/20 chassis, shown here approaching Midland Station in Sheffield. (Roy Marshall)

Eastern National was one of the operators supplied with the dual-purpose variant of the MW body on Bristol MW5G chassis, instead of the more usual MW6G. 216 MHK (1401) was one of a batch of three dating from 1959. (Geoffrey Morant, courtesy Richard Morant)

The first style of coach body fitted to the Bristol MW chassis was very similar to many fitted to the earlier Bristol LS. This is Wilts & Dorset RMR 736 (804) new in 1958, seen in their original red below waistline and cream above coach livery. (John May)

Crosville operated a large fleet of Bristol Lodekkas of various different models. This one is 616 LFM (DLG6) an LD6G from a batch which entered service in 1959-1960. (Geoffrey Morant, courtesy Richard Morant)

This Bristol LD6B dating from 1959 was YRU 72 (1433) of Hants & Dorset. For many years bodies supplied to this operator had a distinctive sun visor at the top of the driver's windscreens as seen on this example. (John May)

The Western and Southern National companies also operated many Lodekkas of various models, this one being Western National 503 BTA (1951) an LD6G, which also dated from 1959. (John May)

Thames Valley had a number of Bristol L6B coaches which were lengthened, fitted with Gardner 5LW engines and rebodied with these SC style bodies by ECW. This was FMO 23 (819) one of four so treated in 1959. (John May)

Despite being nationalised, Mansfield District continued to paint its vehicles in its own light green and cream livery, as shown on 567 ERR (531), one of four FS6Gs dating from 1961 pictured in Nottingham. (Roy Marshall)

Another example of a vehicle carrying the Midland General blue and cream livery is this Bristol FS6G 913 MRB (498) from a batch new in 1960. (Geoffrey Morant, courtesy Richard Morant)

The rare 30ft long rear entrance FL version of the Lodekka is shown here by this 70 seat FL6G of Red & White, Chepstow which was 13 AAX (L1360). (Geoffrey Morant, courtesy Richard Morant)

This Bristol MW5G of Durham District Services with dual-purpose body 2918 HN (DBE18) shown here in 1962, was one of five similar vehicles which had been new the previous year. (Geoffrey Morant, courtesy Richard Morant)

The Southern and Western National companies painted coaches employed on express services, in the attractive 'Royal Blue' livery. Shown here is Western National MW6G 615 DDV (2248) new in 1960. (Geoffrey Morant, courtesy Richard Morant)

Another dual-purpose Bristol MW is this 1960 example of United Counties. WBD 144 (144) was one of the more common MW6G version from a batch of five. (Geoffrey Morant, courtesy Richard Morant)

The Bristol SC4LK proved popular with Crosville for use on its many rural services, particularly within Wales. Coach seated 906 OFM (CSG657) is seen here outside Aberystwyth Depot. (Peter Henson, The Omnibus Society)

As well as the double-deck bodies supplied to the two Sheffield JOC fleets, five of these MW style coach bodies were delivered on Leyland L1 chassis. This one being B Fleet 1910 WA (1010) new in 1961. (Geoffrey Morant, courtesy Richard Morant)

United AS of Darlington operated both short and long versions of the forward entrance Lodekka. This is one of the shorter FSF6Bs, 5100 HN (BL100) from a batch new in 1961. (Geoffrey Morant, courtesy Richard Morant)

Another FSF Lodekka is this FSF6G belonging to the United Welsh fleet based in Swansea. 146 ACY (352) is from a mixed delivery of FSF and FLF models new in 1961. (Roy Marshall)

Seen in Newark in 1972 is this Lincolnshire RCC FS5G Lodekka RFE 477 (2502) new in 1962. By this time the five cylinder engine had largely fallen out of favour for double-deckers, except for operators in flat territory such as Lincolnshire. (Roy Marshall)

United AS eventually operated over two hundred Bristol MW5G and MW6G. This MW5G 5045 HN (BU645) was from a batch of standard 45 seater service buses new in 1962. (Geoffrey Morant, courtesy Richard Morant)

The lightweight Bristol SUL4A chassis which superseded the SC4LK from 1960 is depicted here with the much less common coach version of the standard body. Western National 273 KTA (423) is one of fifteen new in 1962. (Geoffrey Morant, courtesy Richard Morant)

London's Victoria Coach Station is the setting for one of Eastern National's smart coach seated forward entrance Lodekkas. FLF6B RWC 608 (2605) is seen here in company with several Standerwick Atlantean coaches. (Harry Hay)

West Yorkshire was a late convert to the Bristol MW6G in service bus form. This is 838 BWY (SMG30) from a batch of twenty new in 1963, seen in Buckden, in a classic Yorkshire Dales setting. (Geoffrey Morant, courtesy Richard Morant)

Following the break-up of the Alexander fleet in 1961, the Midland company, which retained the attractive blue and cream livery, continued to receive forward entrance Lodekkas. TWG 551 (MRD 172) was new in 1962. (Geoffrey Morant, courtesy Richard Morant)

An early example of the new style of coach body for Bristol MW6G chassis is 797 CWU (CUG37) of West Yorkshire RCC, which entered service in 1963. (John May)

The coach body fitted to the rear-engined Bristol RELH6G was essentially a longer version of that fitted to the MW chassis. Bristol OC 870 UAE (2140) depicts this body in its original form, being new in early 1964. (Peter Henson, The Omnibus Society)

Also displaying the distinctive Mansfield District green and cream livery is this 70 seat Bristol FLF6B, AAL 104B (625), one of four delivered in 1964. (Roy Marshall)

Toward the end of the 1960s many Bristol OC single-deckers began to receive this revised livery incorporating more cream, as shown on 1964 MW5G 984 UHW (2592). (Geoffrey Morant, courtesy Richard Morant)

Cumberland were the operator of this MW with standard service bus bodywork. AAO 34B (231), like other Cumberland MWs, was an MW6G, the larger engine being desirable because of the hilly territory in which they operated. (Geoffrey Morant, courtesy Richard Morant)

Several Scottish Bus Group operators were major users of the Lodekka. This one is FS6G 8944 SF (AA944) of Scottish Omnibuses, seen here in the later single shade of green and cream livery adopted by this operator. (Geoffrey Morant, courtesy Richard Morant)

Another SBG operator to favour the Lodekka for some of its double-deck requirements was Western SMT. VCS 376 (B1822) one of the 1963 delivery of the FLF6G model is seen here in Glasgow. (Roy Marshall)

Another example of the Bristol SU, but this time the less common shorter SUS4A version seating 30. This is Bristol OC AHW 226B (307), one of the last pair of this type received by the operator, dating from 1964. (Geoffrey Morant, courtesy Richard Morant)

The other operator to favour the FS5G version of the Lodekka was Eastern Counties, who like Lincolnshire operated in predominantly flat terrain. Seen in Cambridge is FAH 113C (LFS113) from the 1965 delivery. (John May)

| | | | | | | |
|---|---|---|---|---|---|---|
| 13938 | 987 KOO | Bristol FLF6G | 210.068 | H38/32F | 8/63 | Eastern National, Chelmsford (EX) 1651 |
| 13939 | *988 KOO | Bristol FLF6G | 210.069 | H38/32F | 8/63 | Eastern National, Chelmsford (EX) 1652 |
| 13940 | 989 KOO | Bristol FLF6G | 210.075 | H38/32F | 8/63 | Eastern National, Chelmsford (EX) 1653 |
| 13941 | 990 KOO | Bristol FLF6G | 210.076 | H38/32F | 9/63 | Eastern National, Chelmsford (EX) 1654 |
| 13942 | 991 KOO | Bristol FLF6B | 210.097 | H38/32F | 9/63 | Eastern National, Chelmsford (EX) 1655 |
| 13943 | 992 KOO | Bristol FLF6B | 210.098 | H38/32F | 9/63 | Eastern National, Chelmsford (EX) 1656 |
| 13944 | 993 KOO | Bristol FLF6B | 217.048 | H38/32F | 10/63 | Eastern National, Chelmsford (EX) 1657 |
| 13945 | 994 KOO | Bristol FLF6B | 217.049 | H38/32F | 10/63 | Eastern National, Chelmsford (EX) 1658 |
| 13946 | 995 KOO | Bristol FLF6B | 217.050 | H38/32F | 10/63 | Eastern National, Chelmsford (EX) 1659 |
| 13947 | *934 LWC | Bristol FLF6G | 217.068 | H38/32F | 11/63 | Eastern National, Chelmsford (EX) 1660 |
| 13948 | 935 LWC | Bristol FLF6G | 217.069 | H38/32F | 11/63 | Eastern National, Chelmsford (EX) 1661 |
| 13949 | 936 LWC | Bristol FLF6B | 217.076 | H38/32F | 12/63 | Eastern National, Chelmsford (EX) 1662 |
| 13950 | 937 LWC | Bristol FLF6B | 217.077 | H38/32F | 12/63 | Eastern National, Chelmsford (EX) 1663 |
| 13951 | 938 LWC | Bristol FLF6B | 217.078 | H38/32F | 12/63 | Eastern National, Chelmsford (EX) 1664 |
| 13952 | *AVX 956B | Bristol FLF6B | 217.081 | H38/32F | 1/64 | Eastern National, Chelmsford (EX) 1665 |
| 13953 | *AVX 957B | Bristol FLF6G | 217.097 | H38/32F | 1/64 | Eastern National, Chelmsford (EX) 1666 |
| 13954 | *AVX 958B | Bristol FLF6G | 217.099 | H38/32F | 1/64 | Eastern National, Chelmsford (EX) 1667 |
| 13955 | *AVX 959B | Bristol FLF6G | 217.100 | H38/32F | 1/64 | Eastern National, Chelmsford (EX) 1668 |
| 13956 | *AVX 960B | Bristol FLF6B | 217.101 | H38/32F | 1/64 | Eastern National, Chelmsford (EX) 1669 |
| 13957 | BVX 668B | Bristol FLF6B | 217.139 | CH37/18F | 3/64 | Eastern National, Chelmsford (EX) 1671 |
| 13958 | BVX 669B | Bristol FLF6B | 217.140 | CH37/18F | 3/64 | Eastern National, Chelmsford (EX) 1672 |
| 13959 | BVX 667B | Bristol FLF6B | 217.121 | H38/32F | 3/64 | Eastern National, Chelmsford (EX) 1670 |
| 13960 | BVX 670B | Bristol FLF6B | 217.141 | H38/32F | 5/64 | Eastern National, Chelmsford (EX) 1673 |
| 13961 | *BVX 671B | Bristol FLF6G | 217.175 | H38/32F | 5/64 | Eastern National, Chelmsford (EX) 1674 |
| 13962 | *BVX 672B | Bristol FLF6B | 217.176 | H38/32F | 5/64 | Eastern National, Chelmsford (EX) 1675 |
| 13963 | *BVX 673B | Bristol FLF6G | 217.177 | H38/32F | 5/64 | Eastern National, Chelmsford (EX) 1676 |
| 13964 | BVX 674B | Bristol FLF6G | 217.178 | H38/32F | 5/64 | Eastern National, Chelmsford (EX) 1677 |
| 13965 | BVX 675B | Bristol FLF6B | 224.009 | H38/32F | 7/64 | Eastern National, Chelmsford (EX) 1678 |
| 13966 | BVX 676B | Bristol FLF6B | 224.010 | H38/32F | 7/64 | Eastern National, Chelmsford (EX) 1679 |
| 13967 | *BVX 677B | Bristol FLF6B | 224.011 | H38/32F | 7/64 | Eastern National, Chelmsford (EX) 1680 |
| 13968 | BVX 679B | Bristol FLF6B | 224.023 | H38/32F | 7/64 | Eastern National, Chelmsford (EX) 1682 |
| 13969 | BVX 678B | Bristol FLF6G | 224.022 | H38/32F | 7/64 | Eastern National, Chelmsford (EX) 1681 |
| 13970 | *BVX 680B | Bristol FLF6G | 224.024 | H38/32F | 7/64 | Eastern National, Chelmsford (EX) 1683 |
| 13971 | BVX 681B | Bristol FLF6G | 224.025 | H38/32F | 8/64 | Eastern National, Chelmsford (EX) 2805 |
| 13972 | BVX 682B | Bristol FLF6G | 224.026 | H38/32F | 8/64 | Eastern National, Chelmsford (EX) 2806 |
| 13973 | BVX 683B | Bristol FLF6B | 224.029 | H38/32F | 8/64 | Eastern National, Chelmsford (EX) 2807 |
| 13974 | VFE 959 | Bristol FLF6B | 217.056 | H38/32F | 11/63 | Lincolnshire RCC, Lincoln (LC) 2510 |
| 13975 | VFE 960 | Bristol FLF6G | 217.057 | H38/32F | 11/63 | Lincolnshire RCC, Lincoln (LC) 2511 |
| 13976 | 374 RNN | Bristol FLF6G | 217.051 | H38/32F | 11/63 | Mansfield District (NG) 620 |
| 13977 | 375 RNN | Bristol FLF6G | 217.052 | H38/32F | 11/63 | Mansfield District (NG) 621 |
| 13978 | 376 RNN | Bristol FLF6G | 217.082 | H38/32F | 1/64 | Mansfield District (NG) 622 |
| 13979 | 377 RNN | Bristol FLF6G | 217.083 | H38/32F | 12/63 | Mansfield District (NG) 623 |
| 13980 | 378 RNN | Bristol FLF6B | 224.004 | H38/32F | 8/64 | Mansfield District (NG) 624 |
| 13981 | AAL 104B | Bristol FLF6B | 224.031 | H38/32F | 9/64 | Mansfield District (NG) 625 |
| 13982 | 1387 R | Bristol FLF6B | 217.013 | H38/32F | 11/63 | Midland General, Langley Mill (DE) 626 |
| 13983 | *1388 R | Bristol FLF6B | 217.014 | H38/32F | 12/63 | Midland General, Langley Mill (DE) 627 |
| 13984 | *1389 R | Bristol FLF6B | 217.070 | H38/32F | 12/63 | Midland General, Langley Mill (DE) 628 |
| 13985 | *1390 R | Bristol FLF6B | 217.071 | H38/32F | 12/63 | Midland General, Langley Mill (DE) 629 |
| 13986 | 1391 R | Bristol FLF6B | 217.110 | H38/32F | 2/64 | Midland General, Langley Mill (DE) 630 |
| 13987 | 1392 R | Bristol FLF6B | 217.113 | H38/32F | 2/64 | Midland General, Langley Mill (DE) 631 |
| 13988 | *ANU 11B | Bristol FLF6B | 224.030 | H38/32F | 9/64 | Midland General, Langley Mill (DE) 632 |
| 13989 | 426 PTA | Bristol FLF6B | 217.061 | H38/30F | 1/64 | Southern National, Exeter (DN) 2046 |
| 13990 | 427 PTA | Bristol FLF6B | 217.062 | H38/30F | 1/64 | Southern National, Exeter (DN) 2047 |
| 13991 | *428 PTA | Bristol FLF6B | 217.115 | H38/30F | 2/64 | Southern National, Exeter (DN) 2048 |
| 13992 | 429 PTA | Bristol FLF6B | 217.117 | H38/30F | 2/64 | Southern National, Exeter (DN) 2049 |
| 13993 | ATA 119B | Bristol FLF6B | 224.013 | H38/32F | 8/64 | Southern National, Exeter (DN) 2050 |
| 13994 | ATA 120B | Bristol FLF6B | 224.038 | H38/32F | 9/64 | Southern National, Exeter (DN) 2051 |
| 13995 | 839 CRX | Bristol FLF6G | 217.020 | H38/32F | 10/63 | Thames Valley, Reading (BE) D1 |
| 13996 | 840 CRX | Bristol FLF6G | 217.021 | H38/32F | 10/63 | Thames Valley, Reading (BE) D2 |
| 13997 | 841 CRX | Bristol FLF6G | 217.022 | H38/32F | 10/63 | Thames Valley, Reading (BE) D3 |
| 13998 | *ABL 116B | Bristol FLF6B | 217.084 | CH37/28F | 1/64 | Thames Valley, Reading (BE) D4 |
| 13999 | *ABL 117B | Bristol FLF6B | 217.085 | CH37/28F | 1/64 | Thames Valley, Reading (BE) D5 |
| 14000 | *ABL 118B | Bristol FLF6B | 217.086 | CH37/28F | 2/64 | Thames Valley, Reading (BE) D6 |
| 14001 | *ABL 119B | Bristol FLF6B | 217.087 | CH37/28F | 2/64 | Thames Valley, Reading (BE) D7 |

| | | | | | | |
|---|---|---|---|---|---|---|
| 14002 | BRX 141B | Bristol FLF6G | 224.027 | CH37/28F | 8/64 | Thames Valley, Reading (BE) D8 |
| 14003 | *BRX 142B | Bristol FLF6G | 224.028 | H38/32F | 8/64 | Thames Valley, Reading (BE) D9 |
| 14004 | 137 SHN | Bristol FLF6B | 210.077 | H38/32F | 10/63 | United AS, Darlington (DM) BL137 |
| 14005 | 138 SHN | Bristol FLF6B | 210.078 | H38/32F | 10/63 | United AS, Darlington (DM) BL138 |
| 14006 | 139 SHN | Bristol FLF6B | 210.079 | H38/32F | 10/63 | United AS, Darlington (DM) BL139 |
| 14007 | 140 SHN | Bristol FLF6B | 210.080 | H38/32F | 10/63 | United AS, Darlington (DM) BL140 |
| 14008 | 141 SHN | Bristol FLF6B | 217.058 | H38/32F | 11/63 | United AS, Darlington (DM) BL141 |
| 14009 | 142 SHN | Bristol FLF6B | 217.059 | H38/32F | 12/63 | United AS, Darlington (DM) BL142 |
| 14010 | 143 SHN | Bristol FLF6B | 217.060 | H38/32F | 12/63 | United AS, Darlington (DM) BL143 |
| 14011 | 144 SHN | Bristol FLF6B | 217.089 | H38/32F | 1/64 | United AS, Darlington (DM) BL144 |
| 14012 | 145 SHN | Bristol FLF6B | 217.090 | H38/32F | 1/64 | United AS, Darlington (DM) BL145 |
| 14013 | 146 SHN | Bristol FLF6B | 217.091 | H38/32F | 1/64 | United AS, Darlington (DM) BL146 |
| 14014 | 147 SHN | Bristol FLF6B | 217.092 | H38/32F | 1/64 | United AS, Darlington (DM) BL147 |
| 14015 | 148 SHN | Bristol FLF6B | 217.102 | H38/32F | 2/64 | United AS, Darlington (DM) BL148 |
| 14016 | 149 SHN | Bristol FLF6B | 217.106 | H38/32F | 2/64 | United AS, Darlington (DM) BL149 |
| 14017 | 150 SHN | Bristol FLF6B | 217.108 | H38/32F | 4/64 | United AS, Darlington (DM) BL150 |
| 14018 | 151 SHN | Bristol FLF6B | 217.109 | H38/32F | 2/64 | United AS, Darlington (DM) BL151 |
| 14019 | 152 SHN | Bristol FLF6B | 217.167 | H38/32F | 5/64 | United AS, Darlington (DM) BL152 |
| 14020 | 153 SHN | Bristol FLF6B | 217.168 | H38/32F | 6/64 | United AS, Darlington (DM) BL153 |
| 14021 | 154 SHN | Bristol FLF6B | 217.169 | H38/32F | 6/64 | United AS, Darlington (DM) BL154 |
| 14022 | AHN 155B | Bristol FLF6B | 224.032 | H38/32F | 9/64 | United AS, Darlington (DM) BL155 |
| 14023 | AHN 156B | Bristol FLF6B | 224.033 | H38/32F | 9/64 | United AS, Darlington (DM) BL156 |
| 14024 | AHN 157B | Bristol FLF6B | 224.034 | H38/32F | 9/64 | United AS, Darlington (DM) BL157 |
| 14025 | AHN 158B | Bristol FLF6B | 224.035 | H38/32F | 9/64 | United AS, Darlington (DM) BL158 |
| 14026 | 125 FCY | Bristol FLF6B | 210.099 | H38/32F | 11/63 | United Welsh, Swansea (GG) 377 |
| 14027 | 126 FCY | Bristol FLF6B | 210.100 | H38/32F | 10/63 | United Welsh, Swansea (GG) 378 |
| 14028 | 127 FCY | Bristol FLF6G | 217.080 | H38/32F | 12/63 | United Welsh, Swansea (GG) 379 |
| 14029 | 128 FCY | Bristol FLF6G | 217.088 | H38/32F | 12/63 | United Welsh, Swansea (GG) 380 |
| 14030 | 129 FCY | Bristol FLF6G | 217.112 | H38/32F | 3/64 | United Welsh, Swansea (GG) 381 |
| 14031 | 130 FCY | Bristol FLF6G | 217.114 | H38/32F | 3/64 | United Welsh, Swansea (GG) 382 |
| 14032 | 131 FCY | Bristol FLF6G | 217.163 | H38/32F | 5/64 | United Welsh, Swansea (GG) 383 |
| 14033 | 132 FCY | Bristol FLF6G | 224.036 | H38/32F | 10/64 | United Welsh, Swansea (GG) 384 |
| 14034 | 133 FCY | Bristol FLF6G | 224.037 | H38/32F | 10/64 | United Welsh, Swansea (GG) 385 |
| 14035 | 400 PTA | Bristol FLF6G | 217.017 | H38/30F | 11/63 | Western National, Exeter (DN) 2020 |
| 14036 | 401 PTA | Bristol FLF6B | 217.018 | H38/30F | 11/63 | Western National, Exeter (DN) 2021 |
| 14037 | 402 PTA | Bristol FLF6B | 217.019 | H38/30F | 11/63 | Western National, Exeter (DN) 2022 |
| 14038 | 403 PTA | Bristol FLF6B | 217.047 | H38/30F | 11/63 | Western National, Exeter (DN) 2023 |
| 14039 | 404 PTA | Bristol FLF6G | 217.063 | H38/30F | 12/63 | Western National, Exeter (DN) 2024 |
| 14040 | 405 PTA | Bristol FLF6G | 217.064 | H38/30F | 12/63 | Western National, Exeter (DN) 2025 |
| 14041 | 406 PTA | Bristol FLF6B | 217.065 | H38/30F | 12/63 | Western National, Exeter (DN) 2026 |
| 14042 | 407 PTA | Bristol FLF6B | 217.072 | H38/30F | 12/63 | Western National, Exeter (DN) 2027 |
| 14043 | 408 PTA | Bristol FLF6B | 217.073 | H38/30F | 12/63 | Western National, Exeter (DN) 2028 |
| 14044 | *409 PTA | Bristol FLF6B | 217.103 | H38/30F | 3/64 | Western National, Exeter (DN) 2029 |
| 14045 | 410 PTA | Bristol FLF6B | 217.104 | H38/32F | 3/64 | Western National, Exeter (DN) 2030 |
| 14046 | *412 PTA | Bristol FLF6B | 217.107 | H38/32F | 2/64 | Western National, Exeter (DN) 2032 |
| 14047 | 411 PTA | Bristol FLF6B | 217.105 | H38/32F | 3/64 | Western National, Exeter (DN) 2031 |
| 14048 | 413 PTA | Bristol FLF6B | 217.138 | H38/32F | 3/64 | Western National, Exeter (DN) 2033 |
| 14049 | *414 PTA | Bristol FLF6B | 217.147 | H38/32F | 4/64 | Western National, Exeter (DN) 2034 |
| 14050 | 415 PTA | Bristol FLF6B | 217.148 | H38/32F | 4/64 | Western National, Exeter (DN) 2035 |
| 14051 | *416 PTA | Bristol FLF6B | 217.149 | H38/32F | 5/64 | Western National, Exeter (DN) 2036 |
| 14052 | 417 PTA | Bristol FLF6B | 217.179 | H38/32F | 6/64 | Western National, Exeter (DN) 2037 |
| 14053 | *418 PTA | Bristol FLF6B | 217.180 | H38/32F | 6/64 | Western National, Exeter (DN) 2038 |
| 14054 | 419 PTA | Bristol FLF6B | 217.181 | H38/32F | 6/64 | Western National, Exeter (DN) 2039 |
| 14055 | ATA 121B | Bristol FLF6B | 224.012 | H38/32F | 8/64 | Western National, Exeter (DN) 2040 |
| 14056 | ATA 122B | Bristol FLF6B | 224.040 | H38/32F | 10/64 | Western National, Exeter (DN) 2041 |
| 14057 | ATA 123B | Bristol FLF6B | 224.041 | H38/32F | 10/64 | Western National, Exeter (DN) 2042 |
| 14058 | ATA 124B | Bristol FLF6B | 224.046 | H38/32F | 10/64 | Western National, Exeter (DN) 2043 |
| 14059 | ATA 125B | Bristol FLF6B | 224.047 | H38/32F | 10/64 | Western National, Exeter (DN) 2044 |
| 14060 | ATA 126B | Bristol FLF6B | 224.048 | H38/32F | 10/64 | Western National, Exeter (DN) 2045 |
| 14061 | 467 BMR | Bristol FLF6G | 217.015 | H38/32F | 10/63 | Wilts & Dorset, Salisbury (WI) 658 |
| 14062 | 468 BMR | Bristol FLF6G | 217.016 | H38/32F | 10/63 | Wilts & Dorset, Salisbury (WI) 659 |
| 14063 | 469 BMR | Bristol FLF6G | 217.161 | H38/32F | 5/64 | Wilts & Dorset, Salisbury (WI) 660 |
| 14064 | 470 BMR | Bristol FLF6G | 217.162 | H38/32F | 5/64 | Wilts & Dorset, Salisbury (WI) 661 |
| 14065 | AHR 244B | Bristol FLF6G | 224.021 | H38/32F | 8/64 | Wilts & Dorset, Salisbury (WI) 662 |

| | | | | | | | |
|---|---|---|---|---|---|---|---|
| 14066 | AHR 246B | Bristol FLF6G | 224.039 | H38/32F | 9/64 | Wilts & Dorset, Salisbury (WI) 663 |
| 14067 | 981 UHW | Bristol MW5G | 213.115 | B45F | 2/64 | Bristol OC (GL) 2588 |
| 14068 | 982 UHW | Bristol MW5G | 213.116 | B45F | 2/64 | Bristol OC (GL) 2589 |
| 14069 | 983 UHW | Bristol MW5G | 213.117 | B45F | 2/64 | Bristol OC (GL) 2590 |
| 14070 | 984 UHW | Bristol MW5G | 213.118 | B45F | 2/64 | Bristol OC (GL) 2591 |
| 14071 | 985 UHW | Bristol MW5G | 213.131 | B45F | 2/64 | Bristol OC (GL) 2592 |
| 14072 | 986 UHW | Bristol MW5G | 213.132 | B45F | 3/64 | Bristol OC (GL) 2593 |
| 14073 | 987 UHW | Bristol MW5G | 213.133 | B45F | 3/64 | Bristol OC (GL) 2594 |
| 14074 | 988 UHW | Bristol MW5G | 213.134 | B45F | 3/64 | Bristol OC (GL) 2595 |
| 14075 | *AAE 52B | Bristol MW5G | 213.193 | B45F | 9/64 | Bristol OC (GL) 2596 |
| 14076 | *AAE 53B | Bristol MW5G | 213.194 | B45F | 9/64 | Bristol OC (GL) 2597 |
| 14077 | *AAE 54B | Bristol MW5G | 213.195 | B45F | 9/64 | Bristol OC (GL) 2598 |
| 14078 | *AAE 55B | Bristol MW5G | 213.196 | B45F | 9/64 | Bristol OC (GL) 2599 |
| 14079 | *AHW 787B | Bristol MW5G | 213.214 | B45F | 11/64 | Bristol OC (GL) 2600 |
| 14080 | *AHW 788B | Bristol MW5G | 213.215 | B45F | 11/64 | Bristol OC (GL) 2601 |
| 14081 | 6334 FM | Bristol MW6G | 213.127 | B45F | 3/64 | Crosville MS, Chester (CH) SMG497 |
| 14082 | 6335 FM | Bristol MW6G | 213.128 | B45F | 3/64 | Crosville MS, Chester (CH) SMG498 |
| 14083 | 6336 FM | Bristol MW6G | 213.129 | B45F | 3/64 | Crosville MS, Chester (CH) SMG499 |
| 14084 | 6337 FM | Bristol MW6G | 213.130 | B45F | 3/64 | Crosville MS, Chester (CH) SMG500 |
| 14085 | AFM 108B | Bristol MW6G | 213.185 | B45F | 8/64 | Crosville MS, Chester (CH) SMG501 |
| 14086 | AFM 109B | Bristol MW6G | 213.186 | B45F | 8/64 | Crosville MS, Chester (CH) SMG502 |
| 14087 | AFM 110B | Bristol MW6G | 213.187 | B45F | 8/64 | Crosville MS, Chester (CH) SMG503 |
| 14088 | AFM 111B | Bristol MW6G | 213.188 | B45F | 8/64 | Crosville MS, Chester (CH) SMG504 |
| 14089 | BFM 436B | Bristol MW6G | 213.201 | B45F | 11/64 | Crosville MS, Chester (CH) SMG505 |
| 14090 | BFM 437B | Bristol MW6G | 213.202 | B45F | 12/64 | Crosville MS, Chester (CH) SMG506 |
| 14091 | BFM 438B | Bristol MW6G | 213.203 | B45F | 12/64 | Crosville MS, Chester (CH) SMG507 |
| 14092 | BFM 439B | Bristol MW6G | 213.204 | B45F | 12/64 | Crosville MS, Chester (CH) SMG508 |
| 14093 | BFM 440B | Bristol MW6G | 213.208 | B45F | 12/64 | Crosville MS, Chester (CH) SMG509 |
| 14094 | 425 LAO | Bristol MW6G | 213.103 | B45F | 12/63 | Cumberland MS, Whitehaven (CU) 227 |
| 14095 | 426 LAO | Bristol MW6G | 213.104 | B45F | 12/63 | Cumberland MS, Whitehaven (CU) 228 |
| 14096 | 155 SHN | Bristol MW6G | 213.181 | B45F | 7/64 | United AS, Darlington (DM) BU712 |
| 14097 | 156 SHN | Bristol MW6G | 213.182 | B45F | 7/64 | United AS, Darlington (DM) BU713 |
| 14098 | AHN 414B | Bristol MW6G | 213.205 | B45F | 11/64 | United AS, Darlington (DM) BU714 |
| 14099 | 600 ENG | Bristol MW5G | 213.107 | B45F | 12/63 | Eastern Counties, Norwich (NK) LM600 |
| 14100 | 601 ENG | Bristol MW5G | 213.108 | B45F | 12/63 | Eastern Counties, Norwich (NK) LM601 |
| 14101 | AAH 102B | Bristol MW5G | 213.109 | B45F | 1/64 | Eastern Counties, Norwich (NK) LM602 |
| 14102 | AAH 103B | Bristol MW5G | 213.110 | B45F | 1/64 | Eastern Counties, Norwich (NK) LM603 |
| 14103 | AAH 911B | Bristol MW5G | 213.135 | B45F | 3/64 | Eastern Counties, Norwich (NK) LM604 |
| 14104 | AAH 912B | Bristol MW5G | 213.136 | B45F | 2/64 | Eastern Counties, Norwich (NK) LM605 |
| 14105 | AAH 913B | Bristol MW5G | 213.137 | B45F | 3/64 | Eastern Counties, Norwich (NK) LM606 |
| 14106 | AAH 914B | Bristol MW5G | 213.138 | B45F | 3/64 | Eastern Counties, Norwich (NK) LM607 |
| 14107 | BVF 608B | Bristol MW5G | 213.189 | B45F | 8/64 | Eastern Counties, Norwich (NK) LM608 |
| 14108 | BVF 609B | Bristol MW5G | 213.190 | B45F | 8/64 | Eastern Counties, Norwich (NK) LM609 |
| 14109 | BVF 610B | Bristol MW5G | 213.191 | B45F | 8/64 | Eastern Counties, Norwich (NK) LM610 |
| 14110 | BVF 611B | Bristol MW5G | 213.192 | B45F | 8/64 | Eastern Counties, Norwich (NK) LM611 |
| 14111 | CPW 612B | Bristol MW5G | 213.206 | B45F | 11/64 | Eastern Counties, Norwich (NK) LM612 |
| 14112 | CPW 613B | Bristol MW5G | 213.207 | B45F | 11/64 | Eastern Counties, Norwich (NK) LM613 |
| 14113 | CPW 614B | Bristol MW5G | 213.216 | B45F | 11/64 | Eastern Counties, Norwich (NK) LM614 |
| 14114 | CPW 615B | Bristol MW5G | 213.217 | B45F | 11/64 | Eastern Counties, Norwich (NK) LM615 |
| 14115 | 563 HWO | Bristol MW6G | 213.119 | B45F | 1/64 | Red & White, Chepstow (MH) U163 |
| 14116 | 564 HWO | Bristol MW6G | 213.120 | B45F | 1/64 | Red & White, Chepstow (MH) U263 |
| 14117 | 565 HWO | Bristol MW6G | 213.121 | B45F | 1/64 | Red & White, Chepstow (MH) U363 |
| 14118 | 566 HWO | Bristol MW6G | 213.122 | B45F | 2/64 | Red & White, Chepstow (MH) U463 |
| 14119 | *AAX 11B | Bristol MW6G | 213.139 | B45F | 3/64 | Red & White, Chepstow (MH) U563 |
| 14120 | *AAX 12B | Bristol MW6G | 213.140 | B45F | 3/64 | Red & White, Chepstow (MH) U663 |
| 14121 | *AAX 13B | Bristol MW6G | 213.197 | B45F | 10/64 | Red & White, Chepstow (MH) U763 |
| 14122 | *AAX 14B | Bristol MW6G | 213.198 | B45F | 10/64 | Red & White, Chepstow (MH) U863 |
| 14123 | *AAX 15B | Bristol MW6G | 213.199 | B45F | 10/64 | Red & White, Chepstow (MH) U963 |
| 14124 | *AAX 16B | Bristol MW6G | 213.200 | B45F | 10/64 | Red & White, Chepstow (MH) U1063 |
| 14125 | *AAX 17C | Bristol MW6G | 213.211 | B45F | 4/65 | Red & White, Chepstow (MH) U1163 |
| 14126 | *AAX 18C | Bristol MW6G | 213.212 | B45F | 4/65 | Red & White, Chepstow (MH) U1263 |
| 14127 | *AAX 19C | Bristol MW6G | 213.213 | B45F | 4/65 | Red & White, Chepstow (MH) U1363 |
| 14128 | *AAX 20C | Bristol MW6G | 213.220 | B45F | 4/65 | Red & White, Chepstow (MH) U1463 |
| 14129 | 902 THN | Bristol MW6G | 213.111 | B45F | 12/63 | United AS, Darlington (DM) BU702 |

| | | | | | | |
|---|---|---|---|---|---|---|
| 14130 | 903 THN | Bristol MW6G | 213.112 | B45F | 12/63 | United AS, Darlington (DM) BU703 |
| 14131 | 904 THN | Bristol MW6G | 213.123 | B45F | 3/64 | United AS, Darlington (DM) BU704 |
| 14132 | 905 THN | Bristol MW6G | 213.124 | B45F | 3/64 | United AS, Darlington (DM) BU705 |
| 14133 | 906 THN | Bristol MW6G | 213.125 | B45F | 3/64 | United AS, Darlington (DM) BU706 |
| 14134 | 907 THN | Bristol MW6G | 213.126 | B45F | 3/64 | United AS, Darlington (DM) BU707 |
| 14135 | 908 THN | Bristol MW6G | 213.141 | B45F | 4/64 | United AS, Darlington (DM) BU708 |
| 14136 | 909 THN | Bristol MW6G | 213.142 | B45F | 6/64 | United AS, Darlington (DM) BU709 |
| 14137 | 910 THN | Bristol MW6G | 213.179 | B45F | 7/64 | United AS, Darlington (DM) BU710 |
| 14138 | 911 THN | Bristol MW6G | 213.180 | B45F | 7/64 | United AS, Darlington (DM) BU711 |
| 14139 | 699 FWW | Bristol MW6G | 213.113 | B45F | 2/64 | West Yorkshire RCC, Harrogate (WR) SMG33 |
| 14140 | 700 FWW | Bristol MW6G | 213.114 | B45F | 2/64 | West Yorkshire RCC, Harrogate (WR) SMG34 |
| 14141 | AWU 463B | Bristol MW6G | 213.183 | B45F | 7/64 | West Yorkshire RCC, Harrogate (WR) SMG35 |
| 14142 | AWU 464B | Bristol MW6G | 213.184 | B45F | 8/64 | West Yorkshire RCC, Harrogate (WR) SMG36 |
| 14143 | AWU 465B | Bristol MW6G | 213.209 | B45F | 11/64 | West Yorkshire RCC, Harrogate (WR) SMG37 |
| 14144 | AWU 466B | Bristol MW6G | 213.210 | B45F | 11/64 | West Yorkshire RCC, Harrogate (WR) SMG38 |
| 14145 | BNO 101B | Bristol RELH6G | 212.038 | DP47F | 1/64 | Eastern National, Chelmsford (EX) 591 |
| 14146 | BNO 102B | Bristol RELH6G | 212.039 | DP47F | 1/64 | Eastern National, Chelmsford (EX) 592 |
| 14147 | BNO 103B | Bristol RELH6G | 212.040 | DP47F | 4/64 | Eastern National, Chelmsford (EX) 593 |
| 14148 | BNO 104B | Bristol RELH6G | 212.041 | DP47F | 4/64 | Eastern National, Chelmsford (EX) 594 |
| 14149 | BNO 105B | Bristol RELH6G | 212.042 | DP47F | 4/64 | Eastern National, Chelmsford (EX) 595 |
| 14150 | BNO 106B | Bristol RELH6G | 212.043 | DP47F | 3/64 | Eastern National, Chelmsford (EX) 596 |
| 14151 | BNO 107B | Bristol RELH6G | 212.044 | DP47F | 3/64 | Eastern National, Chelmsford (EX) 597 |
| 14152 | BNO 108B | Bristol RELH6G | 212.045 | DP47F | 4/64 | Eastern National, Chelmsford (EX) 598 |
| 14153 | WFE 415 | Bristol RELH6G | 212.046 | DP47F | 2/64 | Lincolnshire RCC, Lincoln (LC) 2678 |
| 14154 | WFE 416 | Bristol RELH6G | 212.047 | DP47F | 2/64 | Lincolnshire RCC, Lincoln (LC) 2679 |
| 14155 | 1384 R | Bristol RELH6G | 212.048 | DP51F | 5/64 | Midland General, Langley Mill (DE) 30 |
| 14156 | 1385 R | Bristol RELH6G | 212.049 | DP51F | 5/64 | Midland General, Langley Mill (DE) 31 |
| 14157 | 1386 R | Bristol RELH6G | 212.050 | DP51F | 5/64 | Midland General, Langley Mill (DE) 32 |
| 14158 | 250 FRP | Bristol RELH6G | 212.032 | DP47F | 1/64 | United Counties, Northampton (NO) 250 |
| 14159 | *ABD 251B | Bristol RELH6G | 212.051 | DP47F | 3/64 | United Counties, Northampton (NO) 251 |
| 14160 | *ABD 252B | Bristol RELH6G | 212.052 | DP47F | 3/64 | United Counties, Northampton (NO) 252 |
| 14161 | ABD 253B | Bristol RELH6G | 212.058 | DP47F | 3/64 | United Counties, Northampton (NO) 253 |
| 14162 | 101 VHN | Bristol RELH6G | 212.033 | C43F | 1/64 | United AS, Darlington (DM) BRC1 |
| 14163 | 102 VHN | Bristol RELH6G | 212.034 | C43F | 1/64 | United AS, Darlington (DM) BRC2 |
| 14164 | 103 VHN | Bristol RELH6G | 212.035 | C43F | 1/64 | United AS, Darlington (DM) BRC3 |
| 14165 | 104 VHN | Bristol RELH6G | 212.036 | C43F | 1/64 | United AS, Darlington (DM) BRC4 |
| 14166 | 105 VHN | Bristol RELH6G | 212.037 | C43F | 2/64 | United AS, Darlington (DM) BRC5 |
| 14167 | 106 VHN | Bristol RELH6G | 212.053 | C43F | 4/64 | United AS, Darlington (DM) BRC6 |
| 14168 | 107 VHN | Bristol RELH6G | 212.054 | C43F | 4/64 | United AS, Darlington (DM) BRC7 |
| 14169 | 108 VHN | Bristol RELH6G | 212.055 | C43F | 4/64 | United AS, Darlington (DM) BRC8 |
| 14170 | 109 VHN | Bristol RELH6G | 212.056 | C43F | 4/64 | United AS, Darlington (DM) BRC9 |
| 14171 | 110 VHN | Bristol RELH6G | 212.057 | C43F | 4/64 | United AS, Darlington (DM) BRC10 |
| 14172 | *AAO 34B | Bristol MW6G | 213.105 | B45F | 5/64 | Cumberland MS, Whitehaven (CU) 229 |
| 14173 | *AAO 35B | Bristol MW6G | 213.106 | B45F | 5/64 | Cumberland MS, Whitehaven (CU) 230 |
| 14174 | AHN 102B | Bristol RELL6G | 222.001 | B54F | 9/64 | United AS, Darlington (DM) BR2 |
| 14175 | AHN 103B | Bristol RELL6G | 222.002 | B54F | 9/64 | United AS, Darlington (DM) BR3 |
| 14176 | AHN 118B | Bristol RELL6G | 222.047 | B54F | 10/64 | United AS, Darlington (DM) BR18 |
| 14177 | AHN 619B | Bristol RELL6G | 222.048 | B54F | 11/64 | United AS, Darlington (DM) BR19 |
| 14178 | AHN 623B | Bristol RELL6G | 222.054 | B54F | 11/64 | United AS, Darlington (DM) BR23 |
| 14179 | | | | | | Not built |
| 14180 | | | | | | Not built |
| 14181 | | | | | | Not built |
| 14182 | *AFE 471B | Bristol RELL6G | 222.036 | B54F | 10/64 | Lincolnshire RCC, Lincoln (LC) 1201 |
| 14183 | *AFE 472B | Bristol RELL6G | 222.037 | B54F | 10/64 | Lincolnshire RCC, Lincoln (LC) 1202 |
| 14184 | *AFE 473B | Bristol RELL6G | 222.051 | B54F | 10/64 | Lincolnshire RCC, Lincoln (LC) 1203 |
| 14185 | *AFE 474B | Bristol RELL6G | 222.052 | B54F | 12/64 | Lincolnshire RCC, Lincoln (LC) 1204 |
| 14186 | CBL 355B | Bristol RELL6G | 222.028 | B54F | 9/64 | Thames Valley, Reading (BE) S306 |
| 14187 | CBL 356B | Bristol RELL6G | 222.029 | B54F | 9/64 | Thames Valley, Reading (BE) S307 |
| 14188 | CBL 357B | Bristol RELL6G | 222.030 | B54F | 10/64 | Thames Valley, Reading (BE) S308 |
| 14189 | AHN 104B | Bristol RELL6G | 222.031 | B54F | 10/64 | United AS, Darlington (DM) BR4 |
| 14190 | AHN 105B | Bristol RELL6G | 222.032 | B54F | 10/64 | United AS, Darlington (DM) BR5 |
| 14191 | AHN 106B | Bristol RELL6G | 222.033 | B54F | 10/64 | United AS, Darlington (DM) BR6 |
| 14192 | AHN 107B | Bristol RELL6G | 222.034 | B54F | 10/64 | United AS, Darlington (DM) BR7 |
| 14193 | AHN 108B | Bristol RELL6G | 222.035 | B54F | 10/64 | United AS, Darlington (DM) BR8 |

| 14194 | AHN 109B | Bristol RELL6G | 222.038 | B54F | 10/64 | United AS, Darlington (DM) BR9 |
|---|---|---|---|---|---|---|
| 14195 | AHN 110B | Bristol RELL6G | 222.039 | B54F | 10/64 | United AS, Darlington (DM) BR10 |
| 14196 | AHN 111B | Bristol RELL6G | 222.040 | B54F | 10/64 | United AS, Darlington (DM) BR11 |
| 14197 | AHN 112B | Bristol RELL6G | 222.041 | B54F | 10/64 | United AS, Darlington (DM) BR12 |
| 14198 | AHN 113B | Bristol RELL6G | 222.042 | B54F | 10/64 | United AS, Darlington (DM) BR13 |
| 14199 | AHN 114B | Bristol RELL6G | 222.043 | B54F | 10/64 | United AS, Darlington (DM) BR14 |
| 14200 | AHN 115B | Bristol RELL6G | 222.044 | B54F | 10/64 | United AS, Darlington (DM) BR15 |
| 14201 | AHN 116B | Bristol RELL6G | 222.045 | B54F | 10/64 | United AS, Darlington (DM) BR16 |
| 14202 | AHN 117B | Bristol RELL6G | 222.046 | B54F | 10/64 | United AS, Darlington (DM) BR17 |
| 14203 | AHN 620B | Bristol RELL6G | 222.049 | B54F | 11/64 | United AS, Darlington (DM) BR20 |
| 14204 | AHN 621B | Bristol RELL6G | 222.050 | B54F | 11/64 | United AS, Darlington (DM) BR21 |
| 14205 | AHN 622B | Bristol RELL6G | 222.053 | B54F | 11/64 | United AS, Darlington (DM) BR22 |
| 14206 | AHN 624B | Bristol RELL6G | 222.055 | B54F | 11/64 | United AS, Darlington (DM) BR24 |
| 14207 | AHN 625B | Bristol RELL6G | 222.056 | B54F | 11/64 | United AS, Darlington (DM) BR25 |
| 14208 | AHN 626B | Bristol RELL6G | 222.057 | B54F | 11/64 | United AS, Darlington (DM) BR26 |
| 14209 | AHN 627B | Bristol RELL6G | 222.058 | B54F | 11/64 | United AS, Darlington (DM) BR27 |
| 14210 | AHN 628B | Bristol RELL6G | 222.059 | B54F | 11/64 | United AS, Darlington (DM) BR28 |
| 14211 | AHN 629B | Bristol RELL6G | 222.060 | B54F | 11/64 | United AS, Darlington (DM) BR29 |
| 14212 | AHN 630B | Bristol RELL6G | 222.061 | B54F | 12/64 | United AS, Darlington (DM) BR30 |
| 14213 | AHN 631B | Bristol RELL6G | 222.062 | B54F | 12/64 | United AS, Darlington (DM) BR31 |
| 14214 | BYG 756B | Bristol RELL6G | 222.025 | B54F | 10/64 | West Yorkshire RCC, Harrogate (WR) SRG1 |
| 14215 | BYG 757B | Bristol RELL6G | 222.026 | B54F | 10/64 | West Yorkshire RCC, Harrogate (WR) SRG2 |
| 14216 | BYG 758B | Bristol RELL6G | 222.027 | B54F | 10/64 | West Yorkshire RCC, Harrogate (WR) SRG3 |
| 14217 | 843 THY | Bristol SUS4A | 218.012 | B30F | 9/63 | Bristol OC (GL) 303 |
| 14218 | 844 THY | Bristol SUS4A | 218.013 | B30F | 9/63 | Bristol OC (GL) 304 |
| 14219 | 845 THY | Bristol SUS4A | 218.014 | B30F | 9/63 | Bristol OC (GL) 305 |
| 14220 | 846 THY | Bristol SUS4A | 218.015 | B30F | 9/63 | Bristol OC (GL) 306 |
| 14221 | 859 DYG | Bristol SUL4A | 218.006 | B36F | 7/63 | York-West Yorkshire, Harrogate (WR) YSMA7 |
| 14222 | 860 DYG | Bristol SUL4A | 218.007 | B36F | 7/63 | York-West Yorkshire, Harrogate (WR) YSMA8 |
| 14223 | 861 DYG | Bristol SUL4A | 218.008 | B36F | 8/63 | York-West Yorkshire, Harrogate (WR) YSMA9 |
| 14224 | 862 DYG | Bristol SUL4A | 218.009 | B36F | 8/63 | York-West Yorkshire, Harrogate (WR) YSMA10 |
| 14225 | 863 DYG | Bristol SUL4A | 218.010 | B36F | 8/63 | York-West Yorkshire, Harrogate (WR) YSMA11 |
| 14226 | 864 DYG | Bristol SUL4A | 218.011 | B36F | 8/63 | York-West Yorkshire, Harrogate (WR) YSMA12 |
| 14227 | 458 ADL | Bristol SUL4A | 190.058 | B36F | 5/63 | Southern Vectis, Newport (IW) 845 |
| 14228 | 459 ADL | Bristol SUL4A | 190.059 | B36F | 5/63 | Southern Vectis, Newport (IW) 846 |
| 14229 | 460 ADL | Bristol SUL4A | 190.060 | B36F | 5/63 | Southern Vectis, Newport (IW) 847 |
| 14230 | 461 ADL | Bristol SUL4A | 218.001 | B36F | 6/63 | Southern Vectis, Newport (IW) 848 |
| 14231 | 462 ADL | Bristol SUL4A | 218.002 | B36F | 6/63 | Southern Vectis, Newport (IW) 849 |
| 14232 | 463 ADL | Bristol SUL4A | 218.003 | B36F | 6/63 | Southern Vectis, Newport (IW) 850 |
| 14233 | 464 ADL | Bristol SUL4A | 218.004 | B36F | 6/63 | Southern Vectis, Newport (IW) 851 |
| 14234 | *465 ADL | Bristol SUL4A | 218.005 | B36F | 6/63 | Southern Vectis, Newport (IW) 852 |
| 14235 | 3652 FG | Bristol FS6G | 214.001 | H33/27RD | 5/63 | W Alexander (Fife), Kirkcaldy (FE) FRD166 |
| 14236 | 3653 FG | Bristol FS6G | 214.002 | H33/27RD | 5/63 | W Alexander (Fife), Kirkcaldy (FE) FRD167 |
| 14237 | 3654 FG | Bristol FS6G | 214.003 | H33/27RD | 5/63 | W Alexander (Fife), Kirkcaldy (FE) FRD168 |
| 14238 | 3655 FG | Bristol FS6G | 214.004 | H33/27RD | 5/63 | W Alexander (Fife), Kirkcaldy (FE) FRD169 |
| 14239 | 3656 FG | Bristol FS6G | 214.005 | H33/27RD | 5/63 | W Alexander (Fife), Kirkcaldy (FE) FRD170 |
| 14240 | 3657 FG | Bristol FS6G | 214.023 | H33/27RD | 5/63 | W Alexander (Fife), Kirkcaldy (FE) FRD171 |
| 14241 | 3658 FG | Bristol FS6G | 214.024 | H33/27RD | 5/63 | W Alexander (Fife), Kirkcaldy (FE) FRD172 |
| 14242 | 3659 FG | Bristol FS6G | 214.025 | H33/27RD | 5/63 | W Alexander (Fife), Kirkcaldy (FE) FRD173 |
| 14243 | 3660 FG | Bristol FS6G | 214.026 | H33/27RD | 6/63 | W Alexander (Fife), Kirkcaldy (FE) FRD174 |
| 14244 | 3661 FG | Bristol FS6G | 214.027 | H33/27RD | 5/63 | W Alexander (Fife), Kirkcaldy (FE) FRD175 |
| 14245 | 3662 FG | Bristol FS6G | 214.041 | H33/27RD | 7/63 | W Alexander (Fife), Kirkcaldy (FE) FRD176 |
| 14246 | 3663 FG | Bristol FS6G | 214.042 | H33/27RD | 7/63 | W Alexander (Fife), Kirkcaldy (FE) FRD177 |
| 14247 | 3664 FG | Bristol FS6G | 214.043 | H33/27RD | 7/63 | W Alexander (Fife), Kirkcaldy (FE) FRD178 |
| 14248 | 3665 FG | Bristol FS6G | 214.044 | H33/27RD | 7/63 | W Alexander (Fife), Kirkcaldy (FE) FRD179 |
| 14249 | 3666 FG | Bristol FS6G | 214.045 | H33/27RD | 7/63 | W Alexander (Fife), Kirkcaldy (FE) FRD180 |
| 14250 | 3667 FG | Bristol FS6G | 214.055 | H33/27RD | 8/63 | W Alexander (Fife), Kirkcaldy (FE) FRD181 |
| 14251 | 3668 FG | Bristol FS6G | 214.056 | H33/27RD | 8/63 | W Alexander (Fife), Kirkcaldy (FE) FRD182 |
| 14252 | 3669 FG | Bristol FS6G | 214.057 | H33/27RD | 8/63 | W Alexander (Fife), Kirkcaldy (FE) FRD183 |
| 14253 | 3670 FG | Bristol FS6G | 214.058 | H33/27RD | 8/63 | W Alexander (Fife), Kirkcaldy (FE) FRD184 |
| 14254 | 3671 FG | Bristol FS6G | 214.059 | H33/27RD | 8/63 | W Alexander (Fife), Kirkcaldy (FE) FRD185 |
| 14255 | 8943 SF | Bristol FS6G | 214.006 | H33/27RD | 5/63 | Scottish Omnibuses, Edinburgh (MN) AA943 |
| 14256 | 8944 SF | Bristol FS6G | 214.007 | H33/27RD | 5/63 | Scottish Omnibuses, Edinburgh (MN) AA944 |
| 14257 | 8945 SF | Bristol FS6G | 214.008 | H33/27RD | 5/63 | Scottish Omnibuses, Edinburgh (MN) AA945 |

| | | | | | | |
|---|---|---|---|---|---|---|
| 14258 | 8946 SF | Bristol FS6G | 214.009 | H33/27RD | 5/63 | Scottish Omnibuses, Edinburgh (MN) AA946 |
| 14259 | 8947 SF | Bristol FS6G | 214.010 | H33/27RD | 5/63 | Scottish Omnibuses, Edinburgh (MN) AA947 |
| 14260 | 8948 SF | Bristol FS6G | 214.031 | H33/27RD | 6/63 | Scottish Omnibuses, Edinburgh (MN) AA948 |
| 14261 | 8949 SF | Bristol FS6G | 214.032 | H33/27RD | 6/63 | Scottish Omnibuses, Edinburgh (MN) AA949 |
| 14262 | 8950 SF | Bristol FS6G | 214.033 | H33/27RD | 6/63 | Scottish Omnibuses, Edinburgh (MN) AA950 |
| 14263 | 8951 SF | Bristol FS6G | 214.034 | H33/27RD | 6/63 | Scottish Omnibuses, Edinburgh (MN) AA951 |
| 14264 | 8952 SF | Bristol FS6G | 214.035 | H33/27RD | 6/63 | Scottish Omnibuses, Edinburgh (MN) AA952 |
| 14265 | 8953 SF | Bristol FS6G | 214.046 | H33/27RD | 7/63 | Scottish Omnibuses, Edinburgh (MN) AA953 |
| 14266 | 8954 SF | Bristol FS6G | 214.047 | H33/27RD | 7/63 | Scottish Omnibuses, Edinburgh (MN) AA954 |
| 14267 | 8955 SF | Bristol FS6G | 214.048 | H33/27RD | 7/63 | Scottish Omnibuses, Edinburgh (MN) AA955 |
| 14268 | 8956 SF | Bristol FS6G | 214.050 | H33/27RD | 9/63 | Scottish Omnibuses, Edinburgh (MN) AA956 |
| 14269 | 8957 SF | Bristol FS6G | 214.051 | H33/27RD | 7/63 | Scottish Omnibuses, Edinburgh (MN) AA957 |
| 14270 | 8958 SF | Bristol FS6G | 214.060 | H33/27RD | 7/63 | Scottish Omnibuses, Edinburgh (MN) AA958 |
| 14271 | 8959 SF | Bristol FS6G | 214.061 | H33/27RD | 7/63 | Scottish Omnibuses, Edinburgh (MN) AA959 |
| 14272 | 8960 SF | Bristol FS6G | 214.062 | H33/27RD | 7/63 | Scottish Omnibuses, Edinburgh (MN) AA960 |
| 14273 | VWG 353 | Bristol FLF6G | 210.070 | H38/32F | 5/63 | W Alexander (Midland), Falkirk (SN) MRD173 |
| 14274 | VWG 354 | Bristol FLF6G | 210.071 | H38/32F | 5/63 | W Alexander (Midland), Falkirk (SN) MRD174 |
| 14275 | VWG 355 | Bristol FLF6G | 210.072 | H38/32F | 5/63 | W Alexander (Midland), Falkirk (SN) MRD175 |
| 14276 | VWG 356 | Bristol FLF6G | 210.073 | H38/32F | 6/63 | W Alexander (Midland), Falkirk (SN) MRD176 |
| 14277 | VWG 357 | Bristol FLF6G | 210.074 | H38/32F | 6/63 | W Alexander (Midland), Falkirk (SN) MRD177 |
| 14278 | VWG 358 | Bristol FLF6G | 210.081 | H38/32F | 6/63 | W Alexander (Midland), Falkirk (SN) MRD178 |
| 14279 | VWG 359 | Bristol FLF6G | 210.082 | H38/32F | 6/63 | W Alexander (Midland), Falkirk (SN) MRD179 |
| 14280 | VWG 360 | Bristol FLF6G | 210.083 | H38/32F | 6/63 | W Alexander (Midland), Falkirk (SN) MRD180 |
| 14281 | VWG 361 | Bristol FLF6G | 210.084 | H38/32F | 6/63 | W Alexander (Midland), Falkirk (SN) MRD181 |
| 14282 | VWG 362 | Bristol FLF6G | 210.085 | H38/32F | 7/63 | W Alexander (Midland), Falkirk (SN) MRD182 |
| 14283 | VWG 363 | Bristol FLF6G | 210.092 | H38/32F | 7/63 | W Alexander (Midland), Falkirk (SN) MRD183 |
| 14284 | VWG 364 | Bristol FLF6G | 210.093 | H38/32F | 7/63 | W Alexander (Midland), Falkirk (SN) MRD184 |
| 14285 | *VCS 351 | Bristol FLF6G | 210.094 | H38/32F | 7/63 | Western SMT, Kilmarnock (AR) B1797 |
| 14286 | VCS 352 | Bristol FLF6G | 210.095 | H38/32F | 7/63 | Western SMT, Kilmarnock (AR) B1798 |
| 14287 | VCS 353 | Bristol FLF6G | 210.096 | H38/32F | 7/63 | Western SMT, Kilmarnock (AR) B1799 |
| 14288 | *VCS 354 | Bristol FLF6G | 217.008 | H38/32F | 7/63 | Western SMT, Kilmarnock (AR) B1800 |
| 14289 | VCS 355 | Bristol FLF6G | 217.009 | H38/32F | 7/63 | Western SMT, Kilmarnock (AR) B1801 |
| 14290 | VCS 366 | Bristol FLF6G | 217.010 | H38/32F | 8/63 | Western SMT, Kilmarnock (AR) B1812 |
| 14291 | VCS 367 | Bristol FLF6G | 217.011 | H38/32F | 8/63 | Western SMT, Kilmarnock (AR) B1813 |
| 14292 | VCS 368 | Bristol FLF6G | 217.012 | H38/32F | 8/63 | Western SMT, Kilmarnock (AR) B1814 |
| 14293 | VCS 369 | Bristol FLF6G | 217.023 | H38/32F | 8/63 | Western SMT, Kilmarnock (AR) B1815 |
| 14294 | VCS 356 | Bristol FLF6G | 217.024 | H38/32F | 8/63 | Western SMT, Kilmarnock (AR) B1802 |
| 14295 | VCS 357 | Bristol FLF6G | 217.025 | H38/32F | 9/63 | Western SMT, Kilmarnock (AR) B1803 |
| 14296 | VCS 358 | Bristol FLF6G | 217.026 | H38/32F | 10/63 | Western SMT, Kilmarnock (AR) B1804 |
| 14297 | VCS 359 | Bristol FLF6G | 217.027 | H38/32F | 12/63 | Western SMT, Kilmarnock (AR) B1805 |
| 14298 | VCS 360 | Bristol FLF6G | 217.033 | H38/32F | 12/63 | Western SMT, Kilmarnock (AR) B1806 |
| 14299 | VCS 370 | Bristol FLF6G | 217.034 | H38/32F | 12/63 | Western SMT, Kilmarnock (AR) B1816 |
| 14300 | VCS 371 | Bristol FLF6G | 217.035 | H38/32F | 8/63 | Western SMT, Kilmarnock (AR) B1817 |
| 14301 | VCS 372 | Bristol FLF6G | 217.036 | H38/32F | 8/63 | Western SMT, Kilmarnock (AR) B1818 |
| 14302 | VCS 373 | Bristol FLF6G | 217.037 | H38/32F | 8/63 | Western SMT, Kilmarnock (AR) B1819 |
| 14303 | VCS 361 | Bristol FLF6G | 217.038 | H38/32F | 8/63 | Western SMT, Kilmarnock (AR) B1807 |
| 14304 | VCS 362 | Bristol FLF6G | 217.039 | H38/32F | 9/63 | Western SMT, Kilmarnock (AR) B1808 |
| 14305 | VCS 363 | Bristol FLF6G | 217.040 | H38/32F | 9/63 | Western SMT, Kilmarnock (AR) B1809 |
| 14306 | VCS 364 | Bristol FLF6G | 217.041 | H38/32F | 9/63 | Western SMT, Kilmarnock (AR) B1810 |
| 14307 | VCS 365 | Bristol FLF6G | 217.042 | H38/32F | 9/63 | Western SMT, Kilmarnock (AR) B1811 |
| 14308 | VCS 374 | Bristol FLF6G | 217.043 | H38/32F | 9/63 | Western SMT, Kilmarnock (AR) B1820 |
| 14309 | VCS 375 | Bristol FLF6G | 217.044 | H38/32F | 10/63 | Western SMT, Kilmarnock (AR) B1821 |
| 14310 | VCS 376 | Bristol FLF6G | 217.045 | H38/32F | 10/63 | Western SMT, Kilmarnock (AR) B1822 |
| 14311 | VCS 377 | Bristol FLF6G | 217.046 | H38/32F | 10/63 | Western SMT, Kilmarnock (AR) B1823 |
| 14312 | FGM 171 | Bristol FLF6G | 217.001 | H38/32F | 7/63 | Central SMT, Motherwell (LK) BE171 |
| 14313 | FGM 172 | Bristol FLF6G | 217.002 | H38/32F | 7/63 | Central SMT, Motherwell (LK) BE172 |
| 14314 | FGM 173 | Bristol FLF6G | 217.003 | H38/32F | 7/63 | Central SMT, Motherwell (LK) BE173 |
| 14315 | FGM 174 | Bristol FLF6G | 217.004 | H38/32F | 7/63 | Central SMT, Motherwell (LK) BE174 |
| 14316 | FGM 175 | Bristol FLF6G | 217.005 | H38/32F | 7/63 | Central SMT, Motherwell (LK) BE175 |
| 14317 | FGM 176 | Bristol FLF6G | 217.028 | H38/32F | 7/63 | Central SMT, Motherwell (LK) BE176 |
| 14318 | FGM 177 | Bristol FLF6G | 217.029 | H38/32F | 8/63 | Central SMT, Motherwell (LK) BE177 |
| 14319 | FGM 178 | Bristol FLF6G | 217.030 | H38/32F | 8/63 | Central SMT, Motherwell (LK) BE178 |
| 14320 | FGM 179 | Bristol FLF6G | 217.031 | H38/32F | 8/63 | Central SMT, Motherwell (LK) BE179 |
| 14321 | FGM 180 | Bristol FLF6G | 217.032 | H38/32F | 8/63 | Central SMT, Motherwell (LK) BE180 |

| | | | | | | | |
|---|---|---|---|---|---|---|---|
| 14322 | FGM 160 | Bristol FSF6G | 215.001 | H34/26F | 9/63 | Central SMT, Motherwell (LK) | B160 |
| 14323 | FGM 161 | Bristol FSF6G | 215.002 | H34/26F | 9/63 | Central SMT, Motherwell (LK) | B161 |
| 14324 | FGM 162 | Bristol FSF6G | 215.003 | H34/26F | 9/63 | Central SMT, Motherwell (LK) | B162 |
| 14325 | FGM 163 | Bristol FSF6G | 215.004 | H34/26F | 9/63 | Central SMT, Motherwell (LK) | B163 |
| 14326 | FGM 164 | Bristol FSF6G | 215.005 | H34/26F | 9/63 | Central SMT, Motherwell (LK) | B164 |
| 14327 | FGM 165 | Bristol FSF6G | 215.006 | H34/26F | 9/63 | Central SMT, Motherwell (LK) | B165 |
| 14328 | FGM 166 | Bristol FSF6G | 215.007 | H34/26F | 9/63 | Central SMT, Motherwell (LK) | B166 |
| 14329 | FGM 167 | Bristol FSF6G | 215.008 | H34/26F | 9/63 | Central SMT, Motherwell (LK) | B167 |
| 14330 | FGM 168 | Bristol FSF6G | 215.009 | H34/26F | 9/63 | Central SMT, Motherwell (LK) | B168 |
| 14331 | FGM 169 | Bristol FSF6G | 215.010 | H34/26F | 9/63 | Central SMT, Motherwell (LK) | B169 |
| 14332 | FGM 170 | Bristol FSF6G | 215.011 | H34/26F | 9/63 | Central SMT, Motherwell (LK) | B170 |
| 14333 | AMS 3B | Bristol FLF6G | 217.131 | H38/32F | 3/64 | W Alexander (Midland), Falkirk (SN) | MRD185 |
| 14334 | AMS 4B | Bristol FLF6G | 217.132 | H38/32F | 3/64 | W Alexander (Midland), Falkirk (SN) | MRD186 |
| 14335 | AMS 5B | Bristol FLF6G | 217.135 | H38/32F | 3/64 | W Alexander (Midland), Falkirk (SN) | MRD187 |
| 14336 | AMS 6B | Bristol FLF6G | 217.136 | H38/32F | 3/64 | W Alexander (Midland), Falkirk (SN) | MRD188 |
| 14337 | AMS 7B | Bristol FLF6G | 217.137 | H38/32F | 3/64 | W Alexander (Midland), Falkirk (SN) | MRD189 |
| 14338 | AMS 8B | Bristol FLF6G | 217.151 | H38/32F | 4/64 | W Alexander (Midland), Falkirk (SN) | MRD190 |
| 14339 | AMS 9B | Bristol FLF6G | 217.152 | H38/32F | 4/64 | W Alexander (Midland), Falkirk (SN) | MRD191 |
| 14340 | AMS 10B | Bristol FLF6G | 217.153 | H38/32F | 4/64 | W Alexander (Midland), Falkirk (SN) | MRD192 |
| 14341 | AMS 11B | Bristol FLF6G | 217.183 | H38/32F | 6/64 | W Alexander (Midland), Falkirk (SN) | MRD193 |
| 14342 | AMS 12B | Bristol FLF6G | 217.184 | H38/32F | 6/64 | W Alexander (Midland), Falkirk (SN) | MRD194 |
| 14343 | XCS 946 | Bristol FLF6G | 217.127 | H38/30F | 3/64 | Western SMT, Kilmarnock (AR) | B1925 |
| 14344 | XCS 947 | Bristol FLF6G | 217.128 | H38/30F | 3/64 | Western SMT, Kilmarnock (AR) | B1926 |
| 14345 | XCS 948 | Bristol FLF6G | 217.129 | H38/30F | 3/64 | Western SMT, Kilmarnock (AR) | B1927 |
| 14346 | XCS 949 | Bristol FLF6G | 217.130 | H38/30F | 3/64 | Western SMT, Kilmarnock (AR) | B1928 |
| 14347 | *XCS 950 | Bristol FLF6G | 217.133 | H38/30F | 4/64 | Western SMT, Kilmarnock (AR) | B1929 |
| 14348 | XCS 951 | Bristol FLF6G | 217.134 | H38/30F | 4/64 | Western SMT, Kilmarnock (AR) | B1930 |
| 14349 | XCS 952 | Bristol FLF6G | 217.142 | H38/30F | 4/64 | Western SMT, Kilmarnock (AR) | B1931 |
| 14350 | *XCS 953 | Bristol FLF6G | 217.143 | H38/30F | 4/64 | Western SMT, Kilmarnock (AR) | B1932 |
| 14351 | XCS 954 | Bristol FLF6G | 217.144 | H38/30F | 4/64 | Western SMT, Kilmarnock (AR) | B1933 |
| 14352 | XCS 955 | Bristol FLF6G | 217.145 | H38/30F | 4/64 | Western SMT, Kilmarnock (AR) | B1934 |
| 14353 | XCS 956 | Bristol FLF6G | 217.146 | H38/30F | 4/64 | Western SMT, Kilmarnock (AR) | B1935 |
| 14354 | XCS 957 | Bristol FLF6G | 217.154 | H38/30F | 5/64 | Western SMT, Kilmarnock (AR) | B1936 |
| 14355 | XCS 958 | Bristol FLF6G | 217.155 | H38/30F | 5/64 | Western SMT, Kilmarnock (AR) | B1937 |
| 14356 | XCS 959 | Bristol FLF6G | 217.156 | H38/30F | 5/64 | Western SMT, Kilmarnock (AR) | B1938 |
| 14357 | XCS 960 | Bristol FLF6G | 217.157 | H38/30F | 5/64 | Western SMT, Kilmarnock (AR) | B1939 |
| 14358 | XCS 961 | Bristol FLF6G | 217.158 | H38/30F | 5/64 | Western SMT, Kilmarnock (AR) | B1940 |
| 14359 | XCS 962 | Bristol FLF6G | 217.159 | H38/30F | 5/64 | Western SMT, Kilmarnock (AR) | B1941 |
| 14360 | XCS 963 | Bristol FLF6G | 217.160 | H38/30F | 5/64 | Western SMT, Kilmarnock (AR) | B1942 |
| 14361 | *AAG 62B | Bristol FLF6G | 217.170 | H38/30F | 6/64 | Western SMT, Kilmarnock (AR) | B1943 |
| 14362 | *AAG 63B | Bristol FLF6G | 217.171 | H38/30F | 6/64 | Western SMT, Kilmarnock (AR) | B1944 |
| 14363 | *AAG 64B | Bristol FLF6G | 217.172 | H38/30F | 6/64 | Western SMT, Kilmarnock (AR) | B1945 |
| 14364 | *AAG 65B | Bristol FLF6G | 217.173 | H38/30F | 6/64 | Western SMT, Kilmarnock (AR) | B1946 |
| 14365 | *AAG 66B | Bristol FLF6G | 217.174 | H38/30F | 6/64 | Western SMT, Kilmarnock (AR) | B1947 |
| 14366 | *AAG 67B | Bristol FLF6G | 217.185 | H38/32F | 6/64 | Western SMT, Kilmarnock (AR) | B1948 |
| 14367 | *AAG 68B | Bristol FLF6G | 217.186 | H38/32F | 6/64 | Western SMT, Kilmarnock (AR) | B1949 |
| 14368 | *AAG 118B | Bristol FLF6G | 217.187 | H38/32F | 7/64 | Western SMT, Kilmarnock (AR) | B1950 |
| 14369 | *AAG 119B | Bristol FLF6G | 217.188 | H38/32F | 7/64 | Western SMT, Kilmarnock (AR) | B1951 |
| 14370 | *AAG 120B | Bristol FLF6G | 217.189 | H38/32F | 7/64 | Western SMT, Kilmarnock (AR) | B1952 |
| 14371 | *AAG 121B | Bristol FLF6G | 217.190 | H38/32F | 7/64 | Western SMT, Kilmarnock (AR) | B1953 |
| 14372 | *AAG 122B | Bristol FLF6G | 217.191 | H38/32F | 7/64 | Western SMT, Kilmarnock (AR) | B1954 |
| 14373 | *AAG 123B | Bristol FLF6G | 217.194 | H38/30F | 6/64 | Western SMT, Kilmarnock (AR) | B1955 |
| 14374 | *AAG 124B | Bristol FLF6G | 224.001 | H38/32F | 7/64 | Western SMT, Kilmarnock (AR) | B1956 |
| 14375 | *AAG 125B | Bristol FLF6G | 224.002 | H38/32F | 7/64 | Western SMT, Kilmarnock (AR) | B1957 |
| 14376 | BXA 451B | Bristol FS6G | 214.134 | H33/27RD | 3/64 | W Alexander (Fife), Kirkcaldy (FE) | FRD186 |
| 14377 | BXA 452B | Bristol FS6G | 214.135 | H33/27RD | 3/64 | W Alexander (Fife), Kirkcaldy (FE) | FRD187 |
| 14378 | BXA 453B | Bristol FS6G | 214.136 | H33/27RD | 3/64 | W Alexander (Fife), Kirkcaldy (FE) | FRD188 |
| 14379 | BXA 454B | Bristol FS6G | 214.137 | H33/27RD | 3/64 | W Alexander (Fife), Kirkcaldy (FE) | FRD189 |
| 14380 | BXA 455B | Bristol FS6G | 214.142 | H33/27RD | 4/64 | W Alexander (Fife), Kirkcaldy (FE) | FRD190 |
| 14381 | BXA 456B | Bristol FS6G | 214.143 | H33/27RD | 4/64 | W Alexander (Fife), Kirkcaldy (FE) | FRD191 |
| 14382 | BXA 457B | Bristol FS6G | 214.146 | H33/27RD | 4/64 | W Alexander (Fife), Kirkcaldy (FE) | FRD192 |
| 14383 | BXA 458B | Bristol FS6G | 214.147 | H33/27RD | 4/64 | W Alexander (Fife), Kirkcaldy (FE) | FRD193 |
| 14384 | BXA 459B | Bristol FS6G | 214.148 | H33/27RD | 4/64 | W Alexander (Fife), Kirkcaldy (FE) | FRD194 |
| 14385 | BXA 460B | Bristol FS6G | 214.149 | H33/27RD | 4/64 | W Alexander (Fife), Kirkcaldy (FE) | FRD195 |

| 14386 | BXA 461B | Bristol FS6G | 214.150 | H33/27RD | 4/64 | W Alexander (Fife), Kirkcaldy (FE) FRD196 |
|---|---|---|---|---|---|---|
| 14387 | *BXA 462B | Bristol FS6G | 214.186 | H33/27RD | 6/64 | W Alexander (Fife), Kirkcaldy (FE) FRD197 |
| 14388 | BXA 463B | Bristol FS6G | 214.187 | H33/27RD | 6/64 | W Alexander (Fife), Kirkcaldy (FE) FRD198 |
| 14389 | BXA 464B | Bristol FS6G | 214.188 | H33/27RD | 6/64 | W Alexander (Fife), Kirkcaldy (FE) FRD199 |
| 14390 | AGM 681B | Bristol FS6G | 214.164 | H33/27RD | 4/64 | Central SMT, Motherwell (LK) B181 |
| 14391 | AGM 682B | Bristol FS6G | 214.165 | H33/27RD | 4/64 | Central SMT, Motherwell (LK) B182 |
| 14392 | AGM 683B | Bristol FS6G | 214.166 | H33/27RD | 4/64 | Central SMT, Motherwell (LK) B183 |
| 14393 | AGM 684B | Bristol FS6G | 214.167 | H33/27RD | 4/64 | Central SMT, Motherwell (LK) B184 |
| 14394 | AGM 685B | Bristol FS6G | 214.168 | H33/27RD | 5/64 | Central SMT, Motherwell (LK) B185 |
| 14395 | AGM 686B | Bristol FS6G | 214.175 | H33/27RD | 5/64 | Central SMT, Motherwell (LK) B186 |
| 14396 | AGM 687B | Bristol FS6G | 214.176 | H33/27RD | 5/64 | Central SMT, Motherwell (LK) B187 |
| 14397 | AGM 688B | Bristol FS6G | 214.177 | H33/27RD | 5/64 | Central SMT, Motherwell (LK) B188 |
| 14398 | AGM 689B | Bristol FS6G | 214.178 | H33/27RD | 5/64 | Central SMT, Motherwell (LK) B189 |
| 14399 | AGM 690B | Bristol FS6G | 214.179 | H33/27RD | 5/64 | Central SMT, Motherwell (LK) B190 |
| 14400 | AGM 691B | Bristol FS6G | 214.180 | H33/27RD | 5/64 | Central SMT, Motherwell (LK) B191 |
| 14401 | AGM 692B | Bristol FS6G | 214.184 | H33/27RD | 5/64 | Central SMT, Motherwell (LK) B192 |
| 14402 | AGM 693B | Bristol FS6G | 214.185 | H33/27RD | 5/64 | Central SMT, Motherwell (LK) B193 |
| 14403 | AGM 694B | Bristol FS6G | 214.192 | H33/27RD | 5/64 | Central SMT, Motherwell (LK) B194 |
| 14404 | AGM 695B | Bristol FS6G | 214.193 | H33/27RD | 6/64 | Central SMT, Motherwell (LK) B195 |
| 14405 | AGM 696B | Bristol FS6G | 214.194 | H33/27RD | 6/64 | Central SMT, Motherwell (LK) B196 |
| 14406 | AGM 697B | Bristol FS6G | 214.195 | H33/27RD | 6/64 | Central SMT, Motherwell (LK) B197 |
| 14407 | AGM 698B | Bristol FS6G | 214.196 | H33/27RD | 6/64 | Central SMT, Motherwell (LK) B198 |
| 14408 | AGM 699B | Bristol FS6G | 214.197 | H33/27RD | 6/64 | Central SMT, Motherwell (LK) B199 |
| 14409 | AGM 700B | Bristol FS6G | 214.198 | H33/27RD | 6/64 | Central SMT, Motherwell (LK) B200 |
| 14410 | AGM 701B | Bristol FS6G | 214.199 | H33/27RD | 6/64 | Central SMT, Motherwell (LK) B201 |
| 14411 | AGM 702B | Bristol FS6G | 214.200 | H33/27RD | 6/64 | Central SMT, Motherwell (LK) B202 |
| 14412 | AGM 703B | Bristol FS6G | 223.005 | H33/27RD | 6/64 | Central SMT, Motherwell (LK) B203 |
| 14413 | AGM 704B | Bristol FS6G | 223.006 | H33/27RD | 6/64 | Central SMT, Motherwell (LK) B204 |
| 14414 | AGM 705B | Bristol FS6G | 223.007 | H33/27RD | 6/64 | Central SMT, Motherwell (LK) B205 |
| 14415 | AGM 706B | Bristol FS6G | 223.008 | H33/27RD | 7/64 | Central SMT, Motherwell (LK) B206 |
| 14416 | AGM 707B | Bristol FS6G | 223.009 | H33/27RD | 7/64 | Central SMT, Motherwell (LK) B207 |
| 14417 | AGM 708B | Bristol FS6G | 223.010 | H33/27RD | 7/64 | Central SMT, Motherwell (LK) B208 |
| 14418 | AGM 709B | Bristol FS6G | 223.011 | H33/27RD | 7/64 | Central SMT, Motherwell (LK) B209 |
| 14419 | AGM 710B | Bristol FS6G | 223.012 | H33/27RD | 7/64 | Central SMT, Motherwell (LK) B210 |
| 14420 | AGM 711B | Bristol FS6G | 223.013 | H33/27RD | 7/64 | Central SMT, Motherwell (LK) B211 |
| 14421 | AGM 712B | Bristol FS6G | 223.014 | H33/27RD | 7/64 | Central SMT, Motherwell (LK) B212 |
| 14422 | AGM 713B | Bristol FS6G | 223.015 | H33/27RD | 7/64 | Central SMT, Motherwell (LK) B213 |
| 14423 | AGM 714B | Bristol FS6G | 223.016 | H33/27RD | 7/64 | Central SMT, Motherwell (LK) B214 |
| 14424 | AGM 715B | Bristol FS6G | 223.017 | H33/27RD | 7/64 | Central SMT, Motherwell (LK) B215 |
| 14425 | AFS 11B | Bristol FS6G | 214.138 | H33/27RD | 3/64 | Scottish Omnibuses, Edinburgh (MN) AA11 |
| 14426 | AFS 12B | Bristol FS6G | 214.139 | H33/27RD | 3/64 | Scottish Omnibuses, Edinburgh (MN) AA12 |
| 14427 | AFS 13B | Bristol FS6G | 214.140 | H33/27RD | 3/64 | Scottish Omnibuses, Edinburgh (MN) AA13 |
| 14428 | AFS 14B | Bristol FS6G | 214.141 | H33/27RD | 3/64 | Scottish Omnibuses, Edinburgh (MN) AA14 |
| 14429 | AFS 15B | Bristol FS6G | 214.144 | H33/27RD | 3/64 | Scottish Omnibuses, Edinburgh (MN) AA15 |
| 14430 | AFS 16B | Bristol FS6G | 214.145 | H33/27RD | 3/64 | Scottish Omnibuses, Edinburgh (MN) AA16 |
| 14431 | AFS 17B | Bristol FS6G | 214.155 | H33/27RD | 3/64 | Scottish Omnibuses, Edinburgh (MN) AA17 |
| 14432 | AFS 18B | Bristol FS6G | 214.156 | H33/27RD | 4/64 | Scottish Omnibuses, Edinburgh (MN) AA18 |
| 14433 | AFS 19B | Bristol FS6G | 214.157 | H33/27RD | 3/64 | Scottish Omnibuses, Edinburgh (MN) AA19 |
| 14434 | AFS 20B | Bristol FS6G | 214.158 | H33/27RD | 4/64 | Scottish Omnibuses, Edinburgh (MN) AA20 |
| 14435 | AFS 21B | Bristol FS6G | 214.159 | H33/27RD | 4/64 | Scottish Omnibuses, Edinburgh (MN) AA21 |
| 14436 | 4218 FM | Bristol MW6G | 213.151 | C39F | 5/64 | Crosville MS, Chester (CH) CMG510 |
| 14437 | 4219 FM | Bristol MW6G | 213.152 | C39F | 5/64 | Crosville MS, Chester (CH) CMG511 |
| 14438 | 4221 FM | Bristol MW6G | 213.153 | C39F | 5/64 | Crosville MS, Chester (CH) CMG512 |
| 14439 | 4222 FM | Bristol MW6G | 213.157 | C39F | 5/64 | Crosville MS, Chester (CH) CMG513 |
| 14440 | 4223 FM | Bristol MW6G | 213.158 | C39F | 5/64 | Crosville MS, Chester (CH) CMG514 |
| 14441 | 7281 FM | Bristol MW6G | 213.163 | C39F | 5/64 | Crosville MS, Chester (CH) CMG515 |
| 14442 | 7282 FM | Bristol MW6G | 213.164 | C39F | 5/64 | Crosville MS, Chester (CH) CMG516 |
| 14443 | 7283 FM | Bristol MW6G | 213.165 | C39F | 5/64 | Crosville MS, Chester (CH) CMG517 |
| 14444 | 7284 FM | Bristol MW6G | 213.166 | C39F | 5/64 | Crosville MS, Chester (CH) CMG518 |
| 14445 | 7619 FM | Bristol MW6G | 213.174 | C39F | 5/64 | Crosville MS, Chester (CH) CMG519 |
| 14446 | 7622 FM | Bristol MW6G | 213.175 | C39F | 5/64 | Crosville MS, Chester (CH) CMG520 |
| 14447 | 7623 FM | Bristol MW6G | 213.176 | C39F | 5/64 | Crosville MS, Chester (CH) CMG521 |
| 14448 | 7624 FM | Bristol MW6G | 213.177 | C39F | 5/64 | Crosville MS, Chester (CH) CMG522 |
| 14449 | 7625 FM | Bristol MW6G | 213.178 | C39F | 5/64 | Crosville MS, Chester (CH) CMG523 |

| | | | | | | |
|---|---|---|---|---|---|---|
| 14450 | APW 824B | Bristol MW6G | 213.145 | C39F | 5/64 | Eastern Counties, Norwich (NK) LS824 |
| 14451 | APW 825B | Bristol MW6G | 213.146 | C39F | 5/64 | Eastern Counties, Norwich (NK) LS825 |
| 14452 | APW 826B | Bristol MW6G | 213.147 | C39F | 5/64 | Eastern Counties, Norwich (NK) LS826 |
| 14453 | APW 827B | Bristol MW6G | 213.148 | C39F | 5/64 | Eastern Counties, Norwich (NK) LS827 |
| 14454 | APW 828B | Bristol MW6G | 213.149 | C39F | 5/64 | Eastern Counties, Norwich (NK) LS828 |
| 14455 | APW 829B | Bristol MW6G | 213.160 | C39F | 5/64 | Eastern Counties, Norwich (NK) LS829 |
| 14456 | APW 830B | Bristol MW6G | 213.161 | C39F | 5/64 | Eastern Counties, Norwich (NK) LS830 |
| 14457 | APW 831B | Bristol MW6G | 213.162 | C39F | 5/64 | Eastern Counties, Norwich (NK) LS831 |
| 14458 | APW 832B | Bristol MW6G | 213.167 | C39F | 5/64 | Eastern Counties, Norwich (NK) LS832 |
| 14459 | APW 833B | Bristol MW6G | 213.168 | C39F | 5/64 | Eastern Counties, Norwich (NK) LS833 |
| 14460 | APW 834B | Bristol MW6G | 213.169 | C39F | 6/64 | Eastern Counties, Norwich (NK) LS834 |
| 14461 | APW 835B | Bristol MW6G | 213.170 | C39F | 6/64 | Eastern Counties, Norwich (NK) LS835 |
| 14462 | BNO 115B | Bristol MW6G | 213.143 | C39F | 3/64 | Eastern National, Chelmsford (EX) 599 |
| 14463 | BNO 116B | Bristol MW6G | 213.144 | C39F | 3/64 | Eastern National, Chelmsford (EX) 600 |
| 14464 | BNO 117B | Bristol MW6G | 213.159 | C39F | 4/64 | Eastern National, Chelmsford (EX) 601 |
| 14465 | AEL  2B | Bristol MW6G | 213.154 | C39F | 4/64 | Hants & Dorset, Bournemouth (HA) 894 |
| 14466 | AEL  3B | Bristol MW6G | 213.155 | C39F | 4/64 | Hants & Dorset, Bournemouth (HA) 895 |
| 14467 | AEL  4B | Bristol MW6G | 213.156 | C39F | 4/64 | Hants & Dorset, Bournemouth (HA) 896 |
| 14468 | AEL  5B | Bristol MW6G | 213.173 | C39F | 5/64 | Hants & Dorset, Bournemouth (HA) 897 |
| 14469 | BPU 22B | Bristol MW6G | 213.150 | C39F | 4/64 | Tillings Transport, London WC1 (LN) |
| 14470 | BPU 23B | Bristol MW6G | 213.171 | C39F | 5/64 | Tillings Transport, London WC1 (LN) |
| 14471 | BPU 24B | Bristol MW6G | 213.172 | C39F | 5/64 | Tillings Transport, London WC1 (LN) |
| 14472 | 971 WAE | Bristol RELH6G | 212.059 | C45F | 5/64 | Bristol OC (GL) 2125 |
| 14473 | 972 WAE | Bristol RELH6G | 212.060 | C45F | 5/64 | Bristol OC (GL) 2126 |
| 14474 | 973 WAE | Bristol RELH6G | 212.068 | C45F | 6/64 | Bristol OC (GL) 2127 |
| 14475 | 974 WAE | Bristol RELH6G | 212.069 | C45F | 6/64 | Bristol OC (GL) 2128 |
| 14476 | 975 WAE | Bristol RELH6G | 212.082 | C45F | 7/64 | Bristol OC (GL) 2129 |
| 14477 | 976 WAE | Bristol RELH6G | 212.083 | C45F | 7/64 | Bristol OC (GL) 2130 |
| 14478 | 977 WAE | Bristol RELH6G | 212.086 | C45F | 7/64 | Bristol OC (GL) 2131 |
| 14479 | 978 WAE | Bristol RELH6G | 212.087 | C45F | 7/64 | Bristol OC (GL) 2132 |
| 14480 | 979 WAE | Bristol RELH6G | 212.090 | C45F | 7/64 | Bristol OC (GL) 2133 |
| 14481 | *980 WAE | Bristol RELH6G | 212.091 | C45F | 7/64 | Bristol OC (GL) 2134 |
| 14482 | 7285 FM | Bristol RELH6G | 212.062 | C47F | 6/64 | Crosville MS, Chester (CH) CRG524 |
| 14483 | 7286 FM | Bristol RELH6G | 212.063 | C47F | 6/64 | Crosville MS, Chester (CH) CRG525 |
| 14484 | AFM 101B | Bristol RELH6G | 212.084 | C47F | 6/64 | Crosville MS, Chester (CH) CRG526 |
| 14485 | AFM 102B | Bristol RELH6G | 212.085 | C47F | 6/64 | Crosville MS, Chester (CH) CRG527 |
| 14486 | AFM 103B | Bristol RELH6G | 212.092 | C47F | 6/64 | Crosville MS, Chester (CH) CRG528 |
| 14487 | AFM 104B | Bristol RELH6G | 212.093 | C47F | 6/64 | Crosville MS, Chester (CH) CRG529 |
| 14488 | AEL  6B | Bristol RELH6G | 212.074 | C47F | 5/64 | Hants & Dorset, Bournemouth (HA) 898 |
| 14489 | AEL  7B | Bristol RELH6G | 212.075 | C47F | 6/64 | Hants & Dorset, Bournemouth (HA) 899 |
| 14490 | WVL 514 | Bristol RELH6G | 212.078 | C47F | 7/64 | Lincolnshire RCC, Lincoln (LC) 2821 |
| 14491 | *WVL 515 | Bristol RELH6G | 212.079 | C47F | 7/64 | Lincolnshire RCC, Lincoln (LC) 2822 |
| 14492 | 841 SUO | Bristol RELH6G | 212.064 | C45F | 6/64 | Southern National, Exeter (DN) 2361 |
| 14493 | 842 SUO | Bristol RELH6G | 212.070 | C45F | 6/64 | Southern National, Exeter (DN) 2362 |
| 14494 | ATA 105B | Bristol RELH6G | 212.080 | C45F | 7/64 | Southern National, Exeter (DN) 2363 |
| 14495 | ATA 106B | Bristol RELH6G | 212.081 | C45F | 7/64 | Southern National, Exeter (DN) 2364 |
| 14496 | *837 SUO | Bristol RELH6G | 212.061 | C45F | 5/64 | Western National, Exeter (DN) 2351 |
| 14497 | 838 SUO | Bristol RELH6G | 212.065 | C45F | 6/64 | Western National, Exeter (DN) 2352 |
| 14498 | 839 SUO | Bristol RELH6G | 212.066 | C45F | 6/64 | Western National, Exeter (DN) 2353 |
| 14499 | 840 SUO | Bristol RELH6G | 212.067 | C45F | 6/64 | Western National, Exeter (DN) 2354 |
| 14500 | 393 TUO | Bristol RELH6G | 212.076 | C45F | 6/64 | Western National, Exeter (DN) 2355 |
| 14501 | 394 TUO | Bristol RELH6G | 212.077 | C45F | 6/64 | Western National, Exeter (DN) 2356 |
| 14502 | ATA 101B | Bristol RELH6G | 212.088 | C45F | 7/64 | Western National, Exeter (DN) 2357 |
| 14503 | ATA 102B | Bristol RELH6G | 212.089 | C45F | 7/64 | Western National, Exeter (DN) 2358 |
| 14504 | ATA 103B | Bristol RELH6G | 212.094 | C45F | 7/64 | Western National, Exeter (DN) 2359 |
| 14505 | ATA 104B | Bristol RELH6G | 212.095 | C45F | 7/64 | Western National, Exeter (DN) 2360 |
| 14506 | XFE 440 | Bristol RELH6G | 222.013 | C47F | 7/64 | Lincolnshire RCC, Lincoln (LC) 2680 |
| 14507 | XFE 441 | Bristol RELH6G | 222.014 | C47F | 7/64 | Lincolnshire RCC, Lincoln (LC) 2681 |
| 14508 | 157 SHN | Bristol RELH6G | 212.096 | C43F | 7/64 | United AS, Darlington (DM) BRC11 |
| 14509 | 158 SHN | Bristol RELH6G | 212.097 | C43F | 7/64 | United AS, Darlington (DM) BRC12 |
| 14510 | 13 XHN | Bristol RELH6G | 222.003 | C43F | 7/64 | United AS, Darlington (DM) BRC13 |
| 14511 | 14 XHN | Bristol RELH6G | 222.010 | C43F | 7/64 | United AS, Darlington (DM) BRC14 |
| 14512 | 15 XHN | Bristol RELH6G | 222.011 | C43F | 7/64 | United AS, Darlington (DM) BRC15 |
| 14513 | 16 XHN | Bristol RELH6G | 222.012 | C43F | 7/64 | United AS, Darlington (DM) BRC16 |

| | | | | | | |
|---|---|---|---|---|---|---|
| 14514 | 917 XHN | Bristol RELH6G | 222.015 | C43F | 8/64 | United AS, Darlington (DM) BRC17 |
| 14515 | 918 XHN | Bristol RELH6G | 222.016 | C43F | 8/64 | United AS, Darlington (DM) BRC18 |
| 14516 | AHN 119B | Bristol RELH6G | 222.017 | C43F | 9/64 | United AS, Darlington (DM) BRC19 |
| 14517 | AHN 120B | Bristol RELH6G | 222.018 | C43F | 9/64 | United AS, Darlington (DM) BRC20 |
| 14518 | BBD 254B | Bristol RELH6G | 222.007 | C47F | 7/64 | United Counties, Northampton (NO) 254 |
| 14519 | BBD 255B | Bristol RELH6G | 222.008 | C47F | 7/64 | United Counties, Northampton (NO) 255 |
| 14520 | BBD 256B | Bristol RELH6G | 222.009 | C47F | 8/64 | United Counties, Northampton (NO) 256 |
| 14521 | BBD 257B | Bristol RELH6G | 222.019 | C47F | 9/64 | United Counties, Northampton (NO) 257 |
| 14522 | BBD 258B | Bristol RELH6G | 222.020 | C47F | 9/64 | United Counties, Northampton (NO) 258 |
| 14523 | BBD 259B | Bristol RELH6G | 222.021 | C47F | 9/64 | United Counties, Northampton (NO) 259 |
| 14524 | AWR 401B | Bristol RELH6G | 212.071 | DP47F | 5/64 | West Yorkshire RCC, Harrogate (WR) ERG1 |
| 14525 | AWR 402B | Bristol RELH6G | 212.072 | DP47F | 5/64 | West Yorkshire RCC, Harrogate (WR) ERG2 |
| 14526 | AWR 403B | Bristol RELH6G | 212.073 | DP47F | 5/64 | West Yorkshire RCC, Harrogate (WR) ERG3 |
| 14527 | AWR 404B | Bristol RELH6G | 222.022 | DP47F | 10/64 | West Yorkshire RCC, Harrogate (WR) ERG4 |
| 14528 | AWR 405B | Bristol RELH6G | 222.023 | DP47F | 10/64 | West Yorkshire RCC, Harrogate (WR) ERG5 |
| 14529 | AWR 406B | Bristol RELH6G | 222.024 | DP47F | 10/64 | West Yorkshire RCC, Harrogate (WR) ERG6 |
| 14530 | JHK 456C | Bristol MW5G | 213.218 | DP43F | 1/65 | Eastern National, Chelmsford (EX) 1432 |
| 14531 | JHK 457C | Bristol MW5G | 213.219 | DP43F | 1/65 | Eastern National, Chelmsford (EX) 1433 |
| 14532 | JHK 458C | Bristol MW5G | 213.221 | DP43F | 1/65 | Eastern National, Chelmsford (EX) 1434 |
| 14533 | BNN 101C | Bristol MW6G | 213.226 | DP43F | 5/65 | Mansfield District (NG) 213 |
| 14534 | BNN 102C | Bristol MW6G | 213.227 | DP43F | 5/65 | Mansfield District (NG) 214 |
| 14535 | BNN 103C | Bristol MW6G | 213.228 | DP43F | 5/65 | Mansfield District (NG) 215 |
| 14536 | DNU 11C | Bristol MW6G | 213.222 | DP43F | 5/65 | Midland General, Langley Mill (DE) 291 |
| 14537 | DNU 12C | Bristol MW6G | 213.223 | DP43F | 5/65 | Midland General, Langley Mill (DE) 292 |
| 14538 | DNU 13C | Bristol MW6G | 213.224 | DP43F | 5/65 | Midland General, Langley Mill (DE) 293 |
| 14539 | DNU 14C | Bristol MW6G | 213.225 | DP43F | 5/65 | Midland General, Langley Mill (DE) 294 |
| 14540 | AHN 901B | Bristol SUL4A | 226.003 | B36F | 12/64 | United AS, Darlington (DM) S1 |
| 14541 | AHN 902B | Bristol SUL4A | 226.004 | B36F | 12/64 | United AS, Darlington (DM) S2 |
| 14542 | CHN 3C | Bristol SUL4A | 226.005 | B36F | 1/65 | United AS, Darlington (DM) S3 |
| 14543 | CHN 4C | Bristol SUL4A | 226.006 | B36F | 1/65 | United AS, Darlington (DM) S4 |
| 14544 | CHN 5C | Bristol SUL4A | 226.007 | B36F | 1/65 | United AS, Darlington (DM) S5 |
| 14545 | EWT 384C | Bristol SUL4A | 226.008 | B36F | 1/65 | West Yorkshire RCC, Harrogate (WR) SMA15 |
| 14546 | EWT 385C | Bristol SUL4A | 226.009 | B36F | 1/65 | West Yorkshire RCC, Harrogate (WR) SMA16 |
| 14547 | EWT 382C | Bristol SUL4A | 226.010 | B36F | 1/65 | West Yorkshire RCC, Harrogate (WR) SMA13 |
| 14548 | EWT 383C | Bristol SUL4A | 226.011 | B36F | 1/65 | West Yorkshire RCC, Harrogate (WR) SMA14 |
| 14549 | EWT 386C | Bristol SUL4A | 226.012 | B36F | 1/65 | West Yorkshire RCC, Harrogate (WR) SMA17 |
| 14550 | EWT 387C | Bristol SUL4A | 226.013 | B36F | 1/65 | West Yorkshire RCC, Harrogate (WR) SMA18 |
| 14551 | AHW 226B | Bristol SUS4A | 226.001 | B30F | 12/64 | Bristol OC (GL) 307 |
| 14552 | AHW 227B | Bristol SUS4A | 226.002 | B30F | 12/64 | Bristol OC (GL) 308 |
| 14553 | *AHT 718B | Bristol FLF6B | 224.081 | H38/32F | 11/64 | Bristol OC (GL) C7162 |
| 14554 | AHT 719B | Bristol FLF6B | 224.082 | H38/32F | 11/64 | Bristol OC (GL) C7163 |
| 14555 | AHT 717B | Bristol FLF6B | 224.077 | H38/32F | 11/64 | Bristol OC (GL) C7161 |
| 14556 | AHT 720B | Bristol FLF6B | 224.083 | H38/32F | 11/64 | Bristol OC (GL) C7164 |
| 14557 | AAE 261B | Bristol FLF6G | 224.049 | H38/32F | 10/64 | Bristol OC (GL) 7156 |
| 14558 | AAE 262B | Bristol FLF6G | 224.050 | H38/32F | 10/64 | Bristol OC (GL) 7157 |
| 14559 | *AAE 263B | Bristol FLF6G | 224.051 | H38/32F | 10/64 | Bristol OC (GL) 7158 |
| 14560 | AAE 264B | Bristol FLF6G | 224.052 | H38/32F | 10/64 | Bristol OC (GL) 7159 |
| 14561 | AAE 265B | Bristol FLF6G | 224.053 | H38/32F | 10/64 | Bristol OC (GL) 7160 |
| 14562 | *AHY 981B | Bristol FLF6B | 224.097 | H38/32F | 12/64 | Bristol OC (GL) 7165 |
| 14563 | AHY 982B | Bristol FLF6B | 224.098 | H38/32F | 12/64 | Bristol OC (GL) 7166 |
| 14564 | AHY 983B | Bristol FLF6B | 224.099 | H38/32F | 12/64 | Bristol OC (GL) 7167 |
| 14565 | AHY 984B | Bristol FLF6B | 224.100 | H38/32F | 12/64 | Bristol OC (GL) 7168 |
| 14566 | BHU 401C | Bristol FLF6G | 224.118 | H38/32F | 1/65 | Bristol OC (GL) G7172 |
| 14567 | BHU 402C | Bristol FLF6G | 224.119 | H38/32F | 1/65 | Bristol OC (GL) G7173 |
| 14568 | BHU 18C | Bristol FLF6G | 224.111 | H38/32F | 1/65 | Bristol OC (GL) G7169 |
| 14569 | BHU 19C | Bristol FLF6G | 224.112 | H38/32F | 1/65 | Bristol OC (GL) G7170 |
| 14570 | BHU 20C | Bristol FLF6G | 224.117 | H38/32F | 1/65 | Bristol OC (GL) G7171 |
| 14571 | AAO 575B | Bristol FLF6G | 224.058 | H38/32F | 11/64 | Cumberland MS, Whitehaven (CU) 525 |
| 14572 | CAO 649B | Bristol FLF6G | 224.059 | H38/32F | 11/64 | Cumberland MS, Whitehaven (CU) 526 |
| 14573 | CRM 211B | Bristol FLF6G | 224.095 | H38/32F | 12/64 | Cumberland MS, Whitehaven (CU) 527 |
| 14574 | CRM 472C | Bristol FLF6G | 224.096 | H38/32F | 1/65 | Cumberland MS, Whitehaven (CU) 528 |
| 14575 | FWC 426B | Bristol FLF6B | 224.060 | H38/32F | 10/64 | Eastern National, Chelmsford (EX) 2808 |
| 14576 | *FWC 427B | Bristol FLF6B | 224.061 | H38/32F | 10/64 | Eastern National, Chelmsford (EX) 2809 |
| 14577 | FWC 428B | Bristol FLF6B | 224.062 | H38/32F | 10/64 | Eastern National, Chelmsford (EX) 2810 |

| | | | | | | | |
|---|---|---|---|---|---|---|---|
| 14578 | FWC 429B | Bristol FLF6B | 224.067 | H38/32F | 10/64 | Eastern National, Chelmsford (EX) 2811 |
| 14579 | GNO 788B | Bristol FLF6G | 224.072 | H38/32F | 11/64 | Eastern National, Chelmsford (EX) 2812 |
| 14580 | GNO 789B | Bristol FLF6G | 224.073 | H38/32F | 11/64 | Eastern National, Chelmsford (EX) 2813 |
| 14581 | GNO 790B | Bristol FLF6G | 224.074 | H38/32F | 11/64 | Eastern National, Chelmsford (EX) 2814 |
| 14582 | *GNO 791B | Bristol FLF6G | 224.075 | H38/32F | 11/64 | Eastern National, Chelmsford (EX) 2815 |
| 14583 | *HEV 994B | Bristol FLF6G | 224.101 | H38/32F | 12/64 | Eastern National, Chelmsford (EX) 2816 |
| 14584 | HEV 995B | Bristol FLF6G | 224.102 | H38/32F | 12/64 | Eastern National, Chelmsford (EX) 2817 |
| 14585 | HEV 996B | Bristol FLF6G | 224.103 | H38/32F | 12/64 | Eastern National, Chelmsford (EX) 2818 |
| 14586 | *HEV 997B | Bristol FLF6G | 224.104 | H38/32F | 12/64 | Eastern National, Chelmsford (EX) 2819 |
| 14587 | ANN 566B | Bristol FLF6B | 224.084 | H38/32F | 12/64 | Mansfield District (NG) 646 |
| 14588 | ANN 567B | Bristol FLF6B | 224.085 | H38/32F | 12/64 | Mansfield District (NG) 647 |
| 14589 | BRB 492B | Bristol FLF6G | 224.063 | H38/32F | 11/64 | Midland General, Langley Mill (DE) 633 |
| 14590 | BRB 493B | Bristol FLF6G | 224.064 | H38/32F | 11/64 | Midland General, Langley Mill (DE) 634 |
| 14591 | DNU 15C | Bristol FLF6B | 224.107 | H38/32F | 1/65 | Notts & Derby, Langley Mill (DE) 635 |
| 14592 | AFM 112B | Bristol FLF6B | 217.197 | CH37/18F | 8/64 | Crosville MS, Chester (CH) DFB149 |
| 14593 | *AFM 113B | Bristol FLF6B | 217.198 | CH37/18F | 8/64 | Crosville MS, Chester (CH) DFB150 |
| 14594 | AFM 114B | Bristol FLF6B | 217.199 | CH37/18F | 8/64 | Crosville MS, Chester (CH) DFB151 |
| 14595 | AFM 115B | Bristol FLF6B | 217.200 | CH37/18F | 8/64 | Crosville MS, Chester (CH) DFB152 |
| 14596 | AFM 116B | Bristol FLF6B | 224.003 | CH37/18F | 8/64 | Crosville MS, Chester (CH) DFB153 |
| 14597 | DNU 16C | Bristol FLF6B | 224.108 | H38/32F | 1/65 | Notts & Derby, Langley Mill (DE) 636 |
| 14598 | AUO 522B | Bristol FLF6B | 224.088 | H38/32F | 12/64 | Southern National, Exeter (DN) 2052 |
| 14599 | AUO 523B | Bristol FLF6B | 224.089 | H38/32F | 12/64 | Southern National, Exeter (DN) 2053 |
| 14600 | BUO 202B | Bristol FLF6G | 224.109 | H38/32F | 12/64 | Southern National, Exeter (DN) 2054 |
| 14601 | BUO 203B | Bristol FLF6G | 224.110 | H38/32F | 12/64 | Southern National, Exeter (DN) 2055 |
| 14602 | BDL 576B | Bristol FLF6G | 224.042 | H38/32F | 9/64 | Southern Vectis, Newport (DN) 600 |
| 14603 | BDL 577B | Bristol FLF6G | 224.043 | H38/32F | 9/64 | Southern Vectis, Newport (DN) 601 |
| 14604 | BDL 578B | Bristol FLF6G | 224.044 | H38/32F | 9/64 | Southern Vectis, Newport (DN) 602 |
| 14605 | BDL 579B | Bristol FLF6G | 224.045 | H38/32F | 10/64 | Southern Vectis, Newport (DN) 603 |
| 14606 | *BDL 580B | Bristol FLF6G | 224.054 | H38/32F | 10/64 | Southern Vectis, Newport (IW) 604 |
| 14607 | *BDL 581B | Bristol FLF6G | 224.055 | H38/32F | 10/64 | Southern Vectis, Newport (IW) 605 |
| 14608 | BDL 582B | Bristol FLF6G | 224.056 | H38/32F | 10/64 | Southern Vectis, Newport (IW) 606 |
| 14609 | BDL 583B | Bristol FLF6G | 224.057 | H38/32F | 10/64 | Southern Vectis, Newport (IW) 607 |
| 14610 | CMO 833B | Bristol FLF6G | 224.065 | H38/32F | 10/64 | Thames Valley, Reading (BE) D10 |
| 14611 | CMO 834B | Bristol FLF6G | 224.066 | H38/32F | 10/64 | Thames Valley, Reading (BE) D11 |
| 14612 | CMO 835B | Bristol FLF6G | 224.076 | H38/32F | 11/64 | Thames Valley, Reading (BE) D12 |
| 14613 | CMO 836B | Bristol FLF6G | 224.090 | H38/32F | 11/64 | Thames Valley, Reading (BE) D13 |
| 14614 | AHN 459B | Bristol FLF6B | 224.068 | H38/32F | 11/64 | United AS, Darlington (DM) BL159 |
| 14615 | AHN 460B | Bristol FLF6B | 224.069 | H38/32F | 11/64 | United AS, Darlington (DM) BL160 |
| 14616 | AHN 461B | Bristol FLF6B | 224.080 | H38/32F | 12/64 | United AS, Darlington (DM) BL161 |
| 14617 | AHN 462B | Bristol FLF6B | 224.086 | H38/32F | 12/64 | United AS, Darlington (DM) BL162 |
| 14618 | AHN 463B | Bristol FLF6B | 224.087 | H38/32F | 12/64 | United AS, Darlington (DM) BL163 |
| 14619 | CHN 64C | Bristol FLF6B | 224.113 | H38/32F | 1/65 | United AS, Darlington (DM) L164 |
| 14620 | CHN 65C | Bristol FLF6B | 224.114 | H38/32F | 1/65 | United AS, Darlington (DM) L165 |
| 14621 | CHN 66C | Bristol FLF6B | 224.115 | H38/32F | 1/65 | United AS, Darlington (DM) L166 |
| 14622 | CHN 67C | Bristol FLF6B | 224.116 | H38/32F | 1/65 | United AS, Darlington (DM) L167 |
| 14623 | AUO 514B | Bristol FLF6B | 224.070 | H38/32F | 11/64 | Western National, Exeter (DN) 2067 |
| 14624 | AUO 515B | Bristol FLF6B | 224.071 | H38/32F | 11/64 | Western National, Exeter (DN) 2068 |
| 14625 | AUO 516B | Bristol FLF6B | 224.078 | H38/32F | 11/64 | Western National, Exeter (DN) 2069 |
| 14626 | *AUO 517B | Bristol FLF6B | 224.079 | H38/32F | 11/64 | Western National, Exeter (DN) 2070 |
| 14627 | AUO 518B | Bristol FLF6G | 224.091 | H38/32F | 12/64 | Western National, Exeter (DN) 2071 |
| 14628 | AUO 519B | Bristol FLF6G | 224.092 | H38/32F | 12/64 | Western National, Exeter (DN) 2072 |
| 14629 | AUO 520B | Bristol FLF6G | 224.093 | H38/32F | 12/64 | Western National, Exeter (DN) 2073 |
| 14630 | AUO 521B | Bristol FLF6G | 224.094 | H38/32F | 12/64 | Western National, Exeter (DN) 2074 |
| 14631 | *BUO 150B | Bristol FLF6G | 224.105 | H38/32F | 1/65 | Western National, Exeter (DN) 2075 |
| 14632 | BUO 201B | Bristol FLF6G | 224.106 | H38/32F | 1/65 | Western National, Exeter (DN) 2076 |
| 14633 | CNJ 60B | Bristol FS6G | 223.052 | H33/27RD | 9/64 | Brighton, Hove & District (ES) 60 |
| 14634 | CNJ 61B | Bristol FS6G | 223.053 | H33/27RD | 9/64 | Brighton, Hove & District (ES) 61 |
| 14635 | DAP 62C | Bristol FS6B | 223.107 | H33/27RD | 1/65 | Brighton, Hove & District (ES) 62 |
| 14636 | DAP 63C | Bristol FS6B | 223.108 | H33/27RD | 1/65 | Brighton, Hove & District (ES) 63 |
| 14637 | DAP 64C | Bristol FS6B | 223.109 | H33/27RD | 1/65 | Brighton, Hove & District (ES) 64 |
| 14638 | BFM 433B | Bristol FS6G | 223.046 | H33/27RD | 10/64 | Crosville MS, Chester (CH) DFG163 |
| 14639 | BFM 434B | Bristol FS6G | 223.047 | H33/27RD | 10/64 | Crosville MS, Chester (CH) DFG164 |
| 14640 | BFM 435B | Bristol FS6G | 223.048 | H33/27RD | 10/64 | Crosville MS, Chester (CH) DFG165 |
| 14641 | BFM 887B | Bristol FS6B | 223.071 | H33/27RD | 11/64 | Crosville MS, Chester (CH) DFB169 |

| 14642 | BFM 889B | Bristol FS6B | 223.072 | H33/27RD | 11/64 | Crosville MS, Chester (CH) DFB170 |
| 14643 | CFM 340B | Bristol FS6B | 223.090 | H33/27RD | 12/64 | Crosville MS, Chester (CH) DFB171 |
| 14644 | CFM 341B | Bristol FS6B | 223.091 | H33/27RD | 12/64 | Crosville MS, Chester (CH) DFB172 |
| 14645 | CFM 342B | Bristol FS6B | 223.092 | H33/27RD | 12/64 | Crosville MS, Chester (CH) DFB173 |
| 14646 | CFM 343B | Bristol FS6B | 223.098 | H33/27RD | 12/64 | Crosville MS, Chester (CH) DFB174 |
| 14647 | CFM 901C | Bristol FS6G | 223.095 | H33/27RD | 1/65 | Crosville MS, Chester (CH) DFG166 |
| 14648 | CFM 902C | Bristol FS6G | 223.096 | H33/27RD | 1/65 | Crosville MS, Chester (CH) DFG167 |
| 14649 | CFM 903C | Bristol FS6G | 223.097 | H33/27RD | 1/65 | Crosville MS, Chester (CH) DFG168 |
| 14650 | CNG 287B | Bristol FS5G | 223.049 | H33/27RD | 9/64 | Eastern Counties, Norwich (NK) LFS87 |
| 14651 | CNG 288B | Bristol FS5G | 223.050 | H33/27RD | 9/64 | Eastern Counties, Norwich (NK) LFS88 |
| 14652 | CNG 289B | Bristol FS5G | 223.051 | H33/27RD | 10/64 | Eastern Counties, Norwich (NK) LFS89 |
| 14653 | CNG 290B | Bristol FS5G | 223.063 | H33/27RD | 10/64 | Eastern Counties, Norwich (NK) LFS90 |
| 14654 | CNG 291B | Bristol FS5G | 223.064 | H33/27RD | 10/64 | Eastern Counties, Norwich (NK) LFS91 |
| 14655 | CNG 292B | Bristol FS5G | 223.065 | H33/27RD | 11/64 | Eastern Counties, Norwich (NK) LFS92 |
| 14656 | CVF 293B | Bristol FS5G | 223.066 | H33/27RD | 11/64 | Eastern Counties, Norwich (NK) LFS93 |
| 14657 | CVF 294B | Bristol FS5G | 223.067 | H33/27RD | 11/64 | Eastern Counties, Norwich (NK) LFS94 |
| 14658 | CVF 295B | Bristol FS5G | 223.070 | H33/27RD | 11/64 | Eastern Counties, Norwich (NK) LFS95 |
| 14659 | CVF 296B | Bristol FS5G | 223.074 | H33/27RD | 11/64 | Eastern Counties, Norwich (NK) LFS96 |
| 14660 | CVF 297B | Bristol FS5G | 223.075 | H33/27RD | 11/64 | Eastern Counties, Norwich (NK) LFS97 |
| 14661 | DAH 398B | Bristol FS5G | 223.076 | H33/27RD | 12/64 | Eastern Counties, Norwich (NK) LFS98 |
| 14662 | DAH 399B | Bristol FS5G | 223.077 | H33/27RD | 12/64 | Eastern Counties, Norwich (NK) LFS99 |
| 14663 | DAH 400B | Bristol FS5G | 223.078 | H33/27RD | 12/64 | Eastern Counties, Norwich (NK) LFS100 |
| 14664 | BEL 677B | Bristol FS6G | 223.054 | H33/27RD | 10/64 | Hants & Dorset, Bournemouth (HA) 1504 |
| 14665 | BEL 678B | Bristol FS6G | 223.055 | H33/27RD | 10/64 | Hants & Dorset, Bournemouth (HA) 1505 |
| 14666 | BEL 679B | Bristol FS6G | 223.056 | H33/27RD | 10/64 | Hants & Dorset, Bournemouth (HA) 1506 |
| 14667 | BEL 680B | Bristol FS6G | 223.057 | H33/27RD | 10/64 | Hants & Dorset, Bournemouth (HA) 1507 |
| 14668 | *BRU 138B | Bristol FS6B | 223.084 | H33/27RD | 11/64 | Hants & Dorset, Bournemouth (HA) 1508 |
| 14669 | BRU 139B | Bristol FS6B | 223.085 | H33/27RD | 11/64 | Hants & Dorset, Bournemouth (HA) 1509 |
| 14670 | BRU 140B | Bristol FS6B | 223.086 | H33/27RD | 11/64 | Hants & Dorset, Bournemouth (HA) 1510 |
| 14671 | BRU 141B | Bristol FS6B | 223.087 | H33/27RD | 11/64 | Hants & Dorset, Bournemouth (HA) 1511 |
| 14672 | *CEL 860C | Bristol FS6G | 223.103 | H33/27RD | 1/65 | Hants & Dorset, Bournemouth (HA) 1512 |
| 14673 | *CEL 861C | Bristol FS6G | 223.104 | H33/27RD | 1/65 | Hants & Dorset, Bournemouth (HA) 1513 |
| 14674 | *CEL 862C | Bristol FS6G | 223.110 | H33/27RD | 1/65 | Hants & Dorset, Bournemouth (HA) 1514 |
| 14675 | AFE 89B | Bristol FS5G | 223.061 | H33/27RD | 12/64 | Lincolnshire RCC, Lincoln (LC) 2518 |
| 14676 | AFE 90B | Bristol FS5G | 223.062 | H33/27RD | 12/64 | Lincolnshire RCC, Lincoln (LC) 2519 |
| 14677 | AFE 921C | Bristol FS5G | 223.079 | H33/27RD | 1/65 | Lincolnshire RCC, Lincoln (LC) 2520 |
| 14678 | AFE 922C | Bristol FS5G | 223.080 | H33/27RD | 1/65 | Lincolnshire RCC, Lincoln (LC) 2521 |
| 14679 | CNV 663B | Bristol FS6B | 223.058 | H33/27RD | 10/64 | United Counties, Northampton (NO) 663 |
| 14680 | CNV 664B | Bristol FS6B | 223.059 | H33/27RD | 10/64 | United Counties, Northampton (NO) 664 |
| 14681 | CNV 665B | Bristol FS6B | 223.060 | H33/27RD | 11/64 | United Counties, Northampton (NO) 665 |
| 14682 | CNV 666B | Bristol FS6B | 223.073 | H33/27RD | 11/64 | United Counties, Northampton (NO) 666 |
| 14683 | CNV 667B | Bristol FS6B | 223.081 | H33/27RD | 11/64 | United Counties, Northampton (NO) 667 |
| 14684 | CNV 668B | Bristol FS6B | 223.082 | H33/27RD | 11/64 | United Counties, Northampton (NO) 668 |
| 14685 | CNV 669B | Bristol FS6B | 223.083 | H33/27RD | 12/64 | United Counties, Northampton (NO) 669 |
| 14686 | CNV 670B | Bristol FS6B | 223.099 | H33/27RD | 12/64 | United Counties, Northampton (NO) 670 |
| 14687 | CNV 671B | Bristol FS6B | 223.100 | H33/27RD | 12/64 | United Counties, Northampton (NO) 671 |
| 14688 | CNV 672B | Bristol FS6B | 223.101 | H33/27RD | 12/64 | United Counties, Northampton (NO) 672 |
| 14689 | CNV 673B | Bristol FS6B | 223.102 | H33/27RD | 12/64 | United Counties, Northampton (NO) 673 |
| 14690 | BWN 53C | Bristol FS6G | 223.093 | H33/27RD | 3/65 | United Welsh, Swansea (GG) 389 |
| 14691 | BWN 54C | Bristol FS6G | 223.094 | H33/27RD | 4/65 | United Welsh, Swansea (GG) 390 |
| 14692 | DWU 679B | Bristol FS6B | 223.068 | H33/27RD | 11/64 | West Yorkshire RCC, Harrogate (WR) DX180 |
| 14693 | DWW 336B | Bristol FS6B | 223.069 | H33/27RD | 11/64 | West Yorkshire RCC, Harrogate (WR) DX181 |
| 14694 | DYG 222B | Bristol FS6B | 223.105 | H33/27RD | 12/64 | West Yorkshire RCC, Harrogate (WR) DX182 |
| 14695 | DYG 223B | Bristol FS6B | 223.106 | H33/27RD | 12/64 | West Yorkshire RCC, Harrogate (WR) DX183 |
| 14696 | DWY 498B | Bristol FS6B | 223.088 | H33/27RD | 12/64 | York-West Yorkshire, Harrogate (WR) YDX190 |
| 14697 | EWT 401C | Bristol FS6B | 223.089 | H33/27RD | 1/65 | York-West Yorkshire, Harrogate (WR) YDX191 |
| 14698 | *BHW 93C | Bristol MW5G | 213.230 | DP41F | 2/65 | Bristol OC (GL) 2025 |
| 14699 | *BHW 94C | Bristol MW5G | 213.231 | DP41F | 2/65 | Bristol OC (GL) 2026 |
| 14700 | *BHW 95C | Bristol MW5G | 213.232 | DP41F | 2/65 | Bristol OC (GL) 2027 |
| 14701 | *BHW 96C | Bristol MW5G | 213.233 | DP41F | 2/65 | Bristol OC (GL) 2028 |
| 14702 | BHU 91C | Bristol MW6G | 225.001 | DP39F | 2/65 | Bristol OC (GL) 2137 |
| 14703 | BHU 92C | Bristol MW6G | 225.002 | DP39F | 2/65 | Bristol OC (GL) 2138 |
| 14704 | BHU 93C | Bristol MW6G | 225.003 | DP39F | 2/65 | Bristol OC (GL) 2139 |
| 14705 | BHU 94C | Bristol MW6G | 225.004 | DP39F | 2/65 | Bristol OC (GL) 2140 |

| | | | | | | | |
|---|---|---|---|---|---|---|---|
| 14706 | BHU | 95C | Bristol MW6G | 225.005 | DP39F | 2/65 | Bristol OC (GL) 2141 |
| 14707 | BHU | 96C | Bristol MW6G | 225.006 | DP39F | 2/65 | Bristol OC (GL) 2142 |
| 14708 | BHU | 97C | Bristol MW6G | 225.016 | DP39F | 2/65 | Bristol OC (GL) 2143 |
| 14709 | DNU | 19C | Bristol MW6G | 213.229 | DP43F | 5/65 | Midland General, Langley Mill (DE) 295 |
| 14710 | DNU | 20C | Bristol MW6G | 213.234 | DP43F | 5/65 | Midland General, Langley Mill (DE) 296 |
| 14711 | DNU | 21C | Bristol MW6G | 213.239 | DP43F | 5/65 | Midland General, Langley Mill (DE) 297 |
| 14712 | *BDV | 244C | Bristol SUL4A | 226.014 | B36F | 2/65 | Southern National, Exeter (DN) 663 |
| 14713 | *BDV | 245C | Bristol SUL4A | 226.015 | B36F | 2/65 | Southern National, Exeter (DN) 664 |
| 14714 | BDV | 246C | Bristol SUL4A | 226.016 | B36F | 2/65 | Southern National, Exeter (DN) 665 |
| 14715 | BDV | 247C | Bristol SUL4A | 226.017 | B36F | 2/65 | Southern National, Exeter (DN) 666 |
| 14716 | BDV | 248C | Bristol SUL4A | 226.018 | B36F | 2/65 | Western National, Exeter (DN) 667 |
| 14717 | BDV | 249C | Bristol SUL4A | 226.019 | B36F | 2/65 | Western National, Exeter (DN) 668 |
| 14718 | BDV | 250C | Bristol SUL4A | 226.020 | B36F | 2/65 | Western National, Exeter (DN) 669 |
| 14719 | *BDV | 251C | Bristol SUL4A | 226.021 | B36F | 3/65 | Western National, Exeter (DN) 670 |
| 14720 | BDV | 252C | Bristol SUL4A | 226.022 | B36F | 3/65 | Western National, Exeter (DN) 671 |
| 14721 | *BDV | 253C | Bristol SUL4A | 226.023 | B36F | 3/65 | Western National, Exeter (DN) 672 |
| 14722 | BDV | 254C | Bristol SUL4A | 226.024 | B36F | 3/65 | Western National, Exeter (DN) 673 |
| 14723 | BDV | 255C | Bristol SUL4A | 226.025 | B36F | 4/65 | Western National, Exeter (DN) 674 |
| 14724 | DPM | 65C | Bristol FS6G | 223.122 | H33/27RD | 2/65 | Brighton, Hove & District (ES) 65 |
| 14725 | DPM | 66C | Bristol FS6G | 223.123 | H33/27RD | 2/65 | Brighton, Hove & District (ES) 66 |
| 14726 | DPM | 67C | Bristol FS6G | 223.124 | H33/27RD | 2/65 | Brighton, Hove & District (ES) 67 |
| 14727 | ENJ | 68C | Bristol FS6B | 223.140 | H33/27RD | 4/65 | Brighton, Hove & District (ES) 68 |
| 14728 | ENJ | 69C | Bristol FS6B | 223.141 | H33/27RD | 4/65 | Brighton, Hove & District (ES) 69 |
| 14729 | ENJ | 70C | Bristol FS6B | 223.142 | H33/27RD | 4/65 | Brighton, Hove & District (ES) 70 |
| 14730 | FAP | 71C | Bristol FS6G | 228.012 | H33/27RD | 8/65 | Brighton, Hove & District (ES) 71 |
| 14731 | FAP | 72C | Bristol FS6G | 228.014 | H33/27RD | 8/65 | Brighton, Hove & District (ES) 72 |
| 14732 | DFM | 211C | Bristol FS6G | 223.128 | H33/27RD | 3/65 | Crosville MS, Chester (CH) DFG175 |
| 14733 | DFM | 212C | Bristol FS6G | 223.129 | H33/27RD | 3/65 | Crosville MS, Chester (CH) DFG176 |
| 14734 | EFM | 628C | Bristol FS6B | 223.138 | H33/27RD | 6/65 | Crosville MS, Chester (CH) DFB177 |
| 14735 | EFM | 629C | Bristol FS6B | 223.139 | H33/27RD | 7/65 | Crosville MS, Chester (CH) DFB178 |
| 14736 | EFM | 630C | Bristol FS6G | 223.150 | H33/27RD | 7/65 | Crosville MS, Chester (CH) DFG181 |
| 14737 | EFM | 631C | Bristol FS6G | 228.001 | H33/27RD | 7/65 | Crosville MS, Chester (CH) DFG182 |
| 14738 | EFM | 632C | Bristol FS6G | 228.010 | H33/27RD | 8/65 | Crosville MS, Chester (CH) DFG183 |
| 14739 | EFM | 633C | Bristol FS6G | 228.011 | H33/27RD | 8/65 | Crosville MS, Chester (CH) DFG184 |
| 14740 | GFM | 179C | Bristol FS6B | 228.035 | H33/27RD | 10/65 | Crosville MS, Chester (CH) DFB179 |
| 14741 | GFM | 180C | Bristol FS6B | 228.036 | H33/27RD | 10/65 | Crosville MS, Chester (CH) DFB180 |
| 14742 | GFM | 185C | Bristol FS6G | 228.022 | H33/27RD | 10/65 | Crosville MS, Chester (CH) DFG185 |
| 14743 | GFM | 186C | Bristol FS6G | 228.023 | H33/27RD | 10/65 | Crosville MS, Chester (CH) DFG186 |
| 14744 | GFM | 187C | Bristol FS6G | 228.028 | H33/27RD | 10/65 | Crosville MS, Chester (CH) DFG187 |
| 14745 | GFM | 188C | Bristol FS6G | 228.032 | H33/27RD | 10/65 | Crosville MS, Chester (CH) DFG188 |
| 14746 | GFM | 189C | Bristol FS6G | 228.033 | H33/27RD | 11/65 | Crosville MS, Chester (CH) DFG189 |
| 14747 | GFM | 190C | Bristol FS6G | 228.034 | H33/27RD | 11/65 | Crosville MS, Chester (CH) DFG190 |
| 14748 | GFM | 191C | Bristol FS6G | 228.042 | H33/27RD | 11/65 | Crosville MS, Chester (CH) DFG191 |
| 14749 | GFM | 192C | Bristol FS6G | 228.043 | H33/27RD | 11/65 | Crosville MS, Chester (CH) DFG192 |
| 14750 | GFM | 193C | Bristol FS6G | 228.044 | H33/27RD | 12/65 | Crosville MS, Chester (CH) DFG193 |
| 14751 | GFM | 194C | Bristol FS6G | 228.045 | H33/27RD | 12/65 | Crosville MS, Chester (CH) DFG194 |
| 14752 | GFM | 195C | Bristol FS6G | 228.051 | H33/27RD | 12/65 | Crosville MS, Chester (CH) DFG195 |
| 14753 | GFM | 196C | Bristol FS6G | 228.052 | H33/27RD | 12/65 | Crosville MS, Chester (CH) DFG196 |
| 14754 | GFM | 197C | Bristol FS6G | 228.053 | H33/27RD | 12/65 | Crosville MS, Chester (CH) DFG197 |
| 14755 | GFM | 198C | Bristol FS6G | 228.054 | H33/27RD | 12/65 | Crosville MS, Chester (CH) DFG198 |
| 14756 | *DNG | 401C | Bristol FS5G | 223.112 | H33/27RD | 1/65 | Eastern Counties, Norwich (NK) LFS101 |
| 14757 | DNG | 402C | Bristol FS5G | 223.113 | H33/27RD | 1/65 | Eastern Counties, Norwich (NK) LFS102 |
| 14758 | DNG | 403C | Bristol FS5G | 223.114 | H33/27RD | 1/65 | Eastern Counties, Norwich (NK) LFS103 |
| 14759 | DNG | 404C | Bristol FS5G | 223.115 | H33/27RD | 1/65 | Eastern Counties, Norwich (NK) LFS104 |
| 14760 | DNG | 105C | Bristol FS5G | 223.130 | H33/27RD | 3/65 | Eastern Counties, Norwich (NK) LFS105 |
| 14761 | DNG | 106C | Bristol FS5G | 223.131 | H33/27RD | 4/65 | Eastern Counties, Norwich (NK) LFS106 |
| 14762 | DNG | 107C | Bristol FS5G | 223.132 | H33/27RD | 4/65 | Eastern Counties, Norwich (NK) LFS107 |
| 14763 | DVF | 108C | Bristol FS5G | 223.135 | H33/27RD | 5/65 | Eastern Counties, Norwich (NK) LFS108 |
| 14764 | ENG | 109C | Bristol FS5G | 223.145 | H33/27RD | 6/65 | Eastern Counties, Norwich (NK) LFS109 |
| 14765 | ENG | 110C | Bristol FS5G | 223.146 | H33/27RD | 6/65 | Eastern Counties, Norwich (NK) LFS110 |
| 14766 | EVF | 111C | Bristol FS5G | 223.147 | H33/27RD | 6/65 | Eastern Counties, Norwich (NK) LFS111 |
| 14767 | FAH | 112C | Bristol FS5G | 228.005 | H33/27RD | 7/65 | Eastern Counties, Norwich (NK) LFS112 |
| 14768 | FAH | 113C | Bristol FS5G | 228.006 | H33/27RD | 7/65 | Eastern Counties, Norwich (NK) LFS113 |
| 14769 | FAH | 114C | Bristol FS5G | 228.007 | H33/27RD | 7/65 | Eastern Counties, Norwich (NK) LFS114 |

| 14770 | FAH 115C | Bristol FS5G | 228.013 | H33/27RD | 9/65 | Eastern Counties, Norwich (NK) LFS115 |
|---|---|---|---|---|---|---|
| 14771 | FAH 116C | Bristol FS5G | 228.020 | H33/27RD | 9/65 | Eastern Counties, Norwich (NK) LFS116 |
| 14772 | FAH 117C | Bristol FS5G | 228.021 | H33/27RD | 9/65 | Eastern Counties, Norwich (NK) LFS117 |
| 14773 | FAH 118C | Bristol FS5G | 228.029 | H33/27RD | 10/65 | Eastern Counties, Norwich (NK) LFS118 |
| 14774 | FPW 319C | Bristol FS5G | 228.030 | H33/27RD | 10/65 | Eastern Counties, Norwich (NK) LFS119 |
| 14775 | FPW 320C | Bristol FS5G | 228.031 | H33/27RD | 10/65 | Eastern Counties, Norwich (NK) LFS120 |
| 14776 | FVF 421C | Bristol FS5G | 228.048 | H33/27RD | 11/65 | Eastern Counties, Norwich (NK) LFS121 |
| 14777 | FVF 422C | Bristol FS5G | 228.049 | H33/27RD | 11/65 | Eastern Counties, Norwich (NK) LFS122 |
| 14778 | FVF 423C | Bristol FS5G | 228.050 | H33/27RD | 11/65 | Eastern Counties, Norwich (NK) LFS123 |
| 14779 | GNG 124C | Bristol FS5G | 228.055 | H33/27RD | 11/65 | Eastern Counties, Norwich (NK) LFS124 |
| 14780 | GNG 125C | Bristol FS5G | 228.056 | H33/27RD | 11/65 | Eastern Counties, Norwich (NK) LFS125 |
| 14781 | GNG 126C | Bristol FS5G | 228.057 | H33/27RD | 11/65 | Eastern Counties, Norwich (NK) LFS126 |
| 14782 | *CEL 863C | Bristol FS6G | 223.111 | H33/27RD | 1/65 | Hants & Dorset, Bournemouth (HA) 1515 |
| 14783 | CLJ 867C | Bristol FLF6B | 224.156 | H38/32F | 2/65 | Hants & Dorset, Bournemouth (HA) 1516 |
| 14784 | *CLJ 868C | Bristol FLF6B | 224.163 | H38/32F | 2/65 | Hants & Dorset, Bournemouth (HA) 1517 |
| 14785 | CLJ 869C | Bristol FLF6B | 224.198 | H38/32F | 5/65 | Hants & Dorset, Bournemouth (HA) 1518 |
| 14786 | CLJ 870C | Bristol FLF6B | 224.199 | H38/32F | 5/65 | Hants & Dorset, Bournemouth (HA) 1519 |
| 14787 | CLJ 871C | Bristol FLF6B | 224.200 | H38/32F | 5/65 | Hants & Dorset, Bournemouth (HA) 1520 |
| 14788 | *DEL 891C | Bristol FLF6B | 229.085 | H38/32F | 6/65 | Hants & Dorset, Bournemouth (HA) 1521 |
| 14789 | DEL 892C | Bristol FLF6B | 229.086 | H38/32F | 6/65 | Hants & Dorset, Bournemouth (HA) 1522 |
| 14790 | DEL 893C | Bristol FLF6B | 229.087 | H38/32F | 6/65 | Hants & Dorset, Bournemouth (HA) 1523 |
| 14791 | DEL 894C | Bristol FLF6G | 229.120 | H38/32F | 7/65 | Hants & Dorset, Bournemouth (HA) 1524 |
| 14792 | DEL 895C | Bristol FLF6G | 229.121 | H38/32F | 7/65 | Hants & Dorset, Bournemouth (HA) 1525 |
| 14793 | DEL 896C | Bristol FLF6G | 229.122 | H38/32F | 7/65 | Hants & Dorset, Bournemouth (HA) 1526 |
| 14794 | EEL 890C | Bristol FLF6G | 229.158 | H38/32F | 9/65 | Hants & Dorset, Bournemouth (HA) 1527 |
| 14795 | *EEL 891C | Bristol FLF6G | 229.182 | H38/32F | 10/65 | Hants & Dorset, Bournemouth (HA) 1528 |
| 14796 | EEL 892C | Bristol FLF6G | 229.183 | H38/32F | 10/65 | Hants & Dorset, Bournemouth (HA) 1529 |
| 14797 | EEL 893C | Bristol FLF6G | 229.201 | H38/32F | 10/65 | Hants & Dorset, Bournemouth (HA) 1530 |
| 14798 | *EEL 894C | Bristol FLF6G | 229.202 | H38/32F | 10/65 | Hants & Dorset, Bournemouth (HA) 1531 |
| 14799 | BFE 814C | Bristol FS5G | 228.002 | H33/27RD | 7/65 | Lincolnshire RCC, Lincoln (LC) 2524 |
| 14800 | BFE 815C | Bristol FS5G | 228.003 | H33/27RD | 7/65 | Lincolnshire RCC, Lincoln (LC) 2525 |
| 14801 | BVL 286C | Bristol FS5G | 228.004 | H33/27RD | 7/65 | Lincolnshire RCC, Lincoln (LC) 2526 |
| 14802 | BVL 287C | Bristol FS5G | 228.037 | H33/27RD | 12/65 | Lincolnshire RCC, Lincoln (LC) 2528 |
| 14803 | BVL 288C | Bristol FS5G | 228.038 | H33/27RD | 12/65 | Lincolnshire RCC, Lincoln (LC) 2529 |
| 14804 | BVL 289C | Bristol FS5G | 228.039 | H33/27RD | 12/65 | Lincolnshire RCC, Lincoln (LC) 2530 |
| 14805 | DNV 674C | Bristol FS6B | 223.119 | H33/27RD | 2/65 | United Counties, Northampton (NO) 674 |
| 14806 | DNV 675C | Bristol FS6B | 223.120 | H33/27RD | 2/65 | United Counties, Northampton (NO) 675 |
| 14807 | DNV 676C | Bristol FS6B | 223.121 | H33/27RD | 2/65 | United Counties, Northampton (NO) 676 |
| 14808 | DNV 677C | Bristol FS6B | 223.125 | H33/27RD | 2/65 | United Counties, Northampton (NO) 677 |
| 14809 | DNV 678C | Bristol FS6B | 223.133 | H33/27RD | 4/65 | United Counties, Northampton (NO) 678 |
| 14810 | DNV 679C | Bristol FS6B | 223.134 | H33/27RD | 4/65 | United Counties, Northampton (NO) 679 |
| 14811 | EBD 680C | Bristol FS6B | 223.136 | H33/27RD | 5/65 | United Counties, Northampton (NO) 680 |
| 14812 | EBD 681C | Bristol FS6B | 223.137 | H33/27RD | 6/65 | United Counties, Northampton (NO) 681 |
| 14813 | EBD 682C | Bristol FS6B | 223.148 | H33/27RD | 7/65 | United Counties, Northampton (NO) 682 |
| 14814 | ENV 683C | Bristol FS6B | 223.149 | H33/27RD | 7/65 | United Counties, Northampton (NO) 683 |
| 14815 | ENV 684C | Bristol FS6B | 228.015 | H33/27RD | 8/65 | United Counties, Northampton (NO) 684 |
| 14816 | ENV 685C | Bristol FS6B | 228.016 | H33/27RD | 10/65 | United Counties, Northampton (NO) 685 |
| 14817 | ENV 686C | Bristol FS6B | 228.017 | H33/27RD | 9/65 | United Counties, Northampton (NO) 686 |
| 14818 | ENV 687C | Bristol FS6B | 228.018 | H33/27RD | 9/65 | United Counties, Northampton (NO) 687 |
| 14819 | ENV 688C | Bristol FS6B | 228.019 | H33/27RD | 10/65 | United Counties, Northampton (NO) 688 |
| 14820 | ENV 689C | Bristol FS6B | 228.024 | H33/27RD | 10/65 | United Counties, Northampton (NO) 689 |
| 14821 | ENV 690C | Bristol FS6B | 228.025 | H33/27RD | 10/65 | United Counties, Northampton (NO) 690 |
| 14822 | EWY 272C | Bristol FS6B | 223.126 | H33/27RD | 3/65 | West Yorkshire RCC, Harrogate (WR) DX184 |
| 14823 | EWY 273C | Bristol FS6B | 223.127 | H33/27RD | 3/65 | West Yorkshire RCC, Harrogate (WR) DX185 |
| 14824 | GWU 809C | Bristol FS6B | 223.143 | H33/27RD | 6/65 | West Yorkshire RCC, Harrogate (WR) DX186 |
| 14825 | GWW 111C | Bristol FS6B | 223.144 | H33/27RD | 6/65 | West Yorkshire RCC, Harrogate (WR) DX187 |
| 14826 | HWW 477C | Bristol FS6B | 228.026 | H33/27RD | 10/65 | West Yorkshire RCC, Harrogate (WR) DX188 |
| 14827 | HWW 478C | Bristol FS6B | 228.027 | H33/27RD | 10/65 | West Yorkshire RCC, Harrogate (WR) DX189 |
| 14828 | HWY 523C | Bristol FS6B | 228.040 | H33/27RD | 10/65 | West Yorkshire RCC, Harrogate (WR) DX199 |
| 14829 | HWY 829C | Bristol FS6B | 228.041 | H33/27RD | 11/65 | West Yorkshire RCC, Harrogate (WR) DX200 |
| 14830 | HWY 524C | Bristol FS6B | 228.046 | H33/27RD | 10/65 | West Yorkshire RCC, Harrogate (WR) DX201 |
| 14831 | HWY 830C | Bristol FS6B | 228.047 | H33/27RD | 11/65 | West Yorkshire RCC, Harrogate (WR) DX202 |
| 14832 | JWT 402C | Bristol FS6B | 228.060 | H33/27RD | 12/65 | West Yorkshire RCC, Harrogate (WR) DX203 |
| 14833 | JWT 350C | Bristol FS6B | 228.061 | H33/27RD | 12/65 | West Yorkshire RCC, Harrogate (WR) DX204 |

| | | | | | | |
|---|---|---|---|---|---|---|
| 14834 | JWT 351C | Bristol FS6B | 228.062 | H33/27RD | 12/65 | West Yorkshire RCC, Harrogate (WR) DX205 |
| 14835 | EWU 113C | Bristol FS6B | 223.116 | H33/27RD | 2/65 | York-West Yorkshire, Harrogate (WR) YDX192 |
| 14836 | EWU 114C | Bristol FS6B | 223.117 | H33/27RD | 2/65 | York-West Yorkshire, Harrogate (WR) YDX193 |
| 14837 | EWU 875C | Bristol FS6B | 223.118 | H33/27RD | 2/65 | York-West Yorkshire, Harrogate (WR) YDX194 |
| 14838 | GYG 614C | Bristol FS6B | 228.008 | H33/27RD | 8/65 | York-West Yorkshire, Harrogate (WR) YDX195 |
| 14839 | GYG 615C | Bristol FS6B | 228.009 | H33/27RD | 8/65 | York-West Yorkshire, Harrogate (WR) YDX196 |
| 14840 | JWR 411C | Bristol FS6B | 228.058 | H33/27RD | 12/65 | York-West Yorkshire, Harrogate (WR) YDX197 |
| 14841 | JWR 412C | Bristol FS6B | 228.059 | H33/27RD | 12/65 | York-West Yorkshire, Harrogate (WR) YDX198 |
| 14842 | FPM 73C | Bristol FLF6G | 229.174 | H38/32F | 10/65 | Brighton, Hove & District (ES) 73 |
| 14843 | FPM 74C | Bristol FLF6G | 229.175 | H38/32F | 10/65 | Brighton, Hove & District (ES) 74 |
| 14844 | *FPM 75C | Bristol FLF6G | 229.176 | H38/32F | 10/65 | Brighton, Hove & District (ES) 75 |
| 14845 | BHU 975C | Bristol FLF6B | 224.147 | H38/32F | 2/65 | Bristol OC (GL) C7175 |
| 14846 | *BHU 976C | Bristol FLF6B | 224.148 | H38/32F | 2/65 | Bristol OC (GL) C7176 |
| 14847 | BHU 977C | Bristol FLF6B | 224.154 | H38/32F | 2/65 | Bristol OC (GL) C7177 |
| 14848 | BHU 978C | Bristol FLF6B | 224.155 | H38/32F | 2/65 | Bristol OC (GL) C7178 |
| 14849 | BHU 979C | Bristol FLF6B | 224.174 | H38/32F | 3/65 | Bristol OC (GL) C7186 |
| 14850 | BHU 980C | Bristol FLF6B | 224.177 | H38/32F | 4/65 | Bristol OC (GL) C7187 |
| 14851 | CHT 539C | Bristol FLF6B | 224.191 | H38/32F | 5/65 | Bristol OC (GL) C7196 |
| 14852 | CHT 540C | Bristol FLF6B | 229.060 | H38/32F | 6/65 | Bristol OC (GL) C7197 |
| 14853 | *CHT 541C | Bristol FLF6B | 229.061 | H38/32F | 7/65 | Bristol OC (GL) C7198 |
| 14854 | *CHY 417C | Bristol FLF6B | 229.062 | H38/32F | 7/65 | Bristol OC (GL) C7199 |
| 14855 | CHY 418C | Bristol FLF6B | 229.105 | H38/32F | 7/65 | Bristol OC (GL) C7200 |
| 14856 | CHY 419C | Bristol FLF6B | 229.111 | H38/32F | 7/65 | Bristol OC (GL) C7201 |
| 14857 | CHY 420C | Bristol FLF6B | 229.112 | H38/32F | 8/65 | Bristol OC (GL) C7202 |
| 14858 | DHW 987C | Bristol FLF6B | 229.155 | H38/32F | 9/65 | Bristol OC (GL) C7207 |
| 14859 | DHW 988C | Bristol FLF6B | 229.163 | H38/32F | 9/65 | Bristol OC (GL) C7208 |
| 14860 | DHW 989C | Bristol FLF6B | 229.164 | H38/32F | 9/65 | Bristol OC (GL) C7209 |
| 14861 | DHW 990C | Bristol FLF6B | 229.165 | H38/32F | 10/65 | Bristol OC (GL) C7210 |
| 14862 | DHW 991C | Bristol FLF6B | 229.166 | H38/32F | 10/65 | Bristol OC (GL) C7211 |
| 14863 | EHT 106C | Bristol FLF6G | 229.170 | H38/32F | 10/65 | Bristol OC (GL) C7217 |
| 14864 | EHT 107C | Bristol FLF6G | 229.171 | H38/32F | 11/65 | Bristol OC (GL) C7218 |
| 14865 | EHT 108C | Bristol FLF6G | 229.172 | H38/32F | 11/65 | Bristol OC (GL) C7219 |
| 14866 | EHT 116C | Bristol FLF6G | 229.203 | H38/32F | 11/65 | Bristol OC (GL) C7227 |
| 14867 | EHT 117C | Bristol FLF6G | 229.204 | H38/32F | 11/65 | Bristol OC (GL) C7228 |
| 14868 | EHT 851C | Bristol FLF6G | 229.205 | H38/32F | 12/65 | Bristol OC (GL) C7229 |
| 14869 | EHU 583C | Bristol FLF6G | 229.227 | H38/32F | 12/65 | Bristol OC (GL) C7237 |
| 14870 | EHU 584C | Bristol FLF6G | 229.228 | H38/32F | 12/65 | Bristol OC (GL) C7238 |
| 14871 | BHY 715C | Bristol FLF6G | 224.175 | H38/32F | 3/65 | Cheltenham District (GL) 7184 |
| 14872 | BHY 716C | Bristol FLF6G | 224.176 | H38/32F | 4/65 | Cheltenham District (GL) 7185 |
| 14873 | *EHT 109C | Bristol FLF6G | 229.173 | H38/32F | 11/65 | Cheltenham District (GL) 7220 |
| 14874 | *EHT 110C | Bristol FLF6G | 229.181 | H38/32F | 11/65 | Cheltenham District (GL) 7221 |
| 14875 | BHU 98C | Bristol FLF6G | 224.120 | H38/32F | 2/65 | Bristol OC (GL) G7174 |
| 14876 | BHW 671C | Bristol FLF6G | 224.143 | H38/32F | 2/65 | Bristol OC (GL) 7179 |
| 14877 | BHW 672C | Bristol FLF6G | 224.151 | H38/32F | 2/65 | Bristol OC (GL) 7180 |
| 14878 | BHW 673C | Bristol FLF6G | 224.152 | H38/32F | 3/65 | Bristol OC (GL) 7181 |
| 14879 | BHW 674C | Bristol FLF6G | 224.153 | H38/32F | 3/65 | Bristol OC (GL) 7182 |
| 14880 | BHW 675C | Bristol FLF6G | 224.157 | H38/32F | 3/65 | Bristol OC (GL) 7183 |
| 14881 | CHT 531C | Bristol FLF6B | 224.185 | H38/32F | 5/65 | Bristol OC (GL) 7188 |
| 14882 | CHT 532C | Bristol FLF6B | 224.186 | H38/32F | 5/65 | Bristol OC (GL) 7189 |
| 14883 | CHT 533C | Bristol FLF6B | 224.187 | H38/32F | 5/65 | Bristol OC (GL) 7190 |
| 14884 | CHT 534C | Bristol FLF6B | 224.194 | H38/32F | 5/65 | Bristol OC (GL) 7191 |
| 14885 | CHT 535C | Bristol FLF6B | 224.195 | H38/32F | 6/65 | Bristol OC (GL) 7192 |
| 14886 | CHT 536C | Bristol FLF6B | 224.196 | H38/32F | 6/65 | Bristol OC (GL) 7193 |
| 14887 | CHT 537C | Bristol FLF6B | 224.197 | H38/32F | 6/65 | Bristol OC (GL) 7194 |
| 14888 | CHT 538C | Bristol FLF6B | 229.035 | H38/32F | 6/65 | Bristol OC (GL) 7195 |
| 14889 | DHT 783C | Bristol FLF6B | 229.116 | H38/32F | 8/65 | Bristol OC (GL) 7203 |
| 14890 | *DHT 784C | Bristol FLF6B | 229.137 | H38/32F | 8/65 | Bristol OC (GL) 7204 |
| 14891 | DHT 785C | Bristol FLF6B | 229.141 | H38/32F | 8/65 | Bristol OC (GL) 7205 |
| 14892 | DHW 981C | Bristol FLF6B | 229.142 | H38/32F | 8/65 | Bristol OC (GL) 7206 |
| 14893 | DHW 982C | Bristol FLF6G | 229.159 | H38/32F | 9/65 | Bristol OC (GL) 7212 |
| 14894 | *DHW 983C | Bristol FLF6G | 229.160 | H38/32F | 10/65 | Bristol OC (GL) 7213 |
| 14895 | *DHW 984C | Bristol FLF6G | 229.161 | H38/32F | 10/65 | Bristol OC (GL) 7214 |
| 14896 | DHW 985C | Bristol FLF6G | 229.162 | H38/32F | 10/65 | Bristol OC (GL) 7215 |
| 14897 | DHW 986C | Bristol FLF6B | 229.187 | H38/32F | 10/65 | Bristol OC (GL) 7216 |

| | | | | | | | |
|---|---|---|---|---|---|---|---|
| 14898 | EHT 115C | Bristol FLF6B | 229.197 | H38/32F | 11/65 | Bristol OC (GL) 7226 |
| 14899 | EHT 111C | Bristol FLF6G | 229.189 | H38/32F | 11/65 | Bristol OC (GL) 7222 |
| 14900 | EHT 112C | Bristol FLF6G | 229.190 | H38/32F | 11/65 | Bristol OC (GL) 7223 |
| 14901 | EHT 113C | Bristol FLF6G | 229.191 | H38/32F | 11/65 | Bristol OC (GL) 7224 |
| 14902 | EHT 114C | Bristol FLF6G | 229.192 | H38/32F | 11/65 | Bristol OC (GL) 7225 |
| 14903 | EHT 852C | Bristol FLF6G | 229.206 | H38/32F | 11/65 | Bristol OC (GL) 7230 |
| 14904 | EHT 856C | Bristol FLF6G | 229.217 | H38/32F | 12/65 | Bristol OC (GL) 7234 |
| 14905 | EHT 857C | Bristol FLF6G | 229.218 | H38/32F | 12/65 | Bristol OC (GL) 7235 |
| 14906 | EHT 858C | Bristol FLF6G | 229.219 | H38/32F | 12/65 | Bristol OC (GL) 7236 |
| 14907 | *EHW 191C | Bristol FLF6G | 229.239 | H38/32F | 12/65 | Bristol OC (GL) 7239 |
| 14908 | FHT 15D | Bristol FLF6G | 229.240 | H38/32F | 1/66 | Bristol OC (GL) 7240 |
| 14909 | FHT 16D | Bristol FLF6G | 229.243 | H38/32F | 1/66 | Bristol OC (GL) 7241 |
| 14910 | FHT 17D | Bristol FLF6G | 229.244 | H38/32F | 1/66 | Bristol OC (GL) 7242 |
| 14911 | *EHT 853C | Bristol FLF6G | 229.212 | H38/32F | 12/65 | Bristol OC (GL) G7231 |
| 14912 | EHT 854C | Bristol FLF6G | 229.213 | H38/32F | 12/65 | Bristol OC (GL) G7232 |
| 14913 | EHT 855C | Bristol FLF6G | 229.214 | H38/32F | 12/65 | Bristol OC (GL) G7233 |
| 14914 | | | | | | Not built |
| 14915 | | | | | | Not built |
| 14916 | | | | | | Not built |
| 14917 | | | | | | Not built |
| 14918 | | | | | | Not built |
| 14919 | DFM 201C | Bristol FLF6B | 224.166 | H38/32F | 3/65 | Crosville MS, Chester (CH) DFB199 |
| 14920 | EFM 634C | Bristol FLF6B | 229.117 | H38/32F | 7/65 | Crosville MS, Chester (CH) DFB200 |
| 14921 | EFM 635C | Bristol FLF6B | 229.118 | H38/32F | 7/65 | Crosville MS, Chester (CH) DFB201 |
| 14922 | GFM 202C | Bristol FLF6B | 229.188 | H38/32F | 10/65 | Crosville MS, Chester (CH) DFB202 |
| 14923 | GFM 203C | Bristol FLF6B | 229.193 | H38/32F | 10/65 | Crosville MS, Chester (CH) DFB203 |
| 14924 | DAO 201C | Bristol FLF6G | 224.142 | H38/32F | 2/65 | Cumberland MS, Whitehaven (CU) 529 |
| 14925 | DAO 202C | Bristol FLF6G | 229.113 | H38/32F | 8/65 | Cumberland MS, Whitehaven (CU) 530 |
| 14926 | DAO 203C | Bristol FLF6G | 229.114 | H38/32F | 8/65 | Cumberland MS, Whitehaven (CU) 531 |
| 14927 | DAO 204C | Bristol FLF6G | 229.131 | H38/32F | 9/65 | Cumberland MS, Whitehaven (CU) 532 |
| 14928 | *JHK 452C | Bristol FLF6B | 224.123 | H38/32F | 1/65 | Eastern National, Chelmsford (EX) 2820 |
| 14929 | JHK 454C | Bristol FLF6B | 224.131 | H38/32F | 1/65 | Eastern National, Chelmsford (EX) 2822 |
| 14930 | *JHK 455C | Bristol FLF6B | 224.132 | H38/32F | 1/65 | Eastern National, Chelmsford (EX) 2823 |
| 14931 | *JHK 462C | Bristol FLF6B | 224.137 | H38/32F | 1/65 | Eastern National, Chelmsford (EX) 2827 |
| 14932 | JHK 453C | Bristol FLF6G | 224.130 | H38/32F | 1/65 | Eastern National, Chelmsford (EX) 2821 |
| 14933 | JHK 459C | Bristol FLF6G | 224.133 | H38/32F | 1/65 | Eastern National, Chelmsford (EX) 2824 |
| 14934 | JHK 460C | Bristol FLF6G | 224.134 | H38/32F | 1/65 | Eastern National, Chelmsford (EX) 2825 |
| 14935 | JHK 461C | Bristol FLF6G | 224.135 | H38/32F | 3/65 | Eastern National, Chelmsford (EX) 2826 |
| 14936 | *KNO 949C | Bristol FLF6B | 224.178 | CH37/22F | 3/65 | Eastern National, Chelmsford (EX) 2608 |
| 14937 | KNO 950C | Bristol FLF6B | 224.179 | CH37/22F | 3/65 | Eastern National, Chelmsford (EX) 2609 |
| 14938 | KNO 951C | Bristol FLF6B | 224.180 | H38/32F | 3/65 | Eastern National, Chelmsford (EX) 2828 |
| 14939 | KNO 952C | Bristol FLF6B | 224.184 | H38/32F | 3/65 | Eastern National, Chelmsford (EX) 2829 |
| 14940 | KNO 954C | Bristol FLF6G | 229.027 | H38/32F | 5/65 | Eastern National, Chelmsford (EX) 2831 |
| 14941 | KNO 955C | Bristol FLF6G | 229.028 | H38/32F | 5/65 | Eastern National, Chelmsford (EX) 2832 |
| 14942 | KNO 953C | Bristol FLF6G | 229.026 | H38/32F | 5/65 | Eastern National, Chelmsford (EX) 2830 |
| 14943 | LWC 659C | Bristol FLF6B | 229.094 | H38/32F | 6/65 | Eastern National, Chelmsford (EX) 2833 |
| 14944 | LWC 660C | Bristol FLF6B | 229.095 | H38/32F | 6/65 | Eastern National, Chelmsford (EX) 2834 |
| 14945 | LWC 661C | Bristol FLF6B | 229.102 | H38/32F | 6/65 | Eastern National, Chelmsford (EX) 2835 |
| 14946 | LWC 662C | Bristol FLF6G | 229.145 | H38/32F | 8/65 | Eastern National, Chelmsford (EX) 2836 |
| 14947 | LWC 663C | Bristol FLF6G | 229.146 | H38/32F | 8/65 | Eastern National, Chelmsford (EX) 2837 |
| 14948 | LWC 664C | Bristol FLF6G | 229.147 | H38/32F | 9/65 | Eastern National, Chelmsford (EX) 2838 |
| 14949 | LWC 665C | Bristol FLF6G | 229.148 | H38/32F | 8/65 | Eastern National, Chelmsford (EX) 2839 |
| 14950 | LWC 666C | Bristol FLF6G | 229.149 | H38/32F | 8/65 | Eastern National, Chelmsford (EX) 2840 |
| 14951 | MVX 878C | Bristol FLF6B | 229.177 | H38/32F | 9/65 | Eastern National, Chelmsford (EX) 2841 |
| 14952 | MVX 879C | Bristol FLF6B | 229.178 | H38/32F | 9/65 | Eastern National, Chelmsford (EX) 2842 |
| 14953 | MVX 880C | Bristol FLF6B | 229.194 | H38/32F | 10/65 | Eastern National, Chelmsford (EX) 2843 |
| 14954 | MVX 881C | Bristol FLF6B | 229.195 | H38/32F | 10/65 | Eastern National, Chelmsford (EX) 2844 |
| 14955 | MVX 882C | Bristol FLF6B | 229.196 | H38/32F | 10/65 | Eastern National, Chelmsford (EX) 2845 |
| 14956 | MVX 883C | Bristol FLF6G | 229.198 | H38/32F | 10/65 | Eastern National, Chelmsford (EX) 2846 |
| 14957 | MVX 884C | Bristol FLF6G | 229.199 | H38/32F | 10/65 | Eastern National, Chelmsford (EX) 2847 |
| 14958 | MVX 885C | Bristol FLF6G | 229.200 | H38/32F | 10/65 | Eastern National, Chelmsford (EX) 2848 |
| 14959 | NTW 942C | Bristol FLF6G | 229.224 | H38/32F | 11/65 | Eastern National, Chelmsford (EX) 2849 |
| 14960 | NTW 943C | Bristol FLF6G | 229.225 | H38/32F | 11/65 | Eastern National, Chelmsford (EX) 2850 |
| 14961 | *NTW 944C | Bristol FLF6G | 229.226 | H38/32F | 11/65 | Eastern National, Chelmsford (EX) 2851 |

| | | | | | | | |
|---|---|---|---|---|---|---|---|
| 14962 | EEL 895C | Bristol FLF6G | 229.210 | H38/32F | 10/65 | Hants & Dorset, Bournemouth (HA) 1532 |
| 14963 | EEL 896C | Bristol FLF6G | 229.211 | H38/32F | 11/65 | Hants & Dorset, Bournemouth (HA) 1533 |
| 14964 | AVL 216C | Bristol FLF6G | 224.126 | H38/32F | 5/65 | Lincolnshire RCC, Lincoln (LC) 2522 |
| 14965 | AVL 217C | Bristol FLF6G | 224.127 | H38/32F | 5/65 | Lincolnshire RCC, Lincoln (LC) 2523 |
| 14966 | BVL 45C | Bristol FLF6G | 229.115 | H38/32F | 7/65 | Lincolnshire RCC, Lincoln (LC) 2527 |
| 14967 | CFE 230C | Bristol FLF6G | 229.207 | H38/32F | 12/65 | Lincolnshire RCC, Lincoln (LC) 2531 |
| 14968 | *CFE 231C | Bristol FLF6G | 229.208 | H38/32F | 12/65 | Lincolnshire RCC, Lincoln (LC) 2532 |
| 14969 | BNN 291C | Bristol FLF6G | 224.121 | H38/32F | 2/65 | Mansfield District (NG) 648 |
| 14970 | BNN 292C | Bristol FLF6G | 224.122 | H38/32F | 2/65 | Mansfield District (NG) 649 |
| 14971 | DNU 687C | Bristol FLF6G | 224.136 | H38/32F | 3/65 | Notts & Derby, Langley Mill (DE) 639 |
| 14972 | DAL 305C | Bristol FLF6B | 229.126 | H38/32F | 7/65 | Mansfield District (NG) 650 |
| 14973 | DAL 307C | Bristol FLF6B | 229.134 | H38/32F | 8/65 | Mansfield District (NG) 652 |
| 14974 | DAL 308C | Bristol FLF6G | 229.138 | H38/32F | 9/65 | Mansfield District (NG) 653 |
| 14975 | DAL 309C | Bristol FLF6G | 229.139 | H38/32F | 9/65 | Mansfield District (NG) 654 |
| 14976 | DNU 685C | Bristol FLF6G | 224.128 | H38/32F | 2/65 | Notts & Derby, Langley Mill (DE) 637 |
| 14977 | DNU 686C | Bristol FLF6G | 224.129 | H38/32F | 2/65 | Notts & Derby, Langley Mill (DE) 638 |
| 14978 | DNU 688C | Bristol FLF6B | 224.168 | H38/32F | 3/65 | Notts & Derby, Langley Mill (DE) 640 |
| 14979 | DNU 689C | Bristol FLF6B | 224.169 | H38/32F | 3/65 | Notts & Derby, Langley Mill (DE) 641 |
| 14980 | FNU 411C | Bristol FLF6B | 229.119 | H38/32F | 8/65 | Midland General, Langley Mill (DE) 642 |
| 14981 | FNU 412C | Bristol FLF6B | 229.125 | H38/32F | 8/65 | Midland General, Langley Mill (DE) 643 |
| 14982 | DAL 306C | Bristol FLF6G | 229.132 | H38/32F | 7/65 | Mansfield District (NG) 651 |
| 14983 | *FNU 413C | Bristol FLF6G | 229.133 | H38/32F | 9/65 | Midland General, Langley Mill (DE) 644 |
| 14984 | *FNU 414C | Bristol FLF6G | 229.156 | H38/32F | 10/65 | Midland General, Langley Mill (DE) 645 |
| 14985 | BDV 264C | Bristol FLF6B | 224.164 | H38/32F | 2/65 | Southern National, Exeter (DN) 2056 |
| 14986 | BDV 265C | Bristol FLF6B | 224.165 | H38/32F | 2/65 | Southern National, Exeter (DN) 2057 |
| 14987 | BDV 266C | Bristol FLF6B | 224.181 | H38/32F | 3/65 | Southern National, Exeter (DN) 2058 |
| 14988 | *BDV 267C | Bristol FLF6G | 224.182 | H38/32F | 5/65 | Southern National, Exeter (DN) 2059 |
| 14989 | BDV 268C | Bristol FLF6G | 224.183 | H38/32F | 5/65 | Southern National, Exeter (DN) 2060 |
| 14990 | BOD 21C | Bristol FLF6B | 229.103 | H38/32F | 7/65 | Southern National, Exeter (DN) 2061 |
| 14991 | BOD 22C | Bristol FLF6B | 229.104 | H38/32F | 7/65 | Southern National, Exeter (DN) 2062 |
| 14992 | BOD 23C | Bristol FLF6G | 229.130 | H38/32F | 8/65 | Southern National, Exeter (DN) 2063 |
| 14993 | *BOD 24C | Bristol FLF6G | 229.140 | H38/32F | 8/65 | Southern National, Exeter (DN) 2064 |
| 14994 | BOD 25C | Bristol FLF6B | 229.185 | H38/32F | 9/65 | Southern National, Exeter (DN) 2065 |
| 14995 | BOD 26C | Bristol FLF6B | 229.186 | H38/32F | 9/65 | Southern National, Exeter (DN) 2066 |
| 14996 | CDL 476C | Bristol FLF6G | 224.141 | H38/32F | 3/65 | Southern Vectis, Newport (IW) 608 |
| 14997 | CDL 477C | Bristol FLF6G | 229.034 | H38/32F | 5/65 | Southern Vectis, Newport (IW) 609 |
| 14998 | CDL 478C | Bristol FLF6G | 229.041 | H38/32F | 5/65 | Southern Vectis, Newport (IW) 610 |
| 14999 | CDL 479C | Bristol FLF6G | 229.068 | H38/32F | 6/65 | Southern Vectis, Newport (IW) 611 |
| 15000 | *CDL 480C | Bristol FLF6G | 229.069 | H38/32F | 6/65 | Southern Vectis, Newport (IW) 612 |

**Notes:**

```
10493-10631  }
10643-10649  }
10664        }
10668-10670  } Not allocated as a result of the cutback in the 1958 orders, although body numbers
10677-10700  } 10715-16 were re-allocated in 1960 as shown.
10705-10708  }
10715-10719  }
```

10001 (997 CHN): Chassis new 8/47 registered HHN 213 with ECW (1371) B35R body; rebuilt to LL5G specification prior to rebodying; replacement body was 8ft wide on the 7ft 6in wide chassis.

10002 (998 CHN): Chassis new 9/47 registered JHN 326 with ECW (2018) B35R body; rebuilt to LL5G specification prior to rebodying; replacement body was 8ft wide on the 7ft 6in wide chassis.

10012 (KLA 91): Chassis new 7/49 with Strachan FC24F body.

10013 (KLA 90): Chassis new 7/49 with Strachan FC24F body.

10014 (KLA 89): Chassis new 7/49 with Strachan FC24F body.

10015 (KGX 941): Chassis new 7/49 with Strachan FC24F body.

10016 (KGX 940): Chassis new 7/49 with Strachan FC24F body.

10103 (752 GFM): Chassis new 8/53 registered SFM 2 with ECW (6942) C39F body; rebuilt and rebodied following an accident and re-registered 752 GFM.

10123 (GM 9287): Re-registered TVS 367 with Strathclyde Regional Council (XSC) 8/93.

10131 (3003 AH): Re-registered FRE 699A with St Margaret Ward High School, Stoke-on-Trent (XST) c9/80; reverted to original registration 3003 AH with Burnside, Norwich (preservationist) 4/15.

10225 (287 HFM): Re-registered SH 40420 with Rappold Classic AG, Neuhausen (O-CH) 1988.

10240 (296 HFM): Re-registered ACA 230A 11/84.

10348 (SWN 159): Re-registered ACY 178A 4/86 then ACY 307A 3/88 with South Wales Transport Ltd, Swansea (WG); reverted to original registration SWN 159 with Davies, Llanelli (preservationist) by6/03.

10435 (928 JHN): Originally allocated registration 528 JHN.

10436 (929 JHN): Originally allocated registration 529 JHN; re-registered XYJ 717 with unidentified preservationist by2/97.

10437 (930 JHN): Originally allocated registration 530 JHN.

10438 (931 JHN): Originally allocated registration 531 JHN.

10439 (932 JHN): Originally allocated registration 532 JHN.

10440 (933 JHN): Originally allocated registration 533 JHN.

10441 (934 JHN): Originally allocated registration 534 JHN.

10442 (935 JHN): Originally allocated registration 535 JHN.

10443 (936 JHN): Originally allocated registration 536 JHN.

10633 (JAO 837): Chassis new 10/49 with ACB C31F body.

10720 (JUO 985): Chassis new 1948 with Beadle (567) C31F body; rebuilt to LL6B specification prior to rebodying.

10721 (JUO 980): Chassis new 1948 as Southern National, Exeter (DN) 1215 with Beadle (562) C31F body; rebuilt to LL6B specification prior to rebodying.

10722 (JUO 978): Chassis new 1948 with Beadle (560) C31F body; rebuilt to LL6B specification prior to rebodying.

10723 (JUO 982): Chassis new 1948 with Beadle (564) C31F body; rebuilt to LL6B specification prior to rebodying.

10724 (JUO 988): Chassis new 1948 with Beadle (570) C31F body; rebuilt to LL6B specification prior to rebodying.

10725 (JUO 979): Chassis new 1948 as Southern National, Exeter (DN) 1214 with Beadle (561) C31F body; rebuilt to LL6B specification prior to rebodying.

10726 (JUO 989): Chassis new 1948 with Beadle (571) C31F body; rebuilt to LL6B specification prior to rebodying.

10727 (JUO 986): Chassis new 1948 with Beadle (568) C31F body; rebuilt to LL6B specification prior to rebodying.

10728 (JUO 984): Chassis new 1948 with Beadle (566) C31F body; rebuilt to LL6B specification prior to rebodying.

10729 (JUO 981): Chassis new 1948 with Beadle (563) C31F body; rebuilt to LL6B specification prior to rebodying.

10730 (JUO 983): Chassis new 1948 with Beadle (565) C31F body; rebuilt to LL6B specification prior to rebodying.

10731 (JUO 987): Chassis new 1948 with Beadle (569) C31F body; rebuilt to LL6B specification prior to rebodying.

10732 (DMO 665): Chassis new 2/48 with Vincent C32F body; fitted with Gardner 5LW engine and rebuilt to LL5G specification prior to rebodying.

10733 (DMO 666): Chassis new 9/47 with Windover (6664) C32F body; fitted with Gardner 5LW engine and rebuilt to LL5G specification type prior to rebodying.

10734 (DMO 667): Chassis new 10/47 with Windover (6665) C32F body; fitted with Gardner 5LW engine and rebuilt to LL5G specification type prior to rebodying.

10735 (DMO 668): Chassis new 3/48 with Vincent C32F body; fitted with Gardner 5LW engine and rebuilt to LL5G specification prior to rebodying.

10736 (DMO 664): Chassis new 9/47 with Windover (6663) C32F body; fitted with Gardner 5LW engine and rebuilt to LL5G specification type prior to rebodying.

10737 (DMO 669): Chassis new 10/47 with Windover (6666) C32F body; fitted with Gardner 5LW engine and rebuilt to LL5G specification type prior to rebodying.

10738 (JUO 944): Chassis new 1948 with Beadle (559) C31F body; rebuilt to LL6B specification prior to rebodying.

10739 (JUO 934): Chassis new 1948 with Beadle (549) C31F body; rebuilt to LL6B specification prior to rebodying.

10740 (HOD 27): Chassis new 1948 with Beadle C31F body; rebuilt to LL6A specification prior to rebodying.

10741 (JUO 939): Chassis new 1948 with Beadle (554) C31F body; rebuilt to LL6B specification prior to rebodying.

10742 (JUO 938): Chassis new 1948 with Beadle (553) C31F body; rebuilt to LL6B specification prior to rebodying.

10743 (JUO 932): Chassis new 1948 with Beadle (547) C31F body; rebuilt to LL6B specification prior to rebodying.

10744 (JUO 937): Chassis new 1948 with Beadle (552) C31F body; rebuilt to LL6B specification prior to rebodying.
10745 (JUO 936): Chassis new 1948 with Beadle (551) C31F body; rebuilt to LL6B specification prior to rebodying.
10746 (JUO 933): Chassis new 1948 with Beadle (548) C31F body; rebuilt to LL6B specification prior to rebodying.
10747 (JUO 943): Chassis new 1948 with Beadle (558) C31F body; rebuilt to LL6B specification prior to rebodying.
10748 (JUO 940): Chassis new 1948 with Beadle (555) C31F body; rebuilt to LL6B specification prior to rebodying.
10749 (JUO 942): Chassis new 1948 with Beadle (557) C31F body; rebuilt to LL6B specification prior to rebodying.
10750 (JUO 941): Chassis new 1948 with Beadle (556) C31F body; rebuilt to LL6B specification prior to rebodying.
10751 (JUO 935): Chassis new 1948 with Beadle (550) C31F body; rebuilt to LL6B specification prior to rebodying.
10802 (SWS 739): Re-registered T1I.018 at an unknown date and U 46278 by8/88 with B & T Fuller, San Antonio, TX (O-USA).
10805 (SWS 742): Re-registered U 46276 with B & T Fuller, San Antonio, TX (O-USA) by 8/88.
10806 (SWS 743): Re-registered T1I.017 at an unknown date and U 46277 by8/88 with B & T Fuller, San Antonio, TX (O-USA).
10808 (SWS 745): Re-registered B13123 with Double Decker PDX, Portland, OR (O-USA) by9/11.
10863 (990 EHW): Re-registered W756.400 with Music Man, Wien (O-A) by6/84.
10892 (434 FHW): Re-registered BJ-68-DS with unknown owner (O-NL) 3/84.
10903 (611 LFM): Re-registered ACA 216A 10/84.
10913 (629 LFM): Re-registered ACA 195A 8/84, then ACA 544A 7/86 with GE & WRS Walker, Anderton (CH).
10917 (617 LFM): Re-registered 40963 with Fairclough Emirates McAlpine Ltd, Dubai (O-UAE) 7/77.
10930 (XAO 604): Re-registered SG 2945 as mobile carpet showroom (O-CH) 3/74.
10934 (XAO 608): Re-registered 1036 WB 95 with Pompes Guinard, Courbevoie (O-F) 8/77; re-registered 6070 XH 77 with Raiga-Clemenceau, Fontainbleau (O-F) 4/87.
10965 (YRU  65): Re-registered DT 61 505 with JF Biler {Londonbus.dk}, Hjortshoj (O-DK) by2006.
10967 (YRU  67): Re-registered 40961 with Fairclough Emirates McAlpine Ltd, Dubai (O-UAE) 7/77.
11015 ( 20 AAX): Re-registered as follows with National Welsh, Cardiff (SG):- AAX 312A 3/86; AAX 451A 1/87; AAX 466A 2/87; AAX 516A 6/87; AAX 529A 7/87; AAX 562A 9/87; AAX 589A 10/87; AAX 600A 12/87; AAX 630A 1/88; AKG 134A 3/88; AKG 162A 7/88; AKG 197A 8/88; AKG 232A 11/88; AKG 282A 2/89; AKG 296A 3/89 and AKG 307A 5/89.
11018 (SDL 267): Re-registered WSJ 325 with C Sullivan, Borehamwood (preservationist) 6/98; re-registered W.0375 c1/99 and O1V 2951 at an unknown date with Inter Catering, Praha (O-CZ).
11072 (504 BTA): Re-registered TFO 467 with C Ireland, Kingston upon Hull (dealer) 6/96.
11077 (509 BTA): Re-registered CER 571 with Windjammer Cruises, Honolulu, HI (O-USA) 7/77.
11082 (514 BTA): Re-registered 8024 H with D Trone, unknown location, IL (O-USA) by1987.
11086 (518 BTA): Re-registered AAL 969A with Nottinghamshire County Council, Worksop (NG) c7/87.
11120 (348 MFM): Re-registered 4BH9122 with Sir Alfred McAlpine (O-SUD) by11/76.
11123 (351 MFM): Re-registered 4BH9123 with Sir Alfred McAlpine (O-SUD) by11/76.
11148 (1262 EV): Re-registered NNW 626A with Cementation, Pipeline & Mechanical Services, Darlington (XDM) c5/86.
11176 (NVL 165): Re-registered AFE 245A 3/85.
11241 (TWN 114): Had a special low height body for operation under a low bridge at Pontrhydyfen.
11242 (TWN 115): Had a special low height body for operation under a low bridge at Pontrhydyfen.
11282 (206 KFM): Re-registered ACA 578A c7/86.
11380 (NFE 449): Re-registered AJI 3307 with S Twell, Ingham (dealer) 5/72.
11389 (670 COD): Re-registered 6351 as Guernseybus Ltd (CI) 143 5/83.
11400 (FMO  22): Chassis new 3/50 with Windover (6846) C33F body; fitted with Gardner 5LW engine and rebuilt to LL5G specification prior to rebodying.
11401 (FMO  24): Chassis new 3/50 with Windover (6858) C33F body; fitted with Gardner 5LW engine and rebuilt to LL5G specification prior to rebodying.
11402 (FMO  21): Chassis new 3/50 with Windover (6845) C33F body; fitted with Gardner 5LW engine and rebuilt to LL5G specification prior to rebodying.
11403 (FMO  23): Chassis new 3/50 with Windover (6857) C33F body; fitted with Gardner 5LW engine and rebuilt to LL5G specification prior to rebodying.
11533 (728 JHY): Re-registered 05-DB-34 with Krekelberg Hotel, Bemelin (O-NL) 2/78.
11542 (706 JHY): Re-registered 21 RN 50 with MoD (Royal Navy) (GOV) 4/78; reverted to original registration with Wood, Crediton (dealer) 1/83.

11548 (504 BRM): Re-registered 14-19-FB with Endys Dubbeldedekkerservice, Woudenburg (O-NL) 9/74.

11549 (505 BRM): Re-registered ACA 303A with GE & WRS Walker, Anderton (CH) 5/85.

11571 (RPN 10): Re-registered XWV 588A 8/90; re-registered ZH 459496 with J & M Pfiffner {Londag}, Wädenswil (O-CH) 12/90.

11572 (RPN 11): Re-registered XUF 594A 10/86.

11573 (SPM 21): Re-registered XWV 586A 8/90; re-registered ZH 487258 with J & M Pfiffner {Londag}, Wädenswil (O-CH) 5/91.

11574 (SPM 22): Re-registered XWV 602A 9/90; re-registered ZH 763972 with P Hasler, Wädenswil (O-CH) 8/91; re-registered ZH 67787 with unidentified owner (O-CH) by10/98; re-registered 674 UYG with A Colby, Dereham as a caravan 8/14.

11576 (308 PFM): Re-registered 9015 CGT with RG Publicidad en Movimento SL, Barcelona (O-E) by3/03.

11587 (319 PFM): Re-registered AFM 402A 9/91; reverted to original registration 319 PFM with Wirral Borough Council as preserved vehicle 5/10.

11617 (5678 EL): Re-registered 8774 HY 46 with unknown owner (O-F) 8/82.

11623 (OVL 473): Re-registered LDS 448A with Stagecoach (Scotland) Ltd (TE) 11/89; re-registered PVS 315 with R & C Gibbons, Maidstone (preservationists); reverted to original registration OVL 473 with M Rolley, Quainton (preservationist) 12/95.

11624 (OVL 474): Re-registered 8023H with D Trone, Unknown location, IL (O-USA) by1987; re-registered 469H (IL) with Jumer Hotels, Bettendorf, IA and Peoria, IL (O-USA) by1999.

11655 (TDL 998): Re-registered ABK 832A 6/86; reverted to original registration TDL 998 4/87.

11718 (264 SFM): Re-registered PCB 494 with Wascana Centre, Regina, SK (O-USA) by11/85.

11726 ( 80 TVX): Re-registered AHJ 142A as Cedric Garages (Wivenhoe) Ltd (EX) 11 2/84; re-registered 22015 with Red Rover Ltd, West Hartford, MA (O-USA) by10/90; re-registered BC4458 with New York Double Deck Tours, NY (O-USA) 5 11/93.

11746 (462 FTT): Delivered 11/60 but not taxed until 5/61.

11747 (463 FTT): Delivered 11/60 but not taxed until 5/61.

11748 (464 FTT): Delivered 11/60 but not taxed until 6/61.

11749 (465 FTT): Delivered 12/60 but not taxed until 6/61; re-registered AG 18171 with Kontiki Garage AG, Neuenhof (O-CH) 6/84.

11750 (466 FTT): Delivered 12/60 but not taxed until 6/61.

11754 (470 FTT): Re-registered U445A by3/91, U5201A by3/92 with London Double Decker Bus Co, Miami, FL {O-USA).

11756 (472 FTT): Re-registered 7732 MF 69 with unknown owner (O-F) 3/82.

11760 (OVL 488): Noted with incorrect registration 05-DB-34 with Vianen, location unknown (O-NL) 11/78.

11766 ( 5 AAX ): Re-registered as follows with National Welsh, Cardiff (SG):- AAX 311A 3/86; AAX 450A 1/87; AAX 465A 2/87; AAX 489A 3/87; AAX 515A 6/87; AAX 528A 8/87; AAX 563A 9/87; AAX 590A 10/87; AAX 601A 12/87; AAX 631A 1/88; AKG 196A 8/88; AKG 231A 11/88; AKG 271A 2/89; AKG 293A 3/89; AKG 310A 5/89.

11828 (2723 VX): Re-registered BFW 314B with Hanson, Goole (HE) 3/82.

11912 (WCY 696): Had a special low height body for operation under a low bridge at Pontrhydyfen.

11913 (WCY 697): Had a special low height body for operation under a low bridge at Pontrhydyfen.

11914 (WCY 698): Had a special low height body for operation under a low bridge at Pontrhydyfen.

11915 (WCY 701): Had a special low height body for operation under a low bridge at Pontrhydyfen.

11916 (WCY 702): Had a special low height body for operation under a low bridge at Pontrhydyfen.

11917 (WCY 703): Had a special low height body for operation under a low bridge at Pontrhydyfen.

11918 (WCY 704): Had a special low height body for operation under a low bridge at Pontrhydyfen.

11919 (WCY 705): Had a special low height body for operation under a low bridge at Pontrhydyfen.

11925 (302 PFM): Re-registered TYJ 424 with PMT Ltd, Stoke on Trent (ST) 6/93.

11981 (237 SFM): Had an experimental fibreglass body.

12009 (LAH 448E): Body partly completed and retained by BCV for test purposes until 1967; body completed as H38/32F (rebuild R897) as Eastern Counties, Norwich (NK) FLF348 for whom it was first registered LAH 448E 3/67; re-registered 3B09135 with Top Deck Travel, Hollywood, CA (O-USA) by7/84.

12036 (346 EDV): Re-registered 31903 as Guernsey Railways (CI) 130 4/80.

12046 (356 EDV): Re-registered 31907 as Guernsey Railways (CI) 134 4/80.

12059 (314 EDV): Delivered 9/60 but did not enter service until 4/61 following modifications at ECW.

12060 (315 EDV): Delivered 9/60 but did not enter service until 4/61 following modifications at ECW.

12061 (316 EDV): Delivered 9/60 but did not enter service until 4/61 following modifications at ECW.

12062 (317 EDV): Delivered 9/60 but did not enter service until 4/61 following modifications at ECW.

12067 (LYM 731): Chassis new 5/51 with ECW (5480) C39F body

12068 (LYM 728): Chassis new 5/51 with ECW (5482) C39F body

12069 (LYM 729): Chassis new 5/51 with ECW (5483) C39F body

12070 (LYM 730): Chassis new 5/51 with ECW (5481) C39F body

12071 (LYM 732): Chassis new 5/51 with ECW (5484) C39F body

12072 (KEL 65): Chassis new 4/50 with Portsmouth Aviation C28F body; fitted with Gardner 5LW engine and rebuilt to LL5G specification prior to rebodying.

12073 (KEL 66): Chassis new 4/50 with Portsmouth Aviation C28F body; fitted with Gardner 5LW engine and rebuilt to LL5G specification prior to rebodying.

12074 (JRU 66): Chassis new 12/49 with Portsmouth Aviation C32R body; rebuilt to LL6A specification prior to rebodying.

12075 (JRU 67): Chassis new 12/49 with Portsmouth Aviation C32R body; rebuilt to LL6A specification prior to rebodying.

12076 (JRU 68): Chassis new 12/49 with Portsmouth Aviation C32R body; rebuilt to LL6A specification prior to rebodying.

12077 (JRU 69): Chassis new 12/49 with Portsmouth Aviation C32R body; rebuilt to LL6A specification prior to rebodying.

12078 (WJB 223): Re-registered T3522 with Holiday Inn, Dallas-Fort Worth Airport South, TX (O-USA) c1987.

12106 (RWG 372): First entered service with W Alexander (Fife), Kirkcaldy (FE)

12115 (RWG 381): First entered service with W Alexander (Fife), Kirkcaldy (FE)

12116 (RWG 382): First entered service with W Alexander (Fife), Kirkcaldy (FE)

12159 (RAG 403): Re-registered BFX 414A with McLintock, Wareham as a caravan by8/88; re-registered BD5.025 with Hammerson Mississauga Inc, Mississauga, ON (O-CDN) 7/89; re-registered BF9.671 1994 and HVS 652 at an unknown date and BL8.131 by10/08 with Duke of Kent Tours, Mississauga, ON (O-CDN); re-registered 333.8BF with Bus & Boat Company, Toronto, ON (O-CDN) by9/12.

12174 (404 LHT): Re-registered Q507 VHR with unidentified owner as a caravan by1/98.

12176 (406 LHT): Re-registered VSV 444 with unidentified owner as a caravan 8/85; reverted to original registration 406 LHT with P Hughes, Hartley (preservationist) 12/87.

12179 (428 UFM): Re-registered KFF 353 as North Western Road Car Co Ltd (1986) (MY) 919 11/94.

12180 (429 UFM): Re-registered ACA 107A 3/84.

12181 (430 UFM): Re-registered ACA 125A 3/84.

12206 (RFE 461): Re-registered BLV 654A with unidentified owner as a mobile caravan by8/91.

12218 Intended for Thames Valley.

12222 ( 4 BXB ): Re-registered FRE 999A with Newcastle High School (XST) 5/84.

12239 ( 55 GUO): Re-registered JVS 293 with unknown owner, Oxford as a caravan c1/91.

12286 (866 NHT): Re-registered XSL 228A with Stagecoach (South) Ltd, Lewes (ES) 101 3/90.

12289 (869 NHT): Re-registered FAS 962 with Mac Tours Ltd, Edinburgh (LO) 26 7/02; reverted to original registration 869 NHT with M Walker & M Curtis (preservationists) 4/03.

12290 (806 MHW): Re-registered VŽ 186-GH with Autobusni Promet, Varazdin (O-HR) by6/95.

12301 (803 MHW): Re-registered A1044 with Great Knight Tours, Atlanta, GA (O-USA) c1984.

12315 (878 VFM): Re-registered ACA 218A 10/84.

12333 (109 DRM): Re-registered AAO 547A 4/90; reverted to original registration with 550 Group, Workington (preservationists) 3/01.

12339 ( 52 JAL): Re-registered E77D with British Bus Club, Pleasant Mount, PA (O-USA) by9/07.

12346 ( 59 JAL): Re-registered 14749 with Maxwell Silverman's Toolhouse, Worcester, MA (O-USA) by1998.

12347 ( 60 JAL): Re-registered 3M65158 with Lake Tahoe Cruises, CA (O-USA) 3 by10/88.

12351 (444 SNU): Re-registered 106XAR with unknown owner, Fairfield area, CA (O-USA) by1989.

12356 (449 SNU): Re-registered 1GNA543 with Grosvenor Bus Lines, San Francisco, CA (O-USA) 199 by5/83.

12418 (4384 LJ): Noted in Wien (O-A) re-registered OVS 461 1/10.

12445 (2028 YG): Re-registered BH-50-XZ with Kleyn Trucks, Vuren (O-NL) 1983.

12448 (2031 YG): Carried incorrect registration BE-21-03 with Gijsbers, Tilburg (O-NL) by10/98, re-registered BE-35-26 10/98, carried incorrect registration BS-04-96 with Delta, Wapenveld (O-NL) by8/10.

12452 (813 MHW): Re-registered 2B19091 at an unknown date and 5664 BA with Top Deck Travel, Hollywood, CA (O-USA) 1981.

12458 (823 MHW): Re-registered ABH 7534 with Double Decker Bus Co, Denver, CO (O-USA) by8/99.

12462 (205 NAE): Re-registered C4537 with R Alen Stanford (O-AG) by12/99.

12471 (817 MHW): Re-registered C4571 with Bank of Antigua (O-AG) by12/97.

12476 (827 MHW): Re-registered GGA225 with Great Knight Tours, Atlanta, GA (O-USA) c1984.

12485 (900 VFM): Re-registered DCR.946 with Evangelische Stichting, Zelgate (O-B) 1979; re-registered SJJ.006 with Aspekt Mobiel bvba, Zandhoven (O-B) 11/99.

12521 (184 XNO): Re-registered ACA 507A by6/86 and ACA 979A 2/88 with GE & WRS Walker, Anderton (CH).

12533 (5091 HN): Re-registered 7603 with Boston University, Boston, MA (O-USA) by1993.

12559 (134 HUO): Re-registered AXP 725 with Windjammer Cruises, Honolulu, HI (O-USA) by3/80.

12560 (135 HUO): Re-registered EWN 936 then GGG 537 at unknown dates, 952 ELK by10/87 with River Rouge Line, Winnipeg, MB (O-CDN).

12561 (136 HUO): Re-registered ETH 162, EEE 217 at unknown dates with River Rouge Line, Winnipeg, MB (O-CDN).

12562 (137 HUO): Re-registered EEE 214 at an unknown date with River Rouge Line, Winnipeg, MB (O-CDN).

12564 (139 HUO): Re-registered ULR.136 with Robinsons Barley Water, location unknown (O-AUS) 8/82; re-registered BANK.03 with Banksia Tours, Banksia Park, SA (O-AUS) by8/84.

12565 (140 HUO): Re-registered CBJ 928 with Windjammer Cruises, Honolulu, HI (O-USA) by3/80.

12608 (805 MHW): Re-registered LUX 202 with Jayhawk Bookstore, Lawrence, KS (O-USA) c1995; re-registered MVR2691 with Great Knight Tours, Atlanta, GA (O-USA) by8/00.

12685 (135 ACY): Had a special low height body for operation under a low bridge at Pontrhydyfen.

12686 (136 ACY): Had a special low height body for operation under a low bridge at Pontrhydyfen.

12687 (137 ACY): Had a special low height body for operation under a low bridge at Pontrhydyfen.

12688 (138 ACY): Had a special low height body for operation under a low bridge at Pontrhydyfen.

12689 (139 ACY): Had a special low height body for operation under a low bridge at Pontrhydyfen.

12690 (140 ACY): Had a special low height body for operation under a low bridge at Pontrhydyfen.

12739 (RFE 482): Re-registered OWJ 339A with H Cawthorne, Darton (preservationist) c3/86; re-registered NVL 165 9/91 and then reverted to original registration RFE 482 with Lincolnshire RCC, Lincoln (LC) 6/00.

12755 (430 HDV): Re-registered 31908 as Guernsey Railways (CI) 135 4/80.

12760 (417 HDV): Re-registered 31905 as Guernsey Railways (CI) 132 4/80.

12775 (EDL 14): Chassis new 4/46 with ECW (1240) B35R body.

12776 (EDL 15): Chassis new 4/46 with ECW (1241) B35R body.

12777 (KEL 67): Chassis new 5/50 with Portsmouth Aviation C28F body; fitted with Bristol AVW engine and rebuilt to LL6B specification prior to rebodying.

12778 (KEL 401): Chassis new 6/50 with Portsmouth Aviation C28F body; fitted with Bristol AVW engine and rebuilt to LL6B specification prior to rebodying.

12779 (KEL 402): Chassis new 6/50 with Portsmouth Aviation C28F body; fitted with Bristol AVW engine and rebuilt to LL6B specification prior to rebodying.

12780 (KEL 405): Chassis new 5/50 with Portsmouth Aviation C28F body; fitted with Bristol AVW engine and rebuilt to LL6B specification prior to rebodying.

12781 (KEL 403): Chassis new 6/50 with Portsmouth Aviation C28F body; fitted with Bristol AVW engine and rebuilt to LL6B specification prior to rebodying.

12782 (KEL 404): Chassis new 6/50 with Portsmouth Aviation C28F body; fitted with Bristol AVW engine and rebuilt to LL6B specification prior to rebodying.

12840 (EDL 16): Chassis new 4/46 with ECW (1242) B35R body.

12848 ( 12 DLY): Re-registered CFD 777B with Nationwide Coaches Ltd, Lanark (SC) 1/83.

12869 (675 AAM): Re-registered PFO 256 with an unidentified owner as mobile caravan 12/95.

12877 (286 KTA): Re-registered 31916 as Guernsey Railways (CI) 154 6/80; reverted to original registration 286 KTA with C Billington, Holyport (preservationist) c5/87.

12879 (752 BWN): Re-registered OFU 438 with unidentified owner as a stock car transporter c1975.

12882 (268 KTA): Re-registered 31915 as Guernsey Railways (CI) 153 6/80; reverted to original registration 268 KTA with J Widdowson, Sheffield as a caravan by4/93.

12885 (271 KTA): Re-registered 31918 as Guernsey Railways (CI) 156 7/80; re-registered 10558 4/85; reverted to original registration 271 KTA with F Elliott, Golborne (preservationist) c3/87.

12886 (272 KTA): Re-registered 31914 as Guernsey Railways (CI) 152 5/80.

12892 (278 KTA): Re-registered 31917 as Guernsey Railways (CI) 155 6/80.

12894 (280 KTA): Re-registered 31920 as Guernsey Railways (CI) 157 10/80; reverted to original registration 280 KTA with C Billington, Holyport (preservationist) by1/95.

12896 (XPM 41): Re-registered AFE 170A with Lincolnshire RCC, Lincoln (LC) 2350 8/84;

12897 (XPM 42): Re-registered AFE 171A with Lincolnshire RCC, Lincoln (LC) 2351 8/84;

12908 (1205 FM): Re-registered ACA 553A 6/86.

12916 (716 GRM): Re-registered ACA 411A with GE & WRS Walker, Anderton (CH) by2/86.

12935 ( 50 CNG): Re-registered LAH 577A by2/91.

12960 ( 6 EWO): Re-registered RAG 409 with Argas Persicus Travel Ltd, London SW5 (LN) 3/80; re-registered Q795 DPF 4/92, then reverted to previous registration RAG 409 5/92 with Top Deck Travel Group Ltd, Horsell (SR).

12983 (285 BWU): Re-registered 96.20.FA with Gray Line of Victoria Ltd, Victoria, BC (O-CDN) by9/79.

12984 (950 BWR): Re-registered K-ZD 800 with Bibi-Wenburg, Cologne (O-D) by9/83.

12991 (957 BWR): Re-registered 3672JE with Marguerite Tours Ltd, Victoria, BC (O-CDN) by8/80.

13005 (683 AAM): Re-registered VN-36-51 with Beyer, Hoofddorp (O-NL) 1980.

13013 (691 AAM): Re-registered 79-DB-25 with Van Wijk, Leeuwarden (O-NL) 7/78.

13014 (692 AAM): Re-registered 10-HB-79 2/79 and BB-15-VF 7/81 with Van Wijk, Leeuwarden (O-NL).

13016 (694 AAM): Re-registered 98-GB-37 with unknown owner (O-NL) 5/79; noted with registration BE-43-42 with ECP, Ridderkerk (O-NL) 1/06.

13046 (501 OHU): Believed re-registered BE4119 with New York Double Deck Tours, NY (O-USA) 18 by11/96.

13057 (520 OHU): Re-registered 879 BW 91 with P Lenech, Paris (O-F) 6/80.

13066 (535 OHU): Re-registered YND 602A with Reed's School of Motoring, Hyde (GM) 7/91.

13071 (542 OHU): Re-registered U70 IDN with Gateway Bus Tours, Miami, FL (O-USA) by2003.

13075 (538 OHU): Re-registered ABX 172A as Silcox Motor Coach Co Ltd, Pembroke Dock (PE) 20 3/87; re-registered 5127 with Savannah College of Art & Design, Savannah, GA (O-USA) by1998.

13076 (506 OHU): Re-registered Y 2533 with Gray Line Tours, Seattle, WA (O-USA) 9/77; re-registered 8551FW with Gray Line of Victoria Ltd, BC (O-CDN) by8/81; re-registered 919 FYD with Dbl Decker Tours, Regina, SK (O-USA) by6/09.

13086 (530 OHU): Re-registered BHU 218A as Badgerline Ltd (AV) W177 by9/88

13089 (547 OHU): Re-registered 101 with Carthage City Tours, Carthage, MO (O-USA) by8/99.

13095 (511 OHU): Re-registered JSK 492 as Cheltenham & Gloucester (GL) RM1 2/92; re-registered LAS 948 with Rampton, Reading (preservationist) by9/02.

13108 (147 YFM): Re-registered LDS 406A with Teen Challenge, Glasgow (XSC) as mobile exhibition by2/91.

13121 (558 BNG): Re-registered BE-21-03 8/95 with unknown owner (O-NL) 8/95.

13139 (JWC 711): Re-registered NVS 695 with C Ireland, Kingston upon Hull (dealer) c1992; re-registered M-ZU 3492 with Creative Marketing, Munich (O-D) by5/03.

13149 (RWC 607): Re-registered GF-XR 1 with Der Blickfang, Sassenburg (O-D) by5/97.

13152 (RWC 605): Re-registered MFK 98E with Gulf Breeze Media, Fort Walton Beach, FL (O-USA) by3/98; re-registered H77 XXN with Philly-ing Station, Pensacola, FL (O-USA) by9/03.

13161 (VWC  52): Re-registered AAE 8859 with Crane Bus Service, Lusaka (O-Z) 2/82.

13171 (244 MNN): Re-registered SMPC-B with Henderson {Scottish Meat Pie Co}, Burbank, CA (O-USA) by6/88.

13179 (527 VRB): Re-registered GEN BANK with General Bank of Commerce, Los Angeles, CA (O-USA) 2/81; re-registered 3M65158 with Lake Tahoe Cruises, Lake Tahoe, CA (O-USA) 1 by10/88; re-registered 3N62113 with Cupertino Bike Shop, Cupertino, CA (O-USA) by1991.

13180 (528 VRB): Re-registered 3N62113 with Mellor, Dixon, CA (O-USA) by1991; re-registered BD5319 6/94, BC3645 9/94, BD5327 6/95 with New York Double Decker Tours, NY (O-USA) 4.

13182 (530 VRB): Re-registered MA-0067-N with Benaimedena Attraciones SA {Tivoli World}, Arroyo de la Miel (O-E) c4/80.

13183 (531 VRB): Re-registered 75685 with Dubai Aluminium, Dubai (O-UAE) by1979.

13185 (533 VRB): Re-registered 75742 with Dubai Aluminium, Dubai (O-UAE) by1979.

13186 (534 VRB): Re-registered 3963FX with Pacific North West Bus Co, Vancouver, BC (O-CDN) 5/79; re-registered 6916JV with Royal Blue Line, Saanichton, BC (O-CDN) by5/06.

13187 (535 VRB): Re-registered 3972FX with Pacific North West Bus Co, Vancouver, BC (O-CDN) 5/79; re-registered 6916JV by5/06 and 6485KW by9/07 with Royal Blue Line, Saanichton, BC (O-CDN).

13241 (803 KDV): Re-registered PBA 156, PBA 171 at unknown dates, 223 PBA by10/87 with River Rouge Line, Winnipeg, MB (O-CDN).

13242 (804 KDV): Re-registered BE-21-77 with Stairway Promotions, Assen (O-NL) 8/95.

13245 (807 KDV): Re-registered EWN 934, GGG 612 at unknown dates, 901 ELK by10/87 with River Rouge Line, Winnipeg, MB (O-CDN); re-registered 77X 878 with Ludington MTA, Ludington, MI (O-USA) c1995; re-registered 031 956 with Holiday Inn, East Tawas, MI (O-USA) by8/99.

13249 (811 KDV): Re-registered 257YYO with Coach House, San Juan Capistrano, CA (O-USA) by2000.

13251 (813 KDV): Re-registered SH 5078 with Rapold Classic AG, Neuhausen (O-CH) by6/92.

13256 (818 KDV): Re-registered 1-9232 with Surfview Resort, Cannon Beach, OR (O-USA) by9/97.

13267 (7686 LJ): Re-registered 1DOT312 with Ewing, Valencia, CA (O-USA) by9/09.

13269 (MOO 178): Originally allocated registration MOO 174.

13270 (MOO 179): Originally allocated registration MOO 175.

13271 (MOO 973): Originally allocated registration MOO 176.

13272 (MOO 974): Originally allocated registration MOO 177.

13273 (MOO 975): Originally allocated registration MOO 178.

13274 (MOO 976): Originally allocated registration MOO 179.

13312 (878 RAE): Re-seated to DP41F before entering service

13315 (921 RAE): Re-seated to DP41F before entering service

13316 (922 RAE): Re-seated to DP41F before entering service

13319 (925 RAE): Re-seated to DP41F before entering service

13320 (926 RAE): Re-seated to DP41F before entering service

13333 (939 RAE): Re-seated to DP41F before entering service

13488 (KEL 406): Chassis new 7/50 with Portsmouth Aviation C28F body; fitted with Bristol AVW engine and rebuilt to LL6B specification prior to rebodying.

13489 (KEL 407): Chassis new 7/50 with Portsmouth Aviation C28F body; fitted with Bristol AVW engine and rebuilt to LL6B specification prior to rebodying.

13490 (KEL 408): Chassis new 7/50 with Portsmouth Aviation C28F body; fitted with Bristol AVW engine and rebuilt to LL6B specification prior to rebodying.

13491 (KEL 409): Chassis new 7/50 with Portsmouth Aviation C28F body; fitted with Bristol AVW engine and rebuilt to LL6B specification prior to rebodying.

13492 (KEL 410): Chassis new 8/50 with Portsmouth Aviation C28F body; fitted with Bristol AVW engine and rebuilt to LL6B specification prior to rebodying.

13493 (KEL 411): Chassis new 9/50 with Portsmouth Aviation C28F body; fitted with Bristol AVW engine and rebuilt to LL6B specification prior to rebodying.

13591 (TCS 176): Re-registered RREDBUS with Big Red Bus, Elk Grove, CA (O-USA) by9/01.

13596 (TCS 181): Re-registered 45-NB-97 with de Voog, Leiden (O-NL) 8/79; re-registered BJ-19-JZ with NBBS, Leiden (O-NL) by3/96.

13679 (AOO  18B): Originally allocated registration NWC  18

13721 (AVX 961B): Originally allocated registration 939 LWC.

13722 (AVX 962B): Originally allocated registration 940 LWC.

13723 (AVX 963B): Originally allocated registration 941 LWC.

13724 (AVX 964B): Originally allocated registration 942 LWC.

13725 (AVX 965B): Originally allocated registration 943 LWC.

13726 (AVX 966B): Originally allocated registration 944 LWC.

13727 (AVX 967B): Originally allocated registration 945 LWC.

13736 (OWT 241E): Body partly completed and retained by BCV as a development vehicle until late 1966; fitted with a Gardner 6HLX engine, body completed as C47F (rebuild R882) as West Yorkshire RCC, Harrogate (WR) CRG1 for whom it was first registered as OWT 241E 2/67.

13766 (4226 FM): Re-registered EM-RY 92 with Reigeler Braurei, Reigel (O-D) by2/03.

13784 ( 68 DNG): Re-registered NWR 297A with unknown owner by1/95; re-registered BE-20-61 with Stairway Promotions, Assen (O-NL) 8/95.

13802 (BNG 886B): Re-registered BE-15-54 with London Party Bus, Amstenrade (O-NL) 5/94.

13816 (ALJ 574B): Re-registered 21540 with Red Rover Ltd., West Hartford, MA (O-USA) by10/90.

13831 (AAX  21B): Originally allocated registration 169 HAX; re-registered Y167CY197 with Drive Bus, Moscow (O-RUS) 2012.

13832 (AAX  22B): Originally allocated registration 170 HAX.

13833 (AAX  23B): Originally allocated registration 171 HAX.

13834 (AAX  24B): Originally allocated registration 172 HAX.

13835 (AAX  25B): Originally allocated registration 173 HAX.

13874 (AWU 467B): Originally allocated registration 576 EWX.

13886 (808 SHW): Re-registered 26689 with Williamson Transportation, Marietta, GA (O-USA) by4/88; re-registered LTR 7298 with Double Deck Coffee Co, Asheville, NC (O-USA) by8/00.

13888 (810 SHW): Re-registered T-4974 with Dyson, Waco, TX (O-USA) by5/02.

13890 (822 SHW): Re-registered 3ZK035 with Kupd Radio Station, Tempe, AZ (O-USA) c11/91.

13892 (818 SHW): Re-registered ZH 572731 with J & M Pfiffner {Londag}, Wädenswil (O-CH) 1988.

13905 (804 SHW): Re-registered ADE 146A as Silcox Motor Coach Co Ltd, Pembroke Dock (PE) 29 by7/89; re-registered KGH 891A and RAG 409 4/92; reverting to previous registration KGH 891A with Top Deck Travel Group Ltd, Horsell (SR) c5/92;

13906 (805 SHW): Noted in Torino carrying registration KFF 466 10/03.

13911 (828 SHW): Re-registered SKH 717B with C Ireland, Kingston upon Hull (dealer) 3/07.

13917 (838 SHW): Re-registered 3L93324 with Tahoe Queen, South Lake Tahoe, CA (O-USA) 1 by10/88.

13919 (840 SHW): Re-registered PS08882 with Salem Academy, Salem, OR (O-USA) by9/11.

13925 (847 SHW): Re-registered X60.A25 with Nottingham's Seafood Company, Long Branch, NJ (O-USA) by5/01; re-registered BA40206 with a refreshment stand, Wind Gap, PA (O-USA) by9/05.

13926 (AAE  51B): Originally allocated registration 848 SHW

13931 (816 SHW): Re-registered BHT 693A 5/86; re-registered BHW  38A by3/92.

13935 (AAO  36B): Re-registered BHN 928B with Howgill Street Playgroup, Whitehaven (XCA) 11/85.

13939 (988 KOO): Re-registered 035AFW with Double Decker Tours, Reno, NV (O-USA) by1988.

13947 (934 LWC): Re-registered 190 BBL with L Seargent {Double Deck Tours}, Reno, NV (O-USA) by3/88.

13952 (AVX 956B): Originally allocated registration 727 WWC.

13953 (AVX 957B): Originally allocated registration 728 WWC.

13954 (AVX 958B): Originally allocated registration 729 WWC; re-registered AAE 6541 with Crane Bus Service, Lusaka (O-Z) 9/81.

13955 (AVX 959B): Originally allocated registration 730 WWC.

13956 (AVX 960B): Originally allocated registration 731 WWC.

13961 (BVX 671B): Re-registered AAE 3833 with Ridge Roadways, Lusaka (O-Z) 1981.

13962 (BVX 672B): Re-registered AAD 9325 with Ridge Roadways, Lusaka (O-Z) 1981.

13963 (BVX 673B): Re-registered AAE 8860 with Crane Bus Service, Lusaka (O-Z) 2/82.
13967 (BVX 677B): Re-registered AAE 6544 with Crane Bus Service, Lusaka (O-Z) 9/81.
13970 (BVX 680B): Re-registered 5134 with Savannah College of Art & Design, Savannah, GA (O-USA) by2003.
13983 (1388 R): Re-registered 2047GB with Marguerite Tours Ltd, Victoria, BC (O-CDN) 5/78; re-registered 7668XT with Youth for Christ, Matsqui Village, BC (O-CDN) by9/11.
13984 (1389 R): Re-registered 2046GB with Marguerite Tours Ltd, Victoria, BC (O-CDN) 5/78.
13985 (1390 R): Re-registered 0329FC with Marguerite Tours Ltd, Victoria, BC (O-CDN) 5/78; re-registered 5KKR949 with Qutermous, Pleasanton, CA (O-USA) by5/05.
13988 (ANU 11B): Re-registered BA 24890 with Philadelphia Tours, Philadelphia, PA (O-USA) by9/88; re-registered BD3575 6/94, BD5319 9/94, BE4156 11/96 with New York Double Deck Tours, NY (O-USA) 8.
13991 (428 PTA): Re-registered BOC 362B with unknown owner, Birmingham as a training bus (XWM) 6/90; re-registered BG-LP-44 with Prins Classic Transport, Opijnen (O-NL) 6/98.
13998 (ABL 116B): Originally allocated registration 842 CRX.
13999 (ABL 117B): Originally allocated registration 843 CRX.
14000 (ABL 118B): Originally allocated registration 844 CRX.
14001 (ABL 119B): Originally allocated registration 845 CRX.
14003 (BRX 142B): Re-registered 3ZJ-750 with The Pointe Resort Hotel, Phoenix, AZ (O-USA) by3/91; re-registered 3ZN-547 with Rodriguez, Phoenix, AZ (O-USA) by12/98.
14044 (409 PTA): Re-registered 3973FX with Pacific North West Bus Co, Vancouver, BC (O-CDN) c11/76; re-registered 6917JV by5/06, 1882KS by9/07 with Royal Blue Line, Saanichton, BC (O-CDN).
14046 (412 PTA): Re-registered 6664FB with Pacific North West Bus Co, Vancouver, BC (O-CDN) c11/76; re-registered 6918JV by5/06, 1881KS by9/07 with Royal Blue Line, Saanichton, BC (O-CDN).
14049 (414 PTA): Re-registered 1BZT 532 with unknown owner, CA (O-USA) by1985.
14051 (416 PTA): Re-registered 1NKL 103 with unknown owner, CA (O-USA) by1991; re-registered 2M49273 with Roscoes Auto Sales, Panorama City, CA (O-USA) 1991.
14053 (418 PTA): Re-registered Y 2463 with Gray Line Tours, Seattle, WA (O-USA) 6/77; re-registered 8558FW with Gray Line of Victoria Ltd, Victoria, BC (O-CDN) by8/81.
14075 (AAE 52B): Originally allocated registration 989 UHW.
14076 (AAE 53B): Originally allocated registration 990 UHW.
14077 (AAE 54B): Originally allocated registration 991 UHW.
14078 (AAE 55B): Originally allocated registration 992 UHW.
14079 (AHW 787B): Originally allocated registration 993 UHW.
14080 (AHW 788B): Originally allocated registration 994 UHW.
14119 (AAX 11B): Originally allocated registration 567 HWO.
14120 (AAX 12B): Originally allocated registration 568 HWO.
14121 (AAX 13B): Originally allocated registration 569 HWO.
14122 (AAX 14B): Originally allocated registration 570 HWO.
14123 (AAX 15B): Originally allocated registration 571 HWO.
14124 (AAX 16B): Originally allocated registration 572 HWO.
14125 (AAX 17C): Originally allocated registration 573 HWO.
14126 (AAX 18C): Originally allocated registration 574 HWO.
14127 (AAX 19C): Originally allocated registration 575 HWO.
14128 (AAX 20C): Originally allocated registration 576 HWO.
14159 (ABD 251B): Originally allocated registration 251 FRP.
14160 (ABD 252B): Originally allocated registration 252 FRP.
14172 (AAO 34B): Originally allocated registration 427 LAO.
14173 (AAO 35B): Originally allocated registration 428 LAO.
14182 (AFE 471B): Originally allocated registration XFE 760.
14183 (AFE 472B): Originally allocated registration XFE 761.
14184 (AFE 473B): Originally allocated registration XFE 762.
14185 (AFE 474B): Originally allocated registration XFE 763.
14234 (465 ADL): Re-registered BHN 328B for RL Wade & Son, St Helen Auckland (XDM) 1982.
14285 (VCS 351): Re-registered 48740 with Dubai Aluminium, Dubai (O-UAE) by1979.
14288 (VCS 354): Re-registered FUT.848 with A de Sadeleer {Imperial}, Brussels (O-B) by5/96.
14347 (XCS 950): Re-registered FYE.803 with Hannes, Vlasmeer (O-B) by4/97.
14350 (XCS 953): Re-registered 18812 with Dubai Aluminium, Dubai (O-UAE) by1979.
14361 (AAG 62B): Originally allocated registration XCS 964; re-registered 13107 with Dubai Aluminium, Dubai (O-UAE) by1979.
14362 (AAG 63B): Originally allocated registration XCS 965.
14363 (AAG 64B): Originally allocated registration XCS 966.
14364 (AAG 65B): Originally allocated registration XCS 967.
14365 (AAG 66B): Originally allocated registration XCS 968.

14366 (AAG  67B): Originally allocated registration XCS 969.
14367 (AAG  68B): Originally allocated registration XCS 970.
14368 (AAG 118B): Originally allocated registration XCS 971.
14369 (AAG 119B): Originally allocated registration XCS 972; re-registered 03-MB-85 with de Jong, Leiden (O-NL) 3/79.
14370 (AAG 120B): Originally allocated registration XCS 973.
14371 (AAG 121B): Originally allocated registration XCS 974.
14372 (AAG 122B): Originally allocated registration XCS 975.
14373 (AAG 123B): Originally allocated registration XCS 976.
14374 (AAG 124B): Originally allocated registration XCS 977.
14375 (AAG 125B): Originally allocated registration XCS 978.
14387 (BXA 462B): Re-registered O186AB77 between 2005 and 2009, then E415PA199 between 2009 and 2012 with Liggett Ducat, Moscow (O-RUS); re-registered Y166CY197 2012 then P414AB50 by6/13 with Drive Bus, Moscow (O-RUS).
14481 (980 WAE): Re-registered 46437 with Richard Costain, Dubai (O-UAE) GT159 (4/77?).
14491 (WVL 515): Re-registered BFW 523B 1/88.
14496 (837 SUO): Re-registered ARU  99A with H Miller, Horsham (WS) 11/97; reverted to original registration 837 SUO with S Graham, Runcorn (preservationist) 12/04.
14553 (AHT 718B): Re-registered DAY 787 with AC Day {Mr Lift Fork Lift Truck Hire), Almondbury (XGL) by5/82; re-registered DFH 110B with unknown owner at an unknown date.
14559 (AAE 263B): Re-registered B-LN 862 with information unit, theatre Shakespeare & Rock 'n' Roll, Berlin (O-D) by1/98.
14562 (AHY 981B): Re-registered GR 79000 with J & M Pfiffner {Londag}, Wädenswil (O-CH) 11/84.
14576 (FWC 427B): Re-registered 5044 SF 49 with O Poncin {Le Courrier de l'Ouest}, Billancourt (O-F) 3/82; 5852 ST 83 with unknown owner (O-F) at an unknown date; 9461 XG 33 with Fieldbus, Varades (O-F) 6/99; 3855 X 22 with Publibus, Lezardrieux (O-F) c5/06; CC 400 CL with E Belliot {Red Connection Restaurant}, St Nazaire (O-F) 1/12.
14582 (GNO 791B): Re-registered 461 ETN 75 with unknown owner (O-F) 3/82.
14583 (HEV 994B): Re-registered FAZ.457 with unknown owner (O-B) by10/96.
14586 (HEV 997B): Re-registered U5422A with London Double Decker Bus Co, Maimi, FL (O-USA) by3/91; re-registered BA34092 with Piccadilly Tours, Philadelphia, PA (O-USA) by1993.
14593 (AFM 113B): Re-registered 89-ZB-03 with AAF Siemons, Zundert (O-NL) 12/81.
14606 (BDL 580B): Re-registered ICD 49Z with Koa Kampgrounds, Kissimmee, FL (O-USA) by10/94.
14607 (BDL 581B): Re-registered 12151J, 11175J at unknown dates, 26592H by1991, all with Chicago Motor Coach Co, Chicago, IL (O-USA).
14626 (AUO 517B): Re-registered UYF 283 with an unknown horse farm, West Miami, FL (O-USA) by1982.
14631 (BUO 150B): Re-registered S CHIFF 1 with Dr E Berer {Salzburg Highlights}, Salzburg (O-A) 7/10.
14668 (BRU 138B): Re-registered 24-FB-49 with unknown owner (O-NL) 8/78; re-registered F-CZ 485 (NB German registration) with City Lounge, Sarajevo (O-BIH) by4/15.
14672 (CEL 860C): Originally allocated registration BRU 142B.
14673 (CEL 861C): Originally allocated registration BRU 143B.
14674 (CEL 862C): Originally allocated registration BRU 144B.
14698 (BHW  93C): Originally intended for Eastern National, Chelmsford (EX) as JHK 459C (1435).
14699 (BHW  94C): Originally intended for Eastern National, Chelmsford (EX) as JHK 460C (1436).
14700 (BHW  95C): Originally intended for Eastern National, Chelmsford (EX) as JHK 461C (1437).
14701 (BHW  96C): Originally intended for Eastern National, Chelmsford (EX) as JHK 462C (1438).
14712 (BDV 244C): Re-registered 31910 as Guernsey Railways (CI) 142 11/81.
14713 (BDV 245C): Re-registered 31910 as Guernsey Railways (CI) 137 4/80.
14719 (BDV 251C): Re-registered 31912 as Guernsey Railways (CI) 139 4/80.
14721 (BDV 253C): Re-registered 31904 as Guernsey Railways (CI) 131 4/80.
14756 (DNG 401C): Re-registered PZB 592B with Wlodarczyk Electronics, Warsaw (O-PL) c12/91.
14782 (CEL 863C): Originally allocated registration CEL 247B.
14784 (CLJ 868C): Re-registered BNH.485 with RJ Harmer (Fun Decker Coachlines/Tours), The Basin, VIC (O-AUS) 1982; re-registered EBJ.088 with London Transport Bus Tours, Aspendale, VIC (O-AUS) by1991.
14788 (DEL 891C): Re-registered S 557 PJ with Babylon Night Club, Salzburg (O-A) by1/12.
14795 (EEL 891C): Re-registered BE-41-05 with R Stiphout, Maastricht (O-NL) 4/00.
14798 (EEL 894C): Re-registered AG 16950 with Kontiki Reisen, Baden (O-CH) 1990; re-registered ZH 99817 with J & M Pfiffner {Londag}, Basserdorf (O-CH) 3/98.
14844 (FPM  75C): Re-registered KYL.161 by1/94, then NXN.664 with Antique Auto Busverhuur bvba, Brasschaat (O-B) by5/95.
14846 (BHU 976C): Re-registered BD7 534 with Gray Coach Lines, Toronto, ON (O-CDN) 2/91.

14853 (CHT 541C): Re-registered RLE.147 with F Bruyninckx {London Ceremony Bus}, Kapellen (O-B) c2/98.

14854 (CHY 417C): Re-registered NXH 79S with Koa Luxury Kampground, Kissimmee, FL (O-USA) by10/94; displayed BSG WV SWB with Bus Station Grille, Charleston, WV (O-USA) 6/00.

14873 (EHT 109C): Re-registered AG 17357 with Bols-Cynar-Ballantines AG, Zurich (O-CH) 6/84; re-registered SO 20000 at an unknown date.

14874 (EHT 110C): Re-registered ZH 572732 with J & M Pfiffner {Londag}, Wädenswil (O-CH) 1987; re-registered L N 1965 H with Sachsichen Oldtimer Busflotte, Leipzig (O-D) by12/10.

14890 (DHT 784C): Re-registered AG 15821 with Kontiki Reisen, Baden (O-CH) (1984?); re-registered ZH 99817 with J & M Pfiffner {Londag}, Basserdorf (O-CH) 1996.

14894 (DHW 983C): Re-registered BE1 954 with Hiawathaland Tours, Sault Ste. Marie, ON (O-CDN) by1990.

14895 (DHW 984C): Re-registered MDM 313 with L Werklin, Visby (O-S) 6/86.

14907 (EHW 191C): Re-registered CAX.155 12/95, then HFJ.061 at an unknown date, with F Bruyninckx {London Ceremony Bus}, Kapellen (O-B) 12/95; re-registered BE-38-68 with Snow-Planet BV, Nijmegen (O-NL) 9/99.

14911 (EHT 853C): Re-registered T11-024 with Fuller Double Decker, San Antonio, TX (O-USA) by8/88.

14928 (JHK 452C): Re-registered 3298DX with Great Knight Tours, Atlanta, GA (O-USA) by2000.

14930 (JHK 455C): Re-registered BE-48-36 with Prins Classic Transport, Opijnen (O-NL) 6/02.

14931 (JHK 462C): Re-registered DE8081 with London Double Decker Bus Co, Maimi, FL (O-USA) by1984.

14936 (KNO 949C): Re-registered 2B32152 with Top Deck Travel Ltd, Hollywood,CA (O-USA) 5/83; re-registered 6191H with Chicago Motor Coach Co, Chicago, IL (O-USA) by8/92.

14961 (NTW 944C): Re-registered 6603 SJ 34 with S Calazel {Publicite Promotion D'eglantine}, Hérault (O-F) 3/81.

14968 (CFE 231C): Re-registered  BE-20-05 with unknown operator (O-NL) 7/95.

14983 (FNU 413C): Re-registered OCL.609 with M Wouters {Miss Titi}, Leroux (O-B) c4/96.

14984 (FNU 414C): Re-registered 16720 with Dubai Aluminium, Dubai (O-UAE) by1979.

14988 (BDV 267C): Re-registered VD 1561 with Riviera Voyages, Vevey (O-CH) by1/03.

14993 (BOD  24C): Re-registered OCL.609 with Wouters {Miss Titi}, Leroux (O-B) as fish & chip bar by4/96.

15000 (CDL 480C): Re-registered C4538 with R Alen Stanford (O-AG) by12/99.

## Delivery Dates

| No. | Date | No. | Date | No. | Date | No. | Date | No. | Date | No. | Date |
|---|---|---|---|---|---|---|---|---|---|---|---|
| 10001 | 10.5.57 | 10063 | 3.4.58 | 10125 | 24.6.58 | 10187 | 1.11.58 | 10249 | 14.2.59 | 10311 | 30.5.58 |
| 10002 | 17.5.57 | 10064 | | 10126 | 24.6.58 | 10188 | 14.11.58 | 10250 | 21.2.59 | 10312 | 6.6.58 |
| 10003 | | 10065 | | 10127 | 27.6.58 | 10189 | 14.11.58 | 10251 | 3.4.59 | 10313 | 23.10.5 |
| 10004 | 14.6.57 | 10066 | | 10128 | 27.6.58 | 10190 | 28.11.58 | 10252 | 3.4.59 | 10314 | 23.10.5 |
| 10005 | 14.6.57 | 10067 | | 10129 | 5.12.58 | 10191 | 6.12.58 | 10253 | 25.4.59 | 10315 | 2.1.59 |
| 10006 | 14.6.57 | 10068 | 20.3.58 | 10130 | 12.12.58 | 10192 | 7.2.59 | 10254 | 22.5.59 | 10316 | 9.1.59 |
| 10007 | 14.6.57 | 10069 | 26.3.58 | 10131 | 22.12.58 | 10193 | 3.1.59 | 10255 | 22.5.59 | 10317 | 24.10.5 |
| 10008 | 17.6.57 | 10070 | 26.3.58 | 10132 | 14.3.58 | 10194 | 28.2.59 | 10256 | 30.5.59 | 10318 | 17.10.5 |
| 10009 | 7.3.58 | 10071 | 26.3.58 | 10133 | 14.3.58 | 10195 | 28.2.59 | 10257 | 4.6.59 | 10319 | 31.10.5 |
| 10010 | 29.8.58 | 10072 | 24.4.58 | 10134 | 6.3.58 | 10196 | 7.3.59 | 10258 | 4.6.59 | 10320 | 31.10.5 |
| 10011 | 29.8.58 | 10073 | 25.4.58 | 10135 | 23.5.58 | 10197 | 2.5.59 | 10259 | 11.4.59 | 10321 | 7.11.58 |
| 10012 | 5.7.57 | 10074 | 2.5.58 | 10136 | 30.5.58 | 10198 | 2.5.59 | 10260 | 11.4.59 | 10322 | 7.11.58 |
| 10013 | 12.7.57 | 10075 | 30.5.58 | 10137 | 30.5.58 | 10199 | 22.5.59 | 10261 | 11.4.59 | 10323 | 21.11.58 |
| 10014 | 19.5.57 | 10076 | 24.5.58 | 10138 | 6.6.58 | 10200 | 22.5.59 | 10262 | 25.4.59 | 10324 | 21.11.58 |
| 10015 | 25.7.57 | 10077 | 31.5.58 | 10139 | 18.7.58 | 10201 | 22.5.59 | 10263 | 17.4.59 | 10325 | 28.11.58 |
| 10016 | 22.7.57 | 10078 | 6.6.58 | 10140 | 11.7.58 | 10202 | 30.5.59 | 10264 | 17.4.59 | 10326 | 31.12.58 |
| 10017 | 21.2.58 | 10079 | 6.6.58 | 10141 | 25.7.58 | 10203 | 27.9.58 | 10265 | 27.3.58 | 10327 | 31.12.58 |
| 10018 | 21.2.58 | 10080 | 20.6.58 | 10142 | 18.7.58 | 10204 | 4.10.58 | 10266 | 18.4.58 | 10328 | 31.12.58 |
| 10019 | 21.2.58 | 10081 | | 10143 | 25.4.58 | 10205 | 11.10.58 | 10267 | 23.4.58 | 10329 | 2.6.59 |
| 10020 | 4.3.58 | 10082 | | 10144 | 23.5.58 | 10206 | 11.10.58 | 10268 | 26.4.58 | 10330 | 29.5.59 |
| 10021 | 4.3.58 | 10083 | | 10145 | 4.7.58 | 10207 | 11.10.58 | 10269 | 21.2.59 | 10331 | 24.10.58 |
| 10022 | 4.3.58 | 10084 | 15.4.58 | 10146 | 27.6.58 | 10208 | 1.11.58 | 10270 | 27.2.59 | 10332 | 31.10.58 |
| 10023 | 14.3.58 | 10085 | 14.3.58 | 10147 | | 10209 | 7.11.58 | 10271 | 27.2.59 | 10333 | 7.11.58 |
| 10024 | 21.3.58 | 10086 | 11.3.59 | 10148 | | 10210 | 7.11.58 | 10272 | 24.10.58 | 10334 | 7.11.58 |
| 10025 | 11.4.58 | 10087 | 14.3.58 | 10149 | 19.6.58 | 10211 | 15.11.58 | 10273 | 17.10.58 | 10335 | 14.11.58 |
| 10026 | 3.4.58 | 10088 | 21.3.58 | 10150 | 20.6.58 | 10212 | 21.11.58 | 10274 | 17.10.58 | 10336 | 31.1.59 |
| 10027 | 18.4.58 | 10089 | 21.3.58 | 10151 | 20.6.58 | 10213 | 6.12.58 | 10275 | 18.11.58 | 10337 | 9.1.59 |
| 10028 | 11.4.58 | 10090 | 28.3.58 | 10152 | 20.6.58 | 10214 | 12.12.58 | 10276 | 21.11.58 | 10338 | 9.1.59 |
| 10029 | 18.4.58 | 10091 | 28.3.58 | 10153 | 20.6.58 | 10215 | 24.1.59 | 10277 | 21.11.58 | 10339 | 27.2.59 |
| 10030 | 28.4.58 | 10092 | 28.3.58 | 10154 | 4.7.58 | 10216 | 31.1.59 | 10278 | 28.11.58 | 10340 | 6.3.59 |
| 10031 | 2.5.58 | 10093 | 3.4.58 | 10155 | 27.6.58 | 10217 | 3.1.59 | 10279 | 9.1.59 | 10341 | 6.3.59 |
| 10032 | 24.4.58 | 10094 | 3.4.58 | 10156 | 27.6.58 | 10218 | 3.1.59 | 10280 | 9.1.59 | 10342 | 5.6.59 |
| 10033 | 2.5.58 | 10095 | 3.4.58 | 10157 | 18.8.58 | 10219 | 24.1.59 | 10281 | 26.5.59 | 10343 | 7.11.58 |
| 10034 | 9.5.58 | 10096 | 3.4.58 | 10158 | 21.8.58 | 10220 | 31.1.59 | 10282 | 17.10.58 | 10344 | 28.11.58 |
| 10035 | 2.5.58 | 10097 | 11.4.58 | 10159 | 21.8.58 | 10221 | 14.2.59 | 10283 | 17.10.58 | 10345 | 9.1.59 |
| 10036 | 13.6.58 | 10098 | 24.4.58 | 10160 | 29.8.58 | 10222 | 27.2.59 | 10284 | 5.12.58 | 10346 | 10.4.59 |
| 10037 | 5.3.58 | 10099 | 28.4.58 | 10161 | 29.8.58 | 10223 | | 10285 | 5.12.58 | 10347 | 22.5.59 |
| 10038 | 5.3.58 | 10100 | 28.4.58 | 10162 | 29.8.58 | 10224 | 3.10.58 | 10286 | 24.1.59 | 10348 | 22.5.59 |
| 10039 | 5.3.58 | 10101 | 9.5.58 | 10163 | 15.9.58 | 10225 | 3.10.58 | 10287 | 17.1.59 | 10349 | 5.6.59 |
| 10040 | 12.3.58 | 10102 | 16.5.58 | 10164 | 15.9.58 | 10226 | 13.10.58 | 10288 | 20.3.59 | 10350 | 12.12.58 |
| 10041 | 12.3.58 | 10103 | 18.7.58 | 10165 | 15.9.58 | 10227 | 20.10.58 | 10289 | 17.4.59 | 10351 | 12.12.58 |
| 10042 | 12.3.58 | 10104 | 13.2.59 | 10166 | 22.9.58 | 10228 | 31.10.58 | 10290 | 29.5.59 | 10352 | 15.11.58 |
| 10043 | 20.3.58 | 10105 | 13.2.59 | 10167 | 22.9.58 | 10229 | 31.10.58 | 10291 | 5.6.59 | 10353 | 22.11.58 |
| 10044 | 20.3.58 | 10106 | 13.2.59 | 10168 | 22.9.58 | 10230 | 3.11.58 | 10292 | 31.10.58 | 10354 | 6.12.58 |
| 10045 | 3.4.58 | 10107 | 25.3.58 | 10169 | | 10231 | 6.11.58 | 10293 | 31.10.58 | 10355 | 6.12.58 |
| 10046 | 2.4.58 | 10108 | 9.4.58 | 10170 | | 10232 | 20.11.58 | 10294 | 4.11.58 | 10356 | 3.1.59 |
| 10047 | 23.5.58 | 10109 | 9.4.58 | 10171 | | 10233 | 10.11.58 | 10295 | 14.11.58 | 10357 | 10.1.59 |
| 10048 | 30.5.58 | 10110 | 18.4.58 | 10172 | | 10234 | 14.11.58 | 10296 | 7.11.58 | 10358 | 10.1.59 |
| 10049 | 6.6.58 | 10111 | 18.4.58 | 10173 | | 10235 | 24.11.58 | 10297 | 16.1.59 | 10359 | 10.1.59 |
| 10050 | 14.6.58 | 10112 | 25.4.58 | 10174 | 25.4.59 | 10236 | 5.12.58 | 10298 | 16.1.59 | 10360 | 31.1.59 |
| 10051 | 13.1.59 | 10113 | 2.5.58 | 10175 | 25.4.59 | 10237 | 27.11.58 | 10299 | 23.1.59 | 10361 | 31.1.59 |
| 10052 | 22.12.58 | 10114 | 9.5.58 | 10176 | 30.4.59 | 10238 | 20.11.58 | 10300 | 5.6.59 | 10362 | 7.2.59 |
| 10053 | 19.12.58 | 10115 | 2.5.58 | 10177 | 30.4.59 | 10239 | 1.12.58 | 10301 | 5.6.59 | 10363 | 7.2.59 |
| 10054 | 22.12.58 | 10116 | 12.5.58 | 10178 | 1.5.59 | 10240 | 1.12.58 | 10302 | 10.10.58 | 10364 | 14.2.59 |
| 10055 | 19.12.58 | 10117 | 12.5.58 | 10179 | 22.5.59 | 10241 | 12.12.58 | 10303 | 10.10.58 | 10365 | 26.2.59 |
| 10056 | 13.1.59 | 10118 | 20.5.58 | 10180 | 28.5.59 | 10242 | 12.12.58 | 10304 | 30.12.58 | 10366 | 26.2.59 |
| 10057 | 31.12.58 | 10119 | 12.5.58 | 10181 | 28.5.59 | 10243 | 5.1.59 | 10305 | 30.12.58 | 10367 | 26.2.59 |
| 10058 | 2.1.59 | 10120 | 20.5.58 | 10182 | 18.10.58 | 10244 | 5.1.59 | 10306 | 14.11.58 | 10368 | 13.6.59 |
| 10059 | 31.12.58 | 10121 | 27.5.58 | 10183 | 25.10.58 | 10245 | 5.1.59 | 10307 | 14.11.58 | 10369 | 13.6.59 |
| 10060 | 3.4.58 | 10122 | 12.6.58 | 10184 | 25.10.58 | 10246 | 13.2.59 | 10308 | 21.11.58 | 10370 | 5.12.58 |
| 10061 | 3.4.58 | 10123 | 19.6.58 | 10185 | 25.10.58 | 10247 | 31.1.59 | 10309 | 30.5.58 | 10371 | 5.12.58 |
| 10062 | 3.4.58 | 10124 | 24.6.58 | 10186 | 1.11.58 | 10248 | 13.2.59 | 10310 | 6.6.58 | 10372 | 5.12.58 |

| | | | | | | | | | |
|---|---|---|---|---|---|---|---|---|---|
| 10373 | 8.12.58 | 10437 | 23.1.59 | 10501 | | 10565 | | 10629 | | 10693 | |
| 10374 | 9.1.59 | 10438 | 30.1.59 | 10502 | | 10566 | | 10630 | | 10694 | |
| 10375 | 9.1.59 | 10439 | 27.2.59 | 10503 | | 10567 | | 10631 | | 10695 | |
| 10376 | 16.1.59 | 10440 | 27.2.59 | 10504 | | 10568 | | 10632 | 20.6.58 | 10696 | |
| 10377 | 16.1.59 | 10441 | 27.2.59 | 10505 | | 10569 | | 10633 | 5.12.58 | 10697 | |
| 10378 | 2.2.59 | 10442 | 5.6.59 | 10506 | | 10570 | | 10634 | 29.5.58 | 10698 | |
| 10379 | 19.2.59 | 10443 | 9.6.59 | 10507 | | 10571 | | 10635 | 29.5.58 | 10699 | |
| 10380 | 23.2.59 | 10444 | 31.10.58 | 10508 | | 10572 | | 10636 | 30.5.58 | 10700 | |
| 10381 | 15.6.59 | 10445 | 3.11.58 | 10509 | | 10573 | | 10637 | 30.5.58 | 10701 | 28.3.58 |
| 10382 | 12.6.59 | 10446 | 10.11.58 | 10510 | | 10574 | | 10638 | 12.6.58 | 10702 | 28.3.58 |
| 10383 | 15.6.59 | 10447 | 14.11.58 | 10511 | | 10575 | | 10639 | 12.6.58 | 10703 | 31.3.58 |
| 10384 | 19.6.59 | 10448 | 2.1.59 | 10512 | | 10576 | | 10640 | 20.6.58 | 10704 | 31.3.58 |
| 10385 | 23.6.59 | 10449 | 9.1.59 | 10513 | | 10577 | | 10641 | 27.6.58 | 10705 | |
| 10386 | 23.6.59 | 10450 | 13.2.59 | 10514 | | 10578 | | 10642 | 27.6.58 | 10706 | |
| 10387 | 12.12.58 | 10451 | 13.2.59 | 10515 | | 10579 | | 10643 | | 10707 | |
| 10388 | 12.12.58 | 10452 | 28.11.58 | 10516 | | 10580 | | 10644 | | 10708 | |
| 10389 | 12.12.58 | 10453 | 28.11.58 | 10517 | | 10581 | | 10645 | | 10709 | 11.4.58 |
| 10390 | 19.12.58 | 10454 | 28.11.58 | 10518 | | 10582 | | 10646 | | 10710 | 11.4.58 |
| 10391 | 19.12.58 | 10455 | 9.1.59 | 10519 | | 10583 | | 10647 | | 10711 | 18.4.58 |
| 10392 | 19.12.58 | 10456 | 9.1.59 | 10520 | | 10584 | | 10648 | | 10712 | 25.4.58 |
| 10393 | 2.1.59 | 10457 | 20.1.59 | 10521 | | 10585 | | 10649 | | 10713 | 15.4.58 |
| 10394 | 2.1.59 | 10458 | 6.2.59 | 10522 | | 10586 | | 10650 | 4.7.58 | 10714 | 2.5.58 |
| 10395 | 13.2.59 | 10459 | 6.2.59 | 10523 | | 10587 | | 10651 | 11.7.58 | 10715 | 8.4.60 |
| 10396 | 6.2.59 | 10460 | 6.2.59 | 10524 | | 10588 | | 10652 | 25.3.58 | 10716 | 8.4.60 |
| 10397 | 20.2.59 | 10461 | 27.2.59 | 10525 | | 10589 | | 10653 | 25.3.58 | 10717 | |
| 10398 | 20.2.59 | 10462 | 5.3.59 | 10526 | | 10590 | | 10654 | 1.4.58 | 10718 | |
| 10399 | 20.2.59 | 10463 | 12.6.59 | 10527 | | 10591 | | 10655 | 2.4.58 | 10719 | |
| 10400 | 6.3.59 | 10464 | 12.6.59 | 10528 | | 10592 | | 10656 | 10.4.58 | 10720 | 29.8.58 |
| 10401 | 2.7.59 | 10465 | 26.6.59 | 10529 | | 10593 | | 10657 | 2.5.58 | 10721 | 5.9.58 |
| 10402 | 2.7.59 | 10466 | 26.6.59 | 10530 | | 10594 | | 10658 | 25.4.58 | 10722 | 5.9.58 |
| 10403 | 2.7.59 | 10467 | 26.6.59 | 10531 | | 10595 | | 10659 | 9.5.58 | 10723 | 5.9.58 |
| 10404 | 12.12.58 | 10468 | 10.7.59 | 10532 | | 10596 | | 10660 | 16.5.58 | 10724 | 12.9.58 |
| 10405 | 12.12.58 | 10469 | 3.11.58 | 10533 | | 10597 | | 10661 | 27.6.58 | 10725 | 12.9.58 |
| 10406 | 12.12.58 | 10470 | 14.11.58 | 10534 | | 10598 | | 10662 | 27.6.58 | 10726 | 12.9.58 |
| 10407 | 21.11.58 | 10471 | 14.11.58 | 10535 | | 10599 | | 10663 | 27.6.58 | 10727 | 19.9.58 |
| 10408 | 21.11.58 | 10472 | 17.11.58 | 10536 | | 10600 | | 10664 | | 10728 | 19.9.58 |
| 10409 | 25.11.58 | 10473 | 17.11.58 | 10537 | | 10601 | | 10665 | 13.6.58 | 10729 | 19.9.58 |
| 10410 | 25.11.58 | 10474 | 17.11.58 | 10538 | | 10602 | | 10666 | 20.6.58 | 10730 | 26.9.58 |
| 10411 | 28.11.58 | 10475 | 21.11.58 | 10539 | | 10603 | | 10667 | 27.6.58 | 10731 | 26.9.58 |
| 10412 | 20.1.59 | 10476 | 24.11.58 | 10540 | | 10604 | | 10668 | | 10732 | 23.5.58 |
| 10413 | 23.1.59 | 10477 | 24.11.58 | 10541 | | 10605 | | 10669 | | 10733 | 23.5.58 |
| 10414 | 27.2.59 | 10478 | 24.11.58 | 10542 | | 10606 | | 10670 | | 10734 | 30.5.58 |
| 10415 | 16.6.59 | 10479 | 12.6.59 | 10543 | | 10607 | | 10671 | 20.6.58 | 10735 | 30.5.58 |
| 10416 | 22.12.58 | 10480 | 16.1.59 | 10544 | | 10608 | | 10672 | 20.6.58 | 10736 | 13.6.58 |
| 10417 | 22.12.58 | 10481 | 16.1.59 | 10545 | | 10609 | | 10673 | 4.7.58 | 10737 | 13.6.58 |
| 10418 | 22.12.58 | 10482 | 29.5.59 | 10546 | | 10610 | | 10674 | 4.7.58 | 10738 | 20.6.58 |
| 10419 | 17.1.59 | 10483 | 5.6.59 | 10547 | | 10611 | | 10675 | 11.7.58 | 10739 | 27.6.58 |
| 10420 | 17.1.59 | 10484 | 26.11.58 | 10548 | | 10612 | | 10676 | 11.7.58 | 10740 | 11.7.58 |
| 10421 | 31.1.59 | 10485 | 3.12.58 | 10549 | | 10613 | | 10677 | | 10741 | 4.7.58 |
| 10422 | 7.2.59 | 10486 | 3.12.58 | 10550 | | 10614 | | 10678 | | 10742 | 25.7.58 |
| 10423 | 7.2.59 | 10487 | 3.12.58 | 10551 | | 10615 | | 10679 | | 10743 | 25.7.58 |
| 10424 | 7.2.59 | 10488 | 22.12.58 | 10552 | | 10616 | | 10680 | | 10744 | 11.7.58 |
| 10425 | 21.2.59 | 10489 | 26.1.59 | 10553 | | 10617 | | 10681 | | 10745 | 25.7.58 |
| 10426 | 21.2.59 | 10490 | 2.2.59 | 10554 | | 10618 | | 10682 | | 10746 | 22.8.58 |
| 10427 | 7.3.59 | 10491 | 13.2.59 | 10555 | | 10619 | | 10683 | | 10747 | 15.8.58 |
| 10428 | 7.3.59 | 10492 | 15.12.58 | 10556 | | 10620 | | 10684 | | 10748 | 22.8.58 |
| 10429 | 11.7.59 | 10493 | | 10557 | | 10621 | | 10685 | | 10749 | 29.8.58 |
| 10430 | 28.11.58 | 10494 | | 10558 | | 10622 | | 10686 | | 10750 | 22.8.58 |
| 10431 | 6.1.59 | 10495 | | 10559 | | 10623 | | 10687 | | 10751 | 29.8.58 |
| 10432 | 6.1.59 | 10496 | | 10560 | | 10624 | | 10688 | | 10752 | 19.1.59 |
| 10433 | 6.1.59 | 10497 | | 10561 | | 10625 | | 10689 | | 10753 | 19.1.59 |
| 10434 | 6.1.59 | 10498 | | 10562 | | 10626 | | 10690 | | 10754 | 20.1.59 |
| 10435 | 23.1.59 | 10499 | | 10563 | | 10627 | | 10691 | | 10755 | 20.1.59 |
| 10436 | 30.1.59 | 10500 | | 10564 | | 10628 | | 10692 | | 10756 | 20.1.59 |

| | | | | | | | | | | | |
|---|---|---|---|---|---|---|---|---|---|---|---|
| 10757 | 2.2.59 | 10821 | 31.12.58 | 10885 | 20.6.59 | 10949 | 27.10.59 | 11013 | 6.11.59 | 11077 | 9.10.5 |
| 10758 | 5.2.59 | 10822 | 31.12.58 | 10886 | 20.6.59 | 10950 | 27.10.59 | 11014 | 13.1.61 | 11078 | 9.10.5 |
| 10759 | 9.2.59 | 10823 | 12.2.59 | 10887 | 27.6.59 | 10951 | 30.10.59 | 11015 | 13.1.61 | 11079 | 20.11.5 |
| 10760 | 16.2.59 | 10824 | 12.2.59 | 10888 | 27.6.59 | 10952 | 12.4.60 | 11016 | 8.5.59 | 11080 | 20.11.5 |
| 10761 | 16.2.59 | 10825 | 12.2.59 | 10889 | 24.10.59 | 10953 | 22.4.60 | 11017 | 20.5.59 | 11081 | 20.11.5 |
| 10762 | 23.2.59 | 10826 | 12.2.59 | 10890 | 30.10.59 | 10954 | 3.7.59 | 11018 | 8.5.59 | 11082 | 20.11.5 |
| 10763 | 23.2.59 | 10827 | 13.3.59 | 10891 | 31.10.59 | 10955 | 3.7.59 | 11019 | 20.5.59 | 11083 | 27.11.5 |
| 10764 | 2.3.59 | 10828 | 13.3.59 | 10892 | 31.10.59 | 10956 | 26.6.59 | 11020 | 20.5.59 | 11084 | 27.11.5 |
| 10765 | 5.3.59 | 10829 | 20.3.59 | 10893 | 6.11.59 | 10957 | 3.7.59 | 11021 | 5.6.59 | 11085 | 27.11.5 |
| 10766 | 5.3.59 | 10830 | 20.3.59 | 10894 | 14.11.59 | 10958 | 24.7.59 | 11022 | 12.6.59 | 11086 | 26.4.60 |
| 10767 | 2.3.59 | 10831 | 10.4.59 | 10895 | 12.3.60 | 10959 | 21.8.59 | 11023 | 23.6.59 | 11087 | 29.4.60 |
| 10768 | 9.3.59 | 10832 | 17.4.59 | 10896 | 19.3.60 | 10960 | 21.8.59 | 11024 | 7.7.59 | 11088 | 28.8.59 |
| 10769 | 9.3.59 | 10833 | 10.4.59 | 10897 | 12.3.60 | 10961 | 21.8.59 | 11025 | 10.7.59 | 11089 | 2.10.59 |
| 10770 | 11.3.59 | 10834 | 17.4.59 | 10898 | 12.3.60 | 10962 | 21.8.59 | 11026 | 24.7.59 | 11090 | 2.10.59 |
| 10771 | 19.3.59 | 10835 | 17.4.59 | 10899 | 12.9.59 | 10963 | 2.10.59 | 11027 | 24.7.59 | 11091 | 9.10.59 |
| 10772 | 19.3.59 | 10836 | 28.4.59 | 10900 | 12.9.59 | 10964 | 2.10.59 | 11028 | 28.7.59 | 11092 | 20.11.5 |
| 10773 | 23.3.59 | 10837 | 11.5.59 | 10901 | 12.9.59 | 10965 | 9.10.59 | 11029 | 4.9.59 | 11093 | 9.1.60 |
| 10774 | 25.3.59 | 10838 | 14.5.59 | 10902 | 12.9.59 | 10966 | 9.10.59 | 11030 | 4.9.59 | 11094 | 14.8.59 |
| 10775 | 23.3.59 | 10839 | 14.5.59 | 10903 | 14.7.59 | 10967 | 16.10.59 | 11031 | 11.9.59 | 11095 | 14.8.59 |
| 10776 | 23.3.59 | 10840 | 19.5.59 | 10904 | 16.7.59 | 10968 | 27.11.59 | 11032 | 30.10.59 | 11096 | 28.8.59 |
| 10777 | 20.4.59 | 10841 | 1.5.59 | 10905 | 16.7.59 | 10969 | 20.11.59 | 11033 | 30.10.59 | 11097 | 26.3.60 |
| 10778 | 27.4.59 | 10842 | 8.5.59 | 10906 | 22.7.59 | 10970 | 4.12.59 | 11034 | 30.10.59 | 11098 | 26.3.60 |
| 10779 | 27.4.59 | 10843 | 14.5.59 | 10907 | 16.7.59 | 10971 | 4.12.59 | 11035 | 6.11.59 | 11099 | 4.3.60 |
| 10780 | 28.4.59 | 10844 | 14.5.59 | 10908 | 13.8.59 | 10972 | 4.12.59 | 11036 | 6.11.59 | 11100 | 31.3.60 |
| 10781 | 27.4.59 | 10845 | 10.3.59 | 10909 | 13.8.59 | 10973 | 20.4.60 | 11037 | 13.11.59 | 11101 | 8.4.60 |
| 10782 | 27.1.59 | 10846 | 10.3.59 | 10910 | 3.9.59 | 10974 | 2.4.60 | 11038 | 13.11.59 | 11102 | 1.9.59 |
| 10783 | 6.2.59 | 10847 | 17.3.59 | 10911 | 31.8.59 | 10975 | 22.4.60 | 11039 | 26.4.60 | 11103 | 6.11.59 |
| 10784 | 27.1.59 | 10848 | 12.4.60 | 10912 | 24.9.59 | 10976 | 25.3.59 | 11040 | 26.4.60 | 11104 | 25.7.59 |
| 10785 | 27.1.59 | 10849 | 22.4.60 | 10913 | 21.9.59 | 10977 | 25.3.59 | 11041 | 24.7.59 | 11105 | 25.7.59 |
| 10786 | 30.1.59 | 10850 | 22.4.60 | 10914 | 28.9.59 | 10978 | 12.6.59 | 11042 | 24.7.59 | 11106 | 26.9.59 |
| 10787 | 30.1.59 | 10851 | 6.5.60 | 10915 | 28.9.59 | 10979 | 12.6.59 | 11043 | 14.8.59 | 11107 | 26.9.59 |
| 10788 | 30.1.59 | 10852 | 26.4.60 | 10916 | 21.9.59 | 10980 | 10.7.59 | 11044 | 4.9.59 | 11108 | 26.9.59 |
| 10789 | 13.2.59 | 10853 | 10.5.60 | 10917 | 21.9.59 | 10981 | 20.7.59 | 11045 | 11.9.59 | 11109 | 3.10.59 |
| 10790 | 13.2.59 | 10854 | 6.5.60 | 10918 | 6.10.59 | 10982 | 11.9.59 | 11046 | 18.9.59 | 11110 | 3.10.59 |
| 10791 | 17.2.59 | 10855 | 6.6.60 | 10919 | 1.10.59 | 10983 | 11.9.59 | 11047 | 2.10.59 | 11111 | 6.11.59 |
| 10792 | 20.2.59 | 10856 | 10.6.60 | 10920 | 9.11.59 | 10984 | 30.10.59 | 11048 | 2.10.59 | 11112 | 8.11.59 |
| 10793 | 17.2.59 | 10857 | 1.9.59 | 10921 | 23.11.59 | 10985 | 6.11.59 | 11049 | 30.10.59 | 11113 | 6.11.59 |
| 10794 | 20.2.59 | 10858 | 1.9.59 | 10922 | 23.11.59 | 10986 | 11.3.60 | 11050 | 30.10.59 | 11114 | 14.11.59 |
| 10795 | 27.2.59 | 10859 | 5.9.59 | 10923 | 14.3.60 | 10987 | 18.3.60 | 11051 | 6.11.59 | 11115 | 12.12.59 |
| 10796 | 13.3.59 | 10860 | 5.9.59 | 10924 | 28.3.60 | 10988 | 21.8.59 | 11052 | 27.11.59 | 11116 | 30.1.60 |
| 10797 | 13.3.59 | 10861 | 5.9.59 | 10925 | 7.3.60 | 10989 | 21.8.59 | 11053 | 27.11.59 | 11117 | 12.3.60 |
| 10798 | 13.3.59 | 10862 | 12.9.59 | 10926 | 7.3.60 | 10990 | 23.10.59 | 11054 | 27.11.59 | 11118 | 19.3.60 |
| 10799 | 13.3.59 | 10863 | 12.9.59 | 10927 | 28.3.60 | 10991 | 30.10.59 | 11055 | 4.3.60 | 11119 | 17.8.59 |
| 10800 | 3.4.59 | 10864 | 12.9.59 | 10928 | 9.6.59 | 10992 | 23.10.59 | 11056 | 11.3.60 | 11120 | 17.8.59 |
| 10801 | 3.4.59 | 10865 | 12.9.59 | 10929 | 12.6.59 | 10993 | 10.7.59 | 11057 | 10.7.59 | 11121 | 24.8.59 |
| 10802 | 8.4.59 | 10866 | 24.10.59 | 10930 | 9.6.59 | 10994 | 10.7.59 | 11058 | 10.7.59 | 11122 | 1.10.59 |
| 10803 | 8.4.59 | 10867 | 2.7.60 | 10931 | 4.9.59 | 10995 | 17.7.59 | 11059 | 28.8.59 | 11123 | 6.10.59 |
| 10804 | 14.4.59 | 10868 | 2.7.60 | 10932 | 17.8.59 | 10996 | 17.7.59 | 11060 | 28.8.59 | 11124 | 1.10.59 |
| 10805 | 8.5.59 | 10869 | 2.7.60 | 10933 | 13.8.59 | 10997 | 28.8.59 | 11061 | 25.9.59 | 11125 | 8.10.59 |
| 10806 | 1.5.59 | 10870 | 2.7.60 | 10934 | 3.9.59 | 10998 | 18.9.59 | 11062 | 30.9.59 | 11126 | 23.11.59 |
| 10807 | 1.5.59 | 10871 | 15.7.60 | 10935 | 3.9.59 | 10999 | 18.9.59 | 11063 | 30.9.59 | 11127 | 30.11.59 |
| 10808 | 8.5.59 | 10872 | 20.8.60 | 10936 | 16.10.59 | 11000 | 25.9.59 | 11064 | 13.11.59 | 11128 | 14.12.59 |
| 10809 | 4.12.58 | 10873 | 20.8.60 | 10937 | 16.10.59 | 11001 | 18.9.59 | 11065 | 13.11.59 | 11129 | 30.11.59 |
| 10810 | 4.12.58 | 10874 | 3.9.60 | 10938 | 19.6.59 | 11002 | 23.10.59 | 11066 | 13.11.59 | 11130 | 1.2.60 |
| 10811 | 4.12.58 | 10875 | 27.8.60 | 10939 | 2.7.59 | 11003 | 27.11.59 | 11067 | 18.3.60 | 11131 | 19.1.60 |
| 10812 | 5.12.58 | 10876 | 3.9.60 | 10940 | 17.8.59 | 11004 | 20.11.59 | 11068 | 18.3.60 | 11132 | 26.1.60 |
| 10813 | 5.12.58 | 10877 | 10.9.60 | 10941 | 17.8.59 | 11005 | 20.11.59 | 11069 | 3.7.59 | 11133 | 2.2.60 |
| 10814 | 12.12.58 | 10878 | 30.7.59 | 10942 | 28.8.59 | 11006 | 25.3.60 | 11070 | 26.6.59 | 11134 | 9.10.59 |
| 10815 | 5.12.58 | 10879 | 6.6.59 | 10943 | 9.10.59 | 11007 | 6.6.59 | 11071 | 26.6.59 | 11135 | 9.10.59 |
| 10816 | 12.12.58 | 10880 | 13.6.59 | 10944 | 9.10.59 | 11008 | 20.6.59 | 11072 | 26.6.59 | 11136 | 9.10.59 |
| 10817 | 19.12.58 | 10881 | 20.6.59 | 10945 | 16.10.59 | 11009 | 19.9.59 | 11073 | 28.8.59 | 11137 | 11.9.59 |
| 10818 | 19.12.58 | 10882 | 13.6.59 | 10946 | 16.10.59 | 11010 | 24.10.59 | 11074 | 4.9.59 | 11138 | 4.9.59 |
| 10819 | 19.12.58 | 10883 | 20.6.59 | 10947 | 19.10.59 | 11011 | 30.10.59 | 11075 | 4.9.59 | 11139 | 14.9.59 |
| 10820 | 19.12.58 | 10884 | 20.6.59 | 10948 | 19.10.59 | 11012 | 30.10.59 | 11076 | 9.10.59 | 11140 | 14.9.59 |

| | | | | | | | | | | | |
|---|---|---|---|---|---|---|---|---|---|---|---|
| 11141 | 19.10.59 | 11205 | 16.10.59 | 11269 | 25.9.59 | 11333 | 3.4.59 | 11397 | 24.2.60 | 11461 | 4.3.60 |
| 11142 | 23.10.59 | 11206 | 23.10.59 | 11270 | 25.9.59 | 11334 | 3.4.59 | 11398 | 18.2.60 | 11462 | 15.3.60 |
| 11143 | 26.10.59 | 11207 | 23.10.59 | 11271 | 25.9.59 | 11335 | 4.5.59 | 11399 | 18.2.60 | 11463 | 15.3.60 |
| 11144 | 6.11.59 | 11208 | 23.10.59 | 11272 | 28.7.59 | 11336 | 7.5.59 | 11400 | 13.2.59 | 11464 | 25.3.60 |
| 11145 | 23.10.59 | 11209 | 30.10.59 | 11273 | 17.7.59 | 11337 | 7.5.59 | 11401 | 13.2.59 | 11465 | 25.3.60 |
| 11146 | 6.11.59 | 11210 | 13.11.59 | 11274 | 28.7.59 | 11338 | 6.7.59 | 11402 | 17.2.59 | 11466 | 1.4.60 |
| 11147 | 6.11.59 | 11211 | 20.11.59 | 11275 | 28.7.59 | 11339 | 17.8.59 | 11403 | 17.2.59 | 11467 | 1.4.60 |
| 11148 | 3.11.59 | 11212 | 8.12.59 | 11276 | 14.8.59 | 11340 | 20.7.59 | 11404 | | 11468 | 14.4.60 |
| 11149 | 3.11.59 | 11213 | 24.11.59 | 11277 | 23.4.59 | 11341 | 28.9.59 | 11405 | | 11469 | 14.4.60 |
| 11150 | 3.11.59 | 11214 | 20.11.59 | 11278 | 23.4.59 | 11342 | 1.10.59 | 11406 | | 11470 | 14.4.60 |
| 11151 | 9.11.59 | 11215 | 27.11.59 | 11279 | 29.4.59 | 11343 | 9.10.59 | 11407 | 27.6.59 | 11471 | 29.4.60 |
| 11152 | 2.2.60 | 11216 | 20.11.59 | 11280 | 29.4.59 | 11344 | 9.10.59 | 11408 | 27.6.59 | 11472 | 29.4.60 |
| 11153 | 5.2.60 | 11217 | 4.12.59 | 11281 | 22.5.59 | 11345 | 8.2.60 | 11409 | 27.6.59 | 11473 | 15.12.59 |
| 11154 | 5.2.60 | 11218 | 4.12.59 | 11282 | 22.5.59 | 11346 | 8.2.60 | 11410 | 27.6.59 | 11474 | 15.12.59 |
| 11155 | 12.2.60 | 11219 | 8.12.59 | 11283 | 22.5.59 | 11347 | 8.2.60 | 11411 | 4.7.59 | 11475 | 18.12.59 |
| 11156 | 12.2.60 | 11220 | 4.12.59 | 11284 | 25.5.59 | 11348 | 8.2.60 | 11412 | 4.7.59 | 11476 | 18.12.59 |
| 11157 | 30.10.59 | 11221 | 4.12.59 | 11285 | 26.5.59 | 11349 | 29.2.60 | 11413 | 4.7.59 | 11477 | 18.12.59 |
| 11158 | 13.11.59 | 11222 | 4.12.59 | 11286 | 26.5.59 | 11350 | 8.3.60 | 11414 | 11.7.59 | 11478 | 18.12.59 |
| 11159 | 13.11.59 | 11223 | 11.12.59 | 11287 | 25.3.59 | 11351 | 8.3.60 | 11415 | 4.7.59 | 11479 | 7.1.60 |
| 11160 | 1.1.60 | 11224 | 11.12.59 | 11288 | 25.3.59 | 11352 | 7.3.60 | 11416 | 11.7.59 | 11480 | 7.1.60 |
| 11161 | 1.1.60 | 11225 | 8.1.60 | 11289 | 1.5.59 | 11353 | 29.5.59 | 11417 | 4.7.59 | 11481 | 7.1.60 |
| 11162 | 1.1.60 | 11226 | 8.1.60 | 11290 | 4.5.59 | 11354 | 29.5.59 | 11418 | 21.11.60 | 11482 | 7.1.60 |
| 11163 | 1.4.59 | 11227 | 8.1.60 | 11291 | 6.5.59 | 11355 | 12.6.59 | 11419 | 8.11.60 | 11483 | 22.1.60 |
| 11164 | 2.6.59 | 11228 | 15.1.60 | 11292 | 12.5.59 | 11356 | 12.6.59 | 11420 | 11.11.60 | 11484 | 22.1.60 |
| 11165 | 18.9.59 | 11229 | 15.1.60 | 11293 | 14.4.59 | 11357 | 24.8.59 | 11421 | 10.11.60 | 11485 | 22.1.60 |
| 11166 | 18.9.59 | 11230 | 15.1.60 | 11294 | 14.4.59 | 11358 | 28.8.59 | 11422 | 25.11.60 | 11486 | 29.1.60 |
| 11167 | 22.9.59 | 11231 | 15.1.60 | 11295 | 17.4.59 | 11359 | 23.8.59 | 11423 | 11.12.59 | 11487 | 29.1.60 |
| 11168 | 24.7.59 | 11232 | 22.1.60 | 11296 | 17.4.59 | 11360 | 2.10.59 | 11424 | 11.12.59 | 11488 | 5.2.60 |
| 11169 | 24.7.59 | 11233 | 12.2.60 | 11297 | 21.4.59 | 11361 | 16.10.59 | 11425 | 11.12.59 | 11489 | 5.2.60 |
| 11170 | 24.7.59 | 11234 | 12.2.60 | 11298 | 21.4.59 | 11362 | 13.11.59 | 11426 | 15.12.59 | 11490 | 5.2.60 |
| 11171 | 6.11.59 | 11235 | 19.2.60 | 11299 | 29.5.59 | 11363 | 3.6.60 | 11427 | 15.12.59 | 11491 | 12.2.60 |
| 11172 | 10.11.59 | 11236 | 19.2.60 | 11300 | 26.6.59 | 11364 | 4.5.59 | 11428 | 4.1.60 | 11492 | 12.2.60 |
| 11173 | 10.11.59 | 11237 | 19.2.60 | 11301 | 26.6.59 | 11365 | 8.5.59 | 11429 | 4.1.60 | 11493 | 23.2.60 |
| 11174 | 1.1.60 | 11238 | 19.2.60 | 11302 | 14.4.59 | 11366 | 4.5.59 | 11430 | 5.1.60 | 11494 | 23.2.60 |
| 11175 | 8.1.60 | 11239 | 26.2.60 | 11303 | 21.4.59 | 11367 | 15.5.59 | 11431 | 5.1.60 | 11495 | 23.2.60 |
| 11176 | 8.1.60 | 11240 | 26.2.60 | 11304 | 2.5.59 | 11368 | 15.5.59 | 11432 | 19.1.60 | 11496 | 23.2.60 |
| 11177 | 12.1.60 | 11241 | 23.10.59 | 11305 | 2.5.59 | 11369 | 22.5.59 | 11433 | 13.1.60 | 11497 | 20.2.60 |
| 11178 | 13.8.59 | 11242 | 23.10.59 | 11306 | 9.5.59 | 11370 | 10.7.59 | 11434 | 19.1.60 | 11498 | 15.1.60 |
| 11179 | 14.8.59 | 11243 | 21.8.59 | 11307 | 9.5.59 | 11371 | 17.7.59 | 11435 | 13.1.60 | 11499 | 15.1.60 |
| 11180 | 5.9.59 | 11244 | 21.8.59 | 11308 | 9.5.59 | 11372 | 17.7.59 | 11436 | 20.1.60 | 11500 | 21.1.60 |
| 11181 | 5.9.59 | 11245 | 23.6.59 | 11309 | 15.5.59 | 11373 | 20.7.59 | 11437 | 20.1.60 | 11501 | 21.1.60 |
| 11182 | 14.11.59 | 11246 | 23.6.59 | 11310 | 9.5.59 | 11374 | 28.8.59 | 11438 | 22.2.60 | 11502 | 29.1.60 |
| 11183 | 14.11.59 | 11247 | 26.6.59 | 11311 | 15.5.59 | 11375 | 15.9.59 | 11439 | 1.3.60 | 11503 | 6.4.60 |
| 11184 | 21.11.59 | 11248 | 23.6.59 | 11312 | 22.5.59 | 11376 | 15.9.59 | 11440 | 22.2.60 | 11504 | 6.4.60 |
| 11185 | 28.11.59 | 11249 | 26.6.59 | 11313 | 22.5.59 | 11377 | 25.9.59 | 11441 | 1.3.60 | 11505 | 6.4.60 |
| 11186 | 5.12.59 | 11250 | 28.8.59 | 11314 | 30.5.59 | 11378 | 29.1.60 | 11442 | 1.3.60 | 11506 | 6.4.60 |
| 11187 | 5.12.59 | 11251 | 28.8.59 | 11315 | 30.5.59 | 11379 | 22.1.60 | 11443 | 3.4.60 | 11507 | 27.5.60 |
| 11188 | 5.12.59 | 11252 | 10.7.59 | 11316 | 5.4.59 | 11380 | 29.1.60 | 11444 | 11.4.60 | 11508 | 13.1.61 |
| 11189 | 5.12.59 | 11253 | 10.7.59 | 11317 | 7.4.59 | 11381 | 5.2.60 | 11445 | 5.4.60 | 11509 | 13.1.61 |
| 11190 | 5.12.59 | 11254 | 10.7.59 | 11318 | 7.4.59 | 11382 | 19.2.60 | 11446 | 11.4.60 | 11510 | 3.2.61 |
| 11191 | 5.12.59 | 11255 | 17.7.59 | 11319 | 3.4.59 | 11383 | 26.2.60 | 11447 | 11.4.60 | 11511 | 3.2.61 |
| 11192 | 13.2.60 | 11256 | 17.7.59 | 11320 | 3.4.59 | 11384 | 22.1.60 | 11448 | 19.4.60 | 11512 | 10.2.61 |
| 11193 | 13.2.60 | 11257 | 10.7.59 | 11321 | 8.4.59 | 11385 | 22.1.60 | 11449 | 23.4.60 | 11513 | 15.10.60 |
| 11194 | 20.2.60 | 11258 | 17.7.59 | 11322 | 8.4.59 | 11386 | 22.1.60 | 11450 | 2.5.60 | 11514 | 22.10.60 |
| 11195 | 20.2.60 | 11259 | 28.8.59 | 11323 | 8.4.59 | 11387 | 25.2.60 | 11451 | 2.5.60 | 11515 | 22.10.60 |
| 11196 | 3.7.59 | 11260 | 4.9.59 | 11324 | 15.4.59 | 11388 | 25.2.60 | 11452 | 11.5.60 | 11516 | 29.10.60 |
| 11197 | 10.7.59 | 11261 | 28.8.59 | 11325 | 15.4.59 | 11389 | 25.2.60 | 11453 | 9.2.60 | 11517 | 26.10.60 |
| 11198 | 10.7.59 | 11262 | 4.9.59 | 11326 | 24.4.59 | 11390 | 25.2.60 | 11454 | 9.2.60 | 11518 | 29.10.60 |
| 11199 | 17.7.59 | 11263 | 4.9.59 | 11327 | 24.4.59 | 11391 | 22.1.60 | 11455 | 12.2.60 | 11519 | 5.11.60 |
| 11200 | 17.7.59 | 11264 | 4.9.59 | 11328 | 23.3.59 | 11392 | 24.1.60 | 11456 | 26.2.60 | 11520 | 29.10.60 |
| 11201 | 17.7.59 | 11265 | 10.9.59 | 11329 | 1.4.59 | 11393 | 24.1.60 | 11457 | 12.2.60 | 11521 | 4.2.61 |
| 11202 | 18.9.59 | 11266 | 10.9.59 | 11330 | 23.3.59 | 11394 | 24.1.60 | 11458 | 26.2.60 | 11522 | 4.2.61 |
| 11203 | 23.9.59 | 11267 | 10.9.59 | 11331 | 26.3.59 | 11395 | 24.1.60 | 11459 | 4.3.60 | 11523 | 4.2.61 |
| 11204 | 16.10.59 | 11268 | 25.9.59 | 11332 | 26.3.59 | 11396 | 18.2.60 | 11460 | 26.2.60 | 11524 | 4.2.61 |

| | | | | | | | | | | | |
|---|---|---|---|---|---|---|---|---|---|---|---|
| 11525 | 4.2.61 | 11589 | 20.5.60 | 11653 | 26.5.61 | 11717 | 8.12.60 | 11781 | 9.7.60 | 11845 | 17.3.61 |
| 11526 | 17.9.60 | 11590 | 18.5.60 | 11654 | 26.5.61 | 11718 | 13.12.60 | 11782 | 9.7.60 | 11846 | 14.3.61 |
| 11527 | 14.1.61 | 11591 | 18.5.60 | 11655 | 13.5.60 | 11719 | 13.12.60 | 11783 | 15.7.60 | 11847 | 17.3.61 |
| 11528 | 21.1.61 | 11592 | 15.7.60 | 11656 | 13.5.60 | 11720 | 15.12.60 | 11784 | 1.10.60 | 11848 | 22.7.60 |
| 11529 | 21.1.61 | 11593 | 21.7.60 | 11657 | 28.6.60 | 11721 | 22.11.60 | 11785 | 1.10.60 | 11849 | 22.7.60 |
| 11530 | 21.1.61 | 11594 | 11.8.60 | 11658 | 1.7.60 | 11722 | 22.11.60 | 11786 | 8.10.60 | 11850 | 14.10.60 |
| 11531 | 21.1.61 | 11595 | 22.7.60 | 11659 | 20.6.60 | 11723 | 28.11.60 | 11787 | 8.10.60 | 11851 | 21.10.6 |
| 11532 | 11.2.61 | 11596 | 18.8.60 | 11660 | 22.7.60 | 11724 | 5.12.60 | 11788 | 8.10.60 | 11852 | 10.11.6 |
| 11533 | 11.2.61 | 11597 | 26.8.60 | 11661 | 6.8.60 | 11725 | 12.12.60 | 11789 | 11.10.60 | 11853 | 10.11.6 |
| 11534 | 11.2.61 | 11598 | 23.8.60 | 11662 | 22.7.60 | 11726 | 11.11.60 | 11790 | 5.11.60 | 11854 | 3.2.61 |
| 11535 | 10.2.61 | 11599 | 27.3.61 | 11663 | 13.8.60 | 11727 | 11.11.60 | 11791 | 5.11.60 | 11855 | 3.2.61 |
| 11536 | 11.2.61 | 11600 | 27.3.61 | 11664 | 3.9.60 | 11728 | 15.11.60 | 11792 | 5.11.60 | 11856 | 22.7.60 |
| 11537 | 10.2.61 | 11601 | 27.3.61 | 11665 | 3.9.60 | 11729 | 15.11.60 | 11793 | 12.11.60 | 11857 | 12.8.60 |
| 11538 | 17.9.60 | 11602 | 16.6.61 | 11666 | 21.4.61 | 11730 | 25.11.60 | 11794 | 12.11.60 | 11858 | 22.11.6 |
| 11539 | 17.9.60 | 11603 | 12.6.61 | 11667 | 28.4.61 | 11731 | 28.11.60 | 11795 | 10.12.60 | 11859 | 22.11.6 |
| 11540 | 24.9.60 | 11604 | 20.6.61 | 11668 | 28.4.61 | 11732 | 24.11.60 | 11796 | 17.12.60 | 11860 | 20.12.6 |
| 11541 | 8.10.60 | 11605 | 3.5.60 | 11669 | 27.6.61 | 11733 | 28.11.60 | 11797 | 17.12.60 | 11861 | 22.12.6 |
| 11542 | 24.9.60 | 11606 | 3.5.60 | 11670 | 23.6.61 | 11734 | 24.11.60 | 11798 | 17.12.60 | 11862 | 12.7.60 |
| 11543 | 15.10.60 | 11607 | 6.5.60 | 11671 | 7.7.61 | 11735 | 25.11.60 | 11799 | 28.1.61 | 11863 | 12.7.60 |
| 11544 | 1.10.60 | 11608 | 1.7.60 | 11672 | 10.6.60 | 11736 | 29.11.60 | 11800 | 28.1.61 | 11864 | 23.8.60 |
| 11545 | 15.10.60 | 11609 | 8.7.60 | 11673 | 10.6.60 | 11737 | 2.12.60 | 11801 | 28.1.61 | 11865 | 23.8.60 |
| 11546 | 8.10.60 | 11610 | 19.8.60 | 11674 | 2.9.60 | 11738 | 8.12.60 | 11802 | 28.1.61 | 11866 | 23.8.60 |
| 11547 | 15.10.60 | 11611 | 12.8.60 | 11675 | 26.8.60 | 11739 | 29.11.60 | 11803 | 25.2.61 | 11867 | 26.8.60 |
| 11548 | 8.11.60 | 11612 | 26.8.60 | 11676 | 26.8.60 | 11740 | 8.12.60 | 11804 | 25.2.61 | 11868 | 26.8.60 |
| 11549 | 29.10.60 | 11613 | 2.9.60 | 11677 | 24.2.61 | 11741 | 9.12.60 | 11805 | 4.3.61 | 11869 | 2.9.60 |
| 11550 | 30.10.60 | 11614 | 9.9.60 | 11678 | 24.2.61 | 11742 | 9.12.60 | 11806 | 4.3.61 | 11870 | 2.9.60 |
| 11551 | 22.10.60 | 11615 | 21.2.61 | 11679 | 10.3.61 | 11743 | 16.12.60 | 11807 | 14.7.60 | 11871 | 6.9.60 |
| 11552 | 22.10.60 | 11616 | 21.2.61 | 11680 | 10.3.61 | 11744 | 21.12.60 | 11808 | 14.7.60 | 11872 | 16.9.60 |
| 11553 | 4.11.60 | 11617 | 21.2.61 | 11681 | 10.3.61 | 11745 | 17.1.61 | 11809 | 19.7.60 | 11873 | 16.9.60 |
| 11554 | 4.11.60 | 11618 | 20.6.61 | 11682 | 20.5.60 | 11746 | 22.11.60 | 11810 | 19.7.60 | 11874 | 23.9.60 |
| 11555 | 4.11.60 | 11619 | 23.6.61 | 11683 | 20.5.60 | 11747 | 22.11.60 | 11811 | 6.10.60 | 11875 | 27.9.60 |
| 11556 | 25.11.60 | 11620 | 17.6.60 | 11684 | 27.5.60 | 11748 | 25.11.60 | 11812 | 17.10.60 | 11876 | 11.10.60 |
| 11557 | 11.11.60 | 11621 | 24.6.60 | 11685 | 20.8.60 | 11749 | 30.11.60 | 11813 | 1.11.60 | 11877 | 11.10.60 |
| 11558 | 4.11.60 | 11622 | 30.6.60 | 11686 | 20.8.60 | 11750 | 16.12.60 | 11814 | 8.11.60 | 11878 | 11.10.60 |
| 11559 | 2.2.61 | 11623 | 1.7.60 | 11687 | 27.8.60 | 11751 | 18.11.60 | 11815 | 29.12.60 | 11879 | 21.10.60 |
| 11560 | 2.2.61 | 11624 | 15.7.60 | 11688 | 27.8.60 | 11752 | 18.11.60 | 11816 | 29.12.60 | 11880 | 21.10.60 |
| 11561 | 2.2.61 | 11625 | 15.7.60 | 11689 | 3.9.60 | 11753 | 18.11.60 | 11817 | 9.1.61 | 11881 | 21.10.60 |
| 11562 | 10.2.61 | 11626 | 8.7.60 | 11690 | 10.9.60 | 11754 | 6.12.60 | 11818 | 10.1.61 | 11882 | 25.10.60 |
| 11563 | 10.2.61 | 11627 | 15.8.60 | 11691 | 12.5.61 | 11755 | 6.12.60 | 11819 | 20.2.61 | 11883 | 28.10.60 |
| 11564 | 10.2.61 | 11628 | 15.8.60 | 11692 | 12.5.61 | 11756 | 6.12.60 | 11820 | 20.2.61 | 11884 | 8.11.60 |
| 11565 | 10.2.61 | 11629 | 23.8.60 | 11693 | 26.5.61 | 11757 | 30.12.60 | 11821 | 23.2.61 | 11885 | 25.11.60 |
| 11566 | 17.2.61 | 11630 | 28.4.61 | 11694 | 9.6.61 | 11758 | 3.1.61 | 11822 | 27.2.61 | 11886 | 25.11.60 |
| 11567 | 17.2.61 | 11631 | 28.4.61 | 11695 | 9.6.61 | 11759 | 30.12.60 | 11823 | 1.11.60 | 11887 | 25.11.60 |
| 11568 | 28.2.61 | 11632 | 2.5.61 | 11696 | 22.6.61 | 11760 | 6.1.61 | 11824 | 1.11.60 | 11888 | 2.12.60 |
| 11569 | 24.2.61 | 11633 | 30.6.61 | 11697 | 23.6.61 | 11761 | 6.1.61 | 11825 | 17.1.61 | 11889 | 2.12.60 |
| 11570 | 24.5.60 | 11634 | 5.7.61 | 11698 | 23.6.61 | 11762 | 16.12.60 | 11826 | 20.1.61 | 11890 | 2.12.60 |
| 11571 | 27.5.60 | 11635 | 24.6.60 | 11699 | 1.7.60 | 11763 | 21.12.60 | 11827 | 20.1.61 | 11891 | 30.12.60 |
| 11572 | 27.5.60 | 11636 | 24.6.60 | 11700 | 9.7.60 | 11764 | 21.12.60 | 11828 | 12.8.60 | 11892 | 6.1.61 |
| 11573 | 15.7.60 | 11637 | 21.6.60 | 11701 | 10.3.61 | 11765 | 21.12.60 | 11829 | 15.7.60 | 11893 | 4.1.61 |
| 11574 | 15.7.60 | 11638 | 6.7.60 | 11702 | 10.3.61 | 11766 | 21.12.60 | 11830 | 12.8.60 | 11894 | 11.1.61 |
| 11575 | 17.5.60 | 11639 | 21.6.60 | 11703 | 1.7.60 | 11767 | 23.12.60 | 11831 | 22.7.60 | 11895 | 13.1.61 |
| 11576 | 23.5.60 | 11640 | 24.6.60 | 11704 | 1.7.60 | 11768 | 23.12.60 | 11832 | 28.10.60 | 11896 | 3.2.61 |
| 11577 | 23.5.60 | 11641 | 24.2.61 | 11705 | 8.3.61 | 11769 | 23.12.60 | 11833 | 14.10.60 | 11897 | 7.2.61 |
| 11578 | 7.6.60 | 11642 | 24.2.61 | 11706 | 8.3.61 | 11770 | 23.12.60 | 11834 | 14.10.60 | 11898 | 14.2.61 |
| 11579 | 9.6.60 | 11643 | 28.2.61 | 11707 | 15.11.60 | 11771 | 23.12.60 | 11835 | 21.10.60 | 11899 | 10.2.61 |
| 11580 | 17.6.60 | 11644 | 3.3.61 | 11708 | 21.11.60 | 11772 | 30.12.60 | 11836 | 11.11.60 | 11900 | 10.2.61 |
| 11581 | 25.8.60 | 11645 | 8.7.60 | 11709 | 15.11.60 | 11773 | 6.1.61 | 11837 | 11.11.60 | 11901 | 10.2.61 |
| 11582 | 22.8.60 | 11646 | 22.7.60 | 11710 | 21.11.60 | 11774 | 30.12.60 | 11838 | 15.11.60 | 11902 | 14.2.61 |
| 11583 | 30.3.61 | 11647 | 22.8.60 | 11711 | 23.11.60 | 11775 | 6.1.61 | 11839 | 12.12.60 | 11903 | 21.2.61 |
| 11584 | 30.3.61 | 11648 | 22.7.60 | 11712 | 23.11.60 | 11776 | 6.1.61 | 11840 | 24.1.61 | 11904 | 21.2.61 |
| 11585 | 1.5.61 | 11649 | 12.5.61 | 11713 | 8.12.60 | 11777 | 10.1.61 | 11841 | 26.1.61 | 11905 | 24.2.61 |
| 11586 | 6.6.61 | 11650 | 12.5.61 | 11714 | 8.12.60 | 11778 | 10.1.61 | 11842 | 24.1.61 | 11906 | 3.3.61 |
| 11587 | 9.6.61 | 11651 | 19.5.61 | 11715 | 5.12.60 | 11779 | 10.1.61 | 11843 | 7.2.61 | 11907 | 10.3.61 |
| 11588 | 9.6.61 | 11652 | 19.5.61 | 11716 | 5.12.60 | 11780 | 9.7.60 | 11844 | 10.3.61 | 11908 | 17.3.61 |

| | | | | | | | | | | | |
|---|---|---|---|---|---|---|---|---|---|---|---|
| 11909 | 17.3.61 | 11973 | 5.7.60 | 12037 | 25.11.60 | 12101 | 24.4.61 | 12165 | 7.7.61 | 12229 | 5.5.61 |
| 11910 | 24.3.61 | 11974 | 1.7.60 | 12038 | 8.12.60 | 12102 | 25.4.61 | 12166 | 14.7.61 | 12230 | 5.5.61 |
| 11911 | 24.3.61 | 11975 | 8.7.60 | 12039 | 8.12.60 | 12103 | 25.4.61 | 12167 | 7.7.61 | 12231 | 9.6.61 |
| 11912 | 31.8.60 | 11976 | 22.6.60 | 12040 | 27.1.61 | 12104 | 1.5.61 | 12168 | 7.7.61 | 12232 | 13.6.61 |
| 11913 | 31.8.60 | 11977 | 22.6.60 | 12041 | 10.2.61 | 12105 | 4.5.61 | 12169 | 14.7.61 | 12233 | 21.4.61 |
| 11914 | 28.10.60 | 11978 | 24.6.60 | 12042 | 3.2.61 | 12106 | 9.5.61 | 12170 | 19.4.61 | 12234 | 21.4.61 |
| 11915 | 28.10.60 | 11979 | 24.6.60 | 12043 | 10.2.61 | 12107 | 6.5.61 | 12171 | 19.4.61 | 12235 | 29.3.61 |
| 11916 | 6.12.60 | 11980 | 23.6.60 | 12044 | 10.2.61 | 12108 | 13.5.61 | 12172 | 19.4.61 | 12236 | 24.3.61 |
| 11917 | 6.12.60 | 11981 | 15.9.60 | 12045 | 17.2.61 | 12109 | 13.5.61 | 12173 | 30.3.61 | 12237 | 7.4.61 |
| 11918 | 13.12.60 | 11982 | 17.10.60 | 12046 | 28.2.61 | 12110 | 17.5.61 | 12174 | 7.4.61 | 12238 | 5.4.61 |
| 11919 | 13.12.60 | 11983 | 17.10.60 | 12047 | 3.3.61 | 12111 | 10.5.61 | 12175 | 7.4.61 | 12239 | 28.4.61 |
| 11920 | 7.5.60 | 11984 | 8.11.60 | 12048 | 24.2.61 | 12112 | 27.6.61 | 12176 | 19.5.61 | 12240 | 28.4.61 |
| 11921 | 7.5.60 | 11985 | 22.12.60 | 12049 | 14.3.60 | 12113 | 24.6.61 | 12177 | 19.5.61 | 12241 | 2.6.61 |
| 11922 | 7.5.60 | 11986 | 20.12.60 | 12050 | 10.3.60 | 12114 | 30.6.61 | 12178 | 24.6.61 | 12242 | 5.6.61 |
| 11923 | 7.5.60 | 11987 | 9.1.61 | 12051 | 8.4.60 | 12115 | 6.7.61 | 12179 | 9.5.61 | 12243 | 5.5.61 |
| 11924 | 7.5.60 | 11988 | 9.1.61 | 12052 | 19.4.60 | 12116 | 8.7.61 | 12180 | 31.5.61 | 12244 | 5.5.61 |
| 11925 | 30.5.60 | 11989 | 10.1.61 | 12053 | 19.4.60 | 12117 | 20.7.61 | 12181 | 26.5.61 | 12245 | 5.5.61 |
| 11926 | 3.6.60 | 11990 | 10.1.61 | 12054 | 20.4.60 | 12118 | 26.5.61 | 12182 | 31.5.61 | 12246 | 27.6.61 |
| 11927 | 3.6.60 | 11991 | 14.3.61 | 12055 | 20.4.60 | 12119 | 26.5.61 | 12183 | 2.6.61 | 12247 | 28.6.61 |
| 11928 | 3.6.60 | 11992 | 20.3.61 | 12056 | 21.4.60 | 12120 | 30.5.61 | 12184 | 5.7.61 | 12248 | 30.6.61 |
| 11929 | 7.6.60 | 11993 | 20.3.61 | 12057 | 21.4.60 | 12121 | 2.6.61 | 12185 | 29.6.61 | 12249 | 9.5.61 |
| 11930 | 8.4.60 | 11994 | 28.3.61 | 12058 | 13.5.60 | 12122 | 30.6.61 | 12186 | 23.6.61 | 12250 | 18.5.61 |
| 11931 | 19.4.60 | 11995 | 21.3.61 | 12059 | 16.9.60 | 12123 | 30.6.61 | 12187 | 23.6.61 | 12251 | 12.5.61 |
| 11932 | 19.4.60 | 11996 | 29.3.61 | 12060 | 16.9.60 | 12124 | 19.7.61 | 12188 | 23.6.61 | 12252 | 30.6.61 |
| 11933 | 14.5.60 | 11997 | 22.6.60 | 12061 | 22.9.60 | 12125 | 7.3.61 | 12189 | 14.4.61 | 12253 | 30.6.61 |
| 11934 | 14.5.60 | 11998 | 22.6.60 | 12062 | 23.9.60 | 12126 | 7.3.61 | 12190 | 14.4.61 | 12254 | 7.7.61 |
| 11935 | 14.5.60 | 11999 | 22.6.60 | 12063 | 9.9.60 | 12127 | 14.3.61 | 12191 | 17.4.61 | 12255 | 24.3.61 |
| 11936 | 14.5.60 | 12000 | 28.10.60 | 12064 | 9.11.60 | 12128 | 14.3.61 | 12192 | 12.5.61 | 12256 | 29.3.61 |
| 11937 | 24.5.60 | 12001 | 4.11.60 | 12065 | 16.9.60 | 12129 | 14.3.61 | 12193 | 9.5.61 | 12257 | 30.3.61 |
| 11938 | 17.6.60 | 12002 | 28.10.60 | 12066 | 16.9.60 | 12130 | 29.3.61 | 12194 | 19.5.61 | 12258 | 13.4.61 |
| 11939 | 17.6.60 | 12003 | 11.11.60 | 12067 | 10.5.60 | 12131 | 24.3.61 | 12195 | 25.4.61 | 12259 | 20.4.61 |
| 11940 | 17.6.60 | 12004 | 11.11.60 | 12068 | 10.5.60 | 12132 | 30.3.61 | 12196 | 28.4.61 | 12260 | 14.2.61 |
| 11941 | 17.6.60 | 12005 | 15.11.60 | 12069 | 25.5.60 | 12133 | 29.3.61 | 12197 | 6.6.61 | 12261 | 21.2.61 |
| 11942 | 24.6.60 | 12006 | 1.3.61 | 12070 | 25.5.60 | 12134 | 14.4.61 | 12198 | 6.6.61 | 12262 | 14.2.61 |
| 11943 | 20.5.60 | 12007 | 7.3.61 | 12071 | 27.5.60 | 12135 | 28.4.61 | 12199 | 9.6.61 | 12263 | 21.2.61 |
| 11944 | 20.5.60 | 12008 | 10.3.61 | 12072 | 22.3.60 | 12136 | 28.4.61 | 12200 | 16.5.61 | 12264 | 21.2.61 |
| 11945 | 27.5.60 | 12009 | ---- | 12073 | 22.3.60 | 12137 | 28.4.61 | 12201 | 5.5.61 | 12265 | 14.3.61 |
| 11946 | 20.5.60 | 12010 | 27.5.60 | 12074 | 29.3.60 | 12138 | 5.5.61 | 12202 | 5.5.61 | 12266 | 14.3.61 |
| 11947 | 27.5.60 | 12011 | 27.5.60 | 12075 | 29.3.60 | 12139 | 5.5.61 | 12203 | 16.6.61 | 12267 | 14.7.61 |
| 11948 | 3.6.60 | 12012 | 31.5.60 | 12076 | 8.4.60 | 12140 | 26.5.61 | 12204 | 16.6.61 | 12268 | 21.7.61 |
| 11949 | 22.3.60 | 12013 | 31.5.60 | 12077 | 12.4.60 | 12141 | 6.6.61 | 12205 | 20.6.61 | 12269 | 21.7.61 |
| 11950 | 22.3.60 | 12014 | 6.6.60 | 12078 | 20.12.60 | 12142 | 5.6.61 | 12206 | 17.3.61 | 12270 | 25.7.61 |
| 11951 | 25.3.60 | 12015 | 10.6.60 | 12079 | 20.12.60 | 12143 | 12.6.61 | 12207 | 14.4.61 | 12271 | 25.7.61 |
| 11952 | 5.4.60 | 12016 | 17.1.61 | 12080 | 13.1.60 | 12144 | 6.7.61 | 12208 | 21.4.61 | 12272 | 2.3.62 |
| 11953 | 1.4.60 | 12017 | 24.1.61 | 12081 | 20.1.61 | 12145 | 6.7.61 | 12209 | 14.4.61 | 12273 | 2.3.62 |
| 11954 | 1.4.60 | 12018 | 24.1.61 | 12082 | 27.1.61 | 12146 | 13.7.61 | 12210 | 16.5.61 | 12274 | 6.4.62 |
| 11955 | 14.4.60 | 12019 | 27.1.61 | 12083 | 19.7.61 | 12147 | 13.7.61 | 12211 | 16.5.61 | 12275 | 30.3.62 |
| 11956 | 14.4.60 | 12020 | 27.9.60 | 12084 | 14.7.61 | 12148 | 20.7.61 | 12212 | 19.5.61 | 12276 | 6.4.62 |
| 11957 | 29.4.60 | 12021 | 14.10.60 | 12085 | 28.7.61 | 12149 | 20.7.61 | 12213 | 13.6.61 | 12277 | 17.3.62 |
| 11958 | 11.3.60 | 12022 | 5.10.60 | 12086 | 28.7.61 | 12150 | 15.3.61 | 12214 | 13.6.61 | 12278 | 24.3.62 |
| 11959 | 25.3.60 | 12023 | 14.10.60 | 12087 | 28.7.61 | 12151 | 15.3.61 | 12215 | 11.4.61 | 12279 | 17.3.62 |
| 11960 | 18.3.60 | 12024 | 6.12.60 | 12088 | 24.11.61 | 12152 | 17.3.61 | 12216 | 7.4.61 | 12280 | 17.3.62 |
| 11961 | 25.3.60 | 12025 | 9.12.60 | 12089 | 24.11.61 | 12153 | 19.4.61 | 12217 | 15.5.61 | 12281 | 17.3.62 |
| 11962 | 8.4.60 | 12026 | 9.12.60 | 12090 | 24.11.61 | 12154 | 19.4.61 | 12218 | | 12282 | 24.3.62 |
| 11963 | 8.4.60 | 12027 | 16.12.60 | 12091 | 16.2.61 | 12155 | 19.4.61 | 12219 | 18.5.61 | 12283 | 24.3.62 |
| 11964 | 14.7.60 | 12028 | 23.9.60 | 12092 | 16.2.61 | 12156 | 24.4.61 | 12220 | 18.5.61 | 12284 | 13.10.61 |
| 11965 | 19.7.60 | 12029 | 23.9.60 | 12093 | 7.3.61 | 12157 | 28.4.61 | 12221 | 1.9.61 | 12285 | 13.10.61 |
| 11966 | 8.4.60 | 12030 | 23.9.60 | 12094 | 13.3.61 | 12158 | 19.5.61 | 12222 | 13.9.61 | 12286 | 3.11.61 |
| 11967 | | 12031 | 27.9.60 | 12095 | 27.3.61 | 12159 | 19.5.61 | 12223 | 18.9.61 | 12287 | 3.11.61 |
| 11968 | | 12032 | 5.10.60 | 12096 | 20.3.61 | 12160 | 26.5.61 | 12224 | 26.5.61 | 12288 | 10.11.61 |
| 11969 | | 12033 | 27.9.60 | 12097 | 30.3.61 | 12161 | 14.6.61 | 12225 | 2.6.61 | 12289 | 17.11.61 |
| 11970 | | 12034 | 5.10.60 | 12098 | 10.4.61 | 12162 | 16.6.61 | 12226 | 2.6.61 | 12290 | 29.9.61 |
| 11971 | 1.7.60 | 12035 | 18.11.60 | 12099 | 27.3.61 | 12163 | 16.6.61 | 12227 | 20.6.61 | 12291 | 27.4.62 |
| 11972 | 29.6.60 | 12036 | 25.11.60 | 12100 | 24.4.61 | 12164 | 30.6.61 | 12228 | 20.6.61 | 12292 | 14.4.62 |

| | | | | | | | | | | | |
|---|---|---|---|---|---|---|---|---|---|---|---|
| 12293 | 27.4.62 | 12357 | 21.5.62 | 12421 | 6.2.62 | 12485 | 11.9.61 | 12549 | 9.1.62 | 12613 | 3.11.61 |
| 12294 | 27.4.62 | 12358 | 29.9.61 | 12422 | 3.11.61 | 12486 | 27.11.61 | 12550 | 9.1.62 | 12614 | 10.11.61 |
| 12295 | 27.4.62 | 12359 | 19.9.61 | 12423 | 10.11.61 | 12487 | 27.11.61 | 12551 | 11.1.62 | 12615 | 17.11.61 |
| 12296 | 27.4.62 | 12360 | 19.9.61 | 12424 | 17.11.61 | 12488 | 4.12.61 | 12552 | 12.1.62 | 12616 | 10.11.61 |
| 12297 | 19.5.62 | 12361 | 19.9.61 | 12425 | 17.11.61 | 12489 | 11.12.61 | 12553 | 25.8.61 | 12617 | 19.12.61 |
| 12298 | 25.5.62 | 12362 | 29.9.61 | 12426 | 2.2.62 | 12490 | 10.12.61 | 12554 | 18.8.61 | 12618 | 19.12.61 |
| 12299 | 19.5.62 | 12363 | 29.9.61 | 12427 | 2.2.62 | 12491 | 10.12.61 | 12555 | 26.7.61 | 12619 | 11.12.61 |
| 12300 | 25.5.62 | 12364 | 6.10.61 | 12428 | 12.5.61 | 12492 | 8.1.62 | 12556 | 28.7.61 | 12620 | 19.12.61 |
| 12301 | 6.10.61 | 12365 | 6.10.61 | 12429 | 5.5.61 | 12493 | 8.1.62 | 12557 | 18.8.61 | 12621 | 18.1.62 |
| 12302 | 30.10.61 | 12366 | 16.2.62 | 12430 | 3.11.61 | 12494 | 8.1.62 | 12558 | 18.8.61 | 12622 | 26.1.62 |
| 12303 | 18.9.61 | 12367 | 23.2.62 | 12431 | 3.11.61 | 12495 | 22.1.62 | 12559 | 15.12.61 | 12623 | 26.1.62 |
| 12304 | 19.9.61 | 12368 | 2.3.62 | 12432 | 10.11.61 | 12496 | 12.1.62 | 12560 | 15.12.61 | 12624 | 26.1.62 |
| 12305 | 6.10.61 | 12369 | 23.2.62 | 12433 | 17.11.61 | 12497 | 22.1.62 | 12561 | 12.12.61 | 12625 | 24.9.62 |
| 12306 | 9.10.61 | 12370 | 2.3.62 | 12434 | 10.11.61 | 12498 | 22.1.62 | 12562 | 22.12.61 | 12626 | 21.9.62 |
| 12307 | 9.10.61 | 12371 | 12.9.61 | 12435 | 17.11.61 | 12499 | 31.7.61 | 12563 | 22.12.61 | 12627 | 21.9.62 |
| 12308 | 16.10.61 | 12372 | 8.9.61 | 12436 | 24.11.61 | 12500 | 31.7.61 | 12564 | 22.12.61 | 12628 | 28.9.62 |
| 12309 | 16.10.61 | 12373 | 8.9.61 | 12437 | 9.2.62 | 12501 | 25.7.61 | 12565 | 19.1.62 | 12629 | 11.7.61 |
| 12310 | 10.10.61 | 12374 | 8.9.61 | 12438 | 9.2.62 | 12502 | 4.12.61 | 12566 | 11.1.62 | 12630 | 14.7.61 |
| 12311 | 24.10.61 | 12375 | 12.9.62 | 12439 | 15.2.62 | 12503 | 4.12.61 | 12567 | 28.11.61 | 12631 | 24.11.61 |
| 12312 | 24.10.61 | 12376 | 15.12.61 | 12440 | 13.2.62 | 12504 | 14.7.61 | 12568 | 24.11.61 | 12632 | 24.11.61 |
| 12313 | 24.10.61 | 12377 | 25.12.61 | 12441 | 13.2.62 | 12505 | 21.7.61 | 12569 | 24.11.61 | 12633 | 22.12.61 |
| 12314 | 27.10.61 | 12378 | 15.12.61 | 12442 | 15.2.62 | 12506 | 14.7.61 | 12570 | 28.11.61 | 12634 | 29.12.61 |
| 12315 | 30.10.61 | 12379 | 25.12.61 | 12443 | 15.2.62 | 12507 | 25.8.61 | 12571 | 28.11.61 | 12635 | 15.1.62 |
| 12316 | 27.3.62 | 12380 | 29.12.61 | 12444 | 10.11.61 | 12508 | 25.8.61 | 12572 | 1.12.61 | 12636 | 15.1.62 |
| 12317 | 26.3.62 | 12381 | 15.9.61 | 12445 | 14.11.61 | 12509 | 8.9.61 | 12573 | 17.11.61 | 12637 | 14.7.61 |
| 12318 | 9.4.62 | 12382 | 15.9.61 | 12446 | 23.2.62 | 12510 | 17.11.61 | 12574 | 17.11.61 | 12638 | 14.7.61 |
| 12319 | 9.4.62 | 12383 | 8.9.61 | 12447 | 20.2.62 | 12511 | 1.12.61 | 12575 | 21.7.61 | 12639 | 18.7.61 |
| 12320 | 10.4.62 | 12384 | 8.9.61 | 12448 | 20.2.62 | 12512 | 1.12.61 | 12576 | 21.7.61 | 12640 | 25.7.61 |
| 12321 | 9.4.62 | 12385 | 29.9.61 | 12449 | 17.11.61 | 12513 | 11.12.61 | 12577 | 18.8.61 | 12641 | 8.12.61 |
| 12322 | 16.4.62 | 12386 | 29.9.61 | 12450 | 14.11.61 | 12514 | 8.12.61 | 12578 | 18.8.61 | 12642 | 1.12.61 |
| 12323 | 16.4.62 | 12387 | 29.9.61 | 12451 | 14.11.61 | 12515 | 10.12.61 | 12579 | 29.8.61 | 12643 | 27.7.62 |
| 12324 | 3.5.62 | 12388 | 20.10.61 | 12452 | 8.12.61 | 12516 | 10.12.61 | 12580 | 27.10.61 | 12644 | 27.7.62 |
| 12325 | 7.5.62 | 12389 | 31.10.61 | 12453 | 15.12.61 | 12517 | 10.12.61 | 12581 | 27.10.61 | 12645 | 11.7.61 |
| 12326 | 14.5.62 | 12390 | 20.10.61 | 12454 | 15.12.61 | 12518 | 10.12.61 | 12582 | 10.11.61 | 12646 | 18.7.61 |
| 12327 | 14.5.62 | 12391 | 31.10.61 | 12455 | 15.12.61 | 12519 | 22.12.61 | 12583 | 3.11.61 | 12647 | 1.9.61 |
| 12328 | 14.5.62 | 12392 | 26.10.61 | 12456 | 15.12.61 | 12520 | 12.1.62 | 12584 | 17.11.61 | 12648 | 1.9.61 |
| 12329 | 31.5.62 | 12393 | 2.11.61 | 12457 | 19.12.61 | 12521 | 2.2.62 | 12585 | 17.11.61 | 12649 | 20.10.61 |
| 12330 | 31.5.62 | 12394 | 2.11.61 | 12458 | 19.12.61 | 12522 | 2.2.62 | 12586 | 24.11.61 | 12650 | 20.10.61 |
| 12331 | 31.5.62 | 12395 | 2.11.61 | 12459 | 8.12.61 | 12523 | 2.2.62 | 12587 | 1.12.61 | 12651 | 14.11.61 |
| 12332 | 31.5.62 | 12396 | 2.11.61 | 12460 | 12.1.62 | 12524 | 18.8.61 | 12588 | 8.12.61 | 12652 | 17.11.61 |
| 12333 | 10.4.61 | 12397 | 9.11.61 | 12461 | 19.1.62 | 12525 | 25.8.61 | 12589 | 1.12.61 | 12653 | 24.11.61 |
| 12334 | 15.4.61 | 12398 | 9.11.61 | 12462 | 19.1.62 | 12526 | 25.8.61 | 12590 | 8.12.61 | 12654 | 24.11.61 |
| 12335 | 25.4.61 | 12399 | 16.11.61 | 12463 | 19.1.62 | 12527 | 21.12.61 | 12591 | 8.12.61 | 12655 | 28.12.61 |
| 12336 | 25.4.61 | 12400 | 16.11.61 | 12464 | 1.9.61 | 12528 | 22.12.61 | 12592 | 12.1.62 | 12656 | 15.12.61 |
| 12337 | 27.4.61 | 12401 | 19.1.62 | 12465 | 1.9.61 | 12529 | 22.12.61 | 12593 | 12.1.62 | 12657 | 15.12.61 |
| 12338 | 29.9.61 | 12402 | 19.1.62 | 12466 | 1.9.61 | 12530 | 5.1.62 | 12594 | 16.1.62 | 12658 | 28.12.61 |
| 12339 | 6.10.61 | 12403 | 19.1.62 | 12467 | 8.9.61 | 12531 | 16.1.62 | 12595 | 19.1.62 | 12659 | 12.1.62 |
| 12340 | 6.10.61 | 12404 | 26.1.62 | 12468 | 1.9.61 | 12532 | 12.1.62 | 12596 | 19.1.62 | 12660 | 12.1.62 |
| 12341 | 20.10.61 | 12405 | 26.1.62 | 12469 | 8.9.61 | 12533 | 16.1.62 | 12597 | 26.1.62 | 12661 | 12.1.62 |
| 12342 | 6.3.62 | 12406 | 26.1.62 | 12470 | 1.12.61 | 12534 | 23.1.62 | 12598 | 21.7.62 | 12662 | 12.1.62 |
| 12343 | 9.3.62 | 12407 | 1.2.62 | 12471 | 1.12.61 | 12535 | 26.1.62 | 12599 | 28.7.62 | 12663 | 26.1.62 |
| 12344 | 9.3.62 | 12408 | 1.2.62 | 12472 | 1.12.61 | 12536 | 23.1.62 | 12600 | 17.8.62 | 12664 | 24.8.62 |
| 12345 | 25.4.62 | 12409 | 2.2.62 | 12473 | 15.12.61 | 12537 | 23.1.62 | 12601 | 17.8.62 | 12665 | 24.8.62 |
| 12346 | 25.4.62 | 12410 | 2.2.62 | 12474 | 12.1.62 | 12538 | 23.1.62 | 12602 | 17.8.62 | 12666 | 24.8.62 |
| 12347 | 4.5.62 | 12411 | 27.10.61 | 12475 | 12.1.62 | 12539 | 2.3.62 | 12603 | 24.8.62 | 12667 | 28.8.62 |
| 12348 | 29.9.61 | 12412 | 7.11.61 | 12476 | 16.1.62 | 12540 | 2.3.62 | 12604 | 31.8.62 | 12668 | 31.8.62 |
| 12349 | 29.9.61 | 12413 | 3.11.61 | 12477 | 16.1.62 | 12541 | 1.9.61 | 12605 | 31.8.62 | 12669 | 21.9.62 |
| 12350 | 9.11.61 | 12414 | 26.1.62 | 12478 | 16.1.62 | 12542 | 1.9.61 | 12606 | 31.8.62 | 12670 | 19.9.62 |
| 12351 | 13.10.61 | 12415 | 30.1.62 | 12479 | 28.8.61 | 12543 | 6.9.61 | 12607 | 8.9.62 | 12671 | 28.9.62 |
| 12352 | 13.10.61 | 12416 | 30.1.62 | 12480 | 17.8.61 | 12544 | 6.9.61 | 12608 | 30.10.61 | 12672 | 28.9.62 |
| 12353 | 6.3.62 | 12417 | 2.2.62 | 12481 | 28.8.61 | 12545 | 1.12.61 | 12609 | 28.7.61 | 12673 | 2.10.62 |
| 12354 | 9.3.62 | 12418 | 2.2.62 | 12482 | 17.8.61 | 12546 | 8.12.61 | 12610 | 27.7.61 | 12674 | 5.10.62 |
| 12355 | 9.3.62 | 12419 | 2.2.62 | 12483 | 28.8.61 | 12547 | 15.12.61 | 12611 | 28.7.61 | 12675 | 14.7.61 |
| 12356 | 21.5.62 | 12420 | 6.2.62 | 12484 | 4.9.61 | 12548 | 22.12.61 | 12612 | 18.8.61 | 12676 | 28.7.61 |

| | | | | | | | | | | | |
|---|---|---|---|---|---|---|---|---|---|---|---|
| 12677 | 31.10.61 | 12741 | 25.8.61 | 12805 | 3.5.62 | 12869 | 15.5.62 | 12933 | 3.5.63 | 12997 | 30.11.62 |
| 12678 | 31.10.61 | 12742 | 29.8.61 | 12806 | 31.5.62 | 12870 | 19.4.62 | 12934 | 2.5.63 | 12998 | 21.9.62 |
| 12679 | 8.12.61 | 12743 | | 12807 | 1.6.62 | 12871 | 13.4.62 | 12935 | 13.6.63 | 12999 | 21.9.62 |
| 12680 | 8.12.61 | 12744 | | 12808 | 8.6.62 | 12872 | 19.4.62 | 12936 | 14.6.63 | 13000 | 25.9.62 |
| 12681 | 29.12.61 | 12745 | | 12809 | 8.6.62 | 12873 | 27.4.62 | 12937 | 10.7.63 | 13001 | 25.9.62 |
| 12682 | 29.12.61 | 12746 | | 12810 | 9.4.62 | 12874 | 4.5.62 | 12938 | 10.7.63 | 13002 | 2.10.62 |
| 12683 | 14.9.62 | 12747 | | 12811 | 9.4.62 | 12875 | 27.6.62 | 12939 | 10.7.63 | 13003 | 16.11.62 |
| 12684 | 14.9.62 | 12748 | 20.10.61 | 12812 | 10.4.62 | 12876 | 27.6.62 | 12940 | 10.7.63 | 13004 | 16.11.62 |
| 12685 | 18.7.61 | 12749 | 20.10.61 | 12813 | 10.4.62 | 12877 | 29.6.62 | 12941 | 28.9.62 | 13005 | 16.11.62 |
| 12686 | 30.6.61 | 12750 | 3.11.61 | 12814 | 11.5.62 | 12878 | 4.7.62 | 12942 | 29.9.62 | 13006 | 23.11.62 |
| 12687 | 30.6.61 | 12751 | 27.10.61 | 12815 | 11.5.62 | 12879 | 15.6.62 | 12943 | 28.9.62 | 13007 | 23.11.62 |
| 12688 | 30.6.61 | 12752 | 24.11.61 | 12816 | 11.5.62 | 12880 | 15.6.62 | 12944 | 28.9.62 | 13008 | 4.12.62 |
| 12689 | 12.7.61 | 12753 | 1.12.61 | 12817 | 15.6.62 | 12881 | 15.6.62 | 12945 | 28.9.62 | 13009 | 4.12.62 |
| 12690 | 12.7.61 | 12754 | 1.12.61 | 12818 | 4.5.62 | 12882 | 21.6.62 | 12946 | 23.11.62 | 13010 | 4.12.62 |
| 12691 | 1.9.61 | 12755 | 8.12.61 | 12819 | 9.5.62 | 12883 | 20.6.62 | 12947 | 16.11.62 | 13011 | 26.4.63 |
| 12692 | 1.9.61 | 12756 | 8.12.61 | 12820 | 4.5.62 | 12884 | 19.6.62 | 12948 | 16.11.62 | 13012 | 1.5.63 |
| 12693 | 24.11.61 | 12757 | 15.9.61 | 12821 | 15.5.62 | 12885 | 29.6.62 | 12949 | 3.5.63 | 13013 | 26.4.63 |
| 12694 | 24.11.61 | 12758 | 15.9.61 | 12822 | 15.5.62 | 12886 | 29.6.62 | 12950 | 10.5.63 | 13014 | 8.5.63 |
| 12695 | 29.12.61 | 12759 | 19.9.61 | 12823 | 8.6.62 | 12887 | 29.6.62 | 12951 | 19.7.63 | 13015 | 17.5.63 |
| 12696 | 5.1.62 | 12760 | 29.9.61 | 12824 | 23.2.62 | 12888 | 6.7.62 | 12952 | 23.11.62 | 13016 | 24.5.63 |
| 12697 | 21.8.62 | 12761 | 6.10.61 | 12825 | 23.2.62 | 12889 | 11.7.62 | 12953 | 23.11.62 | 13017 | 19.7.63 |
| 12698 | 21.8.62 | 12762 | 7.11.61 | 12826 | 28.2.62 | 12890 | 4.7.62 | 12954 | 26.11.62 | 13018 | 28.9.62 |
| 12699 | 7.9.62 | 12763 | 28.11.61 | 12827 | 28.2.62 | 12891 | 6.7.62 | 12955 | 28.9.62 | 13019 | 2.10.62 |
| 12700 | 7.9.62 | 12764 | 17.11.61 | 12828 | 19.4.62 | 12892 | 6.7.62 | 12956 | 28.9.62 | 13020 | 12.10.62 |
| 12701 | 18.9.61 | 12765 | 24.11.61 | 12829 | 19.4.62 | 12893 | 6.7.62 | 12957 | 5.10.62 | 13021 | 5.10.62 |
| 12702 | 12.9.61 | 12766 | 14.6.61 | 12830 | 19.4.62 | 12894 | 11.7.62 | 12958 | 5.10.62 | 13022 | 9.10.62 |
| 12703 | 18.9.61 | 12767 | 14.6.61 | 12831 | 19.4.62 | 12895 | 19.7.62 | 12959 | 30.11.62 | 13023 | 12.10.62 |
| 12704 | 25.9.61 | 12768 | 16.6.61 | 12832 | 19.4.62 | 12896 | 28.9.62 | 12960 | 30.11.62 | 13024 | 5.10.62 |
| 12705 | 2.10.61 | 12769 | 16.6.61 | 12833 | 1.6.62 | 12897 | 21.9.62 | 12961 | 23.11.62 | 13025 | 9.10.62 |
| 12706 | 10.10.61 | 12770 | 25.5.61 | 12834 | 1.6.62 | 12898 | 5.10.62 | 12962 | 18.4.63 | 13026 | 9.10.62 |
| 12707 | 10.10.61 | 12771 | 26.5.61 | 12835 | 1.6.62 | 12899 | 8.10.62 | 12963 | 25.4.63 | 13027 | 9.10.62 |
| 12708 | 10.10.61 | 12772 | 2.6.61 | 12836 | 1.6.62 | 12900 | 11.11.62 | 12964 | 25.4.63 | 13028 | 10.10.62 |
| 12709 | 10.10.61 | 12773 | 6.6.61 | 12837 | 18.5.62 | 12901 | 8.11.62 | 12965 | 19.4.63 | 13029 | 23.10.62 |
| 12710 | 16.10.61 | 12774 | 9.6.61 | 12838 | 18.5.62 | 12902 | 8.11.62 | 12966 | 28.6.63 | 13030 | 12.10.62 |
| 12711 | 30.10.61 | 12775 | 12.5.61 | 12839 | 18.4.62 | 12903 | 22.11.62 | 12967 | 26.7.62 | 13031 | 12.10.62 |
| 12712 | 24.10.61 | 12776 | 16.5.61 | 12840 | 13.4.62 | 12904 | 22.11.62 | 12968 | 26.7.62 | 13032 | 23.10.62 |
| 12713 | 11.9.61 | 12777 | 19.5.61 | 12841 | | 12905 | 29.11.62 | 12969 | 26.7.62 | 13033 | 26.10.62 |
| 12714 | 18.9.61 | 12778 | 26.5.61 | 12842 | | 12906 | 30.11.62 | 12970 | 31.7.62 | 13034 | 16.10.62 |
| 12715 | 14.7.61 | 12779 | 2.6.61 | 12843 | | 12907 | 11.4.62 | 12971 | 31.7.62 | 13035 | 19.10.62 |
| 12716 | 21.7.61 | 12780 | 2.6.61 | 12844 | | 12908 | 11.4.62 | 12972 | 11.9.62 | 13036 | 26.10.62 |
| 12717 | 21.7.61 | 12781 | 20.6.61 | 12845 | 13.4.62 | 12909 | 9.4.62 | 12973 | 18.9.62 | 13037 | 19.10.62 |
| 12718 | 3.10.61 | 12782 | 23.6.61 | 12846 | 19.4.62 | 12910 | 28.5.62 | 12974 | 21.9.62 | 13038 | 30.10.62 |
| 12719 | 3.10.61 | 12783 | 13.10.62 | 12847 | 3.4.62 | 12911 | 28.5.62 | 12975 | 21.9.62 | 13039 | 30.10.62 |
| 12720 | 5.10.61 | 12784 | 20.10.62 | 12848 | 3.4.62 | 12912 | 5.6.62 | 12976 | 30.11.62 | 13040 | 30.10.62 |
| 12721 | 5.10.61 | 12785 | 20.10.62 | 12849 | 10.4.62 | 12913 | 5.6.62 | 12977 | 26.4.63 | 13041 | 5.10.62 |
| 12722 | 13.10.61 | 12786 | 25.10.62 | 12850 | 23.2.62 | 12914 | 7.6.62 | 12978 | 25.6.63 | 13042 | 12.10.62 |
| 12723 | 13.10.61 | 12787 | 25.10.62 | 12851 | 23.2.62 | 12915 | 17.9.62 | 12979 | 25.6.63 | 13043 | 9.10.62 |
| 12724 | 13.10.61 | 12788 | 19.4.62 | 12852 | 23.2.62 | 12916 | 17.9.62 | 12980 | 28.6.63 | 13044 | 9.10.62 |
| 12725 | 17.10.61 | 12789 | 9.4.62 | 12853 | 23.2.62 | 12917 | 17.9.62 | 12981 | 5.7.63 | 13045 | 12.10.62 |
| 12726 | 17.10.61 | 12790 | 9.4.62 | 12854 | 9.3.62 | 12918 | 12.11.62 | 12982 | 26.7.63 | 13046 | 1.6.62 |
| 12727 | 18.8.61 | 12791 | 10.4.62 | 12855 | 13.3.62 | 12919 | 12.11.62 | 12983 | 26.7.63 | 13047 | 9.6.62 |
| 12728 | 24.8.61 | 12792 | 3.5.62 | 12856 | 16.3.62 | 12920 | 12.11.62 | 12984 | 14.9.62 | 13048 | 9.6.62 |
| 12729 | 25.8.61 | 12793 | 26.4.62 | 12857 | 16.3.62 | 12921 | 17.9.62 | 12985 | 26.9.62 | 13049 | 9.6.62 |
| 12730 | 26.10.61 | 12794 | 19.4.62 | 12858 | 13.3.62 | 12922 | 14.9.62 | 12986 | 26.9.62 | 13050 | 15.6.62 |
| 12731 | 27.10.61 | 12795 | 22.6.62 | 12859 | 1.6.62 | 12923 | 21.9.62 | 12987 | 28.9.62 | 13051 | 20.10.62 |
| 12732 | 2.11.61 | 12796 | 22.6.62 | 12860 | 1.6.62 | 12924 | 4.10.62 | 12988 | 28.9.62 | 13052 | 20.10.62 |
| 12733 | 18.12.61 | 12797 | 22.6.62 | 12861 | 4.6.62 | 12925 | 19.10.62 | 12989 | 5.12.62 | 13053 | 20.10.62 |
| 12734 | 15.12.61 | 12798 | 23.2.62 | 12862 | 8.6.62 | 12926 | 27.11.62 | 12990 | 5.12.62 | 13054 | 27.10.62 |
| 12735 | 29.12.61 | 12799 | 23.2.62 | 12863 | 15.6.62 | 12927 | 23.11.62 | 12991 | 7.12.62 | 13055 | 27.10.62 |
| 12736 | 28.7.61 | 12800 | 2.3.62 | 12864 | 3.4.62 | 12928 | 23.11.62 | 12992 | 7.12.62 | 13056 | 15.2.63 |
| 12737 | 28.7.61 | 12801 | 2.3.62 | 12865 | 3.4.62 | 12929 | 29.4.63 | 12993 | 7.12.62 | 13057 | 15.2.63 |
| 12738 | 18.8.61 | 12802 | 2.3.62 | 12866 | 3.4.62 | 12930 | 29.4.63 | 12994 | 16.11.62 | 13058 | 16.2.63 |
| 12739 | 18.8.61 | 12803 | 9.3.62 | 12867 | 11.5.62 | 12931 | 30.4.63 | 12995 | 16.11.62 | 13059 | 15.2.63 |
| 12740 | 25.8.61 | 12804 | 5.3.62 | 12868 | 11.5.62 | 12932 | 30.4.63 | 12996 | 30.11.62 | 13060 | 23.2.63 |

| | | | | | | | | | | | |
|---|---|---|---|---|---|---|---|---|---|---|---|
| 13061 | 23.2.63 | 13125 | 15.6.62 | 13189 | 17.8.62 | 13253 | 26.2.63 | 13317 | 28.2.63 | 13381 | 11.4.63 |
| 13062 | 2.3.63 | 13126 | 15.6.62 | 13190 | 4.9.62 | 13254 | 26.2.63 | 13318 | 28.2.63 | 13382 | 19.4.63 |
| 13063 | 2.3.63 | 13127 | 15.6.62 | 13191 | 7.9.62 | 13255 | 16.2.63 | 13319 | 9.3.63 | 13383 | 19.4.63 |
| 13064 | 2.3.63 | 13128 | 19.6.62 | 13192 | 8.9.62 | 13256 | 16.2.63 | 13320 | 16.3.63 | 13384 | 12.7.63 |
| 13065 | 9.3.63 | 13129 | 26.6.62 | 13193 | 4.9.62 | 13257 | 16.2.63 | 13321 | 18.5.63 | 13385 | 12.7.63 |
| 13066 | 9.3.63 | 13130 | 24.8.62 | 13194 | 8.9.62 | 13258 | 19.2.63 | 13322 | 24.5.63 | 13386 | 12.7.63 |
| 13067 | 9.3.63 | 13131 | 28.8.62 | 13195 | 21.12.62 | 13259 | 19.2.63 | 13323 | 7.6.63 | 13387 | 19.7.63 |
| 13068 | 9.3.63 | 13132 | 24.8.62 | 13196 | 21.12.62 | 13260 | 20.2.63 | 13324 | 14.6.63 | 13388 | 19.7.63 |
| 13069 | 16.3.63 | 13133 | 28.8.62 | 13197 | 18.1.63 | 13261 | 1.3.63 | 13325 | 14.6.63 | 13389 | 25.7.63 |
| 13070 | 16.3.63 | 13134 | 4.9.62 | 13198 | 18.1.63 | 13262 | 19.4.63 | 13326 | 22.6.63 | 13390 | 26.9.63 |
| 13071 | 16.3.63 | 13135 | 24.8.62 | 13199 | 14.2.63 | 13263 | 14.12.62 | 13327 | 14.6.63 | 13391 | 11.10.6 |
| 13072 | 16.3.63 | 13136 | 4.9.62 | 13200 | 1.3.63 | 13264 | 11.12.62 | 13328 | 14.6.63 | 13392 | 23.10.6: |
| 13073 | 22.3.63 | 13137 | 7.9.62 | 13201 | 29.3.63 | 13265 | 11.12.62 | 13329 | 22.6.63 | 13393 | 25.10.6: |
| 13074 | 3.11.62 | 13138 | 25.10.62 | 13202 | 27.6.62 | 13266 | 14.12.62 | 13330 | 22.6.63 | 13394 | 28.2.63 |
| 13075 | 10.11.62 | 13139 | 26.10.62 | 13203 | 29.6.62 | 13267 | 18.12.62 | 13331 | 28.6.63 | 13395 | 26.2.63 |
| 13076 | 17.8.62 | 13140 | 25.10.62 | 13204 | 29.6.62 | 13268 | 18.12.62 | 13332 | 28.6.63 | 13396 | 1.3.63 |
| 13077 | 17.8.62 | 13141 | 23.10.62 | 13205 | 29.6.62 | 13269 | 13.7.62 | 13333 | 28.6.63 | 13397 | 8.3.63 |
| 13078 | 24.8.62 | 13142 | 26.10.62 | 13206 | 29.6.62 | 13270 | 13.7.62 | 13334 | 5.7.63 | 13398 | 21.6.63 |
| 13079 | 24.8.62 | 13143 | 26.10.62 | 13207 | 8.9.62 | 13271 | 13.7.62 | 13335 | 5.7.63 | 13399 | 21.6.63 |
| 13080 | 24.8.62 | 13144 | 30.10.62 | 13208 | 11.9.62 | 13272 | 20.7.62 | 13336 | 19.7.63 | 13400 | 13.2.63 |
| 13081 | 16.2.63 | 13145 | 21.12.62 | 13209 | 18.9.62 | 13273 | 24.7.62 | 13337 | 7.8.63 | 13401 | 13.2.63 |
| 13082 | 23.2.63 | 13146 | 18.12.62 | 13210 | 3.11.62 | 13274 | 17.8.62 | 13338 | 19.7.63 | 13402 | 19.2.63 |
| 13083 | 23.2.63 | 13147 | 25.1.63 | 13211 | 26.10.62 | 13275 | 28.8.62 | 13339 | 9.8.63 | 13403 | 22.2.63 |
| 13084 | 23.2.63 | 13148 | 1.2.63 | 13212 | 2.11.62 | 13276 | 31.8.62 | 13340 | 9.8.63 | 13404 | 19.2.63 |
| 13085 | 23.2.63 | 13149 | 28.2.63 | 13213 | 28.12.62 | 13277 | 31.8.62 | 13341 | 9.8.63 | 13405 | 22.2.63 |
| 13086 | 2.3.63 | 13150 | 25.2.63 | 13214 | 28.12.62 | 13278 | 7.9.62 | 13342 | 6.12.62 | 13406 | 26.7.63 |
| 13087 | 30.3.63 | 13151 | 1.3.63 | 13215 | 4.1.63 | 13279 | 7.9.62 | 13343 | 14.12.62 | 13407 | 30.8.63 |
| 13088 | 30.3.63 | 13152 | 25.1.63 | 13216 | 28.12.62 | 13280 | 5.10.62 | 13344 | 14.12.62 | 13408 | 30.8.63 |
| 13089 | 22.3.63 | 13153 | 1.2.63 | 13217 | 11.1.63 | 13281 | 5.10.62 | 13345 | 21.12.62 | 13409 | 30.8.63 |
| 13090 | 16.3.63 | 13154 | 15.2.63 | 13218 | 18.1.63 | 13282 | 9.10.62 | 13346 | 17.12.62 | 13410 | 6.9.63 |
| 13091 | 22.3.63 | 13155 | 15.2.63 | 13219 | 6.2.63 | 13283 | 23.10.62 | 13347 | 6.2.63 | 13411 | 20.9.63 |
| 13092 | 9.4.63 | 13156 | 5.3.63 | 13220 | 8.2.63 | 13284 | 26.10.62 | 13348 | 15.2.63 | 13412 | 26.4.63 |
| 13093 | 30.3.63 | 13157 | 5.3.63 | 13221 | 6.2.63 | 13285 | 7.9.62 | 13349 | 19.2.63 | 13413 | 30.4.63 |
| 13094 | 30.3.63 | 13158 | 8.3.63 | 13222 | 15.2.63 | 13286 | 14.9.62 | 13350 | 22.2.63 | 13414 | 3.5.63 |
| 13095 | 31.8.62 | 13159 | 8.3.63 | 13223 | 15.2.63 | 13287 | 14.9.62 | 13351 | 1.3.63 | 13415 | 25.10.63 |
| 13096 | 11.9.62 | 13160 | 15.3.63 | 13224 | 22.2.63 | 13288 | 14.9.62 | 13352 | 25.2.63 | 13416 | 25.10.63 |
| 13097 | 14.9.62 | 13161 | 29.3.63 | 13225 | 29.3.63 | 13289 | 19.7.62 | 13353 | 1.5.63 | 13417 | 1.11.63 |
| 13098 | 11.7.62 | 13162 | 22.3.63 | 13226 | 5.4.63 | 13290 | 19.7.62 | 13354 | 24.5.63 | 13418 | 9.11.62 |
| 13099 | 12.7.62 | 13163 | 11.4.63 | 13227 | 17.8.62 | 13291 | 25.7.62 | 13355 | 23.5.63 | 13419 | 9.11.62 |
| 13100 | 11.7.62 | 13164 | 5.4.63 | 13228 | 24.8.62 | 13292 | 26.7.62 | 13356 | 7.6.63 | 13420 | 27.11.62 |
| 13101 | 12.7.62 | 13165 | 27.7.62 | 13229 | 24.8.62 | 13293 | 26.7.62 | 13357 | 7.6.63 | 13421 | 30.11.62 |
| 13102 | 19.7.62 | 13166 | 27.7.62 | 13230 | 28.8.62 | 13294 | 7.9.62 | 13358 | 5.7.63 | 13422 | 4.12.62 |
| 13103 | 15.11.62 | 13167 | 27.7.62 | 13231 | 31.8.62 | 13295 | 14.9.62 | 13359 | 5.7.63 | 13423 | 14.12.62 |
| 13104 | 28.11.62 | 13168 | 17.8.62 | 13232 | 2.11.62 | 13296 | 21.9.62 | 13360 | 9.7.63 | 13424 | 28.12.62 |
| 13105 | 15.11.62 | 13169 | 31.8.62 | 13233 | 2.11.62 | 13297 | 19.10.62 | 13361 | 9.7.63 | 13425 | 28.12.62 |
| 13106 | 20.11.62 | 13170 | 2.11.62 | 13234 | 9.11.62 | 13298 | 28.10.62 | 13362 | 12.7.63 | 13426 | 28.12.62 |
| 13107 | 20.11.62 | 13171 | 2.11.62 | 13235 | 10.1.63 | 13299 | 19.10.62 | 13363 | 12.7.63 | 13427 | 4.1.63 |
| 13108 | 5.3.63 | 13172 | 21.12.62 | 13236 | 25.1.63 | 13300 | 26.10.62 | 13364 | 3.9.63 | 13428 | 4.1.63 |
| 13109 | 5.3.63 | 13173 | 28.12.62 | 13237 | 5.4.63 | 13301 | 26.10.62 | 13365 | 5.9.63 | 13429 | 11.1.63 |
| 13110 | 8.3.63 | 13174 | 15.1.63 | 13238 | 5.4.63 | 13302 | 26.10.62 | 13366 | 5.9.63 | 13430 | 15.3.63 |
| 13111 | 20.3.63 | 13175 | 11.1.63 | 13239 | 4.7.62 | 13303 | 27.10.62 | 13367 | 10.9.63 | 13431 | 15.3.63 |
| 13112 | 20.3.63 | 13176 | 22.3.63 | 13240 | 29.6.62 | 13304 | 27.10.62 | 13368 | 13.9.63 | 13432 | 22.3.63 |
| 13113 | 26.7.62 | 13177 | 3.4.63 | 13241 | 4.7.62 | 13305 | 3.11.62 | 13369 | 13.9.63 | 13433 | 5.4.63 |
| 13114 | 26.7.62 | 13178 | 20.7.62 | 13242 | 6.7.62 | 13306 | 3.11.62 | 13370 | 20.9.63 | 13434 | 22.3.63 |
| 13115 | 20.7.62 | 13179 | 20.7.62 | 13243 | 11.7.62 | 13307 | 3.11.62 | 13371 | 30.9.63 | 13435 | 29.3.63 |
| 13116 | 19.10.62 | 13180 | 25.7.62 | 13244 | 31.8.62 | 13308 | 10.11.62 | 13372 | 4.1.63 | 13436 | 26.4.63 |
| 13117 | 1.11.62 | 13181 | 26.7.62 | 13245 | 8.9.62 | 13309 | 10.11.62 | 13373 | 4.1.63 | 13437 | 17.5.63 |
| 13118 | 1.11.62 | 13182 | 17.8.62 | 13246 | 8.9.62 | 13310 | 10.11.62 | 13374 | 4.1.63 | 13438 | 7.6.63 |
| 13119 | 7.12.62 | 13183 | 9.1.63 | 13247 | 26.10.62 | 13311 | 19.1.63 | 13375 | 4.1.63 | 13439 | 31.5.63 |
| 13120 | 7.12.62 | 13184 | 11.1.63 | 13248 | 26.10.62 | 13312 | 19.1.63 | 13376 | 11.1.63 | 13440 | 7.6.63 |
| 13121 | 13.12.62 | 13185 | 11.1.63 | 13249 | 2.11.62 | 13313 | 19.1.63 | 13377 | 4.1.63 | 13441 | 7.6.63 |
| 13122 | 14.12.62 | 13186 | 11.1.63 | 13250 | 22.2.63 | 13314 | 19.1.63 | 13378 | 5.4.63 | 13442 | 14.6.63 |
| 13123 | 17.12.62 | 13187 | 9.1.63 | 13251 | 22.2.63 | 13315 | 2.3.63 | 13379 | 5.4.63 | 13443 | 14.6.63 |
| 13124 | 21.12.62 | 13188 | 1.8.62 | 13252 | 22.2.63 | 13316 | 2.3.63 | 13380 | 29.3.63 | 13444 | 7.6.63 |

| | | | | | | | | | | |
|---|---|---|---|---|---|---|---|---|---|---|
| 13445 | 16.8.63 | 13509 | 25.5.62 | 13573 | 23.7.62 | 13637 | 24.12.62 | 13701 | 1.2.63 | 13765 | 20.1.64 |
| 13446 | 16.8.63 | 13510 | 25.5.62 | 13574 | 18.5.62 | 13638 | 11.4.63 | 13702 | 1.2.63 | 13766 | 27.1.64 |
| 13447 | 16.8.63 | 13511 | 15.6.62 | 13575 | 10.5.62 | 13639 | 9.4.63 | 13703 | 29.11.62 | 13767 | 27.1.64 |
| 13448 | 23.8.63 | 13512 | 8.6.62 | 13576 | 10.5.62 | 13640 | 9.4.63 | 13704 | 29.11.62 | 13768 | 27.8.64 |
| 13449 | 16.8.63 | 13513 | 8.6.62 | 13577 | 18.5.62 | 13641 | 5.4.63 | 13705 | 29.11.62 | 13769 | 29.8.64 |
| 13450 | 23.8.63 | 13514 | 15.6.62 | 13578 | 17.5.62 | 13642 | 5.4.63 | 13706 | 14.2.63 | 13770 | 27.8.64 |
| 13451 | 13.9.63 | 13515 | 19.6.62 | 13579 | 17.5.62 | 13643 | 11.4.63 | 13707 | 15.2.63 | 13771 | 4.9.64 |
| 13452 | | 13516 | 22.6.62 | 13580 | 17.5.62 | 13644 | 30.5.63 | 13708 | 19.10.63 | 13772 | 4.9.64 |
| 13453 | 21.5.63 | 13517 | 22.6.62 | 13581 | 23.5.62 | 13645 | 30.5.63 | 13709 | 2.11.63 | 13773 | 21.10.63 |
| 13454 | 21.5.63 | 13518 | 22.6.62 | 13582 | 23.5.62 | 13646 | 31.5.63 | 13710 | 2.11.63 | 13774 | 21.10.63 |
| 13455 | 14.6.63 | 13519 | 23.2.62 | 13583 | 1.6.62 | 13647 | 31.5.63 | 13711 | 2.11.63 | 13775 | 16.3.64 |
| 13456 | 18.6.63 | 13520 | 23.2.62 | 13584 | 1.6.62 | 13648 | 24.5.63 | 13712 | 6.11.63 | 13776 | 16.3.64 |
| 13457 | 18.6.63 | 13521 | 23.2.62 | 13585 | 1.6.62 | 13649 | 17.5.63 | 13713 | 6.11.63 | 13777 | 15.7.64 |
| 13458 | 21.6.63 | 13522 | 27.2.62 | 13586 | 7.6.62 | 13650 | 17.5.63 | 13714 | 25.1.64 | 13778 | 16.8.63 |
| 13459 | 11.1.63 | 13523 | 27.2.62 | 13587 | 7.6.62 | 13651 | 24.5.63 | 13715 | 25.1.64 | 13779 | 16.8.63 |
| 13460 | 11.1.63 | 13524 | 7.3.62 | 13588 | 7.6.62 | 13652 | 20.5.63 | 13716 | 25.1.64 | 13780 | 20.9.63 |
| 13461 | 15.1.63 | 13525 | 7.3.62 | 13589 | 27.6.62 | 13653 | 31.5.63 | 13717 | 15.2.64 | 13781 | 27.9.63 |
| 13462 | 15.1.63 | 13526 | 7.3.62 | 13590 | 20.7.62 | 13654 | 14.11.62 | 13718 | 14.12.63 | 13782 | 4.10.63 |
| 13463 | 18.1.63 | 13527 | 13.3.62 | 13591 | 20.7.62 | 13655 | 14.11.62 | 13719 | 18.1.64 | 13783 | 8.10.63 |
| 13464 | 18.1.63 | 13528 | 13.3.62 | 13592 | 20.7.62 | 13656 | 14.11.62 | 13720 | 18.1.64 | 13784 | 3.10.63 |
| 13465 | 26.4.63 | 13529 | 13.3.62 | 13593 | 18.7.62 | 13657 | 20.11.62 | 13721 | 6.11.63 | 13785 | 25.10.63 |
| 13466 | 10.5.63 | 13530 | 16.3.62 | 13594 | 18.7.62 | 13658 | 23.11.62 | 13722 | 8.11.63 | 13786 | 1.11.63 |
| 13467 | 10.5.63 | 13531 | 16.3.62 | 13595 | 11.7.62 | 13659 | 14.12.62 | 13723 | 15.11.63 | 13787 | 1.11.63 |
| 13468 | 31.5.63 | 13532 | 16.3.62 | 13596 | 18.7.62 | 13660 | 21.12.62 | 13724 | 8.11.63 | 13788 | 1.11.63 |
| 13469 | 28.6.63 | 13533 | 23.3.62 | 13597 | 18.7.62 | 13661 | 21.12.62 | 13725 | 29.11.63 | 13789 | 29.11.63 |
| 13470 | 2.7.63 | 13534 | 20.3.62 | 13598 | 27.7.62 | 13662 | 21.12.62 | 13726 | 29.11.63 | 13790 | 5.12.63 |
| 13471 | 2.7.63 | 13535 | 23.3.62 | 13599 | 27.7.62 | 13663 | 19.2.63 | 13727 | 22.11.63 | 13791 | 6.12.63 |
| 13472 | 2.7.63 | 13536 | 23.3.62 | 13600 | 19.2.63 | 13664 | 19.2.63 | 13728 | 8.1.63 | 13792 | 10.1.64 |
| 13473 | 5.7.63 | 13537 | 20.3.62 | 13601 | 6.3.63 | 13665 | 21.2.63 | 13729 | 14.12.63 | 13793 | 10.1.64 |
| 13474 | 9.7.63 | 13538 | 27.3.62 | 13602 | 22.2.63 | 13666 | 21.2.63 | 13730 | 4.1.64 | 13794 | 14.1.64 |
| 13475 | 4.10.63 | 13539 | 20.3.62 | 13603 | 22.2.63 | 13667 | 2.3.63 | 13731 | 11.1.64 | 13795 | 21.4.64 |
| 13476 | 4.10.63 | 13540 | 27.3.62 | 13604 | 1.3.63 | 13668 | 8.3.63 | 13732 | 11.1.64 | 13796 | 23.4.64 |
| 13477 | 11.10.63 | 13541 | 27.3.62 | 13605 | 15.3.63 | 13669 | 8.3.63 | 13733 | 29.11.63 | 13797 | 22.6.64 |
| 13478 | 11.10.63 | 13542 | 30.3.62 | 13606 | 8.3.63 | 13670 | 23.4.63 | 13734 | 29.11.63 | 13798 | 22.6.64 |
| 13479 | 13.10.62 | 13543 | 30.3.62 | 13607 | 15.3.63 | 13671 | 23.4.63 | 13735 | 3.4.64 | 13799 | 2.7.64 |
| 13480 | 13.10.62 | 13544 | 13.4.62 | 13608 | 22.3.63 | 13672 | 23.4.63 | 13736 | 2.10.63 | 13800 | 3.7.64 |
| 13481 | 13.10.62 | 13545 | 3.4.62 | 13609 | 12.3.63 | 13673 | 30.4.63 | 13737 | | 13801 | 9.7.64 |
| 13482 | 19.10.62 | 13546 | 13.4.62 | 13610 | 19.3.63 | 13674 | 14.5.63 | 13738 | 31.12.63 | 13802 | 23.7.64 |
| 13483 | 19.10.62 | 13547 | 3.4.62 | 13611 | 26.3.63 | 13675 | 28.12.62 | 13739 | 31.12.63 | 13803 | 30.8.63 |
| 13484 | 26.10.62 | 13548 | 17.4.62 | 13612 | 22.3.63 | 13676 | 28.12.62 | 13740 | 13.12.63 | 13804 | 23.8.63 |
| 13485 | 2.11.62 | 13549 | 16.4.62 | 13613 | 26.3.63 | 13677 | 28.12.62 | 13741 | 13.12.63 | 13805 | 6.9.63 |
| 13486 | 26.10.62 | 13550 | 19.4.62 | 13614 | 26.3.63 | 13678 | 8.1.63 | 13742 | 26.3.64 | 13806 | 15.11.63 |
| 13487 | 30.10.62 | 13551 | 3.5.62 | 13615 | 5.4.63 | 13679 | 31.12.62 | 13743 | 9.4.63 | 13807 | 22.11.63 |
| 13488 | 13.4.62 | 13552 | 7.5.62 | 13616 | 9.4.63 | 13680 | 15.3.63 | 13744 | 10.9.63 | 13808 | 22.11.63 |
| 13489 | 19.4.62 | 13553 | 17.5.62 | 13617 | 11.4.63 | 13681 | 15.3.63 | 13745 | 10.9.63 | 13809 | 20.12.63 |
| 13490 | 27.4.62 | 13554 | 14.5.62 | 13618 | 18.4.63 | 13682 | 20.3.63 | 13746 | 13.9.63 | 13810 | 17.12.63 |
| 13491 | 2.5.62 | 13555 | 7.5.62 | 13619 | 11.4.63 | 13683 | 29.3.63 | 13747 | 12.6.64 | 13811 | 17.12.63 |
| 13492 | 9.5.62 | 13556 | 17.5.62 | 13620 | 7.5.63 | 13684 | 29.3.63 | 13748 | 12.6.64 | 13812 | 20.12.63 |
| 13493 | 15.5.62 | 13557 | 21.5.62 | 13621 | 7.5.63 | 13685 | 19.2.63 | 13749 | 16.8.63 | 13813 | 20.3.64 |
| 13494 | 27.3.62 | 13558 | 24.5.62 | 13622 | 10.5.63 | 13686 | 21.2.63 | 13750 | 26.7.63 | 13814 | 13.3.64 |
| 13495 | 27.3.62 | 13559 | 24.5.62 | 13623 | 17.5.63 | 13687 | 23.2.63 | 13751 | 16.8.63 | 13815 | 17.7.64 |
| 13496 | 30.3.62 | 13560 | 24.5.62 | 13624 | 13.5.63 | 13688 | 23.2.63 | 13752 | 11.10.63 | 13816 | 24.7.64 |
| 13497 | 3.4.62 | 13561 | 28.5.62 | 13625 | 23.5.63 | 13689 | 23.2.63 | 13753 | 11.10.63 | 13817 | 14.8.64 |
| 13498 | 27.3.62 | 13562 | 18.6.62 | 13626 | 22.11.63 | 13690 | 25.2.63 | 13754 | 15.10.63 | 13818 | 14.8.64 |
| 13499 | 13.4.62 | 13563 | 19.6.62 | 13627 | 28.11.63 | 13691 | 26.2.63 | 13755 | 15.10.63 | 13819 | 22.11.63 |
| 13500 | 13.4.62 | 13564 | 18.6.62 | 13628 | 6.12.63 | 13692 | 3.5.63 | 13756 | 18.10.63 | 13820 | 26.11.63 |
| 13501 | 18.4.62 | 13565 | 19.6.62 | 13629 | 14.12.63 | 13693 | 26.4.63 | 13757 | 4.11.63 | 13821 | 17.4.64 |
| 13502 | 18.4.62 | 13566 | 25.6.62 | 13630 | 29.11.62 | 13694 | 17.5.63 | 13758 | 25.10.63 | 13822 | 17.4.64 |
| 13503 | 19.4.62 | 13567 | 25.6.62 | 13631 | 27.11.62 | 13695 | 28.5.63 | 13759 | 8.11.63 | 13823 | 21.4.64 |
| 13504 | 27.4.62 | 13568 | 4.7.62 | 13632 | 21.12.62 | 13696 | 21.5.63 | 13760 | 14.11.63 | 13824 | 24.4.64 |
| 13505 | 1.5.62 | 13569 | 11.7.62 | 13633 | 29.11.62 | 13697 | 29.1.63 | 13761 | 14.11.63 | 13825 | 13.9.63 |
| 13506 | 27.4.62 | 13570 | 19.7.62 | 13634 | 21.12.62 | 13698 | 25.1.63 | 13762 | 30.12.63 | 13826 | 20.9.63 |
| 13507 | 11.5.62 | 13571 | 12.7.62 | 13635 | 21.12.62 | 13699 | 25.1.63 | 13763 | 30.12.63 | 13827 | 20.9.63 |
| 13508 | 25.5.62 | 13572 | 23.7.62 | 13636 | 21.12.62 | 13700 | 1.2.63 | 13764 | 20.1.64 | 13828 | 20.11.63 |

| | | | | | | | | | | | |
|---|---|---|---|---|---|---|---|---|---|---|---|
| 13829 | 14.12.63 | 13893 | 21.12.63 | 13957 | 12.3.64 | 14021 | 1.5.64 | 14085 | 29.6.64 | 14149 | 28.2.6 |
| 13830 | 4.1.64 | 13894 | 21.12.63 | 13958 | 16.3.64 | 14022 | 4.9.64 | 14086 | 7.7.64 | 14150 | 2.3.64 |
| 13831 | 11.1.64 | 13895 | 4.1.64 | 13959 | 5.3.64 | 14023 | 28.8.64 | 14087 | 7.7.64 | 14151 | 2.3.64 |
| 13832 | 12.6.64 | 13896 | 22.5.64 | 13960 | 23.5.64 | 14024 | 28.8.64 | 14088 | 13.7.64 | 14152 | 28.2.6 |
| 13833 | 12.6.64 | 13897 | 6.6.64 | 13961 | 8.5.64 | 14025 | 4.9.64 | 14089 | 25.9.64 | 14153 | 19.2.6 |
| 13834 | 25.8.64 | 13898 | 20.6.64 | 13962 | 20.5.64 | 14026 | 4.10.63 | 14090 | 2.10.64 | 14154 | 19.2.6 |
| 13835 | 25.8.64 | 13899 | 20.6.64 | 13963 | 15.5.64 | 14027 | 27.9.63 | 14091 | 2.10.64 | 14155 | 21.2.6 |
| 13836 | 6.9.63 | 13900 | 20.6.64 | 13964 | 15.5.64 | 14028 | 22.11.63 | 14092 | 9.10.64 | 14156 | 14.2.6 |
| 13837 | 30.8.63 | 13901 | 18.7.64 | 13965 | 14.7.64 | 14029 | 26.11.63 | 14093 | 10.10.64 | 14157 | 14.2.6 |
| 13838 | 6.9.63 | 13902 | 6.4.63 | 13966 | 15.7.64 | 14030 | 7.2.64 | 14094 | 4.11.63 | 14158 | 17.1.64 |
| 13839 | 20.9.63 | 13903 | 9.4.63 | 13967 | 15.7.64 | 14031 | 7.2.64 | 14095 | 7.11.63 | 14159 | 21.2.64 |
| 13840 | 20.9.63 | 13904 | 6.4.63 | 13968 | 24.7.64 | 14032 | 21.4.64 | 14096 | 18.6.64 | 14160 | 21.2.64 |
| 13841 | 18.10.63 | 13905 | 20.9.63 | 13969 | 24.7.64 | 14033 | 11.9.64 | 14097 | 26.6.64 | 14161 | 18.3.64 |
| 13842 | 25.10.63 | 13906 | 20.9.63 | 13970 | 27.7.64 | 14034 | 4.9.64 | 14098 | 16.10.64 | 14162 | 10.1.64 |
| 13843 | 25.10.63 | 13907 | 15.2.64 | 13971 | 21.8.64 | 14035 | 11.10.63 | 14099 | 26.11.63 | 14163 | 14.1.64 |
| 13844 | 27.11.63 | 13908 | 15.2.64 | 13972 | 13.8.64 | 14036 | 11.10.63 | 14100 | 28.11.63 | 14164 | 10.1.64 |
| 13845 | 4.12.63 | 13909 | 1.2.64 | 13973 | 14.8.64 | 14037 | 25.10.63 | 14101 | 29.11.63 | 14165 | 17.1.64 |
| 13846 | 17.1.64 | 13910 | 6.2.64 | 13974 | 25.10.63 | 14038 | 25.10.63 | 14102 | 6.12.63 | 14166 | 28.1.64 |
| 13847 | 22.1.64 | 13911 | 8.2.64 | 13975 | 25.10.63 | 14039 | 15.11.63 | 14103 | 4.2.64 | 14167 | 13.3.64 |
| 13848 | 29.1.64 | 13912 | 15.2.64 | 13976 | 18.10.63 | 14040 | 8.11.63 | 14104 | 30.1.64 | 14168 | 13.3.64 |
| 13849 | 29.1.64 | 13913 | 21.3.64 | 13977 | 18.10.63 | 14041 | 22.12.63 | 14105 | 5.2.64 | 14169 | 10.3.64 |
| 13850 | 30.1.64 | 13914 | 18.4.64 | 13978 | 10.12.63 | 14042 | 29.11.63 | 14106 | 17.2.64 | 14170 | 20.3.64 |
| 13851 | 1.5.64 | 13915 | 18.4.64 | 13979 | 10.12.63 | 14043 | 29.11.63 | 14107 | 17.7.64 | 14171 | 20.3.64 |
| 13852 | 8.5.64 | 13916 | 25.4.64 | 13980 | 10.7.64 | 14044 | 9.1.64 | 14108 | 17.7.64 | 14172 | 14.11.63 |
| 13853 | 17.8.64 | 13917 | 27.6.64 | 13981 | 21.8.64 | 14045 | 17.1.64 | 14109 | 21.7.64 | 14173 | 14.11.63 |
| 13854 | 24.7.64 | 13918 | 4.7.64 | 13982 | 11.10.63 | 14046 | 17.1.64 | 14110 | 23.7.64 | 14174 | 11.9.64 |
| 13855 | 17.8.64 | 13919 | 11.7.64 | 13983 | 11.10.63 | 14047 | 23.1.64 | 14111 | 8.10.64 | 14175 | 11.9.64 |
| 13856 | 21.8.64 | 13920 | 11.7.64 | 13984 | 22.11.63 | 14048 | 5.3.64 | 14112 | 9.10.64 | 14176 | 20.10.64 |
| 13857 | 19.8.64 | 13921 | 18.7.64 | 13985 | 22.11.63 | 14049 | 13.3.64 | 14113 | 19.11.64 | 14177 | 20.10.64 |
| 13858 | 27.9.63 | 13922 | 24.7.64 | 13986 | 31.1.64 | 14050 | 20.3.64 | 14114 | 17.11.64 | 14178 | 30.10.64 |
| 13859 | 4.10.63 | 13923 | 18.7.64 | 13987 | 31.1.64 | 14051 | 25.3.64 | 14115 | 8.1.64 | 14179 | |
| 13860 | 27.9.63 | 13924 | 24.7.64 | 13988 | 28.8.64 | 14052 | 15.5.64 | 14116 | 10.1.64 | 14180 | |
| 13861 | 29.11.63 | 13925 | 24.7.64 | 13989 | 1.11.63 | 14053 | 22.5.64 | 14117 | 17.1.64 | 14181 | |
| 13862 | 29.11.63 | 13926 | 15.8.64 | 13990 | 1.11.63 | 14054 | 22.5.64 | 14118 | 14.1.64 | 14182 | 29.9.64 |
| 13863 | 3.1.64 | 13927 | 1.11.63 | 13991 | 7.2.64 | 14055 | 14.8.64 | 14119 | 7.2.64 | 14183 | 29.9.64 |
| 13864 | 3.1.64 | 13928 | 1.11.63 | 13992 | 7.2.64 | 14056 | 11.9.64 | 14120 | 14.2.64 | 14184 | 16.10.64 |
| 13865 | 10.1.64 | 13929 | 1.11.63 | 13993 | 21.7.64 | 14057 | 11.9.64 | 14121 | 4.9.64 | 14185 | 30.10.64 |
| 13866 | 10.1.64 | 13930 | 10.11.63 | 13994 | 29.8.64 | 14058 | 18.9.64 | 14122 | 11.9.64 | 14186 | 19.9.64 |
| 13867 | 15.5.64 | 13931 | 10.11.63 | 13995 | 11.10.63 | 14059 | 11.9.64 | 14123 | 18.9.64 | 14187 | 19.9.64 |
| 13868 | 28.8.64 | 13932 | 13.2.64 | 13996 | 18.10.63 | 14060 | 17.9.64 | 14124 | 19.9.64 | 14188 | 2.10.64 |
| 13869 | 28.8.64 | 13933 | 13.2.64 | 13997 | 18.10.63 | 14061 | 11.10.63 | 14125 | 30.10.64 | 14189 | 18.9.64 |
| 13870 | 28.8.64 | 13934 | 17.2.64 | 13998 | 31.1.64 | 14062 | 8.10.63 | 14126 | 30.10.64 | 14190 | 18.9.64 |
| 13871 | 18.10.63 | 13935 | 3.2.64 | 13999 | 31.1.64 | 14063 | 10.4.64 | 14127 | 30.10.64 | 14191 | 18.9.64 |
| 13872 | 1.11.63 | 13936 | 15.11.63 | 14000 | 7.2.64 | 14064 | 17.4.64 | 14128 | 10.11.64 | 14192 | 20.9.64 |
| 13873 | 8.11.63 | 13937 | 15.11.63 | 14001 | 7.2.64 | 14065 | 14.8.64 | 14129 | 14.11.63 | 14193 | 25.9.64 |
| 13874 | 17.4.64 | 13938 | 30.8.63 | 14002 | 29.8.64 | 14066 | 8.9.64 | 14130 | 14.11.63 | 14194 | 25.9.64 |
| 13875 | 4.9.64 | 13939 | 30.8.63 | 14003 | 22.8.64 | 14067 | 11.1.64 | 14131 | 28.1.64 | 14195 | 2.10.64 |
| 13876 | 4.12.63 | 13940 | 30.8.63 | 14004 | 13.9.63 | 14068 | 21.12.63 | 14132 | 28.1.64 | 14196 | 2.10.64 |
| 13877 | 4.12.63 | 13941 | 6.9.63 | 14005 | 13.9.63 | 14069 | 21.12.63 | 14133 | 30.1.64 | 14197 | 9.10.64 |
| 13878 | 13.12.63 | 13942 | 27.9.63 | 14006 | 13.9.63 | 14070 | 4.1.64 | 14134 | 30.1.64 | 14198 | 9.10.64 |
| 13879 | 13.12.63 | 13943 | 24.9.63 | 14007 | 13.9.63 | 14071 | 18.1.64 | 14135 | 22.2.64 | 14199 | 9.10.64 |
| 13880 | 21.5.64 | 13944 | 22.10.63 | 14008 | 8.11.63 | 14072 | 25.1.64 | 14136 | 26.5.64 | 14200 | 9.10.64 |
| 13881 | 22.5.64 | 13945 | 22.10.63 | 14009 | 8.11.63 | 14073 | 1.2.64 | 14137 | 5.6.64 | 14201 | 16.10.64 |
| 13882 | 22.5.64 | 13946 | 25.10.63 | 14010 | 8.11.63 | 14074 | 8.2.64 | 14138 | 12.6.64 | 14202 | 16.10.64 |
| 13883 | 8.9.64 | 13947 | 12.11.63 | 14011 | 13.12.63 | 14075 | 15.8.64 | 14139 | 12.12.63 | 14203 | 30.10.64 |
| 13884 | 20.9.63 | 13948 | 28.11.63 | 14012 | 13.12.63 | 14076 | 22.8.64 | 14140 | 24.1.64 | 14204 | 30.10.64 |
| 13885 | 20.9.63 | 13949 | 3.12.63 | 14013 | 20.12.63 | 14077 | 22.8.64 | 14141 | 26.6.64 | 14205 | 30.10.64 |
| 13886 | 27.9.63 | 13950 | 4.12.63 | 14014 | 20.12.63 | 14078 | 5.9.64 | 14142 | 3.7.64 | 14206 | 3.11.64 |
| 13887 | 4.10.63 | 13951 | 6.12.63 | 14015 | 8.1.64 | 14079 | 7.11.64 | 14143 | 16.10.64 | 14207 | 3.11.64 |
| 13888 | 4.10.63 | 13952 | 12.12.63 | 14016 | 10.1.64 | 14080 | 7.11.64 | 14144 | 29.10.64 | 14208 | 6.11.64 |
| 13889 | 4.10.63 | 13953 | 12.12.63 | 14017 | 8.1.64 | 14081 | 30.1.64 | 14145 | 24.1.64 | 14209 | 6.11.64 |
| 13890 | 18.1.64 | 13954 | 20.12.63 | 14018 | 8.1.64 | 14082 | 1.2.64 | 14146 | 24.1.64 | 14210 | 13.11.64 |
| 13891 | 22.11.63 | 13955 | 3.1.64 | 14019 | 24.4.64 | 14083 | 18.2.64 | 14147 | 27.2.64 | 14211 | 13.11.64 |
| 13892 | 21.12.63 | 13956 | 7.1.64 | 14020 | 1.5.64 | 14084 | 1.2.64 | 14148 | 28.2.64 | 14212 | 13.11.64 |

| | | | | | | | | | | | |
|---|---|---|---|---|---|---|---|---|---|---|---|
| 14213 | 24.11.64 | 14277 | 29.5.63 | 14341 | 27.3.64 | 14405 | 29.5.64 | 14469 | 20.3.64 | 14533 | 18.12.64 |
| 14214 | 11.9.64 | 14278 | 10.6.63 | 14342 | 1.6.64 | 14406 | 29.5.64 | 14470 | 9.6.64 | 14534 | 18.12.64 |
| 14215 | 11.9.64 | 14279 | 29.5.63 | 14343 | 21.2.64 | 14407 | 29.5.64 | 14471 | 12.6.64 | 14535 | 18.12.64 |
| 14216 | 18.9.64 | 14280 | 29.5.63 | 14344 | 21.2.64 | 14408 | 29.5.64 | 14472 | 2.5.64 | 14536 | 11.12.64 |
| 14217 | 23.8.63 | 14281 | 10.6.63 | 14345 | 28.2.64 | 14409 | 5.6.64 | 14473 | 6.5.64 | 14537 | 11.12.64 |
| 14218 | 23.8.63 | 14282 | 14.6.63 | 14346 | 28.2.64 | 14410 | 9.6.64 | 14474 | 9.5.64 | 14538 | 16.12.64 |
| 14219 | 23.8.63 | 14283 | 14.6.63 | 14347 | 6.3.64 | 14411 | 12.6.64 | 14475 | 9.5.64 | 14539 | 16.12.64 |
| 14220 | 5.9.63 | 14284 | 14.6.63 | 14348 | 6.3.64 | 14412 | 16.6.64 | 14476 | 30.5.64 | 14540 | 27.11.64 |
| 14221 | 25.6.63 | 14285 | 21.6.63 | 14349 | 6.3.64 | 14413 | 16.6.64 | 14477 | 13.6.64 | 14541 | 27.11.64 |
| 14222 | 28.6.63 | 14286 | 5.7.63 | 14350 | 13.3.64 | 14414 | 19.6.64 | 14478 | 13.6.64 | 14542 | 4.12.64 |
| 14223 | 5.7.63 | 14287 | 28.6.63 | 14351 | 20.3.64 | 14415 | 26.6.64 | 14479 | 20.6.64 | 14543 | 4.12.64 |
| 14224 | 9.7.63 | 14288 | 5.7.63 | 14352 | 20.3.64 | 14416 | 23.6.64 | 14480 | 20.6.64 | 14544 | 4.12.64 |
| 14225 | 12.7.63 | 14289 | 5.7.63 | 14353 | 20.3.64 | 14417 | 26.6.64 | 14481 | 25.6.64 | 14545 | 9.12.64 |
| 14226 | 19.7.63 | 14290 | 12.7.63 | 14354 | 3.4.64 | 14418 | 26.6.64 | 14482 | 28.4.64 | 14546 | 9.12.64 |
| 14227 | 17.5.63 | 14291 | 12.7.63 | 14355 | 3.4.64 | 14419 | 30.6.64 | 14483 | 28.4.64 | 14547 | 11.12.64 |
| 14228 | 17.5.63 | 14292 | 12.7.63 | 14356 | 8.4.64 | 14420 | 30.6.64 | 14484 | 13.6.64 | 14548 | 11.12.64 |
| 14229 | 24.5.63 | 14293 | 12.7.63 | 14357 | 3.4.64 | 14421 | 3.7.64 | 14485 | 16.6.64 | 14549 | 11.12.64 |
| 14230 | 6.6.63 | 14294 | 19.7.63 | 14358 | 3.4.64 | 14422 | 7.7.64 | 14486 | 26.6.64 | 14550 | 18.12.64 |
| 14231 | 24.5.63 | 14295 | 19.7.63 | 14359 | 8.4.64 | 14423 | 7.7.64 | 14487 | 29.6.64 | 14551 | 14.11.64 |
| 14232 | 6.6.63 | 14296 | 19.7.63 | 14360 | 8.4.64 | 14424 | 7.7.64 | 14488 | 30.5.64 | 14552 | 21.11.64 |
| 14233 | 11.6.63 | 14297 | 19.7.63 | 14361 | 1.5.64 | 14425 | 25.2.64 | 14489 | 9.6.64 | 14553 | 17.10.64 |
| 14234 | 25.6.63 | 14298 | 11.8.63 | 14362 | 1.5.64 | 14426 | 25.2.64 | 14490 | 30.5.64 | 14554 | 31.10.64 |
| 14235 | 19.4.63 | 14299 | 11.8.63 | 14363 | 8.5.64 | 14427 | 25.2.64 | 14491 | 9.6.64 | 14555 | 31.10.64 |
| 14236 | 22.4.63 | 14300 | 11.8.63 | 14364 | 8.5.64 | 14428 | 28.2.64 | 14492 | 29.5.64 | 14556 | 7.11.64 |
| 14237 | 30.4.63 | 14301 | 23.8.63 | 14365 | 8.5.64 | 14429 | 28.2.64 | 14493 | 26.5.64 | 14557 | 26.9.64 |
| 14238 | 6.5.63 | 14302 | 23.8.63 | 14366 | 29.5.64 | 14430 | 28.2.64 | 14494 | 6.6.64 | 14558 | 26.9.64 |
| 14239 | 6.5.63 | 14303 | 23.8.63 | 14367 | 29.5.64 | 14431 | 13.3.64 | 14495 | 6.6.64 | 14559 | 26.9.64 |
| 14240 | 8.5.63 | 14304 | 23.8.63 | 14368 | 5.6.64 | 14432 | 31.3.64 | 14496 | 28.4.64 | 14560 | 26.9.64 |
| 14241 | 16.5.63 | 14305 | 23.8.63 | 14369 | 5.6.64 | 14433 | 20.3.64 | 14497 | 16.5.64 | 14561 | 26.9.64 |
| 14242 | 16.5.63 | 14306 | 30.8.63 | 14370 | 5.6.64 | 14434 | 20.3.64 | 14498 | 23.5.64 | 14562 | 21.11.64 |
| 14243 | 27.5.63 | 14307 | 30.8.63 | 14371 | 12.6.64 | 14435 | 27.3.64 | 14499 | 23.5.64 | 14563 | 28.11.64 |
| 14244 | 13.5.63 | 14308 | 30.8.63 | 14372 | 12.6.64 | 14436 | 26.3.64 | 14500 | 6.6.64 | 14564 | 28.11.64 |
| 14245 | 24.6.63 | 14309 | 6.9.63 | 14373 | 12.6.64 | 14437 | 3.4.64 | 14501 | 6.6.64 | 14565 | 28.11.64 |
| 14246 | 24.6.63 | 14310 | 6.9.63 | 14374 | 24.6.64 | 14438 | 7.4.64 | 14502 | 30.6.64 | 14566 | 19.12.64 |
| 14247 | 14.6.63 | 14311 | 6.9.63 | 14375 | 19.6.64 | 14439 | 9.4.64 | 14503 | 30.6.64 | 14567 | 19.12.64 |
| 14248 | 5.7.63 | 14312 | 25.6.63 | 14376 | 17.2.64 | 14440 | 9.4.64 | 14504 | 2.7.64 | 14568 | 2.1.65 |
| 14249 | 24.6.63 | 14313 | 1.7.63 | 14377 | 17.2.64 | 14441 | 14.4.64 | 14505 | 2.7.64 | 14569 | 2.1.65 |
| 14250 | 19.7.63 | 14314 | 4.7.63 | 14378 | 17.2.64 | 14442 | 14.4.64 | 14506 | 23.7.64 | 14570 | 2.1.65 |
| 14251 | 26.7.63 | 14315 | 16.7.63 | 14379 | 24.2.64 | 14443 | 21.4.64 | 14507 | 23.7.64 | 14571 | 19.10.64 |
| 14252 | 26.7.63 | 14316 | 9.7.63 | 14380 | 2.3.64 | 14444 | 23.4.64 | 14508 | 10.7.64 | 14572 | 29.10.64 |
| 14253 | 26.7.63 | 14317 | 19.7.63 | 14381 | 2.3.64 | 14445 | 14.5.64 | 14509 | 7.7.64 | 14573 | 27.11.64 |
| 14254 | 26.7.63 | 14318 | 26.7.63 | 14382 | 2.3.64 | 14446 | 14.5.64 | 14510 | 10.7.64 | 14574 | 4.12.64 |
| 14255 | 26.4.63 | 14319 | 26.7.63 | 14383 | 9.3.64 | 14447 | 28.8.64 | 14511 | 21.7.64 | 14575 | 2.10.64 |
| 14256 | 26.4.63 | 14320 | 20.8.63 | 14384 | 9.3.64 | 14448 | 22.5.64 | 14512 | 23.7.64 | 14576 | 2.10.64 |
| 14257 | 26.4.63 | 14321 | 26.7.63 | 14385 | 9.3.64 | 14449 | 26.5.64 | 14513 | 23.7.64 | 14577 | 12.10.64 |
| 14258 | 3.5.63 | 14322 | 20.8.63 | 14386 | 16.3.64 | 14450 | 13.3.64 | 14514 | 14.8.64 | 14578 | 12.10.64 |
| 14259 | 3.5.63 | 14323 | 23.8.63 | 14387 | 11.5.64 | 14451 | 16.3.64 | 14515 | 28.7.64 | 14579 | 13.11.64 |
| 14260 | 31.5.63 | 14324 | 23.8.63 | 14388 | 11.5.64 | 14452 | 18.3.64 | 14516 | 21.8.64 | 14580 | 13.11.64 |
| 14261 | 31.5.63 | 14325 | 3.9.63 | 14389 | 11.5.64 | 14453 | 19.3.64 | 14517 | 21.8.64 | 14581 | 13.11.64 |
| 14262 | 7.6.63 | 14326 | 6.9.63 | 14390 | 9.4.64 | 14454 | 23.3.64 | 14518 | 17.7.64 | 14582 | 17.11.64 |
| 14263 | 7.6.63 | 14327 | 10.9.63 | 14391 | 9.4.64 | 14455 | 20.3.64 | 14519 | 17.7.64 | 14583 | 4.12.64 |
| 14264 | 7.6.63 | 14328 | 10.9.63 | 14392 | 14.4.64 | 14456 | 3.4.64 | 14520 | 24.7.64 | 14584 | 4.12.64 |
| 14265 | 5.7.63 | 14329 | 6.9.63 | 14393 | 17.4.64 | 14457 | 6.4.64 | 14521 | 19.8.64 | 14585 | 4.12.64 |
| 14266 | 5.7.63 | 14330 | 13.9.63 | 14394 | 21.4.64 | 14458 | 24.4.64 | 14522 | 21.8.64 | 14586 | 11.12.64 |
| 14267 | 5.7.63 | 14331 | 17.9.63 | 14395 | 24.4.64 | 14459 | 5.5.64 | 14523 | 26.8.64 | 14587 | 6.11.64 |
| 14268 | 5.7.63 | 14332 | 20.9.63 | 14396 | 28.4.64 | 14460 | 6.5.64 | 14524 | 1.5.64 | 14588 | 6.11.64 |
| 14269 | 12.7.63 | 14333 | 26.2.64 | 14397 | 1.5.64 | 14461 | 7.5.64 | 14525 | 1.5.64 | 14589 | 29.10.64 |
| 14270 | 12.7.63 | 14334 | 24.2.64 | 14398 | 1.5.64 | 14462 | 13.3.64 | 14526 | 1.5.64 | 14590 | 29.10.64 |
| 14271 | 12.7.63 | 14335 | 26.2.64 | 14399 | 1.5.64 | 14463 | 13.3.64 | 14527 | 4.9.64 | 14591 | 27.11.64 |
| 14272 | 12.7.63 | 14336 | 4.3.64 | 14400 | 1.5.64 | 14464 | 10.4.64 | 14528 | 28.8.64 | 14592 | 29.6.64 |
| 14273 | 13.5.63 | 14337 | 4.3.64 | 14401 | 8.5.64 | 14465 | 10.4.64 | 14529 | 18.9.64 | 14593 | 29.6.64 |
| 14274 | 17.5.63 | 14338 | 23.3.64 | 14402 | 12.5.64 | 14466 | 10.4.64 | 14530 | 1.12.64 | 14594 | 3.7.64 |
| 14275 | 17.5.63 | 14339 | 23.3.64 | 14403 | 15.5.64 | 14467 | 21.4.64 | 14531 | 7.12.64 | 14595 | 10.7.64 |
| 14276 | 27.5.63 | 14340 | 25.3.64 | 14404 | 22.5.64 | 14468 | 15.4.64 | 14532 | 1.12.64 | 14596 | 10.7.64 |

| | | | | | | | | | | |
|---|---|---|---|---|---|---|---|---|---|---|
| 14597 | 4.12.64 | 14661 | 4.12.64 | 14725 | 6.2.65 | 14789 | 18.6.65 | 14853 | 5.6.65 | 14917 |
| 14598 | 10.11.64 | 14662 | 16.12.64 | 14726 | 19.2.65 | 14790 | 18.6.65 | 14854 | 5.6.65 | 14918 |
| 14599 | 10.11.64 | 14663 | 16.12.64 | 14727 | 2.4.65 | 14791 | 16.7.65 | 14855 | 26.6.65 | 14919 | 1.2.65 |
| 14600 | 18.12.64 | 14664 | 2.10.64 | 14728 | 9.4.65 | 14792 | 16.7.65 | 14856 | 26.6.65 | 14920 | 2.7.65 |
| 14601 | 18.12.64 | 14665 | 9.10.64 | 14729 | 15.4.65 | 14793 | 23.7.65 | 14857 | 3.7.65 | 14921 | 2.7.65 |
| 14602 | 25.9.64 | 14666 | 9.10.64 | 14730 | 13.8.65 | 14794 | 24.9.65 | 14858 | 27.8.65 | 14922 | 24.9.65 |
| 14603 | 25.9.64 | 14667 | 9.10.64 | 14731 | 27.8.65 | 14795 | 15.10.65 | 14859 | 27.8.65 | 14923 | 24.9.65 |
| 14604 | 25.9.64 | 14668 | 6.11.64 | 14732 | 12.2.65 | 14796 | 15.10.65 | 14860 | 27.8.65 | 14924 | 1.2.65 |
| 14605 | 2.10.64 | 14669 | 6.11.64 | 14733 | 12.2.65 | 14797 | 29.10.65 | 14861 | 11.9.65 | 14925 | 8.7.65 |
| 14606 | 2.10.64 | 14670 | 13.11.64 | 14734 | 21.5.65 | 14798 | 29.10.65 | 14862 | 11.9.65 | 14926 | 8.7.65 |
| 14607 | 9.10.64 | 14671 | 13.11.64 | 14735 | 28.5.65 | 14799 | 2.7.65 | 14863 | 2.10.65 | 14927 | 12.8.65 |
| 14608 | 9.10.64 | 14672 | 18.12.64 | 14736 | 18.6.65 | 14800 | 2.7.65 | 14864 | 9.10.65 | 14928 | 1.1.65 |
| 14609 | 9.10.64 | 14673 | 18.12.64 | 14737 | 25.6.65 | 14801 | 12.7.65 | 14865 | 16.10.65 | 14929 | 15.1.65 |
| 14610 | 31.10.64 | 14674 | 23.12.64 | 14738 | 16.7.65 | 14802 | 1.10.65 | 14866 | 23.10.65 | 14930 | 8.1.65 |
| 14611 | 31.10.64 | 14675 | 9.10.64 | 14739 | 16.7.65 | 14803 | 15.10.65 | 14867 | 23.10.65 | 14931 | 8.1.65 |
| 14612 | 13.11.64 | 14676 | 16.10.64 | 14740 | 10.9.65 | 14804 | 15.10.65 | 14868 | 30.10.65 | 14932 | 29.1.65 |
| 14613 | 13.11.64 | 14677 | 11.12.64 | 14741 | 10.9.65 | 14805 | 25.1.65 | 14869 | 20.11.65 | 14933 | 29.1.65 |
| 14614 | 13.10.64 | 14678 | 16.12.64 | 14742 | 3.9.65 | 14806 | 22.1.65 | 14870 | 20.11.65 | 14934 | 29.1.65 |
| 14615 | 16.10.64 | 14679 | 2.10.64 | 14743 | 10.9.65 | 14807 | 25.1.65 | 14871 | 27.2.65 | 14935 | 5.3.65 |
| 14616 | 6.11.64 | 14680 | 25.9.64 | 14744 | 17.9.65 | 14808 | 29.1.65 | 14872 | 13.3.65 | 14936 | 19.3.65 |
| 14617 | 6.11.64 | 14681 | 2.10.64 | 14745 | 17.9.65 | 14809 | 12.3.65 | 14873 | 16.10.65 | 14937 | 26.3.65 |
| 14618 | 13.11.64 | 14682 | 30.10.64 | 14746 | 1.10.65 | 14810 | 12.3.65 | 14874 | 9.10.65 | 14938 | 19.3.65 |
| 14619 | 4.12.64 | 14683 | 30.10.64 | 14747 | 1.10.65 | 14811 | 30.4.65 | 14875 | 9.1.65 | 14939 | 19.3.65 |
| 14620 | 11.12.64 | 14684 | 4.11.64 | 14748 | 15.10.65 | 14812 | 7.5.65 | 14876 | 6.2.65 | 14940 | 7.5.65 |
| 14621 | 11.12.64 | 14685 | 9.11.64 | 14749 | 15.10.65 | 14813 | 18.6.65 | 14877 | 6.2.65 | 14941 | 7.5.65 |
| 14622 | 11.12.64 | 14686 | 27.11.64 | 14750 | 21.10.65 | 14814 | 25.6.65 | 14878 | 13.2.65 | 14942 | 14.5.65 |
| 14623 | 16.10.64 | 14687 | 27.11.64 | 14751 | 1.11.65 | 14815 | 23.7.65 | 14879 | 13.2.65 | 14943 | 18.6.65 |
| 14624 | 30.10.64 | 14688 | 4.12.64 | 14752 | 5.11.65 | 14816 | 13.8.65 | 14880 | 13.2.65 | 14944 | 28.6.65 |
| 14625 | 30.10.64 | 14689 | 9.12.64 | 14753 | 12.11.65 | 14817 | 13.8.65 | 14881 | 27.3.65 | 14945 | 28.6.65 |
| 14626 | 30.10.64 | 14690 | 18.12.64 | 14754 | 12.11.65 | 14818 | 18.8.65 | 14882 | 3.4.65 | 14946 | 20.8.65 |
| 14627 | 20.11.64 | 14691 | 18.12.64 | 14755 | 22.11.65 | 14819 | 27.8.65 | 14883 | 3.4.65 | 14947 | 20.8.65 |
| 14628 | 20.11.64 | 14692 | 16.10.64 | 14756 | 1.1.65 | 14820 | 27.8.65 | 14884 | 15.4.65 | 14948 | 3.9.65 |
| 14629 | 20.11.64 | 14693 | 29.10.64 | 14757 | 7.1.65 | 14821 | 3.9.65 | 14885 | 8.5.65 | 14949 | 27.8.65 |
| 14630 | 20.11.64 | 14694 | 4.12.64 | 14758 | 14.1.65 | 14822 | 5.2.65 | 14886 | 8.5.65 | 14950 | 27.8.65 |
| 14631 | 18.12.64 | 14695 | 4.12.64 | 14759 | 14.1.65 | 14823 | 5.2.65 | 14887 | 1.5.65 | 14951 | 17.9.65 |
| 14632 | 18.12.64 | 14696 | 17.11.64 | 14760 | 26.2.65 | 14824 | 28.5.65 | 14888 | 8.5.65 | 14952 | 17.9.65 |
| 14633 | 25.9.64 | 14697 | 27.11.64 | 14761 | 26.3.65 | 14825 | 11.6.65 | 14889 | 3.7.65 | 14953 | 1.10.65 |
| 14634 | 2.10.64 | 14698 | 2.1.65 | 14762 | 26.3.65 | 14826 | 3.9.65 | 14890 | 10.7.65 | 14954 | 1.10.65 |
| 14635 | 25.11.64 | 14699 | 2.1.65 | 14763 | 28.4.65 | 14827 | 3.9.65 | 14891 | 20.7.65 | 14955 | 1.10.65 |
| 14636 | 4.12.64 | 14700 | 8.1.65 | 14764 | 17.6.65 | 14828 | 8.10.65 | 14892 | 23.7.65 | 14956 | 22.10.65 |
| 14637 | 9.12.64 | 14701 | 7.1.65 | 14765 | 10.6.65 | 14829 | 15.10.65 | 14893 | 25.9.65 | 14957 | 15.10.65 |
| 14638 | 11.9.64 | 14702 | 7.1.65 | 14766 | 24.6.65 | 14830 | 8.10.65 | 14894 | 18.9.65 | 14958 | 15.10.65 |
| 14639 | 11.9.64 | 14703 | 9.1.65 | 14767 | 1.7.65 | 14831 | 15.10.65 | 14895 | 18.9.65 | 14959 | 12.11.65 |
| 14640 | 11.9.64 | 14704 | 9.1.65 | 14768 | 15.7.65 | 14832 | 20.11.65 | 14896 | 25.9.65 | 14960 | 12.11.65 |
| 14641 | 8.10.64 | 14705 | 15.1.65 | 14769 | 16.7.65 | 14833 | 26.11.65 | 14897 | 25.9.65 | 14961 | 12.11.65 |
| 14642 | 16.10.64 | 14706 | 22.1.65 | 14770 | 20.8.65 | 14834 | 26.11.65 | 14898 | 9.10.65 | 14962 | 22.10.65 |
| 14643 | 16.11.64 | 14707 | 15.1.65 | 14771 | 20.8.65 | 14835 | 1.1.65 | 14899 | 16.10.65 | 14963 | 2.11.65 |
| 14644 | 16.11.64 | 14708 | 30.1.65 | 14772 | 20.8.65 | 14836 | 1.1.65 | 14900 | 23.10.65 | 14964 | 22.1.65 |
| 14645 | 20.11.64 | 14709 | 1.1.65 | 14773 | 9.9.65 | 14837 | 8.1.65 | 14901 | 16.10.65 | 14965 | 22.1.65 |
| 14646 | 27.11.64 | 14710 | 8.1.65 | 14774 | 21.9.65 | 14838 | 9.7.65 | 14902 | 23.10.65 | 14966 | 12.7.65 |
| 14647 | 11.12.64 | 14711 | 8.1.65 | 14775 | 24.9.65 | 14839 | 9.7.65 | 14903 | 26.10.65 | 14967 | 29.10.65 |
| 14648 | 18.12.64 | 14712 | 1.1.65 | 14776 | 22.10.65 | 14840 | 5.11.65 | 14904 | 6.11.64 | 14968 | 29.10.65 |
| 14649 | 18.12.64 | 14713 | 1.1.65 | 14777 | 28.10.65 | 14841 | 5.11.65 | 14905 | 13.11.65 | 14969 | 1.1.65 |
| 14650 | 3.9.64 | 14714 | 8.1.65 | 14778 | 29.10.65 | 14842 | 1.10.65 | 14906 | 6.11.65 | 14970 | 1.1.65 |
| 14651 | 11.9.64 | 14715 | 2.2.65 | 14779 | 11.11.65 | 14843 | 6.10.65 | 14907 | 27.11.65 | 14971 | 5.2.65 |
| 14652 | 15.9.64 | 14716 | 22.1.65 | 14780 | 11.11.65 | 14844 | 6.10.65 | 14908 | 4.12.65 | 14972 | 9.7.65 |
| 14653 | 15.10.64 | 14717 | 28.1.65 | 14781 | 19.11.65 | 14845 | 22.1.65 | 14909 | 10.12.65 | 14973 | 2.7.65 |
| 14654 | 19.10.64 | 14718 | 4.2.65 | 14782 | 1.1.65 | 14846 | 15.1.65 | 14910 | 10.12.65 | 14974 | 13.8.65 |
| 14655 | 27.10.64 | 14719 | 5.2.65 | 14783 | 26.2.65 | 14847 | 15.1.65 | 14911 | 6.11.65 | 14975 | 20.8.65 |
| 14656 | 27.10.64 | 14720 | 25.2.65 | 14784 | 26.2.65 | 14848 | 22.1.65 | 14912 | 6.11.65 | 14976 | 22.1.65 |
| 14657 | 27.10.64 | 14721 | 12.2.65 | 14785 | 14.5.65 | 14849 | 13.3.65 | 14913 | 13.11.65 | 14977 | 29.1.65 |
| 14658 | 3.11.64 | 14722 | 30.3.65 | 14786 | 7.5.65 | 14850 | 13.3.65 | 14914 | | 14978 | 12.2.65 |
| 14659 | 3.11.64 | 14723 | 5.3.65 | 14787 | 14.5.65 | 14851 | 15.4.65 | 14915 | | 14979 | 12.2.65 |
| 14660 | 3.11.64 | 14724 | 6.2.65 | 14788 | 18.6.65 | 14852 | 29.5.65 | 14916 | | 14980 | 9.7.65 |

| | | | | | | | | |
|---|---|---|---|---|---|---|---|---|---|
| 14981 | 9.7.65 | 14985 | 29.1.65 | 14989 | 2.4.65 | 14993 | 23.7.65 | 14997 | 20.5.65 |
| 14982 | 20.8.65 | 14986 | 29.1.65 | 14990 | 6.7.65 | 14994 | 28.9.65 | 14998 | 13.5.65 |
| 14983 | 20.8.65 | 14987 | 19.3.65 | 14991 | 6.7.65 | 14995 | 28.9.65 | 14999 | 8.6.65 |
| 14984 | 10.9.65 | 14988 | 26.3.65 | 14992 | 13.8.65 | 14996 | 5.2.65 | 15000 | 8.6.65 |

# Cross Reference of Registrations to Body Numbers
## (UK and Irish civilian registrations only)

| Reg | Body | Reg | Body | Reg | Body | Reg | Body | Reg | Body |
|---|---|---|---|---|---|---|---|---|---|
| GM 9271 | 10107 | CGM 122 | 12266 | FGM 160 | 14322 | JWC 713 | 13141 | LCS 346 | 10137 |
| GM 9272 | 10108 | CGM 123 | 12118 | FGM 161 | 14323 | JWC 714 | 13142 | LCS 347 | 10138 |
| GM 9273 | 10109 | CGM 124 | 12119 | FGM 162 | 14324 | JWC 715 | 13143 | LCS 348 | 10139 |
| GM 9274 | 10110 | CGM 125 | 12120 | FGM 163 | 14325 | JWC 716 | 13144 | LCS 349 | 10140 |
| GM 9275 | 10111 | CGM 126 | 12121 | FGM 164 | 14326 | JWC 717 | 13145 | LCS 350 | 10141 |
| GM 9276 | 10112 | CGM 127 | 12122 | FGM 165 | 14327 | JWC 718 | 13146 | LCS 351 | 10142 |
| GM 9277 | 10113 | CGM 128 | 12123 | FGM 166 | 14328 | KEL 65 | 12072 | LWC 869 | 13728 |
| GM 9278 | 10114 | CGM 129 | 12124 | FGM 167 | 14329 | KEL 66 | 12073 | LYM 728 | 12068 |
| GM 9279 | 10115 | DGM 430 | 13519 | FGM 168 | 14330 | KEL 67 | 12777 | LYM 729 | 12069 |
| GM 9280 | 10116 | DGM 431 | 13520 | FGM 169 | 14331 | KEL 401 | 12778 | LYM 730 | 12070 |
| GM 9281 | 10117 | DGM 432 | 13521 | FGM 170 | 14332 | KEL 402 | 12779 | LYM 731 | 12067 |
| GM 9282 | 10118 | DGM 433 | 13522 | FGM 171 | 14312 | KEL 403 | 12781 | LYM 732 | 12071 |
| GM 9283 | 10119 | DGM 434 | 13523 | FGM 172 | 14313 | KEL 404 | 12782 | MCS 750 | 10809 |
| GM 9284 | 10120 | DGM 435 | 13524 | FGM 173 | 14314 | KEL 405 | 12780 | MCS 751 | 10810 |
| GM 9285 | 10121 | DGM 436 | 13525 | FGM 174 | 14315 | KEL 406 | 13488 | MCS 752 | 10811 |
| GM 9286 | 10122 | DGM 437 | 13526 | FGM 175 | 14316 | KEL 407 | 13489 | MCS 753 | 10812 |
| GM 9287 | 10123 | DGM 438 | 13527 | FGM 176 | 14317 | KEL 408 | 13490 | MCS 754 | 10813 |
| GM 9288 | 10124 | DGM 439 | 13528 | FGM 177 | 14318 | KEL 409 | 13491 | MCS 755 | 10814 |
| GM 9289 | 10125 | DGM 440 | 13529 | FGM 178 | 14319 | KEL 410 | 13492 | MCS 756 | 10815 |
| GM 9290 | 10126 | DGM 441 | 13530 | FGM 179 | 14320 | KEL 411 | 13493 | MCS 757 | 10816 |
| GM 9291 | 10127 | DGM 442 | 13531 | FGM 180 | 14321 | KFF 353 | 12179 | MCS 758 | 10817 |
| GM 9292 | 10128 | DGM 443 | 13532 | FMO 21 | 11402 | KFF 466 | 13906 | MCS 759 | 10818 |
| GM 9993 | 10845 | DGM 444 | 13534 | FMO 22 | 11400 | KGX 940 | 10016 | MCS 760 | 10819 |
| GM 9994 | 10846 | DGM 445 | 13533 | FMO 23 | 11403 | KGX 941 | 10015 | MCS 761 | 10820 |
| GM 9995 | 10847 | DGM 446 | 13535 | FMO 24 | 11401 | KLA 89 | 10014 | MCS 762 | 10821 |
| OO 9543 | 12810 | DGM 447 | 13536 | HOD 27 | 10740 | KLA 90 | 10013 | MCS 763 | 10822 |
| OO 9544 | 12811 | DGM 448 | 13537 | JAO 837 | 10633 | KLA 91 | 10012 | MCS 764 | 10823 |
| OO 9545 | 12812 | DGM 449 | 13538 | JRU 66 | 12074 | KWG 599 | 10752 | MCS 765 | 10824 |
| OO 9546 | 12813 | DGM 450 | 13539 | JRU 67 | 12075 | KWG 601 | 10753 | MCS 766 | 10825 |
| OO 9547 | 12814 | DGM 451 | 13540 | JRU 68 | 12076 | KWG 602 | 10754 | MCS 767 | 10826 |
| OO 9548 | 12815 | DGM 452 | 13541 | JRU 69 | 12077 | KWG 603 | 10755 | MCS 768 | 10827 |
| OO 9549 | 12816 | DGM 453 | 13542 | JSK 492 | 13095 | KWG 604 | 10149 | MCS 769 | 10828 |
| OO 9550 | 12817 | DGM 454 | 13543 | JUO 932 | 10743 | KWG 605 | 10150 | MCS 770 | 10829 |
|  |  | DGM 455 | 13544 | JUO 933 | 10746 | KWG 606 | 10151 | MCS 771 | 10830 |
| AJI 3307 | 11380 | DGM 456 | 13545 | JUO 934 | 10739 | KWG 607 | 10152 | MCS 772 | 10831 |
| BGM 96 | 11453 | DGM 457 | 13546 | JUO 935 | 10751 | KWG 608 | 10153 | MCS 773 | 10832 |
| BGM 97 | 11454 | DGM 458 | 13547 | JUO 936 | 10745 | KWG 609 | 10154 | MCS 774 | 10833 |
| BGM 98 | 11455 | DGM 459 | 13548 | JUO 937 | 10744 | KWG 610 | 10155 | MCS 775 | 10834 |
| BGM 99 | 11456 | DMO 664 | 10736 | JUO 938 | 10742 | KWG 611 | 10156 | MCS 776 | 10835 |
| BGM 100 | 11457 | DMO 665 | 10732 | JUO 939 | 10741 | KWG 612 | 10157 | MMS 731 | 10760 |
| BGM 101 | 11458 | DMO 666 | 10733 | JUO 940 | 10748 | KWG 613 | 10158 | MMS 732 | 10761 |
| BGM 102 | 11459 | DMO 667 | 10734 | JUO 941 | 10750 | KWG 614 | 10159 | MMS 733 | 10762 |
| BGM 103 | 11460 | DMO 668 | 10735 | JUO 942 | 10749 | KWG 615 | 10160 | MMS 734 | 10763 |
| BGM 104 | 11461 | DMO 669 | 10737 | JUO 943 | 10747 | KWG 616 | 10161 | MMS 735 | 10764 |
| BGM 105 | 11462 | EDL 14 | 12775 | JUO 944 | 10738 | KWG 617 | 10162 | MMS 736 | 10765 |
| BGM 106 | 11463 | EDL 15 | 12776 | JUO 978 | 10722 | KWG 618 | 10163 | MMS 737 | 10766 |
| BGM 107 | 11464 | EDL 16 | 12840 | JUO 979 | 10725 | KWG 619 | 10164 | MMS 738 | 10767 |
| BGM 108 | 11465 | EOO 579 | 13125 | JUO 980 | 10721 | KWG 620 | 10165 | MMS 739 | 10768 |
| BGM 109 | 11466 | EOO 580 | 13126 | JUO 981 | 10729 | KWG 621 | 10166 | MMS 740 | 10769 |
| BGM 110 | 11467 | EOO 581 | 13127 | JUO 982 | 10723 | KWG 622 | 10167 | MMS 741 | 10770 |
| BGM 111 | 11468 | EOO 582 | 13128 | JUO 983 | 10730 | KWG 623 | 10168 | MMS 742 | 10771 |
| BGM 112 | 11469 | EOO 583 | 13129 | JUO 984 | 10728 | KWG 624 | 10756 | MMS 743 | 10772 |
| BGM 113 | 11470 | EOO 584 | 13130 | JUO 985 | 10720 | KWG 626 | 10757 | MMS 744 | 10773 |
| BGM 114 | 11471 | EOO 585 | 13131 | JUO 986 | 10727 | KWG 627 | 10758 | MMS 745 | 10774 |
| BGM 115 | 11472 | EOO 586 | 13132 | JUO 987 | 10731 | KWG 628 | 10759 | MMS 746 | 10775 |
| CGM 116 | 12260 | EOO 587 | 13133 | JUO 988 | 10724 | LAS 948 | 13095 | MMS 747 | 10776 |
| CGM 117 | 12261 | EOO 588 | 13134 | JUO 989 | 10726 | LCS 341 | 10132 | MMS 748 | 10777 |
| CGM 118 | 12262 | EOO 589 | 13135 | JVS 293 | 12239 | LCS 342 | 10133 | MMS 749 | 10778 |
| CGM 119 | 12263 | EOO 590 | 13136 | JWC 710 | 13138 | LCS 343 | 10134 | MMS 750 | 10779 |
| CGM 120 | 12264 | EOO 591 | 13137 | JWC 711 | 13139 | LCS 344 | 10135 | MMS 751 | 10780 |
| CGM 121 | 12265 | FAS 962 | 12289 | JWC 712 | 13140 | LCS 345 | 10136 | MMS 752 | 10781 |

| | | | | | | | | | |
|---|---|---|---|---|---|---|---|---|---|
| MMS 753 | 10836 | NWC 16 | 13677 | OVL 470 | 11620 | RAG 400 | 12156 | RPN 18 | 10852 |
| MMS 754 | 10837 | NWC 17 | 13678 | OVL 471 | 11621 | RAG 401 | 12157 | RPN 19 | 10853 |
| MMS 755 | 10838 | OCS 61 | 11498 | OVL 472 | 11622 | RAG 402 | 12158 | RPN 20 | 10854 |
| MMS 756 | 10839 | OCS 62 | 11499 | OVL 473 | 11623 | RAG 403 | 12159 | RSC 622 | 10017 |
| MMS 757 | 10840 | OCS 63 | 11500 | OVL 474 | 11624 | RAG 404 | 12160 | RSC 623 | 10018 |
| MOO 174 | 12625 | OCS 64 | 11501 | OVL 475 | 11625 | RAG 405 | 12161 | RSC 624 | 10019 |
| MOO 175 | 12626 | OCS 65 | 11502 | OVL 476 | 11626 | RAG 406 | 12162 | RSC 625 | 10020 |
| MOO 176 | 12627 | OCS 66 | 11503 | OVL 477 | 11627 | RAG 407 | 12163 | RSC 626 | 10021 |
| MOO 177 | 12628 | OCS 67 | 11504 | OVL 478 | 11628 | RAG 408 | 12164 | RSC 627 | 10022 |
| MOO 178 | 13269 | OCS 68 | 11505 | OVL 479 | 11629 | RAG 409 | 12165 | RSC 628 | 10023 |
| MOO 179 | 13270 | OCS 69 | 11506 | OVL 480 | 11630 | RAG 409 | 13905 | RSC 629 | 10024 |
| MOO 973 | 13271 | OCS 70 | 11507 | OVL 481 | 11631 | RAG 409 | 12960 | RSC 630 | 10025 |
| MOO 974 | 13272 | OFU 438 | 12879 | OVL 482 | 11632 | RAG 410 | 12166 | RSC 631 | 10026 |
| MOO 975 | 13273 | OMS 209 | 11423 | OVL 483 | 11633 | RAG 411 | 12167 | RSC 632 | 10027 |
| MOO 976 | 13274 | OMS 210 | 11424 | OVL 484 | 11634 | RAG 412 | 12168 | RSC 633 | 10028 |
| NFE 311 | 11302 | OMS 211 | 11425 | OVL 485 | 11757 | RAG 413 | 12169 | RSC 634 | 10029 |
| NFE 312 | 11303 | OMS 212 | 11426 | OVL 486 | 11758 | RFE 461 | 12206 | RSC 635 | 10030 |
| NFE 431 | 11364 | OMS 213 | 11427 | OVL 487 | 11759 | RFE 462 | 12629 | RSC 636 | 10031 |
| NFE 433 | 11365 | OMS 214 | 11428 | OVL 488 | 11760 | RFE 463 | 12630 | RSC 637 | 10032 |
| NFE 434 | 11366 | OMS 215 | 11429 | OVL 489 | 11761 | RFE 464 | 12631 | RSC 638 | 10033 |
| NFE 435 | 11367 | OMS 216 | 11430 | OVL 490 | 12010 | RFE 465 | 12632 | RSC 639 | 10034 |
| NFE 436 | 11368 | OMS 217 | 11431 | OVL 491 | 12011 | RFE 466 | 12633 | RSC 640 | 10035 |
| NFE 437 | 11369 | OMS 218 | 11432 | OVL 492 | 12012 | RFE 467 | 12634 | RSC 641 | 10036 |
| NFE 438 | 11370 | OMS 219 | 11433 | OVL 493 | 12013 | RFE 468 | 12635 | RSC 642 | 10087 |
| NFE 439 | 11371 | OMS 220 | 11434 | OVL 494 | 12014 | RFE 469 | 12636 | RSC 643 | 10088 |
| NFE 440 | 11372 | OMS 221 | 11435 | OVL 495 | 12015 | RFE 470 | 12715 | RSC 644 | 10089 |
| NFE 441 | 11373 | OMS 222 | 11436 | OVL 496 | 12016 | RFE 471 | 12716 | RSC 645 | 10090 |
| NFE 442 | 11374 | OMS 223 | 11437 | OVL 497 | 12017 | RFE 472 | 12717 | RSC 646 | 10091 |
| NFE 443 | 11375 | OMS 224 | 11438 | OVL 498 | 12018 | RFE 473 | 12422 | RSC 647 | 10092 |
| NFE 445 | 11376 | OMS 225 | 11439 | OVL 499 | 12019 | RFE 474 | 12423 | RSC 648 | 10093 |
| NFE 446 | 11377 | OMS 226 | 11440 | OVS 461 | 12418 | RFE 475 | 12424 | RSC 649 | 10094 |
| NFE 447 | 11378 | OMS 227 | 11441 | OWC 606 | 13394 | RFE 476 | 12425 | RSC 650 | 10095 |
| NFE 448 | 11379 | OMS 228 | 11442 | OWC 607 | 13395 | RFE 477 | 12426 | RSC 651 | 10096 |
| NFE 449 | 11380 | OMS 229 | 11443 | OWC 608 | 13396 | RFE 478 | 12427 | RSC 652 | 10097 |
| NFE 450 | 11381 | OMS 230 | 11444 | OWC 609 | 13397 | RFE 479 | 12736 | RSC 653 | 10098 |
| NFE 451 | 11382 | OMS 231 | 11445 | OWC 610 | 13398 | RFE 480 | 12737 | RSC 654 | 10099 |
| NFE 452 | 11383 | OMS 232 | 11446 | OWC 611 | 13399 | RFE 481 | 12738 | RSC 655 | 10100 |
| NFE 928 | 10978 | OMS 233 | 11447 | PDL 514 | 10084 | RFE 482 | 12739 | RSC 656 | 10101 |
| NFE 929 | 10979 | OMS 234 | 11448 | PDL 515 | 10085 | RFE 483 | 12740 | RSC 657 | 10102 |
| NFE 930 | 10980 | OMS 235 | 11449 | PDL 516 | 10309 | RFE 484 | 12741 | RWC 600 | 13147 |
| NFE 931 | 10981 | OMS 236 | 11450 | PDL 517 | 10310 | RFE 485 | 12742 | RWC 601 | 13148 |
| NFE 932 | 10982 | OMS 237 | 11451 | PDL 518 | 10311 | RFU 687 | 10650 | RWC 602 | 13154 |
| NFE 933 | 10983 | OMS 238 | 11452 | PDL 519 | 10312 | RFU 688 | 10651 | RWC 603 | 13155 |
| NFE 934 | 10984 | OPN 801 | 10179 | PFO 256 | 12869 | RFU 689 | 10709 | RWC 604 | 13151 |
| NFE 935 | 10985 | OPN 802 | 10180 | PRX 926 | 10313 | RFU 690 | 10710 | RWC 605 | 13152 |
| NFE 936 | 10986 | OPN 803 | 10181 | PRX 927 | 10314 | RFU 691 | 10711 | RWC 606 | 13153 |
| NFE 937 | 10987 | OPN 804 | 10174 | PRX 928 | 10315 | RFU 692 | 10712 | RWC 607 | 13149 |
| NVL 157 | 11168 | OPN 805 | 10175 | PRX 929 | 10316 | RFU 693 | 10713 | RWC 608 | 13150 |
| NVL 158 | 11169 | OPN 806 | 10176 | PRX 930 | 11316 | RFU 694 | 10714 | RWG 359 | 12093 |
| NVL 159 | 11170 | OPN 807 | 10177 | PRX 931 | 11317 | RHR 852 | 10671 | RWG 360 | 12094 |
| NVL 160 | 11171 | OPN 808 | 10178 | PRX 932 | 11318 | RHR 853 | 10672 | RWG 361 | 12095 |
| NVL 161 | 11172 | ORX 631 | 10652 | PRX 933 | 11319 | RMR 524 | 10673 | RWG 362 | 12096 |
| NVL 162 | 11173 | ORX 632 | 10653 | PVS 315 | 11623 | RMR 736 | 10674 | RWG 363 | 12097 |
| NVL 163 | 11174 | ORX 633 | 10654 | RAG 389 | 12091 | RMR 992 | 10675 | RWG 364 | 12098 |
| NVL 164 | 11175 | ORX 634 | 10655 | RAG 390 | 12092 | RMR 995 | 10676 | RWG 365 | 12099 |
| NVL 165 | 11176 | OVL 461 | 11966 | RAG 391 | 12170 | RPN 9 | 11570 | RWG 366 | 12100 |
| NVL 165 | 12739 | OVL 462 | 11848 | RAG 392 | 12171 | RPN 10 | 11571 | RWG 367 | 12101 |
| NVL 168 | 11177 | OVL 463 | 11849 | RAG 393 | 12172 | RPN 11 | 11572 | RWG 368 | 12102 |
| NVL 613 | 11165 | OVL 464 | 11850 | RAG 394 | 12150 | RPN 12 | 10715 | RWG 369 | 12103 |
| NVL 614 | 11166 | OVL 465 | 11851 | RAG 395 | 12151 | RPN 13 | 10716 | RWG 370 | 12104 |
| NVL 615 | 11167 | OVL 466 | 11852 | RAG 396 | 12152 | RPN 14 | 10848 | RWG 371 | 12105 |
| NVS 695 | 13139 | OVL 467 | 11853 | RAG 397 | 12153 | RPN 15 | 10849 | RWG 372 | 12106 |
| NWC 14 | 13675 | OVL 468 | 11854 | RAG 398 | 12154 | RPN 16 | 10850 | RWG 373 | 12107 |
| NWC 15 | 13676 | OVL 469 | 11855 | RAG 399 | 12155 | RPN 17 | 10851 | RWG 374 | 12108 |

| | | | | | | | | | |
|---|---|---|---|---|---|---|---|---|---|
| RWG 375 | 12109 | SPM 21 | 11573 | TCS 166 | 13581 | TWN 107 | 11062 | UWO 701 | 11304 |
| RWG 376 | 12110 | SPM 22 | 11574 | TCS 167 | 13582 | TWN 108 | 11063 | UWO 702 | 11305 |
| RWG 377 | 12111 | SPM 23 | 10855 | TCS 168 | 13583 | TWN 109 | 11064 | UWO 703 | 11306 |
| RWG 378 | 12112 | SPM 24 | 10856 | TCS 169 | 13584 | TWN 110 | 11065 | UWO 704 | 11307 |
| RWG 379 | 12113 | SPM 25 | 10857 | TCS 170 | 13585 | TWN 111 | 11066 | UWO 705 | 11308 |
| RWG 380 | 12114 | SRP 134 | 10444 | TCS 171 | 13586 | TWN 112 | 11067 | UWO 706 | 11309 |
| RWG 381 | 12115 | SRP 135 | 10445 | TCS 172 | 13587 | TWN 113 | 11068 | UWO 707 | 11310 |
| RWG 382 | 12116 | SRP 136 | 10446 | TCS 173 | 13588 | TWN 114 | 11241 | UWO 708 | 11311 |
| RWG 383 | 12117 | SWN 150 | 10448 | TCS 174 | 13589 | TWN 115 | 11242 | UWO 709 | 11312 |
| RWN 883 | 10661 | SWN 151 | 10449 | TCS 175 | 13590 | TYJ 424 | 11925 | UWO 710 | 11313 |
| RWN 884 | 10662 | SWN 152 | 10450 | TCS 176 | 13591 | UAM 941 | 11103 | UWO 711 | 11314 |
| RWN 885 | 10663 | SWN 153 | 10451 | TCS 177 | 13592 | UAP 28 | 11510 | UWO 712 | 11315 |
| SBD 545 | 10331 | SWN 154 | 10343 | TCS 178 | 13593 | UAP 29 | 11511 | UWW 739 | 10009 |
| SBD 546 | 10332 | SWN 155 | 10344 | TCS 179 | 13594 | UAP 30 | 11512 | UWW 740 | 10010 |
| SBD 547 | 10333 | SWN 156 | 10345 | TCS 180 | 13595 | UAX 556 | 10416 | UWW 741 | 10011 |
| SBD 548 | 10334 | SWN 157 | 10346 | TCS 181 | 13596 | UAX 557 | 10417 | VAO 383 | 10265 |
| SBD 549 | 10335 | SWN 158 | 10347 | TCS 182 | 13597 | UAX 558 | 10418 | VAO 384 | 10266 |
| SBD 550 | 10336 | SWN 159 | 10348 | TCS 183 | 13598 | UAX 559 | 10419 | VAO 385 | 10267 |
| SBD 551 | 10337 | SWN 160 | 10349 | TCS 184 | 13599 | UAX 560 | 10420 | VAO 386 | 10268 |
| SBD 552 | 10338 | SWS 719 | 10782 | TDL 998 | 11655 | UAX 561 | 10421 | VAO 387 | 10269 |
| SBD 553 | 10339 | SWS 720 | 10783 | TDL 999 | 11656 | UAX 562 | 10422 | VAO 388 | 10270 |
| SBD 554 | 10340 | SWS 721 | 10784 | TFO 467 | 11072 | UAX 563 | 10423 | VAO 389 | 10271 |
| SBD 555 | 10341 | SWS 722 | 10785 | TMW 273 | 11102 | UAX 564 | 10424 | VAO 390 | 10632 |
| SBD 556 | 10342 | SWS 723 | 10786 | TPN 26 | 11508 | UAX 565 | 10425 | VAO 391 | 10492 |
| SDL 265 | 11016 | SWS 724 | 10787 | TPN 27 | 11509 | UAX 566 | 10426 | VAP 31 | 12267 |
| SDL 266 | 11017 | SWS 725 | 10788 | TRP 557 | 11041 | UAX 567 | 10427 | VAP 32 | 12268 |
| SDL 267 | 11018 | SWS 726 | 10789 | TRP 558 | 11042 | UAX 568 | 10428 | VAP 33 | 12269 |
| SDL 268 | 11019 | SWS 727 | 10790 | TRP 559 | 11043 | UAX 569 | 10429 | VAP 34 | 12270 |
| SDL 269 | 11020 | SWS 728 | 10791 | TRP 560 | 11044 | UJB 196 | 11949 | VAP 35 | 12271 |
| SFU 304 | 10292 | SWS 729 | 10792 | TRP 561 | 11045 | UJB 197 | 11950 | VAX 501 | 11007 |
| SFU 305 | 10293 | SWS 730 | 10793 | TRP 562 | 11046 | UJB 198 | 11951 | VAX 502 | 11008 |
| SFU 306 | 10294 | SWS 731 | 10794 | TRP 563 | 11047 | UJB 199 | 11952 | VAX 503 | 11009 |
| SFU 307 | 10295 | SWS 732 | 10795 | TRP 564 | 11048 | UJB 200 | 11418 | VAX 504 | 11010 |
| SFU 308 | 10296 | SWS 733 | 10796 | TRP 565 | 11049 | UJB 201 | 11419 | VAX 505 | 11011 |
| SFU 309 | 10051 | SWS 734 | 10797 | TRP 566 | 11050 | UJB 202 | 11420 | VAX 506 | 11012 |
| SFU 310 | 10052 | SWS 735 | 10798 | TRP 567 | 11051 | UJB 203 | 11421 | VAX 507 | 11013 |
| SFU 311 | 10053 | SWS 736 | 10799 | TRP 568 | 11052 | UJB 204 | 11422 | VAX 508 | 11762 |
| SFU 312 | 10054 | SWS 737 | 10800 | TRP 569 | 11053 | URP 600 | 11055 | VAX 509 | 11763 |
| SFU 313 | 10055 | SWS 738 | 10801 | TRP 570 | 11054 | URP 601 | 11056 | VCS 351 | 14285 |
| SFU 314 | 10297 | SWS 739 | 10802 | TVL 305 | 12952 | USC 750 | 11473 | VCS 352 | 14286 |
| SFU 315 | 10298 | SWS 740 | 10803 | TVL 306 | 12953 | USC 751 | 11474 | VCS 353 | 14287 |
| SFU 316 | 10299 | SWS 741 | 10804 | TVL 307 | 12954 | USC 752 | 11475 | VCS 354 | 14288 |
| SFU 317 | 10300 | SWS 742 | 10805 | TVL 308 | 13165 | USC 753 | 11476 | VCS 355 | 14289 |
| SFU 318 | 10301 | SWS 743 | 10806 | TVL 309 | 13166 | USC 754 | 11477 | VCS 356 | 14294 |
| SFU 844 | 10407 | SWS 744 | 10807 | TVL 310 | 13167 | USC 755 | 11478 | VCS 357 | 14295 |
| SFU 845 | 10408 | SWS 745 | 10808 | TVS 367 | 10123 | USC 756 | 11479 | VCS 358 | 14296 |
| SFU 846 | 10409 | SWS 746 | 10841 | TWG 531 | 13549 | USC 757 | 11480 | VCS 359 | 14297 |
| SFU 847 | 10410 | SWS 747 | 10842 | TWG 541 | 13550 | USC 758 | 11481 | VCS 360 | 14298 |
| SFU 848 | 10411 | SWS 748 | 10843 | TWG 542 | 13551 | USC 759 | 11482 | VCS 361 | 14303 |
| SFU 849 | 10056 | SWS 749 | 10844 | TWG 543 | 13552 | USC 760 | 11483 | VCS 362 | 14304 |
| SFU 850 | 10057 | SWV 688 | 11326 | TWG 544 | 13553 | USC 761 | 11484 | VCS 363 | 14305 |
| SFU 851 | 10058 | SWV 689 | 11327 | TWG 545 | 13554 | USC 762 | 11485 | VCS 364 | 14306 |
| SFU 852 | 10059 | TBD 137 | 10447 | TWG 546 | 13555 | USC 763 | 11486 | VCS 365 | 14307 |
| SFU 853 | 10412 | TBD 138 | 10480 | TWG 547 | 13556 | USC 764 | 11487 | VCS 366 | 14290 |
| SFU 854 | 10413 | TBD 139 | 10481 | TWG 548 | 13562 | USC 765 | 11488 | VCS 367 | 14291 |
| SFU 855 | 10414 | TBD 140 | 10482 | TWG 549 | 13563 | USC 766 | 11489 | VCS 368 | 14292 |
| SFU 856 | 10415 | TBD 141 | 10483 | TWG 550 | 13568 | USC 767 | 11490 | VCS 369 | 14293 |
| SHR 440 | 10350 | TCS 159 | 13574 | TWG 551 | 13569 | USC 768 | 11491 | VCS 370 | 14299 |
| SHR 441 | 10351 | TCS 160 | 13575 | TWN 101 | 11325 | USC 769 | 11492 | VCS 371 | 14300 |
| SMO 78 | 11021 | TCS 161 | 13576 | TWN 102 | 11057 | USC 770 | 11493 | VCS 372 | 14301 |
| SMO 79 | 11022 | TCS 162 | 13577 | TWN 103 | 11058 | USC 771 | 11494 | VCS 373 | 14302 |
| SMO 80 | 11023 | TCS 163 | 13578 | TWN 104 | 11059 | USC 772 | 11495 | VCS 374 | 14308 |
| SMO 81 | 11024 | TCS 164 | 13579 | TWN 105 | 11060 | USC 773 | 11496 | VCS 375 | 14309 |
| SMO 82 | 11025 | TCS 165 | 13580 | TWN 106 | 11061 | USC 774 | 11497 | VCS 376 | 14310 |

| | | | | | | | | | |
|---|---|---|---|---|---|---|---|---|---|
| VCS 377 | 14311 | VYO 767 | 11322 | WRX 774 | 12216 | XEL 541 | 10282 | XUO 734 | 10077 |
| VDL 844 | 12428 | VYO 768 | 11323 | WRX 775 | 12217 | XEL 542 | 10283 | XUO 735 | 10078 |
| VDL 845 | 12429 | VYO 769 | 11324 | WSC 845 | 12125 | XEL 543 | 10284 | XUO 736 | 10079 |
| VFE 959 | 13974 | WBD 142 | 11976 | WSC 846 | 12126 | XEL 544 | 10285 | XUO 737 | 10080 |
| VFE 960 | 13975 | WBD 143 | 11977 | WSC 847 | 12127 | XEL 545 | 10286 | XYG 831 | 11094 |
| VFE 961 | 13819 | WBD 144 | 11978 | WSC 848 | 12128 | XEL 546 | 10287 | XYG 832 | 11095 |
| VFE 962 | 13820 | WBD 145 | 11979 | WSC 849 | 12129 | XEL 547 | 10288 | XYG 833 | 11096 |
| VFE 963 | 13821 | WBD 146 | 11980 | WSC 850 | 12130 | XEL 548 | 10289 | XYJ 717 | 10436 |
| VFE 964 | 13822 | WBD 602 | 11657 | WSC 851 | 12131 | XEL 549 | 10290 | YBD 200 | 12229 |
| VFE 965 | 13823 | WBD 603 | 11658 | WSC 852 | 12132 | XEL 550 | 10291 | YBD 201 | 12230 |
| VFE 966 | 13824 | WBD 604 | 11659 | WSC 853 | 12133 | XEL 551 | 10404 | YBD 202 | 12231 |
| VJB 943 | 11856 | WBD 605 | 11660 | WSC 854 | 12134 | XEL 552 | 10405 | YBD 203 | 12232 |
| VJB 944 | 11857 | WBD 606 | 11661 | WSC 855 | 12135 | XEL 553 | 10406 | YCY 809 | 12233 |
| VJB 945 | 11858 | WBD 607 | 11662 | WSC 856 | 12136 | XFE 440 | 14506 | YCY 810 | 12234 |
| VJB 946 | 11859 | WBD 608 | 11663 | WSC 857 | 12137 | XFE 441 | 14507 | YDL 314 | 12967 |
| VJB 947 | 11860 | WBD 609 | 11664 | WSC 858 | 12138 | XMR 942 | 12249 | YDL 315 | 12968 |
| VJB 948 | 11861 | WBD 610 | 11665 | WSC 859 | 12139 | XMR 943 | 12250 | YDL 316 | 12969 |
| VSV 444 | 12176 | WBD 611 | 11666 | WSC 860 | 12140 | XMR 944 | 12251 | YDL 317 | 12970 |
| VVL 730 | 13729 | WBD 612 | 11667 | WSC 861 | 12141 | XMR 945 | 12252 | YDL 318 | 12971 |
| VVL 731 | 13730 | WBD 613 | 11668 | WSC 862 | 12142 | XMR 946 | 12253 | YEL 223 | 10976 |
| VWC 45 | 13156 | WBD 614 | 11669 | WSC 863 | 12143 | XMR 947 | 12254 | YEL 224 | 10977 |
| VWC 46 | 13157 | WBD 615 | 11670 | WSC 864 | 12144 | XMR 948 | 12691 | YEL 225 | 11163 |
| VWC 47 | 13158 | WBD 616 | 11671 | WSC 865 | 12145 | XMR 949 | 12692 | YEL 226 | 11164 |
| VWC 48 | 13159 | WCY 694 | 11953 | WSC 866 | 12146 | XMR 950 | 12693 | YEL 227 | 11299 |
| VWC 49 | 13160 | WCY 695 | 11954 | WSC 867 | 12147 | XMR 951 | 12694 | YEL 228 | 11300 |
| VWC 50 | 13162 | WCY 696 | 11912 | WSC 868 | 12148 | XMR 952 | 12695 | YEL 229 | 11301 |
| VWC 51 | 13164 | WCY 697 | 11913 | WSC 869 | 12149 | XMR 953 | 12696 | YNG 779 | 10634 |
| VWC 52 | 13161 | WCY 698 | 11914 | WSJ 327 | 11018 | XMR 954 | 12697 | YNG 780 | 10635 |
| VWC 53 | 13163 | WCY 701 | 11915 | WVL 514 | 14490 | XMR 955 | 12698 | YNG 781 | 10636 |
| VWG 353 | 14273 | WCY 702 | 11916 | WVL 515 | 14491 | XMR 956 | 12699 | YNG 782 | 10637 |
| VWG 354 | 14274 | WCY 703 | 11917 | WWU 269 | 10484 | XMR 957 | 12700 | YNG 783 | 10638 |
| VWG 355 | 14275 | WCY 704 | 11918 | WWU 270 | 10485 | XPM 41 | 12896 | YNG 784 | 10639 |
| VWG 356 | 14276 | WCY 705 | 11919 | WWU 271 | 10486 | XPM 42 | 12897 | YNG 785 | 10640 |
| VWG 357 | 14277 | WCY 706 | 11672 | WWU 272 | 10487 | XPM 43 | 12898 | YNG 786 | 10641 |
| VWG 358 | 14278 | WCY 707 | 11673 | XAO 600 | 11287 | XPM 44 | 12899 | YNG 787 | 10642 |
| VWG 359 | 14279 | WCY 708 | 11674 | XAO 601 | 11288 | XPM 45 | 13018 | YNV 617 | 12541 |
| VWG 360 | 14280 | WCY 709 | 11675 | XAO 602 | 10928 | XPM 46 | 13019 | YNV 618 | 12542 |
| VWG 361 | 14281 | WCY 710 | 11676 | XAO 603 | 10929 | XPM 47 | 13020 | YNV 619 | 12543 |
| VWG 362 | 14282 | WCY 711 | 11677 | XAO 604 | 10930 | XPM 48 | 13021 | YNV 620 | 12544 |
| VWG 363 | 14283 | WCY 712 | 11678 | XAO 605 | 10931 | XPM 49 | 13022 | YNV 621 | 12545 |
| VWG 364 | 14284 | WCY 713 | 11679 | XAO 606 | 10932 | XPM 50 | 13023 | YNV 622 | 12546 |
| VWO 215 | 11178 | WCY 714 | 11680 | XAO 607 | 10933 | XUO 711 | 10038 | YNV 623 | 12547 |
| VWO 216 | 11179 | WCY 715 | 11681 | XAO 608 | 10934 | XUO 712 | 10037 | YNV 624 | 12548 |
| VWO 217 | 11180 | WFE 415 | 14153 | XAO 609 | 10935 | XUO 713 | 10039 | YNV 625 | 12549 |
| VWO 218 | 11181 | WFE 416 | 14154 | XAO 610 | 11353 | XUO 714 | 10040 | YNV 626 | 12550 |
| VWO 219 | 11182 | WJB 223 | 12078 | XAO 611 | 11354 | XUO 715 | 10042 | YNV 627 | 12551 |
| VWO 220 | 11183 | WJB 224 | 12079 | XCS 946 | 14343 | XUO 716 | 10041 | YNV 628 | 12552 |
| VWO 221 | 11184 | WJB 225 | 12080 | XCS 947 | 14344 | XUO 717 | 10043 | YRU 56 | 10954 |
| VWO 222 | 11185 | WJB 226 | 12081 | XCS 948 | 14345 | XUO 718 | 10044 | YRU 57 | 10955 |
| VWO 223 | 11186 | WJB 227 | 12082 | XCS 949 | 14346 | XUO 719 | 10045 | YRU 58 | 10956 |
| VWO 224 | 11187 | WJB 228 | 12083 | XCS 950 | 14347 | XUO 720 | 10046 | YRU 59 | 10957 |
| VWO 225 | 11188 | WJB 229 | 12084 | XCS 951 | 14348 | XUO 721 | 10047 | YRU 60 | 10958 |
| VWO 226 | 11189 | WJB 230 | 12085 | XCS 952 | 14349 | XUO 722 | 10048 | YRU 61 | 10959 |
| VWO 227 | 11190 | WJB 231 | 12086 | XCS 953 | 14350 | XUO 723 | 10049 | YRU 62 | 10960 |
| VWO 228 | 11191 | WJB 232 | 12087 | XCS 954 | 14351 | XUO 724 | 10050 | YRU 63 | 10961 |
| VWO 229 | 11192 | WJB 233 | 12088 | XCS 955 | 14352 | XUO 725 | 10068 | YRU 64 | 10962 |
| VWO 230 | 11193 | WJB 234 | 12089 | XCS 956 | 14353 | XUO 726 | 10069 | YRU 65 | 10965 |
| VWO 231 | 11194 | WJB 235 | 12090 | XCS 957 | 14354 | XUO 727 | 10070 | YRU 66 | 10966 |
| VWO 232 | 11195 | WNJ 36 | 12272 | XCS 958 | 14355 | XUO 728 | 10071 | YRU 67 | 10967 |
| VWU 232 | 10665 | WNJ 37 | 12273 | XCS 959 | 14356 | XUO 729 | 10072 | YRU 68 | 10963 |
| VWU 233 | 10666 | WNJ 38 | 12274 | XCS 960 | 14357 | XUO 730 | 10073 | YRU 69 | 10964 |
| VWU 234 | 10667 | WNJ 39 | 12275 | XCS 961 | 14358 | XUO 731 | 10074 | YRU 70 | 10968 |
| VYO 765 | 11320 | WNJ 40 | 12276 | XCS 962 | 14359 | XUO 732 | 10075 | YRU 71 | 10969 |
| VYO 766 | 11321 | WRX 773 | 12215 | XCS 963 | 14360 | XUO 733 | 10076 | YRU 72 | 10970 |

| | | | | | | | | | | | |
|---|---|---|---|---|---|---|---|---|---|---|---|
| YRU 73 | 10971 | 3003 AH | 10131 | 1251 EV | 11137 | 1225 FM | 13351 | 4221 FM | 14438 | | |
| YRU 74 | 10972 | 3004 AH | 10370 | 1252 EV | 11138 | 1226 FM | 13352 | 4222 FM | 14439 | | |
| YRU 75 | 10973 | 3005 AH | 10371 | 1253 EV | 11139 | 1227 FM | 13353 | 4223 FM | 14440 | | |
| YRU 76 | 10974 | 3006 AH | 10372 | 1254 EV | 11140 | 1228 FM | 13354 | 4224 FM | 13764 | | |
| YRU 77 | 10975 | 3007 AH | 10373 | 1255 EV | 11141 | 1229 FM | 13355 | 4225 FM | 13765 | | |
| YWB 152 | 10004 | 3008 AH | 10374 | 1256 EV | 11142 | 1231 FM | 13356 | 4226 FM | 13766 | | |
| YWB 153 | 10005 | 3009 AH | 10375 | 1257 EV | 11143 | 1232 FM | 13357 | 4227 FM | 13767 | | |
| YWB 292 | 10006 | 3010 AH | 10376 | 1258 EV | 11144 | 1233 FM | 13358 | 5454 FM | 13626 | | |
| YWB 293 | 10007 | 3011 AH | 10377 | 1259 EV | 11145 | 1234 FM | 13359 | 5455 FM | 13627 | | |
| YWB 294 | 10008 | 3012 AH | 10378 | 1260 EV | 11146 | 1235 FM | 13360 | 5457 FM | 13628 | | |
| YWS 870 | 13494 | 3013 AH | 10379 | 1261 EV | 11147 | 1236 FM | 13361 | 5458 FM | 13629 | | |
| YWS 871 | 13495 | 3014 AH | 10380 | 1262 EV | 11148 | 1237 FM | 13362 | 6334 FM | 14081 | | |
| YWS 872 | 13496 | 3015 AH | 10381 | 1263 EV | 11149 | 1238 FM | 13363 | 6335 FM | 14082 | | |
| YWS 873 | 13497 | 3016 AH | 10382 | 1264 EV | 11150 | 1239 FM | 13364 | 6336 FM | 14083 | | |
| YWS 874 | 13498 | 3017 AH | 10383 | 1265 EV | 11151 | 1241 FM | 13365 | 6337 FM | 14084 | | |
| YWS 875 | 13499 | 3018 AH | 10384 | 1266 EV | 11152 | 1242 FM | 13366 | 7281 FM | 14441 | | |
| YWS 876 | 13500 | 3019 AH | 10385 | 1267 EV | 11153 | 1243 FM | 13367 | 7282 FM | 14442 | | |
| YWS 877 | 13501 | 3020 AH | 10386 | 1268 EV | 11154 | 1244 FM | 13368 | 7283 FM | 14443 | | |
| YWS 878 | 13502 | 5788 AH | 11289 | 1269 EV | 11155 | 1245 FM | 13369 | 7284 FM | 14444 | | |
| YWS 879 | 13503 | 5789 AH | 11290 | 1270 EV | 11156 | 1246 FM | 13370 | 7285 FM | 14482 | | |
| YWS 880 | 13504 | 5790 AH | 11291 | 3652 FG | 14235 | 1247 FM | 13371 | 7286 FM | 14483 | | |
| YWS 881 | 13505 | 5791 AH | 11292 | 3653 FG | 14236 | 2172 FM | 13600 | 7619 FM | 14445 | | |
| YWS 882 | 13506 | 6557 AH | 11355 | 3654 FG | 14237 | 2173 FM | 13601 | 7622 FM | 14446 | | |
| YWS 883 | 13507 | 6558 AH | 11356 | 3655 FG | 14238 | 2174 FM | 13602 | 7623 FM | 14447 | | |
| YWS 884 | 13508 | 6559 AH | 11357 | 3656 FG | 14239 | 2175 FM | 13603 | 7624 FM | 14448 | | |
| YWS 885 | 13509 | 6560 AH | 11358 | 3657 FG | 14240 | 2176 FM | 13604 | 7625 FM | 14449 | | |
| YWS 886 | 13510 | 6561 AH | 11359 | 3658 FG | 14241 | 2177 FM | 13605 | 7015 HK | 10143 | | |
| YWS 887 | 13511 | 6562 AH | 11360 | 3659 FG | 14242 | 2178 FM | 13606 | 7016 HK | 10144 | | |
| YWS 888 | 13512 | 6563 AH | 11361 | 3660 FG | 14243 | 2179 FM | 13607 | 7017 HK | 10145 | | |
| YWS 889 | 13513 | 6564 AH | 11362 | 3661 FG | 14244 | 2181 FM | 13608 | 7018 HK | 10146 | | |
| YWS 890 | 13514 | 9216 AH | 10936 | 3662 FG | 14245 | 2182 FM | 13609 | 1536 HN | 11971 | | |
| YWS 891 | 13515 | 9217 AH | 10937 | 3663 FG | 14246 | 2183 FM | 13610 | 1537 HN | 11972 | | |
| YWS 892 | 13516 | 9459 AH | 11134 | 3664 FG | 14247 | 2184 FM | 13611 | 1538 HN | 11973 | | |
| YWS 893 | 13517 | 9460 AH | 11135 | 3665 FG | 14248 | 2185 FM | 13612 | 1539 HN | 11974 | | |
| YWS 894 | 13518 | 9461 AH | 11136 | 3666 FG | 14249 | 2186 FM | 13613 | 1540 HN | 11975 | | |
| YWT 290 | 11272 | 4655 AP | 13744 | 3667 FG | 14250 | 2187 FM | 13614 | 2057 HN | 11550 | | |
| YWT 291 | 11273 | 4656 AP | 13745 | 3668 FG | 14251 | 2188 FM | 13615 | 2058 HN | 11551 | | |
| YWT 292 | 11274 | 4657 AP | 13746 | 3669 FG | 14252 | 2189 FM | 13616 | 2059 HN | 11552 | | |
| YWT 293 | 11275 | 2714 EL | 11157 | 3670 FG | 14253 | 2191 FM | 13617 | 2060 HN | 11553 | | |
| YWT 294 | 11276 | 2715 EL | 11158 | 3671 FG | 14254 | 2192 FM | 13618 | 2061 HN | 11554 | | |
| YWW 73 | 11088 | 2716 EL | 11159 | 1198 FM | 12900 | 2193 FM | 13619 | 2062 HN | 11555 | | |
| YWW 74 | 11089 | 2717 EL | 11160 | 1199 FM | 12901 | 2194 FM | 13620 | 2063 HN | 11556 | | |
| YWW 75 | 11090 | 2718 EL | 11161 | 1201 FM | 12902 | 2195 FM | 13621 | 2064 HN | 11557 | | |
| YWW 76 | 11091 | 2719 EL | 11162 | 1202 FM | 12905 | 2196 FM | 13622 | 2065 HN | 11558 | | |
| YWW 77 | 11093 | 5666 EL | 11605 | 1203 FM | 12906 | 2197 FM | 13623 | 2066 HN | 11559 | | |
| YWW 78 | 11092 | 5667 EL | 11606 | 1204 FM | 12907 | 2198 FM | 13624 | 2067 HN | 11560 | | |
| | | 5668 EL | 11607 | 1205 FM | 12908 | 2199 FM | 13625 | 2068 HN | 11561 | | |
| 1378 R | 13648 | 5669 EL | 11608 | 1206 FM | 12909 | 4202 FM | 13749 | 2069 HN | 11562 | | |
| 1379 R | 13649 | 5670 EL | 11609 | 1207 FM | 12903 | 4203 FM | 13750 | 2070 HN | 11563 | | |
| 1380 R | 13650 | 5671 EL | 11610 | 1208 FM | 12904 | 4204 FM | 13751 | 2071 HN | 11564 | | |
| 1381 R | 13651 | 5672 EL | 11611 | 1209 FM | 12910 | 4205 FM | 13752 | 2072 HN | 11565 | | |
| 1382 R | 13652 | 5673 EL | 11612 | 1211 FM | 12911 | 4206 FM | 13753 | 2073 HN | 11566 | | |
| 1383 R | 13653 | 5674 EL | 11613 | 1212 FM | 12912 | 4207 FM | 13754 | 2074 HN | 11567 | | |
| 1384 R | 14155 | 5675 EL | 11614 | 1213 FM | 12913 | 4208 FM | 13755 | 2075 HN | 11568 | | |
| 1385 R | 14156 | 5676 EL | 11615 | 1214 FM | 12914 | 4209 FM | 13756 | 2076 HN | 11569 | | |
| 1386 R | 14157 | 5677 EL | 11616 | 1215 FM | 13342 | 4211 FM | 13757 | 2583 HN | 11862 | | |
| 1387 R | 13982 | 5678 EL | 11617 | 1216 FM | 13343 | 4212 FM | 13758 | 2584 HN | 11863 | | |
| 1388 R | 13983 | 5679 EL | 11618 | 1217 FM | 13344 | 4213 FM | 13759 | 2585 HN | 11864 | | |
| 1389 R | 13984 | 5680 EL | 11619 | 1218 FM | 13345 | 4214 FM | 13760 | 2586 HN | 11865 | | |
| 1390 R | 13985 | 6226 EL | 11938 | 1219 FM | 13346 | 4215 FM | 13761 | 2587 HN | 11866 | | |
| 1391 R | 13986 | 6227 EL | 11939 | 1221 FM | 13347 | 4216 FM | 13762 | 2588 HN | 11867 | | |
| 1392 R | 13987 | 6228 EL | 11940 | 1222 FM | 13348 | 4217 FM | 13763 | 2589 HN | 11868 | | |
| 3001 AH | 10129 | 6229 EL | 11941 | 1223 FM | 13349 | 4218 FM | 14436 | 2590 HN | 11869 | | |
| 3002 AH | 10130 | 6230 EL | 11942 | 1224 FM | 13350 | 4219 FM | 14437 | 2591 HN | 11870 | | |

| | | | | | | | | | |
|---|---|---|---|---|---|---|---|---|---|
| 2592 HN | 11871 | 5036 HN | 12648 | 7013 HN | 12872 | 8685 HN | 13435 | 7683 LJ | 13264 |
| 2593 HN | 11872 | 5037 HN | 12649 | 7014 HN | 12873 | 8686 HN | 13436 | 7684 LJ | 13265 |
| 2594 HN | 11873 | 5038 HN | 12650 | 7015 HN | 12874 | 8687 HN | 13437 | 7685 LJ | 13266 |
| 2595 HN | 11874 | 5039 HN | 12651 | 7112 HN | 13202 | 8688 HN | 13438 | 7686 LJ | 13267 |
| 2596 HN | 11875 | 5040 HN | 12652 | 7113 HN | 13203 | 8689 HN | 13439 | 7687 LJ | 13268 |
| 2597 HN | 11876 | 5041 HN | 12653 | 7114 HN | 13204 | 8690 HN | 13440 | 5601 NG | 11589 |
| 2598 HN | 11877 | 5042 HN | 12654 | 7115 HN | 13205 | 8691 HN | 13441 | 5602 NG | 11590 |
| 2599 HN | 11878 | 5043 HN | 12655 | 7116 HN | 13206 | 8692 HN | 13442 | 5603 NG | 11591 |
| 2600 HN | 11879 | 5044 HN | 12656 | 7117 HN | 13207 | 8693 HN | 13443 | 5604 NG | 11592 |
| 2601 HN | 11880 | 5045 HN | 12657 | 7118 HN | 13208 | 8694 HN | 13444 | 5605 NG | 11593 |
| 2602 HN | 11881 | 5046 HN | 12658 | 7119 HN | 13209 | 8695 HN | 13445 | 5606 NG | 11594 |
| 2603 HN | 11882 | 5047 HN | 12659 | 7120 HN | 13210 | 8696 HN | 13446 | 5607 NG | 11595 |
| 2604 HN | 11883 | 5048 HN | 12660 | 7121 HN | 13211 | 8697 HN | 13447 | 5608 NG | 11596 |
| 2605 HN | 11884 | 5049 HN | 12661 | 7122 HN | 13212 | 8698 HN | 13448 | 5609 NG | 11597 |
| 2606 HN | 11885 | 5050 HN | 12662 | 7123 HN | 13213 | 8699 HN | 13449 | 5610 NG | 11598 |
| 2607 HN | 11886 | 5051 HN | 12663 | 7124 HN | 13214 | 8700 HN | 13450 | 5611 NG | 11599 |
| 2608 HN | 11887 | 5052 HN | 12664 | 7125 HN | 13215 | 8701 HN | 13451 | 5612 NG | 11600 |
| 2609 HN | 11888 | 5053 HN | 12665 | 7126 HN | 13216 | 9636 HN | 13453 | 5613 NG | 11601 |
| 2610 HN | 11889 | 5054 HN | 12666 | 7127 HN | 13217 | 9637 HN | 13454 | 5614 NG | 11602 |
| 2611 HN | 11890 | 5055 HN | 12667 | 7128 HN | 13218 | 9638 HN | 13455 | 5615 NG | 11603 |
| 2612 HN | 11891 | 5056 HN | 12668 | 7129 HN | 13219 | 9639 HN | 13456 | 5616 NG | 11604 |
| 2613 HN | 11892 | 5057 HN | 12669 | 7130 HN | 13220 | 9640 HN | 13457 | 6566 NG | 11363 |
| 2614 HN | 11893 | 5058 HN | 12670 | 7131 HN | 13221 | 9641 HN | 13458 | 6567 NG | 11997 |
| 2615 HN | 11894 | 5059 HN | 12671 | 7132 HN | 13222 | 1468 LJ | 12200 | 6568 NG | 11998 |
| 2616 HN | 11895 | 5060 HN | 12672 | 7133 HN | 13223 | 1469 LJ | 12201 | 6569 NG | 11999 |
| 2617 HN | 11896 | 5061 HN | 12673 | 7134 HN | 13224 | 1470 LJ | 12202 | 6570 NG | 12000 |
| 2618 HN | 11897 | 5062 HN | 12674 | 7135 HN | 13225 | 1471 LJ | 12203 | 6571 NG | 12001 |
| 2619 HN | 11898 | 5077 HN | 12371 | 7136 HN | 13226 | 1472 LJ | 12204 | 6572 NG | 12002 |
| 2620 HN | 11899 | 5078 HN | 12372 | 7432 HN | 13285 | 1473 LJ | 12205 | 6573 NG | 12003 |
| 2621 HN | 11900 | 5079 HN | 12373 | 7433 HN | 13286 | 4377 LJ | 12411 | 6574 NG | 12004 |
| 2622 HN | 11901 | 5080 HN | 12374 | 7434 HN | 13287 | 4378 LJ | 12412 | 6575 NG | 12005 |
| 2623 HN | 11902 | 5081 HN | 12375 | 7435 HN | 13288 | 4379 LJ | 12413 | 6576 NG | 12006 |
| 2624 HN | 11903 | 5082 HN | 12376 | 7541 HN | 13275 | 4380 LJ | 12414 | 6577 NG | 12007 |
| 2625 HN | 11904 | 5083 HN | 12377 | 7542 HN | 13276 | 4381 LJ | 12415 | 6578 NG | 12008 |
| 2626 HN | 11905 | 5084 HN | 12378 | 7543 HN | 13277 | 4382 LJ | 12416 | 7792 NG | 11930 |
| 2627 HN | 11906 | 5085 HN | 12379 | 7544 HN | 13278 | 4383 LJ | 12417 | 7793 NG | 11931 |
| 2628 HN | 11907 | 5086 HN | 12380 | 7545 HN | 13279 | 4384 LJ | 12418 | 7794 NG | 11932 |
| 2629 HN | 11908 | 5087 HN | 12529 | 8109 HN | 13041 | 4385 LJ | 12419 | 1117 PW | 12392 |
| 2630 HN | 11909 | 5088 HN | 12530 | 8110 HN | 13042 | 4386 LJ | 12420 | 1118 PW | 12393 |
| 2631 HN | 11910 | 5089 HN | 12531 | 8111 HN | 13043 | 4387 LJ | 12421 | 1119 PW | 12394 |
| 2632 HN | 11911 | 5090 HN | 12532 | 8112 HN | 13044 | 4388 LJ | 12567 | 1120 PW | 12395 |
| 2917 HN | 11823 | 5091 HN | 12533 | 8113 HN | 13045 | 4389 LJ | 12568 | 1121 PW | 12396 |
| 2918 HN | 11824 | 5092 HN | 12534 | 8663 HN | 13280 | 4390 LJ | 12569 | 1122 PW | 12397 |
| 2919 HN | 11825 | 5093 HN | 12535 | 8664 HN | 13281 | 4391 LJ | 12570 | 1123 PW | 12398 |
| 2920 HN | 11826 | 5094 HN | 12536 | 8665 HN | 13282 | 4392 LJ | 12571 | 1124 PW | 12399 |
| 2921 HN | 11827 | 5095 HN | 12537 | 8666 HN | 13283 | 4393 LJ | 12572 | 1125 PW | 12400 |
| 4206 HN | 12224 | 5096 HN | 12538 | 8667 HN | 13284 | 7118 LJ | 12818 | 2926 PW | 12401 |
| 4207 HN | 12225 | 5097 HN | 12539 | 8668 HN | 13418 | 7119 LJ | 12819 | 2927 PW | 12402 |
| 4208 HN | 12226 | 5098 HN | 12540 | 8669 HN | 13419 | 7120 LJ | 12820 | 2928 PW | 12403 |
| 4209 HN | 12227 | 5099 HN | 12358 | 8670 HN | 13420 | 7121 LJ | 12821 | 2929 PW | 12404 |
| 4210 HN | 12228 | 5100 HN | 12359 | 8671 HN | 13421 | 7122 LJ | 12822 | 2930 PW | 12405 |
| 5022 HN | 12675 | 5101 HN | 12360 | 8672 HN | 13422 | 7123 LJ | 12823 | 2931 PW | 12406 |
| 5023 HN | 12676 | 5102 HN | 12361 | 8673 HN | 13423 | 7671 LJ | 12941 | 2932 PW | 12407 |
| 5024 HN | 12677 | 5103 HN | 12362 | 8674 HN | 13424 | 7672 LJ | 12942 | 2933 PW | 12408 |
| 5025 HN | 12678 | 5104 HN | 12363 | 8675 HN | 13425 | 7673 LJ | 12943 | 2934 PW | 12409 |
| 5026 HN | 12679 | 5105 HN | 12364 | 8676 HN | 13426 | 7674 LJ | 12944 | 2935 PW | 12410 |
| 5027 HN | 12680 | 5106 HN | 12365 | 8677 HN | 13427 | 7675 LJ | 12945 | 3804 PW | 12798 |
| 5028 HN | 12681 | 5107 HN | 12366 | 8678 HN | 13428 | 7676 LJ | 12946 | 3805 PW | 12799 |
| 5029 HN | 12682 | 5108 HN | 12367 | 8679 HN | 13429 | 7677 LJ | 12947 | 3806 PW | 12800 |
| 5030 HN | 12683 | 5109 HN | 12368 | 8680 HN | 13430 | 7678 LJ | 12948 | 3807 PW | 12801 |
| 5031 HN | 12684 | 5110 HN | 12369 | 8681 HN | 13431 | 7679 LJ | 12949 | 3808 PW | 12802 |
| 5033 HN | 12645 | 5111 HN | 12370 | 8682 HN | 13432 | 7680 LJ | 12950 | 3809 PW | 12803 |
| 5034 HN | 12646 | 7011 HN | 12870 | 8683 HN | 13433 | 7681 LJ | 12951 | 3810 PW | 12804 |
| 5035 HN | 12647 | 7012 HN | 12871 | 8684 HN | 13434 | 7682 LJ | 13263 | 3811 PW | 12805 |

| | | | | | | | |
|---|---|---|---|---|---|---|---|
| 3812 PW | 12806 | 4824 VF | 12192 | 9769 WU | 11696 | 686 AAM | 13008 | 216 ANN | 10305 |
| 3813 PW | 12807 | 4825 VF | 12193 | 9770 WU | 11697 | 687 AAM | 13009 | 901 AUO | 10452 |
| 3814 PW | 12808 | 4826 VF | 12194 | 9771 WU | 11698 | 688 AAM | 13010 | 902 AUO | 10453 |
| 3815 PW | 12809 | 8001 VF | 12727 | 2223 WW | 11699 | 689 AAM | 13011 | 903 AUO | 10454 |
| 8036 PW | 12921 | 8002 VF | 12728 | 2224 WW | 11700 | 690 AAM | 13012 | 904 AUO | 10455 |
| 8037 PW | 12922 | 8003 VF | 12729 | 2225 WW | 11701 | 691 AAM | 13013 | 905 AUO | 10456 |
| 8038 PW | 12923 | 8004 VF | 12730 | 2226 WW | 11702 | 692 AAM | 13014 | 906 AUO | 10457 |
| 8039 PW | 12924 | 8005 VF | 12731 | 2227 WW | 11703 | 693 AAM | 13015 | 907 AUO | 10458 |
| 8040 PW | 12925 | 8006 VF | 12732 | 2228 WW | 11704 | 694 AAM | 13016 | 908 AUO | 10459 |
| 2688 RU | 13638 | 8007 VF | 12733 | 2229 WW | 11705 | 695 AAM | 13017 | 909 AUO | 10460 |
| 2689 RU | 13639 | 8008 VF | 12734 | 2230 WW | 11706 | 3 AAX | 11764 | 910 AUO | 10461 |
| 2690 RU | 13640 | 8009 VF | 12735 | 8124 WX | 12243 | 4 AAX | 11765 | 911 AUO | 10462 |
| 2691 RU | 13641 | 3384 VW | 11933 | 8125 WX | 12244 | 5 AAX | 11766 | 912 AUO | 10463 |
| 2692 RU | 13642 | 3385 VW | 11934 | 8126 WX | 12245 | 6 AAX | 11767 | 913 AUO | 10464 |
| 2693 RU | 13643 | 3386 VW | 11935 | 8127 WX | 12246 | 7 AAX | 11768 | 914 AUO | 10465 |
| 4688 RU | 13803 | 3387 VW | 11936 | 8128 WX | 12247 | 8 AAX | 11769 | 915 AUO | 10466 |
| 4689 RU | 13804 | 3388 VW | 11937 | 8129 WX | 12248 | 9 AAX | 11770 | 916 AUO | 10467 |
| 4690 RU | 13805 | 2723 VX | 11828 | 7902 WY | 12718 | 10 AAX | 11771 | 917 AUO | 10468 |
| 4691 RU | 13806 | 2724 VX | 11829 | 7903 WY | 12719 | 11 AAX | 11772 | 361 BAX | 12637 |
| 4692 RU | 13807 | 2725 VX | 11830 | 7904 WY | 12720 | 12 AAX | 11773 | 362 BAX | 12638 |
| 4693 RU | 13808 | 2726 VX | 11831 | 7905 WY | 12721 | 13 AAX | 11774 | 363 BAX | 12639 |
| 4694 RU | 13809 | 2727 VX | 11832 | 7906 WY | 12722 | 14 AAX | 11775 | 364 BAX | 12640 |
| 4695 RU | 13810 | 2728 VX | 11833 | 7907 WY | 12723 | 15 AAX | 11776 | 365 BAX | 12641 |
| 4696 RU | 13811 | 2729 VX | 11834 | 7908 WY | 12724 | 16 AAX | 11777 | 366 BAX | 12642 |
| 4697 RU | 13812 | 2730 VX | 11835 | 7909 WY | 12725 | 17 AAX | 11778 | 367 BAX | 12643 |
| 4698 RU | 13813 | 2731 VX | 11836 | 7910 WY | 12726 | 18 AAX | 11779 | 368 BAX | 12644 |
| 4699 RU | 13814 | 2732 VX | 11837 | 2010 YG | 12430 | 19 AAX | 11014 | 536 BBL | 13188 |
| 8943 SF | 14255 | 2733 VX | 11838 | 2011 YG | 12431 | 20 AAX | 11015 | 537 BBL | 13189 |
| 8944 SF | 14256 | 2734 VX | 11839 | 2012 YG | 12432 | 520 ABL | 12839 | 538 BBL | 13190 |
| 8945 SF | 14257 | 2735 VX | 11840 | 2013 YG | 12433 | 135 ACY | 12685 | 539 BBL | 13191 |
| 8946 SF | 14258 | 2736 VX | 11841 | 2014 YG | 12434 | 136 ACY | 12686 | 540 BBL | 13192 |
| 8947 SF | 14259 | 2737 VX | 11842 | 2015 YG | 12435 | 137 ACY | 12687 | 541 BBL | 13193 |
| 8948 SF | 14260 | 2738 VX | 11843 | 2016 YG | 12436 | 138 ACY | 12688 | 542 BBL | 13194 |
| 8949 SF | 14261 | 2739 VX | 11844 | 2017 YG | 12437 | 139 ACY | 12689 | 543 BBL | 13195 |
| 8950 SF | 14262 | 2740 VX | 11845 | 2018 YG | 12438 | 140 ACY | 12690 | 544 BBL | 13196 |
| 8951 SF | 14263 | 2741 VX | 11846 | 2019 YG | 12439 | 141 ACY | 12553 | 545 BBL | 13197 |
| 8952 SF | 14264 | 2742 VX | 11847 | 2020 YG | 12440 | 142 ACY | 12554 | 546 BBL | 13198 |
| 8953 SF | 14265 | 1880 WA | 12255 | 2021 YG | 12441 | 143 ACY | 12381 | 547 BBL | 13199 |
| 8954 SF | 14266 | 1881 WA | 12256 | 2022 YG | 12442 | 144 ACY | 12382 | 548 BBL | 13200 |
| 8955 SF | 14267 | 1882 WA | 12257 | 2023 YG | 12443 | 145 ACY | 12383 | 549 BBL | 13201 |
| 8956 SF | 14268 | 1910 WA | 12258 | 2024 YG | 12449 | 146 ACY | 12384 | 467 BMR | 14061 |
| 8957 SF | 14269 | 1911 WA | 12259 | 2025 YG | 12450 | 147 ACY | 12385 | 468 BMR | 14062 |
| 8958 SF | 14270 | 4506 WU | 11097 | 2026 YG | 12451 | 148 ACY | 12386 | 469 BMR | 14063 |
| 8959 SF | 14271 | 4507 WU | 11098 | 2027 YG | 12444 | 149 ACY | 12387 | 470 BMR | 14064 |
| 8960 SF | 14272 | 4508 WU | 11099 | 2028 YG | 12445 | 150 ACY | 12388 | 473 BMR | 13876 |
| 7401 SP | 13557 | 4509 WU | 11100 | 2029 YG | 12446 | 151 ACY | 12389 | 474 BMR | 13877 |
| 7402 SP | 13558 | 4510 WU | 11101 | 2030 YG | 12447 | 152 ACY | 12390 | 475 BMR | 13878 |
| 7403 SP | 13559 | 7935 WU | 11955 | 2031 YG | 12448 | 153 ACY | 12391 | 476 BMR | 13879 |
| 7404 SP | 13560 | 7936 WU | 11956 | 9168 YG | 12864 | 458 ADL | 14227 | 477 BMR | 13880 |
| 7405 SP | 13561 | 7937 WU | 11957 | 9169 YG | 12865 | 459 ADL | 14228 | 478 BMR | 13881 |
| 7406 SP | 13564 | 9755 WU | 11682 | 9170 YG | 12866 | 460 ADL | 14229 | 479 BMR | 13882 |
| 7407 SP | 13565 | 9756 WU | 11683 | 673 AAM | 12867 | 461 ADL | 14230 | 41 BNG | 12926 |
| 7408 SP | 13566 | 9757 WU | 11684 | 674 AAM | 12868 | 462 ADL | 14231 | 42 BNG | 12927 |
| 7409 SP | 13567 | 9758 WU | 11685 | 675 AAM | 12869 | 463 ADL | 14232 | 43 BNG | 12928 |
| 7410 SP | 13570 | 9759 WU | 11686 | 676 AAM | 12998 | 464 ADL | 14233 | 471 BNG | 13372 |
| 7411 SP | 13571 | 9760 WU | 11687 | 677 AAM | 12999 | 465 ADL | 14234 | 472 BNG | 13373 |
| 7412 SP | 13572 | 9761 WU | 11688 | 678 AAM | 13000 | 130 AMW | 13703 | 473 BNG | 13374 |
| 7413 SP | 13573 | 9762 WU | 11689 | 679 AAM | 13001 | 131 AMW | 13704 | 474 BNG | 13375 |
| 4227 VF | 12186 | 9763 WU | 11690 | 680 AAM | 13002 | 132 AMW | 13705 | 475 BNG | 13376 |
| 4228 VF | 12187 | 9764 WU | 11691 | 681 AAM | 13003 | 133 AMW | 13706 | 476 BNG | 13377 |
| 4229 VF | 12188 | 9765 WU | 11692 | 682 AAM | 13004 | 134 AMW | 13707 | 556 BNG | 13119 |
| 4821 VF | 12189 | 9766 WU | 11693 | 683 AAM | 13005 | 213 ANN | 10302 | 557 BNG | 13120 |
| 4822 VF | 12190 | 9767 WU | 11694 | 684 AAM | 13006 | 214 ANN | 10303 | 558 BNG | 13121 |
| 4823 VF | 12191 | 9768 WU | 11695 | 685 AAM | 13007 | 215 ANN | 10304 | 816 BNG | 13630 |

| | | | | | | | | | |
|---|---|---|---|---|---|---|---|---|---|
| 817 BNG | 13631 | 508 BTA | 11076 | 837 BWY | 13475 | 672 COD | 11391 | 988 DAE | 10369 |
| 818 BNG | 13632 | 509 BTA | 11077 | 838 BWY | 13476 | 673 COD | 11392 | 483 DAH | 13384 |
| 819 BNG | 13633 | 510 BTA | 11078 | 839 BWY | 13477 | 674 COD | 11393 | 484 DAH | 13385 |
| 820 BNG | 13634 | 511 BTA | 11079 | 840 BWY | 13478 | 675 COD | 11394 | 485 DAH | 13386 |
| 821 BNG | 13635 | 512 BTA | 11080 | 1 BXB | 12221 | 676 COD | 11395 | 486 DAH | 13387 |
| 822 BNG | 13636 | 513 BTA | 11081 | 2 BXB | 12219 | 677 COD | 11396 | 487 DAH | 13388 |
| 823 BNG | 13637 | 514 BTA | 11082 | 3 BXB | 12220 | 678 COD | 11397 | 488 DAH | 13389 |
| 477 BPW | 13378 | 515 BTA | 11083 | 4 BXB | 12222 | 679 COD | 11398 | 258 DCY | 13024 |
| 478 BPW | 13379 | 516 BTA | 11084 | 5 BXB | 12223 | 680 COD | 11399 | 259 DCY | 13025 |
| 559 BPW | 13122 | 517 BTA | 11085 | 997 CHN | 10001 | 681 COD | 11384 | 260 DCY | 13026 |
| 560 BPW | 13123 | 518 BTA | 11086 | 998 CHN | 10002 | 682 COD | 11385 | 261 DCY | 13027 |
| 561 BPW | 13124 | 519 BTA | 11087 | 811 CHU | 10182 | 51 CPW | 12936 | 262 DCY | 13028 |
| 501 BRM | 11545 | 479 BVF | 13380 | 812 CHU | 10183 | 52 CPW | 12937 | 263 DCY | 13029 |
| 502 BRM | 11546 | 480 BVF | 13381 | 813 CHU | 10184 | 53 CPW | 12938 | 264 DCY | 13030 |
| 503 BRM | 11547 | 481 BVF | 13382 | 814 CHU | 10185 | 54 CPW | 12939 | 265 DCY | 13031 |
| 504 BRM | 11548 | 482 BVF | 13383 | 815 CHU | 10186 | 55 CPW | 12940 | 266 DCY | 13032 |
| 505 BRM | 11549 | 752 BWN | 12879 | 816 CHU | 10187 | 62 CPW | 13778 | 267 DCY | 13033 |
| 506 BRM | 11721 | 753 BWN | 12880 | 817 CHU | 10188 | 63 CPW | 13779 | 268 DCY | 13034 |
| 507 BRM | 11722 | 803 BWO | 12573 | 818 CHU | 10189 | 64 CPW | 13780 | 269 DCY | 13035 |
| 508 BRM | 11723 | 804 BWO | 12574 | 819 CHU | 10190 | 834 CRX | 13731 | 270 DCY | 13036 |
| 509 BRM | 11724 | 807 BWR | 13482 | 820 CHU | 10191 | 835 CRX | 13732 | 271 DCY | 13037 |
| 510 BRM | 11725 | 808 BWR | 13483 | 821 CHU | 10192 | 839 CRX | 13995 | 272 DCY | 13038 |
| 511 BRM | 11964 | 809 BWR | 13484 | 822 CHU | 10193 | 840 CRX | 13996 | 273 DCY | 13039 |
| 512 BRM | 11965 | 810 BWR | 13485 | 823 CHU | 10194 | 841 CRX | 13997 | 274 DCY | 13040 |
| 147 BRP | 13289 | 811 BWR | 13486 | 824 CHU | 10195 | 101 CWO | 12824 | 615 DDV | 11943 |
| 148 BRP | 13290 | 812 BWR | 13487 | 825 CHU | 10196 | 102 CWO | 12825 | 616 DDV | 11944 |
| 149 BRP | 13291 | 950 BWR | 12984 | 826 CHU | 10197 | 103 CWO | 12826 | 617 DDV | 11945 |
| 150 BRP | 13292 | 951 BWR | 12985 | 827 CHU | 10198 | 104 CWO | 12827 | 618 DDV | 11946 |
| 151 BRP | 13293 | 952 BWR | 12986 | 828 CHU | 10199 | 105 CWO | 12828 | 619 DDV | 11947 |
| 152 BRP | 13294 | 953 BWR | 12987 | 829 CHU | 10200 | 106 CWO | 12829 | 620 DDV | 11948 |
| 153 BRP | 13295 | 954 BWR | 12988 | 830 CHU | 10201 | 107 CWO | 12830 | 621 DDV | 11958 |
| 154 BRP | 13296 | 955 BWR | 12989 | 831 CHU | 10202 | 108 CWO | 12831 | 622 DDV | 11959 |
| 155 BRP | 13297 | 956 BWR | 12990 | 832 CHU | 10203 | 109 CWO | 12832 | 623 DDV | 11960 |
| 156 BRP | 13298 | 957 BWR | 12991 | 833 CHU | 10204 | 110 CWO | 12833 | 624 DDV | 11961 |
| 157 BRP | 13299 | 958 BWR | 12992 | 834 CHU | 10205 | 111 CWO | 12834 | 625 DDV | 11962 |
| 158 BRP | 13300 | 959 BWR | 12993 | 835 CHU | 10206 | 112 CWO | 12835 | 626 DDV | 11963 |
| 159 BRP | 13301 | 274 BWU | 12972 | 836 CHU | 10207 | 113 CWO | 12836 | 9 DLY | 12845 |
| 160 BRP | 13302 | 275 BWU | 12973 | 837 CHU | 10208 | 144 CWR | 12994 | 10 DLY | 12846 |
| 629 BRP | 13227 | 276 BWU | 12974 | 838 CHU | 10209 | 145 CWR | 12995 | 11 DLY | 12847 |
| 630 BRP | 13228 | 277 BWU | 12975 | 839 CHU | 10210 | 146 CWR | 12996 | 12 DLY | 12848 |
| 631 BRP | 13229 | 278 BWU | 12976 | 840 CHU | 10211 | 147 CWR | 12997 | 13 DLY | 12849 |
| 632 BRP | 13230 | 279 BWU | 12977 | 850 CHU | 10212 | 796 CWU | 13697 | 65 DNG | 13781 |
| 633 BRP | 13231 | 280 BWU | 12978 | 851 CHU | 10213 | 797 CWU | 13698 | 66 DNG | 13782 |
| 634 BRP | 13232 | 281 BWU | 12979 | 852 CHU | 10214 | 798 CWU | 13699 | 67 DNG | 13783 |
| 635 BRP | 13233 | 282 BWU | 12980 | 853 CHU | 10215 | 799 CWU | 13700 | 68 DNG | 13784 |
| 636 BRP | 13234 | 283 BWU | 12981 | 854 CHU | 10216 | 800 CWU | 13701 | 69 DNG | 13785 |
| 637 BRP | 13235 | 284 BWU | 12982 | 855 CHU | 10217 | 801 CWU | 13702 | 70 DPW | 13786 |
| 638 BRP | 13236 | 285 BWU | 12983 | 856 CHU | 10218 | 971 DAE | 10352 | 71 DPW | 13787 |
| 639 BRP | 13237 | 821 BWY | 13459 | 857 CHU | 10219 | 972 DAE | 10353 | 72 DPW | 13788 |
| 640 BRP | 13238 | 822 BWY | 13460 | 858 CHU | 10220 | 973 DAE | 10354 | 489 DPW | 13390 |
| 191 BRR | 10988 | 823 BWY | 13461 | 859 CHU | 10221 | 974 DAE | 10355 | 490 DPW | 13391 |
| 192 BRR | 10989 | 824 BWY | 13462 | 860 CHU | 10222 | 975 DAE | 10356 | 491 DPW | 13392 |
| 193 BRR | 10990 | 825 BWY | 13463 | 44 CNG | 12929 | 976 DAE | 10357 | 492 DPW | 13393 |
| 194 BRR | 10991 | 826 BWY | 13464 | 45 CNG | 12930 | 977 DAE | 10358 | 109 DRM | 12333 |
| 195 BRR | 10992 | 827 BWY | 13465 | 46 CNG | 12931 | 978 DAE | 10359 | 110 DRM | 12334 |
| 196 BRR | 11243 | 828 BWY | 13466 | 47 CNG | 12932 | 979 DAE | 10360 | 111 DRM | 12335 |
| 197 BRR | 11244 | 829 BWY | 13467 | 48 CNG | 12933 | 980 DAE | 10361 | 112 DRM | 12336 |
| 501 BTA | 11069 | 830 BWY | 13468 | 49 CNG | 12934 | 981 DAE | 10362 | 113 DRM | 12337 |
| 502 BTA | 11070 | 831 BWY | 13469 | 50 CNG | 12935 | 982 DAE | 10363 | 114 DRM | 12499 |
| 503 BTA | 11071 | 832 BWY | 13470 | 667 COD | 11386 | 983 DAE | 10364 | 115 DRM | 12500 |
| 504 BTA | 11072 | 833 BWY | 13471 | 668 COD | 11387 | 984 DAE | 10365 | 116 DRM | 12501 |
| 505 BTA | 11073 | 834 BWY | 13472 | 669 COD | 11388 | 985 DAE | 10366 | 117 DRM | 12502 |
| 506 BTA | 11074 | 835 BWY | 13473 | 670 COD | 11389 | 986 DAE | 10367 | 118 DRM | 12503 |
| 507 BTA | 11075 | 836 BWY | 13474 | 671 COD | 11390 | 987 DAE | 10368 | 119 DRM | 12713 |

| | | | | | | | | | |
|---|---|---|---|---|---|---|---|---|---|
| 120 DRM | 12714 | 350 EDV | 12040 | 990 EHY | 11113 | 135 FCY | 13734 | 60 GUO | 12208 |
| 834 DYG | 13858 | 351 EDV | 12041 | 991 EHY | 11114 | 136 FCY | 13735 | 61 GUO | 12209 |
| 835 DYG | 13859 | 352 EDV | 12042 | 992 EHY | 11115 | 805 FFM | 10060 | 62 GUO | 12210 |
| 836 DYG | 13860 | 353 EDV | 12043 | 993 EHY | 11116 | 806 FFM | 10061 | 63 GUO | 12211 |
| 837 DYG | 13861 | 354 EDV | 12044 | 994 EHY | 11117 | 807 FFM | 10062 | 64 GUO | 12212 |
| 838 DYG | 13862 | 355 EDV | 12045 | 995 EHY | 11118 | 808 FFM | 10063 | 65 GUO | 12213 |
| 839 DYG | 13863 | 356 EDV | 12046 | 600 ENG | 14099 | 431 FHW | 10889 | 66 GUO | 12214 |
| 840 DYG | 13864 | 357 EDV | 12047 | 601 ENG | 14100 | 432 FHW | 10890 | 917 GUO | 12770 |
| 841 DYG | 13865 | 358 EDV | 12048 | 561 ERR | 11635 | 433 FHW | 10891 | 918 GUO | 12771 |
| 842 DYG | 13866 | 961 EHW | 10879 | 562 ERR | 11636 | 434 FHW | 10892 | 919 GUO | 12772 |
| 859 DYG | 14221 | 962 EHW | 10880 | 563 ERR | 11637 | 435 FHW | 10893 | 920 GUO | 12773 |
| 860 DYG | 14222 | 963 EHW | 10881 | 564 ERR | 11638 | 436 FHW | 10894 | 921 GUO | 12774 |
| 861 DYG | 14223 | 964 EHW | 10882 | 565 ERR | 11639 | 437 FHW | 10895 | 922 GUO | 12766 |
| 862 DYG | 14224 | 965 EHW | 10883 | 566 ERR | 11640 | 438 FHW | 10896 | 923 GUO | 12767 |
| 863 DYG | 14225 | 966 EHW | 10884 | 567 ERR | 11641 | 439 FHW | 10897 | 924 GUO | 12768 |
| 864 DYG | 14226 | 967 EHW | 10885 | 568 ERR | 11642 | 440 FHW | 10898 | 925 GUO | 12769 |
| 641 EBD | 13836 | 968 EHW | 10886 | 569 ERR | 11643 | 250 FRP | 14158 | 374 GWN | 13738 |
| 642 EBD | 13837 | 969 EHW | 10887 | 570 ERR | 11644 | 462 FTT | 11746 | 375 GWN | 13739 |
| 643 EBD | 13838 | 970 EHW | 10888 | 1 EWO | 12955 | 463 FTT | 11747 | 163 HAX | 13825 |
| 644 EBD | 13839 | 971 EHW | 11407 | 2 EWO | 12956 | 464 FTT | 11748 | 164 HAX | 13826 |
| 645 EBD | 13840 | 972 EHW | 11408 | 3 EWO | 12957 | 465 FTT | 11749 | 165 HAX | 13827 |
| 646 EBD | 13841 | 973 EHW | 11409 | 4 EWO | 12958 | 466 FTT | 11750 | 166 HAX | 13828 |
| 647 EBD | 13842 | 974 EHW | 11410 | 5 EWO | 12959 | 467 FTT | 11751 | 167 HAX | 13829 |
| 648 EBD | 13843 | 975 EHW | 11411 | 6 EWO | 12960 | 468 FTT | 11752 | 168 HAX | 13830 |
| 649 EBD | 13844 | 976 EHW | 11412 | 7 EWO | 12961 | 469 FTT | 11753 | 414 HDV | 12757 |
| 650 EBD | 13845 | 977 EHW | 11413 | 8 EWO | 12962 | 470 FTT | 11754 | 415 HDV | 12758 |
| 651 EBD | 13846 | 978 EHW | 11414 | 9 EWO | 12963 | 471 FTT | 11755 | 416 HDV | 12759 |
| 652 EBD | 13847 | 979 EHW | 11415 | 10 EWO | 12964 | 472 FTT | 11756 | 417 HDV | 12760 |
| 653 EBD | 13848 | 980 EHW | 11416 | 11 EWO | 12965 | 699 FWW | 14139 | 418 HDV | 12761 |
| 654 EBD | 13849 | 981 EHW | 11417 | 12 EWO | 12966 | 700 FWW | 14140 | 419 HDV | 12762 |
| 655 EBD | 13850 | 982 EHW | 10878 | 573 EWX | 13871 | 752 GFM | 10103 | 420 HDV | 12763 |
| 276 ECY | 13680 | 983 EHW | 10858 | 574 EWX | 13872 | 301 GHN | 10656 | 421 HDV | 12764 |
| 277 ECY | 13681 | 984 EHW | 10859 | 575 EWX | 13873 | 302 GHN | 10657 | 422 HDV | 12765 |
| 278 ECY | 13682 | 985 EHW | 10860 | 11 FAX | 13400 | 303 GHN | 10658 | 423 HDV | 12748 |
| 279 ECY | 13683 | 986 EHW | 10861 | 12 FAX | 13401 | 304 GHN | 10659 | 424 HDV | 12749 |
| 280 ECY | 13684 | 987 EHW | 10862 | 13 FAX | 13402 | 305 GHN | 10660 | 425 HDV | 12750 |
| 314 EDV | 12059 | 988 EHW | 10899 | 14 FAX | 13403 | 993 GHN | 10317 | 426 HDV | 12751 |
| 315 EDV | 12060 | 989 EHW | 10900 | 15 FAX | 13404 | 994 GHN | 10318 | 427 HDV | 12752 |
| 316 EDV | 12061 | 990 EHW | 10863 | 16 FAX | 13405 | 995 GHN | 10319 | 428 HDV | 12753 |
| 317 EDV | 12062 | 991 EHW | 10864 | 17 FAX | 13406 | 996 GHN | 10320 | 429 HDV | 12754 |
| 318 EDV | 12020 | 992 EHW | 10865 | 18 FAX | 13407 | 997 GHN | 10321 | 430 HDV | 12755 |
| 319 EDV | 12021 | 993 EHW | 10901 | 19 FAX | 13408 | 998 GHN | 10322 | 431 HDV | 12756 |
| 320 EDV | 12022 | 994 EHW | 10902 | 20 FAX | 13409 | 999 GHN | 10323 | 286 HFM | 10224 |
| 321 EDV | 12023 | 995 EHW | 10866 | 21 FAX | 13410 | 709 GRM | 13113 | 287 HFM | 10225 |
| 322 EDV | 12024 | 571 EHY | 10867 | 22 FAX | 13411 | 710 GRM | 13114 | 288 HFM | 10226 |
| 323 EDV | 12025 | 572 EHY | 10868 | 23 FAX | 13654 | 711 GRM | 13115 | 289 HFM | 10227 |
| 324 EDV | 12026 | 573 EHY | 10869 | 24 FAX | 13655 | 712 GRM | 13116 | 290 HFM | 10228 |
| 325 EDV | 12027 | 574 EHY | 10870 | 25 FAX | 13656 | 713 GRM | 13117 | 291 HFM | 10229 |
| 334 EDV | 12063 | 575 EHY | 10871 | 26 FAX | 13657 | 714 GRM | 13118 | 292 HFM | 10230 |
| 335 EDV | 12064 | 576 EHY | 10872 | 27 FAX | 13658 | 715 GRM | 12915 | 293 HFM | 10237 |
| 336 EDV | 12065 | 577 EHY | 10873 | 28 FAX | 13659 | 716 GRM | 12916 | 294 HFM | 10238 |
| 337 EDV | 12066 | 578 EHY | 10874 | 29 FAX | 13660 | 717 GRM | 12917 | 295 HFM | 10239 |
| 338 EDV | 12028 | 579 EHY | 10875 | 30 FAX | 13661 | 718 GRM | 12918 | 296 HFM | 10240 |
| 339 EDV | 12029 | 580 EHY | 10876 | 31 FAX | 13662 | 719 GRM | 12919 | 297 HFM | 10241 |
| 340 EDV | 12030 | 581 EHY | 10877 | 125 FCY | 14026 | 720 GRM | 12920 | 298 HFM | 10242 |
| 341 EDV | 12031 | 981 EHY | 11104 | 126 FCY | 14027 | 51 GUO | 12235 | 612 HFM | 10231 |
| 342 EDV | 12032 | 982 EHY | 11105 | 127 FCY | 14028 | 52 GUO | 12236 | 613 HFM | 10232 |
| 343 EDV | 12033 | 983 EHY | 11106 | 128 FCY | 14029 | 53 GUO | 12237 | 614 HFM | 10233 |
| 344 EDV | 12034 | 984 EHY | 11107 | 129 FCY | 14030 | 54 GUO | 12238 | 615 HFM | 10234 |
| 345 EDV | 12035 | 985 EHY | 11108 | 130 FCY | 14031 | 55 GUO | 12239 | 616 HFM | 10235 |
| 346 EDV | 12036 | 986 EHY | 11109 | 131 FCY | 14032 | 56 GUO | 12240 | 617 HFM | 10236 |
| 347 EDV | 12037 | 987 EHY | 11110 | 132 FCY | 14033 | 57 GUO | 12241 | 618 HFM | 10243 |
| 348 EDV | 12038 | 988 EHY | 11111 | 133 FCY | 14034 | 58 GUO | 12242 | 619 HFM | 10244 |
| 349 EDV | 12039 | 989 EHY | 11112 | 134 FCY | 13733 | 59 GUO | 12207 | 620 HFM | 10245 |

| | | | | | | | | | |
|---|---|---|---|---|---|---|---|---|---|
| 621 HFM | 10247 | 565 HWO | 14117 | 704 JHY | 11526 | 815 KDV | 13253 | 278 KTA | 12892 |
| 622 HFM | 10248 | 566 HWO | 14118 | 705 JHY | 11541 | 816 KDV | 13254 | 279 KTA | 12893 |
| 623 HFM | 10246 | 51 JAL | 12338 | 706 JHY | 11542 | 817 KDV | 13255 | 280 KTA | 12894 |
| 624 HFM | 10249 | 52 JAL | 12339 | 707 JHY | 11543 | 818 KDV | 13256 | 281 KTA | 12895 |
| 625 HFM | 10250 | 53 JAL | 12340 | 708 JHY | 11544 | 819 KDV | 13257 | 282 KTA | 12837 |
| 626 HFM | 10259 | 54 JAL | 12341 | 709 JHY | 11513 | 820 KDV | 13258 | 283 KTA | 12838 |
| 627 HFM | 10260 | 55 JAL | 12342 | 710 JHY | 11514 | 821 KDV | 13259 | 284 KTA | 12875 |
| 628 HFM | 10261 | 56 JAL | 12343 | 711 JHY | 11515 | 822 KDV | 13260 | 285 KTA | 12876 |
| 629 HFM | 10262 | 57 JAL | 12344 | 712 JHY | 11516 | 823 KDV | 13261 | 286 KTA | 12877 |
| 630 HFM | 10263 | 58 JAL | 12345 | 713 JHY | 11517 | 824 KDV | 13262 | 287 KTA | 12878 |
| 631 HFM | 10264 | 59 JAL | 12346 | 714 JHY | 11518 | 190 KFM | 11328 | 420 LAO | 13773 |
| 632 HFM | 10251 | 60 JAL | 12347 | 715 JHY | 11519 | 191 KFM | 11329 | 421 LAO | 13774 |
| 633 HFM | 10252 | 565 JFM | 10488 | 716 JHY | 11520 | 192 KFM | 11330 | 425 LAO | 14094 |
| 634 HFM | 10253 | 566 JFM | 10489 | 717 JHY | 11521 | 193 KFM | 11331 | 426 LAO | 14095 |
| 635 HFM | 10254 | 568 JFM | 10490 | 718 JHY | 11522 | 194 KFM | 11332 | 611 LFM | 10903 |
| 636 HFM | 10255 | 569 JFM | 10491 | 719 JHY | 11527 | 195 KFM | 11333 | 612 LFM | 10904 |
| 637 HFM | 10256 | 523 JHN | 10430 | 720 JHY | 11528 | 196 KFM | 11334 | 613 LFM | 10905 |
| 638 HFM | 10257 | 524 JHN | 10431 | 721 JHY | 11529 | 197 KFM | 11335 | 614 LFM | 10906 |
| 639 HFM | 10258 | 525 JHN | 10432 | 722 JHY | 11530 | 198 KFM | 11336 | 615 LFM | 10907 |
| 10 HHN | 10324 | 526 JHN | 10433 | 723 JHY | 11523 | 199 KFM | 11337 | 616 LFM | 10916 |
| 11 HHN | 10325 | 527 JHN | 10434 | 724 JHY | 11524 | 201 KFM | 11277 | 617 LFM | 10917 |
| 12 HHN | 10326 | 714 JHN | 10104 | 725 JHY | 11525 | 202 KFM | 11278 | 618 LFM | 10918 |
| 13 HHN | 10327 | 715 JHN | 10105 | 726 JHY | 11531 | 203 KFM | 11279 | 619 LFM | 10919 |
| 14 HHN | 10328 | 716 JHN | 10106 | 727 JHY | 11532 | 204 KFM | 11280 | 620 LFM | 10921 |
| 15 HHN | 10329 | 928 JHN | 10435 | 728 JHY | 11533 | 205 KFM | 11281 | 621 LFM | 10922 |
| 16 HHN | 10330 | 929 JHN | 10436 | 729 JHY | 11534 | 206 KFM | 11282 | 622 LFM | 10923 |
| 289 HHU | 11920 | 930 JHN | 10437 | 730 JHY | 11535 | 207 KFM | 11283 | 623 LFM | 10924 |
| 290 HHU | 11921 | 931 JHN | 10438 | 731 JHY | 11536 | 208 KFM | 11284 | 624 LFM | 10908 |
| 291 HHU | 11922 | 932 JHN | 10439 | 732 JHY | 11537 | 209 KFM | 11285 | 625 LFM | 10909 |
| 292 HHU | 11923 | 933 JHN | 10440 | 508 JRA | 11245 | 210 KFM | 11286 | 626 LFM | 10910 |
| 293 HHU | 11924 | 934 JHN | 10441 | 509 JRA | 11246 | 987 KOO | 13938 | 627 LFM | 10911 |
| 259 HNU | 10306 | 935 JHN | 10442 | 510 JRA | 11247 | 988 KOO | 13939 | 628 LFM | 10912 |
| 260 HNU | 10307 | 936 JHN | 10443 | 511 JRA | 11248 | 989 KOO | 13940 | 629 LFM | 10913 |
| 261 HNU | 10308 | 937 JHN | 10479 | 512 JRA | 11249 | 990 KOO | 13941 | 630 LFM | 10914 |
| 262 HNU | 10469 | 511 JHU | 11780 | 513 JRA | 11250 | 991 KOO | 13942 | 631 LFM | 10915 |
| 263 HNU | 10470 | 512 JHU | 11781 | 514 JRA | 11251 | 992 KOO | 13943 | 632 LFM | 10920 |
| 264 HNU | 10471 | 513 JHU | 11782 | 515 JRA | 10993 | 993 KOO | 13944 | 633 LFM | 10925 |
| 265 HNU | 10472 | 514 JHU | 11783 | 516 JRA | 10994 | 994 KOO | 13945 | 634 LFM | 10926 |
| 266 HNU | 10473 | 515 JHU | 11784 | 517 JRA | 10995 | 995 KOO | 13946 | 635 LFM | 10927 |
| 267 HNU | 10474 | 516 JHU | 11785 | 518 JRA | 10996 | 253 KTA | 12850 | 636 LFM | 11338 |
| 268 HNU | 10475 | 517 JHU | 11786 | 519 JRA | 10997 | 254 KTA | 12851 | 637 LFM | 11339 |
| 269 HNU | 10476 | 518 JHU | 11787 | 520 JRA | 10998 | 255 KTA | 12852 | 638 LFM | 11340 |
| 270 HNU | 10477 | 519 JHU | 11788 | 521 JRA | 10999 | 256 KTA | 12853 | 639 LFM | 11341 |
| 271 HNU | 10478 | 520 JHU | 11789 | 522 JRA | 11000 | 257 KTA | 12854 | 640 LFM | 11342 |
| 215 HRO | 10086 | 521 JHU | 11790 | 523 JRA | 11001 | 258 KTA | 12855 | 641 LFM | 11343 |
| 130 HUO | 12555 | 522 JHU | 11791 | 524 JRA | 11002 | 259 KTA | 12856 | 642 LFM | 11344 |
| 131 HUO | 12556 | 523 JHU | 11792 | 525 JRA | 11003 | 260 KTA | 12857 | 643 LFM | 11345 |
| 132 HUO | 12557 | 524 JHU | 11793 | 526 JRA | 11004 | 261 KTA | 12858 | 644 LFM | 11346 |
| 133 HUO | 12558 | 525 JHU | 11794 | 527 JRA | 11005 | 262 KTA | 12859 | 645 LFM | 11347 |
| 134 HUO | 12559 | 526 JHU | 11795 | 528 JRA | 11006 | 263 KTA | 12860 | 646 LFM | 11348 |
| 135 HUO | 12560 | 527 JHU | 11796 | 801 KDV | 13239 | 264 KTA | 12861 | 647 LFM | 11349 |
| 136 HUO | 12561 | 528 JHU | 11797 | 802 KDV | 13240 | 265 KTA | 12862 | 648 LFM | 11350 |
| 137 HUO | 12562 | 529 JHU | 11798 | 803 KDV | 13241 | 266 KTA | 12863 | 649 LFM | 11351 |
| 138 HUO | 12563 | 530 JHU | 11799 | 804 KDV | 13242 | 267 KTA | 12881 | 650 LFM | 11352 |
| 139 HUO | 12564 | 531 JHU | 11800 | 805 KDV | 13243 | 268 KTA | 12882 | 801 LFM | 10701 |
| 140 HUO | 12565 | 532 JHU | 11801 | 806 KDV | 13244 | 269 KTA | 12883 | 802 LFM | 10702 |
| 141 HUO | 12566 | 533 JHU | 11802 | 807 KDV | 13245 | 270 KTA | 12884 | 803 LFM | 10703 |
| 142 HUO | 12524 | 534 JHU | 11803 | 808 KDV | 13246 | 271 KTA | 12885 | 804 LFM | 10704 |
| 143 HUO | 12525 | 535 JHU | 11804 | 809 KDV | 13247 | 272 KTA | 12886 | 442 LHN | 11026 |
| 144 HUO | 12526 | 536 JHU | 11805 | 810 KDV | 13248 | 273 KTA | 12887 | 443 LHN | 11027 |
| 145 HUO | 12527 | 537 JHU | 11806 | 811 KDV | 13249 | 274 KTA | 12888 | 444 LHN | 11028 |
| 146 HUO | 12528 | 701 JHY | 11538 | 812 KDV | 13250 | 275 KTA | 12889 | 445 LHN | 11029 |
| 563 HWO | 14115 | 702 JHY | 11539 | 813 KDV | 13251 | 276 KTA | 12890 | 446 LHN | 11030 |
| 564 HWO | 14116 | 703 JHY | 11540 | 814 KDV | 13252 | 277 KTA | 12891 | 447 LHN | 11031 |

| Reg | No. | Reg | No. | Reg | No. | Reg | No. | Reg | No. |
|---|---|---|---|---|---|---|---|---|---|
| 448 LHN | 11032 | 573 LHN | 11231 | 351 MFM | 11123 | 804 MHW | 12302 | 221 NAE | 12298 |
| 449 LHN | 11033 | 574 LHN | 11232 | 352 MFM | 11124 | 805 MHW | 12608 | 222 NAE | 12299 |
| 450 LHN | 11034 | 575 LHN | 11233 | 353 MFM | 11125 | 806 MHW | 12290 | 223 NAE | 12300 |
| 451 LHN | 11035 | 576 LHN | 11234 | 354 MFM | 11126 | 807 MHW | 12464 | 280 NHK | 11293 |
| 452 LHN | 11036 | 577 LHN | 11235 | 355 MFM | 11127 | 808 MHW | 12465 | 281 NHK | 11294 |
| 453 LHN | 11037 | 578 LHN | 11236 | 356 MFM | 11128 | 809 MHW | 12466 | 282 NHK | 11295 |
| 454 LHN | 11038 | 579 LHN | 11237 | 357 MFM | 11129 | 810 MHW | 12467 | 283 NHK | 11296 |
| 455 LHN | 11039 | 580 LHN | 11238 | 358 MFM | 11130 | 811 MHW | 12468 | 284 NHK | 11297 |
| 456 LHN | 11040 | 581 LHN | 11239 | 359 MFM | 11131 | 812 MHW | 12469 | 285 NHK | 11298 |
| 516 LHN | 11252 | 582 LHN | 11240 | 360 MFM | 11132 | 813 MHW | 12452 | 866 NHT | 12286 |
| 517 LHN | 11253 | 403 LHT | 12173 | 361 MFM | 11133 | 814 MHW | 12453 | 867 NHT | 12287 |
| 518 LHN | 11254 | 404 LHT | 12174 | 201 MHK | 10387 | 815 MHW | 12454 | 868 NHT | 12288 |
| 519 LHN | 11255 | 405 LHT | 12175 | 202 MHK | 10388 | 816 MHW | 12470 | 869 NHT | 12289 |
| 520 LHN | 11256 | 406 LHT | 12176 | 203 MHK | 10389 | 817 MHW | 12471 | 903 OFM | 12049 |
| 521 LHN | 11257 | 407 LHT | 12177 | 204 MHK | 10390 | 818 MHW | 12472 | 904 OFM | 12050 |
| 522 LHN | 11258 | 351 LPU | 10272 | 205 MHK | 10391 | 819 MHW | 12473 | 905 OFM | 12051 |
| 523 LHN | 11259 | 352 LPU | 10273 | 206 MHK | 10392 | 820 MHW | 12455 | 906 OFM | 12052 |
| 524 LHN | 11260 | 353 LPU | 10274 | 207 MHK | 10393 | 821 MHW | 12456 | 907 OFM | 12053 |
| 525 LHN | 11261 | 354 LPU | 10275 | 208 MHK | 10394 | 822 MHW | 12457 | 908 OFM | 12054 |
| 526 LHN | 11262 | 355 LPU | 10276 | 209 MHK | 10395 | 823 MHW | 12458 | 909 OFM | 12055 |
| 527 LHN | 11263 | 356 LPU | 10277 | 210 MHK | 10396 | 824 MHW | 12459 | 910 OFM | 12056 |
| 528 LHN | 11264 | 357 LPU | 10278 | 211 MHK | 10397 | 825 MHW | 12474 | 911 OFM | 12057 |
| 529 LHN | 11265 | 358 LPU | 10279 | 212 MHK | 10398 | 826 MHW | 12475 | 912 OFM | 12058 |
| 530 LHN | 11266 | 359 LPU | 10280 | 213 MHK | 10399 | 827 MHW | 12476 | 501 OHU | 13046 |
| 531 LHN | 11267 | 360 LPU | 10281 | 214 MHK | 10400 | 241 MNN | 13168 | 502 OHU | 13047 |
| 532 LHN | 11268 | 934 LWC | 13947 | 215 MHK | 10401 | 242 MNN | 13169 | 503 OHU | 13048 |
| 533 LHN | 11269 | 935 LWC | 13948 | 216 MHK | 10402 | 243 MNN | 13170 | 504 OHU | 13049 |
| 534 LHN | 11270 | 936 LWC | 13949 | 217 MHK | 10403 | 244 MNN | 13171 | 505 OHU | 13050 |
| 535 LHN | 11271 | 937 LWC | 13950 | 351 MHU | 12575 | 245 MNN | 13172 | 506 OHU | 13076 |
| 538 LHN | 11196 | 938 LWC | 13951 | 352 MHU | 12576 | 246 MNN | 13173 | 507 OHU | 13077 |
| 539 LHN | 11197 | 736 MDV | 13685 | 353 MHU | 12577 | 247 MNN | 13174 | 508 OHU | 13078 |
| 540 LHN | 11198 | 737 MDV | 13686 | 354 MHU | 12578 | 248 MNN | 13175 | 509 OHU | 13079 |
| 541 LHN | 11199 | 738 MDV | 13687 | 355 MHU | 12579 | 249 MNN | 13177 | 510 OHU | 13080 |
| 542 LHN | 11200 | 739 MDV | 13688 | 356 MHU | 12580 | 250 MNN | 13176 | 511 OHU | 13095 |
| 543 LHN | 11201 | 740 MDV | 13689 | 357 MHU | 12581 | 906 MRB | 11645 | 512 OHU | 13096 |
| 544 LHN | 11202 | 741 MDV | 13690 | 358 MHU | 12582 | 907 MRB | 11646 | 513 OHU | 13097 |
| 545 LHN | 11203 | 742 MDV | 13691 | 359 MHU | 12583 | 908 MRB | 11647 | 514 OHU | 13051 |
| 546 LHN | 11204 | 743 MDV | 13692 | 360 MHU | 12584 | 909 MRB | 11648 | 515 OHU | 13052 |
| 547 LHN | 11205 | 744 MDV | 13693 | 361 MHU | 12585 | 910 MRB | 11649 | 516 OHU | 13053 |
| 548 LHN | 11206 | 745 MDV | 13694 | 362 MHU | 12586 | 911 MRB | 11650 | 517 OHU | 13054 |
| 549 LHN | 11207 | 746 MDV | 13695 | 363 MHU | 12587 | 912 MRB | 11651 | 518 OHU | 13055 |
| 550 LHN | 11208 | 747 MDV | 13696 | 364 MHU | 12588 | 913 MRB | 11652 | 519 OHU | 13056 |
| 551 LHN | 11209 | 751 MDV | 13412 | 365 MHU | 12589 | 914 MRB | 11653 | 520 OHU | 13057 |
| 552 LHN | 11210 | 752 MDV | 13413 | 366 MHU | 12590 | 915 MRB | 11654 | 521 OHU | 13058 |
| 553 LHN | 11211 | 753 MDV | 13414 | 367 MHU | 12591 | 201 NAE | 12477 | 522 OHU | 13059 |
| 554 LHN | 11212 | 754 MDV | 13415 | 368 MHU | 12592 | 202 NAE | 12478 | 523 OHU | 13060 |
| 555 LHN | 11213 | 755 MDV | 13416 | 369 MHU | 12593 | 203 NAE | 12460 | 524 OHU | 13061 |
| 556 LHN | 11214 | 756 MDV | 13417 | 370 MHU | 12594 | 204 NAE | 12461 | 525 OHU | 13081 |
| 557 LHN | 11215 | 757 MDV | 13663 | 371 MHU | 12595 | 205 NAE | 12462 | 526 OHU | 13082 |
| 558 LHN | 11216 | 758 MDV | 13664 | 372 MHU | 12596 | 206 NAE | 12463 | 527 OHU | 13083 |
| 559 LHN | 11217 | 759 MDV | 13665 | 373 MHU | 12597 | 207 NAE | 12277 | 528 OHU | 13084 |
| 560 LHN | 11218 | 760 MDV | 13666 | 374 MHU | 12598 | 208 NAE | 12278 | 529 OHU | 13085 |
| 561 LHN | 11219 | 761 MDV | 13667 | 375 MHU | 12599 | 209 NAE | 12279 | 530 OHU | 13086 |
| 562 LHN | 11220 | 762 MDV | 13668 | 376 MHU | 12600 | 210 NAE | 12280 | 531 OHU | 13062 |
| 563 LHN | 11221 | 763 MDV | 13669 | 377 MHU | 12601 | 211 NAE | 12281 | 532 OHU | 13063 |
| 564 LHN | 11222 | 764 MDV | 13670 | 378 MHU | 12602 | 212 NAE | 12282 | 533 OHU | 13064 |
| 565 LHN | 11223 | 765 MDV | 13671 | 379 MHU | 12603 | 213 NAE | 12283 | 534 OHU | 13065 |
| 566 LHN | 11224 | 766 MDV | 13672 | 380 MHU | 12604 | 214 NAE | 12291 | 535 OHU | 13066 |
| 567 LHN | 11225 | 767 MDV | 13673 | 381 MHU | 12605 | 215 NAE | 12292 | 536 OHU | 13067 |
| 568 LHN | 11226 | 768 MDV | 13674 | 382 MHU | 12606 | 216 NAE | 12293 | 537 OHU | 13074 |
| 569 LHN | 11227 | 347 MFM | 11119 | 383 MHU | 12607 | 217 NAE | 12294 | 538 OHU | 13075 |
| 570 LHN | 11228 | 348 MFM | 11120 | 801 MHW | 12284 | 218 NAE | 12295 | 539 OHU | 13068 |
| 571 LHN | 11229 | 349 MFM | 11121 | 802 MHW | 12285 | 219 NAE | 12296 | 540 OHU | 13069 |
| 572 LHN | 11230 | 350 MFM | 11122 | 803 MHW | 12301 | 220 NAE | 12297 | 541 OHU | 13070 |

| | | | | | | | | | |
|---|---|---|---|---|---|---|---|---|---|
| 542 OHU | 13071 | 418 PTA | 14053 | 859 RFM | 11818 | 157 SHN | 14508 | 842 SUO | 14493 |
| 543 OHU | 13072 | 419 PTA | 14054 | 860 RFM | 11819 | 158 SHN | 14509 | 902 THN | 14129 |
| 544 OHU | 13073 | 426 PTA | 13989 | 861 RFM | 11820 | 801 SHW | 13902 | 903 THN | 14130 |
| 545 OHU | 13087 | 427 PTA | 13990 | 862 RFM | 11821 | 802 SHW | 13903 | 904 THN | 14131 |
| 546 OHU | 13088 | 428 PTA | 13991 | 863 RFM | 11822 | 803 SHW | 13904 | 905 THN | 14132 |
| 547 OHU | 13089 | 429 PTA | 13992 | 370 RNN | 13644 | 804 SHW | 13905 | 906 THN | 14133 |
| 548 OHU | 13090 | 861 RAE | 13479 | 371 RNN | 13645 | 805 SHW | 13906 | 907 THN | 14134 |
| 549 OHU | 13091 | 862 RAE | 13480 | 372 RNN | 13646 | 806 SHW | 13884 | 908 THN | 14135 |
| 550 OHU | 13092 | 863 RAE | 13481 | 373 RNN | 13647 | 807 SHW | 13885 | 909 THN | 14136 |
| 551 OHU | 13093 | 864 RAE | 12783 | 374 RNN | 13976 | 808 SHW | 13886 | 910 THN | 14137 |
| 552 OHU | 13094 | 865 RAE | 12784 | 375 RNN | 13977 | 809 SHW | 13887 | 911 THN | 14138 |
| 302 PFM | 11925 | 866 RAE | 12785 | 376 RNN | 13978 | 810 SHW | 13888 | 914 THN | 13936 |
| 303 PFM | 11926 | 867 RAE | 12786 | 377 RNN | 13979 | 811 SHW | 13889 | 915 THN | 13937 |
| 304 PFM | 11927 | 868 RAE | 12787 | 378 RNN | 13980 | 812 SHW | 13927 | 843 THY | 14217 |
| 305 PFM | 11928 | 869 RAE | 13303 | 237 SFM | 11981 | 813 SHW | 13928 | 844 THY | 14218 |
| 306 PFM | 11929 | 870 RAE | 13304 | 238 SFM | 11982 | 814 SHW | 13929 | 845 THY | 14219 |
| 307 PFM | 11575 | 871 RAE | 13305 | 239 SFM | 11983 | 815 SHW | 13930 | 846 THY | 14220 |
| 308 PFM | 11576 | 872 RAE | 13306 | 240 SFM | 11984 | 816 SHW | 13931 | 393 TUO | 14500 |
| 309 PFM | 11577 | 873 RAE | 13307 | 241 SFM | 11985 | 817 SHW | 13891 | 394 TUO | 14501 |
| 310 PFM | 11578 | 874 RAE | 13308 | 242 SFM | 11986 | 818 SHW | 13892 | 80 TVX | 11726 |
| 311 PFM | 11579 | 875 RAE | 13309 | 243 SFM | 11987 | 819 SHW | 13893 | 81 TVX | 11727 |
| 312 PFM | 11580 | 876 RAE | 13310 | 244 SFM | 11988 | 820 SHW | 13894 | 82 TVX | 11728 |
| 313 PFM | 11581 | 877 RAE | 13311 | 245 SFM | 11989 | 821 SHW | 13895 | 83 TVX | 11729 |
| 314 PFM | 11582 | 878 RAE | 13312 | 246 SFM | 11990 | 822 SHW | 13890 | 84 TVX | 11735 |
| 315 PFM | 11583 | 879 RAE | 13313 | 247 SFM | 11991 | 823 SHW | 13907 | 85 TVX | 11736 |
| 316 PFM | 11584 | 880 RAE | 13314 | 248 SFM | 11992 | 824 SHW | 13908 | 86 TVX | 11737 |
| 317 PFM | 11585 | 921 RAE | 13315 | 249 SFM | 11993 | 825 SHW | 13909 | 87 TVX | 11738 |
| 318 PFM | 11586 | 922 RAE | 13316 | 250 SFM | 11994 | 826 SHW | 13910 | 88 TVX | 11739 |
| 319 PFM | 11587 | 923 RAE | 13317 | 251 SFM | 11995 | 827 SHW | 13912 | 89 TVX | 11730 |
| 320 PFM | 11588 | 924 RAE | 13318 | 252 SFM | 11996 | 828 SHW | 13911 | 90 TVX | 11731 |
| 47 PPU | 10938 | 925 RAE | 13319 | 253 SFM | 11707 | 829 SHW | 13913 | 91 TVX | 11732 |
| 48 PPU | 10939 | 926 RAE | 13320 | 254 SFM | 11708 | 830 SHW | 13914 | 92 TVX | 11733 |
| 49 PPU | 10940 | 927 RAE | 13321 | 255 SFM | 11709 | 831 SHW | 13915 | 93 TVX | 11734 |
| 50 PPU | 10941 | 928 RAE | 13322 | 256 SFM | 11710 | 832 SHW | 13916 | 94 TVX | 11740 |
| 51 PPU | 10942 | 929 RAE | 13323 | 257 SFM | 11711 | 833 SHW | 13896 | 95 TVX | 11741 |
| 52 PPU | 10943 | 930 RAE | 13324 | 258 SFM | 11712 | 834 SHW | 13897 | 96 TVX | 11742 |
| 53 PPU | 10944 | 931 RAE | 13325 | 259 SFM | 11713 | 835 SHW | 13898 | 97 TVX | 11743 |
| 54 PPU | 10945 | 932 RAE | 13326 | 260 SFM | 11714 | 836 SHW | 13899 | 98 TVX | 11744 |
| 55 PPU | 10946 | 933 RAE | 13327 | 261 SFM | 11715 | 837 SHW | 13900 | 99 TVX | 11745 |
| 56 PPU | 10947 | 934 RAE | 13328 | 262 SFM | 11716 | 838 SHW | 13917 | 861 UAE | 13708 |
| 57 PPU | 10948 | 935 RAE | 13329 | 263 SFM | 11717 | 839 SHW | 13918 | 862 UAE | 13709 |
| 58 PPU | 10949 | 936 RAE | 13330 | 264 SFM | 11718 | 840 SHW | 13919 | 863 UAE | 13710 |
| 59 PPU | 10950 | 937 RAE | 13331 | 265 SFM | 11719 | 841 SHW | 13920 | 864 UAE | 13711 |
| 60 PPU | 10951 | 938 RAE | 13332 | 266 SFM | 11720 | 842 SHW | 13901 | 865 UAE | 13712 |
| 61 PPU | 10952 | 939 RAE | 13333 | 137 SHN | 14004 | 843 SHW | 13921 | 866 UAE | 13713 |
| 62 PPU | 10953 | 940 RAE | 13334 | 138 SHN | 14005 | 844 SHW | 13922 | 867 UAE | 13714 |
| 400 PTA | 14035 | 941 RAE | 13335 | 139 SHN | 14006 | 845 SHW | 13923 | 868 UAE | 13715 |
| 401 PTA | 14036 | 942 RAE | 13336 | 140 SHN | 14007 | 846 SHW | 13924 | 869 UAE | 13716 |
| 402 PTA | 14037 | 943 RAE | 13337 | 141 SHN | 14008 | 847 SHW | 13925 | 870 UAE | 13717 |
| 403 PTA | 14038 | 944 RAE | 13338 | 142 SHN | 14009 | 441 SNU | 12348 | 427 UFM | 12178 |
| 404 PTA | 14039 | 945 RAE | 13339 | 143 SHN | 14010 | 442 SNU | 12349 | 428 UFM | 12179 |
| 405 PTA | 14040 | 946 RAE | 13340 | 144 SHN | 14011 | 443 SNU | 12350 | 429 UFM | 12180 |
| 406 PTA | 14041 | 947 RAE | 13341 | 145 SHN | 14012 | 444 SNU | 12351 | 430 UFM | 12181 |
| 407 PTA | 14042 | 848 RFM | 11807 | 146 SHN | 14013 | 445 SNU | 12352 | 431 UFM | 12182 |
| 408 PTA | 14043 | 849 RFM | 11808 | 147 SHN | 14014 | 446 SNU | 12353 | 432 UFM | 12183 |
| 409 PTA | 14044 | 850 RFM | 11809 | 148 SHN | 14015 | 447 SNU | 12354 | 433 UFM | 12184 |
| 410 PTA | 14045 | 851 RFM | 11810 | 149 SHN | 14016 | 448 SNU | 12355 | 434 UFM | 12185 |
| 411 PTA | 14047 | 852 RFM | 11811 | 150 SHN | 14017 | 449 SNU | 12356 | 981 UHW | 14067 |
| 412 PTA | 14046 | 853 RFM | 11812 | 151 SHN | 14018 | 450 SNU | 12357 | 982 UHW | 14068 |
| 413 PTA | 14048 | 854 RFM | 11813 | 152 SHN | 14019 | 837 SUO | 14496 | 983 UHW | 14069 |
| 414 PTA | 14049 | 855 RFM | 11814 | 153 SHN | 14020 | 838 SUO | 14497 | 984 UHW | 14070 |
| 415 PTA | 14050 | 856 RFM | 11815 | 154 SHN | 14021 | 839 SUO | 14498 | 985 UHW | 14071 |
| 416 PTA | 14051 | 857 RFM | 11816 | 155 SHN | 14096 | 840 SUO | 14499 | 986 UHW | 14072 |
| 417 PTA | 14052 | 858 RFM | 11817 | 156 SHN | 14097 | 841 SUO | 14492 | 987 UHW | 14073 |

| | | | | | | | | | | | |
|---|---|---|---|---|---|---|---|---|---|---|---|
| 988 UHW | 14074 | 921 VFM | 12708 | 176 XNO | 12513 | ACA 216A | 10903 | AAG 65B | 14364 | | |
| 569 UVX | 12195 | 922 VFM | 12709 | 177 XNO | 12514 | ACA 218A | 12315 | AAG 66B | 14365 | | |
| 570 UVX | 12196 | 923 VFM | 12710 | 178 XNO | 12515 | ACA 230A | 10240 | AAG 67B | 14366 | | |
| 571 UVX | 12197 | 924 VFM | 12711 | 179 XNO | 12516 | ACA 303A | 11549 | AAG 68B | 14367 | | |
| 572 UVX | 12198 | 925 VFM | 12712 | 180 XNO | 12517 | ACA 411A | 12916 | AAG 118B | 14368 | | |
| 573 UVX | 12199 | 101 VHN | 14162 | 181 XNO | 12518 | ACA 507A | 12521 | AAG 119B | 14369 | | |
| 674 UYG | 11574 | 102 VHN | 14163 | 182 XNO | 12519 | ACA 544A | 10913 | AAG 120B | 14370 | | |
| 864 VFM | 12303 | 103 VHN | 14164 | 183 XNO | 12520 | ACA 553A | 12908 | AAG 121B | 14371 | | |
| 865 VFM | 12304 | 104 VHN | 14165 | 184 XNO | 12521 | ACA 578A | 11282 | AAG 122B | 14372 | | |
| 866 VFM | 12305 | 105 VHN | 14166 | 185 XNO | 12523 | ACA 979A | 12521 | AAG 123B | 14373 | | |
| 867 VFM | 12322 | 106 VHN | 14167 | 186 XNO | 12522 | ACY 178A | 10348 | AAG 124B | 14374 | | |
| 868 VFM | 12323 | 107 VHN | 14168 | 137 YFM | 13098 | ACY 307A | 10348 | AAG 125B | 14375 | | |
| 869 VFM | 12306 | 108 VHN | 14169 | 138 YFM | 13099 | ADE 146A | 13905 | AAH 102B | 14101 | | |
| 870 VFM | 12307 | 109 VHN | 14170 | 139 YFM | 13100 | AFE 170A | 12896 | AAH 103B | 14102 | | |
| 871 VFM | 12308 | 110 VHN | 14171 | 140 YFM | 13101 | AFE 171A | 12897 | AAH 124B | 13718 | | |
| 872 VFM | 12309 | 526 VRB | 13178 | 141 YFM | 13102 | AFE 245A | 11176 | AAH 125B | 13719 | | |
| 873 VFM | 12310 | 527 VRB | 13179 | 142 YFM | 13103 | AFM 402A | 11587 | AAH 126B | 13720 | | |
| 874 VFM | 12311 | 528 VRB | 13180 | 143 YFM | 13104 | AHJ 142A | 11726 | AAH 173B | 13789 | | |
| 875 VFM | 12312 | 529 VRB | 13181 | 144 YFM | 13105 | AKG 134A | 11015 | AAH 174B | 13790 | | |
| 876 VFM | 12313 | 530 VRB | 13182 | 145 YFM | 13106 | AKG 162A | 11015 | AAH 175B | 13791 | | |
| 877 VFM | 12314 | 531 VRB | 13183 | 146 YFM | 13107 | AKG 196A | 11766 | AAH 614B | 13792 | | |
| 878 VFM | 12315 | 532 VRB | 13184 | 147 YFM | 13108 | AKG 197A | 11015 | AAH 615B | 13793 | | |
| 879 VFM | 12316 | 533 VRB | 13185 | 148 YFM | 13109 | AKG 231A | 11766 | AAH 616B | 13794 | | |
| 880 VFM | 12317 | 534 VRB | 13186 | 149 YFM | 13110 | AKG 232A | 11015 | AAH 911B | 14103 | | |
| 881 VFM | 12318 | 535 VRB | 13187 | 150 YFM | 13111 | AKG 271A | 11766 | AAH 912B | 14104 | | |
| 882 VFM | 12319 | 971 WAE | 14472 | 151 YFM | 13112 | AKG 282A | 11015 | AAH 913B | 14105 | | |
| 883 VFM | 12320 | 972 WAE | 14473 | 201 YVX | 12613 | AKG 293A | 11766 | AAH 914B | 14106 | | |
| 884 VFM | 12321 | 973 WAE | 14474 | 202 YVX | 12614 | AKG 296A | 11015 | AAL 104B | 13981 | | |
| 885 VFM | 12324 | 974 WAE | 14475 | 203 YVX | 12615 | AKG 307A | 11015 | AAO 34B | 14172 | | |
| 886 VFM | 12325 | 975 WAE | 14476 | 204 YVX | 12616 | AKG 310A | 11766 | AAO 35B | 14173 | | |
| 887 VFM | 12326 | 976 WAE | 14477 | 205 YVX | 12617 | ARU 99A | 14496 | AAO 36B | 13935 | | |
| 888 VFM | 12327 | 977 WAE | 14478 | 206 YVX | 12618 | BFX 414A | 12159 | AAO 37B | 13932 | | |
| 889 VFM | 12328 | 978 WAE | 14479 | 207 YVX | 12619 | BHT 693A | 13931 | AAO 38B | 13933 | | |
| 890 VFM | 12329 | 979 WAE | 14480 | 208 YVX | 12620 | BHU 218A | 13086 | AAO 39B | 13934 | | |
| 891 VFM | 12330 | 980 WAE | 14481 | 209 YVX | 12621 | BHW 38A | 13931 | AAO 573B | 13775 | | |
| 892 VFM | 12331 | 801 WVW | 12504 | 210 YVX | 12622 | BLV 654A | 12206 | AAO 574B | 13776 | | |
| 893 VFM | 12332 | 802 WVW | 12506 | 211 YVX | 12623 | FRE 699A | 10131 | AAO 575B | 14571 | | |
| 894 VFM | 12479 | 803 WVW | 12507 | 212 YVX | 12624 | FRE 999A | 12222 | AAP 51B | 13740 | | |
| 895 VFM | 12480 | 804 WVW | 12609 | | | KGH 891A | 13905 | AAP 52B | 13741 | | |
| 896 VFM | 12481 | 805 WVW | 12610 | AAL 969A | 11086 | LAH 577A | 12935 | AAP 53B | 13742 | | |
| 897 VFM | 12482 | 806 WVW | 12611 | AAO 547A | 12333 | LDS 406A | 13108 | AAP 54B | 13743 | | |
| 898 VFM | 12483 | 807 WVW | 12612 | AAX 311A | 11766 | LDS 448A | 11623 | AAX 11B | 14119 | | |
| 899 VFM | 12484 | 808 XFM | 12788 | AAX 312A | 11015 | NNW 629A | 11148 | AAX 12B | 14120 | | |
| 900 VFM | 12485 | 809 XFM | 12789 | AAX 450A | 11766 | NWR 297A | 13784 | AAX 13B | 14121 | | |
| 901 VFM | 12486 | 810 XFM | 12790 | AAX 451A | 11015 | OWJ 339A | 12739 | AAX 14B | 14122 | | |
| 902 VFM | 12487 | 811 XFM | 12791 | AAX 465A | 11766 | XSL 228A | 12286 | AAX 15B | 14123 | | |
| 903 VFM | 12488 | 812 XFM | 12792 | AAX 466A | 11015 | XUF 594A | 11572 | AAX 16B | 14124 | | |
| 904 VFM | 12489 | 813 XFM | 12793 | AAX 489A | 11766 | XWV 586A | 11573 | AAX 21B | 13831 | | |
| 905 VFM | 12490 | 814 XFM | 12794 | AAX 515A | 11766 | XWV 588A | 11571 | AAX 22B | 13832 | | |
| 906 VFM | 12491 | 815 XFM | 12795 | AAX 516A | 11015 | XWV 602A | 11574 | AAX 23B | 13833 | | |
| 907 VFM | 12492 | 816 XFM | 12796 | AAX 528A | 11766 | YND 602A | 13066 | AAX 24B | 13834 | | |
| 908 VFM | 12493 | 817 XFM | 12797 | AAX 529A | 11015 | AAE 51B | 13926 | AAX 25B | 13835 | | |
| 909 VFM | 12494 | 13 XHN | 14510 | AAX 562A | 11015 | AAE 52B | 14075 | ABD 251B | 14159 | | |
| 910 VFM | 12495 | 14 XHN | 14511 | AAX 563A | 11766 | AAE 53B | 14076 | ABD 252B | 14160 | | |
| 911 VFM | 12496 | 15 XHN | 14512 | AAX 589A | 11015 | AAE 54B | 14077 | ABD 253B | 14161 | | |
| 912 VFM | 12497 | 16 XHN | 14513 | AAX 590A | 11766 | AAE 55B | 14078 | ABD 656B | 13851 | | |
| 913 VFM | 12498 | 917 XHN | 14514 | AAX 600A | 11015 | AAE 261B | 14557 | ABD 657B | 13852 | | |
| 914 VFM | 12701 | 918 XHN | 14515 | AAX 601A | 11766 | AAE 262B | 14558 | ABD 658B | 13853 | | |
| 915 VFM | 12702 | 170 XNO | 12505 | AAX 630A | 11015 | AAE 263B | 14559 | ABD 659B | 13854 | | |
| 916 VFM | 12703 | 171 XNO | 12508 | AAX 631A | 11766 | AAE 264B | 14560 | ABD 660B | 13855 | | |
| 917 VFM | 12704 | 172 XNO | 12509 | ABK 832A | 11655 | AAE 265B | 14561 | ABD 661B | 13856 | | |
| 918 VFM | 12705 | 173 XNO | 12510 | ACA 107A | 12180 | AAG 62B | 14361 | ABD 662B | 13857 | | |
| 919 VFM | 12706 | 174 XNO | 12511 | ACA 125A | 12181 | AAG 63B | 14362 | ABL 116B | 13998 | | |
| 920 VFM | 12707 | 175 XNO | 12512 | ACA 195A | 10913 | AAG 64B | 14363 | ABL 117B | 13999 | | |

| | | | | | | | | | |
|---|---|---|---|---|---|---|---|---|---|
| ABL 118B | 14000 | AGM 707B | 14416 | AHY 981B | 14562 | AVX 960B | 13956 | BNG 884B | 13800 |
| ABL 119B | 14001 | AGM 708B | 14417 | AHY 982B | 14563 | AVX 961B | 13721 | BNG 885B | 13801 |
| AEL 2B | 14465 | AGM 709B | 14418 | AHY 983B | 14564 | AVX 962B | 13722 | BNG 886B | 13802 |
| AEL 3B | 14466 | AGM 710B | 14419 | AHY 984B | 14565 | AVX 963B | 13723 | BNO 101B | 14145 |
| AEL 4B | 14467 | AGM 711B | 14420 | ALJ 573B | 13815 | AVX 964B | 13724 | BNO 102B | 14146 |
| AEL 5B | 14468 | AGM 712B | 14421 | ALJ 574B | 13816 | AVX 965B | 13725 | BNO 103B | 14147 |
| AEL 6B | 14488 | AGM 713B | 14422 | ALJ 575B | 13817 | AVX 966B | 13726 | BNO 104B | 14148 |
| AEL 7B | 14489 | AGM 714B | 14423 | ALJ 576B | 13818 | AVX 967B | 13727 | BNO 105B | 14149 |
| AFE 89B | 14675 | AGM 715B | 14424 | AMS 3B | 14333 | AWR 401B | 14524 | BNO 106B | 14150 |
| AFE 90B | 14676 | AHN 102B | 14174 | AMS 4B | 14334 | AWR 402B | 14525 | BNO 107B | 14151 |
| AFE 471B | 14182 | AHN 103B | 14175 | AMS 5B | 14335 | AWR 403B | 14526 | BNO 108B | 14152 |
| AFE 472B | 14183 | AHN 104B | 14189 | AMS 6B | 14336 | AWR 404B | 14527 | BNO 115B | 14462 |
| AFE 473B | 14184 | AHN 105B | 14190 | AMS 7B | 14337 | AWR 405B | 14528 | BNO 116B | 14463 |
| AFE 474B | 14185 | AHN 106B | 14191 | AMS 8B | 14338 | AWR 406B | 14529 | BNO 117B | 14464 |
| AFM 101B | 14484 | AHN 107B | 14192 | AMS 9B | 14339 | AWU 463B | 14141 | BOC 362B | 13991 |
| AFM 102B | 14485 | AHN 108B | 14193 | AMS 10B | 14340 | AWU 464B | 14142 | BPM 58B | 13747 |
| AFM 103B | 14486 | AHN 109B | 14194 | AMS 11B | 14341 | AWU 465B | 14143 | BPM 59B | 13748 |
| AFM 104B | 14487 | AHN 110B | 14195 | AMS 12B | 14342 | AWU 466B | 14144 | BPU 22B | 14469 |
| AFM 108B | 14085 | AHN 111B | 14196 | ANN 566B | 14587 | AWU 467B | 13874 | BPU 23B | 14470 |
| AFM 109B | 14086 | AHN 112B | 14197 | ANN 567B | 14588 | AWU 468B | 13875 | BPU 24B | 14471 |
| AFM 110B | 14087 | AHN 113B | 14198 | ANU 11B | 13988 | AWU 469B | 13867 | BRB 492B | 14589 |
| AFM 111B | 14088 | AHN 114B | 14199 | AOO 18B | 13679 | AWU 470B | 13868 | BRB 493B | 14590 |
| AFM 112B | 14592 | AHN 115B | 14200 | APW 824B | 14450 | AWU 471B | 13869 | BRM 79B | 13777 |
| AFM 113B | 14593 | AHN 116B | 14201 | APW 825B | 14451 | AWU 472B | 13870 | BRU 138B | 14668 |
| AFM 114B | 14594 | AHN 117B | 14202 | APW 826B | 14452 | BBD 254B | 14518 | BRU 139B | 14669 |
| AFM 115B | 14595 | AHN 118B | 14176 | APW 827B | 14453 | BBD 255B | 14519 | BRU 140B | 14670 |
| AFM 116B | 14596 | AHN 119B | 14516 | APW 828B | 14454 | BBD 256B | 14520 | BRU 141B | 14671 |
| AFS 11B | 14425 | AHN 120B | 14517 | APW 829B | 14455 | BBD 257B | 14521 | BRX 141B | 14002 |
| AFS 12B | 14426 | AHN 155B | 14022 | APW 830B | 14456 | BBD 258B | 14522 | BRX 142B | 14003 |
| AFS 13B | 14427 | AHN 156B | 14023 | APW 831B | 14457 | BBD 259B | 14523 | BUO 150B | 14631 |
| AFS 14B | 14428 | AHN 157B | 14024 | APW 832B | 14458 | BDL 576B | 14602 | BUO 201B | 14632 |
| AFS 15B | 14429 | AHN 158B | 14025 | APW 833B | 14459 | BDL 577B | 14603 | BUO 202B | 14600 |
| AFS 16B | 14430 | AHN 414B | 14098 | APW 834B | 14460 | BDL 578B | 14604 | BUO 203B | 14601 |
| AFS 17B | 14431 | AHN 459B | 14614 | APW 835B | 14461 | BDL 579B | 14605 | BVF 608B | 14107 |
| AFS 18B | 14432 | AHN 460B | 14615 | ATA 101B | 14502 | BDL 580B | 14606 | BVF 609B | 14108 |
| AFS 19B | 14433 | AHN 461B | 14616 | ATA 102B | 14503 | BDL 581B | 14607 | BVF 610B | 14109 |
| AFS 20B | 14434 | AHN 462B | 14617 | ATA 103B | 14504 | BDL 582B | 14608 | BVF 611B | 14110 |
| AFS 21B | 14435 | AHN 463B | 14618 | ATA 104B | 14505 | BDL 583B | 14609 | BVX 667B | 13959 |
| AGM 681B | 14390 | AHN 619B | 14177 | ATA 105B | 14494 | BEL 677B | 14664 | BVX 668B | 13957 |
| AGM 682B | 14391 | AHN 620B | 14203 | ATA 106B | 14495 | BEL 678B | 14665 | BVX 669B | 13958 |
| AGM 683B | 14392 | AHN 621B | 14204 | ATA 119B | 13993 | BEL 679B | 14666 | BVX 670B | 13960 |
| AGM 684B | 14393 | AHN 622B | 14205 | ATA 120B | 13994 | BEL 680B | 14667 | BVX 671B | 13961 |
| AGM 685B | 14394 | AHN 623B | 14178 | ATA 121B | 14055 | BFM 234B | 13768 | BVX 672B | 13962 |
| AGM 686B | 14395 | AHN 624B | 14206 | ATA 122B | 14056 | BFM 235B | 13769 | BVX 673B | 13963 |
| AGM 687B | 14396 | AHN 625B | 14207 | ATA 123B | 14057 | BFM 236B | 13770 | BVX 674B | 13964 |
| AGM 688B | 14397 | AHN 626B | 14208 | ATA 124B | 14058 | BFM 237B | 13771 | BVX 675B | 13965 |
| AGM 689B | 14398 | AHN 627B | 14209 | ATA 125B | 14059 | BFM 238B | 13772 | BVX 676B | 13966 |
| AGM 690B | 14399 | AHN 628B | 14210 | ATA 126B | 14060 | BFM 433B | 14638 | BVX 677B | 13967 |
| AGM 691B | 14400 | AHN 629B | 14211 | AUO 514B | 14623 | BFM 434B | 14639 | BVX 678B | 13969 |
| AGM 692B | 14401 | AHN 630B | 14212 | AUO 515B | 14624 | BFM 435B | 14640 | BVX 679B | 13968 |
| AGM 693B | 14402 | AHN 631B | 14213 | AUO 516B | 14625 | BFM 436B | 14089 | BVX 680B | 13970 |
| AGM 694B | 14403 | AHN 901B | 14540 | AUO 517B | 14626 | BFM 437B | 14090 | BVX 681B | 13971 |
| AGM 695B | 14404 | AHN 902B | 14541 | AUO 518B | 14627 | BFM 438B | 14091 | BVX 682B | 13972 |
| AGM 696B | 14405 | AHR 244B | 14065 | AUO 519B | 14628 | BFM 439B | 14092 | BVX 683B | 13973 |
| AGM 697B | 14406 | AHR 245B | 13883 | AUO 520B | 14629 | BFM 440B | 14093 | BXA 451B | 14376 |
| AGM 698B | 14407 | AHR 246B | 14066 | AUO 521B | 14630 | BFM 887B | 14641 | BXA 452B | 14377 |
| AGM 699B | 14408 | AHT 717B | 14555 | AUO 522B | 14598 | BFM 889B | 14642 | BXA 453B | 14378 |
| AGM 700B | 14409 | AHT 718B | 14553 | AUO 523B | 14599 | BFW 314B | 11828 | BXA 454B | 14379 |
| AGM 701B | 14410 | AHT 719B | 14554 | AVF 579B | 13795 | BFW 523B | 14491 | BXA 455B | 14380 |
| AGM 702B | 14411 | AHT 720B | 14556 | AVF 580B | 13796 | BHN 328B | 14234 | BXA 456B | 14381 |
| AGM 703B | 14412 | AHW 226B | 14551 | AVX 956B | 13952 | BHN 928B | 13935 | BXA 457B | 14382 |
| AGM 704B | 14413 | AHW 227B | 14552 | AVX 957B | 13953 | BNG 881B | 13797 | BXA 458B | 14383 |
| AGM 705B | 14414 | AHW 787B | 14079 | AVX 958B | 13954 | BNG 882B | 13798 | BXA 459B | 14384 |
| AGM 706B | 14415 | AHW 788B | 14080 | AVX 959B | 13955 | BNG 883B | 13799 | BXA 460B | 14385 |

| | | | | |
|---|---|---|---|---|
| BXA 461B 14386 | GNO 790B 14581 | BNN 101C 14533 | DAL 309C 14975 | EBD 682C 14813 |
| BXA 462B 14387 | GNO 791B 14582 | BNN 102C 14534 | DAO 201C 14924 | EEL 890C 14794 |
| BXA 463B 14388 | HEV 994B 14583 | BNN 103C 14535 | DAO 202C 14925 | EEL 891C 14795 |
| BXA 464B 14389 | HEV 995B 14584 | BNN 291C 14969 | DAO 203C 14926 | EEL 892C 14796 |
| BYG 756B 14214 | HEV 996B 14585 | BNN 292C 14970 | DAO 204C 14927 | EEL 893C 14797 |
| BYG 757B 14215 | HEV 997B 14586 | BOD 21C 14990 | DAP 62C 14635 | EEL 894C 14798 |
| BYG 758B 14216 | SKH 717B 13911 | BOD 22C 14991 | DAP 63C 14636 | EEL 895C 14962 |
| CAO 649B 14572 | AAX 17C 14125 | BOD 23C 14992 | DAP 64C 14637 | EEL 896C 14963 |
| CBL 355B 14186 | AAX 18C 14126 | BOD 24C 14993 | DEL 891C 14788 | EFM 628C 14734 |
| CBL 356B 14187 | AAX 19C 14127 | BOD 25C 14994 | DEL 892C 14789 | EFM 629C 14735 |
| CBL 357B 14188 | AAX 20C 14128 | BOD 26C 14995 | DEL 893C 14790 | EFM 630C 14736 |
| CEL 247B 14782 | AFE 921C 14677 | BVL 45C 14966 | DEL 894C 14791 | EFM 631C 14737 |
| CFD 777B 12848 | AFE 922C 14678 | BVL 286C 14801 | DEL 895C 14792 | EFM 632C 14738 |
| CFM 340B 14643 | AVL 216C 14964 | BVL 287C 14802 | DEL 896C 14793 | EFM 633C 14739 |
| CFM 341B 14644 | AVL 217C 14965 | BVL 288C 14803 | DFM 201C 14919 | EFM 634C 14920 |
| CFM 342B 14645 | BDV 244C 14712 | BVL 289C 14804 | DFM 211C 14732 | EFM 635C 14921 |
| CFM 343B 14646 | BDV 245C 14713 | BWN 53C 14690 | DFM 212C 14733 | EHT 106C 14863 |
| CMO 833B 14610 | BDV 246C 14714 | BWN 54C 14691 | DHT 783C 14889 | EHT 107C 14864 |
| CMO 834B 14611 | BDV 247C 14715 | CDL 476C 14996 | DHT 784C 14890 | EHT 108C 14865 |
| CMO 835B 14612 | BDV 248C 14716 | CDL 477C 14997 | DHT 785C 14891 | EHT 109C 14873 |
| CMO 836B 14613 | BDV 249C 14717 | CDL 478C 14998 | DHW 981C 14892 | EHT 110C 14874 |
| CNG 287B 14650 | BDV 250C 14718 | CDL 479C 14999 | DHW 982C 14893 | EHT 111C 14899 |
| CNG 288B 14651 | BDV 251C 14719 | CDL 480C 15000 | DHW 983C 14894 | EHT 112C 14900 |
| CNG 289B 14652 | BDV 252C 14720 | CEL 860C 14672 | DHW 984C 14895 | EHT 113C 14901 |
| CNG 290B 14653 | BDV 253C 14721 | CEL 861C 14673 | DHW 985C 14896 | EHT 114C 14902 |
| CNG 291B 14654 | BDV 254C 14722 | CEL 862C 14674 | DHW 986C 14897 | EHT 115C 14898 |
| CNG 292B 14655 | BDV 255C 14723 | CEL 863C 14782 | DHW 987C 14858 | EHT 116C 14866 |
| CNJ 60B 14633 | BDV 264C 14985 | CFE 230C 14967 | DHW 988C 14859 | EHT 117C 14867 |
| CNJ 61B 14634 | BDV 265C 14986 | CFE 231C 14968 | DHW 989C 14860 | EHT 851C 14868 |
| CNV 663B 14679 | BDV 266C 14987 | CFM 901C 14647 | DHW 990C 14861 | EHT 852C 14903 |
| CNV 664B 14680 | BDV 267C 14988 | CFM 902C 14648 | DHW 991C 14862 | EHT 853C 14911 |
| CNV 665B 14681 | BDV 268C 14989 | CFM 903C 14649 | DNG 105C 14760 | EHT 854C 14912 |
| CNV 666B 14682 | BFE 814C 14799 | CHN 3C 14542 | DNG 106C 14761 | EHT 855C 14913 |
| CNV 667B 14683 | BFE 815C 14800 | CHN 4C 14543 | DNG 107C 14762 | EHT 856C 14904 |
| CNV 668B 14684 | BHU 18C 14568 | CHN 5C 14544 | DNG 401C 14756 | EHT 857C 14905 |
| CNV 669B 14685 | BHU 19C 14569 | CHN 64C 14619 | DNG 402C 14757 | EHT 858C 14906 |
| CNV 670B 14686 | BHU 20C 14570 | CHN 65C 14620 | DNG 403C 14758 | EHU 583C 14869 |
| CNV 671B 14687 | BHU 91C 14702 | CHN 66C 14621 | DNG 404C 14759 | EHU 584C 14870 |
| CNV 672B 14688 | BHU 92C 14703 | CHN 67C 14622 | DNU 11C 14536 | EHW191C 14907 |
| CNV 673B 14689 | BHU 93C 14704 | CHT 531C 14881 | DNU 12C 14537 | ENG 109C 14764 |
| CPW 612B 14111 | BHU 94C 14705 | CHT 532C 14882 | DNU 13C 14538 | ENG 110C 14765 |
| CPW 613B 14112 | BHU 95C 14706 | CHT 533C 14883 | DNU 14C 14539 | ENJ 68C 14727 |
| CPW 614B 14113 | BHU 96C 14707 | CHT 534C 14884 | DNU 15C 14591 | ENJ 69C 14728 |
| CPW 615B 14114 | BHU 97C 14708 | CHT 535C 14885 | DNU 16C 14597 | ENJ 70C 14729 |
| CRM 211B 14573 | BHU 98C 14875 | CHT 536C 14886 | DNU 19C 14709 | ENV 683C 14814 |
| CVF 293B 14656 | BHU 401C 14566 | CHT 537C 14887 | DNU 20C 14710 | ENV 684C 14815 |
| CVF 294B 14657 | BHU 402C 14567 | CHT 538C 14888 | DNU 21C 14711 | ENV 685C 14816 |
| CVF 295B 14658 | BHU 975C 14845 | CHT 539C 14851 | DNU 685C 14976 | ENV 686C 14817 |
| CVF 296B 14659 | BHU 976C 14846 | CHT 540C 14852 | DNU 686C 14977 | ENV 687C 14818 |
| CVF 297B 14660 | BHU 977C 14847 | CHT 541C 14853 | DNU 687C 14971 | ENV 688C 14819 |
| DAH 398B 14661 | BHU 978C 14848 | CHY 417C 14854 | DNU 688C 14978 | ENV 689C 14820 |
| DAH 399B 14662 | BHU 979C 14849 | CHY 418C 14855 | DNU 689C 14979 | ENV 690C 14821 |
| DAH 400B 14663 | BHU 980C 14850 | CHY 419C 14856 | DNV 674C 14805 | EVF 111C 14766 |
| DWU 679B 14692 | BHW 93C 14698 | CHY 420C 14857 | DNV 675C 14806 | EWT 382C 14547 |
| DWW 336B 14693 | BHW 94C 14699 | CLJ 867C 14783 | DNV 676C 14807 | EWT 383C 14548 |
| DWY 498B 14696 | BHW 95C 14700 | CLJ 868C 14784 | DNV 677C 14808 | EWT 384C 14545 |
| DYG 222B 14694 | BHW 96C 14701 | CLJ 869C 14785 | DNV 678C 14809 | EWT 385C 14546 |
| DYG 223B 14695 | BHW 671C 14876 | CLJ 870C 14786 | DNV 679C 14810 | EWT 386C 14549 |
| FWC 426B 14575 | BHW 672C 14877 | CLJ 871C 14787 | DPM 65C 14724 | EWT 387C 14550 |
| FWC 427B 14576 | BHW 673C 14878 | CRM 472C 14574 | DPM 66C 14725 | EWT 401C 14697 |
| FWC 428B 14577 | BHW 674C 14879 | DAL 305C 14972 | DPM 67C 14726 | EWU 113C 14835 |
| FWC 429B 14578 | BHW 675C 14880 | DAL 306C 14982 | DVF 108C 14763 | EWU 114C 14836 |
| GNO 788B 14579 | BHY 715C 14871 | DAL 307C 14973 | EBD 680C 14811 | EWU 875C 14837 |
| GNO 789B 14580 | BHY 716C 14872 | DAL 308C 14974 | EBD 681C 14812 | EWY 272C 14822 |

| | | | | | | | | |
|---|---|---|---|---|---|---|---|---|
| EWY 273C | 14823 | GFM 186C | 14743 | HWY 524C | 14830 | KNO 955C | 14941 | | |
| FAH 112C | 14767 | GFM 187C | 14744 | HWY 829C | 14829 | LWC 659C | 14943 | Q795 DPF | 12960 |
| FAH 113C | 14768 | GFM 188C | 14745 | HWY 830C | 14831 | LWC 660C | 14944 | Q507 VHR | 12174 |
| FAH 114C | 14769 | GFM 189C | 14746 | JHK 452C | 14928 | LWC 661C | 14945 | | |
| FAH 115C | 14770 | GFM 190C | 14747 | JHK 453C | 14932 | LWC 662C | 14946 | Guernsey | |
| FAH 116C | 14771 | GFM 191C | 14748 | JHK 454C | 14929 | LWC 663C | 14947 | | |
| FAH 117C | 14772 | GFM 192C | 14749 | JHK 455C | 14930 | LWC 664C | 14948 | 6351 | 11389 |
| FAH 118C | 14773 | GFM 193C | 14750 | JHK 456C | 14530 | LWC 665C | 14949 | 10558 | 12885 |
| FAP 71C | 14730 | GFM 194C | 14751 | JHK 457C | 14531 | LWC 666C | 14950 | 31903 | 12036 |
| FAP 72C | 14731 | GFM 195C | 14752 | JHK 458C | 14532 | MVX 878C | 14951 | 31904 | 14721 |
| FNU 411C | 14980 | GFM 196C | 14753 | JHK 459C | 14933 | MVX 879C | 14952 | 31905 | 12760 |
| FNU 412C | 14981 | GFM 197C | 14754 | JHK 460C | 14934 | MVX 880C | 14953 | 31907 | 12046 |
| FNU 413C | 14983 | GFM 198C | 14755 | JHK 461C | 14935 | MVX 881C | 14954 | 31908 | 12755 |
| FNU 414C | 14984 | GFM 202C | 14922 | JHK 462C | 14931 | MVX 882C | 14955 | 31910 | 14713 |
| FPM 73C | 14842 | GFM 203C | 14923 | JWR 411C | 14840 | MVX 883C | 14956 | 31910 | 14712 |
| FPM 74C | 14843 | GNG 124C | 14779 | JWR 412C | 14841 | MVX 884C | 14957 | 31912 | 14719 |
| FPM 75C | 14844 | GNG 125C | 14780 | JWT 350C | 14833 | MVX 885C | 14958 | 31914 | 12886 |
| FPW 319C | 14774 | GNG 126C | 14781 | JWT 351C | 14834 | NTW 942C | 14959 | 31915 | 12882 |
| FPW 320C | 14775 | GWU 809C | 14824 | JWT 402C | 14832 | NTW 943C | 14960 | 31916 | 12877 |
| FVF 421C | 14776 | GWW 111C | 14825 | KNO 949C | 14936 | NTW 944C | 14961 | 31917 | 12892 |
| FVF 422C | 14777 | GYG 614C | 14838 | KNO 950C | 14937 | FHT 15D | 14908 | 31918 | 12885 |
| FVF 423C | 14778 | GYG 615C | 14839 | KNO 951C | 14938 | FHT 16D | 14909 | 31920 | 12894 |
| GFM 179C | 14740 | HWW 477C | 14826 | KNO 952C | 14939 | FHT 17D | 14910 | | |
| GFM 180C | 14741 | HWW 478C | 14827 | KNO 953C | 14942 | LAH 448E | 12009 | | |
| GFM 185C | 14742 | HWY 523C | 14828 | KNO 954C | 14940 | OWT 241E | 13736 | | |

# HISTORICAL COUNTY CODES

GOV        Government Department

| | | | |
|---|---|---|---|
| AD | Aberdeenshire | KK | Kirkcudbrightshire |
| AH | Armagh | KN | Kesteven division of Lincolnshire |
| AL | Argyllshire | KS | Kinross-shire |
| AM | Antrim | KT | Kent |
| AR | Ayrshire | LA | Lancashire |
| AS | Angus | LC | Lincoln (City) |
| AY | Isle of Anglesey | LE | Leicestershire |
| BC | Brecknockshire | LI | Lindsey division of Lincolnshire |
| BD | Bedfordshire | LK | Lanarkshire |
| BE | Berkshire | LN | London Postal area |
| BF | Banffshire | LY | Londonderry |
| BK | Buckinghamshire | ME | Merionethshire |
| BU | Buteshire | MH | Monmouthshire |
| BW | Berwickshire | MN | Midlothian |
| CG | Cardiganshire | MO | Montgomeryshire |
| CH | Cheshire | MR | Morayshire |
| CI | Channel Islands | MX | Middlesex |
| CK | Clackmannanshire | ND | Northumberland |
| CM | Cambridgeshire | NG | Nottinghamshire |
| CN | Caernarvonshire | NK | Norfolk |
| CO | Cornwall | NN | Nairnshire |
| CR | Carmarthenshire | NO | Northamptonshire |
| CS | Caithness | NR | North Riding of Yorkshire |
| CU | Cumberland | OK | Orkney Islands |
| DB | Dunbartonshire | OX | Oxfordshire |
| DE | Derbyshire | PB | Peebles-shire |
| DF | Dumfries-shire | PE | Pembrokeshire |
| DH | Denbighshire | PH | Perthshire |
| DM | County Durham | RD | Rutland |
| DN | Devon | RH | Roxburghshire |
| DO | Down | RR | Radnorshire |
| DT | Dorset | RW | Renfrewshire |
| EI | Eire | RY | Ross-shire & Cromarty |
| EK | East Suffolk | SD | Shetland Islands |
| EL | East Lothian | SH | Shropshire |
| ER | East Riding of Yorkshire | SI | Selkirkshire |
| ES | East Sussex | SN | Stirlingshire |
| EX | Essex | SO | Somerset |
| EY | Isle of Ely | SP | Soke of Peterborough |
| FE | Fife | SR | Surrey |
| FH | Fermanagh | ST | Staffordshire |
| FT | Flintshire | SU | Sutherland |
| GG | Glamorgan | TY | Tyrone |
| GL | Gloucestershire | WF | West Suffolk |
| HA | Hampshire | WI | Wiltshire |
| HD | Holland division of Lincolnshire | WK | Warwickshire |
| HN | Huntingdonshire | WL | West Lothian |
| HR | Herefordshire | WN | Wigtownshire |
| HT | Hertfordshire | WO | Worcestershire |
| IM | Isle of Man | WR | West Riding of Yorkshire |
| IV | Inverness | WS | West Sussex |
| IW | Isle of Wight | WT | Westmorland |
| KE | Kincardineshire | YK | York (City) |

Note:    A 'G' prefix (eg GLA) indicates the vehicle had been converted to goods (eg lorry or van) and the operator was a goods operator (in this case, in Lancashire).

# OVERSEAS COUNTRY CODES

| | |
|---|---|
| O-A | Austria |
| O-AG | Antigue & Barbuda |
| O-AUS | Australia |
| O-B | Belgium |
| O-CDN | Canada |
| O-CH | Switzerland |
| O-CZ | Czechia |
| O-D | Germany |
| O-DK | Denmark |
| O-E | Spain |
| O-F | France |
| O-HR | Croatia |
| O-NL | Netherlands/Holland |
| O-PL | Poland |
| O-RUS | Russia |
| O-S | Sweden |
| O-SUD | Sudan |
| O-UAE | United Arab Emirates |
| O-USA | United States of America |
| O-Z | Zambia |